Lecture Notes in Artificial Intelligence   10061

Subseries of Lecture Notes in Computer Science

LNAI Series Editors

Randy Goebel
University of Alberta, Edmonton, Canada
Yuzuru Tanaka
Hokkaido University, Sapporo, Japan
Wolfgang Wahlster
DFKI and Saarland University, Saarbrücken, Germany

LNAI Founding Series Editor

Joerg Siekmann
DFKI and Saarland University, Saarbrücken, Germany

More information about this series at http://www.springer.com/series/1244

Grigori Sidorov · Oscar Herrera-Alcántara (Eds.)

Advances in Computational Intelligence

15th Mexican International Conference
on Artificial Intelligence, MICAI 2016
Cancún, Mexico, October 23–28, 2016
Proceedings, Part I

 Springer

Editors
Grigori Sidorov
Instituto Politécnico Nacional
Centro de Investigación en Computación
Mexico City
Mexico

Oscar Herrera-Alcántara
Universidad Autónoma Metropolitana
Mexico City
Mexico

ISSN 0302-9743 ISSN 1611-3349 (electronic)
Lecture Notes in Artificial Intelligence
ISBN 978-3-319-62433-4 ISBN 978-3-319-62434-1 (eBook)
DOI 10.1007/978-3-319-62434-1

Library of Congress Control Number: 2017940386

LNCS Sublibrary: SL7 – Artificial Intelligence

Printed on acid-free paper

This Springer imprint is published by Springer Nature
The registered company is Springer International Publishing AG
The registered company address is: Gewerbestrasse 11, 6330 Cham, Switzerland

Preface

The Mexican International Conference on Artificial Intelligence (MICAI) is a yearly international conference series that has been organized by the Mexican Society of Artificial Intelligence (SMIA) since 2000. MICAI is a major international artificial intelligence forum and the main event in the academic life of the country's growing artificial intelligence community.

MICAI conferences publish high-quality papers in all areas of artificial intelligence and its applications. The proceedings of the previous MICAI events have been published by Springer in its *Lecture Notes in Artificial Intelligence* series, vols. 1793, 2313, 2972, 3789, 4293, 4827, 5317, 5845, 6437, 6438, 7094, 7095, 7629, 7630, 8265, 8266, 8856, 8857, 9413, and 9414. Since its foundation in 2000, the conference has been growing in popularity and improving in quality.

The proceedings of MICAI 2016 are published in two volumes. The first volume, *Advances in Computational Intelligence*, contains 44 papers structured into seven sections:

- Natural Language Processing
- Social Networks and Opinion Mining
- Fuzzy Logic
- Time Series Analysis and Forecasting
- Planning and Scheduling
- Image Processing and Computer Vision
- Robotics

The second volume, *Advances in Soft Computing*, contains 44 papers structured into ten sections:

- General
- Reasoning and Multi-Agent Systems
- Neural Networks and Deep Learning
- Evolutionary Algorithms
- Machine Learning
- Classification and Clustering
- Optimization
- Data Mining
- Graph-Based Algorithms
- Intelligent Learning Environments

This two-volume set will be of interest for researchers in all areas of artificial intelligence, students specializing in related topics, and for the general public interested in recent developments in artificial intelligence.

The conference received for evaluation 238 submissions by 584 authors from 32 countries: Argentina, Brazil, Canada, Chile, China, Colombia, Costa Rica, Cuba, Czech Republic, Ecuador, France, Germany, Greece, Hungary, India, Iran, Ireland, Israel, Italy, Macao, Mexico, Pakistan, Russia, Serbia, Singapore, South Africa, Spain,

Thailand, Turkey, Ukraine, UK, and USA. Of these submissions, 86 papers were selected for publication in these two volumes after a peer-reviewing process carried out by the international Program Committee. The acceptance rate was 36.1%.

In addition to regular papers, the volumes contain two invited papers by the keynote speaker Vladik Kreinovich (USA):

- "For Multi-Interval-Valued Fuzzy Sets, Centroid Defuzzification Is Equivalent to Defuzzifying Its Interval Hull: A Theorem"
- "Metric Spaces Under Interval Uncertainty: Towards an Adequate Definition"

The international Program Committee consisted of 140 experts from 26 countries: Australia, Azerbaijan, Benin, Brazil, Canada, Colombia, Czech Republic, Finland, France, Germany, Greece, India, Israel, Italy, Japan, Luxembourg, Mexico, Poland, Russia, Singapore, Spain, Sweden, Switzerland, Turkey, UK, and USA.

MICAI 2016 was honored by the presence of renowned experts who gave excellent keynote lectures:

- Efstathios Stamatatos, University of the Aegean, Greece
- Imre J. Rudas, Óbuda University, Hungary
- Vladik Kreinovich, University of Texas at El Paso, USA
- Genoveva Vargas Solar, Centre national de la recherche scientifique, France

In addition, a special talk was given by Ángel Fernando Kuri Morales, ITAM, Mexico.

The technical program of the conference also featured tutorials presented by Félix Castro (UAEH), Miguel González Mendoza (ITESM), Oscar Herrera Alcántara (UAM), Francisco Viveros Jimenez (CIC-IPN), Alexei Morozov (IRE-RAS, Russia), and Ildar Batyrshin (CIC-IPN), among others. Four workshops were held jointly with the conference: the First International Workshop on Genetic Programming, the 9th International Workshop of Hybrid Intelligent Systems (HIS 2016), the Second International Workshop on Intelligent Decision Support Systems for Industry, and the 9th International Workshop on Intelligent Learning Environments (WILE 2016).

The authors of the following papers received the Best Paper Award based on the paper's overall quality, significance, and originality of the reported results:

First place:	"Author Profiling with doc2vec Neural Network-Based Document Embeddings," by Ilia Markov, Helena Gómez-Adorno, Juan-Pablo Posadas-Durán, Grigori Sidorov, and Alexander Gelbukh (Mexico)
	Prize from Springer: € 400; prize from SMIA: € 400
Second place:	"Using a Grammar Checker to Validate Compliance of Processes with Workflow Models," by Roman Barták and Vladislav Kuboň (Czech Republic)
	Prize from Springer: € 300; prize from SMIA: € 300
Third place:	"Neural Network Modelling for Dissolved Oxygen Effects in Extensive Litopenaeus Vannamei Culture," by José Juan Carbajal-Hernández and Luis P. Sánchez-Fernández (Mexico)
	Prize from Springer: € 200; prize from SMIA: € 200

The authors of the following papers selected among all papers of which the first author was a full-time student, excluding the papers listed above, shared the Best Student Paper Award:

First place:	"Relevance of Named Entities in Authorship Attribution," by Germán Ríos-Toledo, Grigori Sidorov, Noé Alejandro Castro-Sánchez, Alondra Nava-Zea, and Liliana Chanona-Hernández (Mexico)
	Prize from Springer: € 50; prize from SMIA: € 50
	"A Compact Representation for Cross-Domain Short Text Clustering," by Alba Núñez-Reyes, Esaú Villatoro-Tello, Gabriela Ramírez-de-la-Rosa, and Christian Sánchez-Sánchez (Mexico)
	Prize from Springer: € 50; prize from SMIA: € 50

The awards included significant monetary prizes sponsored by Springer and by the Mexican Society of Artificial Intelligent (SMIA).

We want to thank everyone involved in the organization of this conference. Firstly, the authors of the papers published in this book: It is their research work that gives value to the book and to the work of the organizers. We thank the track chairs for their hard work, and the Program Committee members and additional reviewers for their great effort in reviewing the submissions.

We would like to thank the Instituto Tecnológico de Cancún (ITCancún) for hosting the workshops and tutorials of MICAI 2016; particularly we thank Socorro Xóchitl Carmona Bareño, Director of the ITCancún, for her support and generosity. We also want to thank the staff of the Instituto Tecnológico de Cancún for their support in the organization of this conference. We gratefully acknowledge the sponsorship received from Springer for monetary prizes handed to the authors of the best papers of the conference. This generous sponsorship demonstrates Springer's strong commitment to the development of science and their sincere interest in the highest quality of the conferences published in their series.

We are deeply grateful to the conference staff and to all members of the Local Committee headed by Fernando Antonio Koh Puga. We acknowledge support received from the project CONACYT 240844. The entire submission, reviewing, and selection process, as well as preparation of the proceedings, was supported free of charge by the EasyChair system (www.easychair.org). Finally, yet importantly, we are very grateful to the staff at Springer for their patience and help in the preparation of this volume.

October 2016

Grigori Sidorov
Oscar Herrera-Alcántara
Obdulia Pichardo-Lagunas
Sabino Miranda-Jiménez

Organization

MICAI 2016 was organized by the Mexican Society of Artificial Intelligence (SMIA, Sociedad Mexicana de Inteligencia Artificial) in collaboration with the Instituto Tecnológico de Cancún (ITCancún), the Centro de Investigación en Computación del Instituto Politécnico Nacional (CIC-IPN), the Universidad Autónoma de México Azcapotzalco (UAM), the Unidad Profesional Interdisciplinaria en Ingeniería y Tecnologías Avanzadas del Instituto Politécnico Nacional (UPIITA-IPN), and INFOTEC.

The MICAI series website is www.MICAI.org. The website of the Mexican Society of Artificial Intelligence, SMIA, is www.SMIA.org.mx. Contact details and additional information can be found on these websites.

Conference Committee

General Chair

Grigori Sidorov   Instituto Politécnico Nacional, Mexico

Program Chairs

Grigori Sidorov	Instituto Politécnico Nacional, Mexico
Oscar Herrera Alcántara	Universidad Autónoma Metropolitana Azcapotzalco, Mexico
Sabino Miranda-Jiménez	INFOTEC, Mexico
Obdulia Pichardo Lagunas	Instituto Politécnico Nacional, Mexico

Workshop Chairs

Obdulia Pichardo Lagunas	Instituto Politécnico Nacional, Mexico
Noé Alejandro Castro Sánchez	Centro Nacional de Investigación y Desarrollo Tecnológico, Mexico

Tutorials Chair

Félix Castro Espinoza   Universidad Autónoma del Estado de Hidalgo, Mexico

Doctoral Consortium Chairs

Miguel Gonzalez Mendoza	Tecnológico de Monterrey CEM, Mexico
Antonio Marín Hernandez	Universidad Veracruzana, Mexico

Keynote Talks Chair

Sabino Miranda Jiménez   INFOTEC, Mexico

Publication Chair

Miguel Gonzalez Mendoza   Tecnológico de Monterrey CEM, Mexico

Financial Chair

Ildar Batyrshin   Instituto Politécnico Nacional, Mexico

Grant Chairs

Grigori Sidorov   Instituto Politécnico Nacional, Mexico
Miguel Gonzalez Mendoza   Tecnológico de Monterrey CEM, Mexico

Organizing Committee Chair

Fernando Antonio   Instituto Tecnológico de Cancún, Mexico
  Koh Puga

Area Chairs

Natural Language Processing

Grigori Sidorov   Instituto Politécnico Nacional, Mexico
Sofía Natalia Galicia Haro   Universidad Nacional Autónoma de México, Mexico
Alexander Gelbukh   Instituto Politécnico Nacional, Mexico

Machine Learning and Pattern Recognition

Alexander Gelbukh   Instituto Politécnico Nacional, Mexico

Data Mining

Miguel Gonzalez-Mendoza   Tecnológico de Monterrey CEM, Mexico
Félix Castro Espinoza   Universidad Autónoma del Estado de Hidalgo, Mexico

Intelligent Tutoring Systems

Alexander Gelbukh   Instituto Politécnico Nacional, Mexico

Evolutionary and Nature-Inspired Metaheuristic Algorithms

Oliver Schütze   CINVESTAV, Mexico
Jaime Mora Vargas   Tecnológico de Monterrey CEM, Mexico

Computer Vision and Image Processing

Oscar Herrera Alcántara   Universidad Autónoma Metropolitana Azcapotzalco,
                            Mexico

Robotics, Planning, and Scheduling

Fernando Martin   Universidad Veracruzana, Mexico
  Montes-Gonzalez

Neural Networks and Hybrid Intelligent Systems

Sergio Ledesma-Orozco   Universidad de Guanajuato, Mexico

Logic, Knowledge-Based Systems, Multi-agent Systems and Distributed AI

Mauricio Osorio   Jose Raymundo Marcial Romero

Fuzzy Systems and Probabilistic Models in Decision-Making

Ildar Batyrshin   Instituto Politécnico Nacional, Mexico

Bioinformatics and Medical Applications

Jesus A. Gonzalez   Instituto Nacional de Astrofísica, Óptica y Electrónica,
                                Mexico
Felipe Orihuela-Espina   Instituto Nacional de Astrofísica, Óptica y Electrónica,
                                Mexico

Program Committee

Juan C. Acosta-Guadarrama   Universidad Autónoma de Ciudad Juárez, Mexico
Fernando Aldana   Universidad Veracruzana, Mexico
Gustavo Arroyo   Instituto de Investigaciones Eléctricas, Mexico
Maria Lucia Barrón-Estrada   Instituto Tecnológico de Culiacán, Mexico
Ildar Batyrshin   Instituto Politécnico Nacional, Mexico
Igor Bolshakov   Russian State University for the Humanities, Russia
Ramon F. Brena   Tecnológico de Monterrey, Mexico
Eduardo Cabal-Yepez   Universidad de Guanajuato, Mexico
Hiram Calvo   Instituto Politécnico Nacional, Mexico
Nicoletta Calzolari   Istituto di Linguistica Computazionale – CNR, Italy
Erik Cambria   Nanyang Technological University, Singapore
Jorge Victor Carrera Trejo   Instituto Politécnico Nacional, Mexico
Maya Carrillo   Instituto Nacional de Astrofísica, Óptica y Electrónica,
                                Mexico
Heydy Castillejos   Universidad Autónoma del Estado de Hidalgo, Mexico
Oscar Castillo   Instituto Tecnológico de Tijuana, Mexico
Felix Castro Espinoza   Universidad Autónoma del Estado de Hidalgo, Mexico
Noé Alejandro   Centro Nacional de Investigación y Desarrollo
  Castro-Sánchez   Tecnológico, Mexico
Hector Ceballos   Tecnológico de Monterrey, Mexico
Gustavo Cerda-Villafana   Universidad de Guanajuato, Mexico
Liliana Chanona-Hernandez   Instituto Politécnico Nacional, Mexico
Stefania Costantini   Università degli Studi dell'Aquila, Italy
Heriberto Cuayahuitl   Heriot-Watt University, UK
Erik Cuevas   Universidad de Guadalajara, Mexico
Guillermo De Ita   Universidad Autónoma de Puebla, Mexico
Asif Ekbal   Indian Institute of Technology Patna, India

Hugo Jair Escalante   Instituto Nacional de Astrofísica, Óptica y Electrónica, Mexico
Ponciano Jorge   Instituto Politécnico Nacional, Mexico
   Escamilla-Ambrosio
Vlad Estivill-Castro   Griffith University, Australia
Gibran Etcheverry   Universidad de Sonora, Mexico
Eugene C. Ezin   Institut de Mathématiques et de Sciences Physiques, Benin
Denis Filatov   Instituto Politécnico Nacional, Mexico
Juan J. Flores   Universidad Michoacana de San Nicolás de Hidalgo, Mexico
Andrea Formisano   Università di Perugia, Italy
Anilu Franco-Arcega   Instituto Nacional de Astrofísica, Óptica y Electrónica, Mexico
Alfredo Gabaldon   General Electric Global Research, USA
Sofia N. Galicia-Haro   Universidad Nacional Autónoma de México, Mexico
Ana Gabriela   Universidad Nacional Autónoma de México, Mexico
   Gallardo-Hernández
Carlos Hugo   Universidad de Guanajuato, Mexico
   Garcia-Capulin
Alexander Gelbukh   Instituto Politécnico Nacional, Mexico
Onofrio Gigliotta   University of Naples Federico II, Italy
Eduardo Gomez-Ramirez   Universidad La Salle, Mexico
Arturo Gonzalez   Universidad de Guanajuato, Mexico
Jesus A. Gonzalez   Instituto Nacional de Astrofísica, Óptica y Electrónica, Mexico
Miguel Gonzalez-Mendoza   Tecnológico de Monterrey CEM, Mexico
Felix F. Gonzalez-Navarro   Universidad Autónoma de Baja California, Mexico
Efren Gorrostieta   Universidad Autónoma de Querétaro, Mexico
Carlos Arturo   CERN, Switzerland
   Gracios-Marin
Joaquin Gutierrez   Centro de Investigaciones Biológicas del Noroeste S.C., Mexico
Rafael Guzman   Universidad de Guanajuato, Mexico
Yasunari Harada   Waseda University, Japan
Rogelio Hasimoto   Centro de Investigación en Matemáticas, Mexico
Antonio Hernandez   Instituto Politécnico Nacional, Mexico
Yasmín Hernández Pérez   Instituto de Investigaciones Eléctricas, Mexico
Alberto Hernández   Universidad Autnoma del Estado de Morelos, Mexico
Oscar Herrera   Universidad Autónoma Metropolitana Azcapotzalco, Mexico
Dieter Hutter   DFKI GmbH, Germany
Pablo H. Ibarguengoytia   Instituto de Investigaciones Eléctricas, Mexico
Oscar G. Ibarra-Manzano   Universidad de Guanajuato, Mexico
Héctor Jiménez Salazar   Universidad Autónoma Metropolitana, Mexico
Laetitia Jourdan   Inria/LIFL/CNRS, France

Pinar Karagoz	Middle East Technical University, Turkey
Ryszard Klempous	Wroclaw University of Technology, Poland
Olga Kolesnikova	Instituto Politécnico Nacional, Mexico
Vladik Kreinovich	University of Texas at El Paso, USA
Angel Kuri-Morales	Instituto Tecnológico Autónomo de México, Mexico
Mathieu Lafourcade	Le Laboratoire d'Informatique, de Robotique et de Microélectronique de Montpellier (UM2/CNRS), France
Ricardo Landa	CINVESTAV Tamaulipas, Mexico
Dario Landa-Silva	University of Nottingham, UK
Bruno Lara	Universidad Autónoma del Estado de Morelos, Mexico
Yulia Ledeneva	Universidad Autónoma del Estado de México, Mexico
Yoel Ledo Mezquita	Universidad de las Américas, Mexico
Eugene Levner	Ashkelon Academic College, Israel
Rocio Lizarraga-Morales	Universidad de Guanajuato, Mexico
Blanca Lopez	Instituto Politécnico Nacional, Mexico
Tanja Magoc	University of Texas at El Paso, USA
J. Raymundo Marcial-Romero	Universidad Autónoma del Estado de México, Mexico
Luis Martí	Universidade Federal Fluminense, Brazil
Lourdes Martínez	Universidad Panamericana, Mexico
Juan Martínez-Miranda	Centro de Investigación Científica y de Educación Superior de Ensenada, Mexico
Miguel Félix Mata Rivera	Instituto Politécnico Nacional, Mexico
Patricia Melin	Instituto Tecnológico de Tijuana, Mexico
Ivan Vladimir Meza Ruiz	Universidad Nacional Autónoma de México, Mexico
Efrén Mezura-Montes	Universidad Veracruzana, Mexico
Mikhail Mikhailov	University of Tampere, Finland
Sabino Miranda-Jiménez	INFOTEC, Mexico
Raul Monroy	Tecnologico de Monterrey CEM, Mexico
Omar Montaño Rivas	Universidad Politécnica de San Luis Potosí, Mexico
Manuel Montes-y-Gómez	Instituto Nacional de Astrofísica, Óptica y Electrónica, Mexico
Carlos Montoro	Universidad de Guanajuato, Mexico
Eduardo Morales	Instituto Nacional de Astrofísica, Óptica y Electrónica, Mexico
Guillermo Morales-Luna	CINVESTAV, Mexico
Masaki Murata	Tottori University, Japan
Michele Nappi	University of Salerno, Italy
Jesús Emeterio Navarro-Barrientos	Society for the Promotion of Applied Computer Science (GFaI e.V.), Germany
Juan Carlos Nieves	Umeå University, Sweden
C. Alberto Ochoa-Zezatti	Universidad Autónoma de Ciudad Juárez, Mexico
Ivan Olmos	Benemérita Universidad Autónoma de Puebla, Mexico
Sonia Ordoñez	Universidad Distrital F.J. de C., Colombia
Partha Pakray	National Institute of Technology Mizoram, India

Ivandre Paraboni	University of Sao Paulo, Brazil
Mario Pavone	University of Catania, Italy
Ted Pedersen	University of Minnesota Duluth, USA
Obdulia Pichardo-Lagunas	Instituto Politécnico Nacional, Mexico
David Pinto	Benemérita Universidad Autónoma de Puebla, Mexico
Hiram Ponce Espinosa	Tecnológico de Monterrey CCM, Mexico
Soujanya Poria	Nanyang Technological University, Singapore
Héctor Pérez-Urbina	Google, USA
Risto Fermin Rangel Kuoppa	Universidad Autónoma Metropolitana Azcapotzalco, Mexico
Iván Salvador Razo-Zapata	Luxembourg Institute of Science and Technology, Luxembourg
Orion Reyes	University of Alberta Edmonton AB, Canada
Alberto Reyes Ballesteros	Instituto de Investigaciones Eléctricas, Mexico
Carlos Alberto Reyes García	Instituto Nacional de Astrofísica, Óptica y Electrónica, Mexico
Arles Rodriguez	Universidad Nacional de Colombia, Colombia
Alejandro Rosales	Instituto Nacional de Astrofísica, Óptica y Electrónica, Mexico
Horacio Rostro Gonzalez	Universidad de Guanajuato, Mexico
Jose Ruiz-Pinales	Universidad de Guanajuato, Mexico
Chaman Sabharwal	Missouri University of Science and Technology, USA
Abraham Sánchez López	Benemérita Universidad Autónoma de Puebla, Mexico
Antonio-José Sánchez-Salmerón	Universitat Politècnica de València, Spain
Jose Santos	University of A Coruña, Spain
Friedhelm Schwenker	Ulm University, Germany
Shahnaz Shahbazova	Azerbaijan Technical University, Azerbaijan
Patrick Siarry	Université de Paris 12, France
Grigori Sidorov	Instituto Politécnico Nacional, Mexico
Bogdan Smolka	Silesian University of Technology, Poland
Juan Humberto Sossa Azuela	Instituto Politécnico Nacional, Mexico
Efstathios Stamatatos	University of the Aegean, Greece
Josef Steinberger	University of West Bohemia, Czech Republic
Alexander Tulupyev	St. Petersburg Institute for Informatics and Automation of Russian Academy of Sciences, Russia
Fevrier Valdez	Instituto Tecnológico de Tijuana, Mexico
Manuel Vilares Ferro	University of Vigo, Spain
Esau Villatoro-Tello	Universidad Autónoma Metropolitana, Mexico
Aline Villavicencio	Universidade Federal do Rio Grande do Sul, Brazil
Francisco Viveros Jiménez	Instituto Politécnico Nacional, Mexico
Panagiotis Vlamos	Ionian University, Greece
Piotr W. Fuglewicz	TiP Sp. z o. o., Poland

Carlos Mario Zapata Jaramillo	Universidad Nacional de Colombia, Colombia
Ramón Zatarain	Instituto Tecnológico de Culiacán, Mexico
Alisa Zhila	IBM, USA
Reyer Zwiggelaar	Aberystwyth University, UK

Additional Reviewers

Adan Enrique Aguilar-Justo
Maria-Yaneli Ameca-Alducin
Andreas Attenberger
Zbigniew Banaszak
Grzegorz Bocewicz
Wojciech Bozejko
Jose Camargo-Orduño
Esteban Castillo
Silvio Ricardo Cordeiro
Víctor Darriba
Dario Della Monica
Saul Dominguez
Víctor Manuel Fernández Mireles
Helena Monserrat Gómez Adorno
Marcos Angel González-Olvera
Mario Graff
César Guerra
Helena Gómez-Adorno
Jorge Hernandez Del Razo
Geovanni Hernandez-Gomez
Luis M. Ledesma-Carrillo
Rocio Lizarraga-Morales
Misael Lopez Ramirez
Adrián Pastor Lopez-Monroy
Joji Maeno
Navonil Majumder
Ilia Markov
María-Guadalupe Martínez-Peñaloza
Mariana-Edith Miranda-Varela
Daniela Moctezuma

Dagmar Monett-Diaz
Alondra Nava-Zea
Felipe Ojeda-Cruz
Felipe De Jesús Ojeda-Cruz
Rosa María Ortega-Mendoza
Nahitt Padilla
José Luis Paredes
Carla Piazza
Edgar Alfredo Portilla-Flores
Claudia E. Ramírez Hernández
Gabriela Ramírez-De-La-Rosa
Francisco J. Ribadas-Pena
Francesco Ricca
Daniel Rivas
Jorge Rodas
Hector Rodriguez Rangel
Carlos Rodriguez-Donate
Mariana Rojas-Delgado
Salvador Ruiz-Correa
Ryan Stansifer
Fernando Sánchez
Kazuhiro Takeuchi
Eric S. Tellez
Alejandro Antonio Torres García
Monica Trejo
Yasushi Tsubota
Roberto Villarejo
Remy Wahnoun
Sławomir Wojciechowski
Miguel Ángel Álvarez Carmona

Organizing Committee

Local Chair

Fernando Antonio   Instituto Tecnológico de Cancún, Mexico
   Koh Puga

Logistics Chair

Oscar Andrés Cárdenas   Instituto Tecnológico de Cancún, Mexico
   Alvarado

Registration Chair

José Israel Cupul Dzib   Instituto Tecnológico de Cancún, Mexico

Publicity and Event Follow-up Chair

Viviana Nasheli   Instituto Tecnológico de Cancún, Mexico
   Andrade Armenta

Members

Alejandro Filiberto Gómez Pérez
Luis Alfonso Marín Priego
Francisco José Arroyo Rodríguez
Juan Carlos Navarrete Montero
Florentino Chimal y Alamilla
Silverio Hernández Chávez
Juan Antonio Ruíz Velazco de la Garza
Octavio Ramírez López
Rosa Hilda Valencia Ruíz
Elisa Malibé Carballo Guillén
Domingo Ramos Hernández
Enrique Alberto Trejo Guzmán
Sixto Raúl Rodríguez Alvarado
Esmeralda Tepixtle Guevara
Juan Miguel Morán García
Emery Concepción Medina Díaz
Georgina Chan Díaz
Oscar San Juan Farfán, Instituto Tecnológico de Cancún, Mexico

Contents – Part I

Social Networks and Opinion Mining

Fuzzy Logic

Invited paper:

Invited paper:

Time Series Analysis and Forecasting

Planning and Scheduling

Best Paper Award, Second Place:

Image Processing and Computer Vision

Robotics

Contents – Part II

Neural Networks and Deep Learning

Best Paper Award, First Place:

Best Paper Award, Third Place:

Evolutionary Algorithms

Machine Learning

Data Mining

Graph-Based Algorit

Intelligent Learning Environments

Natural Language Processing

Relevance of Named Entities in Authorship Attribution

Germán Ríos-Toledo[1]([✉]), Grigori Sidorov[2],
Noé Alejandro Castro-Sánchez[1], Alondra Nava-Zea[1],
and Liliana Chanona-Hernández[3]

[1] Centro Nacional de Investigación y Desarrollo Tecnológico,
Cuernavaca, Morelos, Mexico
{german_rios,ncastro,anz}@cenidet.edu.mx
[2] Centro de Investigación en Computación, Instituto Politécnico Nacional,
Mexico City, Mexico
sidorov@cic.ipn.mx
[3] Instituto Politécnico Nacional, ESIMEZ, Mexico City, Mexico

Abstract. Named entities (NE) are words that refer to names of people, locations, organization, etc. NE are present in every kind of documents: e-mails, letters, essays, novels, poems. Automatic detection of these words is very important task in natural language processing. Sometimes, NE are used in authorship attribution studies as a stylometric feature. The goal of this paper is to evaluate the effect of the presence of NE in texts for the authorship attribution task: are we really detecting the style of an author or are we just discovering the appearance of the same NE. We used the corpus that consists of 91 novels of 7 authors of XVIII century. These authors spoke and wrote English, their native language. All novels belong to fiction genre. The used stylometric features were character n-grams, word n-gram and n-gram of POS tags of various sizes (2-grams, 3-grams, etc.). Five novels were selected for each author, these novels contain between 4 and 7% of the NE. All novels were divided into blocks, each block contains 10,000 terms. Two kinds of experiment were conducted: automatic classification of blocks containing NE and of the same blocks without NE. In some cases, we use only the most frequent n-grams (500, 2,000 and 4,000 n-grams). Three machine learning algorithms were used for classification task: NB, SVM (SMO) and J48. The results show that as a tendency the presence of the NE helps to classify (improvements from 5% to 20%), but there are specific authors when NE do not help and even make the classification worse (about 10% of experimental data).

Keywords: Named entities · Authorship attribution · Machine learning · N-grams

1 Introduction

According to [11], the term "named entity" was coined for the Sixth Message Understanding Conference in 1996. Process of identifying references to names

G. Sidorov and O. Herrera-Alcántara (Eds.): MICAI 2016, Part I, LNAI 10061, pp. 3–15, 2017.
DOI: 10.1007/978-3-319-62434-1_1

(peoples, locations, and organizations) and numerical expressions (date, time, quantities) is called Named Entity Recognition (NER).

Named Entity Recognition is a difficult task. The detailed analysis of the context is required to identify a set of features to infer their presence. In Natural Language Processing (NLP) these features are known as stylometric features, see, for example [16]. For the aim of this paper, three of these types of features are presented in Table 1.

Nadeau [11] describes a set of features for NE recognition in a hypothetic system. In his study, these features are called word-level features, as shown in Table 2.

Tables 1 and 2 show the same types of features used for two different purposes: on the one hand, features in Table 1 are used for the authorship attribution task, meanwhile Table 2 is used for the task of the named entities recognition.

Authorship attribution is a classification task for determining, who is the author of a document. More generally, it is to determine the class (the author) of each element (document). This classification can be content based or topic based. Authorship attribution is a difficult task, because it is not clear what author style is and there are several factors to consider: writing peculiarities, document type (mails, text messages, books, essays, papers, etc.), document length and selected stylometric features. It has applications in areas such as law (dispute the authorship of a book), journalism (identify the author of an article), plagiarism detection (in texts or in program source codes [13, 15])

Table 1. Classification of stylometric features.

Type of features	Description
Character	Alphabetic, numeric, uppercase, lowercase, punctuation marks, character n-grams
Lexical	Word length, sentence length, vocabulary richness (type token ratio V/N), hapax-legomena, hapax-dislegomena, frequent words, word n-grams, spelling mistakes
Syntactic	Rewrite rules, POS tags distribution, syntactic n-grams, chunks, noun phrase, verb phrase, etc.

Table 2. Stylometric features for NE recognition.

Feature	Example
Case	Word starts with a capital letter, word is all uppercased, word in mixed case
Punctuation	Word ends with period, word has internal period or apostrophe, hyphen or ampersand
Digits	Cardinal, ordinal, roman number, word with digits
Character	Possessive mark, first person pronoun, Greek letters
Morphology	Prefix, suffix, singular version, plural, stem
POS	Proper name, verb, noun, foreign word, etc.
Function	n-grams, token length, phrase length

and quantifications of stylistic variations that occur along the literary production of an author. It is assumed that an author has a unique writing style and therefore it is possible to quantify it by a statistical model [4]. Stylometric features are required to develop this model, which includes: punctuation mark, vocabulary richness, frequent word, function words, content word, sentence length, word length, syntactic complexity, n-grams, named entities, among others. In various works, the number of stylometric features (not speaking about n-grams) reached about 1,000 [12], they are also known as style markers.

The aim of this study is to evaluate the performance of the machine learning algorithms with two types of texts: texts containing named entities and further the same texts whose named entities have been deleted. From the corpus of 7 authors with 13 novels per author [13], we chose 5 novels with most frequency of use of named entities. Two versions of each novel was created: one with the named entities and the other without them. At the next step each novel was divided into files with 10,000 terms. For these files, vector space models for each author were created. Classifiers should identify to what author (class) the fragments of the novels belong. These experiments were conducted for all 13 authors.

The rest of the paper is organized as follows. In related works, research on authorship attribution and stylometric features for named entities is presented. Methodology section describes our proposal. The results section presents the data obtained in the experiments. In discussion section the data interpretation is proposed and finally the conclusions are presented.

2 Related Work

Tanguy *et al.* [18] made a study using features commonly applied in authorship attribution. These features were words, word frequencies, cases, morphology, word lengths, writing mistakes, contractions and named entities. Tanguy *et al.* [16] performed experiments on authorship attribution, specifically for genre of fiction. They established that the names of characters are important in this literary genre. For detection of proper names they used a tagger. In both works it is not specified how they used the named entities.

The work [7] made a study about authorship attribution using a stylometric feature they called Local Syntactic Dependencies (LSD) that surround a named entity. The LSD allow to identify grammatical structures that writers use to refer to proper names and thus establish the degree of how writing styles vary when talking about people. The vectors used to represent documents contain the frequencies of occurrences of standard syntactic dependencies and the cosine similarity is applied to determine the attribution of authorship of a document. They indicate that LSD surrounding the named entities can achieve good predictive performance and suggest to use their idea for other types of documents.

Dalen-Oskam [1] performed experiments to analyze the stylistic function of the use of names in literary texts, expecting to compare the use and function of names through the works, genres, time periods, cultures and languages. He states that primary function of names is to identify people, places or objects. Besides it is mentioned that names can play another role in a literary genre (fiction): the names allow to make the fiction more realistic. Manipulation of this element keeps the author's expectation. In one of the experiments it was found that set of texts with the highest percentage of names usage were books for children or young persons. It suggests that probable cause of this high percentage is due to the fact that in this type of texts the names are not replaced by pronouns, probably to facilitate the understanding of the text. However, this hypothesis is not completely confirmed. Their conclusions claim that names can be a stylistic element of comparison between languages.

Stylometric features used in authorship attribution studies should be independent from the literary genre, topic, timing and other factors [7]. Moreover, they argue that features must have a reasonable frequency of occurrence in order to facilitate statistical analysis. The stylometric features which fulfill these considerations are the well-known function words. On the other hand, [5] tries to identify universal features for text categorization using a measure of "stability". They concluded that function words are unstable in sense that such words can be easily replaced with their syntactic equivalents, without affecting meaning of text. So they are an excellent universal feature for text categorization based on style. In this paper, we do not exploit the function words, but in general it is considered that their combinations and sequences are very good stylometric feature.

Another factor influencing degree of loss of accuracy in classifiers is documented in [6]: presentation of speech. Speech can be presented in direct form and indirect form. The choice has implications for lexical and syntactic levels. Leech also indicates that authors have others options such as Free Direct Speech (FDS), Narrative Report of Speech Acts (NRSA) and Free Indirect Speech (FIS). All these forms may occur frequently in genre of fiction.

3 Methodology

3.1 Corpus Selection and Preparation

To carry out this study, we used a corpus of 7 authors of fiction [13]. All authors spoke and wrote in English, all novels were obtained from Gutenberg Project. See Table 3 for details.

All punctuation marks were deleted from the texts using regular expressions, keeping only digits and words. Named Entity Recognition was made on complete novels using a NER module from NLTK. This module produces tags for each word, where the tags related with named entities are Proper Noun Singular (NNP) and Proper Noun Plural (NNPS). For each author, five novels were selected with the largest number of named entities. At the end of this process, there are two sets with the same novels: one containing Named Entities and the other set without them (i.e., we eliminated all NE form one set of novels).

3.2   Creating Samples and Selection of N-Grams

All novels were divided into blocks of 10,000 terms, number of blocks in each novel depends on length of the document. From each block, character n-grams, POS n-grams and word n-grams were extracted with n equal to 1, 2 and 3 (unigrams, 2-grams and 3-grams). N-grams with frequency 1 were discarded. Table 4 shows number of 2-grams and 3-grams used by the authors in their 5 novels.

3.3   Vector Space Model

Further, vector space models were created for each author. Table 5 shows the abstracted representation of the vector space models.

Table 3. Corpus for the study.

Authors	Novels
B. Tarkington	13
C. Dickens	13
F. Marryat	13
G. MacDonald	13
G. Vaisey	13
L. Tracy	13
M. Twain	13

Table 4. N-grams per author.

Authors	2-grams	3-grams
Tarkington	13,749	8,045
Dickens	31,708	24,319
Marryat	19,197	12,290
Macdonald	19,120	10,939
Vaizey	12,574	5,899
Tracy	10,157	4,232
Twain	21,427	12,290

Table 5. Abstracted representation of the vector space model

Features (n-grams)						Novel
B_{11}	B_{12}	B_{13}	B_{14}	...	B_{1m}	Ambersons
B_{21}	B_{22}	B_{23}	B_{24}	...	B_{2m}	Gentleman
...	...	...	...	...	...	....
B_{n1}	B_{n2}	B_{n3}	B_{n4}	...	B_{nm}	Turmoil

We used three profile sizes (500, 2,000 and 4,000). If number of features is greater than a profile size then only the most frequent n-grams were selected, otherwise, all features were used for classification. If we do not mention the profile size, then the number of features is less than 500.

3.4   Classification

Three machine learning algorithms were used in the experiments: NB (Naive Bayes), J48 (in some cases) and SVM (Support Vector Machines). These algorithms are used typically in the NLP tasks. The data was divided into two sets: 80% for training and 20% for test. The aim of the classifiers after training is to determine to what author belong the blocks from the test set. The experiments were conducted for every author. If Named Entities do not affect the classifiers, then there will be no difference using them or discarding them.

4   Results

Figure 1 shows the results using character n-grams for texts with and without NEs. We also present the table for SVM classifier (Table 6).

Figure 2 shows results using POS n-grams.

Figures 3, 4, 5, 6, 7, 8 and 9 show results using word n-grams, texts with and without Named Entities and most frequent n-grams.

5   Discussion

Trend in testing character n-grams was decreasing in accuracy in text without named entities. Nevertheless, George Vaizey shows an increase without NE using 3-grams in all classifiers.

Note that character n-grams is the most widely used baseline for the authorship attribution. The best results are usually achieved using the SVM classifier.

Trend in testing POS tags n-grams was the same and again, George Vaizey shows an increase without NE using 2-grams and 3-grams in all classifiers.

The same pattern was observed in word n-grams: a decrease in accuracy in most instances using text without named entities. Few cases occurred with opposite behavior: Dickens using 3-grams, SVM and 500 features, Marryat using 3-grams, NB and 2,000 features, Macdonald using 3-grams, SVM and 4,000 features, Vaizey using 3-grams, any amount of features in all classifiers and Tracy using 3-grams, J48 and any amount of features.

We also present the comparative table for the SVM classifier (Table 7). Note that in this table we also include the union of all word n-grams as features.

Recall that novels are characterized by n-grams and their frequencies. N-grams are sequences of elements taken in the order that they appear in a text. Consider the sentence *"Enrique Peña Nieto es el presidente de México"* (*Enrique Peña Nieto is the*

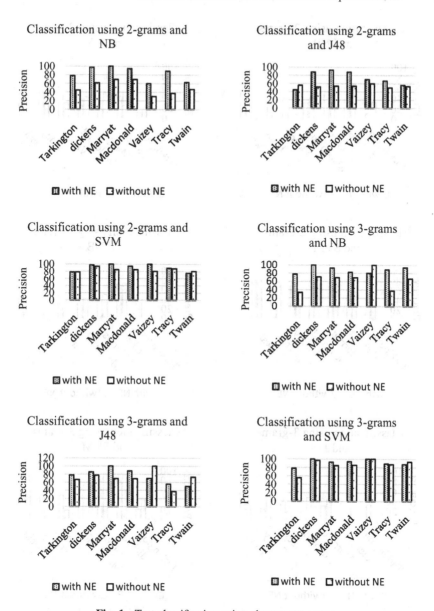

Fig. 1. Test classification using character n-grams

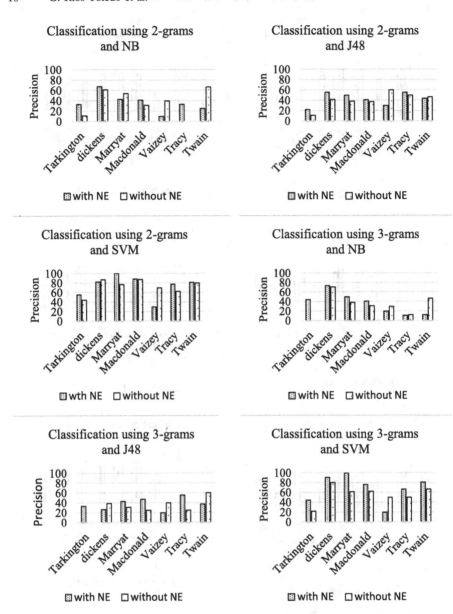

Fig. 2. Test classification using POS n-grams

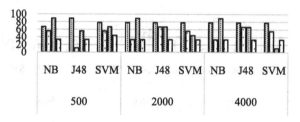

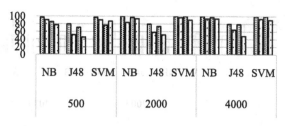

☒ 2 and 3-grams with NE   ☐ 2 and 3-grams without NE

Fig. 3. Test using word n-grams for Tarkington

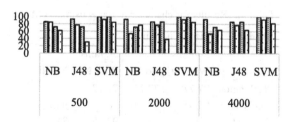

☒ 2 and 3-grams with NE   ☐ 2 and 3-grams without NE

Fig. 4. Test using word n-grams for Dickens

☒ 2 and 3-grams with NE   ☐ 2 and 3-grams without NE

Fig. 5. Test using word n-grams for Marryat

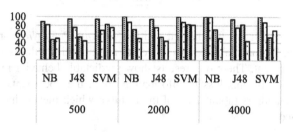

☒ 2 and 3-grams with NE   ☐ 2 and 3-grams without NE

Fig. 6. Test using word n-grams for Macdonald

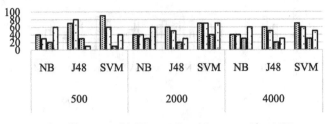

▦ 2 and 3-grams with NE   ▢ 2 and 3-grams without NE

Fig. 7. Test using word n-grams for Vaizey.

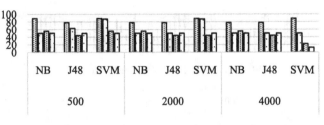

▦ 2 and 3-grams with NE   ▢ 2 and 3-grams without NE

Fig. 8. Test using word n-grams for Tracy.

Table 6. Results for character n-grams using SVM.

Author	Size of n-grams			
	2-grams		3-grams	
	With NE	No NE	With NE	No NE
Tarkington	77.77	77.77	77.77	55.55
Dickens	97.05	93.54	100	96.77
Marryat	100	84.61	92.85	84.61
Macdonald	94.11	84.61	94.11	85.61
Vaizey	100	80.00	100	100
Tracy	88.88	87.50	88.88	87.50
Twain	75.00	80.00	87.50	93.33

president of Mexico). It has two named entities (*Enrique-Peña-Nieto* and *México*). If we used character 2-grams, all n-grams related to these entities will disappear from the vector of the document. Therefore, results show predictable behavior in loss accuracy in classifiers caused by this loss of information about the document. Atypical cases occur for specific authors (about 10% of the results), which means that more detailed studies are needed.

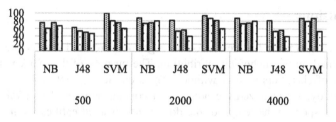

2 and 3-grams with NE   2 and 3-grams without NE

Fig. 9. Test using word n-grams for Twain.

Table 7. Word n-grams per author using SVM ("+NE" means "with NE", "–NE" means "without NE").

Author	Profile size	Size of n-grams							
		1		2		3		Union (1–2–3)	
		+NE	–NE	+NE	–NE	+NE	–NE	+NE	–NE
Tarkington	500	88.88	55.55	77.77	55.55	66.66	44.44	88.88	44.44
	2000	77.77	55.55	77.77	55.55	44.44	33.33	77.77	55.55
	4000	77.77	55.55	77.77	55.55	11.11	33.33	77.77	44.44
Dickens	500	100	93.54	97.05	90.32	76.47	87.09	100	96.77
	2000	100	100	100	96.77	100	90.32	100	96.77
	4000	100	96.77	100	93.54	100	90.32	100	96.77
Marryat	500	100	92.30	100	92.30	100	84.61	100	92.30
	2000	100	92.30	100	92.30	100	84.61	100	92.30
	4000	100	84.61	100	92.30	100	81.81	100	92.30
Macdonald	500	94.11	92.30	94.11	68.75	82.35	75.00	94.11	81.25
	2000	94.11	92.30	100	87.50	82.35	81.25	94.11	93.75
	4000	94.11	84.61	100	87.50	52.84	68.75	94.11	93.75
Vaizey	500	90.00	90.00	90.00	60.00	10.00	40.00	90.00	90.00
	2000	80.00	100	70.00	70.00	40.00	70.00	80.00	90.00
	4000	70.00	90.00	70.00	60.00	30.00	50.00	80.00	90.00
Tracy	500	88.88	87.50	88.88	87.50	55.55	50.00	88.88	87.50
	2000	88.88	87.50	88.88	87.50	44.44	50.00	88.88	87.50
	4000	88.88	87.50	88.88	50.00	22.22	12.50	88.88	62.50
Twain	500	93.75	93.33	100	80.00	75.00	60.00	100	93.33
	2000	100	93.33	93.75	86.66	81.25	60.00	93.75	80.00
	4000	100	93.33	87.50	80.00	87.50	53.33	100	80.00

6 Conclusions

In this work, stylometric features based on n-grams were used for document characterization aimed on the authorship attribution. The purpose of this work is to analyze the behavior of classifiers with or without named entities present in the documents.

In this study, we analyzed the novels that contain between 4 and 7% of named entities with respect to the length of the documents. Named entities are formed by at least one term and they may appear at least once on the text.

Named entities contain important information for a correct classification of a document, but how do they affect the stylistic analysis? That is, if named entities are deleted from the text then generally it occurs a decrease in the accuracy of classifiers. About 90% of the results confirm this fact. By eliminating named entities from texts a number of n-grams and their frequencies disappear from statistical data, consequently there is a loss of important information for correct classification of the documents.

In future work it will be interesting to try word embeddings [2] or graph-based features [3] and analyze the influence of the corpus itself [9]. We will further investigate whether deep learning-based methods [19, 20] and personality detection [8] can improve the performance of our framework.

Acknowledgements. We would like to thank the support of Mexican government (CONACYT project 240844, SNI, SIP IPN projects 20161947, 20161958).

References

1. van Dalen-Oskam, K.: Names in novels: an experiment in computational stylistics. Literary Linguist. Comput. **28**(2), 359–370 (2013)
2. Gómez-Adorno, H., Markov, I., Sidorov, G., Posadas-Durán, J.P., Sanchez-Perez, M.A., Chanona-Hernandez, L.: Improving feature representation based on a neural network for author profiling in social media texts. Comput. Intell. Neurosci. **2016** (2016)
3. Gómez-Adorno, H., Sidorov, G., Pinto, D., Markov, I.: A graph based authorship identification approach. Working Notes Papers of the CLEF 2015 Evaluation Labs. CEUR Workshop Proceedings, vol. 1391. CEUR (2015)
4. Goodman, R., Hahn, M., Marella, M., Ojar, C., Westcott, S.: The use of stylometry for email author identification: a feasibility study. Pace Pacing Clin. Electrophysiol., 1–7 (2007)
5. Koppel, M., Akiva, N., Dagan, I.: A corpus-independent feature set for style-based text categorization. Science, 1263–1276 (2002)
6. Leech, G.N.: Style in Fiction (1982)
7. Lucic, A., Blake, C.L.: A syntactic characterization of authorship style surrounding proper names. Digit. Scholarsh. Humanit. **30**(1), 53–70 (2015)
8. Majumder, N., Poria, S., Gelbukh, A., Cambria, E.: Deep learning based document modeling for personality detection from text. IEEE Intell. Syst. **32**(2), 74–79 (2017)
9. Markov, I., Gómez-Adorno, H., Sidorov, G., Gelbukh, A.: Adapting cross-genre author profiling to language and corpus. Working Notes Papers of the CLEF 2016 Evaluation Labs. CEUR Workshop Proceedings, vol. 1609, pp. 947–955. CLEF and CEUR-WS.org (2016)
10. Mikros, G.K., Argiri, E.K.: Investigating topic influence in authorship attribution, vol. 276 (2007)

11. Nadeau, D.: A survey of named entity recognition and classification. Linguisticae Investigationes **30**, 3–26 (2007)
12. Rudman, J.: The state of authorship attribution studies: some problems and solutions. Comput. Humanit. **31**(4), 351–365 (1997)
13. Sidorov, G., Velasquez, F., Stamatatos, E., Gelbukh, A., Chanona-Hernández, L.: Syntactic n-grams as machine learning features for natural language processing. Expert Syst. Appl. **41** (3), 853–860 (2014)
14. Sidorov, G., Ibarra Romero, M., Markov, I., Guzman Cabrera, R., Chanona-Hernández, L., Velásquez, F.: Automatic detection of similarity of programs in karel programming language based on natural language processing techniques. Computación y Systemas **20**(2), 279–288 (2016)
15. Sidorov, G., Ibarra Romero, M., Markov, I., Guzman Cabrera, R., Chanona-Hernández, L., Velásquez, F.: Measuring similarity between karel programs using character and word n-grams. Program. Comput. Softw. **43** (accepted, 2017)
16. Stamatatos, E.: A survey of modern authorship attribution methods. J. Am. Soc. Inform. Sci. Technol. **60**, 538–556 (2009)
17. Tanguy, L., Sajous, F., Calderone, B., Hathout, N.: Authorship attribution: using rich linguistic features when training data is scarce. Working Notes Papers of the CLEF 2012 Evaluation Labs, pp. 1–12 (2012)
18. Tanguy, L., Urieli, A., Calderone, B., Hathout, N., Sajous, F.: A multitude of linguistically-rich features for authorship attribution. In: CEUR Workshop Proceedings, vol. 1177 (2011)
19. Poria, S., Cambria, E., Gelbukh, A.: Deep convolutional neural network textual features and multiple kernel learning for utterance-level multimodal sentiment analysis. In: EMNLP 2015, pp. 2539–2544 (2015)
20. Poria, S., Chaturvedi, I., Cambria, E., Hussain, A.: Convolutional MKL based multimodal emotion recognition and sentiment analysis. In 2016 IEEE 16th International Conference on Data Mining (ICDM), pp. 439–448 (2016)

A Compact Representation for Cross-Domain Short Text Clustering

Alba Núñez-Reyes[1,2], Esaú Villatoro-Tello[2(✉)], Gabriela Ramírez-de-la-Rosa[2],
and Christian Sánchez-Sánchez[2]

[1] Maestría en Diseño, Información y Comunicación (MADIC),
División de Ciencias de la Comunicación y Diseño,
Universidad Autónoma Metropolitana (UAM) Unidad Cuajimalpa,
Mexico City, Mexico
ar.nunezreyes@gmail.com
[2] Language and Reasoning Research Group, Information Technologies Department,
Universidad Autónoma Metropolitana (UAM) Unidad Cuajimalpa,
Mexico City, Mexico
{evillatoro,gramirez,csanchez}@correo.cua.uam.mx

Abstract. Nowadays, Twitter depicts a rich source of on-line reviews, ratings, recommendations, and other forms of opinion expressions. This scenario has created the compelling demand to develop innovative mechanisms to store, search, organize and analyze all this data automatically. Unfortunately, it is seldom available to have enough labeled data in Twitter, because of the cost of the process or due to the impossibility to obtain them, given the rapid growing and change of this kind of media. To avoid such limitations, *unsupervised categorization strategies* are employed. In this paper we face the problem of cross-domain short text clustering through a compact representation that allows us to avoid the problems that arise with the high dimensionality and sparseness of vocabulary. Our experiments, conducted on a cross-domain scenario using very short texts, indicate that the proposed representation allows to generate high quality groups, according to the value of Silhouette coefficient obtained.

Keywords: Short text clustering · Unsupervised categorization · Cross-domain clustering · Compact text representation · Silhouette coefficient

1 Introduction

Nowadays, microblogging media has become a universal tool for sharing and obtaining information from millions of people. For instance, Twitter represents a rich source of trends, reviews, ratings, recommendations, and many other forms of online opinion expressions. This scenario has created a compelling demand for innovative mechanisms to automatically store, search, organize and analyze all this data. An example of such mechanisms are *topic detection* methods, which implies the automatic discovery of thematic-related groups into free-text documents, namely *tweets*.

© Springer International Publishing AG 2017
G. Sidorov and O. Herrera-Alcántara (Eds.): MICAI 2016, Part I, LNAI 10061, pp. 16–26, 2017.
DOI: 10.1007/978-3-319-62434-1_2

Traditional approaches for topic detection, such as supervised classification strategies, assume that training and test documents are drawn from the same distribution. However, in many cases this scenario is unreal, especially in datasets extracted from Twitter. Thus, the process of using a statistical model trained in one (source) domain, for categorizing information contained in a different (target) domain, requires bridging the gab between the two domains to facilitate the knowledge transfer[1]. Accordingly, *cross-domain clustering* represents an unsupervised process where instances from the target domain are categorized using information obtained from the formed clusters within the source domain [2–5].

In this paper we describe an analysis on the pertinence of using a very compact representation for texts in a cross-domain clustering scenario. Thus, we employed a representation based on the transition point (TP) technique, which dictates that terms surrounding the TP value are closely related to the conceptual content of a document; the TP is located at the middle point between the terms with most and less frequency. Therefore, we hypothesise that the terms whose frequencies are closer to the TP can be used as features to represent a document to transfer the knowledge from one domain to another. Although this technique has been extensively validated for solving Natural Language Processing (NLP) tasks such as text clustering [6] and text classification [7]; a common characteristic among these research works is that experiments were performed using formal documents, *i.e.*, news reports, books, articles, abstracts, etc. Currently, to the best of our knowledge, there is no formal study regarding the evaluation on the pertinence of a representation based on TP for a scenario with the following characteristics: *(i)* documents are very short texts, specifically Twitter posts, *(ii)* documents belong to a very dynamic and constantly growing environment, and, *(iii)* a proposal where a representation that fits to the distribution of unknown domains is used, *i.e.*, cross-domain topic detection. According to these observations, our research looks for answers to the following questions: *how useful is a compact document representation based on the TP for topics detection in Twitter?* and, *to what extent can be improved the clustering quality of tweets, by means of the acquired knowledge from other domains?*

The rest of the paper is organized as follows. Section 2 describes recent approaches in domain adaptation for text clustering in short texts. Section 3 explains our experimental methodology, and Sect. 4 presents the obtained results. Finally, Sect. 5 depicts our conclusions and some ideas for future work.

2   Related Work

Several approaches have been proposed for the automatic topic detection problem. The most popular proposal considers the application of *supervised strategies* to infer a classification function from a training hand-labelled set (*i.e., source* domain), and then, the learnt function is used for predicting the category of new unlabeled documents (*i.e., target* domain) [8]. As expected, the more the number of labeled documents, the better the results in the target distribution,

---

[1] A research problem known as *domain adaptation* [1].

and consequently the categorization performance. Unfortunately, as we previously mentioned, for many real life tasks, such as Twitter data analysis, having enough labeled data is uncommon, and often, too expensive or some times even impossible to obtain given the rapid growing and change of such media. As a consequence of this limitations, *unsupervised strategies* are employed.

In the work described in [9], authors proposed a method that allows the identification of news topics in Twitter. In general the system works as follows: *(i)* tweets are obtained by means of querying specific keywords, then, *(ii)* a supervised classifier distinguishes between news-tweets and junk-tweets, *(iii)* news-tweets are clustered into topics using a leader-follower algorithm, which requires a set of initial handpicked tweets to lead the algorithm; and finally, *(iv)* a geo-tag is assigned to tweets for visualizing the results to the user. A key difference between this work and ours is that we do not require training documents, neither a set of manually picked tweets for building the groups.

In Atefeh et al. [10], authors provide an extensive review of several methods for topic detection in Twitter media. Generally speaking, the topic detection methods are categorized based on the following characteristics: *(i)* whether the topics are known a priori or not, *(ii)* if the employed approach is supervised, unsupervised or hybrid, and, *(iii)* if a retrospective analysis is needed or if the recently acquired data need to be analysed to discover new topics. Most of the works described in [10] employ a traditional Bag-of-Terms representation, in which the terms vary from the full vocabulary to specific named entities and even to some other probabilistic representations (*e.g.,* language models). Regarding similarity metrics, the most common are: Euclidean distance, Pearson's correlation coefficient, cosine similarity and others like Hellinger distance and clustering index. It is worth mentioning that most of these works assume an in-domain scenario, *i.e.,* data were drawn from the same distribution. Contrastingly, our experiments are conducted on a cross-domain configuration, and our proposal of a compact representation depicts a balance between the high dimensionality and the sparseness of vocabulary.

Concerning to the cross-domain clustering, there has been a lesser amount of research, and even less for cross-domain text clustering [3,5]. In [3] the authors propose learning from a subspace of common knowledge while at the same time clustering both the source domain and target domain, such that the data distribution of different domains are similar when projected in the subspace. In [5] authors propose an iterative clustering method that allows transfer the knowledge of distributions of clusters from the source domain to the target domain, in addition, its approach uses a density based method for clustering the target domain. In these works, the employed datasets for experimentation are formal documents (*e.g.,* news reports) and the number of groups in both domains have to be known a priori. In our work, we use more challenging data, namely tweets, and, as in real life, the number of existing clusters in both domains are unknown.

In summary, most of the previous work apply either a supervised or an unsupervised categorization strategy that assumes a similar distribution of the data, hence most of the reported experiments are performed under an in-domain scenario using large-formal documents. On the contrary, our proposal faces the problem of cross-domain clustering by means of using a compact representation that efficiently deals with the vocabulary high dimensionality and sparseness of short text documents.

3   Experimental Methodology

In this section we describe our proposed methodology for tackling the problem of cross-domain short text clustering. Firstly, we explain the pre-processing operations applied to our data, then we briefly report how the compact representation was computed; and finally, we describe the employed clustering method as well as the evaluation metric considered for reporting our experimental results.

3.1   Pre-processing Stage

As pre-processing steps we applied the following operations to each tweet contained in the employed dataset: *(1)* tweets are transformed to lowercase; *(2)* user mentions (*i.e.*, @USER), hashtags (*i.e.*, #HASHTAG), and outgoing links are deleted from the tweet; *(3)* all punctuation mark as well as emoticons are deleted; *(4)* a stemming process is applied using the Porter algorithm [11]; and, *(5)* all stopwords are removed.

3.2   Document Representation

As mentioned before, we propose to use a compact representation for tackling the problem of cross-domain short texts clustering. Accordingly, we employed the Transition Point (TP) technique as a key aspect in our proposed solution. It is known that the TP depicts a frequency value that divides the vocabulary of a document into those terms with high and low frequency values respectively. This technique is based on the Zipf law of word occurrences [12,13]. From these studies it is possible to hypothesise that those terms whose frequency value is closer to the *tp* factor, are strongly related to the main conceptual content of a document, and therefore are good elements for its representation. A typical formula for computing the *tp* value is shown in expression 1.

$$tp_T = \frac{\sqrt{8 * I_1 + 1} - 1}{2} \tag{1}$$

where I_1 represents the number of hapax[2] contained in the collection vocabulary. Once the *tp* is defined, a document is then represented by means of a BoW-like[3] technique considering only those words near to the *tp* frequency value. In our experiments, we employ a fixed percentage of terms near to the *tp* frequency value, particularly 40%.

---

[2] A word that occurs just once within a text.
[3] Bag-of-Words representation.

As described in [6], the *tp* technique has been employed as a term selection strategy in different NLP related tasks. However, as far as we know, it has never been applied for representing Twitter posts, for the task of cross-domain clustering.

3.3 Clustering Method

As the main clustering method we employed the well known k-means algorithm. The k-means algorithm is an iterative approach that executes two basic steps: first, assigns documents to existing centroids and second, reduces the divergence by the re-estimation of the centroids based on the current assignment of documents.

Although the k-means method has the disadvantage of requiring a manually-set parameter by the user, *i.e.*, the number of groups (k), we decided to use this algorithm since it has demonstrated to be an effective method for many clustering related tasks [14]. The used similarity metric was the Euclidean distance[4].

3.4 Evaluation

Given that the number of existing topics within the data are unknown, supervised evaluation metrics such as *accuracy, F-score, precision* or *recall* can not be applied. Nevertheless, it is necessary to measure the quality of formed groups, aiming at determining the clustering tendencies of the data, *i.e.*, distinguishing whether (or not) a random structure actually exists in the data.

Accordingly, as evaluation measure we employ the popular metric of silhouette coefficient [15], which combines the concepts of cohesion and separation for each point of a clusters. As it is known, the cluster's cohesion measures how closely the objects in a cluster are related among them. Whilst cluster's separation measures how well a cluster is distinguished from other clusters. The silhouette coefficient value varies from -1 to 1. A negative silhouette value depicts an undesirable result, meaning a bad clustering; on the contrary, positive values define a better quality in the clustering result, which is a preferable performance.

4   Empirical Evaluation and Results

In order to answer our stated research questions, we employed a dataset of tweets in English and Spanish gathered for the Online Reputation Laboratory (RepLap[5]). For the experiments we used the subset belonging to the topic detection task in its 2013 edition [16]. This dataset contains tweets from four different domains: Automotive (Au), Banking (Ba), Music (Mu) and University (Un). In Table 1 some statistics of this dataset are shown.

From Table 1 can be observed some interesting facts regarding the nature of the dataset. For instance, the comparison of the data across domains shows that

---

[4] We employed the k-means as implemented in http://scikit-learn.org/.
[5] http://nlp.uned.es/replab2013/.

Table 1. Statistics for the dataset used for the experimental evaluation. *Au*, *Ba*, *Mu* and *Un* refer to Automotive, Banking, Music and University, respectively.

	Spanish				English			
	Au	*Ba*	*Mu*	*Un*	*Au*	*Ba*	*Mu*	*Un*
Avg. words per tweet	9.9	10.1	9.9	10.0	10.6	11.3	10.0	10.9
Avg. vocabulary per tweet	9.5	9.8	9.5	9.7	10.0	10.8	9.5	10.4
Avg. tweet length (chars.)	63.8	69.5	62.2	68.7	60.6	66.4	56.6	65.9
Avg. words length per tweet	6.4	6.9	6.3	6.9	5.7	5.9	5.6	6.1
Total number of tweets	5735	6552	8288	1056	33453	14378	33016	17863

tweets from the Banking domain have more words than the rest of the domains (in both languages); however the size of the vocabulary per tweet, in average, is similar across the four domains. Another interesting statistic is that tweets in Spanish have less number of words than tweets in English, but the number of English tweets is four times the sample in Spanish. Additionally, notice that the smaller domain (according to the number of tweets) in Spanish is University; while the smaller domain in English is Banking followed by University.

For the empirical evaluation two main set of experiments were designed. The first set evaluates the pertinence of the proposed representation, *i.e.* the TP approach, in a in-domain clustering scenario. The second set of experiments evaluates if the representation learned from a source domain, is able to produce quality clusters in a target domain, *i.e.*, cross-domain clustering. Following subsections describe the setup configuration as well as the obtained results.

4.1   In-Domain Clustering Experiments

The main goal of this set of experiments is to find out if the compact representation, based on the TP, is useful for topic detection in Twitter. As mentioned in Sect. 3.3, as clustering algorithm we employed the k-means method, using six different values of $k = \{5, 10, 15, 20, 25, 30\}$.

We established the maximum number of groups $k = 30$ because we considered this number small enough for a posterior analysis of the data by an online reputation manager; otherwise, the analysis could become very tedious. It is important to mention that RepLab organizers provided information regarding the number of *named entities* contained in each domain, for instance, some of the entities contained in the Automotive domain are: Nissan, Honda, BMW, etc. The quantity of entities in each domain is: 10 for Music, 11 for Banking, 19 for University and 21 for Automotive. Although this information was known a priori, it was not used in our experiments, but provides a referential parameter regarding the number of clusters that may be useful in a real case scenario.

As we are proposing a compact representation, we selected as a baseline a representation based on the *bag-of-words* (BOW) technique. As known, this type of representation considers the entire vocabulary for representing each document.

Results for *in-domain* experiments, both for Spanish and English languages, can be seen in Tables 2 and 3 respectively. Obtained results are reported in terms of the silhouette coefficient (SC). Notice that we compare the quality of the formed clusters for the two types of representation, *BOW* and *TP*, for each domain, as well as for the 6 different values of k. According to the SC values, the proposed compact representation outperforms the baseline representation. Interestingly, we can observe a difference between SC values for Spanish and English languages, mainly for University and Banking domains, where the quality of formed groups is better in Spanish than in English. This difference may has been caused by the size of the datasets between the two languages. In consequence, the number of elements contained into the clusters formed for the English data is bigger and thus the clusters may contain tweets with a higher diversity of topics.

4.2 Cross-Domain Clustering Experiments

Previous experiments demonstrate that the employed compact representation improves the performance of the clustering in very short texts. Taking this into

Table 2. Silhouette coefficient values for in-domain clustering for tweets in Spanish language. In the third row, the vector's dimension for each type of representation.

k	Automotive		Banking		Music		University	
	BOW	*TP*	*BOW*	*TP*	*BOW*	*TP*	*BOW*	*TP*
	13944	86	14284	79	14089	114	4419	22
5	0.008	0.109	0.031	0.197	0.029	0.143	0.028	0.251
10	0.012	0.129	0.035	0.205	0.037	0.143	0.026	0.371
15	−0.007	0.137	0.018	0.200	0.04	0.178	0.013	0.407
20	−0.016	0.142	0.013	0.217	0.038	**0.179**	0.020	0.452
25	0.007	0.152	0.021	0.224	0.016	0.179	0.020	0.483
30	−0.219	**0.163**	−0.004	**0.233**	0.024	0.178	−0.002	**0.503**

Table 3. Silhouette coefficient values for in-domain clustering for tweets in English language. In the third row, the vector's dimension for each type of representation.

k	Automotive		Banking		Music		University	
	BOW	*TP*	*BOW*	*TP*	*BOW*	*TP*	*BOW*	*TP*
	30358	527	17988	310	22356	502	22593	327
5	0.120	0.061	0.01	0.085	0.023	**0.126**	0.010	0.083
10	**0.130**	0.088	0.021	0.089	0.028	0.120	0.021	**0.095**
15	0.102	0.094	0.003	0.079	0.030	0.060	0.005	0.067
20	0.017	0.064	0.019	**0.091**	0.030	0.072	0.019	0.078
25	−0.116	0.002	0.016	0.090	0.040	0.118	0.016	0.059
30	0.113	0.009	0.003	0.090	0.024	0.088	−0.003	0.056

account, for the next set of experiments we used the *TP* strategy for representing documents. The goal of the *cross-domain* clustering scenario is to determinate the robustness of the acquired knowledge from a source domain into a target domain. Results for the cross-domain experiments are shown in Tables 4 and 5 for Spanish and English languages respectively.

Table 4. Silhouette coefficient values for cross-domain clustering for tweets in Spanish language. The target domain is given in the first row and the source domain is indicated by *Au*, *Ba*, *Mu* and *Un* to refer to Automotive, Banking, Music and University, respectively.

k	Automotive			Banking			Music			University		
	Ba	*Mu*	*Un*	*Au*	*Mu*	*Un*	*Au*	*Ba*	*Un*	*Au*	*Ba*	*Mu*
5	0.27	0.27	0.65	0.24	0.26	0.67	0.25	0.29	0.66	0.24	0.28	0.29
10	0.30	0.29	0.81	0.27	0.31	0.80	0.27	0.33	0.82	0.27	0.32	0.30
15	0.32	0.32	0.87	0.31	0.33	0.86	0.30	0.36	0.87	0.30	0.36	0.32
20	0.35	0.34	0.89	0.32	0.38	0.88	0.32	0.38	0.89	0.33	0.37	0.36
25	0.38	0.35	0.90	0.35	0.40	0.90	0.33	0.42	0.91	0.37	0.42	0.39
30	0.40	0.37	**0.92**	0.37	0.43	**0.91**	0.36	0.44	**0.93**	0.38	**0.43**	0.42

Table 5. Silhouette coefficient values for cross-domain clustering for tweets in English language. The target domain is given in the first row and the source domain is indicated by *Au*, *Ba*, *Mu* and *Un* to refer to Automotive, Banking, Music and University, respectively.

k	Automotive			Banking			Music			University		
	Ba	*Mu*	*Un*	*Au*	*Mu*	*Un*	*Au*	*Ba*	*Un*	*Au*	*Ba*	*Mu*
5	0.13	**0.14**	0.12	0.10	0.14	0.10	0.10	0.13	0.13	0.11	**0.15**	0.13
10	0.11	0.12	0.13	0.10	**0.15**	0.10	0.11	0.11	0.12	0.11	0.12	0.11
15	0.11	0.13	0.10	0.09	**0.15**	0.11	0.09	0.11	0.13	0.10	0.13	0.09
20	0.13	0.13	0.10	0.11	0.13	0.11	0.12	0.13	0.12	0.10	0.13	0.13
25	0.13	0.12	0.11	0.10	0.14	0.12	0.10	0.13	0.12	0.11	0.14	0.12
30	**0.14**	0.13	0.11	0.10	0.13	0.12	0.09	**0.14**	**0.14**	0.10	0.14	0.13

Several observations can be made from these results; firstly, similarly to the in-domain experiments, the quality of the clusters are better for Spanish than for English. The advantage of representing a domain in terms of another one is significantly better for the Spanish language. For example, for the *Music* (Mu) domain, the best in-domain performance was of $SC = 0.179$ with $k = 20$ (see Table 2), whilst for the cross-domain scenario the obtained result is $SC = 0.930$

Table 6. Silhouette coefficient values for cross-domain clustering of two source domains for Spanish language. The target domain is given in the first row and the source domain is indicated by *Au*, *Ba*, *Mu* and *Un* to refer to Automotive, Banking, Music and University, respectively. The - symbol indicates that the target domain does not contain any terms from the source domain.

k	Automotive			Banking			Music			University		
	BaMu	*BaUn*	*MuUn*	*AuMu*	*AuUn*	*MuUn*	*AuBa*	*AuUn*	*BaUn*	*AuBa*	*AuMu*	*BaMu*
5	0.24	0.25	0.26	0.26	0.21	0.25	-	0.22	0.30	-	0.22	0.23
10	0.26	0.28	0.29	0.26	0.24	0.30	-	0.26	0.30	-	0.24	0.30
15	0.28	0.31	0.31	0.25	0.28	0.34	-	0.28	0.35	-	0.27	0.26
20	0.28	0.34	0.33	0.28	0.29	0.37	-	0.29	0.36	-	0.28	0.31
25	0.31	0.37	0.34	0.29	0.31	0.39	-	0.31	0.40	-	0.31	0.34
30	0.31	**0.38**	0.36	0.32	0.32	**0.41**	-	0.33	**0.41**	-	0.31	**0.36**

with $k = 30$ (see Table 4). The latter means that formed groups have good cohesion and good separability when knowledge from the University domain is considered to categorize tweets about Music.

In general, the knowledge extracted from the University domain turns out to be the best source domain for the Spanish language, however it was not the same for the English tweets. In Table 5 can been noticed that the improvement of using knowledge from other domains is smaller. For instance, SC values for the in-domain clusters formed for the Banking domain is $SC = 0.091$ with $k = 20$ (see Table 3). However, when using Music as source domain, the quality of the formed clusters in the Banking data is improved by 6%, *i.e.*, $SC = 0.15$ with $k = 15$ (see Table 5). In addition, notice that for the Spanish experiments, the better results are more consistent with $k = 30$; contrastingly, for the English data there is not a clear tendency for the k value.

4.3   Are the More Domains the Better?

Our performed experiments in a *cross-domain* scenario indicate that the *TP* representation depicts an effective approach for detecting topics across different target domains. Hence, we design a third set of experiments aiming to explore to what extent the quality of the clustering can increase, when more than one domain are used as source data.

To perform this set of experiments, the compact vocabulary (based on the TP) was unified from two and from three source domains, then the combined vocabulary was used to represent one target domain. The obtained results for these experiments in Spanish tweets are shown in Tables 6 and 7. In general, it is not possible to further improve the quality of the formed groups (see Table 4), however, the obtained performance still is better that when the in-domain clustering is performed (see Table 2). We think that the produced detriment is due to the inclusion of noisy terms when more source domains are considered.

Table 7. Silhouette coefficient values for cross-domain clustering of three source domains for Spanish language. The target domain is given in the first row and the source domain is indicated by *Au*, *Ba*, *Mu* and *Un* to refer to Automotive, Banking, Music and University, respectively.

k	Automotive	Banking	Music	University
	BaMuUn	*AuMuUn*	*AuBaUn*	*AuBaMu*
5	0.23	0.22	0.26	0.25
10	0.24	0.26	0.30	0.24
15	0.26	0.27	0.31	0.21
20	0.27	0.29	0.33	0.27
25	0.29	0.31	0.35	**0.29**
30	**0.30**	**0.32**	**0.38**	0.25

5   Conclusions

In this paper we tackled the problem of cross-domain short text clustering, particularly topic detection in Twitter posts. We carried out a study on the pertinence of using a compact document representation, specifically a term selection method based on the Transition Point technique, which establishes that terms surrounding the transition point are good terms for capturing the conceptual content of a document.

Two research questions were stated at the beginning of this paper. First, we were interested in validating the usefulness of the TP representation for topic detection in Twitter. The performed experiments showed that the proposed compact representation allows to produce high quality groups, particularly for tweets in Spanish language. Second, we were interested in evaluating if the proposed representation was suitable to identify topics under a cross-domain scenario, *i.e.*, if the TP facilitates the knowledge transfer between the source and target domains. Our experiments showed that the proposed methodology produces high quality groups under a *cross-domain* scenario, specially for tweets in Spanish. Finally, an additional experiment, showed that the combination of the knowledge extracted from two or three domains, is not useful for improving the clustering results in the target domain.

As future work, we want to explore the sensitivity of the proposed compact representation to the number of selected terms by the TP technique. Furthermore, we want to incorporate contextual information, namely, word n-grams. Our intuition is that if some contextual information is added, specially for English tweets, the quality of the formed clusters could be improved. Additionally, we intent to determine the pertinence of the proposed representation for solving non-thematic text classification tasks, such as author profiling problems (*e.g.*, age, gender, and personality recognition), where not enough/reliable labeled data are available.

Acknowledgments. This work was partially funded by CONACyT: through project grant 258588, the Thematic Networks program (Language Technologies Thematic Network projects 260178, 271622), and scholarship number 587804. We also thank to UAM Cuajimalpa and SNI-CONACyT for their support.

References

1. Li, Q.: Literature survey: domain adaptation algorithms for natural language processing. Department of Computer Science, The Graduate Center, The City University of New York, pp. 8–10 (2012)
2. Dai, W., Yang, Q., Xue, G.-R., Yu, Y.: Self-taught clustering. In: Proceedings of the 25th International Conference on Machine Learning, ICML 2008, pp. 200–207. ACM, New York (2008)
3. Gu, Q., Zhou, J.: Learning the shared subspace for multi-task clustering and transductive transfer classification. In: 2009 Ninth IEEE International Conference on Data Mining, pp. 159–168, December 2009
4. Bhattacharya, I., Godbole, S., Joshi, S., Verma, A.: Cross-guided clustering: transfer of relevant supervision across tasks. ACM Trans. Knowl. Discov. Data **6**, 9:1–9:28 (2012)
5. Samanta, S., Selvan, A.T., Das, S.: Cross-domain clustering performed by transfer of knowledge across domains. In: 2013 Fourth National Conference on Computer Vision, Pattern Recognition, Image Processing and Graphics (NCVPRIPG), pp. 1–4, December 2013
6. Pinto, D., Jiménez-Salazar, H., Rosso, P.: Clustering abstracts of scientific texts using the transition point technique. In: Gelbukh, A. (ed.) CICLing 2006. LNCS, vol. 3878, pp. 536–546. Springer, Heidelberg (2006). doi:10.1007/11671299_55
7. Moyotl-Hernández, E., Jiménez-Salazar, H.: Enhancement of DTP feature selection method for text categorization. In: Gelbukh, A. (ed.) CICLing 2005. LNCS, vol. 3406, pp. 719–722. Springer, Heidelberg (2005). doi:10.1007/978-3-540-30586-6_80
8. Sebastiani, F.: Machine learning in automated text categorization. ACM Comput. Surv. **34**, 1–47 (2002)
9. Sankaranarayanan, J., Samet, H., Teitler, B.E., Lieberman, M.D., Sperling, J.: Twitterstand: news in tweets. In: Proceedings of the 17th ACM SIGSPATIAL International Conference on Advances in Geographic Information Systems, GIS 2009, pp. 42–51. ACM, New York (2009)
10. Atefeh, F., Khreich, W.: A survey of techniques for event detection in twitter. Comput. Intell. **31**, 132–164 (2015)
11. Porter, M.F.: An algorithm for suffix stripping. Program **14**(3), 130–137 (1980)
12. Zipf, G.: Human Behaviour and the Principle of Least-Effort. Addison-Wesley, Cambridge (1949)
13. Booth, A.D.: A law of occurrences for words of low frequency. Inf. Control **10**(4), 386–393 (1967)
14. Aggarwal, C.C., Zhai, C.: A survey of text clustering algorithms. In: Aggarwal, C., Zhai, C. (eds.) Mining Text Data, pp. 77–128. Springer US, Boston (2012)
15. Rousseeuw, P.J.: Silhouettes: graphical aid to the interpretation and validation of cluster analysis. J. Comput. Appl. Math. **20**, 53–65 (1987)
16. Amigó, E., et al.: Overview of replab 2013: evaluating online reputation monitoring systems. In: Forner, P., Müller, H., Paredes, R., Rosso, P., Stein, B. (eds.) CLEF 2013. LNCS, vol. 8138, pp. 333–352. Springer, Heidelberg (2013). doi:10.1007/978-3-642-40802-1_31

Characteristics of Most Frequent Spanish Verb-Noun Combinations

Olga Kolesnikova[1]([⊠]) and Alexander Gelbukh[2]

[1] ESCOM, Instituto Politécnico Nacional, 07738 Mexico City, Mexico
kolesolga@mail.com
[2] CIC, Instituto Politécnico Nacional, 07738 Mexico City, Mexico
http://www.gelbukh.com

Abstract. We study most frequent Spanish verb-noun combinations retrieved from the Spanish Web Corpus. We present the statistics of these combinations and analyze the degree of cohesiveness of their components. For the verb-noun combinations which turned out to be collocations, we determined their semantics in the form of lexical functions. We also observed what word senses are most typical for polysemous words in the verb-noun combinations under study and determined the level of generalization which characterizes the semantics of words in the combinations, that is, at what level of the hyperonymy-hyponymy tree they are located. The data collected by us can be used in various applications of natural language processing, especially, in predictive models in which most frequent cases are taken into account.

Keywords: Verb-noun combinations · Frequency · Collocations · Lexical functions · Hyperonymy

1 Introduction

Knowledge of lexical, syntactic, and semantic relations among words is important in many tasks of natural language processing, such as text analysis and generation, knowledge extraction, opinion mining (Cambria et al. 2014, 2016, Poria et al. 2013a, b, 2015, 2016c; Majumder et al. 2017), text summarization, question answering (Pakray 2010, 2011a, b), machine translation, polarity identification (Poria et al. 2017a, b, Chikersal et al. 2015), information retrieval (Poria et al. 2016a, b), among others.

In this paper, the focus of our research is on various characteristics and properties of Spanish most frequent verb-noun combinations of the pattern 'verb + noun as direct object'.

Verb-noun combinations in general are very common in any natural language, so a correct analysis of them accounts for an accurate understanding of large portions of texts. Therefore, we expect that our closer attention to most frequent verb-noun phrases will provide significant information useful for text automatic analysis as well as text automatic generation.

The objective of our study is four-fold. First, we aim at determining the degree of cohesiveness in verb-noun pairs, that is, we want to identify, what pairs are free combinations and what pairs are collocations. Second, we are to analyze the semantics

© Springer International Publishing AG 2017
G. Sidorov and O. Herrera-Alcántara (Eds.): MICAI 2016, Part I, LNAI 10061, pp. 27–40, 2017.
DOI: 10.1007/978-3-319-62434-1_3

of collocations in terms of lexical functions (Mel'čuk 1996, 2015). Third, we intend to observe what word senses are typical for polysemous words in most frequent verb-noun pairs, and fourth, determine the level of generalization of all words in our data, that is, at what level of hyperonymy-hyponymy tree they are located.

The rest of the paper is organized as follows. In Sect. 2 we describe the data under our analysis, in Sect. 3 we present the results of our observations, and Sect. 4 contains concluding remarks and ideas for future work.

2 Data

To fulfill the objectives of our work defined in the Introduction, we used the list of all verb-noun combinations extracted automatically from the Spanish Web Corpus in the SketchEngine (Kilgarriff et al. 2014; https://www.sketchengine.co.uk/).

The Spanish Web Corpus was compiled using a list of URLs provided by Serge Sharoff at the University of Leeds using the method described in (Sharoff 2006), designed to produce a general language resource. This corpus contains 116,900,060 tokens, it was part-of-speech tagged and lemmatized by means of the TreeTagger, a language-independent tool (Schmid 1995).

The number of verb-noun pairs retrieved from the Spanish Web Corpus was 997,575, and the list of these pairs was ordered by frequency in a descending way. Table 1 presents the initial part of this list. To give more examples of the list, we arranged them into three columns. For each verb-noun pair, its frequency in the Spanish Web Corpus is given.

Since the TreeTagger does not ensure 100% accuracy, the list includes erroneous pairs: in some of them, non-literal symbols are encountered (like « no in Table 1); there are also word pairs which do not correspond to the pattern 'verb + noun as direct object' like *decir no* (say no) in Table 1, and other pairs corresponding to non-expectant syntactic patters, see the discussion in Sect. 3.2.

There are other more complicated erroneous cases involving syntactic ambiguity: for instance, the pairs *haber estado* and *haber hecho* from Table 1 can be interpreted in Spanish as 'verb + noun' as well as 'verb + past participle'. *Haber estado* can be translated as 'had stayed' or 'had a state', and *haber hecho*, as 'had done' or 'had a fact'. It seems that the TreeTagger made a union of both options, therefore, the frequencies of *haber estado* and *haber hecho* do not correspond to the frequencies of these combinations in the interpretation 'verb + noun as direct object'. Further on, for the purpose of observing semantic characteristics of the data, we removed the erroneous combinations from the list.

As the original list is very big and includes almost a million of pairs (997,574 pairs to be exact), it seemed feasible for us to select a smaller portion of this list for a detailed semantic analysis, so we chose the first 1000 pairs. In these pairs, we found 61 erroneous combinations due to the TreeTagger errors mentioned above. After removing these errors, finally we obtained a list of 939 most frequent Spanish verb-noun combinations. All our observations and study described in the following sections was performed on this list.

Table 1. The initial section of the list of all verb-noun pairs of the Spanish Web Corpus ordered by frequency; for each pair its frequency is given; to present a larger part of the list, it was arranged in three columns

dar cuenta	9236	tener posibilidad	1603	prestar servicio	951
formar parte	7454	tener éxito	1596	hacer mes	950
tener lugar	6680	abrir puerta	1591	tener cuenta	944
tener derecho	5255	dar respuesta	1576	tomar parte	939
hacer falta	4827	merecer pena	1521	enviar mensaje	929
dar lugar	4180	tener carácter	1479	« La	927
hacer referencia	3252	tener suerte	1475	decir cosa	924
hacer año	3211	tener conocimiento	1396	decir no	922
tener problema	3075	jugar papel	1394	leer libro	910
hacer tiempo	3059	tener importancia	1372	ocupar lugar	905
tomar decisión	2781	hacer caso	1370	dar importancia	899
tener acceso	2773	llegar momento	1293	dar impresión	898
tener razón	2768	tener interés	1245	dar\decir cuenta	897
llamar atención	2698	poner fin	1235	tener vida	892
tener sentido	2563	publicar comentario	1232	solucionar problema	884
haber estado	2430	tomar medida	1216	dar nombre	874
hacer cosa	2374	hacer esfuerzo	1202	tener dificultad	873
tener miedo	2226	correr riesgo	1159	tener gana	871
haber hecho	2168	caber duda	1145	dar resultado	871
tener oportunidad	2137	decir verdad	1132	hacer cargo	870
dar paso	2100	tener experiencia	1114	contar historia	870
hacer uso	2081	tener necesidad	1102	desempeñar papel	869
resolver problema	1939	obtener información	1091	dar gracia	864
tener tiempo	1905	« no	1086	ganar dinero	863
tener efecto	1905	dar vida	1086	dar razón	861
prestar atención	1883	hacer pregunta	1075	satisfacer necesidad	858
tener relación	1849	hacer daño	1074	realizar estudio	854
tener capacidad	1847	iniciar sesión	1062	establecer relación	847
tener valor	1769	hacer trabajo	1035	adoptar medida	846
valer pena	1765	pasar día	1026	producir efecto	840
tener idea	1734	pasar año	1000	dar origen	840
tener hijo	1685	pasar tiempo	988	tomar conciencia	839
dar vuelta	1653	hacer día	971	tener obligación	839

3   Semantic Characteristics

3.1   Collocations and Compositional Combinations

First, we analyzed manually the degree of cohesion in the list of 939 most frequent verb-noun pairs described in Sect. 2 and found that 202 of 939 pairs are free combinations, i.e. fully compositional phrases, so the other 737 pairs (78% of 939 pairs)

turned out to be restricted lexical combinations, i.e., collocations. This fact confirms the conclusion of other researchers that collocations very frequently form a big part of the language we employ today: for example, Sag et al. (2002) state that 41% of the WordNet entries (Miller et al. 1993, Miller 1995, WordNet 3.1 online: http://wordnet. princeton.edu/) are collocations, also, Nakagawa and Mori (2003) affirm that depending on a specific domain, collocations can comprise up to 85% of vocabulary in texts; consequently, the correct analysis of collocations is an important task in NLP. In our analysis, we observed that 78% of most frequent Spanish verb-noun phrases are collocations.

3.2   Lexical Functions in Collocations

In 737 pairs found in the list of the first 939 most frequent Spanish verb-noun pairs described in Sect. 2, we manually determined their lexical functions (Mel'čuk 1996, 2015). Lexical function (LF) is a formalized representation of semantic and structural patterns of collocations, it is a mapping from the base of a collocation to its collocate. This mapping captures the selectional preference of words functioning as bases in collocations.

More formally, LF is a function in the mathematical sense defined as a correspondence of a word w_0 called the LF argument to a set of words $\{w_1, w_2, \ldots, w_n\}$ in which each word w_i, $1 \leq i \leq n$, has a particular (and the same) lexical relation with the argument w_0; so using mathematical notation, LF is represented as $\mathrm{LF}(w_0) = \{w_i\}, 1 \leq i \leq n$.

For the names of LFs, abbreviated Latin words are used; these words convey the meaning represented by LFs. Besides, LFs capture the basic syntactic and predicate-argument structure of sentences in which collocation belonging to these functions are used. In Table 2, we give the definitions of some LFs we found in our list of 737 most frequent Spanish verb-noun collocations. The definitions are borrowed from (Fontenelle 1994, 1996, 1997; Mel'čuk 1998; Kahane and Polguere 2001; Song 2006; Lemnitzer and Geyken 2015).

To explain and illustrate the formalism of LF in a more detailed way, we will use as an example the lexical function which we observed to be most frequent in the 737 verb-noun collocations mentioned above. This LF is termed Oper1, from Latin *operari* = do, carry out, so the value of Oper1 lexicalizes the action of carrying out of what is denoted by the noun, the Oper1 argument. For instance, if the argument of Oper1 is the noun *decision*, the respective Oper1 value is *make*: Oper1(*decision*) = *make*. This is the functional manner to represent the collocation *make a decision*. Other verb-noun collocations of Oper1 are *pursue a goal, make an error, apply a measure, give a smile, take a walk, have lunch, deliver a lecture, make an announcement, lend support, put up resistance, give an order.*

Besides, 1 in Oper1 means that the word, used to lexicalize the semantic role of agent of the action expressed by the verb (agent is numbered as the first participant of an action), functions as the grammatical subject in sentences, where *make a decision* is used. Finally, summing up the semantic and syntactic aspects of Oper1, we can conclude that this LF represents the pattern *Agent performs w_0 (w_0 is the argument of a

Table 2. Definitions of lexical functions found in most frequent Spanish verb-noun collocations. The names of the functions are abbreviated Latin words (in italics) which represent their semantics; sb stands for somebody, sth stands for something

LF	Name etymology and semantics
Oper	*operari*, to do, perform, carry out, experience (an emotion)
Func	*functionare*, to function
Real	*realis*, real, fulfill the requirement of sb/sth
Incep	*incipere*, to begin
Cont	*continuare*, to continue
Fin	*finire*, to cease
Perm	*permittere*, to permit, allow, do nothing which would cause that a situation stops occurring
Caus	*causare*, to cause, do something so that a situation begins occurring
Manif	*manifestare*, to manifest, sb/sth manifests itself, becomes apparent in sb/sth
Perf	*perfectus, complete, finished*, the action reaches its natural limit
Liqu	*liquidare*, to liquidate, do something so that a situation stops occurring
Plus	more, to a greater extent than sth else
Minus	less, to a lesser extent than sth else
Anti	*antonymum*, antonym
Copul	*copula*, a verb with the meaning of a copula (to be)

lexical function) as it can be seen in the sentence *The president made a decision.* A further explanation of LF notation can be found in (Mel'čuk 1996).

Table 2 includes those LFs which are called simple, since they denote unitary semantic elements. Simple LFs can be combined to represent more than two semantic units, such functions are called complex. Tables 3 and 4 include both simple and complex LFs.

Table 3 presents the results of our analysis of the list of most frequent Spanish verb-noun pairs (939 pairs) with respect to two criteria. First, we distinguished restricted lexical co-occurrence or collocations from free combinations; this we discussed in Sect. 3.1. As we mentioned there, we found 202 free word combinations (FC in Table 3) and, respectively, 737 collocations. Second, we manually determined lexical functions in collocations, having detected 36 different LFs. For each function, we present the number of their pairs (in the column denoted by # in Table 3). Also, in the same table, we give frequency in corpus for each lexical function, having summed up the corpus frequencies of all pairs belonging to this function—these data are located in the column denoted as Freq.

In is interesting to observe in Table 3, that verb-noun collocations of Oper1 are more frequently met in corpus than free word combinations. Certainly, this conclusion was made based on a sample of only 939 most frequent verb-noun pairs, however, it provides some insight on restricted versus free lexical usage.

It can also be seen in Table 3, that the causative semantics is very frequently met in corpus: it is conveyed by such LFs as CausFunc0, CausFunc1, Caus2Func1, CausPlusFunc0, CausPlusFunc1, Caus1Oper1, Caus1Func1, CausManifFunc0, CausMinusFunc0, CausPerfFunc0, and CausMinusFunc1—totally, 11 lexical functions include causation as their semantic element. These 11 functions embrace 242 pairs (about 26% of all 939 pairs in the list), and their total frequency in corpus is 101,282 (about 24% of the total frequency of all 939 pairs which equals 420,049).

In Table 4 we gave the description of semantic and structural properties of the first nine lexical functions from Table 3. This description is prepared in the form of patterns which convey the basic semantics and structure of utterances in which the verb-noun collocations belonging to the respective lexical functions are used in texts. These patterns can be used for LF recognition in corpora as well as for text generation purposes. In the patterns, the noun which functions as the LF argument is denoted as w_0. To illustrate the LF patterns in Table 4, we give examples of the same LFs from our list of verb-noun pairs in Table 5.

Table 3. Lexical functions (LF) in the list of 939 most frequent Spanish verb-noun combinations: Freq is frequency in the Spanish Web Corpus, # is the number of pairs in the list; for comparison; the table also includes the data on free combinations (FC)

LF	Freq	#	LF	Freq	#
Oper1	165319	280	Caus1Oper1	1280	2
FC	70211	202	Caus1Func1	1085	3
CausFunc1	45688	90	IncepFunc0	1052	3
CausFunc0	40717	112	PermOper1	910	3
Real1	19191	61	CausManifFunc0	788	2
Func0	17393	25	CausMinusFunc0	746	3
IncepOper1	11805	25	Oper3	520	1
Oper2	8967	30	LiquFunc0	514	2
Caus2Func1	8242	16	IncepReal1	437	2
ContOper1	5354	16	Real3	381	1
Manif	3339	13	PlusOper1	370	1
Copul	2345	9	CausPerfFunc0	290	1
CausPlusFunc0	2203	7	AntiReal3	284	1
Func1	1848	4	MinusReal1	265	1
PerfOper1	1736	4	AntiPermOper1	258	1
CausPlusFunc1	1548	5	ManifFunc0	240	1
Real2	1547	3	CausMinusFunc1	229	1
FinOper1	1476	6	FinFunc0	178	1
PerfFunc0	1293	1			

At this point we resume the discussion of TreeTagger accuracy started in Sect. 2 and will add, that although we intended to extract combinations 'verb + noun as a direct object' from the Spanish Web Corpus, other combinations (beside pairs with orthographic inconsistencies) were also retrieved due to the TreeTagger faults. These combinations included phrases of the structure 'noun as subject + verb'. Such phrases can have different semantics, but there is one lexical function termed Func0 which captures one particular semantics of this structure, namely, 'w_0 functions', see Table 4.

Table 4. Semantic and structural patterns of most frequent lexical functions found in 737 verb-noun collocations, w_0 represents the noun in a collocation

LF	Pattern
Oper1	Agent performs w_0
CausFunc1	Non-agent participant causes w_0 to realize the inherent objective associated with it
CausFunc0	Agent causes the realization of w_0
Real1	Agent does with regard to w_0 that which is normally expected of him/her to realize the inherent purpose associated with w_0
Func0	w_0 functions
IncepOper1	Agent begins to perform w_0
Oper2	Agent undergoes w_0
Caus2Func1	Non-agent participant causes w_0 to be experienced by another participant
ContOper1	Agent continues to perform w_0

Table 5. Examples from the list of 939 most frequent verb-noun pairs for the lexical functions in Table 4

LF	Examples
Oper1	*tener problema, tener oportunidad, tener efecto, hacer uso, hacer daño, prestar atención, prestar servicio, jugar papel, correr riesgo, realizar estudio, adoptar medida, pedir perdón, pedir permiso, dar salto, dar testimonio, decir palabra, presentar problema, añadir comentario, ocupar posición*
CausFunc1	*dar lugar, dar paso, abrir paso, proporcionar información, dejar lugar, ofrecer servicio, ofrecer solución, causar daño, establecer base, establecer contacto, despertar interés, poner límite*
CausFunc0	*formar parte, producir efecto, escribir libro, desarrollar actividad, encontrar respuesta, dar fruto, elaborar plan, declara guerra, impartir curso*
Real1	*resolver problema, satisfacer necesidad, seguir instrucción, corregir error, utilizar programa, usar sistema, contestar pregunta, aprovechar oportunidad, cumplir condición*
Func0	*existir problema, existir posibilidad, caber duda, quedar duda, pasar siglo*
IncepOper1	*iniciar sesión, asumir responsabilidad, adquirir importancia, encontrar trabajo, tomar posición, adoptar actitud, asumir papel, abordar problema*
Oper2	*obtener resultado, obtener beneficio, recibir información, recibir premio, recibir carta, tener apoyo, sufrir consecuencia, sufrir daño, escuchar voz, tomar sol*
Caus2Func1	*llamar atención, dar impresión, dar asco, imponer pena, dar vergüenza, costar trabajo, sacar provecho*
ContOper1	*mantener relación, mantener contacto, seguir vida, llevar vida, seguir camino, guardar relación, guardar silencio*

In Table 3 it can be seen that we found 25 samples of this function in the first 1000 most frequent Spanish verb-noun pairs described in Sect. 2. Some examples of Func0 are included in Table 5 with the ordering 'verb + noun', as they were found in the list.

However, in the Spanish Web Corpus these phrases were used also in the reversed order according to the structure 'noun as subject + verb'.

It is obvious that due to some inconsistencies of the TreeTagger, noun as a direct object was confused with its function as a subject in an utterance. Here we will also mention that the TreeTagger showed an accuracy of 86.46% on words with a rate of ambiguity 5 in the University of Stuttgart corpus (Volk and Scheider 1998) and an accuracy of 96.36% on Penn-Treebank in (Schmid 2013). However, its accuracy is reported as low as 71% in (Derczynski et al. 2016). As we will see in Table 6, the rate of ambiguity of some nouns is rather high, so this can be one of the reasons of the TreeTagger confusion. However, in the case of the erroneous extraction of 'noun as subject + verb' combinations, we took advantage of them to study the characteristics of the lexical function Func0.

3.3 Word Senses

In this section we present the results of our observations on the word senses performed on the list of most frequent Spanish verb-noun pairs. Remember, we chose the first 1000 pairs extracted automatically from the Spanish Web Corpus. After deleting 61 erroneous pairs due to automatic POS tagging and lemmatizing errors, 939 pairs were left. Then, all verbs and nouns were disambiguated manually with the Spanish WordNet senses. For some meanings, this dictionary did not have definitions—such meanings were found in 39 pairs.

Therefore, for our analysis of word senses we finally got 900 pairs. Table 6 presents the data on word senses of these most frequent verb-noun pairs. The notation we used in this table is the following: s# is the sense number, #v is the number of verbs, and #n is the number of nouns.

In Table 6, in the first column, we give the statistics of word senses for all 900 verb-noun pairs which include free combinations as well as collocations. Word senses of verbs and nouns are presented in separate columns.

Then, in the second column, we put the data for the most frequent lexical function Oper1: the argument to this function is a noun, and the value is the verb convening the semantics of performing the action expressed by the noun. In the list under study, we have 266 pairs of Oper1 annotated with word senses.

In the third column of Table 6, we present word senses for verbs and nouns of two lexical functions—CausFunc0 and CausFunc1. With the purpose of having a bigger number of pairs to derive more accurate statistics, we put together the pairs of both functions since they have very close semantics: the verb as the value of these functions conveys the meaning of causing the realization of the action lexicalized by the noun. In total, we had 198 verb-noun pairs of CausFunc0 and CausFunc1 together.

Considering that it would be interesting to make observations on word senses contrasting collocations with free combinations, in the last column of Table 6 we present the data for word senses of verbs and nouns in free combinations (FC), and we had 196 such pairs.

Table 6. Word senses of most frequent Spanish verb-noun pairs, s# is sense number, #v is the number of verbs, and #n is the number of nouns

Verbs in all 900 pairs		Nouns in all 900 pairs		Oper1:266 pairs				CausFunc0 and CausFunc1:198 pairs				FC:196 pairs			
s#	#v	s#	#n	s#	#v	s#	#n	s#	#v	s#	#n	s#	#v	s#	#n
1	404	1	479	1	112	1	124	1	45	1	103	1	123	1	130
2	205	2	197	2	54	2	74	2	58	2	36	2	41	2	34
3	65	3	110	3	33	3	40	3	6	3	28	3	9	3	14
4	57	4	33	4	2	4	10	4	27	4	9	4	13	4	3
5	16	5	28	5	1	5	7	5	6	5	8	5	4	5	7
6	34	6	24	6	22	6	5	6	4	6	8	6	3	6	3
7	4	7	15	7	0	7	3	7	0	7	4	7	1	7	0
8	3	8	2	8	1	8	0	8	0	8	0	8	1	8	1
9	63	9	4	9	2	9	0	9	51	9	2	9	0	9	2
10	0	10	0	10	0	10	0	10	0			10	0	10	0
11	9	11	3	11	1	11	2	11	0			11	0	11	0
12	1	12	3	12	1	12	0	12	0			12	0	12	1
13	0	13	0	13	0	13	0	13	0			13	0	13	0
14	0	14	0	14	0	14	0	14	0			14	0	14	0
15	37	15	1	15	37	15	0	15	0			15	0	15	1
16	1	16	1			16	1	16	0			16	1		
17	1							17	1						

We will remark here that Table 6 shows the statistics without taking into account how many times one and the same word is encountered in different pairs, this we is left for future study.

As it can be observed in Table 6, the figures for all 900 pairs seem to be distributed according to the Zipf's law (Woodroofe and Hill 1975) with a very few exceptions. Most verbs and nouns are used in their first sense which is commonly associated with their typical or autosemantic sense. The autosemantic sense is defined as the meaning which can be understood of a word outside any context (Hausmann 1979, 2004). The majority of sense 1 is seen also for Oper1, for free combinations, and for the nouns of causative lexical functions. The only exception is the verbs of CausFunc0 and Caus-Func1: their most observed senses are 2 and 9. Sense 2 belongs to the verbs *abrir* (open), *desarrollar* (develop), *formar* (form), *hacer* (do), *provocar* (provoke), *consti-tuir* (construct), *establecer* (establish), *sentar* (sit), *interponer* (interpose), *publicar* (publish). Sense 9 was observed only in one case: of the verb *dar* (give). Both senses express the causative semantics corresponding to CausFunc0/CausFunc1.

3.4   Generalization Level

Our observations on the generalization level of the words in 900 Spanish verb-noun combinations described in Sect. 3.3 are summed up in Table 7. The data is organized in the same manner as in Table 6. In the first column we give the statistics for all 900 verb-noun pairs, then the next two columns present the results for Oper1 and for two causative functions, CausFunc0 and CausFunc1, grouped together. The last column gives the results on free combinations, in order to compare them with collocations of Oper1 and the causative functions.

Table 7. Number of hypernyms in most frequent Spanish verb-noun pairs, #h is the number of hypernyms, #v is the number of verbs, and #n is the number of nouns

Verbs in all 900 pairs		Nouns in all 900 pairs		Oper1:266 pairs				CausFunc0 and CausFunc1:198 pairs				FC:196 pairs			
#h	#v	#h	#n	#h	#v	#h	#n	#h	#v	#h	#n	#h	#v	#h	#n
0	336	0	6	0	165	0	2	0	15	0	2	0	84	0	1
1	353	1	40	1	78	1	14	1	113	1	4	1	70	1	8
2	102	2	104	2	4	2	35	2	41	2	26	2	16	2	14
3	61	3	207	3	14	3	53	3	14	3	42	3	11	3	51
4	31	4	171	4	5	4	61	4	8	4	30	4	9	4	33
5	6	5	159			5	41	5	3	5	38	5	3	5	38
6	7	6	114			6	38	6	4	6	26	6	2	6	22
7	2	7	48			7	11			7	13	7	1	7	13
8	0	8	16			8	6			8	2			8	6
9	2	9	5			9	1			9	2			9	2
		10	11			10	3			10	4			10	3
		11	0			11	0			11	0			11	0
		12	3			1	1			12	2			12	0
		13	6							13	2			13	3
		14	0							14	0			14	0
		15	7							15	3			15	1
		16	2							16	2			16	0
		17	0											17	0
		18	0											18	0
		19	0											19	0
		20	1											20	1

It can be seen in Table 7, that almost all verbs in the 900 verb-noun pairs express very general semantics, since they have none or very few hypernyms. The same cannot be said about the nouns in these pairs: most of them are located at levels from two to six in the hyperonymy-hyponymy trees of the Spanish WordNet.

Concerning the difference between collocations and free combinations, it is notable that the verbs of Oper1 represent most general concepts: the verbs in 165 of 266 pairs have no hypernyms (62% of 266 Oper1 pairs), and the verbs in 78 pairs have only one hypernym (29%), making totally 91% of all Oper1 verbs.

Oper1 verbs contrast with the verbs in free combinations, where only about 78% have zero or one hypernym. The verbs of the causative functions CausFunc0 and CausFunc1 are less general and more specific: only 64% of the verbs have zero or one hypernym. Speaking about the nouns in all verb-noun pairs, it is seen that they represent more specific concepts: many nouns have three, four, or five hypernyms.

The data we collected can be used in many natural language processing task. Here we will only mention one of them: word sense disambiguation (WSD). This task consists in assigning each word in a text its sense number from a list of senses. One of the issues in this task is that many words have very big list of senses, especially those words which are frequently used in texts. Table 8 gives an idea of how complex the WSD task is for some common verbs. Also, Table 9 shows that these verbs cannot be ignored: their disambiguation is important due to their frequency in texts.

Continuing with our example of disambiguation of common Spanish verbs in Tables 8 and 9, we will add that the knowledge of most typical senses and the number of hypernyms (which limits significantly the search in the list of senses) can help in this complex task of disambiguation.

Table 8. Number of senses of some common Spanish verbs in DRAE (Diccionario de la lengua española, 22 edition, 2001, Dictionary of the Spanish Language); English equivalents are given in parenthesis

Verb	Number of senses
pasar (pass)	64
picar (bite)	57
hacer (do)	56
dar (give)	53
echar (throw)	48
cargar (carry)	46
tomar (take)	39

Table 9. Frequency of Spanish verbs in the Spanish Web Corpus; the second column contains the number of occurrences of the verbs and the third column display the same data with respect to the corpus size

Verb	Frequency in Spanish Web Corpus	Percentage with respect to all words in Spanish Web Corpus
hacer (do)	323,621	0.28%
dar (give)	160,489	0.14%
poner (put)	76,475	0.07%
tomar (take)	45,462	0.04%

4 Conclusions and Future Work

In this paper we reported the results of our study of most frequent Spanish verb-noun combination found in the Spanish Web Corpus located in the Sketch Engine (Kilgarriff et al. 2014; https://www.sketchengine.co.uk/). The Spanish Web Corpus contains 116,900,060 tokens. The list of extracted verb-noun combinations included 997,575 pairs. For our detailed study were selected the first 1000 pairs.

Using these data, we analyzed the degree of cohesiveness between the verb and the noun in a pair and found that the majority of pairs were collocations. We also determined the semantic and structural characteristics of collocations in terms of their lexical functions (Mel'čuk 1996, 2015). We found that the most frequently met lexical function is Oper1 which represents the pattern 'Agent performs the action expressed by the noun of a collocation'. Interestingly, Oper1 verb-noun pairs are more frequent than free (fully compositional) verb-noun combinations.

We also observed what word senses were most typical for polysemous words in the verb-noun combinations under study and determined the level of generalization which characterizes the semantics of words in the combinations, that is, at what level of the hyperonymy-hyponymy tree they are located. We found that the level of generalization of verbs in collocations is higher than that in free combinations.

We believe that the data collected by us can be used in various applications of natural language processing, especially, in predictive models in which most frequent cases are taken into account.

As future work, we aim at analyzing other important features of verb-noun combinations as well as perform a study of a bigger number of this type of phrases so typical in any natural language.

Acknowledgements. The authors are grateful to Vojtěch Kovář for providing us with the list of most frequent verb-noun pairs from the Spanish Web Corpus of the Sketch Engine, www.sketchengine.co.uk. The authors also appreciate the support of Mexican Government which made it possible to complete this work: SNI-CONACYT, BEIFI-IPN, SIP-IPN: grants 20162064, 20161958, and 20162204, and the EDI Program. We give special thanks to Dr. Noé Alejandro Castro-Sánchez for collecting the statistics of verb senses in Diccionario de la lengua española (DRAE).

References

Cambria, E., Poria, S., Gelbukh, A., Kwok, K.: Sentic API: a common-sense based API for concept-level sentiment analysis. In: Proceedings of the 4th Workshop on Making Sense of Microposts, co-located with the 23rd International World Wide Web Conference (WWW 2014). CEUR Workshop Proceedings, vol. 1141, pp. 19–24 (2014)

Cambria, E., Poria, S., Bajpai, R., Schuller, B.: SenticNet 4: A semantic resource for sentiment analysis based on conceptual primitives. In COLING 2016, The 26th International Conference on Computational Linguistics, pp. 2666–2677 (2016)

Chikersal, P., Poria, S., Cambria, E., Gelbukh, A., Siong, C.E.: Modelling public sentiment in Twitter: using linguistic patterns to enhance supervised learning. In: Gelbukh, A. (ed.) CICLing 2015. LNCS, vol. 9042, pp. 49–65. Springer, Cham (2015). doi:10.1007/978-3-319-18117-2_4

Derczynski, L., Lukasik, M., Srijith, P.K., Bontcheva, K., Hepple, M., Lobo, T.P., Radzimski, M.: D6. 2.1 Evaluation Report-Interim Results (2016)

Fontenelle, T.: Using lexical functions to discover metaphors. In: Proceedings of the 6th EURALEX International Congress, pp. 271–278 (1994)

Fontenelle, T.: Ergativity, collocations and lexical functions. In: Gellerstam, M., et al. (eds.), pp. 209–222 (1996)

Fontenelle, T.: Using a bilingual dictionary to create semantic networks. Int. J. Lexicogr. 10(4), 275–303 (1997)

Hausmann, F.J.: Un dictionnaire des collocations est-il possible? Travaux de Linguistique et de Littérature Strasbourg 17(1), 187–195 (1979)

Hausmann, F.J.: Was sind eigentlich Kollokationen. In: Wortverbindungen-mehr oder weniger fest, pp. 309–334 (2004)

Kahane, S., Polguere, A.: Formal foundation of lexical functions. In: Proceedings of ACL/EACL 2001 Workshop on Collocation, pp. 8–15 (2001)

Kilgarriff, A., Baisa, V., Bušta, J., Jakubíček, M., Kovář, V., Michelfeit, J., Suchomel, V.: The sketch engine: ten years on. Lexicography 1(1), 7–36 (2014)

Lemnitzer, L., Geyken, A.: Semantic modeling of collocations for lexicographic purposes. J. Cogn. Sci. 16(3), 200–223 (2015)

Majumder, N., Poria, S., Gelbukh, A., Cambria, E.: Deep learning based document modeling for personality detection from text. IEEE Intell. Syst. 32(2), 74–79 (2017)

Mel'čuk, I.A.: Lexical functions: a tool for the description of lexical relations in a lexicon. In: Wanner, L. (ed.) Lexical Functions in Lexicography and Natural Language Processing, pp. 37–102. John Benjamins Academic Publishers, Amsterdam and Philadelphia (1996)

Mel'čuk, I.A.: Collocations and lexical functions. In: Cowie, A.P. (ed.) Phraseology. Theory, Analysis, and Applications, pp. 25–53. Clarendon Press, Oxford (1998)

Mel'čuk, I.A.: Semantics: From Meaning to Text, vol. 3. John Benjamins Publishing Company, Amsterdam and Philadelphia (2015)

Miller, G.A.: WordNet: a lexical database for English. Commun. ACM 38(11), 39–41 (1995)

Miller, G.A., Leacock, C., Tengi, R., Bunker, R.T.: A semantic concordance. In: Proceedings of the Workshop on Human Language Technology Association for Computational Linguistics, pp. 303–308 (1993)

Nakagawa, H., Mori, T.: Automatic term recognition based on statistics of compound nouns and their components. Terminology 9(2), 201–219 (2003)

Pakray, P., Pal, S., Poria, S., Bandyopadhyay, S., Gelbukh, A.: JU_CSE_TAC: textual entailment recognition system at TAC RTE-6. In: System Report. Text Analysis Conference, Recognizing Textual Entailment Track (TAC RTE). Notebook (2010)

Pakray, P., Neogi, S., Bhaskar, P., Poria, S., Bandyopadhyay, S., Gelbukh, A.: A textual entailment system using anaphora resolution. In: System Report. Text Analysis Conference, Recognizing Textual Entailment Track (TAC RTE). Notebook (2011a)

Pakray, P., Poria, S., Bandyopadhyay, S., Gelbukh, A.: Semantic textual entailment recognition using UNL. POLIBITS 43, 23–27 (2011)

Poria, S., Gelbukh, A., Agarwal, B., Cambria, E., Howard, N.: Common sense knowledge based personality recognition from text. In: Castro, F., Gelbukh, A., González, M. (eds.) MICAI 2013. LNCS, vol. 8266, pp. 484–496. Springer, Heidelberg (2013a). doi:10.1007/978-3-642-45111-9_42

Poria, S., Gelbukh, A., Hussain, A., Howard, N., Das, D., Bandyopadhyay, S.: Enhanced SenticNet with affective labels for concept-based opinion mining. IEEE Intell. Syst. **28**(2), 31–38 (2013b)

Poria, S., Cambria, E., Gelbukh, A., Bisio, F., Hussain, A.: Sentiment data flow analysis by means of dynamic linguistic patterns. IEEE Comput. Intell. Mag. **10**(4), 26–36 (2015)

Poria, S., Cambria, E., Hazarika, D., Vij, P.: A deeper look into sarcastic tweets using deep convolutional neural networks. In: The 26th International Conference on Computational Linguistics, COLING 2016, pp. 1601–1612 (2016a)

Poria, S., Cambria, E., Gelbukh, A.: Aspect extraction for opinion mining with a deep convolutional neural network. Knowl.-Based Syst. **108**, 42–49 (2016b)

Poria, S., Chaturvedi, I., Cambria, E., Hussain, A.: Convolutional MKL based multimodal emotion recognition and sentiment analysis. In: 2016 IEEE 16th International Conference on Data Mining (ICDM), pp. 439–448 (2016c)

Poria, S., Cambria, E., Bajpai, R., Hussain, A.: A review of affective computing: from unimodal analysis to multimodal fusion. Inf. Fusion **37**, 98–125 (2017a)

Poria, S., Peng, H., Hussain, A., Howard, N., Cambria, E.: Ensemble application of convolutional neural networks and multiple kernel learning for multimodal sentiment analysis. Neurocomputing (2017b, in press)

Sag, I.A., Baldwin, T., Bond, F., Copestake, A., Flickinger, D.: Multiword expressions: a pain in the neck for NLP. In: Gelbukh, A. (ed.) CICLing 2002. LNCS, vol. 2276, pp. 1–15. Springer, Heidelberg (2002). doi:10.1007/3-540-45715-1_1

Schmid, H.: Improvements in part-of-speech tagging with an application to German. In: Proceedings of the ACL SIGDAT-Workshop (1995)

Schmid, H.: Probabilistic part-of-speech tagging using decision trees. In: New Methods in Language Processing, p. 154. Routledge (2013)

Sharoff, S.: Creating general-purpose corpora using automated search engine queries. In: WaCky, pp. 63–98 (2006)

Song, S.H.: Zur Korrespondenz der NV-Kollokationen im Deutschen und Koreanischen. 언어학 **44**, 37–57 (2006)

Volk, M., Scheider, G.: Comparing a statistical and a rule-based tagger for German. In: Computers, Linguistics, and Phonetics Between Language and Speech. Proceedings of 4th Conference on Natural Language Processing-KONVENS 1998 (1998)

Woodroofe, M., Hill, B.: On Zipf's law. J. Appl. Prob. **12**, 425–434 (1975)

Sentence Paraphrase Graphs: Classification Based on Predictive Models or Annotators' Decisions?

Ekaterina Pronoza[1], Elena Yagunova[1(✉)], and Nataliya Kochetkova[2]

[1] St. Petersburg State University,
7/9 Universitetskaya Nab., St. Petersburg, Russian Federation
katpronoza@gmail.com, iagounova.elena@gmail.com
[2] National Research University Higher School of Economics,
20 Myasnitskaya ul., Moscow, Russian Federation
natalia_k_11@mail.ru

Abstract. As part of our project ParaPhraser on the identification and classification of Russian paraphrase, we have collected a corpus of more than 8000 sentence pairs annotated as precise, loose or non-paraphrases. The corpus is annotated via crowdsourcing by naïve native Russian speakers, but from the point of view of the expert, our complex paraphrase detection model can be more successful at predicting paraphrase class than a naive native speaker.

Our paraphrase corpus is collected from news headlines and therefore can be considered a summarized news stream describing the most important events. By building a graph of paraphrases, we can detect such events.

In this paper we construct two such graphs: based on the current human annotation and on the complex model prediction. The structure of the graphs is compared and analyzed and it is shown that the model graph has larger connected components which give a more complete picture of the important events than the human annotation graph. Predictive model appears to be better at capturing full information about the important events from the news collection than human annotators.

Keywords: Paraphrase graph · Sentential paraphrase · News stream · Connected components · Central nodes · Predictive model

1 Introduction

This paper is a part of the project ParaPhraser on the collection, identification and classification of sentential paraphrase in Russian language [12]. We have already collected a corpus of more than 8000 pairs of sentences annotated as precise, loose or non-paraphrases via crowdsourcing (we distinguish 3 classes of paraphrases).

Our annotators are native Russian speakers, a few of them are linguistic specialists but most are naïve Russian speakers. From the point of view of the expert, our complex paraphrase detection model [14] can be even more successful at predicting paraphrase class than a naive native speaker.

G. Sidorov and O. Herrera-Alcántara (Eds.): MICAI 2016, Part I, LNAI 10061, pp. 41–52, 2017.
DOI: 10.1007/978-3-319-62434-1_4

The corpus consists of pairs of news headlines: different official Russian media sources are parsed every day, and pairs of headlines are compared and collected in real time. The corpus can be considered a news stream describing the most important events, and this resource (and similar resources in general) can also be used to track and analyze these events (and this, we believe, is another reason why the corpus can be useful for such tasks as information extraction and news threads analysis). And such events can be detected by building a paraphrase graph.

Paraphrase graph is a graph the nodes of which are sentences, and the edges are paraphrase relations (i.e., an edge exists between a pair of nodes if these two nodes contain paraphrases). In such paraphrase graph, the largest connected components correspond to the most important events. The corpus has its crowdsourced paraphrase annotation, but, as sometimes this annotation is disputable and inferior to the prediction of the model, we are going to check whether the graph based on such prediction is also more informative than the native annotation in terms of the events coverage.

In this paper we construct paraphrase graphs in two main ways: based on paraphrase relations annotated by the naive speakers and on paraphrase relations predicted by the models (which is a combination of shallow, semantic and distributive models). We analyze and compare the structure of the graphs. It is shown that the graph based on the complex model prediction has larger connected components than the graph based on the decisions of the annotators. Moreover, the largest connected components of the "model" graph are usually denser than those of the "annotators" graph and are able to show a more complete picture of the events occurring in the world. We believe that predictive model is better at capturing full information about the important events from the news collection than the annotators.

2 Related Work

There exist a substantial number of paraphrase resources, on the sentence and phrase levels, in paraphrase community, most of which are for the English language [3–5, 17]. Such corpora can be used for paraphrase identification, text summarization, information extraction, information retrieval, question answering and other natural language processing tasks. Some of the corpora, those which are collected from the news texts, can be also considered a reflection of the news stream, especially when represented as a paraphrase graph. We are not aware of the examples of such usage of paraphrase resources (and that is why we decided to address this issue) but nevertheless there are works proposing similar ideas.

In [8] an approach closest to ours is proposed. The authors propose an effective algorithm of decomposing collections of news texts into semantically coherent threads (threads of relevant articles). They actually solve a graph decomposition problem, but the distance between the documents is calculated simply using Term-Document Matrix, and no linguistic resources or methods are applied.

An approach to clustering abstracts is proposed in [1]. It is based on the grouping of keywords and the use of document similarity measure. But the authors, unlike us, work with scientific abstracts.

In [7] the authors solve the problem of determining the main topics of a document. For each topic in the dictionary the documents are compared with the "ideal" document, and the "ideal" document for a concept is one that contains only the keywords belonging to this concept, in the proportion to their occurrences in the training corpus.

In [10] a modified Suffix Tree (or Trie) method is applied to the clustering problem. The author works with a sample of the Norwegian Newspaper Corpus [11], and the modification of the Trie algorithm is reported to be successful.

Unlike the described approaches, ours is based on the usage of a paraphrase resource as a news collection, and we construct a graph of events using a paraphrase corpus, so this graph is also a paraphrase graph.

3 Data

Our data is represented by the Russian sentential paraphrase corpus ParaPhraser. It is constantly growing and at the moment its size is 8072 sentence pairs. Each sentence pair is annotated with one of the three paraphrase classes: the corpus consists of 1862 precise, 3257 loose and 2953 non-paraphrases (23%/40%/37%). The corpus is not a general purpose one. It is intended to be useful for information extraction and text summarization. Such tasks require paraphrases of different granularity, and that is why we distinguish 3 classes of paraphrases.

The corpus is collected from news headlines: pairs of headlines from 7 different media sources (Lenta.ru, RBC, RIA, RT, RG, etc.) are collected and compared in real time. For each pair of headlines published on the same day a metric is calculated. This metric can be described as an extended unsupervised matrix similarity metric [6], or a variant of soft cosine measure [15] for each pair of sentences. The sentences with the value of the metric above the threshold are included in the corpus. Then the sentences are annotated by the native speakers via the online interface. Each pair of sentences in the corpus is tagged by at least 3 annotators. Finally, sentence pairs receive their paraphrase class which is calculated as the median of the scores given by the annotators provided that there are no opposite decisions, like non-paraphrase and precise paraphrase. Such restriction is quite important because the average level of agreement between all pairs of the annotators in the project in general is quite low (Kohen's Cappa less than 60%), and we cannot possibly include all the annotated sentence pairs in the corpus. But we believe that the described class calculation procedure makes the annotation acceptably reliable, although our annotators are mostly naïve Russian speakers which often offer inconsistent decisions on paraphrases.

As for the linguistic characteristics of the corpus, there is a phenomenon which complicates both the work of the annotators and the development of the paraphrase classifier. Its name is presupposition. Indeed, annotators often disagree on the paraphrase class of the sentences with presupposition, and predictive models, according to the previous research, tend to misclassify them [14]. However, from the point of view of an expert, on some sentence pairs a classifier gives a better prediction than the annotators. Let us consider, for example, the following pair of sentences:

- В Альпах разбился снегоход с российскими туристами. /In the Alps, a snow-mobile with Russian tourists crashed./
- Группа туристов разбилась на снегоходе в Альпах. /A group of tourists cra-shed on a snowmobile in the Alps./

According to the decision of the annotators, this pair of sentences is a precise paraphrase, which is disputable. But for a naïve Russian speaker a news report about tourists may be identical to the one about Russian tourists. As reported in [14], two predictive models out of three annotated this pair of sentence as loose paraphrase, which we believe it is.

4 Paraphrase Graphs

Paraphrase graph is a graph where nodes are formed by the sentences, and paraphrase relations between the sentences are the edges.

In this paper we propose the construction of paraphrase graphs to detect the most important events from the news stream in two ways: by using a paraphrase corpus (i.e., the annotation made by the naïve native speakers) and by using a model which predicts paraphrase class.

There are 3 classes of paraphrases in the ParaPhraser corpus, two of them being actually paraphrases (precise and loose). In a paraphrase graph, sentences form the nodes, and an edge is drawn between each pair of nodes if there exist a paraphrase relation between the corresponding pair of sentences (no matter precise or loose).

Connected components in such paraphrase graph refer to the different events, and central nodes within each connected component are the sum and substance of the corresponding events. We compare the main characteristics of the two graphs and the structure of the components which refer to the same events in the two graphs.

We construct paraphrase graph, firstly, on the annotated subcorpus, with the classes marked by the naïve Russian speakers, and secondly, on the subcorpus of paraphrases with classes predicted by the paraphrase classification model.

The corpus is divided into two consecutive parts: the graphs are constructed on the second part, and the model is trained on the first part (training and testing set are not chosen randomly, because in a splitting into consecutive parts any possible chains of events are not lost). The second part of the corpus, as a news stream, reflects the events which happened since 2015, and the first part of the corpus refers to 2013–2014. It is also important to note that we do not employ any other data apart from the corpus because we need to compare the graphs on the same data, and the data should be annotated.

Our predictive model is a Gradient Tree Boosting classifier with 3 types of features corresponding to the 3 types of similarity measures: shallow features, semantic features and distributive features, and with optimized settings (optimization was conducted on the development set (20% of the training set) using standard tools provided by scikit-learn[1] library for python). Due to space limits, we cannot give a full description

---

[1] http://scikit-learn.org.

of the features, but all the details can be found in [14]. The only difference from [14] is that we drop some of the semantic features which make rather small contribution to the model performance but are costly in terms of calculation time (these are the features which involve searching for synonyms of the synonyms of the synonyms, etc.). Shallow features are based in string or lexical overlap and include traditional ones like n-grams overlap, BLEU, edit distance, etc., as well as those introduced in [13], which are calculated based on the characteristics of what is left in the two sentences after the removal of overlapping words (e.g., the portion of notional/capitalized words, the portion of overlapping substrings left in the two sentences after such procedure, etc.). Semantic features are represented by the improved version of the metric which was used for corpus construction and features based on the similarities between the sentences with removed overlapping words: the portion of synonyms, words with the same root, synonyms of the words with the same root, etc. These features are calculated using two semantic resources: YARN – Yet Another RussNet [2] and the dictionary of word formation by Tikhonov [16]. And finally, distributional features are calculated as cosine distance and other vector distance measures (we use 44 of them) on the word vectors of the sentences. We employ skip-gram model implemented in Word2vec [9] to calculate such features.

5 Results. Discussion

We start this section with the results of the paraphrase classification model performance (Gradient Tree Boosting used for paraphrase class prediction). As described in Sect. 4, we trained the model on the first half of the corpus, and then predicted the paraphrase class of the sentence pairs from the second half[2]. Its accuracy score equals 0.5542. Precision, recall and F1-score are shown in Table 1.

Table 1. Paraphrase classification results

Class	Precision	Recall	F1-score
−1	0.7954	0.4126	0.5434
0	0.4774	0.7701	0.5894
1	0.5544	0.4030	0.4667
Average	0.6193	0.5542	0.5465

The model evidently needs improvement, but it is not the goal of this part of our research (we leave it for future work).[3] It can be seen from Table 1 that the highest

---

[2] Since the second half of the corpus is already annotated, actually we do not need any prediction here, but to be able to compare the graphs we have to construct them on the same data, and that is why we use model prediction.

[3] Moreover, we only work with news headlines, and better results in the detection of the same events could be achieved by taking into account the bodies of the news reports as well. We believe that current results (i.e., model performance) are acceptable for building adequate paraphrase graph based on the corpus.

recall value is reached for the class of loose paraphrases, while the highest precision for the class of non-paraphrases. Indeed, the model uses a combination of shallow, semantic and distributional feature sets, and the first one (shallow) is the most high-performing and important one. As it was shown in [13], shallow model tends to mistake non-paraphrases for loose-paraphrases. When it concerns graphs construction, it means that the described model can identify chains of events missed by human annotators, but it also might cause noise.

As described in Sect. 4, we split paraphrase corpus into two consecutive parts, and built two graphs based on the second part of the corpus.

Firstly, we constructed a graph based on the annotators' decisions. The graph is visualized using yEd[4] software (see Fig. 1).

Fig. 1. Paraphrase graph based on the annotators' decisions (a fragment)

This graph consists of 4086 nodes and 2434 edges. It has 1815 connected components, most of which are of a small size (2 or 3 nodes). Such small subgraphs are of no interest to us, unlike the larger ones, like those in the left upper corner of the picture (see Fig. 1), which evidently correspond to some important events.

Secondly, we constructed a graph based on the prediction of the model. This graph is also visualized using yEd (see Fig. 2).

The second graph is larger than the first one (4790 nodes and 3205 edges, 1913 connected components) because it includes more sentences than the first one (i.e., the model reveals more paraphrase relations than the annotators). Like the first graph, it has a large number of small connected components, and a few large ones. But the large components of the second graph, according to the visualization, are larger than those of the first graph.

At this part of the research we compare both main characteristics of the two constructed graphs and characteristics of their corresponding largest connected components. Characteristics of the two graphs are as follows: average node degree of the "annotators" and "model" are 1.18 and 1.32 respectively, density equals 0.00029 and 0.00028 and average clustering coefficient equals 0.0446 and 0.0464.

---

[4] https://www.yworks.com/products/yed.

Fig. 2. Paraphrase graph based on the model prediction (a fragment)

It can be seen that the "annotators" graph is a little denser than the "model" graph, however, its average node degree and average clustering coefficient are lower than the corresponding characteristics of the "model" graph. The difference in density can be explained by the fact that compared to the "annotators" graph in the "model" graph a hundred of small connected components are added (obviously, without any edges between them and the other components, which reduces density). The differences between average node degree and average clustering coefficient differences imply that in the "model" graph the nodes tend to cluster together more than in the "annotators" graph, and its connected components are larger and "fuller" in the coverage of the corresponding events than those of the "annotators" graph. But to be convinced of this, a more thorough analysis of the connected components is required.

We analyzed top-50 largest connected components of the "model" graph in comparison with the "annotators" graph to see whether the components corresponding to the same events are really larger in the "model" graph as it can be seen from the Figs. 1 and 2. We also tracked central nodes (the nodes with the largest degree within each component) to see whether they are different in the corresponding connected components of the two graphs. Corresponding connected components were tracked automatically using a simple condition: two connected components from different graphs are considered to refer to the same event if at least half of the sentences from the "annotators" graph component is present in the "model" graph component.

According to the automatic analysis of the top-50 largest connected components, out of 50 connected components of the "model" graph, 42 (84%) are larger than the corresponding components of the "annotators" graph, 23 (46%) connected components correspond to 2 or more "annotators" components each, 10 (20%) connected components correspond to several "annotators" components each by mistake (false positives).

Out of the 10 mistakes, in 6 cases absolutely different events are mentioned in the "annotators" connected components (e.g., the death of Nemtsov and the collapse of Oceanarium), and in the other 4 different aspects of the same events are described (e.g., various reports about missing people as a result of the earthquake).

A few of the connected components in the "model" graph should have been combined into a single component, but they are not (they can be called false negatives).

They include connected components describing the following two events: the run of the Night Wolves and changes in currency exchange rates.

In general, it can be concluded that the "model" graph gives more complete information about the events than the "annotators" graph. Both false positives and false negatives are caused by the nature of the model (it is strongly dependent on words overlap). False positive rate is quite high (20%), but such mistakes are not critical for our task, unlike false negatives, and false negative rate is quite low (only 2 events out of 50 connected components). The improvement can only be achieved by looking into deep semantic structure of the sentences which is beyond the scope of this part of our research.

To illustrate such conclusions with examples, we provide top-5 connected components of the two graphs and compare them in detail (see Table 2). In Table 2, CND and AvgND in the header denote Central Node Degree and Average Node Degree respectively, Order refers to the number of nodes in the connected components, i.e., the number of its nodes, "#" denotes the number of the connected component (they are numbered in descending order by size in both graphs).

We need to explain the denotation in Table 2. Some numbers in the second column are marked with asterisk. It means that in the corresponding graph there are several connected components referring to the event in question (events are in the "Topic" column), and only the number of the largest one is given. In this case, size, the maximal and average node degrees (and maximal node degree is actually the degree of the central node within a connected component) are given for each connected component, separated by semicolon. The only exception is in the components referring to the meeting of Putin and Kerry: there are a lot of very small such connected components in the "annotators" graph, and we only consider the largest one of them. And a single asterisk in the connected component about a new earthquake in Nepal ("annotators" graph) means that the number of the component is so large (because its size is the smallest possible size of a connected component in the graph: only 2 nodes) that we can neglect it as it is far from being in top-5 largest components.

It can be seen that in most cases a connected component in the "model" graph is larger than a connected component in the "annotators" graph. It can also be noted that the "model" components are usually formed by joining several "annotators" components referring to the same topic and adding some details, but nevertheless central nodes often stay the same from graph to graph in the corresponding components (see, for example, the earthquake in Nepal components). Such tendency can be explained by both the nature of the model and the nature of the data: news headlines are usually laconic, and the simplest ones happen to be central nodes in the "annotators" graph; at the same time, the most important features of the model are the shallow features which roughly speaking compare the sentences, and it means that the shortest and simplest sentences are likely to have the largest node degrees. However, the model has its drawbacks: based on the n-grams overlap, it can join absolutely different events together (for example, fire in Orel, evacuation of people from Mi-8 and clashes in Peru in the 4th largest "annotators" connected component). Sometimes "model" components can miss some nodes, for example, the component with headlines about "Progress M-27M" lacks one node which is present in the "annotators" graph. But taking into account all the described characteristics of the connected components of the two

Table 2. Top-5 largest connected components of the graphs based on the annotators' decisions (1) and on the model prediction (2)

Graph	#	Topic	Order	Central node(s)	CND	AvgND
Annotators	1	Earthquake in Nepal	41	The number of victims of the earthquake in Nepal has exceeded 2260 people	11	4
Model	1	Earthquake in Nepal + avalanche on Everest (#2 in the annotators' graph) + a few sentences about other disasters	113	The number of victims of the earthquake in Nepal has exceeded 2260 people	18	4
Annotators	3	"Immortal regiment" march	9	The "Immortal regiment" march was attended by 12 million Russians	3	1
Model	7	"Immortal regiment" march	14	The "Immortal regiment" march was attended by 12 million Russians	6	2
Annotators	4	The space truck "Progress M-27M"	7	The space truck "Progress M-27M" burned out over the Pacific Ocean	3	5
Model	57	The space truck "Progress M-27M"	6	The space truck "Progress M-27M" burned out over the Pacific Ocean	3	4
				The spacecraft "Progress" burned out over the Pacific Ocean		
				"Progress M-27M" has ceased to exist over the Pacific Ocean		
Annotators	5	Evacuation from Nepal by a Russian aircraft	7	Russian plane evacuates 128 people from Nepal	3	2
				EMERCOM of Russia evacuated 128 people from Nepal		
Model	9	Evacuation from Nepal by a Russian aircraft	11	EMERCOM of Russia evacuated 128 people from Nepal	4	2
Annotators	7*	Elections in Kazakhstan	6; 2	CEC: Nazarbayev gaining 97.7% of the vote in the presidential elections	3; 1	2; 1
				The CEC announced Nazarbayev's victory in the elections in Kazakhstan		
				The counting of votes in the presidential elections in Kazakhstan has started		
				The voting in the presidential elections in Kazakhstan has ended		

(continued)

Table 2. (*continued*)

Graph	#	Topic	Order	Central node(s)	CND	AvgND
Model	2	Elections in Kazakhstan	28	The voting in the presidential elections in Kazakhstan has ended		
Annotators	*	A new earthquake in Nepal	2	36 people became victims of a new earthquake in Nepal	1	1
				The number of victims of a new earthquake in Nepal has risen to 36 people		
Model	3	A new earthquake in Nepal	25	36 people became victims of a new earthquake in Nepal	7	3
Annotators	14*	Fire and explosions at the fireworks store in Orel + Hard landing of Mi-8 on Kamchatka + Clashes in Peru (3 different connected components)	6; 2; 2	Fire and explosions occurred at the fireworks store in Orel	4; 1; 1	1; 1; 1
				People from Mi-8 which committed a hard landing on Kamchatka, have been evacuated		
				The crew and passengers of Mi-8 are evacuated on Kamchatka		
				One person was killed, 21 injured in collisions at a meeting in Peru		
				One person was killed as a result of the collisions at a meeting in Peru		
Model	4	Fire and explosions at the fireworks store in Orel + Hard landing of Mi-8 on Kamchatka + Clashes in Peru	21	Fire and explosions occurred at the fireworks store in Orel	9	2
Annotators	33*	The meeting of Putin and Kerry	4	Putin will met Kerry in Sochi on Tuesday	2	1
				Peskov announced an appointment between Putin and Kerry in Sochi		
Model	5	The meeting of Putin and Kerry	19	The meeting of Putin and Kerry has started in Sochi	8	2

graphs, we can conclude that in general the "model" connected components give a more complete picture of the described events from the news stream than the respective connected components of the "annotators" graph.

6   Conclusion

In this paper we have presented the results of our research which is a part of the project ParaPhraser. This is a project on the collection, identification and classification of sentential paraphrase in Russian language. We have already collected a corpus of more than 8000 pairs of sentences. We distinguish 3 classes of paraphrases: precise, loose or non-paraphrases, and the annotation is a result of the crowdsourcing. Our annotators are mostly naïve native Russian speakers, and the introduction of the expert annotation above the naïve one if one of our future work directions. We have also experimented with paraphrase classification and have built a model based on the combination of shallow, semantic and distributive similarity measures. From the point of view of the expert, such complex model can be even more successful at predicting paraphrase class than a naive native speaker.

The corpus consists of pairs of news headlines which are collected from different official Russian media sources in real time every day. The corpus can be considered a news stream describing the most important events occurring in the world. We believe that such resource can be useful not only for paraphrase identification, but also for information extraction, text summarization and news threads analysis. If we build a graph based on the paraphrase relations from the corpus, the largest connected components of such graph will correspond to the most important events.

In this paper we have constructed two such paraphrase graphs: based on paraphrase relations annotated by the naive speakers and on paraphrase relations predicted by the models. We have compared the main characteristics of the graphs and their largest connected components and it can be concluded that the graph based on the model prediction is more successful at reflecting the most important events of the news stream (than the graph based on the decisions of the annotators): its connected components provide more complete information and details about the events in question.

Acknowledgements. The authors acknowledge St.-Petersburg State University for the research grant 30.38.305.2014.

References

1. Alexandrov, M., Gelbukh, A., Rosso, P.: An approach to clustering abstracts. In: Montoyo, A., Muñoz, R., Métais, E. (eds.) NLDB 2005. LNCS, vol. 3513, pp. 275–285. Springer, Heidelberg (2005). doi:10.1007/11428817_25
2. Braslavski, P., Ustalov, D., Mukhin, M.: A spinning wheel for YARN: user interface for a crowdsourced thesaurus. In: Proceedings of the Demonstrations at the 14th Conference of the European Chapter of the Association for Computational Linguistics, Gothenburg, Sweden, pp. 101–104 (2014)
3. Clough, P., Gaizauskas, R., Piao, S., Wilks, Y.: METER: MEasuring TExt Reuse. In: Isabelle, P. (ed.) Proceedings of the Fortieth Annual Meeting on Association for Computational Linguistics, pp. 152–159. Association for Computational Linguistics, Philadelphia (2002)

4. Cohn, T., Callison-Burch, C., Lapata, M.: Constructing corpora for the development and evaluation of paraphrase systems. Comput. Linguist. Arch. **34**(4), 597–614 (2008)
5. Dolan, B., Quirk, C., Brockett, C.: Unsupervised construction of large paraphrase corpora: exploiting massively parallel news sources. In: Proceedings of the 20th International Conference on Computational Linguistics (COLING 2004), Geneva, Switzerland, pp. 350–356 (2004)
6. Fernando, S., Stevenson, M.: A semantic similarity approach to paraphrase detection. In: 11th Annual Research Colloqium on Computational Linguistics UK (CLUK 2008) (2008)
7. Gelbukh, A., Sidorov, G., Guzmán-Arenas, A.: A method of describing document contents through topic selection. In: Proceedings of the String Processing and Information Retrieval Symposium and International Workshop on Groupware, pp. 73–80 (1999)
8. Guha, R., Kumar R., Sivakumar, D., Sundaram, R.: Unweaving a web of documents. In: Proceedings of the Eleventh ACM SIGKDD International Conference on Knowledge Discovery in Data Mining, pp. 574–579 (2005)
9. Mikolov, T., Chen, K., Corrado, G., Dean, J.: Efficient estimation of word representations in vector space (2013). http://arxiv.org/abs/1301.3781/
10. Moe, R.E.: Clustering in a news corpus. In: Sojka, P., Horák, A., Kopeček, I., Pala, K. (eds.) TSD 2014. LNCS, vol. 8655, pp. 301–307. Springer, Cham (2014). doi:10.1007/978-3-319-10816-2_37
11. Norwegian Newspaper Corpus. http://avis.uib.no/om-aviskorpuset/english
12. Pronoza, E., Yagunova, E., Pronoza, A.: Construction of a Russian paraphrase corpus: unsupervised paraphrase extraction. In: Braslavski, P., Markov, I., Pardalos, P., Volkovich, Y., Ignatov, Dmitry I., Koltsov, S., Koltsova, O. (eds.) RuSSIR 2015. CCIS, vol. 573, pp. 146–157. Springer, Cham (2016). doi:10.1007/978-3-319-41718-9_8
13. Pronoza, E., Yagunova, E.: Low-level features for paraphrase identification. In: Sidorov, G., Galicia-Haro, Sofía N. (eds.) MICAI 2015. LNCS, vol. 9413, pp. 59–71. Springer, Cham (2015). doi:10.1007/978-3-319-27060-9_5
14. Pronoza, E., Yagunova, E.: Comparison of sentence similarity measures for Russian paraphrase identification. In: Artificial Intelligence and Natural Language and Information Extraction, Social Media and Web Search FRUCT Conference (AINL-ISMW FRUCT), pp. 74–82 (2015)
15. Sidorov, G., Gelbukh, A., Gómez-Adorno, H., Pinto, D.: Soft similarity and soft cosine measure: similarity of features in vector space model. Computación y Sistemas **18**(3), 491–504 (2014)
16. Tihonov, A. N.: Slovoobrazovatelnij Slovar' Russkogo Yazika v Dvuh Tomah: Ok 145000 Slov. Moscow, Russkiy Yazik, vol. 1, 854 p.; vol. 2, 885 p. (1985)
17. Xu, W., Ritter, A., Grishman, R.: Gathering and generating paraphrases from twitter with application to normalization. In: Proceedings of the Sixth Workshop on Building and Using Comparable Corpora, Sofia, Bulgaria, pp. 121–128, August 2013

Mathematical Model of an Ontological-Semantic Analyzer Using Basic Ontological-Semantic Patterns

Anastasia Mochalova$^{(\boxtimes)}$ and Vladimir Mochalov

IKIR FEB RAS, Mirnaya str. 7., 684034 Paratunka, Kamchatka Region, Russia
{a.mochalova,vmochalov}@ikir.ru
http://www.ikir.ru

Abstract. In this work we propose a mathematical model of a Russian-text semantic analyzer based on semantic rules. We provide a working algorithm of the semantic analyzer and demonstrate some examples of its software implementation in Java language. According to the developed algorithm, the text that proceeds to the input of the semantic analyzer is gradually reduced: some syntaxemes from the analyzed text, in accordance with semantic rules, are added to a queue with priority; then on each iteration the syntaxeme corresponding to the highest priority element is removed from the text. When a syntaxeme is removed from the text, the corresponding element is removed from the queue. Priority definition for a queue element bases on the value of the group priority of the semantic dependence which is described by a semantic rule, as well as on the position in the analyzed syntaxeme corresponding to the queue element.

Keywords: Semantic analyzer · Semantic relations · Automated text processing

1 Introduction

Development of informational technologies has led to increase in digital texts volumes. Consequently, the problems of automated text processing become more and more urgent. Semantic analysis is one of the basic problems of machine text analysis. The task of semantic text analysis arises when solving the following problems of automated text processing in development of question answering systems and information retrieval systems, in classification systems and estimation of texts resemblance, in plagiarism and authorship detection, in problems of semantic matching in search, disambiguation and information retrieval and some others. A lot of works are devoted to the listed problems, for instance [1–11] etc. In this work we propose a mathematical model of semantic text analysis, describe the operation algorithm of the analyzer that was constructed according to this model and software implementation of a prototype of semantic analysis system.

G. Sidorov and O. Herrera-Alcántara (Eds.): MICAI 2016, Part I, LNAI 10061, pp. 53–66, 2017.
DOI: 10.1007/978-3-319-62434-1_5

One of the most commonly used methods of automated text processing is its comparison with various patterns. For example, in work [12] the author describes a method to automatically construct ontologies basing on lexical-semantic patterns. The method of syntactic patterns based on case grammar conception of Ch. Fillmore described in works [13,14] is used for automated transformation of knowledge structures stored in a database into natural language texts. Such patterns are also used to formalize text information which is described by the author of [15]. The author proposes a method for automated pattern formation to identify entities and events, as well as algorithms to form a graph of syntactic-semantic relation using syntactic-semantic patterns, the construction of which is suggested to be automatized. Syntactic patterns for named groups compilation are used to extract collocation terms [16,17].

One of effective methods to extract semantic relations is the lexical patterns method [18,19]. Marti Hearst [18] has shown that this method demonstrates the "adequate enough" result for identification of subsumption relations. patterns are another inherent part of machine search in a documents collection as well as other areas of automated text analysis. Although all aforementioned patterns differ from one another, as well as their purposes, they still have one characteristic in common: they are compared to a natural-language text which is kept immutable during the whole operation of comparison with all patterns. In this work we propose a method to compare a text with basic semantic patterns that results in formed semantic dependencies linking the parts of the analyzed sentence. A peculiar feature of this algorithm and its difference from aforementioned methods of comparing text with patterns is that the analyzed sentence fed to the input of the semantic analyzer is gradually reduced during the analysis: some parts of the sentence are removed from the following analysis under certain conditions described in basic semantic patterns. The proposed model of a semantic analyzer suggests manual formation of basic semantic patterns, though the number of such patterns is significantly smaller than the number of patterns for comparison in classical algorithms that do not imply gradual reduction of the analyzed text. Due to moderate number of basic semantic patterns, the work of the semantic analyzer is significantly accelerated.

1.1 Semantic Relation

By semantic relation we shall mean some general linkage that a native-speaking person sees in the text. This linkage is binary, that is, it comes from one semantic node to another [20]. As semantic nodes being the arguments of semantic relations we will consider syntaxemes (a syntaxeme is a minimal further undivisible semantic-syntactic entity of the Russian language acting both as a carrier of elementary (categorial semantic) sense and as a constructive element of more complex syntactic constructions [21]) or a tuple of syntaxemes (an ordered set of fixed length). We will call two different semantic nodes α and β from the same sentence to be connected by a semantic relation named R (define $R(\alpha, \beta)$), if there is some binary relation between α and β. [20] For certain semantic nodes

α, β and relation R we choose direction in such way that the formula $R(\alpha, \beta)$ would be equivalent to one of two following assertions:

1. "β is R for α"
2. "question R can be asked from α to β"

Examples of semantic relations equivalent to the first assertion:

- Action (собака [dog], начинать лаять [start barking]);
- Attribute (дом [home], родной [sweet]);
- Time (заходить [come], минута [for a minute]).
- Action characteristic (разоделись [dressed up], в пух и прах [to the nines]);

Examples of semantic relations equivalent to the second assertion:

- With whom (прийти [come], с другом [with a friend]);
- Why (уронил [dropped], нарочно [intentionally]);
- Whose (шарф [scarf], мамин [mother's]);

In the current software implementation, all semantic relations are divided into 17 groups (further in the paper we call them semantic groups); each semantic group is associated with a certain natural number from the interval $[1, 17]$. This number is further called a priority of a semantic group.

1.2 Onto-Semantic Graph

By onto-semantic graph (*onto* from the word "ontology") we shall mean a graph $G = (V, E)$ where each vertex $v_i \in V$ corresponds to some initial form of a syntaxeme from T which, in its turn, corresponds to some class or an object of the ontology, and each edge $e_i \in E$ corresponds to a semantic relation between two syntaxemes from T.

In Fig. 1 we provide an example of an onto-semantic graph constructed on analyzed text T presented by the sentence *"Время от времени в Великом Новгороде усиливалась княжеская власть. [From time to time the princely power in Velikiy Novgorod would increase.]"*. The vertices of the onto-semantic graph $G = (V, E)$ constructed on the analyzed text T will be the syntaxemes allocated in the sentence T in normal form: $V = \{v_1 = $"Время от времени *[from time to time]*", $v_2 = $"(в) Великий Новгород *[(in) Velikiy Novgorod]*", $v_3 = $"усиливаться *[increase]*", $v_4 = $" княжеский *[princely]*", $v_5 = $власть *"[power]"*$\}$. Graph edges will correspond to the semantic relations:

1. Action (власть *[power]*, усиливаться *[increase]*)
2. Attribute (власть *[power]*, княжеский *[princely]*)
3. Time (усиливаться *[increase]*, время от времени *[from time to time]*)
4. Location (усиливаться *[increase]*, Великий Новгород *[Velikiy Novgorod]*)

In curly brackets we specify the corresponding names of parent classes for each vertex of the onto-semantic graph.

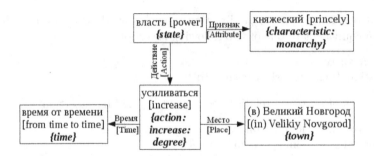

Fig. 1. Example of an onto-semantic graph

2 Mathematical Model of the Onto-Semantic Analyzer

2.1 Problem Statement

By the problem of semantic analyzer we will understand the task of constructing a set $R = \{R_1(t_{1_1}, t_{1_2}), ..., R_r(t_{r_1}, t_{r_2})\}$ of semantic relations found in the analyzed text T, presented as a tuple of syntaxemes t_i: $T = [t_1, ..., t_n]$ where each syntaxeme t_i is put into correspondence with set $p(t_i)$, the elements of which define the name of the syntaxeme, its morphological and ontological characteristics.

In such way, T is the **input data**, and R is the **output data of the model**.

2.2 Problem Solution

Queue with priority

In classical definition, a queue with priority is defined as an abstract data type allowing to keep pairs (key, value) and supporting the following operations [22]:

- *Init*—initialization of a new empty queue;
- *Insert*—inserting a new element to a queue;
- *Remove*—removal and return of the queue element with the highest priority;
- *isEmpty*—checking the queue for elements occurrence.

Within this work, we define a queue with priority as a set $Q = \{q_1, ..., q_k\}$ consisting of elements q_i presented by triples $q_i = (x_{i_1}, x_{i_2}, x_{i_3})$ where x_{i_1} is a tuple of syntaxeme names from T, x_{i_2} is the priority of a semantic group, x_{i_3} is the maximal sequential number in T of a syntaxeme from x_{i_1}. We assign to to each element q_i of queue Q its priority $h(q_i)$. Define the queue element with the highest priority as $q^{max} = (x_1^{max}, x_2^{max}, x_3^{max})$, and the maximal priority value as $h^{max} = h(q^{max})$.

Let us define the priority of the element $q_i = (x_{i_1}, x_{i_2}, x_{i_3})$ of queue Q in such way that the element with the minimal priority value of the semantic group (x_{i_2}) will always have the highest priority. In case queue Q contains several elements with equal minimal value x_{i_2}, we choose the one with the maximal position of the syntaxeme x_{i_3} (that is, the one to the right). One may show that when calculating the priority of each element of the queue using formula

$$h(q_i) = h(x_{i_1}, x_{i_2}, x_{i_3}) = L \cdot x_{i_2} - x_{i_3},$$

where L is the product of the maximal possible values x_{i_2} and x_{i_3}, the queue element satisfying conditions of the highest priority will have the highest priority.

Let us define the operation $Init$ to initialize a new empty queue:

$$Init(Q) = Q = \varnothing$$

Define the operation $Insert$ to insert a new element (x_1, x_2, x_3) to queue Q in such way that if the sequential number of this element matches the sequential number of some element (x_1^*, x_2^*, x_3^*) from Q ($x_3 = x_3^*$), and priority of the semantic group of such element of Q is less than the inserted element ($x_2 > x_2^*$), then we replace the element of Q with the inserted element: $Q \cup (x_1, x_2, x_3) \setminus (x_1^*, x_2^*, x_3^*)$, otherwise we just add the new element to Q:

$$Insert(Q, (x_1, x_2, x_3)) = \begin{cases} Q \cup (x_1, x_2, x_3) \setminus (x_1^*, x_2^*, x_3^*), \text{ if} & \begin{cases} \exists (x_1^*, x_2^*, x_3^*): \\ (x_1^*, x_2^*, x_3^*) \in Q \\ \wedge \\ (x_2 > x_2^*) \\ \wedge \\ (x_3 = x_3^*) \end{cases} \\ Q, & \text{if} \begin{cases} \exists (x_1^*, x_2^*, x_3^*): \\ (x_1^*, x_2^*, x_3^*) \in Q \\ \wedge \\ (x_2 > x_2^*) \\ \wedge \\ (x_3 = x_3^*) \end{cases} \\ Q \cup (x_1, x_2, x_3), & \text{if} \begin{cases} \nexists (x_1^*, x_2^*, x_3^*): \\ (x_1^*, x_2^*, x_3^*) \in Q \\ \wedge \\ (x_3 = x_3^*) \end{cases} \end{cases}$$

Assign two actions to the operation $Remove$: return the queue element with the highest priority and removal of this element from the queue:

1. $Remove(Q) = q^{max}$
2. $Q \setminus q^{max}$

Define the operation of checking the queue for elements occurrence in classical way:

$$isEmpty(Q) = \begin{cases} 1, \text{ if} & Q = \varnothing \\ 0, \text{ else} \end{cases}$$

Search for semantic relations

We propose to search for a set of semantic relations R with help of basic onto-semantic rules $Rul = \{rul_1, ..., rul_m\}$, where rul_i is the i-th one.

Basic onto-semantic rules have the form of "If A, then B". We call the left side of the rule (A) the basic onto-semantic pattern.

Each basic semantic rule rul_i is a tuple of four elements:

$$rul_i = [PT_i, R_i(\alpha_i, \beta_i), del_i, sp_i] \text{ where:}$$

1. PT_i—is a tuple $[p(t_i^1), p(t_i^2), ..., p(t_i^s)]$, each element of which is in its turn a tuple of three elements: $p(t_i^j) = [name_i^j, morphP_i^j, ontP_i^j]$ where $name_i^j$—is the name of syntaxeme t_i^j, while $morphP_i^j$ and $ontP_i^j$ are sets of morphological and ontological characteristics of the system correspondingly;
2. $R_i(\alpha_i, \beta_i)$—is the semantic relation named R_i, connecting two semantic nodes α_i and β_i, where α_i and β_i are defined by the tuples of the corresponding sequential numbers of the syntaxemes from PT_i;
3. del_i—is the set of sequential numbers of syntaxemes in PT_i;
4. sp_i—is the priority value of semantic group of semantic relation R_i.

The underlying idea of the mathematical model of semantic analyzer is that we search the analyzed text T for a tuple of sequential syntaxemes matching a basic onto-semantic pattern PT_i. In case such match with pattern PT_i takes place, we form semantic relation R_i, the first and the second arguments of which consist of the tuples of syntaxemes from T corresponding to sequential numbers of the tuples α_i and β_i in PT_i correspondingly. In addition (in case the set del_i is not empty), an element $(t_{del}, sp_i, pos(t_{del}))$ is being added to Q, where t_{del} is the tuple of syntaxemes from T that correspond in PT_i to the elements with sequential numbers from del; $pos(t_{del})$ is a sequential number of a syntaxeme in T that corresponds in PT_i to an element with sequential number equal to the maximal element from the set del. We then add this element to the queue. After one has found all possible semantic relations in the analyzed text T that could be defined by Rul, we remove the element with the highest priority from the queue. The syntaxeme corresponding to this element is removed from T, and search for semantic patterns from Rul is performed again. This process is continued until the queue with priority becomes empty and at the same time there is no single basic semantic pattern in the analyzed text.

In Fig. 2 we present an example of an ontological-semantic rule rul_i using which one can find in the analyzed text a semantic relation between any (-) verb ($\mathcal{\varepsilon}$) with any ontological characteristics (-) and any (-) noun (C) that has ontological characteristic "время [time]" (*врем*).

In order to formalize such model we define some concepts used in it. We will call the elements $p(t_i^j)$ of the basic semantic pattern PT_i the characteristic of syntaxeme t_i^j. We will call characteristics of two syntaxemes

$$p(t_\alpha) = [name_\alpha, morphP_\alpha, ontP_\alpha] \text{ and } p(t_\beta) = [name_\beta, morphP_\beta, ontP_\beta]$$

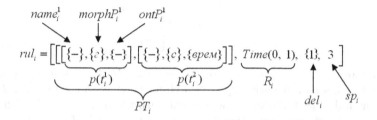

Fig. 2. Example of a basic ontological-semantic rule

noncontradictory (denote as $p(t_\alpha) \subset p(t_\beta)$) if the names of the syntaxemes match, and morphological and ontological characteristics of the syntaxemes t_α and t_β match correspondingly:

$$p(t_\alpha) \subset p(t_\beta) \Leftrightarrow \begin{cases} (name_\alpha = name_\beta) \\ \wedge \\ (morphP_\alpha \subset morphP_\beta) \\ \wedge \\ (ontP_\alpha \subset ontP_\beta) \end{cases}$$

We define function In to search for a tuple $[t_j, t_{j+1}, ..., t_{j+s-1}]$ of s elements which are sequential syntaxemes from T matching the basic semantic pattern $PT_i = [p(t_i^1), p(t_i^2), ..., p(t_i^s)]$:

$$In(T, PT_i) = \begin{cases} 1, & \text{if } \exists [t_j, t_{j+1}, ..., t_{j+s-1}] \in T : p(t_i^\xi) \subset p(t_{j+\xi-1}), \ \xi \in 1..s \\ 0, & \text{else} \end{cases}$$

In order to solve the problem of searching semantic relations R in the analyzed text T for each basic onto-semantic rule $rul_i = [PT_i, R_i(\alpha_i, \beta_i), del_i, sp_i]$, we perform the check for occurrence of the basic onto-semantic pattern PT_i in T. If such pattern PT_i is found in T, then we add semantic relation $R_i(t_{i_1}, t_{i_2})$ defined in PT_i with arguments defined in the same pattern to the set of found semantic relations R; we add the element $(t_{del}, sp_i, pos(t_{del}))$ to the queue Q with priority.

$$(In(T, PT_i) = 1) \Rightarrow \begin{cases} R \cup R_i(t_{i_1}, t_{i_2}) \\ Insert(Q, (t_{del}, sp_i, pos(t_{del}))) \end{cases}$$

Next, we check the queue Q for elements occurrence: if the set Q is empty then search for semantic relations R in the analyzed text T is stopped.

We define the q^{max} element of the queue Q with the highest priority:

$$(x_1^{max}, x_2^{max}, x_3^{max}) = q^{max}$$

In case the set Q is non-empty, the element q^{max} with the highest priority is removed from the queue Q, and the syntaxeme corresponding to q^{max} is removed from the analyzed text T:

$$\left(isEmpty(Q) = 0\right) \Rightarrow \begin{cases} Q \setminus q^{max} \\ T \setminus x_1^{max} \end{cases}$$

We perform search for basic semantic patterns PT_i from Rul again in text T reduced by a semantic entity x_1^{max}. Search for basic semantic patterns PT_i in T with the following removal of the element with the highest priority from the queue is continued until semantic relations cease to occur in T and the queue Q becomes empty. As the output data, we then have the produced set of semantic relations R.

$$\left. \begin{array}{c} \left(In(T, PT_i) = 0\right) \\ \bigwedge \\ (isEmpty(Q) = 0) \end{array} \right\} \Rightarrow \text{Return } R$$

3   Software Implementation of the Semantic Analyzer

During our work we developed and implemented in software the operation algorithm of the semantic analyzer for a Russian-language text. This algorithm is described step-by-step in paper [3]. The program is implemented in Java language.

Table 1. Examples of semantic relations

Name of semantic relation	Example	Found semantic relation
Time	опоздать на час [to be one hour late]	Time(опаздывать [to be late], на час [one hour])
Action	учитель говорит [the teacher speaks]	Action(учитель [the teacher], говорить [to speak])
Whom	поймал рыбу [caught a fish]	Whom(поймать [to catch], рыбу [a fish])
Number	семеро козлят [seven goatlings]	Number(козлят [goatlings], семь [seven])
Location	переехали в деревню [moved to a village]	Location(переезжать [to move], деревня [village])
Property	добрый человек [kind person]	Property(человек [person], добрый [kind])
Belong	мамин шарф [mother's scarf]	Belong(шарф [scarf], мама [mother])
Reason	опоздать из-за аварии [to be late due to a crash]	Reason(опоздать [to be late], из-за авария [due to a crash])
For whom	зайти за другом [to come for a friend]	For whom(заходить [to come], за друг [for a friend])
About what	говорить о погоде [to speak about the weather]	About what(говорить [to speak], о погода [about the weather])

To accelerate the work of the program, we decided to employ the expert system Drools 6 [23] which uses PHREAK, the algorithm of fast comparison with patterns. Using Drools, the system retrieves basic semantic patterns. The testing has shown that the speed of software implementation of the semantic analyzer (the working algorithm of which is proposed in the paper) increased

Table 2. Work stages of the semantic analyzer

Diagram (first):

В чем [In what] Действие [Action] Признак [Property] Признак [Property]

7 сентября [On September 7] [0] | в Великом Новгороде [in Velikiy Novgorod] [1] | в чаепитии [in a tea ceremony] [2] | поучаствовали [participated] [3] | посетители [visitors] [4] | традиционной [of a traditional] [5] | ярмарки [fair] [6] | медовой [of honey] [7] | продукции [production] [8]

Место [Place]   Время [Time]   Чего [Belong]   Чего [Belong]

Found semantic relationship	Operations on Q	Elements of Q
In what (participated, in a tea ceremony)	Insert (Q, (in a tea ceremony, 4, 2))	(in a tea ceremony, 4, 2)
Action(visitors, participated)	Insert (Q, (participated, 15, 3))	(in a tea ceremony, 4, 2), (participated, 15, 3)
Property(fair, of a traditional)	Insert (Q, (of a traditional, 1, 5))	(in a tea ceremony, 4, 2), (participated, 15, 3), (of a traditional, 1, 5)
Property(production, of honey)	Insert (Q, (of honey, 1, 7))	(in a tea ceremony, 4, 2), (participated, 15, 3), (of a traditional, 1, 5), (of honey, 1, 7)
	Remove (Q, (of honey, 1, 7))	(in a tea ceremony, 4, 2), (participated, 15, 3), (of a traditional, 1, 5)

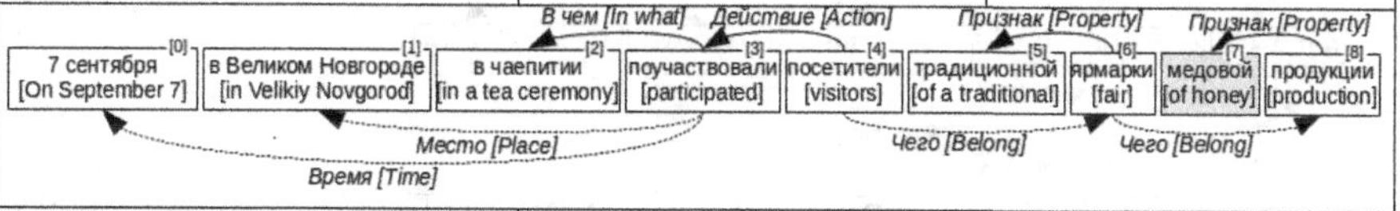

Diagram (second):

В чем [In what] Действие [Action] Признак [Property] Чего [Belong]

7 сентября [On September 7] [0] | в Великом Новгороде [in Velikiy Novgorod] [1] | в чаепитии [in a tea ceremony] [2] | поучаствовали [participated] [3] | посетители [visitors] [4] | традиционной [of a traditional] [5] | ярмарки [fair] [6] | продукции [production] [8]

Место [Place]   Время [Time]   Чего [Belong]

Found semantic relationship	Operations on Q	Elements of Q
Belong(fair, productionl)	Insert(Q, (production, 2, 8))	(in a tea ceremony, 4, 2), (participated, 15, 3), (of a traditional, 1, 5), (production, 2, 8)
	Remove (Q, (of a traditional, 1, 5))	(in a tea ceremony, 4, 2), (participated, 15, 3), (production, 2, 8)

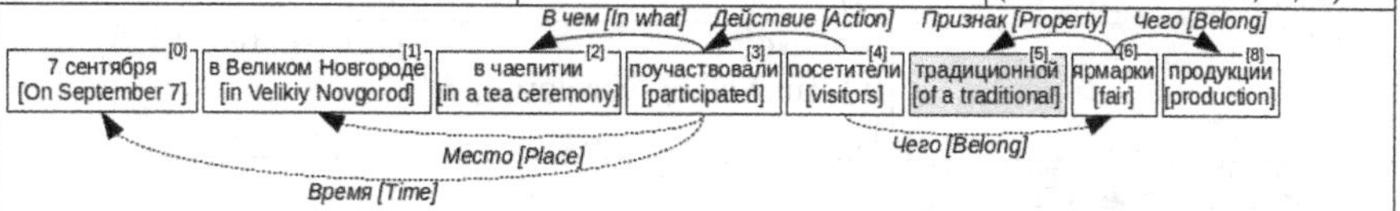

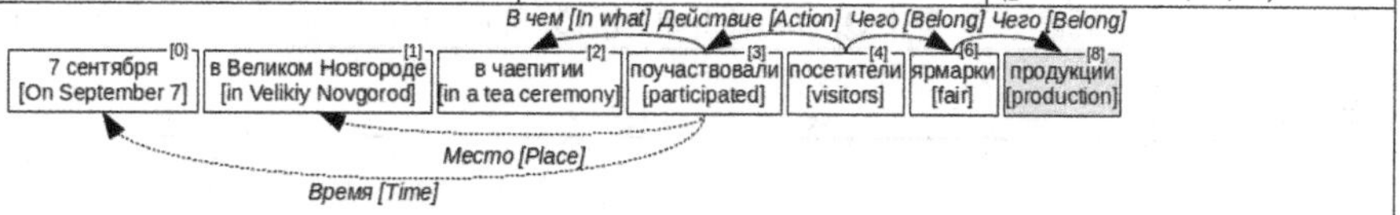

Diagram (third):

В чем [In what] Действие [Action] Чего [Belong] Чего [Belong]

7 сентября [On September 7] [0] | в Великом Новгороде [in Velikiy Novgorod] [1] | в чаепитии [in a tea ceremony] [2] | поучаствовали [participated] [3] | посетители [visitors] [4] | ярмарки [fair] [6] | продукции [production] [8]

Место [Place]   Время [Time]

Table 2. (*continued*)

Belong(visitors, fair)	Insert (Q, (fair, 2, 6))	(in a tea ceremony, 4, 2), (participated, 15, 3), (production, 2, 8), (fair, 2, 6)
	Remove (Q, (production, 2, 8))	(in a tea ceremony, 4, 2), (participated, 15, 3), (fair, 2, 6)

Diagram: В чем [In what] Действие [Action] Чего [Belong] — boxes: [0] 7 сентября [On September 7], [1] в Великом Новгороде [in Velikiy Novgorod], [2] в чаепитии [in a tea ceremony], [3] поучаствовали [participated], [4] посетители [visitors], [6] ярмарки [fair]; Место [Place]; Время [Time]

	Remove(Q, (fair, 2, 6))	(in a tea ceremony, 4, 2), (participated, 15, 3)

Diagram: В чем [In what] Действие [Action] — boxes: [0] 7 сентября [On September 7], [1] в Великом Новгороде [in Velikiy Novgorod], [2] в чаепитии [in a tea ceremony], [3] поучаствовали [participated], [4] посетители [visitors]; Место [Place]; Время [Time]

	Remove (Q, (in a tea ceremony, 4, 2))	(participated, 15, 3)

Diagram: Место [Place] Действие [Action] — boxes: [0] 7 сентября [On September 7], [1] в Великом Новгороде [in Velikiy Novgorod], [3] поучаствовали [participated], [4] посетители [visitors]; Время [Time]

Location (participated, in Velikiy Novgorod)	Insert (Q, (in Velikiy Novgorod, 3, 1))	(participated, 15, 3), (in Velikiy Novgorod, 3, 1)
	Remove (Q, (in Velikiy Novgorod, 3, 1))	(participated, 15, 3)

Diagram: Время [Time] Действие [Action] — boxes: [0] 7 сентября [On September 7], [3] поучаствовали [participated], [4] посетители [visitors]

Time (participated, on September 7)	Insert (Q, (on September 7, 7, 0))	(participated, 15, 3), (on September 7, 7, 0)
	Remove (Q, (on September 7, 7, 0))	(participated, 15, 3)

Diagram: Действие [Action] — boxes: [3] поучаствовали [participated], [4] посетители [visitors]

	Remove (Q, (participated, 15, 3))	Q = {}

Diagram: box: [4] посетители [visitors]

on the average by a factor of 7 when using Drools. As an example, the software implementation of the semantic analyzer using Drools in the writing "The Golden Pot" by E.T.A. Hoffmann identified 9566 semantic relations in 6930 ms. The testing was implemented on a processor Intel Core i3 M 350 CPU 2.27 GHz in the operating system Ubuntu 12.04.

As of the third party software, the developed system employs only the third party program Mystem 3.0 [24] the results of which are used in the morphological analyzer module together with the rules for disposal of morphological omonymy that were manually developed by the authors, the digital version of grammatical dictionary by A.A. Zaliznyak [25] and the module of automatic definition of non-vocabulary words (implemented in software by the authors according to the algorithm proposed in [26]).

In the work course, we have implemented a prototype of a Russian-language object-oriented ontology which is currently presented as a MySQL database (such method of ontology data storage was chosen due to convenient integration between MySQL and Java, the programming language which was used for the semantic analyzer proposed in this work). From the data of such base we form the set of ontological characteristics $ontP_i^j$ used in description of mathematical model of the semantic analyzer. The ontology was filled using ideographic dictionaries [27–30]; some ontological data were entered manually. The same dictionaries are employed in the developed system for allocating syntaxemes in text.

In current implementation of the semantic analyzer 217 semantic relations are used, and 196 among them were produced using prepositions. All these semantic relations are divided into 17 semantic groups each having a certain priority assigned. In Table 1 we present some semantic relations used in the system.

In Table 2 we provide an example of step-by-step work of the semantic analyzer that takes the sentence "7 сентября в Великом Новгороде в чаепитии поучаствовали посетители традиционной ярмарки медовой продукции

[Visitors of a traditional fair of honey production participated in a tea ceremony on September 7 in Velikiy Novgorod.]" as its input. With dashed lines we mark semantic relations that are present in the analyzed text but have not been discovered up to the present stage. With solid lines we mark discovered up to the present stage (using onto-semantic patterns) semantic relations. With gray color we emphasize the syntaxemes to be removed from the analyzed text (they correspond to the element of the queue Q that has the highest priority).

4   Conclusion

Most existing software developments of semantic analyzers are English-language-oriented. The problem of development of a semantic analyzer for a Russian-language text is considerably more complicated than a similar problem oriented to English-language. It is related to several factors. Firstly, the Russian language is considerably more complex than English (it is one of the most complex languages in the world) and, unlike English, it does not have strict word order in a sentence. For this reason, it is impossible to use the working algorithms of English-language semantic analyzers for development of a Russian-language one. Secondly, there are no open Russian-language linguistic databases comparable in completeness with known open English databases like WordNet [32] or DBpedia [33] which could be used in the work of semantic analyzer.

In this work we propose an heuristic mathematical model of a semantic analyzer of a Russian-language text. All mathematical expressions and formulas used in it have been obtained experimentally. Testing of the developed Russian-language semantic analyzer has demonstrated that provided the large enough amount of ontological-semantic rules used in the work of the analyzer, the quality of the program work (i.e. the total number of found semantic relations, the numbers of correctly and erroneously defined semantic relations) is comparable with the results of the most known freely distributed Russian-language semantic analyzer developed by the group Aot.ru [31] and oriented to the Russian language. What is more, the work speed of the proposed analyzer exceeds the work speed of the analyzer developed by Aot.ru group in 42 times in average. Software implementation of the proposed analyzer is used as a component module in a Russian-language question answering system described in work [2].

Acknowledgments. The work was implemented with financial support from the Russian Foundation for the Humanities as part of research project № 15-04-12029—Software development of an electronic resource with an online version of a Russian-language question answering system.

References

1. Sun, R., Jiang, J., Fan, Y., Hang, T., Tat-seng, C., Kan, C.M.Y.: Using syntactic and semantic relation analysis in question answering. In: Proceedings of TREC (2005)
2. Kuznetsov, V.A., Mochalov, V.A., Mochalova, A.V.: Ontological-semantic text analysis and the question answering system using data from ontology. ICACT Trans. Adv. Commun. Technol. (TACT) 4(4), 651–658 (2015)
3. Mochalova, A.: Search for answers in ontological-semantic graph. In: Proceedings of the AINL-ISMW FRUCT, Saint-Petersburg, Russia, ITMO University, FRUCT, pp. 174–180, 9–14 November 2015
4. Hsu, M.-H., Tsai, M.-F., Chen, H.-H.: Query expansion with ConceptNet and WordNet: an intrinsic comparison. In: Ng, H.T., Leong, M.-K., Kan, M.-Y., Ji, D. (eds.) AIRS 2006. LNCS, vol. 4182, pp. 1–13. Springer, Heidelberg (2006). doi:10. 1007/11880592_1
5. Panchenko, A., Beaufort, R., Naets, H., Fairon, C.: Towards detection of child sexual abuse media: categorization of the associated filenames. In: Serdyukov, P., Braslavski, P., Kuznetsov, S.O., Kamps, J., Rüger, S., Agichtein, E., Segalovich, I., Yilmaz, E. (eds.) ECIR 2013. LNCS, vol. 7814, pp. 776–779. Springer, Heidelberg (2013). doi:10.1007/978-3-642-36973-5_82
6. Mihalcea, R., Corley, C., Strapparava, C.: Corpus-based and knowledge-based measures of text semantic similarity. In: AAAI 2006, pp. 775–780 (2006)
7. Tsatsaronis, G., Varlamis, I., Vazirgiannis, M.: Text relatedness based on a word thesaurus. J. Artif. Intell. Res. **37**, 1–39 (2010)

8. Patwardhan, S., Banerjee, S., Pedersen, T.: Using measures of semantic relatedness for word sense disambiguation. In: Gelbukh, A. (ed.) CICLing 2003. LNCS, vol. 2588, pp. 241–257. Springer, Heidelberg (2003). doi:10.1007/3-540-36456-0_24

9. Li, H., Xu, J.: Semantic matching in search. Found. Trends Inf. Retr. **7**(5), 343–469 (2014)

10. Gupta, M., Bendersky, M.: Information retrieval with verbose queries. Found. Trends Inf. Retr. **9**(3–4), 209–354 (2015)

11. Gómez-Adorno, H., Sidorov, G., Pinto, D., Vilariño, D., Gelbukh, A.: Automatic authorship detection using textual patterns extracted from integrated syntactic graphs. Sensors **16** (2016)

12. Rabchevskiy, E.A.: Automated construction of ontologies basin on lexical-syntactic patterns for information retrieval. In: Proceedings of 11th All-Russian Scientific Conference "Digital Libraries: Prospective Methods and Technologies, Digital Collections" – RCDL 2009, Petrozavodsk, pp. 69–77 (2009). (in Russian)

13. Fillmore, C.: The Case for Case. New in foreign linguistics, Issue X, pp. 369–495. Progress, Moscow (1981). (in Russian)

14. Fillmore, C.: The case for case reopened. New in Foreign Linguistics, Issue X, pp. 496–530. Progress, Moscow (1981). (in Russian)

15. Chubinidze, K.A.: A method of syntactic-semantic patterns and its application in information technology of texts interpretation. Ph.D. thesis, Technical Sciences, Moscow (2006). (in Russian)

16. Bol'shakov, I.A.: Which word collocations should be stored in dictionaries? In: Proceedings of the International Workshop Dialog 2002 on Computer Linguistics and Its Applications, Protvino, vol. 2. pp. 61–69 (2002). (in Russian)

17. Zagorul'ko, Y.A., Sidorova, E.A.: The system to extract subject terminology from text basing on lexical-syntactic patterns. In: Proceedings of XIII International Conference Problems of management and modeling in complex systems, pp. 506–511. Samara Research Center of the RAS, Samara (2011). (in Russian)

18. Hearst, M.A.: Automatic acquisition of hyponyms from large text corpora. In: Proceedings of the 14th International Conference on Computational Linguistics, pp. 539–545 (1992)

19. Lyons, J.: Introduction to Theoretical Linguistics, chap. 10, 544 p. Progress, Moscow (1978). (in Russian)

20. Sokirko, A.V.: Semantic dictionaries and natural language processing. Ph.D. thesis, Moscow, Russia (2001). (in Russian)

21. Zolotova, G.A.: Syntactic dictionary. The repertoire of the elementary units of Russian syntax. Nauka, Moscow (1988). (in Russian)

22. Downey, A.B.: Think Python: How to Think Like Computer Scientist, 300 p. O'Reilly Media (2012)

23. Drools Documentation [Digital resourse]. http://docs.jboss.org/drools/release/6.0.1.Final/drools-docs/html_single. Accessed 2 July 2016

24. About mystem program [Digital resourse]. Russian language: http://api.yandex.ru/mystem. Accessed 17 June 2016

25. Zaliznyak, A.A.: The grammatical dictionary of the Russian language. Inflection, 880 p. (1980). (in Russian)

26. Zelenkov, Y.G., Segalovich, I.V., Titov, V.A.: A probabilistic model of morphological omonymy disposal basing on normalising substitutions and positions of neighbor words. In: Computer Linguistics and Intellectual Technologies, pp. 188–197 (2005). (in Russian)

27. The large explanatory dictionary of Russian nouns: ideographic description. In: Babenko, L.G. (ed.) Synonyms and Antonyms, 864 p. AST-PRESS KNIGA (2005). (in Russian)
28. The large explanatory dictionary of Russian verbs: Ideographic description. In: Babenko, L.G. (ed.) Synonyms and Antonyms. English equivalents, 576 p. AST-PRESS KNIGA (2007). (in Russian)
29. Efremova, T.F.: Explanatory dictionary of auxiliary parts of speech of the Russian language, 862 p. Russian language (2001). (in Russian)
30. Baranov, O.S.: Ideographic dictionary of the Russian language. ETS Publishing House, 820 p. (1995). (in Russian)
31. Automatic text processing [Digital resourse]. Russian language: http://www.aot.ru. Accessed 23 May 2016
32. WordNet. https://wordnet.princeton.edu/. Accessed 14 Feb 2016
33. DBpedia. http://wiki.dbpedia.org. Accessed 14 Feb 2016

CookingQA: A Question Answering System Based on Cooking Ontology

Riyanka Manna[1], Partha Pakray[2], Somnath Banerjee[1], Dipankar Das[1],
and Alexander Gelbukh[3(✉)]

[1] Department of Computer Science and Engineering,
Jadavpur University, Kolkata, India
riyankamanna16@gmail.com, sb.cse.ju@gmail.com,
dipankar.dipnil2005@gmail.com
[2] Department of Computer Science and Engineering,
National Institute of Technology Mizoram, Aizawl, India
parthapakray@gmail.com
[3] Centro de Investigación en Computación (CIC),
Instituto Politécnico Nacional (IPN), Mexico City, Mexico
gelbukh@gelbukh.com
http://www.gelbukh.com

Abstract. We present an approach to develop a Question Answering (QA) system over cooking recipes that makes use of Cooking Ontology management. QA systems are designed to satisfy the user's specific information need whereas ontology is the conceptualization of knowledge and it exhibits the hierarchical structure. The system is an Information retrieval (IR) based system where the various tasks to be handled like question classification, answer pattern recognition, indexing, final answer generation. Our proposed QA System use Apache Lucene for document retrieval. All cooking related documents are indexed using Apache Lucene. Stop words are removed from each cooking related question and formed the query words which are identified to retrieve the most relevant document using Lucene. Relevant paragraphs are selected from the retrieved documents based on the *tf-idf* of the matching query words along with n-gram overlap of the paragraph with the original question. This paper also presents a way to develop an ontology model in such a way that the queries can be processed with the help of the ontology knowledge base and generate the exact answer.

1 Introduction

Question Answering (QA) is an important research area in Natural Language Processing. It provides an answer-driven approach to information access. The task of a QA system is to find the answer to a question basing on a large collection of documents where questions are submitted in place of keyword-based query and relevant answers are returned in place of documents. The most popular classes of technique for QA are open-domain and restricted-domain systems. Open-domain question answering (ODQA) deals with questions about nearly everything and can only rely on general ontology. In contrast, restricted-domain question answering (RDQA) deals with

G. Sidorov and O. Herrera-Alcántara (Eds.): MICAI 2016, Part I, LNAI 10061, pp. 67–78, 2017.
DOI: 10.1007/978-3-319-62434-1_6

questions under a specific domain like railways, jobs, agriculture, automobiles, medicine or cooking.

Our QA system is intended for the cooking domain. In cooking recipe domain, the textual data contains a set of queries that show how to prepare dishes, what is the preparation time, etc. The extraction of important information (e.g., components, ingredients, processing etc.) from a recipe becomes essential to the people in general and to the people in specific such as chefs, house-wives, nutritionists etc.

This QA system is based on Information Retrieval (IR) and also will use the Cooking Ontology for answering of a particular question. An ontology is helpful in this context of a QA system. Ontology is commonly used as a structure for capturing knowledge about a certain topic via providing relevant concepts and relations between the entities. Ontology has a different meaning in the field of AI or knowledge sharing. The work [1] gives the following meaning in the AI field: For AI systems, what "exists" is that which can be represented. When the knowledge of a domain is represented in a declarative formalism, the set of objects that can be represented is called the universe of discourse. This set of objects, and the describable relationships among them, are reflected in the representational vocabulary with which a knowledge based program represents knowledge. Thus, in the context of AI, we can describe the ontology of a program by defining a set of representational terms. In such an ontology, definitions associate the names of entities in the universe of discourse (e.g., classes, relations, functions, or other objects) with human readable text describing what the names mean, and formal axioms that constrain the interpretation and well-formed use of these terms.

Formally, an ontology is in instantiation of a logical theory. An ontology is a structured web of words and concepts which are connected with each other. The top of an ontology are the concepts, and concepts can have more specific concepts. This determines the structure of the ontology. Ontologies are a fundamental data structure for conceptualizing knowledge. Ontology evaluation is an important issue that must be addressed if ontologies are to be widely adopted in question answering system Ontology construction is an iterative process and involves the following steps [2]:

- Design: Specifies the scope and purpose of the ontology. Also reveals the relationship among classes and subclasses.
- Development: Decides whether construction of ontology has to be done from scratch or to reuse an existing ontology.
- Integration: Combine the developed ontology with the already existing one.
- Validation and Feedback: The completeness of the constructed ontology is verified with the help of automated tools or by seeking the opinion of the experts.
- Iteration: Repeat the process and incorporate the changes given by the expert.

An ontology provides a common understanding of specific domains that can be communicated between people and application systems. Ontology consists of four main components to represent a domain. They are:

1. Concept or class: It represents a set of entities within a domain.
2. Relation: specifies the interaction among concepts.

3. Instance: indicates the concrete example of concepts within the domain.
4. Axioms: denote a statement that is always true.

The rest of the paper is structured as follows: we start with a discussion of the related work in Sect. 2. We propose the cooking ontology in Sect. 3. The class hierarchy and conceptual relation for ontology is described in Sect. 4. In Sect. 5, we discuss the reusability of the ontology. Section 6 discusses the proposed architecture of the research problem and finally in Sect. 7, we end with a conclusion.

2 Related Work

The main aim of Question Answering is to find the exact answers to natural language question from a large collection of documents. In general Question Answering systems that combine the IR with extraction techniques to detect a set of candidates and then use some selection strategy to generate the final answers. The research problem we have attempted in this work is procedural question answering. In general, a "procedure" is a specified series of actions or operations or a set of commands which have to be executed in order to obtain a goal. Less precisely speaking, the word "procedure" can indicate a sequence of activities, task, steps, decisions, calculations and processes, that when undertaken in the sequence laid down produces the described results, product or outcome. Therefore, procedural texts compose of a sequence of instructions in order to reach a goal and range from apparently simple cooking recipes to large maintenance manuals. It also includes documents as diverse as teaching texts, medical notices, social behaviour recommendations, directions for use, assembly notices, do-it-yourself notices, itinerary guides, advice texts, savoir-faire guides etc. [19, 20]. So, the questions of procedural text are as diverse as its range of diversity. In our perspective, procedural questions will be of much growing interest to the non-technical as well as technical staff. Statistics also showed that procedural questions is the second largest set of queries formed to web search engines after factoid questions [21]. This is confirmed by another detailed study carried out by [22].

During ontology construction, concepts are modelled as classes or sub classes, the relations are represented as is-a, part-of and so on that exists between classes and sub classes. Instances are the values of the attributes of the class that describes the necessary properties. The work on the ontology field goes back to the beginning of 1990. The first ontologies were built from scratch and made available in order to demonstrate their usefulness. Gruber's [1] work was the first to describe the role of ontologies in supporting knowledge sharing activities, and presented a set of guidelines for the development of ontologies.

The paper [3] explores the question recommendation and answer extraction is in question answering system. The system uses the statistical language model to find out user interest distribution, and develop the user list of question recommendation. This paper also analyses the candidate answers, calculates the similarity between the question and the answer with the help of multiple syntactic and semantic features, and then gets the probable answer list, so the user can more easily choose the best required answer. According to [4] an IR based question answering system is developed which analyses user questions, retrieves service documents from an inverted index and ranks them with a customized scoring function. The QA system is designed to generate direct answers to questions in German concerning governmental services. The system successfully maintains ambiguous questions with the help of retrieval methods, task trees and a rule-based approach.

A machine-learning approach [5] is described to develop some components of a question answering system i.e., POS tagger, a shallow parser, a named entity recognition module, and a module for finding the aim of the question. These modules are used for analysing the questions and also for analysing the selected passages which may contain the exact answer. Question analyser extracts the syntactic and semantic features using these three components and saves them in question analysis records. Passage retriever uses this information to extract relevant passages. Answer selector compare the question-analysis record and retrieved passages and generate the final answer with the help of these three learning components. A new system [6] is introduced, i.e., Text2KB, that enriches question answering over a knowledge base by using external text data. This work develops a novel techniques for using external text to improve the performance of the Knowledge base Question Answering (KBQA) approach. Unstructured text resources can be effectively utilized for knowledge base question answering to improve query understanding, candidate answer generation and ranking. This approach bridges the gap between Text-QA and KBQA worlds, introducing an important step forward towards combining unstructured and structured data for question answering.

An ontology based cooking system [7] was developed to integrate a question answering system. The paper gives details on the steps performed for the building process, which mainly consisted in: specification, knowledge acquisition, conceptualization, implementation and evaluation. The ontology comprehends four main modules covering the key concepts of the cooking domain – actions, food, recipes, and utensils – and three auxiliary modules – units and measures, equivalencies and plate types. The knowledge model was then formalized using Protégé, which is an open-source ontology editor and framework for building intelligent systems. A Food-Oriented Ontology-Driven system [8] was presented for food or menu planning in a restaurant, clinic/hospital, or at home. The ontology contains specifications of ingredients, substances, nutrition facts, recommended daily intakes for different regions, dishes, and menus.

An Ontology Design Pattern for Cooking Recipes [9] present a description and result of an ontology modelling. The aim of the model is to bridge heterogeneity across representational choices by developing a content ontology design pattern which is general enough to allow for the integration of information from different web sites. The concrete OWL ontology was created using Protégé.

In [10] proposed a model for the instructional structure and criteria to identify its main components: titles, instructions, warnings and prerequisites. The main aim of this research, besides a contribution to text processing, was to be able to answer procedural questions (How-to? questions), where the answer was a well-formed portion of a text, not a small set of words as for factoid questions.

In [11] addressed the parsing and analysing argumentative structures in procedural texts. The pattern matching based query classification for procedural QA has proposed in [12].

For our experiment we have used Protégé[1] as the tool of choice for setting up the ontology.

3   Cooking Ontology

Our ontology is based on the requirement analysis of cooking domain. The concepts therein provide a schematic view of the particulars involved in the domain. The relationships between the concepts or classes comprehend the real world interaction among various modules of ontology.

This model describes the following process:

1. identification of concepts or classes;
2. classification of groups of concepts in classification trees;
3. description of properties or attributes of classes;
4. relationships between the classes.

Concepts within these hierarchies were associated through IS-A relations. Attribute-based relations were used to associate concepts from the several hierarchies. The scope of the ontology is described through some basic questions that are called competency questions. The ontology building process will start through finding the answers to these competency questions.

CQ1: Method-oriented
- CQ1.1: How to make the dish x?
- CQ1.2: Help me to cook the dish x?
- CQ1.3: What are the tips to cook x?

CQ2: Time-oriented
- CQ2.1: What is the preparation time to cook X?
- CQ2.2: What is the cooking time of X?
- CQ2.3: What is the total time make the dish X?

CQ3: Ingredient-oriented
- CQ3.1: What are the ingredients to make X?
- CQ3.2: What is the quantity of a particular ingredient to make x?
- CQ3.3: What are the quantities to use when making recipe X for 4 persons?

CQ4: Utensil-oriented
- CQ4.1: Which utensils can we use to make the recipe X?
- CQ4.2: Which recipes can be made using the oven?

Our ontology has been designed on the basis of the answers to these questions. However, more implicit questions will be answered as the development of cooking

---

[1] protege.stanford.edu.

ontology will take into complete structure. Our proposed cooking ontology has shown in Fig. 1.

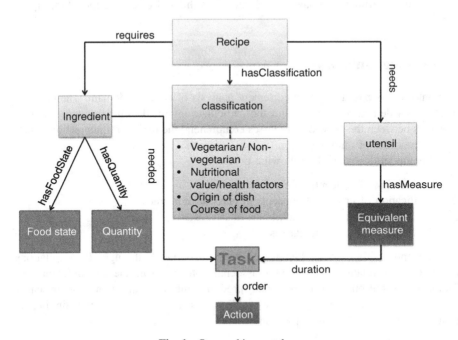

Fig. 1. Our cooking ontology

4   Class Hierarchy and Conceptual Relation

The ontology building process has mainly three areas namely ingredients, classification and utensil. The ingredients class groups the type and list of ingredients that falls under the recipe classes. The ingredient class has subclasses as food state and quantity. The food state subclass describes the state of food product i.e. it is raw or boiled or grated or mashed. The quantity subclass describes the required quantity of ingredients to make the dish. The utensil class similarly mention the required utensil name and it has the subclass equivalence measure that is also related to the specific ingredient. Suppose if anybody wants to make "*kheer*" and wants to know how many cups are in one litre of milk? And how much rice will need with one litre of milk? Another concept in class hierarchy is classification which provides the type representation of recipes according to different criteria. First classification is the dish is vegetarian or non-vegetarian, i.e., according to the major ingredient that is used. Second type is origin of the dish, i.e., it is Indian/Italian/Chinese/Mexican, etc.

The third type is according to its nutritional value such as it is low calorie recipes for weight loss or recipes for high blood pressure or recipes for diabetic patients or recipes for pregnancy. The other type is course of food i.e. is it breakfast/salads/starters/snacks/soups/main course/dessert. The list is not at all exhaustive as different information at every stage of the application can be added in the hierarchy, in the process of ontology development.

The ontology will have several relations existing among the classes/concepts. There is a relation between recipe and ingredient is 'requires' which describes the required ingredients for a specific recipe. The recipe maintains a relation with utensil namely 'needs' which provides the needed utensil name. The recipe and classification maintains a relation called 'hasClassification' that holds the different classification criteria. There is a relation between ingredient and food state is 'hasFoodstate' that describes the state of the food- material and another relation between ingredient and quantity is 'hasQuantity' that specifies the required quantity to make the dish. The utensil has a relation with equivalent measure is 'hasMeasure' that specifies the measurement of utensil. The needed ingredient and required equivalent utensil maintains a relation 'duration' and perform the desired task. Finally some ordered tasks form the final action.

5   Considerations for Re-usability

As ontology design and development is a long process which demands huge amount of time and effort, so its re-usability is equally important with its application orientation. In the proposed design most of the concepts related to cooking recipe has an implicit use in related domains. The classes 'ingredients', 'utensils' & 'classification' can be used in such ontologies which poses such kind of interaction with cooking recipe.

The concepts of ontology and relations among them are represented by the Web Ontology Language (OWL) in a suitable format for interaction with any semantic web interface. The ontology can further be improved by the semantic web community which shares the OWL platform. The application queries can easily be mapped to the ontology for the required domain knowledge using the OWL representation.

6   System Architecture

In this work, we have addressed a challenging restricted-domain procedural question answering task: cooking recipes. This work is based on Ontology-Based Information Extraction (OBEI) which is an emerged subfield of Information Extraction. In OBEI, usually the information extraction process uses the ontologies to generate the output. Information extraction retrieves information for a particular domain and the concepts of that domain is explicitly specify by ontology.

Our system is based on information retrieval, question classification, answer pattern generation, and information extraction techniques.

Question-answering systems made it possible to ask questions and retrieve answers using natural language queries. An ontology-based automated question answering system [13] on software test documents domain allows users to enter a question about the domain by means of natural language and returns exact answer of the questions (Fig. 2).

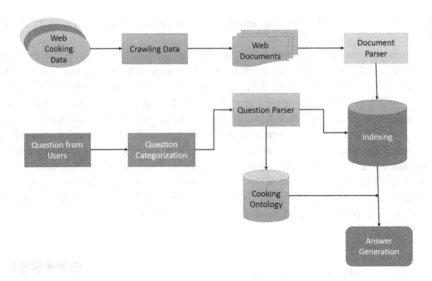

Fig. 2. System architecture

Our system is divided in to various modules. The modules are described in the subsequent subsections.

A. Crawler: A web crawler is a relatively simple automated program, or script that methodically scans or "crawls" through Internet pages to create an index of the data it's looking for. Alternative names for a web crawler include web spider, web robot, crawler, and automatic indexer. A focused crawler or topical crawler is a web crawler that attempts to download only web pages that are relevant to a pre-defined topic or set of topics. Topical crawling generally assumes that only the topic is given, while focused crawling also assumes that some labelled examples of relevant and not relevant pages are available. The importance of a page for a crawler can also be expressed as a function of the similarity of a page to a given query. Focused crawlers or topical crawlers attempt to download pages that are similar to each other.

Initially, we prepare a seed-list which contains the URLs of the webpages which contains cooking recipes. The focused crawler picks a URL from this seed-list and fetches the webpage. After fetching the cooking recipes webpage, the fetched page passes to 'document-identifier'. The 'document-identifier' validates the fetched page. If the page is legitimate cooking recipe document, the page is stored in the 'database'. Usually, a relevant webpage contains the URLs which are also cooking recipes web-pages. A 'link-extractor' is used to fetch those relevant URLs. After extracting the URLs by the link-extractor from the relevant webpages, the extracted URLs are added to the seed-list for crawling if it is not present in the 'processed-list' (Fig. 3).

A URL is also discarded if it is unnecessary. A list of unnecessary link words is maintained to verify the extracted links. The unnecessary link words contains 'about us', 'sitemap', etc.

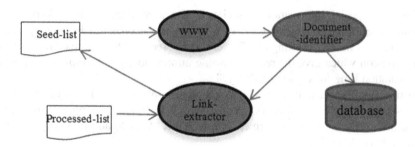

Fig. 3. Crawling from seed list

B. Indexing: The collected corpus is will in HTML format. All the crawled HTML data extracts will extract first using by HTML Parser. The HTML Parser extracts the sentences from the document. After parsing the documents, the indexing is performed using Lucene which is an open source full text search tool.

C. Question Categorization: This module is very important to satisfy the user's need. The main objective of this module is to take a user's query of an information need expressed in natural language and seek an answer from the cooking document collection. In order to answer user's queries accurately, it must accurately classify the question. The reason is intuitive: a question contains all the information to retrieve the answer. Pattern matching based [12, 14] or machine learning based [15, 16] or hybrid based [17, 18] question classification approaches can be applied to correctly categorize the user's queries.

In pattern matching based classification approach, surface patterns are identified from the corpora. The type of the answers is then extracted from retrieved documents using these patterns. External knowledge is crucial in pattern matching based classification. Without the help of external knowledge, surface pattern methods suffer from limited ability to exclude answers that are in irrelevant semantic classes, especially when using smaller or heterogeneous corpora.

In machine learning based question classification approaches, machine learning algorithms such as support vector machine, maximum entropy model, etc. are applied to lexical, syntactic and semantic features. To classify the question. It is noted that machine learning based approaches achieved higher accuracies than pattern based approaches.

Hybrid approaches combines pattern based approaches as well as machine learning based approaches. Studies showed that often hybrid approach is suitable for the question classification task.

The proposed research work is at initial stage of development. Therefore, initially we adopt the question classes proposed in [12]. In [12], the following seven question classes for cooking recipes are proposed:

1. Prerequisites Associated: In cooking recipe, ingredients are the prerequisites. For example, 'What are the ingredients for cooking chilly chicken?'
2. Direction Associated: The user wants an ordered set of instructions in order to reach a goal. For example 'How to prepare tea?'

3. Extra or Special Information Associated: The user often wants to know some optional information that may be very useful to the cooking. In cooking recipe "preparation time", "cooking time", "servings", "serve with" are the extra or special information which give the reader valuable information. For example, "what is the preparation time for cooking fish fry?"

4. Justification Associated: Often the cooking data contains text like "Add about three cups of chilled water to adjust the consistency". Therefore, this type of instruction justifies an action to the performer. For example, "Why to add three cups of child water in cooking rice?"

5. Advice Associated: Often users retrieve the advice or suggestions instruction using advice associated questions. For example, "what are the suggestions for cooking chilly chicken?"

6. Warning Associated: Cooking data often contains some action instructions that must be followed carefully to reach the goal or to avoid risk factors. The outcome of the procedure highly depends on this action instruction and unsuccessful action may lead to damage or harm. For example, "What are the instructions must follow for preparing tea?"

7. Simple Instruction Associated: More often a cooking instruction has no support and considered as simple instruction or instruction with empty support [10]. For example, "Add the chili powder, salt and tomatoes.", "Heat oil in pan, fry the onions and green chilies." Therefore, queries on these action instructions are aimed to extract the timing of action. For example, the query could be "When to add chili powder in cooking chilly chicken?"

D. Query Word Identification and Sentence Retrieval: In this step, query is formed and the relevant sentences are retrieved. After indexing has been done, the queries have to be processed to retrieve relevant sentences from the associated documents. Each query is processed to identify the query words for submission to Lucene. Each hypothesis has been submitted to Lucene after removing stop words. A stop word list is maintained to identify the stop words. After discarding the stop words from the query, the remaining words are identified as the query words. Query words may appear in inflected forms in the question.

E. Ontology Development for Cooking Recipes: An ontology is helpful in this QA system. The ontology field has started the beginning of 1990. From those early years, ontology building methodologies have evolved, and several have been proposed in order to achieve the current state of the art in ontology design. Ontology has a different meaning in the field of Artificial Intelligence (AI) or knowledge sharing.

The ontology is specialised in relations between words, such as ingredients and what kind of actions you can perform on them and what will be the result of that action. This could help in the analysis of questions or the corpus and it could spot ambiguity and could ask for clarification. For example, *"Which instrument is required for frying egg?"*. By the ontology could be answered. In this entire research, ontology for cooking recipe will make which will help to answer the particular question. In the entire research one ontology database will construct and follow some step to build ontology like collection of recipe, annotate, extract and mining recipe data, then convert into ontology format.

The ontology contains information about the prerequisites, ingredients, procedure, some special information such as serving time, cooking time etc. of a recipe.

7 Conclusion and Future Works

We have presented a question-answering system based on a domain ontology for a challenging specific domain: cooking recipes. Our system is implemented in Apache Nutch[2]. We added a combinational searching technique that produces a set of queries by several combinations of all the keywords occurring in the user query.

Classifying the user's query strongly impacts the performance of the proposed research work. As the patterns of the user's queries have the ability of deciding the question type correctly, we will try to develop a query classification based on pattern matching. We will also perform machine learning based approaches for query classification.

References

1. Gruber, T.: A translation approach to portable ontology specifications. Knowl. Acquis. **5**(2), 199–220 (1993)
2. Ismail, M.A., Yaacob, M., Kareem, S.A.: Ontology Construction: An Overview. National Convention of Educational Technology, 9th–11th September (2006)
3. Xianfeng, Y.: Question recommendation and answer extraction in question answering community. Int. J. Database Theor. Appl. **9**(1), 35–44 (2016)
4. Schwarzer, M., et al.: An Interactive e-Government Question Answering System (2016)
5. Roth, D., et al.: Learning Components for A Question-Answering System. In: TREC (2001)
6. Savenkov, D., Eugene, A.: When a knowledge base is not enough: question answering over knowledge bases with external text data. In: Proceedings of the 39th International ACM SIGIR Conference on Research and Development in Information Retrieval. ACM (2016)
7. Batista, F., Pardal, J.P., Mamede, P.V.N., Ribeiro, R.: Ontology construction: cooking domain. Artif. Intell. Methodol. Appl. **41**, 1–30 (2006)
8. Snae, C., Bruckner, M.: FOODS: a food-oriented ontology-driven system. In: 2nd IEEE International Conference on Digital Ecosystems and Technologies, DEST 2008, pp. 168–176. IEEE, February 2008
9. Sam, M., Krisnadhi, A.A., Wang, C., Gallagher, J., Hitzler, P.: An ontology design pattern for cooking recipes: classroom created. In: Proceedings of the 5th International Conference on Ontology and Semantic Web Patterns, vol. 1302, pp. 49–60. CEUR-WS. org (2014)
10. Delpech, E.: Investigating the structure of procedural texts for answering how-to questions. In: Language Resources and Evaluation Conference, LREC 2008, p. 544, May 2008

---

[2] https://nutch.apache.org/

11. Fontan, L., Saint-Dizier, P.: Analyzing the explanation structure of procedural texts: Dealing with advice and warnings. In: Proceedings of the 2008 Conference on Semantics in Text Processing, pp. 115–127. Association for Computational Linguistics, September 2008

12. Banerjee, S., Bandyopadhyay, S.: Question classification and answering from procedural text in English. In: 24th International Conference on Computational Linguistics, p. 11 (2012)

13. Serhatli, M., Alpaslan, F.N.: An ontology based question answering system on software test document domain. World Acad. Sci. Eng. Technol. 54(09) (2009)

14. Hovy, E., Hermjakob, U., Ravichandran, D.: A question/answer typology with surface text patterns. In: Proceedings of the Second International Conference on Human Language Technology Research, pp. 247–251. Morgan Kaufmann Publishers Inc., March 2002

15. Li, X., Roth, D.: Learning question classifiers: the role of semantic information. Nat. Lang. Eng. 12(03), 229–249 (2006)

16. Zhang, D., Lee, W.S.: Question classification using support vector machines. In: Proceedings of the 26th Annual International ACM SIGIR Conference on Research and Development in Information Retrieval, pp. 26–32. ACM, July 2003

17. Silva, J., Coheur, L., Mendes, A.C., Wichert, A.: From symbolic to sub-symbolic information in question classification. Artif. Intell. Rev. 35(2), 137–154 (2011)

18. Huang, Z., Thint, M., Qin, Z.: Question classification using head words and their hypernyms. In: Proceedings of the Conference on Empirical Methods in Natural Language Processing, pp. 927–936. Association for Computational Linguistics, October 2008

19. Aouladomar, F., Saint-Dizier, P.: An exploration of the diversity of natural argumentation in instructional Texts. In: 5th International Workshop on Computational Models of Natural Argument, IJCAI, Edinburgh, (2005)

20. Aouladomar, F.: Towards answering procedural questions. In: Proceedings of IJCAI Workshop on Knowledge and Reasoning for Answering Questions, pp. 21–31 (2005)

21. De Rijke, M.: Question answering: what's next? In: Sixth International Workshop on Computational Semantics, Tilburg (2005)

22. Yin, L.: Topic analysis and answering procedural questions, Information Technology Research Institute Technical Report Series, ITRI-04-14, University of Brighton, UK (2004)

LEXIK. An Integrated System for Specialized Terminology

Gerardo Sierra[1], Jorge Lázaro[2(✉)], and Gemma Bel-Enguix[1]

[1] Grupo de Ingeniería Lingüística, Universidad Nacional Autónoma de México,
Mexico City, Mexico
{gsierram,gbele}@iingen.unam.mx
[2] Facultad de Filosofía y Letras, Benemérita Universidad Autónoma de Puebla,
Puebla, Mexico
jlazaroh@iingen.unam.mx

Abstract. The paper presents LEXIK, an intelligent terminological architecture that is able to efficiently obtain specialized lexical resources for elaborating dictionaries and providing lexical support for different expert tasks. LEXIK is designed as a powerful tool to create a rich knowledge base for lexicography. It will process big amounts of data in a modular system, that combines several applications and techniques for terminology extraction, definition generation, example extraction and term banks, that have been partially developed so far. Such integration is a challenge for the area, which lacks an integrated system for extracting and defining terms from a non-preprocessed corpus.

1 Motivation and Introduction

In the 21st century, knowledge and science have become very specialized domains, where the increasing amount of data, the new possibilities offered by computers and the interaction among scientists have led to a very fragmented paradigm that needs, however, constant communication and collaboration between disciplines in order to reach new theoretical advances and applications.

This scenario urges the creation of dictionaries and electronic resources such as lexical knowledge bases, thesauri or terminological databases in different areas of knowledge. A possible solution for the current situation of lexicography and terminology is the design and building of automatic tools that integrate the modules to process all the steps that are needed to generate a terminological products.

We propose LEXIK as a system that can help both, lexicographers and final users, to efficiently obtain specialized lexical resources that can be used to elaborate dictionaries and provide lexical support in different expert tasks. LEXIK is a powerful tool to create a rich knowledge base for lexicography, providing as result a wide repository of corpora, terminology, definitions and examples of different specialised domains. For this purpose, LEXIK is able to process big amounts of data in an integrated system.

G. Sidorov and O. Herrera-Alcántara (Eds.): MICAI 2016, Part I, LNAI 10061, pp. 79–91, 2017.
DOI: 10.1007/978-3-319-62434-1_7

LEXIK will combine several different applications and techniques that have been partially developed so far. This is a challenge for the area, which lacks an integrated system for extracting and defining terms from a non-preprocessed corpus.

2   State-of-the-Art

LEXIK is a system that integrates several tools; some of them have been already developed by the work group and others are not implemented yet. As these tools are products of the language engineering and the results among each one depend on several factors, LEXIK will use well tested systems, all assessed within the state-of-the-art in order to complement the research ongoing, as it is stated below.

2.1   Terminology Extraction

A term is a lexical unit which represents a concept from a specialized domain. Term detection and extraction are essential for the continuous development of domains, as they are used in dictionaries, text indexing, translation databases, thesauri, among other resources. However, these tasks, done by terminologists, have become harder as the development of the human knowledge increased and new domains appeared. Moreover, since first quarter of the 20th century, it was seen the acute necessity of automatically detecting and extracting the terms for certain disciplines [8].

Terminology, in fact, was one of the first domains of linguistics in having access to computers, specially to create terminological banks [12]. Nonetheless, it was not until the last decade of the 20th century that the automatic terminological extraction had started to show interesting results. Since then, several systems and tools have been developed for terminologists.

In order to explain the different terminological extractors, these have been classified into 3 types according to the knowledge used: linguistic, statistical and hybrid.

Linguistic-based systems are those where the linguistic patterns and structures are used to determine whether a word (or set of them) may be considered as a term. Being more specific, they make use of the morphological and syntactical analysis of sentences/phrases, and rules. Using this kind of knowledge, we can name TERMINO [11], LEXTER [6], NOTIONS [13].

With respect to the statistical-based systems, they make use of words probability, frequency, and co-occurrence in order to detect the terms. Among these systems, we can highlight ANA [14,24]. Although, these kind extractors have the advantage to be language independent, unlike the linguistic-based ones, they tend to have problems with no so frequent terms.

Hybrid systems are those based on the use of more than two knowledge resources in order to extract terms. The knowledge resources can be linguistic (rules, patterns, structures), statistical (frequency, probability), external (dictionaries, ontologies, folksonomies). Some examples of these systems are: NEURAL [17], Termext [5], YATE [30]. As well, in the last years, systems that include, for example, pre-validation of terms [31] or the use of Machine Learning [10] have been developed. In this research Termext will be our main term extractor since it is a tool developed in our workgroup and it is being scaled for English and French.

2.2 Definition Extraction

In the last few years automatic extraction of definitions from textual data has become a common research topic in several domains of Natural Language Processing. The 1st International Workshop on Definition Extraction [26] provided a forum for interaction among members of different research communities, a means for participants to increase their knowledge and understanding of the potential of definition extraction and a means for promoting definition extraction as a consolidated domain of NLP. The findings include:

(a) Definition extraction as a methodological resource for fields as different as computational semantics, information extraction, text mining, ontology development, WEB semantics and e-learning; and
(b) The conception of definition extraction as a self-challenging task, in particular in computational lexicography and terminography, fields oriented towards the design and implementation of electronic tools such as lexical knowledge bases, machine-readable dictionaries, terminological databases, thesauri, machine translation systems or question-answering systems.

There are currently many authors that have proposed different methodologies for identifying candidates to definitions, considering both linguistic and statistical points of view. Among other system we can find:

– Definder [19] is a rule-based system for the automatic extraction of definitions from medical texts in English.
– GlossExtractor [29] works on the Web, mainly online glossaries and Web specialised documents, for the automatic extraction of definitions, but starting from a list of predefined terms.
– DefExplorer [22] for definition extraction of Web documents for the Chinese Language.
– DefExt [15]. Extracts definitions from a given corpus using a semi-supervised approach. It learns from training data based on features previously shown to be useful for the task (linguistic features, lexicographic information and statistical features).
– Describe [25] will be our main definition extraction system. It is a very important tool which it has been developed for several years in the Linguistic Engineering Group. It exploits specialised documents of WEB for definition extraction by integrating a complex methodology based on verbal patterns identification and by using a method to cluster and organize the results.

2.3 Example Extractors

- GDEX (Good Example Extraction). GDEX or Good Example Extraction [18] its a system that tries to be a model of semi-automatic extraction of examples from large textual corpora. In former models, examples mainly followed many of the criteria of different lexicography manuals and treaties on dictionaries. With this classic methodology as working principal, it is not unusual that some researchers designed tools to support the semi-automatic extraction of examples, consisting in obtaining concordances for collocations that were stored and analyzed by human agents, one-by-one, in order to find a good example. GDEXs method, however, retrieves classified concordances and presents them in order of importance. In order to classify them this way, it assigns weights obtained from a list that students have previously rated (based on their linguistic knowledge) and which is then evaluated in a way that the system selects the same options as students, creating rules to select the best collocation.
- GENEX (Générateur d'éxamples) [21] Its a tool developed to extract examples of terms from a specialized definition by using the semantic closeness between certain fragments of texts. This process was based on the combination of the successive extraction of concordances and collocations with the determination of the semantic closeness by the Mutual Information method and Cosine calculus. Results have proven that a good example is almost always associated to the definition of the word to which it is making reference, and that it can be extracted automatically by the consecutive restriction of semantic fields applied to fragments of general language corpora. This has the advantage of presenting a conceptual reformulation of what is said in the definition by using highly informative textual fragments, but with a less formal register. Nowadays it is working in Spanish and French-Spanish (with a translator module). It is being scaled for work in English and Spanish-French-English with a complex translator module to generate examples in any of that three languages. This will be our main example extractor system.

2.4 Term Banks

There is a great variety of users of term banks to satisfy different needs and get answers for specific requirements in a short time. First of all, professionals from specialised areas, such as terminologists, lexicographers, communication theorists, documentalists, language engineers. And of course the final user, the ordinary public who looks for information about specialised terms in an specific domain. Several public institutions, universities, technical societies and representatives of the private sector have been interested in creating accessible terminology resources. Some of the most well known are:

- The EuroTermBank[1] was launched by 8 partners from 7 European Union countries. It is a centralized online terminology databank for 27 languages

---
[1] http://www.eurotermbank.com.

interlinked to other terminology banks and resources. The terminology data bank collects, harmonizes and disseminates dispersed terminology resources.

- TERMIUM Plus[2] was developed in 1970 by the Université de Montréal and now it is maintained by the Translation Bureau, under the Government of Canada. It is one of the largest terminology and linguistic data banks in the world (more than four million terms in English, French, Spanish and Portuguese). It provides terms, abbreviations, definitions and usage examples in a wide range of specialized fields.
- Terminology Forum & Terminology Collection was established in 1994 by Anita Nuopponen at the University of Vaasa, Finland[3]. It provides online glossaries and termbanks from different fields as well as on general language dictionaries in various languages.
- SABTEF[4] was created in 2009 by the Universidad Nacional Autnoma de Mexico. It is a system for the capture and classification of terminological data according to the requirements of the user.

3   Architecture of LEXIK

As explained above, LEXIK is a system that integrates several tools: GECO (corpus management system), TERMEX (meaning extractor), DESCRIBE (definition extractor), GENEX (example extractor), and SABTEF (term bank).

The input for LEXIK is a set of domain-relevant documents. These documents are submitted to Geco, which is a corpus management system with several functions developed by the Language Engineering Group. It identifies the language of the documents and applies a part-of-speech tagging for each one. Geco also asks the user if the documents are copyrighted or are free to use. In the first case, people are not allowed to see the documents, otherwise it is possible to download the documents either in plain text or tagged.

Once the documents are ready, Termex extracts the terms in them and their ranking. The list of terms is available to the users. For each one, Describe finds a set of definitions in the web. Describe extracts four types of definitions: functional, extensional, analytical and synonymical. These definitions, though, are not grouped by semantic sense. The next module, Defgen, clusters the extracted definitions according to their word sense, and from each cluster a single definition is generated. Genex searches in the web examples for each one of the definitions of the term. Finally, the list of terms with their generated definition and examples, once approved by the user, are submitted to the term bank SABTEF.

The process and working of these modules together can be seen in Fig. 1.

---

[2] http://www.btb.termiumplus.gc.ca/.
[3] http://www.uva.fi/en/sites/terminology/.
[4] http://www.corpus.unam.mx/SABTEF/.

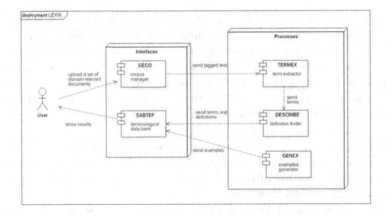

Fig. 1. LEXIK architecture

3.1   Geco

Geco is a Web application whose main objective is to manage a set of text documents in order to be used as a client app[5]. That is, to be used as an entry by other applications intended to several objectives such as the intelligent word processing, text mining, statistic analysis, linguistic studies, among others. Its main features are:

- Integration of a database in which documents are stored, with the possibility of associating each document to a series of metadata that will allow categorizing it later. For uploading the files a regular folder system is used.
- Uploaded documents are being processed by certain programs, such as a tokenizer and a Part-Of-Speech tagger.
- Documents that have been uploaded by users can optionally be shared with other users, while the folders can be collaboratives.
- Uploaded documents lead to one or more projects. One project is a collection of specialized texts which may contain files from one or more folders. Projects constitute the fundamental unit that is exposed to client applications, acting as the catalog for entry data for them.
- Users can create a public web portal to make their projects known. Portal visitors will be able to directly use the client applications that the website creator has specified.

   GECO provides a user interface through which you can upload files and manage folders and projects. This interface allows for (1) uploading new files to the system; (2) browsing through the folders; (3) creating projects determining which documents belong to the project; (4) accessing the client applications through a catalog; (5) building the design and portal contents for each project.

---

[5] http://www.corpus.unam.mx/geco.

3.2 Termex

Termex is an hybrid term recognition system that involves both a statistical and a strong linguistic process[6]. It is based on the C-value/NC-value algorithm which is the base of the Termine suite to recognize multiword term candidates from specialised documents in English [17]. Termex is an hybrid term recognition system that involves both a statistical and a strong linguistic process. But some linguistic and functional adaptations were carried out over different stages of the algorithm [5].

Considering that it is a rule-based algorithm, a linguistic study of patterns of the terms in Spanish was carried out, as well as the creation of a stop-list near to 200 nouns and adjectives. In such a way, regarding to the original algorithm, Termex allows to handle candidates of one word and improves precision and recall, i.e., it lets retrieve better real terms, while retrieve most of the terms in the corpus.

This hybrid (linguistic-statistical) algorithm is divided into two main stages: C-value and NC-value.

By the C-value algorithm an input corpus of specialised texts is processed to recognises noun phrases and generate a list of candidate terms. This list is ranked according to its termhood, i.e., the potential of each candidate of being a real term. For this purpose, the algorithm considers: (a) The frequency of the candidate in the entire corpus. (b) The frequency of the candidate when it appears nested in longer candidates. (c) The number of those longer candidates. (d) The length of the candidate (in words).

$$C - value = \begin{cases} c \times f(a) & \text{if } a \notin nested \\ c \times \left(f(a) - \dfrac{1}{P(Ta)} \displaystyle\sum_{b \in T} f(b) \right) & \text{otherwise} \end{cases} \quad (1)$$

where $c = i + \log_2 |a|$.

As real terms with length $= 1$ used to appear too far in the bottom of the output list, after a lot of bad longer candidates, then it was defined $i = 1$, which produces better rankings.

On the other hand, the NC-value method extends C-value by considering the candidates context with a context weighting factor. Term context words are those appearing in the neighbourhood of the candidates. Only nouns, adjectives and verbs were considered as context words. A list of obtained context words is obtained and ranked according to their relevance over the terms. This relevance is based on the number of terms that appear in their contexts. The higher this number, the higher the probability that the word is related to real terms.

3.3 Describe

Describe exploits the Web in the sense of searching in every kind of documents the possible definitions for a specific term. Describe uses ECODE [1],

---

[6] www.corpus.unam.mx/termext.

a system that searches for definitional contexts in Spanish from defining verbal patterns which introduce three types of definitions: analytical, extensional and functional[7]. The aim of Describe is to give definitions from the three mentioned types for a certain term needed. Because of this purpose, the system indexes the defining information on the Web and processes it to identify and deliver the definitions properly organized [25].

Thus, the first step of Describe is the extraction of definitional context candidates through ECODE, as follows:

- The extraction of definitional context candidates by using a grammar of verbal patterns with some specific parameters: the definitional verbs to search for and the nexus. The grammar also includes constraints on the verbal times and grammatical person in which each verb can occur, as well as the different positions for each verb where the term can occur in a definitional context.
- The filtering of non-relevant candidates (i.e. non definitional contexts), by using a set of linguistic and contextual rules to determine those cases where no definitional contexts are found.
- The automatic identification of their constituent elements (i.e. the term and its definition), by making use of a decision tree [2].
- Finally, an automatic ranking of the results, by using a set of heuristic rules to identify those candidates that follow a prototypical structure of terms and definitions.

As a term could have different definitions from different domains or different meanings, the second step of Describe is to join them according to its domain or meaning. This clustering process [23] uses a non supervised method with the object of making groups of definitions automatically that share similar semantic characteristics. This method includes:

- Binary representation of definitions. The definitions are represented through vectors. Each entry of the vector take a value, called weight, which represents the importance of a word in the definition. As we front the problem of unitary frequencies in the vocabulary, i.e., a word appears in a definition only once, the method considers a distance measure for binary vectors.
- Hierarchic clustering. The clustering algorithm applied finally used an agglomerated hierarchic algorithm and the method of nearby neighbor or complete linkage [28]. The later generates small clusters, highly cohesive and well delimited. It increases the precision of the clusters, more than any other method.
- Textual energy as similarity distance. The measure of similitude used between the definitions is based on a method called Textual Energy [16]. This technique has been conceived since the beginning to work with texts, therefore it is excellent for binary representations. Besides, the technique does not need marks or tags of any kind and is language independent.

---

[7] http://www.describe.com.mx.

– The energetic distance. The energetic distance is an array containing the distance between any two documents. By using the energetic distance as criteria each iteration, it is possible to use this array in combination with a clustering algorithm to generate the structure of groups.

Describe is still in a development phase, but a prototype can be tested at www.describe.com.mx. Although the clustering algorithm generates small clusters, highly cohesive and well delimited, currently Describe prototype only shows definitional context. The clustering algorithm is being improved so far [3].

3.4   Genex

The Genex system works on the basis of an association measure called *lexicometrical density* [21]. This measure is a direct product of the notion of *semantic saturation*. *Semantic saturation* is a theoretical budget which basically states that ideally a person knows a term in all its instances, its definitions, its contexts, and all the conceptual variants that it may have within a specialized discourse. If we include the above within the *Communicative Theory of Terminology* [7], with which we are working, this would be the same as saying that a person knows enough to cover all the sides of the polyhedron which represents the concept of a term, that is, the person would ideally fulfill the *Polyhedral principle* [9]. To measure *semantic saturation* it is essential to acknowledge that the example is closely related to the definition of the term, and that the terms elements should appear ideally in the former, but not in a strict word order or under the same lexical rules. That is, there may be variation. Precisely this relation measures the *lexicometrical density*. The items that are measured in the example are those words present in the definition excluding defining verbs or function words. The term, in this theory, is an essential element.

The instance in the example of words from the definition addresses two main issues. On the one hand, the inclusion of the term in the example gives the fragment a conceptual nucleus around which the elements of the definition revolve, which will ultimately be satellites and limits to the significance of that term. If seen in this way, the combination of the words of a definition in a new non-defining structure allows the terms activation context [20] to continue operating. A terms activation context is a theoretical concept that allows seeing any given word within a context where it acquires a specialized value. This is, a context where it is already being used as a term. This kind of context is thus a fragment which makes a given word a member of a particular semantic field. These fragments, however, are usually simple collocations of the given word. From this perspective, applying another filter is needed in order to find complex collocations.

In this theory not every context is a sentence. To give cohesion to the fragment which could potentially work as an example, only those that contain a verb semantically close to term will be chosen. This verb can exist a priori in the definition (a verb other than definitional) or may be the result of a search made within the working corpus through the Mutual Information measure [32]. This filter allows finding complex collocations of the terms to exemplify.

As can be seen, the first part of the *lexicometrical density* calculates how much information a textual fragment has and how much semantic proximity it has with another fragment, so that the former can complement the latter at the conceptual level. In our case, we consider a definition to be a vector formed by its conforming elements, all the words. The second vector, the closest one, would be a potential example. This association is made through the cosine measure [4,27]. The cosine determines that a sentence is semantically close by the amount of information it contains, but does not take into account its length. Thus it is not difficult to infer that many of the fragments extracted with this methodology were too long, even more than the definitions to which they were associated. Therefore, we decided to choose only those fragments with high scores, but with fewer tokens. Having determined this restriction, we can consider that *lexicometrical density* is the product of the cosine value of a sentence (any with words from the definition) regarding another one (the same definition) by the inverse of the logarithm of its length. That is, the second part of the algorithm associated with this formula extracts the shorter sentences but which contain as much information as possible. Graphically, the formula to determine this is as follows:

$$score_i = \cos\left(sentence_i, q\right) \times \frac{1}{\log\left(sentence_i\right)} \tag{2}$$

The Genex system uses four basic resources:

- A general language dictionary
- A good-size set of corpora (± 1 billion words)
- A morphological tagger (*TreeTagger*)
- A program to calculate Mutual Information

Genex's general architecture is shown in Fig. 2.

3.5   Sabtef

SABTEF was designed as an flexible administration system for databank terms, a tool for specialized queries with the aim of supporting terminological tasks. It currently covers so far the areas of disasters and destructive phenomena, physics, engineering, language engineering, linguistics, corpora, and veterinary and zoology[8].

One of the main features of the development is that it is connected to several data bases, whose content is managed by means of a web application. Therefore, it is possible to create different terminological banks depending on the required topic. SABTEF also accepts different mechanisms of search: by index, keyword, or restricting the search area.

An improvement that is ongoing is the design of an interface able to include the examples in the definition of the terms.

---

[8] http://www.corpus.unam.mx/SABTEF.

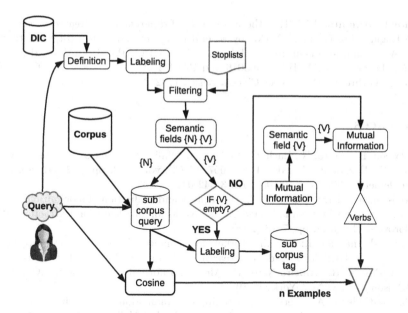

Fig. 2. GENEX architecture

4   Conclusions

LEXIK will be a milestone in terminology and lexicography, because it will be able to process big amounts of data in an integrated system. LEXIK comes to cover an area that has been developed only partially. The main objectives for designing such structure are the following:

- To implement an integrated system able to extract a list of terms with definitions and examples from any collection of specialized texts.
- To explore lexicographic techniques that can be used in real-time, with online, non previously designed databases, in a way that the lexicographic resources are always updated, taking into account the current state of the language.
- To make available efficient tools for term extraction, definition generation and exemplification that work in parallel in French, English and Spanish.
- To make the work easy of lexicographers automatizing most of the tasks that implies the confection of specialized dictionaries.
- To develop open source tools for computational linguistics, that can be free and friendly for users.

LEXIK allows us to envision a future of actual intelligent computational terminology, in which final users can create dictionaries *ad hoc*, use the resources made by others and collaborate in improving the term banks. For that, it is necessary to create a single online application with the capabilities for elaboration of dictionaries, corpus management, online collaboration and multi-lingual modules. LEXIK can be the first development offering all this.

Acknowledgments. LEXIK is the integration of different tools created at the Language Engineering Group, UNAM, by several undergraduate and postgraduate students. An acknowledgment to all of them. Also to DGAPA, UNAM by the funds through the projects PAPIIT IN403016 and PAPIIT AN400117, and to CONACYT by the funds through the project Ciencia Básica 178248.

References

1. Alarcón, R., Sierra, G., Bach, C.: ECODE: a definition extraction system. In: Vetulani, Z., Uszkoreit, H. (eds.) LTC 2007. LNCS, vol. 5603, pp. 382–391. Springer, Heidelberg (2009). doi:10.1007/978-3-642-04235-5_33
2. Alarcón, R., Sierra, G., Bach, C.: Description and evaluation of a definition extraction system for Spanish language. In: 1st Workshop on Definition Extraction 2009, Borovets, Bulgaria, pp. 7–13 (2009)
3. Arroyo-Fernández, I.: Learning kernels for semantic clustering: a deep approach. In: NAACL-HLT 2015 Student Research Workshop (SRW), pp. 79–87 (2015)
4. Baeza-Yates, R., Ribeiro-Neto, B.: Modern Information Retrieval. ACM Press Addison-Wesley, New York (1999)
5. Barrón-Cedeño, A., Sierra, G., Drouin, P., Ananiadou, S.: An improved automatic term recognition method for Spanish. In: Gelbukh, A. (ed.) CICLing 2009. LNCS, vol. 5449, pp. 125–136. Springer, Heidelberg (2009). doi:10.1007/978-3-642-00382-0_10
6. Bourigault, D.: LEXTER, un Logiciel d'EXtraction de Terminologie. Application à l'acquisition des connaissances à partir de textes. Ph.D. tesis, Ecole des Hautes Etudes en Sciences Sociales, Paris (1994)
7. Cabré, T.: La terminología: representación y comunicación. Institut Universitari de Lingüística Aplicada, Universitat Pompeu Fabra, Elementos para una teoría de base comunicativa y otros artículos, Barcelona (1999)
8. Cabré, M.T., Estopá, R., Vivaldi, J.: Automatic Term Detection: A Review of Current Systems. Recent Advances in Computational Terminology, pp. 53–88. John Benjamins Publishing Company, Amsterdam/Philadelphia (2001)
9. Cabré, T.: El principio de poliedricidad: la articulación de lo discursivo, lo cognitivo y lo lingüístico en terminología (I), pp. 9–36, Ibérica (2008)
10. da Silva Conrado, M., Pardo, T.A.S., Rezende, S.O.A.: Machine learning approach to automatic term extraction using a rich feature set. In: HLT-NAACL, pp. 16–23 (2013)
11. David, S., Plante, P.: Le progiciel TERMINO: de la nécessité d'une analyse morphosyntaxique pour le dépouillement terminologique des textes. In: Proceedings of the Montreal Colloquium Les industries de la langue: perspectives des années 1990, vol. 1, pp. 71–88 (1991)
12. Drouin, P.: Acquisition automatique de termes: simuler le travail du terminologue. Ela. Etudes de linguistique appliquée **4**, 417–427 (2015)
13. Drouin, P., Ladouceur, J.: Lidentification automatique de descripteurs complexes dans des textes de spcialité. In: Proceedings of the Workshop on Compound Nouns: Multilingual Aspects of Nominal Composition, pp. 8–28 (1994)
14. Enguehard, C., Pantera, L.: Automatic natural acquisition of a terminology. J. Quant. Linguist. **2**(1), 27–32 (1994)
15. Espinosa-Anke, L., Carlini, R., Saggion, H., Ronzano, F.: A semi supervised definition extraction tool (2016). arXiv:1606.02514

16. Fernández, S., SanJuan, E., Torres-Moreno, J.M.: Textual energy of associative memories: performant applications of enertex algorithm in text summarization and topic segmentation. In: Gelbukh, A., Kuri Morales, Á.F. (eds.) MICAI 2007. LNCS, vol. 4827, pp. 861–871. Springer, Heidelberg (2007). doi:10.1007/978-3-540-76631-5_82

17. Frantzi, K., Ananiadou, S.: Statistical measures for terminological extraction. Working paper of the Department of Computing of Manchester Metropolitan University (1995)

18. Kilgarriff, A., Husák, M., McAdam, K., Rundell, M., Rychly, P.: GDEX automatically finding good dictionary examples in a corpus. In: Proceedings of the XIII EURALEX International Congress (2008)

19. Klavans, J.L., Muresan, S.: Evaluation of the DEFINDER system for fully automatic glossary construction. In: Proceedings of the AMIA Symposium, pp. 324–328 (2001)

20. Kuguel, I.: La activación del significado especializado. In: Lorente, M., Estopá, R., Freixa, J., Martí, J., Tebé, C. (eds.) Estudis de lingüística aplicada en honor de M. Teresa Cabré Castellv. Series del Institut Universitari de Lingüística Aplicada, Barcelona (2007)

21. Lázaro, J.A.: El ejemplo en terminología, caracterización y extracción automática. Ph.D. thesis, Universitat Pompeu Fabra (2015)

22. Leu, F-Y., Ko, C.C.: An automated term definition extraction using the web corpus in Chinese language. In: International Conference on Natural Language Processing and Knowledge Engineering, NLP-KE 2007. IEEE (2007)

23. Molina, A.: Agrupamiento automático de contextos definitorios. Master thesis, UNAM (2009)

24. Pantel, P., Lin, D.: A statistical corpus-based term extractor. In: En 14th Biennial Conference of the Canadian Society for Computational Studies of Intelligence, Ottawa, Canada (2001)

25. Sierra, G., Alarcón, R., Molina, A., Aldana, E.: Web exploitation for definition extraction. En Chávez, E., Morán, E.F.A. (eds.) 2009 Latin American Web Congress, pp. 217–223. IEEE, Los Alamitos (2009). ISBN 978-0-7695-3856-3

26. Sierra, G., Pozzi, M., Torres Moreno, J.M.: 1st International Workshop on Definition Extraction, Borovets, Bulgaria, 18 de septiembre (2009)

27. Sparck-Jones, K.: A statistical interpretation of term specificity and its application in retrieval. J. Doc. 28(1), 11–21 (1972)

28. Sørensen, T.: A method of establishing groups of equal amplitude in plant sociology based on similarity of species content and its application to analyses of the vegetation on Danish commons. Biol. Skr. 5, 1–34 (1948). Denmark

29. Velardi, P., Navigli, R., D'Amadio, P.: Mining the web to create specialized glossaries. IEEE Intell. Syst. 5, 18–25 (2008)

30. Vivaldi, J.: Extracción de candidatos a término mediante combinación de estrategias heterogéneas. Ph.D. thesis, Universidad Politécnica de Catalua, Barcelona (2001)

31. Vivaldi, J., Rodríguez, H.: Using Wikipedia for term extraction in the biomedical domain: first experiences. Procesamiento del Lenguaje Natural 45, 251–254 (2010)

32. Ward Church, K., Hanks, P.: Word association mutual information and lexicography. Comput. Linguist. 16(1), 22–29 (1990)

Linguistic Restrictions in Automatic Translation from Written Spanish to Mexican Sign Language

Obdulia Pichardo-Lagunas[(✉)], Bella Martínez-Seis,
Alejandro Ponce-de-León-Chávez, Carlos Pegueros-Denis,
and Ricardo Muñoz-Guerrero

Instituto Politécnico Nacional, Unidad Profesional Interdisciplinaria
en Ingeniería y Tecnologías Avanzadas, Mexico City, Mexico
{opichardol,bcmartinez}@ipn.mx

Abstract. This document shows the lexical and syntactic study made to evaluate the distinguishing features of the Mexican Sign Language (MSL), it also shows the work accomplished in a model for automatic translation from written Spanish to MSL. The aims of this work were to encourage the conditions of a greater social inclusion of deaf and hearing impaired people, it also looked and contributed to the creation of linguistic resources in order to support further studies of Mexican Sign Language. This project allowed the development of a corpora of signs of MSL, an small interlingua collocations dictionary between Spanish an MSL, and a dictionary of synonyms in MSL. There were identified essentials cases of MSL with regard to Spanish. The application was developed using the system of translation by rules, and lexical and syntactic transfer. It required the design of a model with validation of basic syntactic structures and equivalences rules in Spanish.

1 Introduction

Deaf and hearing impaired people have strong difficulties trying to communicate with hearing persons. Although deaf and hearing people belong to the same community, each group has its own language. Sign language is indeed the main language of deaf people. In Mexico, according to National Institute of Geography and Statistic, 60% of total deaf people use the Mexican Sign Language (MSL) but only 20% can read and write in Spanish. Deaf people are more vulnerable, they do not have the same opportunities as hearing people. They do not have access to information and to education in the same way as hearing people do.

Software tools that support communication between deaf and hearing people are needed and should be treated like any translation problem. Today, the progress of new technologies, offers remarkable opportunities to develop applications to solve this kind of problems.

A sign language uses bodily communication to convey meaning *mainly the hands*. It combines the orientation and movement of the hands, the arms, facial expressions, and characteristics of their environment. Like any problem of automatic translation, the development of software applications need resources.

© Springer International Publishing AG 2017
G. Sidorov and O. Herrera-Alcántara (Eds.): MICAI 2016, Part I, LNAI 10061, pp. 92–104, 2017.
DOI: 10.1007/978-3-319-62434-1_8

The MSL does not have neither official dictionaries, nor lexical or syntactic norms. It was officially recognized until 2011. One of the objectives of this project is the creation of corpora, it can be use as a basis of the automatic translation system. Moreover, this article proposes the creation of a machine translation system based on rules incorporating characteristics observed in the analysis of the relation between the Spanish writing and Sign Language of Mexico.

The rest of the paper is organized as follows. Section 2 introduces sign languages and some of their features identified in the development of this work. The methodology employed in order to build the translation is presented in Sect. 3. In this section we also present the creation of two corpus: one of selected synonyms and another of collocations and locutions. Section 4 describes the characteristics of the experiments and the results of them. The conclusions of the paper are in Sect. 5.1, and finally Sect. 5.2 shows the future tasks for our work.

2 Sign Languages and Features Identified

Sign language is the natural language of the deaf people. It is considered an agraphic and a three-dimensional language. Sign languages have their own rules, are not a copy of the oral languages and are not representations of spoken languages although the influence of the dominant spoken language is undeniable [14]. There are different sign languages depending on the country or even in different areas of the same country.

It is important to consider that even though sign languages have been recognized officially, the influence of the dominant language in the place of origin is unquestionable. In the case of Mexico the use of Spanish is essential to have access to education and public services.

However, deaf people cannot understand the Spanish in the same way that listeners. As would happen with the speakers of a different language, do not always have a mental picture of words–they have signs which are associated with concepts–. They only apply the rules of MSL, and do not know the meaning of Spanish syntactic rules, also, they are unfamiliar with the use of linguistics constructions in different languages.

Deaf people who can read and write in Spanish usually use a variation of the MSL called Signed Spanish. This alternative try to use signs keeping the lexicon and syntactic rules of Spanish.

Looking at the problem of automatic translation is important to consider some of the fundamental differences between spoken language and sign language:

- The spoken languages are sequential unlike the MSL where a sign, a facial expression or body movement can be performed simultaneously, each with its own semantic contribution.
- Other important difference is the order of the elements in sentences:

Spanish	SVO (subject-verb-object)
MSL	SOV (subject-object-verb)

– In MSL are unused articles, except in the case of Spanish signed.

Spanish: $[O[_{SN}[_{Det}El][_{N}niño]][_{SV}[_{V}juega][_{SN}[_{N}pelota]]]]$ (the boy plays ball)
MSL: $[O[_{SN}[_{N}niño]][_{SV}[_{SN}[_{N}pelota]][_{V}juega]]]$ (boy ball play)

– MSL describes the plural form incorporating the sign of *many* of its singular form of expression.

Spanish $[O[_{SN}[_{Det}Los][_{N}niños]][_{SV}[_{V}juegan][_{SN}[_{N}pelota]]]]$ (the boys plays ball)
MSL $[O[_{SN}[_{N}niño][_{ADV}muchos]][_{SV}[_{SN}[_{N}pelota]][_{V}jugar]]]$ (boys many plays ball)

– The MSL incorporates the sign of "woman" to designate feminine nouns

Spanish $[O[_{SN}[_{Det}La][_{N}tía]][_{SV}[_{V}calienta][_{SN}[_{Det}la][_{N}sopa]]]]$ (Aunt heated soup)
MSL $[O[_{SN}[_{N}tío][_{N}mujer]][_{SV}[_{SN}[_{N}sopa][_{V}calentar]]]]$ (uncle+ woman+soup+heat)

– Are common cases of homonyms

Spanish	noun *Fuego* (fire)
MSL	verb *Quemar* (burn)

Where *fire* and *burn* use the same sign.
– In Spanish it is common use linguistic resources like locutions and collocations, both cases relate to compositions of words associated with a concept. In MSL the notion related to these concepts it is reduced to a single sign. This situation can also apply to some proper names.

Jugar canicas (Play marbles)
Azú rey (Royal blue)
Ciudad Victoria

3   Automatic Translation from Written Spanish to MSL in Present Tense

The system is focus on a restricted vocabulary given by the book *Manos con Voz*, some selected syntactic trees, and sentences in present tense. The proposed translation uses tree main corpus: the dictionary of signs with Spanish words, a corpus of collocations and locutions of MSL, and a corpus of synonyms. As we can see in Fig. 1, we first tag the words in the multiple sentences, then we made some reductions given by selected stop words, and finally the lexical, syntactic, and semantic restrictions are performed.

In the first part we describe the vocabulary that was used, and is also presented as a contribution a corpus of synonyms, and a corpus of collocations and locutions. Second, we explained how we got the tag of each word and its importance. In the third part, we show our study ans analysis of reductions of Spanish to MSL, and then other reduction given by the lexical parts.

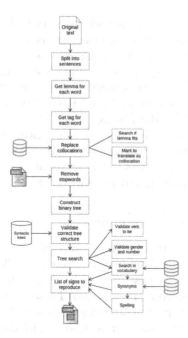

Fig. 1. Process of the automatic translation

3.1   The Corpus

MSL is a language that lacks of a formal standard. It is complicated to find a list of words that can be considered the full corpus MSL. The vocabulary considered in this software is taken from the book *Manos Con Voz* which is the closest there is to a dictionary of MSL. The words that are not found in the dictionary of 1790 signs, are searched in a corpus of synonyms or spelled as it is done in the "spoken" MSL.

We created a corpus of synonyms. We collected 206 signs with synonyms of Spanish words. It allowed us to increase the original dictionary. It is important to understand that a word can be synonym of another word in Spanish, but do not in MSL. For example *correr*(run) and *volar*(fly) in Spanish can used as synonyms; but they are not synonyms in the corresponding sign. Nevertheless, words like *caminar* (walk) has the same sign as: *andar*, *pasear*, and *transitar*. In the other hand the sign of *vino* (wine) is also used for a drunk person.

We also developed a corpus of 37 collocations and locutions that were identified in the restricted vocabulary. Those will be explained in Sect. 3.6.

3.2   Lemmatizer and Tagger

In order to perform the lexical analysis of a text, it is necessary to break the sentence down into simpler parts, and grow the complexity of its structure as the analysis is performed. In order to do so, the first step is to split the whole text into sentences which in turn are split into words. Despite of not being the simplest part of the language (those are the characters), they are simple enough to provide sufficient information to start the analysis. Freeling takes care of this task and while it parses the sentence to do the tokenization, it takes into account the role that each word has in the sentence to build as much context as possible to provide the part of the speech and the lemma of each word. The part of the speech tag is based on the EAGLE tags.

The importance of this step is related to the identification of the correct sign, for example if the word *vino* is tagged as a noun, we know it refers to the wine, but if it is tagged as a verb, it refers to the action of arrive. In this case the same word correspond to different signs depending on the tag.

3.3   Reductions and Interpretation

During pre-process, the system already knows the part of the speech of each word, and which set of words should be considered as collocations (See Sect. 3.6) to perform the translation. Not every word is required to get the main idea of a sentence and some of them could be removed. These words are called stopwords. As in the MSL the vocabulary is more reduced than in the spoken language, it is in fact mandatory to remove some of these words which do not have a sign in their corpus, simply, because they are not needed. One of the most frequent reductions found in this study is the omission of articles, moreover, after analysing a corpus of sentences, we defined which stopwords should be removed, which of them are not, and which of them are transform to a different sign.

- **Preposition.** We only kept *bajo* (under), *contra* (against), *sobre* (over), *entre* (between), *por* (by), and *sin* (without). In formal translation we also kept *ante* (in front), *con* (with), *de* (of), *en* (in), and *para* (for). In addition, *encima de* (over) is converted to *sobre* (over).
- **Personal pronoun** are kept. We only remove the personal pronouns of objects like: *lo, las,* and *le.*
- **Possessive pronoun.** The following transformations are performed:
  - *mías, míos,* and *mía* are transformed into *mío* (mine)
  - *suyo,* and *tuyos* are transformed into *tuyo* (yours)
  - *nuestro,* and *nuestras* are transformed into *nosotros* (ours)
- **Demonstrative pronoun.** Those are transform to three distances: near, half distance, and far. It was not implemented on this system because of the three-dimensional limitation.
- **Indefinite pronoun.** We only kept *algo* (some), *bastante* (a lot), *nadie* (no body), *otro* (an other), and *nada* (nothing).
- **Articles** are removed.

3.4   Lexical Restrictions

MSL has less registered words than Spanish. The vocabulary that we used to perform the automatic translation is restricted to the generated corpus (see Sect. 3.1). It is known that verb, adverbs, substantives, and adjectives are not consider stopwords. Nevertheless, MLS does not use some other words because of the needed velocity to express an idea. In order to perform the proposed automatic translation to MSL, we detected some other words that will be removed:

- **Possessive adjective.** We only kept: *su* (yours), *mi* (mine), *tu* (your), *nuestros* (ours).
- **Demonstrative adjective.** They are removed.
- **Indefinite adjective.** They are removed.
- **Adverbs of time.** We only kept: *ahora* (now), *antes* (before), *mañana* (tomorrow), *tarde* (afternoon), *anoche* (last night), *cuando* (when), *después* (after), *pronto* (soon), *siempre* (always), *ayer* (yesterday), *anteayer* (the day before yesterday), *temprano* (early), and *hoy* (today); moreover *ya* (already) is converted to *ahora* (now).
- **Adverbs of place:** We only kept *arriba* (up), *encima* (over), *afuera* (outside), *ahí* (there), *aquí* (here), *cerca* (near), *abajo* (down), *dentro* (inside), *junto* (next to), *detrás* (behind), *lejos de* (far away), *fuera* (outside), *adelante* (ahead), *enfrente* (in front), *debajo* (under), and *atrás* (behind); moreover, *allí* (yonder) is converted to *ahí* (there).
- **Adverbs of degree.** We only kept: *menos* (less), *mitad* (half), *más* (more), *cuanto* (as much as), *poco* (few), *muy* (very), and *algo* (some); moreover *medio* (middle) is converted to *mitad* (half); *excepto* (except), and *salvo* (but) are converted to *no* (not); *tan* (as) is converted to *igual* (equal); and *tanto* (so much) is converted to *mucho* (much).
- **Adverbs of manner.** We only kept *bien* (well), *mal* (wrong), *cómo* (as), *despacio* (slow), *cuál* (which), and *aprisa* (hurry); moreover *apenas* (barely) is converted to *ahora* (now).
- **Adverbs of affirmation.** Only *sí* (yes), and *cierto* (true) are kept.
- **Adverbs of negation.** Only *no* (not) is kept; and *nada* (nothing), *tampoco* (neither), *nunca* (never), *jamás* (at no time) are translated to *no* (not).
- **Adverbs of doubt** are removed.

3.5 Syntactic Restrictions

Structure Analysis, Generation and Validation. We have to treat MSL as a whole different language apart from Spanish because, as a matter of fact, it is. In order to make the automatic translation, first we constructed syntactic trees for each sentences. For example in Fig. 2, the sentence *El té está muy caliente* is transformed into the tree of the Fig. 2A. The word *está* (is) is the conjugation in present tense of the third person. The adverb *bastante* is transform into the adverb *muy* because of the common use in MSL. In the sentence (Fig. 2b) *Mi tío baila en la fiesta*, the verb *baila* (dances) is transform to *bailar* (to dance).

The way the sentences are built in this language is very different as the way they are built in Spanish, because of this we can not make a direct translation from Spanish keeping its grammatical structure. There are two ways we can express a Spanish sentence in MSL: **formal** and **informal**, to make the

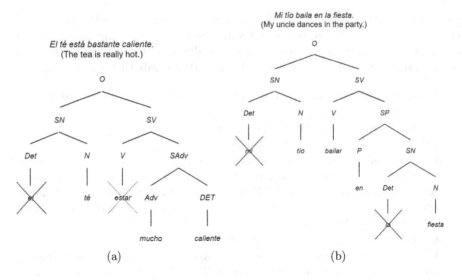

Fig. 2. Syntactic trees in Spanish for automatic translation to MSL

transformation from Spanish to these mentioned structures the approach chosen is to construct a tree out of the original Spanish structure (after replacing collocations and removing stopwords) and over this tree make a *in-order* tree search to obtain the formal structure in MSL, and *post-order* to obtain the informal structure. For the formal translation, we read the syntactic tree of Fig. 2 as: $[_O[_{SN}[_N té]][_{SV}[_V estar][_{SAdv}[_{Adv} muy][_{Adj} caliente]]]]$ omitting the article. For the informal translation, we read the tree as: $[_O[_{SN}[_N té]][_{SAdv}[_{Adv} muy][_{Adj} caliente]]]$ omitting the article and the verb to be. The sentence *Mi tío baila en la fiesta* is read in formal MLS as $[_O[_{SN}[_N tío]][_{SV}[_V bailar][_{SPrep}[_{Prep} en][_{SN}[_N fiesta]]]]]$, and in infomal MLS as: $[_O[_{SN}[_N tío]][_{SV}[_{SPrep}[_{Prep} en][_{SN}[_N fiesta]][_V bailar]]]]$.

As we know there are countless ways to form a sentence in a given language, and Spanish is not the exception, that is why there are pre validated syntactic structures that the system validates when the tree is constructed. If a non valid structure is detected then a direct translation word by word will be made without taking into account the construction of the tree. The accepted tree structures are 16 with similar grammatical structures as:

1. (a) $O \rightarrow SNSV$
   (b) $SN \rightarrow DetN$
   (c) $SV \rightarrow V Adj$
2. (a) $O \rightarrow SNSV$
   (b) $SN \rightarrow Det$
   (c) $SV \rightarrow V Adj$
3. (a) $O \rightarrow SNSV$
   (b) $SN \rightarrow DetDetN$
   (c) $SV \rightarrow VSN$

    (d) $SN \rightarrow DetN$
4. (a) $0 \rightarrow SV$
    (b) $SV \rightarrow VSN$
    (c) $SN \rightarrow DetN$
5. (a) $0 \rightarrow SNSV$
    (b) $SN \rightarrow DetN$
    (c) $SV \rightarrow VSAdv$
    (d) $SAdv \rightarrow AdvAdj$
6. (a) $0 \rightarrow SVSPrep$
    (b) $SV \rightarrow DetV$
    (c) $SPrep \rightarrow PrepSN$
    (d) $SN \rightarrow DetN$

Syntactic Tree Reading, and Search in Corpus. The construction of the tree is a step close to the end but not the last one, before translating there is one consideration that needs to be made.

In MSL there are very few feminine nouns so usually there is the necessity to add the word 'woman' to a masculine noun to make the transformation to feminine, e.g. boy + woman = girl. It is a similar situation with the plural nouns, the word "many" needs to be included to transform a single noun to a plural noun e.g. boy + woman + many = girls.

Once the gender and number of the nouns is checked then the system can proceed to translate. As mentioned before there is no formal standard for MSL and the vocabulary to make the translation is rather short, if a word is not found within our vocabulary there are two dictionaries of synonyms that are checked for equivalences to the unfound word: Spanish - MSL and MSL - MSL. If a synonym is not found then the word is spelled letter by letter.

The result of the process described above is a list of signs (full words or the spelling of the word) which will be reproduced one after the other.

3.6   Semantic Restrictions

The semantic restrictions considered for this approach are focus on the collocation analysis and a selection of synonyms. As in any spoken language, there are *idioms* which are sets of words that mean something different when they are used together than when they are used separately, it is necessary to take similar considerations on the MSL because some common expressions such as *jugar canicas* (*"play marbles"* in English) are represented by a single sign on the MSL rather than saying one word after the other one.

To deal with these situations, we have a special dictionary of collocations and locutions with a lemma that represents its main idea (e.g. a collocation can be a verb, a noun, etc.). When a combination of words is found in the dictionary, it is marked to be translated as a collocation or locution on the following modules. In this sense, we constructed a dictionary that considers a group of words in Spanish which are represented by just one sign in MSL, and also a group of signs that correspond to one word.

4   Performance Evaluation

Sentences were deeply analyse and test in the constructed system. As we have said, the system performs two different translations: a formal translation which is based on signed Spanish, and the informal translation that is based on MLS everyday use; we test them separately. First, we evaluate the reduction given by the stop words, the syntactic structures, the lexical restrictions, and the correctness of the chosen sign. Second, we used the metric BLEU to evaluate the translation.

In order to perform the tests, we ask teachers of MSL in *Casa de Cultura del Sordo* to create common sentences, those sentences use the grammar structure that we selected. We ask some advanced students to translate the sentences, and we selected as the correct translation the one that was more commonly used by them. It allowed us to have a list of sentences with the correct translation. We compared the system with other translators that use Spanish, taking into consideration that the signs differs from one region to another, we do not evaluate the selection of the sign, we only evaluate the order and the corresponding word.

The formal translation (signed Spanish) follows the same structure as Spanish. Nevertheless, we got exceeded expectations for the informal translation because of the higher omission of words. In general both of them showed good translations getting exactly the correct translation. We got about 85.71% of totally correct translations in formal and informal, while other automatic translation systems got a lower performance as we can see in Fig. 3. HETA [15] uses CSL (Colombia Sign Language), and SIGNSLATOR [17] uses ESL (Spain Sign Language), this one has a lot of similarities [10] with MSL.

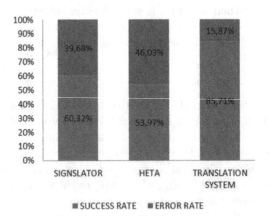

Fig. 3. Comparison of our approach for automatic translation with other translators

The reduction, given by the stopwords and by the lexical restrictions, was successfully when removing or transforming. It has a good performance even when the words are confused. For example, the word *nada* can be interpret as the adverb of negation *nothing*, or as a conjugation of the verb *swim*. In the first case the word should be transform to *no*, and in the second one to *nadar*. The system not only looks for the stopwords, but also check theirs tags.

The transformation of collocations has two main challenges. First, the collocation should be storage by its normal form, then searching collocations in the sentences was made by lemmas; for example *jugar canicas* can be found in a sentence like *jugamos canicas*. Second, we had to identify if the sentence really refers to that collocation, for example the collocation *bajo las escaleras* refers to the action of going down stairs, but we can find it in the sentence *El libro está bajo las escaleras* (The book is under the stairs) where the meaning refers to a place instead of an action. Because of the tagging process, the system makes correctly the difference.

We detected specific complications associated with the tagging. The grammatical structure subject+verb+adverb was the most affected because it identifies verbs as substantive or adjective, it causes that the shown signs in MSL do not correspond to the semantic of the sentences. There is also a difficulty in verbs which act as a substantive in a sentences. For example in the sentence "Running is important for good health" the main verb identified was *run* instead of *is*. Another issue with the tagging is given by the confusion of verbs and adjectives, for example in the sentence *La abuela limpia la casa*, the word *limpia* is a verb but the given tag is adjective.

Some semantic issues were consider as it is done with collocations and synonyms. Nevertheless there are some Spanish words with a different meaning according to the context, these are called homonyms. For example the word *toma* could mean *take* or *drink*, it depends on the context. The system can not identified the real meaning, then the sign can be or not correct. For example the word *rico* is an adjective but it can refers to a delicious meal or to a rich people.

BLEU is a metrics propose by Papineni et al., to report high correlation with human judgements of quality. The central idea of this metric is "The closer a machine translation is to a professional human translation, the better it is" [13]. The metric calculates scores for individual segments, then averages these scores over the whole corpus for a final rate. BLEU is given by:

$$BLEU = BP \cdot \exp(\sum_{n=1}^{N} w_n \log p_n), \tag{1}$$

where the brevity penalty is

$$BP = \begin{cases} 1 & if\ c > r \\ e^{(1-r/c)} & if\ c \leq r \end{cases} \tag{2}$$

and the brevity penalty is given when the candidate is smaller that the reference.

The evaluation of the automatic translators was using BLEU with some adjustments considering some characteristics of the objective language for example: in MSL the sentences have less words than in Spanish, because it is important to express the idea with the less possible signs. This aspect is not evaluated by

BLEU because it gives a higher score to n-grama but do not penalize it when there are unnecessary terms. Then, we modify it to penalize the extra-words in the candidate translation; then the BP will be given by:

$$BP_t = \begin{cases} e^{(1-c/r)} \ if \ c > r \\ e^{(1-r/c)} \ if \ c \leq r. \end{cases} \qquad (3)$$

In Table 1 we appreciate that the proposed automatic translation system got better results in average compare to other translator systems. We evaluate the performance in each grammatical structure given in Sect. 3.5. We got the same performance as Singslator in the structure number four, this one has not a explicit subject and both systems translate it correctly.

Table 1. Experimental results.

Grammar structure	Singslator		HETAH		Our system	
	AVG	DEV	AVG	DEV	AVG	DEV
1	0.835	**0.030**	0.895	0.084	**0.967**	0.060
2	0.872	0.153	0.930	0.094	**0.983**	**0.031**
3	0.969	0.058	0.666	0.375	**0.978**	**0.041**
4	**0.958**	**0.075**	0.807	0.251	**0.958**	**0.075**
5	0.865	**0.000**	0.723	0.289	**0.933**	0.107

In Fig. 4 we appreciate the difference between correct translation according to BLEU, we can see that the performance in all cases is much higher that in Fig. 3 because BLEU does not evaluates the order of the words.

We got better results than other existing translators, but the test was focus on analysing the behaviour of our automatic translation. We detected some problems in the semantic aspect and tagging process, some of them were solved with the analysis of the word and its tag. The preprocessing given by the reductions allowed us to have a better translation. Also the deep study in some synonyms and structures help us to separate two different translations.

5   Conclusions and Future Work

5.1   Conclusions

The proposed translation system got better results than the baseline tools because most of them only use a directed translation. They do not evaluate the tag of words, and in some cases they do not skip the article, or do not consider the gender and number of the elements involved.

The used syntactic trees were proposed considering that deaf people uses simple syntactic structures to communicate. Also, the restricted vocabulary in

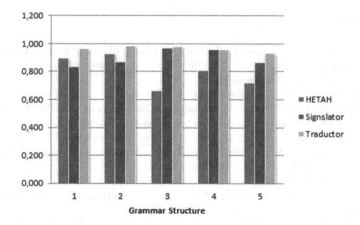

Fig. 4. Comparison of our approach for automatic translation with other translators using the metric of BLEU

MSL allowed us to identified collocations, locutions, and proper names that improves the translation.

The use of synonyms increases the lexicon of Spanish words using the same set of signs. Nevertheless, not all the synonyms in Spanish can be used like synonyms is MSL, as a consequence those synonyms were validated.

As in any translation system the semantic aspect is difficult to handle. There is also a challenge with homonyms that can be solve with a bigger context. We identified some error in the tagging phase which can also be solve with larger sentences.

5.2 Future Work

The inventory of syntactic structures in MSL limits the number of available translation of sentences. It is necessary to extend the number of structures and the lexicon.

With the collection of examples and their validations, we are able to make statistical translation. Then we should collect the sentences introduced in the system with a validation.

In order to handle different tenses, there should be a deeper study in this sense. In Spanish we have many different tenses while in MLS there are just tree basic ones.

References

1. Baldassarri, S., Royo-Santas, F.: Traductor de Español a LSE basado en reglas gramaticales y morfológicas. In: Actas del VIII Congreso Internacional de Interacción Persona Ordenador, Zaragoza, España (2007)
2. Calvo-Hernández, M., Tamez-Guerra, R.: Diccionario Español-Lenguade Señas Mexicana (DIELSEME) Estudio introductorio al léxico de la LSM. Secretaría de Educación Pública, Dirección de Educación Especial (2010)
3. Carreras, X., Chao, I., Padro, L., Padró, M.: Freeling: an open-source suite of language analyzers. In: Proceedings of the 4th International Conference of Language Resources and Evaluation (LREC 2004) (2004)
4. Cruz-Aldrete, M.: Gramática de la Lengua de Señas Mexicana, tesis doctorado en Lingüística, Centro de Estudios Lingüísticos y Literarios-El Colegio de México, México (2008)
5. Dreuw, P., Stein, D., Deselaers, T., Rybach, D., Zahedi, M., Bungeroth, J., Ney, H.: Spoken language processing techniques for sign language recognition and translation. Technol. Disabil. **20**, 121–133 (2008)
6. Dreuw, P., Forster, J., Gweth, Y., Stein, D., Ney, H., Martinez, G., Hoyoux, T.: Signspeak–understanding, recognition, and translation of sign languages. In: 4th Workshop on the Representation and Processing of Sign Languages: Corpora and Sign Language Technologies (2010)
7. Fridman-Mintz, B.: Reflexiones sobre las etnias sordas. In: Congreso iberoamericano de educación bilingüe para sordos, Paraguay (2012)
8. Huerta, A., Ibáñez, E., San-Segundo, R., Fernández, F., Barra, R., D'Haro, L.F.: Primera experiencia de traducción automática de voz en lengua de signos (2015)
9. Lopez-Garcia, L., Rodriguez, R., Cervantes, M., Zamora-Martinez, S., San Esteban-Sosa, S.: Mis manos que hablan, lengua de señas para sordos. Trillas, Mexico (2013)
10. Ludeña, V.L., San-Segundo, R., del Habla, G.D.T.: Statistical Methods for Improving Spanish into Spanish Sign Language Translation (2006)
11. Maher, J., Sacks, O.: Seeing in Sign: The works of William Stokoe, 1st edn. Gallaudet University Press, Washington (1996)
12. Manning, C., Schütze, H.: Foundations of Statistical Natural Language Processing. MIT Press, Cambridge (1999)
13. Papineni, K., Roukos, S., Ward, T., Zhu, W.J.: BLEU: a method for automatic evaluation of machine translation. In: Proceedings of the 40th Annual Meeting on Association for Computational Linguistics, pp. 311–318. Association for Computational Linguistics, July 2002
14. Pichardo-Lagunas, O., Martinez-Seis, B.: Resource Creation for Automatic Translation System from Texts in Spanish into Mexican Sign Language. Notes of MICAI 2015 (2015)
15. Rodríguez, J.: Fundación HETAH. HETAH (2016). http://www.hetah.net/traductor?ids=es. Accessed 12 June 2016
16. Fleischman, M.S., González-Pérez, R.: Manos con voz, Diccionario de lengua de señas mexicana, 1st edn. Consejo Nacional para Prevenir la Discriminación, Mexico (2011)
17. Signslator.com: Signslator (2016). http://www.signslator.com/. Accessed 12 June 2016
18. Stein, D., Dreuw, P., Ney, H., Morrissey, S., Way, A.: Hand in hand: automatic sign language to English translation (2007)

Intra-document and Inter-document Redundancy in Multi-document Summarization

Pabel Carrillo-Mendoza[✉], Hiram Calvo[✉], and Alexander Gelbukh[✉]

CIC, Instituto Politécnico Nacional,
Avenue Juan de Dios Bátiz, 07738 Mexico City, Mexico
pabel.cm@gmail.com, hcalvo@cic.ipn.mx,
gelbukh@gelbukh.com

Abstract. Multi-document summarization differs from single-document summarization in excessive redundancy of mentions of some events or ideas. We show how the amount of redundancy in a document collection can be used for assigning importance to sentences in multi-document extractive summarization: for instance, an idea could be important if it is redundant across documents because of its popularity; on the other hand, an idea could be important if it is not redundant across documents because of its novelty. We propose an unsupervised graph-based technique that, based on proper similarity measures, allows us to experiment with intra-document and inter-document redundancy. Our experiments on DUC corpora show promising results.

Keywords: Multi-document summarization · Graph-based methods · Unsupervised summarization · Doc2vec · Intra-document redundancy · Per-document redundancy · Inter-document redundancy · Cross-documents redundancy

1 Introduction

In the task of generic summarization, no assumptions are made about the genre or domain of the materials that need to be summarized [1]. In this setting, the importance of information is determined only with respect to the content of the input itself. Nevertheless, the concept of importance is vague, it is still difficult to define what a generic summary must contain. In some cases, the summarization algorithm can use some clues to determine importance, such as in query-focused, comparative or update summarization: in these approaches, a sentence is considered important if it matches a specific query, if it is the most discriminative sentence by representing the characteristics of a document group, or if it shows information different from what was previously known. However, one may need a general panorama of what the text says, so in this case what should we consider important to show to the user? This is why we propose a different perspective to search for information in multiple documents based on redundancy.

© Springer International Publishing AG 2017
G. Sidorov and O. Herrera-Alcántara (Eds.): MICAI 2016, Part I, LNAI 10061, pp. 105–115, 2017.
DOI: 10.1007/978-3-319-62434-1_9

One can give relevance to an idea depending on how redundant it is across documents, i.e., inter-document redundancy, or how redundant it is within each document, i.e., intra-document redundancy. For example, one can say that an idea is important if it is redundant across all documents (such as popular information), or that it is important if it is not mentioned across all documents (as the concept of the inverse document frequency, that if it is mentioned by everyone then it is not relevant because everyone knows about it), or that an idea is important if it is redundant only in one document but not on all of them (if only one author thinks it is important maybe it is, as valuable rare information). All these ideas could be valid on different areas such as medicine, news, geography, politics, etc.

The multi-document summarization task is mostly concerned with eliminating redundancy in the information, but instead, we take advantage of this redundancy as relevant information. Of course at the end redundancy should be eliminated from the final summary, but this information on sentences was not ignored.

2 Related Work

Text analysis techniques can be broadly classified into knowledge-based [2] and statistical-based [3] ones. Recently, concept-based methods have been gaining popularity, especially in the fields of sentiment analysis [4,5] and sarcasm detection [6]. Many of these techniques have been used for the automatic summarization task.

All approaches to automatic summarization agree that redundancy should be eliminated from the final summary. Some approximations manage redundancy at the phase of sentence selection by selecting the top n of non-redundant ranked sentences, i.e., avoiding sentences in the summary if their similarity to the previously selected sentences is greater than a given threshold [7,8].

The maximum marginal relevance (MMR) approach [9] searches novelty by penalizing the score of sentences according to their similarity with the already selected sentences for the summary. But as much as they penalize this redundancy, they benefit similarity with a given query. This method is tipically applied during the process of sentence selection for query-focused summarization methods [10,11]. So in this way, the top sentences conforming the final summary are important to the query and are not redundant between themselves (diverse).

Other techniques also penalize redundancy on the computation of the sentence score, but without taking into account the similarity with a given query. For example, Radev et al. [12] penalize a sentence if it overlaps with highest ranked sentences. Or for instance Toutanova et al. [13] use a discount factor on the computation of each feature value of the sentence, where the magnitude of the discount or penalization is related to the similarity with the first selected sentences for the summary.

Some others, instead of penalizing, compensate the non-redundancy or diversity. For example, Parveen and Strube [14] compensate sentences by not sharing the same entities, or as Galanis et al. [15] that compensate sentences by not sharing the same bigrams.

A different approach is to deal with redundancy in previous stages. In graph-based methods this is considered from the construction of the graph. For example, Mihalcea and Tarau [16] establish a maximum threshold of similarity, in this way very similar sentences are not linked with an edge and thereby they do not add importance to a node. Other graph-based approximation is presented by Shen and Li [17], where the summary is represented by the minimum dominating set on a graph built by representing nodes as sentences and edges as similarities, hence leaving out the redundant sentences by looking for the minimum set.

Clustering methods also have been successful in reducing redundancy and representing diversity by grouping sentences which are highly similar to each other into one cluster, thus generating a number of clusters. Once sentences are clustered, sentence selection is performed by selecting a sentence from each cluster. At the end some extra measures have to be executed on the selected sentences to ensure non-redundancy on the final summary [12].

As seen, none of these methods judge the importance of an idea by its absence or presence of redundancy. Their management of redundancy is only focused on avoiding this redundancy on their final summary.

3 Our Method

Given a cluster of texts, we adopt a traditional method to map them into a graph. Sentences of all texts are represented as nodes and edges as the similarity between them, so the edges are weighted with the similarity measure. After this, we also weight nodes to determine which ones are more important according to a certain criterion. This latter is going to be useful for decision making at removing sentences. We adopted the unsupervised method *TextRank* [18] to provide the initial weight of nodes, which is somehow related to redundancy because nodes' weight can be computed as in PageRank, considering also importance of the edges weight: the more strong connections (strong similarities) the node has with other important nodes, the higher score the node will have.

An important resource when building the graph is a proper similarity measure. We did our experiments with the cosine similarity measure on sentences represented on a vector space model, generated by the *Paragraph Vector* method proposed by Le and Mikolov [19], which has shown to give good results in measuring similarity considering context.

Once we have constructed this graph, we proceed to experiment with redundancy. There are nine possible approaches given the combination of intra-document redundancy and inter-document redundancy. These approaches are that: a sentence is relevant if:

1. It is redundant per document and redundant across documents.
2. It is redundant per document and not redundant across documents.
3. It is redundant per document.
4. It is not redundant per document and redundant across documents.

5. It is not redundant per document and not redundant across documents.
6. It is not redundant per document.
7. It is redundant across documents.
8. It is not redundant across documents.
9. Redundancy is not taken into account to provide relevance.

Option 3 and 6 determine the relevance of a sentence based on intra-document redundancy only, inter-document redundancy is irrelevant. Something similar happens to option 7 and 8 but giving relevance based on inter-document redundancy, without taking into account intra-document redundancy. Option 9 is a combination of these two last ideas, by ignoring intra-document and inter-document redundancy, so the redundancy is eliminated without taking it into account to determine the relevance of the sentence.

For choosing which approach to explore, two flags are stated:

- pd: indicating how intra-document redundancy should be managed,
  - pd = 1   *if intra-document redundancy is important,*
  - pd = 0   *if intra-document redundancy is irrelevant,*
  - pd = −1   *if intra-document redundancy is undesired.*

- cd: indicating how inter-document redundancy should be managed,
  - cd = 1   *if inter-document redundancy is important,*
  - cd = 0   *if inter-document redundancy is irrelevant,*
  - cd = −1   *if inter-document redundancy is undesired.*

Having established these approaches, all that follows is the merging of similar nodes on the graph, but taking care of how the relevance of the nodes is being carried on. This merging should be done first by document and then across documents. Starting from the graph with weighted edges and weighted nodes, we present the algorithm for merging:

Step 1. Choose the most similar two nodes on the graph: N_+ and N_-. Being N_+ the node with the highest weight (the important node) and N_- the other node (the less important node).

Step 2. Merge nodes, taking into account the following aspects:
  (a) The text of N_+ remains, while the other is dropped.
  (b) All the edges of N_- must be inherited to N_+ by averaging the weight of its correspondent edges.
  (c) The weight of N_+ is re-computed, depending on the flags:

  $N_+ = N_+ + N_-$ *if redundancy is important (if* pd = 1 *or* cd = 1)
  $N_+ = N_+$ *if redundancy is irrelevant (if* pd = 0 *or* cd = 0)
  $N_+ = N_+ - N_-$ *if redundancy is undesired (if* pd = −1 *or* cd = −1)

Step 3. Repeat step 1 until a similarity threshold is reached.

When merging per document, the two chosen nodes at first step must belong to the same document and the flag taken into account for second step (c) is pd. When merging across documents, the two chosen nodes at first step must belong to different documents and the flag taken into account is cd.

So in this way, the merging increases, ignores, or penalizes the relevance of the node when it finds a similar sentence, giving the flexibility needed to experiment with the nine presented approaches.

4   Experiments and Results

For our experiments, we used the DUC 2004 task 2 and DUC 2007 main task corpora. No data set to train the method was necessary since it is unsupervised. DUC 2004 task 2 provides 50 clusters of 10 documents each and 4 reference summaries for each cluster. In DUC 2007 main task, 45 clusters are provided, each cluster with 25 documents and also with 4 reference summaries. Summaries provided on DUC 2007 are oriented to a topic, while DUC 2004 summaries are completely generic. We compared the summaries generated by our method against those provided by DUC on the same cluster of texts, to assess which of the previous stated redundancy approaches are DUC summaries using.

Table 1. Sentences used to test doc2vec

		Similarity with	
		s3	s4
s1	John Onoda, a spokesman at McDonald's Oak Brook, Ill., headquarters, said it was the first of the chain's outlets in a communist country	0.012	0.149
s2	The restaurant has 350 seats and employs 110 people capable of serving 2500 meals per hour	0.071	0.131
s3	Normally dour citizens broke into grins as they caught the infectious cheerful mood from youthful Soviet staffers hired for their ability to smile and work hard	1.0	−0.081
s4	The world's largest version of the landmark American fast-food chain rang up 30000 meals on 27 cash registers, breaking the opening-day record for McDonald's worldwide, officials said	−0.081	1.0
s5	McDonald's hamburgers, fries and golden arches came to China on Monday when the fast-food chain opened its first restaurant in a nation famed for its distinctive cuisine	0.216	0.123
s6	With seats for 900 and 27 cash registers, it served 30000 people on opening day	0.048	**0.396**
s7	The world's largest McDonald's, with 27 cash registers and a seating capacity of 900, brings to Moscow not only hamburgers, french fries and shakes (called 'milk cocktails' here), but also a living lesson in Western-style marketing	0.055	0.153
s8	At training sessions before opening day, cashiers were taught the importance of greeting customers cheerfully, of saying 'please' and 'thank you' – all of which promises something distinctly different from the typically surly service at most of Moscow's dingy state cafes	**0.240**	0.136

As we said before, we adopted the *Paragraph Vector* method, also known as doc2vec, to create a model so we can generate vectors from the sentences and compare them using a cosine measure. We used the Distributed Memory Model of Paragraph Vectors (PV-DM) model, and we built a neural network with 100 neurons, a window between the predicted word and context words of 8 words, ignoring all words with total frequency lower than 5, and doing 10,000 iterations at the inference stage for computing new sentence vectors. The neural network requires big volumes of texts to be trained, for this mean we used the dataset from "One Billion Word Language Modeling Benchmark" that has almost 1 billion words[1]. Punctuation marks were removed to train the model, so the texts to be represented afterwords in this vector space model are also processed without punctuation marks.

To exemplify the use of the doc2vec-based similarity measure we used, we extracted a few sample sentences from DUC 2002 and compared them. See Table 1. Let us consider sentences $s4$ and $s3$ as a reference to be compared with the other sentences. In the table one can see that the texts of sentence $s3$ and sentence $s8$ refer to a similar idea, while sentences $s4$, $s6$ and $s7$ seem to refer to the same fact. The similarities between them are shown in the rightmost columns of Table 1. The highest values are given to the most similar ideas.

Continuing with our experiments, we tested the merging method on all nine redundancy approaches on the clusters of texts from DUC 2004 and DUC 2007 corpora. The resulting summaries of our method were evaluated against the summaries provided by DUC with the ROUGE method. Results of the recall measure for these experiments, ordered by ROUGE-1 measure in descending order, are presented in Tables 2 and 3.

The thresholds used for these experiments were 0.3 as the minimum and 0.9 as the maximum similarity to generate an edge in the graph, and 0.5 as the similarity where the merging of nodes per and across documents should stop. The reason for using a threshold to generate or not an edge is to avoid having a very complex graph with useless information, i.e., the similarities which do not provide information about redundancy. The upper threshold allows us to eliminate similar ideas whose text is almost the same—with the same words but missing or changing one or two of these words. For valuable redundancy, we do not look for precisely identical sentences but similar ones, expressed in a different way; being this similarity usually unconscious to the writers.

As seen in Table 2, for DUC 2004 the approach that generated the best ROUGE results was number 7, that is, giving relevance to ideas redundant across documents (i.e., inter-document redundancy). Even the next two best approaches, indicate that giving relevance to ideas redundant across documents ($cd = 1$) are the best possible options. Moreover, the approaches where an idea is penalized by being redundant across documents ($cd = -1$) were ranked in the four worst results.

Another interesting pattern to notice is when the cd flag is left static, the pd flag follows the same ranking: first, it is best to ignore intra-document redundancy ($pd = 0$), a less good option is to penalize it ($pd = -1$), and the worst option is to taking it into account to provide relevance ($pd = 1$). A similar case

---

Table 2. ROUGE results on all approaches of redundancy for DUC 2004 texts

Approach	Flags		ROUGE-1	ROUGE-2	ROUGE-SU4
	pd	cd			
7	0	1	**0.3775**	**0.0771**	**0.1283**
4	−1	1	0.3763	0.0765	0.1273
1	1	1	0.3709	0.0754	0.1251
9	0	0	0.3594	0.0719	0.1210
6	−1	0	0.3590	0.0709	0.1198
8	0	−1	0.3560	0.0675	0.1171
5	−1	−1	0.3546	0.0669	0.1162
3	1	0	0.3504	0.0657	0.1137
2	1	−1	0.3471	0.0634	0.1120

happens when the pd flag is left static, being the same rank for the cd flag: the best option is to take into account inter-document redundancy (cd = 1), then ignore this redundancy (cd = 0) and being the worst option to penalize inter-document redundancy (cd = −1).

The more inter-document redundancy is considered as favorable, the better the result is, whereas intra-document redundancy is irrelevant for the importance of the sentence.

Table 3. ROUGE results on all approaches of redundancy for DUC 2007 texts

Approach	Flags		ROUGE-1	ROUGE-2	ROUGE-SU4
	pd	cd			
6	−1	0	**0.4197**	0.1008	0.1558
4	−1	1	0.4194	**0.1037**	**0.1581**
9	0	0	0.4174	0.1019	0.1566
7	0	1	0.4152	0.1026	0.1568
1	1	1	0.4122	0.1017	0.1554
3	1	0	0.4106	0.0981	0.1523
5	−1	−1	0.4105	0.0886	0.1457
8	0	−1	0.4098	0.0910	0.1474
2	1	−1	0.4081	0.0926	0.1478

In the case of DUC 2007, one can see in Table 3 that the best approach is disputed between approaches number 6 and number 4 just by a little difference on the scores, where both penalize the relevance of the sentence if it is redundant per document (i.e., intra-document redundancy). Approach 6 does not take into account inter-document redundancy while approach 4 does. The worst three approaches are when inter-document redundancy is penalized. And the same ranking for the pd flag is observed when the cd flag is left static, that is: the best option is to penalize intra-document redundancy (pd = −1), then ignore this redundancy (pd = 0) and the worst option is giving relevance when intra-document redundancy is present (pd = 1).

In this case, the more intra-document redundancy is penalized, the better the result is, whereas ideas redundant across documents (i.e., inter-document redundancy) could be desirable. In other words, ideas not biased to a single source are better. Considering that DUC 2007 summaries are topic-oriented, one can think that it is more likely to solve a specific query by looking for ideas that are not continuously addressed by a single author.

Even if in this work we did not aim to outperform the best techniques in multi-document summarization, we present a comparison with other techniques on Table 4 just to show that this technique is competent when overcoming well-known baselines. We do not focus on overcoming the best results by now to leave the method as simple and pure as possible. In this way, it is easy to manipulate the graph and provide the flexibility needed to generate different summaries for the same cluster of texts, depending on the redundancy approach. We compare our method on the best approach of redundancy, which was the number 7 (ideas redundant across documents) for DUC 2004, against some baselines and some of the best techniques on DUC 2004.

Table 4. Comparison with baselines on DUC 2004 data

Method	ROUGE-1	ROUGE-2
Random	0.3198	0.0498
Lead	0.3299	0.0634
Coverage	0.3440	0.0768
Our method	0.3775	0.0771
CLASSY 04 (best at DUC 2004)	0.3822	**0.0921**
LexPageRank	**0.3830**	0.0920

The methods we compare to are: random baseline, putting in the summary random sentences (the measure stated in the table is the median of 10 runs); lead-based baseline, where the last sentences of the last (most recent) document in the cluster are taken in the final summary; coverage baseline, where the summaries are composed by the first sentence of each document of the cluster; the best score obtained at DUC 2004; and the LexPageRank method proposed by Erkan and Radev [20]. We show only the recall measure for ROUGE-1 and ROUGE-2, since it is the only available for all of these methods, and also considering that ROUGE-1 is the measure that has been shown to correlate well with human judgements [21]. We do not compare against results on DUC 2007 data because its summaries are topic-oriented while our method is focused on generic summaries.

5   Conclusions

We presented a method that can handle all variations on intra-document redundancy and inter-document redundancy, allowing to generate summaries with popular or diverse information within multiple documents, and in general any information being redundant or non-redundant across documents or per document. This can be useful for some areas where this flexibility is needed to provide a general idea of what multiple texts talk about.

Additionally, we discovered that ideas redundant across documents and non-redundant per document are good to conform a summary from multiple documents. For DUC 2004 gold standard for example, it is important to take ideas that are popular among different sources into the final summary. While for DUC 2007, it is desirable to take popular ideas in the final summary, but most importantly non-redundant per document.

For future work, it is possible to change the way of computing the initial sentences relevance by testing different techniques from TextRank. For example, a supervised technique could improve the results by obtaining the sentence relevance through features of the sentence, and learning the importance of each feature with a given corpus. Furthermore, the readability of the final summary can be enhanced by providing information of the sequence of sentences by inserting directed edges when building the graph with all texts. In addition, we will consider deep learning-based methods for document summarization [22–26]. On the other hand, we will consider textual entailment [27–29] for sentence similarity measure. Multimodal summarization might be also part of our future research [30, 31].

References

1. Nenkova, A., McKeown, K.: Automatic summarization. Found. Trends Inf. Retr. 5(2–3), 103–233 (2011)
2. Cambria, E., Poria, S., Gelbukh, A., Kwok, K.: Sentic API: a common-sense based API for concept-level sentiment analysis. In: Proceedings of the 4th Workshop on Making Sense of Microposts, Co-located with WWW 2014, 23rd International World Wide Web Conference, Number 1141 in CEUR Workshop Proceedings (2014)
3. Poria, S., Gelbukh, A., Agarwal, B., Cambria, E., Howard, N.: Common sense knowledge based personality recognition from text. In: Castro, F., Gelbukh, A., González, M. (eds.) MICAI 2013. LNCS, vol. 8266, pp. 484–496. Springer, Heidelberg (2013). doi:10.1007/978-3-642-45111-9_42
4. Poria, S., Gelbukh, A., Hussain, A., Howard, N., Das, D., Bandyopadhyay, S.: Enhanced SenticNet with affective labels for concept-based opinion mining. IEEE Intell. Syst. 28, 31–38 (2013)

5. Cambria, E., Poria, S., Bajpai, R., Schuller, B.: SenticNet 4: A semantic resource for sentiment analysis based on conceptual primitives. In: 26th International Conference on Computational Linguistics (COLING 2016), Osaka, Japan (2016)
6. Poria, S., Cambria, E., Hazarika, D., Vij, P.: A deeper look into sarcastic tweets using deep convolutional neural networks. In: 26th International Conference on Computational Linguistics (COLING 2016), Osaka, Japan, pp. 1601–1612 (2016)
7. Celikyilmaz, A., Hakkani-Tur, D.: A hybrid hierarchical model for multi-document summarization. In: Proceedings of 48th Annual Meeting of the Association for Computational Linguistics (ACL 2010), Uppsala, Sweden, pp. 815–824 (2010)
8. Prasad Pingali, R.K, Varma, V.: IIIT hyderabad at DUC 2007. In: Proceedings of 7th Document Understanding Conference (DUC 2007), Rochester, NY (2007)
9. Carbonell, J., Goldstein, J.: The use of MMR, diversity-based reranking for reordering documents and producing summaries. In: Proceedings of 21st Annual International ACM SIGIR Conference on Research and Development in Information Retrieval (SIGIR 1998), Melbourne, Australia. pp. 335–336 (1998)
10. Li, Y., Li, S.: Query-focused multi-document summarization: Combining a topic model with graph-based semi-supervised learning. In: Proceedings of 25th International Conference on Computational Linguistics (COLING 2014), Dublin, Ireland, pp. 1197–1207 (2014)
11. Ouyang, Y., Li, W., Li, S., Qin, L.: Applying regression models to query-focused multi-document summarization. Inf. Process. Manag. 47(2), 227–237 (2011)
12. Radev, D.R., Jing, H., Styś, M., Tam, D.: Centroid-based summarization of multiple documents. Inf. Process. Manag. 40(6), 919–938 (2004)
13. Toutanova, K., Brockett, C., Gamon, M., Jagarlamudi, J., Suzuki, H., Vanderwende, L.: The PYTHY summarization system: Microsoft research at DUC 2007. In: Proceedings of 7th Document Understanding Conference(DUC 2007), Rochester, NY (2007)
14. Parveen, D., Strube, M.: Multi-document summarization using bipartite graphs. In: Proceedings of TextGraphs-9: Graph-based Methods for Natural Language Processing, Workshop at EMNLP 2014, Doha, Qatar, pp. 15–24 (2014)
15. Galanis, D., Lampouras, G., Androutsopoulos, I.: Extractive multi-document summarization with integer linear programming and support vector regression. In: Proceedings of 24th International Conference on Computational Linguistics (COLING 2012), Mumbai, India, pp. 911–926 (2012)
16. Mihalcea, R., Tarau, P.: A language independent algorithm for single and multiple document summarization. In: Proceedings of 2nd International Join Conference on Natural Language Processing(IJCNLP 2005), Jeju Island, Korea, pp. 19–24 (2005)
17. Shen, C., Li, T.: Multi-document summarization via the minimum dominating set. In: Proceedings of 23rd International Conference on Computational Linguistics (COLING 2010), Beijing, China, vol. 2, pp. 984–992 (2010)
18. Mihalcea, R., Tarau, P.: TextRank: Bringing order into texts. In: Proceedings of 9th conference on Empirical Methods in Natural Language Processing (EMNLP 2004), Barcelona, Spain, vol. 4, pp. 404–411 (2004)
19. Le, Q., Mikolov, T.: Distributed representations of sentences and documents. In: Proceedings of 31st International Conference on Machine Learning (ICML 2014), Beijing, China, pp. 1188–1196 (2014)
20. Erkan, G., Radev, D.R.: LexPageRank: Prestige in multi-document text summarization. In: Proceedings of 9th conference Empirical Methods in Natural Language Processing (EMNLP 2004), Barcelona, Spain, pp. 365–371 (2004)

21. Lin, C.Y., Hovy, E.: Automatic evaluation of summaries using n-gram co-occurrence statistics. In: Proceedings of 1st Conference of the North American Chapter of the Association for Computational Linguistics on Human Language Technology (HLT-NAACL 2003), Edmonton, Canada, pp. 71–78 (2003)
22. Poria, S., Cambria, E., Gelbukh, A., Bisio, F., Hussain, A.: Sentiment data flow analysis by means of dynamic linguistic patterns. IEEE Comput. Intell. Mag. **10**, 26–36 (2015)
23. Majumder, N., Poria, S., Gelbukh, A., Cambria, E.: Deep learning based document modeling for personality detection from text. IEEE Intell. Syst. **32**, 74–79 (2017)
24. Poria, S., Cambria, E., Bajpai, R., Hussain, A.: A review of affective computing: From unimodal analysis to multimodal fusion. Inf. Fus. **37**, 98–125 (2017)
25. Poria, S., Peng, H., Hussain, A., Howard, N., Cambria, E.: Ensemble application of convolutional neural networks and multiple kernel learning for multimodal sentiment analysis. Neurocomputing, page in press (2017)
26. Chikersal, P., Poria, S., Cambria, E., Gelbukh, A., Siong, C.E.: Modelling public sentiment in twitter: using linguistic patterns to enhance supervised learning. In: Gelbukh, A. (ed.) CICLing 2015. LNCS, vol. 9042, pp. 49–65. Springer, Cham (2015). doi:10.1007/978-3-319-18117-2_4
27. Pakray, P., Neogi, S., Bhaskar, P., Poria, S., Bandyopadhyay, S., Gelbukh, A.: A textual entailment system using anaphora resolution. In: Text Analysis Conference, Recognizing Textual Entailment Track (TAC RTE), System Report. Notebook (2011)
28. Pakray, P., Poria, S., Bandyopadhyay, S., Gelbukh, A.: Semantic textual entailment recognition using UNL. POLIBITS **43**, 23–27 (2011)
29. Pakray, P., Pal, S., Poria, S., Bandyopadhyay, S., Gelbukh, A.: JU CSE TAC: Textual entailment recognition system at TAC RTE-6. In: Text Analysis Conference, Recognizing Textual Entailment Track (TAC RTE), System Report. Notebook (2010)
30. Poria, S., Cambria, E., Gelbukh, A.: Aspect extraction for opinion mining with a deep convolutional neural network. Knowl. Based Syst. **108**, 42–49 (2016)
31. Poria, S., Chaturvedi, I., Cambria, E., Hussain, A.: Convolutional MKL based multimodal emotion recognition and sentiment analysis. In: 16th International Conference on Data Mining (ICDM 2016), pp. 439–448. IEEE (2016)

Indexing and Searching of Judicial Precedents Using Automatic Summarization

Armando Ordóñez[1(✉)], Diego Belalcazar[1], Manuel Calambas[1],
Angela Chacón[2], Hugo Ordoñez[3], and Carlos Cobos[4]

[1] Intelligent Management Systems,
University Foundation of Popayán, Popayán, Colombia
jaordonez@unicauca.edu.co,
{dbelalcazar,mcalambas}@fup.edu.co
[2] Derecho y Tecnología, Corporación Universitaria Autónoma del Cauca,
Popayán, Colombia
achacon@uniautonoma.edu.co
[3] Research Laboratory in Development of Software Engineering,
Universidad San Buenaventura, Cali, Colombia
haordonez@usbcali.edu.co
[4] Information Technology Research Group (GTI),
Universidad del Cauca, Popayán, Colombia
ccobos@unicauca.edu.co

Abstract. With the aim of democratizing access to justice, the Colombian legal system has recognized the importance of judicial precedent. Judicial precedent allows citizens to request judicial decisions based on previous sentences (court rulings). Some tools are provided to search these sentences. These tools are based on keywords and therefore the search may obtain many non-relevant results. The low efficacy of these tools may make it difficult to find the right sentence. Recently, an approach for sentences searching in the Colombian context was presented. This approach explores the full content of the sentences, which leads to high processing times. One solution to this problem may be to generate automatic summaries before performing the search. This paper presents a comparative analysis of algorithms for automatic summaries. The experimental evaluation shows promising results.

Keywords: Automated summary · Legal sentences · Automated search

1 Introduction

Colombian legal System recognizes the importance of jurisprudence, understood as a set of sentences handed down by judges, which can be used as a legal precedent and formal source of law. The law 1437/2011 orders to the judges to consider previous sentences from the Council of State and the constitutional court. This law also created the figure of "extension of jurisprudence" which offers the ordinary citizen the possibility of request authorities to make decisions in one case based on previous and similar cases [1]. This law may lead to an effective democratization of justice.

G. Sidorov and O. Herrera-Alcántara (Eds.): MICAI 2016, Part I, LNAI 10061, pp. 116–126, 2017.
DOI: 10.1007/978-3-319-62434-1_10

In practice, finding previous similar cases must be done in two phases: Firstly, it is necessary to search statements (judgments) on similar cases. The search can be done using available search engines [2, 3]. These search engines use keywords and syntactical matching, which may result in a large set of results. The second phase requires finding the central argument of each sentence that served as the basis for the decision ("ratio decidendi") [4]. Identifying the ratio decidendi requires experts who know the technical legal language. In this connection, although some legal tools exist to expand access to justice, in practice, the sentences identification may become a cumbersome task.

Various approaches have addressed the issue of automatic processing and searching of judgments [5–7]. However, these approaches are not applicable to the particular legal context of the Colombian and Spanish language. Recently, a system for processing judgments supported on natural language processing, and clustering was presented [8]. However, this approach used the full text of the sentences originating a high processing time. An interesting solution to this problem is to conduct the search using summaries of the sentences. The sentences of the Supreme Court contain a brief summary generated manually. However, this summary does not contain all relevant information. Additionally, the content of this summary is not uniform and may vary between sentences. Automatic summarization is used to analyze scientific papers [9], social networks [10] and legal documents [11, 12]. However, few research works can be found to date including implementations with actual jurisprudence in the Colombian context. This paper presents the architecture of the framework for sentences search as well as a comparative analysis of algorithms for automatic summaries.

The rest of the article is organized as follows: Sect. 2 presents a characterization of the Colombian judicial sentences. Section 3 presents the architecture of the framework for sentences indexing and searching. Section 4 presents the comparison of the algorithms for automatic summarization. Section 5 presents the conclusions and future work.

2 Characterization of the Colombian Jurisprudence

In the Colombian legal system, the first step for solving a conflict is to analyze the law. However, judges are also required to review some previous judgments or decisions from the high Courts. This element is known as *judicial precedent*. These decisions are contained in sentences. Next, the structure of the sentences is presented.

2.1 Structure of the Sentences

As far as the judicial precedent is concerned, it should be clarified that the Constitutional Court resolves a particular situation involving exclusively to one or more parts. Therefore its ruling or decision will only affect those subjects. However, to make the decision in a particular case, the Court considered a variety of arguments presented in connection with the conflict. These arguments are known as *ratio decidendi* or *obiter dicta*.

For the Constitutional Court, the *ratio decidendi* is a norm that acquires general nature, and therefore its application becomes mandatory for all cases under similar conditions in order to guarantee the right to equality and the due process. Thus, the analysis of sentences must be focused on finding the *ratio decidendi* of the sentences. There are various types of sentences; the present approach considers the unification sentences, as they are the most relevant for the judicial precedents. The structure of the sentences of unification is comprised parts; "Introduction" and "Body."

2.2   Preface

The preface is the first section of the sentence, and consists of the following parts:

- *Topics*: contains the subject or topic of the whole judicial sentence. Figure 1 describes an example of a sentence, where the topics are capitalized subtitles followed by one hyphen (-), a description and a slash (/).
- *Summary:* this section describes the position and analysis of the court regarding the elements on the subject, the way they were resolved and some general conclusions. For some sentences, at the end of the summary, there is a section called "NOTE RAPPORTEUR" referring other complementary statements or legal documents.
- *Formal source*: Here, some articles and codes supporting the legal process are mentioned.

IMMEDIACY - Criteria for analysis when it comes to tutela against court order dealing with periodic benefits / DECISION OF JURISPRUDENTIAL UNIFICATION – To reach the quality of pensioned or be the person enjoying retirement allocation is not a circumstance which "per se" allows to omit the requirement of immediacy of tutela against court order / TO BE IN SPECIAL SITUATION - The judge must consider special situations of each case for its determination.

Fig. 1.   Topics of the unification sentences (English translation from Colombian sentence)

2.3   Body of the Sentence

It contains the most relevant elements of the sentences.

- *Head:* this part contains elements that can be used to identify the sentences, such as: the authority that issues (Council of State), Chamber, Section responsible for the demand, name of the counselor, place and date of issue, case id (which corresponds to the unique identification of each ruling), actor (who promotes the judgment) and defendant (person or entity).
- *Background:* the facts underlying demand and requests, claims, and arguments presented by the plaintiff (applicant) and the defendant answer.
- *Considerations:* Describes the information about the competence of the court, analysis of charges raised, proven fact, and applicable laws.
- *Decision (judicial ruling):* Final result of the sentences according to the facts, the judgment indicates whether it accepts or rejects the request or application.

Next, the architecture of the framework for searching judicial precedents is presented.

3   Architecture of the Platform for Indexing and Searching Judicial Sentences

The architecture consists of two modules (Fig. 2): indexing module, and the searching module. The indexing module, it is supported in SOLR [13] takes the sentences as input and processes them in order to include them in the database. This processing starts with the segmentation of documents which consist in the division of the text in paragraphs and phrases [14]. Once divided the text into segments, the simplest units or words are identified through the process known as tokenization [15]. Next, the empty words or stop words are removed [16] because these words don't contribute to the search process (articles, pronouns, prepositions, etc.). The remaining words are normalized using techniques of *lemmatization* and *stemming* [17] which consist in reduce the words stem or base.

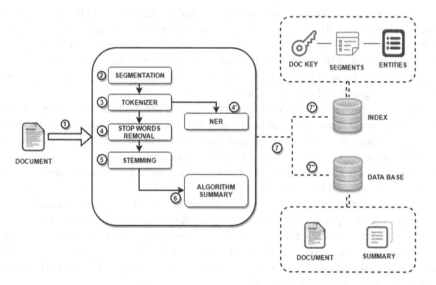

Fig. 2. Description of the process for sentences entry

The final processing tasks include the automatic summarization and identification of entities (Named Entity Recognition). The NER is used for the precise identification of judges, jurisdiction, courts, chambers, and other elements that may help to identify sentences [18]. Identification of entities is performed using an algorithm, which is trained using a configuration script. This script contains sentences segmented by tokens and labels identifying the entities (Fig. 3).

```
 4  useSequences=true
 5  usePrevSequences=true
 6  # the last 4 properties deal with word shape features
 7  useTypeSeqs=true
 8  useTypeSeqs2=true
 9  useTypeySequences=true
10  wordShape=chris2useLC
11  en              0
12  vigencia        0
13  de              0
14  la              0
15  Constitución    law
16  Política        law
17  de              law
18  1991            law
19  ,               0
20  entre           0
21  los             0
```

Fig. 3. Configuration script for the NER

The NER uses an algorithm of conditional random fields (CRF) [19]. Unlike other learning algorithms CRF considers the complete structure of sentences, each token, and its neighbors to determine the precise label. The summary generated as well as the full document are stored in a relational database. On the other hand, an indexes engine is used to support the search module. The index allows managing the information of the entities and segments of each document.

The second part of the architecture corresponds to the module search (Fig. 4). The indexes engine is responsible for processing the search strings entered by the user. Equally, this module returns the segments associated with the search and the summary to which these segments belong The elements of pre-processing module work in the same way as their counterparts in the entry module, with the difference that the processed segments are retrieved during the search process.

The clustering module performs the weighting of the extracted terms of each of the segments. The weighting represents the importance of each of the terms when compared with other segments; this process allows identifying keywords in the content of each document. The weighting tf -idf (described in Eq. (1)) is widely used in information retrieval systems [20] and combines the term frequency factors (Tf) and the inverse frequency of documents (idf)

$$tf - idf_{t,d} = tf_{t,d} idf_t \tag{1}$$

Where the weight is assigned to a term t in a document d such that [20]: (i) The weight is greater when a term t appears many times in a reduced number of documents. (ii) The weight is lower when a term t appears many times in many documents d. (iii) The weight is lower when a term t appears in all documents.

The weighted terms are then organized into a vector model, each segment (phrase) can be seen as a vector of components which corresponds to the terms found during the pre-processing phase [20]. This treatment allows achieving a geometric dimension of

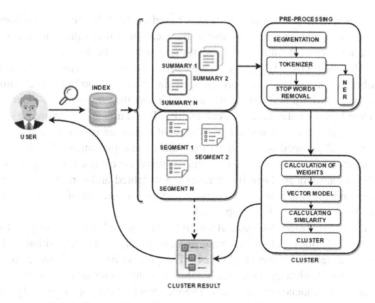

Fig. 4. Description of the process for searching sentences.

the segment, which facilitates calculating the similarity based on Euclidean distance or cosine distances. The vector representation of the sentences allows calculating the similarity between sentences using the similarity of cosines (Eq. 2).

$$Sen(V_{d1}, V_{d2}) = Cos\,\theta = \frac{V_{d1}.V_{d2}}{|V_{d1}||V_{d2}|} \tag{2}$$

Where the numerator represents the inner product of vectors, while the denominator is the product of their Euclidean distances [20]. The result of the similarity of cosines is always positive and is in a range of [0, 1], the value is 1 if the measured segments are exactly identical and 0 when they are totally different [6].

4 Comparison of the Algorithms for Automatic Summarization

One of the most important tasks of the platform is the automatic summarization. This section presents a comparative analysis of the algorithms that can be used for this task.

4.1 Selected Algorithms

- *Edmundson algorithm:* this algorithm uses a reference method (cue method) based on keywords for weighting a phrase. The keywords are divided into bonus words (comparatives, superlatives, and adverbs ending) and stigma words (anaphoric expressions). The keywords detection is based on [21], hence it is considered the frequency of occurrence in a document, the location of the phrases in the document, and the number of documents in which the words can be found [22].

- *Luhn Algorithm* [14, 23]: This algorithm filters the most relevant words in the text (significant words). The words are grouped statistically according to their similarity. Those words with a common prefix and with less than six different characters are considered part of the same lexical family. The number of occurrences of each lexical group is counted, and the non-frequent words are removed. The phrases are weighted and grouped according to the number and proximity of their keywords. The number of words is limited so that a sentence cannot have more than four non-significant words. Then the phrases are weighted and sorted according to the number and proximity of your keywords setting a word limit so that a sentence cannot have more than four stop word.

- *LSA Algorithm (Latent Semantic Analysis):* This method is inspired by LSI (Latent Semantic Indexing) and an algebraic process of matrix decomposition called singular value decomposition (SVD) [24]. The process begins with the creation of a matrix of words-phrases where each column of the vector of the matrix represents the weighted frequency of the terms. The weighting of the phrases is assigned using SVD. The phrase with the highest index value is selected to be included in the summary [25]. One hypothesis states that the more important the sentence is, more semantically closer to the original text it is.

- *Graph-based algorithms:* These algorithms apply the concept of graph-based ordering for weighting the phrases [26, 27]. The document is represented by units of text. The importance of a vertex depends on its number of links to other larger vertex. This method establishes a criterion of relevance and prestige to create the summary.

  - *Lex rank*: In this method, an undirected graph of phrases is built using symmetrical similarities. This method employs cosine similarity and adjacency matrix for graphically representing the phrases [28].
  - *Text rank*: In this algorithm, the vertices are weighted based on the similarity of the graph edges. The weight of each sentence is calculated iteratively until the convergence of the solution is reached [27].

4.2 Experimental Evaluation

For the experimental evaluation, a corpus of sentences and a prototype for automatic summarization were created. The corpus is comprised of 33 jurisprudential unification sentences issued by the State Council. These sentences were selected due to the fact that they can be used as judicial precedents.

Regarding the prototype, it consists of two main modules. The first module allows managing and modifying the algorithms for automatic summarization. The second module supports the processing of different document formats. For the first module, it was used the framework "sumy" [21], and the default configuration is maintained for the execution of algorithms. For the document processing "textract" [29] was used during the implementation.

Diverse tests may be used for evaluation. However, testing in early stages may be done using of intrinsic methods [30]. Therefore at this stage, the content was measured using co-selection tests based on the following metrics: Precision, Recall, and F-score.

On the other hand, a comparison of the automatic summarization with the human summarization was performed. For this purpose, a set of judicial documents were summarized by lawyers. These summaries were performed using an extractive process that allows selecting the most relevant and informative parts of the document generating summaries of around 450 words. The summaries prepared by the experts were compared with the ones generated automatically using the algorithms. This comparison was made using the ROUGE evaluation measures [31]. This evaluation employs a method based on the similarity of N-grams (ROUGE - N) [32] which allows comparing a candidate summary and a set of reference summaries [31] where n represents the length of the N-gram.

For the present approach, 4 sentences were used with ROUGE -1 and ROUGE-2. This decision was taken because the values of ROUGE -1 show low correlation with human evaluation. Conversely, ROUGE-2 shows have a better correlation [33].

4.3 Analysis of the Results

The most important measure for the present evaluation is Recall [34]. However, all the measures were analyzed (Fig. 5).

Tables 1 and 2 shows the values of ROUGE-1 and ROUGE-2 for each algorithm. As can be observed, *Edmundson* reached the best results (38%). These results are due to the fact that this algorithm weights the number of keywords found in a phrase. Hence the superlatives, adverbs, and comparatives are detected in the documents to retrieve and the user request. Consequently, this method increases the weighting of *tf/idf*, thereby making that the document with the higher number of keywords per phrase

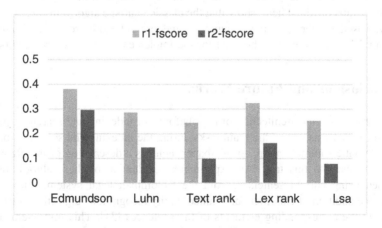

Fig. 5. Summary of results F-score

Table 1. Co-selection measures of the algorithms applied to 4 sentences

Judicial sentence	Algorithm	Type	Rouge-1-recall	Rouge-1-precision	Rouge-1-f score	Rouge-2-recall	Rouges-precision	Rouge-2-f score
05001-23-31-000-1997-0117201(31170)	Edmundson	Heuristic	0,31776	0,34694	0,33171	0,28351	0,28351	0,28351
	Luhn	Heuristic	0,31776	0,34694	0,33171	0,28351	0,28351	0,28351
	Test rank	Graphs	0,14486	0,14904	0,14692	0,05155	0,04926	0,05038
	Lex rank	Graphs	0,14953	0,14884	0,14918	0, 02062	0, 01951	0,02005
	LSA	Semantic	0,21963	0,20889	0,21412	0,03608	0,03196	0,0339
11001-03-15-000-2015-00001-01(AC)	Edmundson	Heuristic	0,33594	0,50588	0,40376	0,31707	0,46429	0,37681
	Luhn	Heuristic	0,25751	0,24444	0,25095	0,05691	0,05263	0,05469
	Text rank	Graphs	0,05469	0,04795	0,05109	0,01626	0,01389	0,01498
	Lex rank	Graphs	0,2S125	0,30252	0,2915	0,06504	0,06897	0,06695
	LSA	Semantic	0,1875	0,16438	0,17518	0,3252	0,02878	0,03053
85001-23-31-000-1999-0395-01(3539-01)	Edmundson	Heuristic	0,52174	0,57534	0,54723	0,41667	0,45139	0,43333
	Luhn	Heuristic	0,40373	0,34211	0,37037	0,19231	0,16043	0,17493
	Text rank	Graphs	0,47205	0,4497	0,46061	0,22436	0,21472	0,21944
	Lex rank	Graphs	0,56522	0,57233	0,56875	0,44231	0,44231	0,44231
	LSA	Semantic	0,44099	0,50355	0,4702	0,20513	0,23358	0,21843
08001-23-33-000-2013-00310-01(ACU)	Edmundson	Heuristic	0,21186	0,28409	0,24272	0,0793	0,10345	0,08978
	Luhn	Heuristic	0,1906S	0,19313	0,1919	0,06608	0,06494	0,0655
	Text rank	Graphs	0,29237	0,34848	0,31797	0,10573	0,12245	0,11348
	Lex rank	Graphs	0,24153	0,36076	0,28934	0,10132	0,14839	0,12042
	LSA	Semantic	0,15678	0,15289	0,15481	0,03524	0,03478	0,03501

Table 2. Average of the co-selection measures

Algorithm	TYPE	R1-Recall	R1-Precision	R1 F-score	R2-Recall	R2-Precisior	R2 F-score
Edmundson	Heuristic	0,346825	0,4280625	0,381355	0,2741375	0,32566	0,2958575
Luhn	Heuristic	0,292495	0,251655	0,2562325	0,1497025	0,1403775	0,1446575
Test rank	Graphs	0,2409925	0,2457925	0,2441475	0,099475	0,10005	0,09957
Lex rank	Graphs	0,309383	0,3461125	0,3246925	0,1573225	0,169795	0,1624325
LSA	Semantic	0,251225	0,2574275	0,2535775	0,0772425	0,052275	0,0794575

becomes the most relevant to users. On the other side, Lex Rank ranked second with 32% of recall, these results of the use of graphs similarity to identify similar phrases. The best values of Precision, Recall, and F-score are those who most approximate to 1 [35]. The results obtained here, show that the classic heuristic algorithms are still valid. Equally, based on the previous evaluation, the present study selected *Edmundson* algorithm. This algorithm will be used for the implementation of the framework.

5   Conclusions and Future Works

This paper presents the architecture of the platform for indexing and searching judicial sentences. Equally as one of the main tasks during the indexing and searching process is the automatic summarization, so this paper includes a description of the algorithms that can be used to this task. An experimental evaluation of these algorithms was performed using current sentences from the Colombian legal system. Future work includes the addition of classifiers or "named- entity recognition" algorithms that allow identifying the corresponding elements of the sentences [31]. This improvement will enable the system to know more effectively the key parts of the document in order to perform a better summary. Also, it will be considered to develop a hybrid algorithm based on the previously analyzed algorithms that improve the recall and precision. This new algorithm may include concepts of meta-heuristics and Deep learning.

References

1. Congreso de Colombia: Código de Procedimiento Administrativo y de lo Contencioso Administrativo. Ley 1437 (2011)
2. Rama Judicial del Poder Publico: "Consulta temática simultánea en las Altas Corporaciones", Sistema de Consulta de Jurisprudencia, (2011). http://190.24.134.114:8080/WebRelatoria/consulta/index.xhtml
3. Consejo de Estado: Consulta de Jurisprudencia - Consejo de Estado. http://190.24.134.114:8080/WebRelatoria/ce/index.xhtml
4. De Goytisolo, J.V.: "El razonamiento judicial", Anales de la Real Academia de Jurisprudencia y Legislación, 39th edn. Madrid, 2009
5. De Colla Furquim, L.O., De Lima, V.L.S.: Clustering and categorization of Brazilian Portuguese legal documents. In: Caseli, H., Villavicencio, A., Teixeira, A., Perdigão, F. (eds.) PROPOR 2012. LNCS, vol. 7243, pp. 272–283. Springer, Heidelberg (2012). doi:10.1007/978-3-642-28885-2_31
6. Raghuveer, K.: Legal documents clustering using latent dirichlet allocation. IAES Int. J. Artif. Intell. 2(1), 34–37 (2012)
7. Lu, Q., Keenan, W., Conrad, J.G., Al-kofahi, K.: Legal document clustering with built-in topic segmentation categories and subject descriptors. In: Proceeding of 11th ACM Inernational Conerence on Information Knowedge Management, pp. 383–392 (2011)
8. Calambás, MA., Ordóñez, A., Chacón, A., Ordoñez, H.: Judicial precedents search supported by natural language processing and clustering. In: Computation Colombian Conference, vol. 10, pp. 372–377 (2015)
9. Visser, W.T., Wieling, M.B.: Sentence-based summarization of scientific documents. Design Implementation. Autumn Report. accessed 29 Nov (2007)
10. Sharifi, B., Hutton, M.-A., Kalita, J.K.: Experiments in microblog summarization. In: 2010 IEEE Second International Conference on Social Computing (SocialCom), pp. 49–56. IEEE (2010)
11. Farzindar, A., Lapalme, G.: LetSum: an automatic Legal Text Summarizing system. In: Legal Knowedge Information System JURIX, pp. 11–18 (2004)
12. Chieze, E., Farzindar, A., Lapalme, G.: An automatic system for summarization and information extraction of legal information. In: Francesconi, E., Montemagni, S., Peters, W., Tiscornia, D. (eds.) Semantic Processing of Legal Texts. LNCS, vol. 6036, pp. 216–234. Springer, Heidelberg (2010). doi:10.1007/978-3-642-12837-0_12
13. Apache Foundation, Apache Lucene: http://lucene.apache.org/core/ Accessed 10 Feb-2015
14. Torres Moreno, J.M.: Single-document summarization. In: Mani, I., Maybury, M.T. (eds.) Advances in Automatic Text Summarization, pp. 59–60. MIT Press, London (2014)
15. Stanford University, The Stanford NLP (Natural Language Processing) Group
16. Stanford University, Dropping common terms: stop words
17. Stanford University, Stemming and lemmatization

18. Dozier, C., Kondadadi, R., Light, M., Vachher, A., Veeramachaneni, S., Wudali, R.: Named entity recognition and resolution in legal text. In: Francesconi, E., Montemagni, S., Peters, W., Tiscornia, D. (eds.) Semantic Processing of Legal Texts. LNCS, vol. 6036, pp. 27–43. Springer, Heidelberg (2010). doi:10.1007/978-3-642-12837-0_2

19. Lafferty, J., McCallum, A., Pereira, F.C.N.: Conditional random fields: Probabilistic models for segmenting and labeling sequence data. In: Proceeding of 18th International Conference Machine Learning (ICML 2001), vol. 8, pp. 282–289 (2001)

20. Manning, C.D., Raghavan, P., Schütze, H.: Introduction to information retrieval. J. Am. Soc. Inf. Sci. Technol. 1, 496 (2008)

21. Belica, M.: sumy 0.4.0: Python Package Index

22. Edmundson, H.P.: New methods in automatic extracting. In: Mani, I., Maybury, M.T. (eds.) Advances in Automatic Text Summarization, pp. 24–26. MIT Press, Cambdidge (1999)

23. Luhn, H.P.: The Automatic Creation of Literature Abstracts. In: Mani, I., Maybury, M.T. (eds.) Advances in Automatic Text Summarization, pp. 15–23. MIT Press, Cambdidge (1999)

24. Steinberger, J., Jezek, K.: Using latent semantic analysis in text summarization and summary evaluation. In: Proceeding of ISIM 2004, pp. 93–100 (2004)

25. Torres Moreno, J.M.: Latent semantic analysis in Automatic Text Summarization, pp. 73–74, London (2014)

26. Torres Moreno, J.M.: Graph-based approaches in Automatic Text Summarization, pp. 76–81, London (2014)

27. Mihalcea, R., Tarau, P.: TextRank: Bringing order into texts (2004)

28. Erkan, G., Radev, D.R.: LexRank: Graph-based lexical centrality as salience in text summarization. J. Artif. Intell. Res. 22, 457–479 (2004)

29. Malmgren, D.: textract 1.4.0: Python Package Index

30. Inderjeet, M.: Summarization evaluation: an overview. Pflege Z. 62(6), 337–341 (2009)

31. Ganesan, K.: ROUGE 2.0 Documentation - Java Package for Evaluation of Summarization Tasks | Kavita Ganesan

32. Steinberger, J., Ježek, K.: Evaluation measures for text summarization. Comput. Inf. 28(2), 251–275 (2012)

33. Liu, F., Liu, Y.: Exploring correlation between ROUGE and human evaluation on meeting summaries. IEEE Trans. Audio. Speech. Lang. Process. 18(1), 187–196 (2010)

34. Powers, D.: Evaluation: From Precision, Recall and F-Factor to ROC, Informedness, Markedness and Correlation. School Informatics Engineering vol. SIE-07-001, pp. 2–5 (2009)

35. Moens, M.F.: Innovative techniques for legal text retrieval. Artif. Intell. Law 9(1), 29–57 (2001)

Discriminatory Capacity of the Most Representative Phonemes in Spanish: An Evaluation for Forensic Voice Comparison

Fernanda López-Escobedo[1]([⊠]) and Luis Alberto Pineda Cortés[2]

[1] Licenciatura en Ciencia Forense, Facultad de Medicina, UNAM,
Circuito de la Investigación Científica SN, CU, 04510 Ciudad de Mexico, Mexico
flopeze@unam.mx
[2] Departamento de Ciencias de la Computación, IIMAS,
UNAM, Circuito Escolar SN, CU, 04510 Ciudad de Mexico, Mexico
www.fernandalopez-escobedo.com

Abstract. In this paper, a study of the discriminatory capacity of the most representative segments for forensic speaker comparison in Mexican Spanish is presented. The study is based on two corpora in order to assess the discriminatory capacity of the fundamental frequency and the three first vocalic formants acoustic parameters for reading and semi-spontaneous speech. We found that the context /sa/ has 73% of discriminatory capacity to classify speakers using the three first formants of the vowel /a/ with a dynamic analysis. We used several statistical techniques and found that the best methodology for the recognition of patterns consists of using linear regression with a quadratic fitting to reduce the number of predictors to a manageable level and apply discriminant analysis on the reduced set. This result is consistent with previous research data despite the methodology for Mexican Spanish had never been used.

Keywords: Pattern recognition · Forensic speech recognition · Linear Discriminant Analysis · Principal Component Analysis · Linear Regression

1 Introduction

Forensic linguistics is a relative recent development area that has the aim to use the linguistic knowledge in order to support legal cases. One of its applications is the forensic voice comparison that consists of comparing an unknown voice sample (criminal voice) to a set of known voice samples (voices of suspects) and select those which share the greater number of acoustics characteristics.

The development of different tools and methodologies to facilitate and optimize forensic voice comparison has become a fundamental aim in forensic phonetic research. This article explores a methodology to improve the discrimination between speaker voices and examines whether the analysis of formant dynamics can be applied to classify a vocalic segment of Mexican Spanish.

© Springer International Publishing AG 2017
G. Sidorov and O. Herrera-Alcántara (Eds.): MICAI 2016, Part I, LNAI 10061, pp. 127–140, 2017.
DOI: 10.1007/978-3-319-62434-1_11

In the forensic field, it is very common to rely on short recordings for speaker comparison; therefore, it is very helpful to study sounds that occur often in a short period of time. Hence, the selection of the sound used in this study is based on the frequency of occurrence of the Spanish phonemes. Several papers [1–7] documented that the vocalic phoneme /a/ is one of the most frequent phonemes in this language. Other sounds, like diphthongs, have a much lower probability of occurrence. Consequently, the sound /a/ was selected for the present study. In addition, this sound was studied in the most frequent syllabic context [8], which is formed by a consonant followed by a vowel (CV). The consonant phonemes preceding /a/ in this syllabic context are also the most frequent consonants in Spanish (i.e., /s/, /t/, /p/, /l/, /n/). If it turns out that these contexts improve the discriminatory potential of /a/ and present stability across different types of speech then they have a high value in Spanish forensic phonetic studies.

The empirical resource used in the present research consisted of two corpora: one in semi-spontaneous and the other in read speech. Speakers in the two corpora were different. All instances of the vocalic phoneme /a/ were segmented and analyzed. For this, two acoustic parameters were used: (1) the fundamental frequency (F0); and, (2) the three first vocalic formants (F1, F2 and F3). Both parameters were studied with two methods that we named static and dynamic. The first is based on the value of the acoustic parameter at the midpoint of the vowel, and the second uses several values of the parameter along the total duration of the vowel. The dynamic method, which takes into account the three first vocalic formants in nine equidistant points, was used to analyze the Australian English diphthong /a/ by McDougall [9]. The same method was used to study intervocalic /r/ in the sequence /ərV/, where the vowels considered were /iː,æː,ɑː,ɔː,uː/ in British English [10]. In 2008, Eriksson and Sullivan [11] examined whether this methodology could be applied to another segment of the same size constituted by /jœː/ in Swedish. In addition, this latter study considered the value of the fourth vocalic formant. In the present investigation, the parameters considered were the fundamental frequency and the three first formants, and each parameter was analyzed with both the static and the dynamic methods. For the dynamic method, the value of both parameters at nine equidistant points along the total duration of /a/ was used.

In order to assess the discriminatory capacity of /a/ in the referred contexts, three statistic techniques were used: Linear Discriminant Analysis (LDA), Principal Components Analysis (PCA) and Linear Regression. The Linear Discriminant Analysis is a statistical technique whose main objective is to identify the characteristics that differentiate between two or more groups of subjects and most of the time is useful to classify new observations as belonging to one group or another [12]. PCA is a statistical technique that reduces the number of original variables through their linear combination, where the reduced set of variables is called 'components'. Finally, the Linear Regression technique consists of an optimal linear model that represents the distribution of the data [13].

McDougall [9, 10] and Eriksson and Sullivan [11] used LDA to determine the discriminatory capacity of the sounds analyzed in their corresponding studies.

In this study, LDA was used to assess the discriminatory capacity of /a/ in all the different contexts of the two corpora, considering the two acoustic parameters and with both the static and the dynamic methods. The higher percentages of classification were obtained with the dynamic method, using the three first formants in the semi-spontaneous speech corpora. In particular, the contexts that best discriminate among speakers were /sa/ and /ta/.

However, LDA yields unstable results when the number of tokens is not above the number of predictors at least by two. For this reason, McDougall [9] proposed an approach to achieve higher percentages of classification with a less number of predictors using different combinations of variables. Later on she proposed a new methodological approach in which the three first formant contours were fitted with a quadratic and a cubic polynomial equation using linear regression, and the parameters of the polynomial fittings were used as predictors in LDA [10]. In this study we also tested McDougall's methodologies, but in addition, we used PCA to reduce the number of variables. In particular, the contexts /sa/ and /ta/ in semi-spontaneous speech corpora were analyzed with all of these methodologies, as these are the best classified contexts.

The overall conclusion of this study is that the contexts /sa/ and /ta/ analyzed with the dynamic method using the three first vocalic formants are frequent enough and have the best discriminatory capacity to classify speakers in semi-spontaneous speech in Mexican Spanish.

2   Empirical Resource

As aforementioned in the introduction, the vocalic segment /a/ was chosen because of its high frequency of occurrence in Spanish. The effect of neighboring sounds was considered so that the /a/ segment was analyzed within a syllabic context formed by CV preceded by the five most frequent consonants in Spanish as shown in Table 1.

Table 1. Occurrence percentage of the five most frequent consonants in Spanish [6]

Non vocalic phonemes	Frequency of ocurrence (%)
/s/	20.99
/t/	10.94
/p/	10.81
/l/	10.39
/n/	10.21

In order to determine whether dynamic measures of vocalic formants and the fundamental frequency can be used as idiosyncratic properties of the speakers' voice independently of the type of speech, the vowel /a/ has been evaluated by making use of two types of corpora: a read speech (RS) corpus and a semi-spontaneous speech (SS) corpus.

The read speech corpus consists of the recorded speech of five male and five female native speakers of Mexican Spanish, 16–36 age range. All ten speakers were born in Mexico City and have completed secondary school. Corpus RS is a subcorpus of corpus DIMEx100 [7] 'designed and collected to support the development of language technologies, especially speech recognition, and also to provide an empirical base for phonetic studies of Mexican Spanish'. It included recordings from 100 Mexican Spanish speakers. The corpus DIMEx100 was collected from the Web. A very large Spanish sentences were extracted and its content was measured according to the perplexity value. The 5,010 sentences with the largest value were selected. Hence, the corpus is complete and phonetically balanced. All 10 speakers in corpus RS read 60 five-to-fifteen word sentences. The list of sentences contains 50 individual sentences for each speaker and 10 equal sentences for all of them. So, corpus RS consists of 510 different sentences. Typical sentences are for instance[1]:

Ofrecemos la mejor calidad y el mejor precio en tinas de hidromasaje
Si acaso, de vez en cuando, pasan como tormentas de verano por mis asquerosos pensamientos
La cuenta la pagaría, por tanto, el último que quedara sentado a la mesa
Para el mes de enero, las fases de la luna son las siguientes
En ágora, estamos convencidos de que la participación ciudadana debe ser libre y voluntaria

The recordings were made in a sound studio at CCADET[2] UNAM[3] with an Audigy Platinum ex (24 bit/96khz/100db SNR) sound blaster. The WaveLab 4.0 program with a sampling format of mono at 16 bits and sampling rate of 44.1 Hz was used. Each speaker was recorded with a single diaphragm studio condenser microphone Behringe B-1.

The semi-spontaneous speech corpus consisted of recordings from three native male and two native female speakers of Mexican Spanish. All speakers participating in SS were different from the ones in read speech corpus. The speakers were between 18 and 30 years old, held a higher education diploma and were born in Mexico City. The recordings consisted of sociolinguistic interviews, based on the criteria and techniques proposed by the Labovian tradition of sociolinguistic variation [14,15]. Recordings were made in a silent room with a MiniDisc Sony MZ-R900 and a lapel microphone. Each speaker's interview lasted from 35 to 45 min.

3   Dynamic Method

In the last two decades, forensic phonetic research has shown an interest in the dynamic characteristics of the acoustic signal [9–11,16–19]. McDougall [9] points

---

[1] The full corpus is available on request to the main author.

[2] Centro de Ciencias Aplicadas y Desarrollo Tecnológico.

[3] Universidad Nacional Autónoma de México.

out that the study of the change undergone by acoustic properties throughout time provides more information about the individual characteristics of a speaker's voice than the measurement of these acoustic features in a single point in time. Previous studies that have considered the dynamic acoustic properties of the signal have been structured around two criteria: length of the analyzed segment and type of alignment. For example, Greisbach, Esser and Weinstock in 1995 [16] compared the discriminatory potential of first and second vocalic formants, both measured in a single point of the segment and in five intervals of equal duration. The analyzed segments were three German vowels ([a:], [e:], [o:]) and three German diphthongs ([ae:], [ao:], [oe:]). Rose in 1999 [17] undertook a study of the word hello produced by six Australian English speakers, by extracting the four first vocalic formants from seven intervals and defining their length in terms of the middle of the first vowel, the middle of the /l/ phoneme and five intervals of equal duration in the /oʊ/ diphthong. It is the criterion of how alignments are made that establishes the main difference between both studies. According with Greisbach, Esser and Weinstock, the alignment is normalized, since the segment is divided into five intervals of equal duration and five frequency measures of each interval are extracted. By contrast, Rose delimits the duration of the interval based on each phoneme's duration; therefore, the alignment is not normalized. In addition, the consideration of the length of the segment establishes another difference between these two studies. Thus, while Greisbach, Esser and Weinstock studies a short segment constituted by a vowel, Rose analyzes a longer stretch of speech. In the latter case, the analyses can be based on a word [17] or on the whole recording [19].

McDougall [9,10] and Eriksson and Sullivan [11] analyzed a short speech segment with a time-normalized alignment. The methodology proposed by McDougall was used to analyze the Australian English diphthong /ai/ and to extract the three first vocalic formants at nine equidistant points. Each of these points was employed as a predictor variable in a Linear Discriminant Analysis (LDA). This analysis allows the classification of each speaker's tokens, drawing from the linear functions based on the information contained in the set of predictor variables. Furthermore, the number of predictors was reduced, since LDA yields unstable results when the number of tokens is not above the number of predictors at least by two. The criterion followed by McDougall was to disregard the variables that display the smallest F-ratio in an ANOVA and to test different combinations of predictor variables in order to determine which one discriminates the speakers better. The best result showed 95% of correct classification versus the 68% obtained with the predictor variables corresponding to the midpoint of the diphthong.

The high rates obtained by McDougall encouraged Eriksson and Sullivan to examine whether the methodology could be applied to Swedish and to another segment of the same size constituted by /jœ:/. In addition, these researchers included the fourth vocalic formant measurement. The nonparametric Kruskal-Wallis test was used instead of ANOVA, as a criterion to reduce the number of predictor variables. Those with the smallest values in the k statistic were excluded from the analysis. Also, the combination of predictors achieved from the nonparametric test was assayed along with the different combinations proposed by McDougall. The best result yielded a classification rate of 88%.

In 2006, McDougall presented another study applying the same methodology for the analysis of a British English segment, formed by intervocalic /r/ in the sequence /ərV/, where the vowels considered were /iː,æː,ɑː,ɔː,uː/, which carried the nuclear stress of the sentence. In this new study, a classification rate of 88% was reached. Additionally, McDougall [10] proposed a new methodological approach in which the three first formant contours of /ai/ diphthong were fitted with a quadratic and a cubic polynomial equation by using the linear regression technique. The three first formant contours of intervocalic /ai/ were fitted with cubic, quartic and quintic polynomial equations thus reducing the number of variables required to describe the dynamics of the formant contours. The parameters of polynomial fittings were used as predictor variables in LDA. The rate yielded with the polynomial fittings was equivalent to the rate yielded with direct measurements used in the first methodological approach. However, the number of predictors used with the polynomial fitting is lower than that of direct measurements. Thus, it opens the possibility of including additional acoustic information from each segment in the analysis.

The results of all these studies show that formant transitions discriminate well between the speakers' voices and can contribute to robust forensic voice comparison. In this study, the vocalic segment /a/ in Mexican Spanish is analyzed by employing the methodology proposed by McDougall in 2004, and the new one reported by this researcher in 2006. Moreover, fundamental frequency transitions are also analyzed in our research work following procedures of several studies [20–24] which agree on their discriminatory potential to undertake forensic voice comparison.

4   Statistical Analysis

The three statistical techniques employed in this study were Linear Discriminant Analysis (LDA), Principal Components Analysis (PCA) and Linear Regression (LR)[4]. LDA is a statistical technique whose main aims are: (a) discrimination, in order to determine the characteristics that differentiate between groups, as well as to find the optimal representation where the observation projection distinguishes between groups; and, (b) classification, which is used to assign a new observation to one of the existing groups, and is based on the original variables [12].

The discriminant functions generated by LDA out of the data are used for the classification process. In a first approach, the whole dataset is used for generating discriminant functions and testing classification ability. However, this approach overestimates the classification since an observation used to generate

---

[4] All statistical analyses were performed with R program. Each statistical analysis was programmed in order to reproduce the methodology proposed in this work.

the discriminant functions is also employed to test their capacity of classification. A better approach is to partition the data in two sets, one for generating
the discriminant functions and the other for testing. In this study, the latter was
employed using different partitions in a leave-one-out cross-validation method.

However, as aforementioned, LDA can only be used with reliability if the
number of tokens exceeds the number of predictor variables by two, which was
not always the case. Hence, we used PCA to reduce the number of variables.
PCA is a technique that maps the original set of variables into an orthogonal
space in which it is possible to model the data as a linear combination in the
reduced set of dimensions called components. The net effect of the model is to
filter out the natural dependency among the variables in the original set [13].

In this study, PCA was carried out with contexts in which the amount of
tokens did not exceed the number of predictor variables in at least by two. The
number of components that explained 80% of the total variance was used as a
predictor variable in LDA. Figure 1 shows the two analysis carried out depending
on the number of tokens obtained.

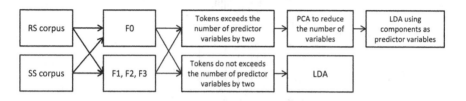

Fig. 1. Type of analysis carried out in each corpus

In addition, we also used the LR method as suggested by McDougall [10].
The LR model specifies that for any value of the independent variable x, the
population mean of the dependent or response variable, y, is described by a
straight line [25]. This model is written as:

$$y = \beta_0 + \beta_1 x + \varepsilon \tag{1}$$

However, it is not always possible to fit the data into a straight line and often
a more general kind of figure is needed. Hence, a polynomial model is frequently
used. This is the case of formant contours, where the nine measures made along
the total duration of vowel /a/ in contexts /sa/ and /ta/ in semi-spontaneous
corpora can be fitted into a polynomial model as follows:

$$y = \beta_o + \beta_1 x + \beta_2 x^2 + \beta_3 x^3 + ... + \beta_m x^m + \varepsilon \tag{2}$$

This model is called an mth-order polynomial in which the m corresponds to
the degree of polynomial. The greater the value of m, the better the fit. However,
models with fewer parameters are preferred. In this study, the F1, F2 and F3
contour of each token of /a/ was fitted with a quadratic and a cubic polynomial.
For the quadratic model, three parameters were used as predictor variables in
LDA and four in the case of the cubic model.

5 Analysis of the Data

All recordings containing /a/ vowels in the contexts defined in section one were analyzed. The beginning and end of each vowel were labeled with Praat [26]. Additionally, a script was created in order to segment the /a/ in ten equal intervals. Finally, the fundamental frequency and the three first vocalic formants in all intervals were extracted, as shown in Fig. 2.

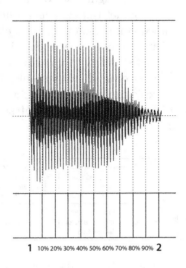

Fig. 2. /a/ vowel divided into ten time intervals of equal duration

The script displays frequency measures for each of the eleven points shown in Fig. 2; however, only nine measurements – represented by the nine percentiles in Fig. 2 – were used; this is, the first and the last measurements were eliminated in order to avoid possible errors at the vowel borders. Consequently, nine predictor variables were obtained for the fundamental frequency and nine more for each of the three first formants. Table 2 shows the predictor variables used in the statistical analysis.

Table 2. Predictor variables obtained for the statistical analysis

	Predictor variables								
	10%	20%	30%	40%	50%	60%	70%	80%	90%
F0	F01	F02	F03	F04	F05	F06	F07	F08	F09
F1	F11	F12	F13	F14	F15	F16	F17	F18	F19
F2	F21	F22	F23	F24	F25	F26	F27	F28	F29
F3	F31	F32	F33	F34	F35	F36	F37	F38	F39

Although the number of tokens per context is the same for all speakers, the number of tokens for each context varies as illustrated in Table 3. In the case of context /sa/, it was not possible to obtain at least five tokens from any of the speakers in RS corpus. However, in SS corpus, the number of tokens analyzed for this context was 24 in all five speakers.

Table 3. Number of occurrences per speaker in each corpus

Context	Number of tokens per speaker in RS	Number of tokens per speaker in SS
/sa/	-	24
/ta/	6	32
/pa/	7	34
/la/	18	32
/na/	7	33

Two Linear Discriminant Analyses were performed for each parameter. LDA analyses were carried out for F0: (1) using the nine predictors obtained from a dynamic measurement, and (2) midpoint measurement that corresponds to the F05 predictor. Additionally, two LDA were performed for the acoustic parameter of the three first formants. One analysis used 27 predictors, while the other, the three central ones (i.e., F15, F25 and F35). A Principal Component Analysis was carried out for both parameters in the dynamic case when the amount of predictor variables did not surpass the number of tokens by at least a factor of two. Then, the components that explain 80% of the total variance were used as predictor variables in LDA as shown in Fig. 1. For instance, the number of tokens in the context /na/ in the RS corpora for F0 was seven (see Table 3) and the number of predictor variables was nine; therefore, PCA was performed before LDA.

In addition, LDA for a number of combinations of predictor variables for the most discriminating contexts /sa/ and /ta/ in semi-spontaneous speech corpus were carried out, along the lines suggested by McDougall [9], as shown in Table 4.

Contexts /sa/ and /ta/ in semi-spontaneous speech corpora were also chosen to test the methodology proposed by McDougall [10]. The F1, F2 and F3 contours of each token of /a/ were fitted with a quadratic and a cubic polynomial. The parameters of these fittings were used as predictor variables in LDA.

Table 4. Different combinations of predictor variables

P	F1	F2	F3	F1+F2	F2+F3	F1+F3	F1+F2+F3	Optimal* F3+F2
1	F15	F25	F35					
2				F15,25	F25,35	F15,35		
3	F11,15,19	F21,25,29	F31,35,39				F15,25,35	
5	F11,13,15, 17,19	F21,23,25, 27,29	F31,33,35, 37,39					
6				F11,15,19, 21,25,29	F21,25,29, 31,35,39	F11,15,19, 31,35,39		F32,33,34, 35,36,26
9	F11,12,13, 14,15,16, 17,18,19	F21,22,23, 24,25,26, 27,28,29	F31,32,33, 34,35,36, 37,38,39					
10				F11,13,15, 17,19,21, 23,25,27, 29	F21,23,25, 27,29,31, 33,35,37, 39	F11,13,15, 17,19,31, 33,35,37, 39		
15							F11,13,15, 17,19,21, 23,25,27, 29,31,33, 35,37,39	
18				F11,12,13, 14,15,16, 17,18,19, 21,22,23, 24,25,26, 27,28,29	F21,22,23, 24,25,26, 27,28,29, 31,32,33, 34,35,36, 37,38,39	F11,12,13, 14,15,16, 17,18,19, 31,32,33, 34,35,36, 37,38,39		
27							F11,12,13, 14,15,16, 17,18,19, 21,22,23, 24,25,26, 27,28,29, 31,32,33, 34,35,36, 37,38,39	

P = Predictors included in each analysis,
*The optimal combination mentioned by Eriksson and Sullivan [11]

6　Results and Conclusions

The results obtained with dynamic and midpoint measurements for each type of genre speech (read and semi-spontaneous) are shown in Table 5.

The F0 parameter in both tables shows that the classification performance of the dynamic and static methods is the same for both corpora. Hence, the methodology applied to the F0 parameter is not useful for forensic voice comparison in Mexican Spanish. However, the dynamic method is better when the three first formants are used.

Table 5. Average of percentage of classification

Parameter	RS corpus (10 speakers)		SS corpus (5 speakers)	
	Dynamic	Static	Dynamic	Static
F0	24	24	43	43
F1, F2, F3	48	42	63	61

Although a direct comparison between the classification rates between the two corpora is not strictly granted, especially because the number of speakers is not the same, it can be appreciated that the classification obtained with the dynamic method is 20% higher in the semi-spontaneous speech corpus.

The results for each particular phonetic context of F1, F2 and F3 with the dynamic method for the semi-spontaneous speech case are shown in Table 6.

Table 6. Percentages of correct classification with dynamic measurements in semi-spontaneous speech corpus

Context	Correct classification (%)
/sa/	66
/ta/	64
/na/	62
/pa/	62
/la/	59

The contexts /sa/ and /ta/ show the best classification performances, and thus were chosen to run other Linear Discriminant Analyses using the different combinations of predictor variables proposed by McDougall [9]. Additionally, the optimal combination proposed by Eriksson and Sullivan [11], and the combination based on the parameters of a polynomial equation proposed by McDougall [10] were tested. The results are shown in Table 7.

The best classification percentage (73%) refers to the /sa/ context using nine predictors of F1, F2 and F3 followed by 72% fitting a quadratic polynomial model to the vocalic formants. For context /ta/, using the same predictors, the best classification percentage was 66%.

A comparison of the best percentage obtained in this study for the /sa/ context (73%) with McDougall's [9] and Eriksson and Sullivan's [11] shows that this percentage is 4% and 22% below the one obtained by Eriksson and Sullivan's [11] and McDougall [9], respectively. However, the method used by McDougall to test the discriminatory capacity of the linear functions overestimates the classification rate as she included the test data within the training data instead of the cross validation method used in the present study and also in that of Eriksson and Sullivan [11] in which test and training data are always kept apart.

Table 7. Correct classification rates obtained in contexts /sa/ and /ta/ using different combinations of predictors in LDA

Combination of formants	Predictors number	Correct classification SS corpus (%)	
		/sa/	/ta/
F1	1	59	53
	3	67	65
	5	65	64
	9	68	62
F2	1	48	35
	3	53	43
	5	48	44
	9	45	44
F3	1	39	27
	3	37	35
	5	37	38
	9	34	36
F1 + F2	2	60	57
	6	63	62
	10	66	64
	18	68	60
F2 + F3	2	53	38
	6	53	52
	10	50	48
	18	49	48
F1 + F3	2	65	47
	6	68	63
	10	62	63
	18	59	60
F1 + F2 + F3	3	64	58
	6	60	56
	9	**73**	**66**
	15	68	65
	27	-	64
Optimal F3 + F2	6	45	41
Quadratic	9	**72**	**66**
Cubic	12	66	65

In this study, one of the best results obtained by fitting the three first formant contours with a polynomial equation using linear regression was reached with the quadratic equation as well as McDougall [10]. A comparison of the best percentages obtained with this methodology shows a difference of 17% between the result reached by McDougall [10] (89%) and the corresponding to this study (72%). However, these results cannot be compared directly as the studies employed different segments in different languages.

The overall conclusion is that the dynamic analysis using only F0, is not informative enough to classify reliably speakers' voices. On the other hand, the dynamic analysis using F1, F2 and F3 improves the classification results over the static method that uses only the midpoint frequency. These results are in accordance with McDougall's [9,10] and Eriksson and Sullivan's [11] findings, which indicate that the dynamic method is better than the static one.

The highest percentages of classification was obtained with two methods: using nine predictors for the three first formants (F11, F15, F19, F21, F25, F29, F31, F35, F39) and fitting a quadratic equation (better than the cubic) using linear regression (i.e., down to nine variables), and applying the discriminant functions (i.e., discriminant analysis) on this reduced set, as suggested by McDougall [10], who obtained up to 89% of classification performance. Both methodologies are better to discriminate between speakers in the RS corpus. It is possible to obtain up to 73% of discrimination rate for the /sa/ context and, therefore, it can be used as evidence for forensic speaker comparison in Mexican Spanish.

Acknowledgements. Authors want to thank Mrs. Josefina Bolado, Head of the Scientific Paper Translation Department, from División de Investigación at Facultad de Medicina, UNAM, for editing the English-language version of this manuscript.

References

1. Zipf, G.K., Rogers, F.M.: Phonemes and Variphones in four present-day Romance Languages and Classical Latin from the viewpoint of dynamic Philology. Archives Néerlandaises de Phonétique Experimentale **15**, 111–147 (1939)
2. Navarro, T.: Estudios de Fonología Española. Syracuse University Press, New York (1946)
3. Alarcos, T.: Estudios de Fonología Española. Gredos, Madrid (1991)
4. Guirao, M., García, J.: Estudio Estadístico del Español. Consejo Nacional de Investigaciones Científicas y Técnicas, Buenos Aires (1993)
5. Pérez, E.: Frecuencia de fonemas. E-rthabla, Revista de Tecnologías del habla **1**, 1–7 (2003). http://gth-www.die.upm.es/numeros/N1/N1_A4.pdf
6. Cuétara, J.: Fonética y fonología del habla espontánea de la ciudad de México. Su aplicación en las tecnologías del habla [disertation]. Universidad Nacional Autónoma de México, México (2004)
7. Pineda, L., Castellanos, H., Cuétara, J., Galescu, L., Juárez, J., Llisterri, J., Pérez, P., Villaseñor, L.: The Corpus DIMEx100: transcription and evaluation. Lang. Resourc. Eval. **44**, 347–370 (2010)

8. Guerra, R.: Estudio estadístico de la sílaba en español. In: Esgueva, M., Cantanero, M. (eds.) Estudios de Fonética, vol. I, pp. 9–112. Consejo Superior de Investigaciones Científicas, Madrid (1983)

9. McDougall, K.: Speaker-specific formant dynamics: an experiment on Australian English /aI/. Int. J. Speech Lang. Law **11**(1), 103–130 (2004)

10. McDougall, K.: Dynamic features of speech and the characterization of speakers: toward a new approach using formant frequencies. Int. J. Speech Lang. Law **13**(1), 89–126 (2006)

11. Eriksson, E., Sullivan, K.: An investigation of the effectiveness of a Swedish glide+vowel segment for speaker discrimination. Forensic Linguist. **5**(1), 51–66 (2008)

12. Pardo, A., Ruiz, M.A.: SPSS 11. Guía Para el Análisis de Datos. McGraw-Hill, Madrid (2002)

13. Rencher, A.: Methods of Multivariate Analysis. John Wiley & Sons Inc., Publication, USA (2002)

14. Labov, W.: Field methods used by the project on linguistic change and variation. In: Baugh, J., Sherzer, J. (eds.) Language in use: Readings in Sociolinguistics. Prentice Hall, New Jersey (1984)

15. Turell, M.: La base teórica y metodológica de la variación lingüística. In: Turell, M. (ed.) La Sociolingüística de la Variación. Promociones y Publicaciones Universitarias, Barcelona (1995)

16. Greisbach, R., Esser, O., Weinstock, C.: Speaker identification by formant contours. In: Braun, A., Köster, J. (eds.) Studies in Forensic Phonetics, pp. 49–55. Wissenschaftlicher Verlag, Trier (1995)

17. Rose, P.: Long- and short-term within-speaker differences in the formants of Australian hello. In: Braun, A., Köster, J. (eds.) Studies in Forensic Phonetics, pp. 49–55. Wissenschaftlicher Verlag, Trier (1995)

18. McDougall, K.: Nolan, F: Discrimination of speakers using the formant dynamics of /u:/ in british English. In: Trouvain, J., Barry, W.J. (eds.) Proceeding of the 16th International Congress on Phonetic Sciences, pp. 1825–1828. Universität des Saarlandes, Saarbrücken (2007)

19. Kinoshita, Y., Ishihara, S., Rose, P.: Exploring the discriminatory potential of F0 distribution parameters in traditional forensic speaker recognition. Int. J. Speech Lang. Law **16**(1), 91–111 (2009)

20. Nolan, F.: The Phonetic Bases of Speech Recognition. Cambridge University Press, Cambridge (1983)

21. Hollien, H.: The Acoustics of Crime. The New Science of Forensic Phonetics. Plenum Press, New York (1990)

22. Jiang, M.: Fundamental frequency vector for a speaker identification system. Forensic Linguist. **3**(1), 95–106 (1996)

23. Jessen, M.: Speaker-specific information in voice quality parameters. Forensic Linguist. **4**(1), 84–103 (1997)

24. Foulkes, P., Barron, A.: Telephone speaker recognition amongst members of a close social network. Forensic Linguist. **7**(2), 180–198 (2000)

25. Freund, R., Wilson, W., Sa, P.: Regression Analysis. Statistical Modeling of a Response Variable. Elsevier, Amsterdam (2006)

26. Boersma, P., Weenink, D.: Praat: doing phonetics by computer [Computer program]. 5.1.25 Version. University of Amsterdam (2010)

A Speech-Based Web Co-authoring Platform for the Blind

Madeeha Batool[1], Mirza Muhammad Waqar[1],
Ana Maria Martinez-Enriquez[2], and Aslam Muhammad[1(✉)]

[1] Department of CSE, University of Engineering and Technology,
Lahore, Lahore, Pakistan
violentspyl01@gmail.com, mirzamwaqar@hotmail.com,
maslam@uet.edu.pk
[2] Department of CS, CINVESTAV-IPN, D.F. Mexico, Mexico
ammartin@cinvestav.mx

Abstract. Today, even in the presence of IT applications built for the blind, they are facing many problems. Either the applications are for individual's use or if offer collaborative writing, they are not up to the mark. In the collaborative writing, for instance, in Microsoft Word Add-In and the Google Docs UI, the authors do not know about changes made in the document. Though the former facilitates this feature through adding comments in the document, but the dynamic actions, e.g. notifications (the user sign-in, editing the document, closing it) and communication option is yet to be considered. We describe a web application for the blind community to work on a shared document from different locations. Users are able to write, read, edit, and update the collaborative document in a controlled way. We aim to enhance the self-reliance among users and improve performance.

Keywords: Collaborative writing · Group awareness notifications · Blind

1 Introduction

According to a recent estimation (2015) by the World Health Organization (WHO) the population of the world is 7.28 billion [3]. Roughly, 285 million are visually impaired and thirty nine million are blind [4]. The population of Pakistan is 149.03 million out of which blind persons are 2 million [2]. They contribute a key role and require equal opportunity to read, write, and to have an employment.

Due to lack of group awareness and coordination facilities, they have to face a lot of problems, e.g., manually they contact each other to know about the status of the currently work. They want to work collaboratively on a shared document where they can communicate, too. Currently, there exist several assistants to support visually disabled persons, for instance, face recognition like Grava Architecture [12]. Avoiding obstacles (holes, slopes) as White Cane [13], similarly Robotic Walker [14] assisting the blind in indoor activities.

Writing and reading using Braille on mobiles and computers is limited to English. Braille Writing Tutor [5] captures the activities of persons using an e-slate and boosts

© Springer International Publishing AG 2017
G. Sidorov and O. Herrera-Alcántara (Eds.): MICAI 2016, Part I, LNAI 10061, pp. 141–152, 2017.
DOI: 10.1007/978-3-319-62434-1_12

the Braille writing expertise. The Indian Language Speech Converter translates the textual input to the native Indian speech, using an Aural QWERTY editor [1].

In Computer Supported Cooperative Writing (CSCW), the functionality for the blind requires extra groupware features to follow the progress of the shared document: a) A text to speech converter through which the blind will be aware about what is updated; b).- Braille for the writing role; c).- An embedded chat messenger for the communication and to get notifications about the history of occurred activities. An example of the existing collaborative writing application is the Microsoft Word Add-In [19].

The aim of our approach is to introduce the collaborative work for a group in which some members can be blind or visually impaired. The joint efforts can enhance their confidence to solve individual problems. Blind Co-Authoring Platform (BCAP) tackles the issues of group awareness and establishes the cooperation, coordination, and communication among members of the group. The goal is to reduce communication barriers for members by the cooperative work. To achieve this goal, a text-to-speech converter is developed to act as a screen reader and give audio alerts about the group activities. Besides a shared document environment has been created.

The paper is organized as follows: Sect. 2 reviews the current research domain. Section 3 describes the results of a survey conducted in the course of this research. Section 4 explains our approach. Section 5 concludes the research, and explains the future of the research.

2   Literature Survey

CSCW is related to the advanced technology that allows users to work collaboratively on a common goal, for instance, Computer Aided Design, multimedia co-editing, tele-diagnosing, e-meeting, email, and communication [15]. There are many collaborative systems for normal people, e.g. EquiText [16], REDUCE [17], PINAS [6].

The groupware functionalities for the blind include cooperation, communication, data sharing, coordination, time, collaboration, space, and awareness. For visually impaired persons, commonly, the screen reader and voice synthesizer are used for interaction with the application. Sometimes, it becomes complex to use, e.g., the serial content and data overhead. Unluckily, in the collaborative environment, visual methods become necessary, such as, who is busy in performing a task continuously? Which part of the document is going to be updated? [7].

Voice Browser for Groupware Systems (VoBG) is a browser application designed particularly for the blind [9]. VoBG includes a groupware system 'Garoon 2' easy to access and use. Basically, VoBG is a client application for Garoon 2, developed in Japan, acting as a task manager and a scheduler between the blind [8]. Garoon 2 is used in a school environment, but its design is complex enough for the novice blind students. VoBG facilitates the display of Web pages but it only receives data. In the earlier version, searching for a specific content in the entire program through reader was not easy, but now with the help of Voice Browser, only titles appear first and when a user selects some title out of topic, it jumps to the related articles [9].

The Google Docs UI for the Blind [10] is a groupware interface that is widely used in homes and organizations. Recently, the modified version has been designed using the World Wide Web Consortium (W3C) source for the blind people with the enhanced accessibility, effectiveness, learnedness, operability, robustness, usability and ease to remove errors, if any. For the visually impaired persons, the interface must be usable and easily accessible. Besides, the group awareness is an essential requirement for blind people, because they face a lot of problems while using the collaborative writing application with the text-to-speech converter. Google Docs is an interactive application that is particularly used for collaborative editing and facilitates the visually disabled people [21]. However, the dynamic actions, like pop-up window, speech alert (user sign-in, editing, closing the document) are not considered in this application.

A Text-to-Speech Synthesizer application converts text into speech based on NLP and Digital Signal Processing (DSP). The blind can easily listen to the writings on personal computers [11]. The interface for the blind (Braille Language Translation System and Text-to-Speech Converter) is proposed through which users remain informed about the current status of the work. Our research has implemented Text-to-Speech Conversion System within the Collaborative Authoring environment.

Microsoft Word Add-In [19, 20] specifically facilitates in finding the changes made in the document and adding the comments in it as well. Similarly, if a user has to accept or reject a comment, he has an option too. Thus, the usability and accessibility features have been targeted in this Add-In. Text can be added, edited and deleted in its document. Every comment can be viewed separately. There is a command bar to choose any Add-In. It also shows a finalized preview of the document when all the revisions are complete. Its great feature is that it supports JAWS 13 version. Besides, it offers alternate speech conversion, if some blind user cannot afford the JAWS screen reader. The comments or revision appears in a pop up window and tells how many paragraphs are there, how many comments are there and likewise, some context of the document. When the users are writing, updating, deleting or changing the text, they are well aware of the use of Command Bar, because it appears on right click at any place in the word document. It saves them from extra overhead and addition in the cost of application is not required.

3   Web Co-authoring for the Blind

Our platform for the visually impaired persons is based on Web co-authoring, XML and SMIL technologies. The access to the Internet has been made efficient. The rules followed by our application for managing updates are in accord with the document and repositories to be used. The system informs the users about the speech alerts through the embedded Text-to-Speech Converter. The goal is to enhance the spirit of cooperation as well as self-reliance among the blind. In order to get the feedback, we inquired to 100 visually persons from different educational institutions about the text-to-speech converter, the group awareness, the cooperation, the communication used, and the role of IT for the blind. The results are illustrated in Table 1. Twenty-one questions were formulated. Each question shows how many persons vote.

The questions have been divided into three categories, i.e. category 1 contains the questions about the group activities. Category 2 explains the questions about technology for the blind and category 3 contains questions about jobs for the blind.

Table 1. Results of questionnaire

Questions	Option 1 (%)	Option 2 (%)	Option 3 (%)
Category 1: questions about group activities			
1 Group activity b/w blind	Yes (100)	No (0)	Rarely (0)
2 Between blind & normal	Yes (85)	No (0)	Rarely (15)
3 Worked on a shared doc.	Yes (0)	No (60)	No idea (40)
4 Group awareness during work	Yes (20)	No (60)	Somehow (20)
5 Interest will develop by	Diff. roles (81)	salary (3)	Restrictions (16)
6 Which way for group work?	CSCW (96)	Old ways (0)	Both (4)
7 If not a common goal, then?	Shared doc. (0)	Separate doc. (100)	Both (0)
8 Group work at same place is	Easy (90)	Difficult (5)	Normal (5)
9 Group work at diff. places is	Easy (40)	Difficult (50)	Normal (10)
10 Issue in group with normal?	Yes (66)	No (16)	Somehow (18)
Category 2: questions about technology for the blind			
11 Need of Text-to-Speech	Yes (100)	No (0)	Somehow (0)
12 Role of technology for blind	Major (100)	Minor (0)	Not (0)
13 Special computers for blind?	Yes (0)	No (0)	S/w is diff. (100)
14 Technology solves issues?	Yes (100)	No (0)	Somehow (0)
15 Achieve group awareness	Manually (80)	By chat/call (20)	By alerts (0)
16 App. For communication?	Skype (84)	Yahoo (16)	Google Talk (0)
17 Preferable technology?	Screen Reader (100)	Sensor (0)	Haptics (0)
Category 3: questions about jobs for the blind			
18 Lack of trust in jobs	Yes (70)	No (10)	Somehow (20)
19 Not encouraged for jobs?	Yes (86)	No (0)	Somehow (4)
20 Online job is better for you?	Yes (42)	No (10)	May be (48)
21 Which job is the best?	Official (7)	Teaching (83)	Some art (11)

The problems faced by the blind have been thoroughly discussed. The solution presents an applicable idea, especially for the blind. The feedback received from the users contains some suggestions:

(1) The automatic shuffling of roles should be there, so that each user may work as a different user each time. (2) The privacy should be strictly maintained. (3) The blind face problem in working on images and tabular format. So, there should be some tool to tackle such issues. (4) Handicapped persons have not worked on a shared document before while 40% persons have no idea about what a shared document means (Question 3, Category 1). (5) 96% of the blind prefer a CSCW application (Question 6, Category 1). (6) They are supposed to have little knowledge about the activities of others. They ask for a platform on which group awareness is enhanced (Questions 4, Category 1). According to them, whenever some group member joins, edits or updates the

document, all others should receive a notification alert as an audio beep appearing on a side of the concerning document. (7) The survey reveals that 100% educated blind people favor using the Text-to-Speech Converter, finding it the best support for understanding Web data. Users propose that speech alerts about the updates should work for each activity. (Question 11, Category 2). Visually impaired people are not trusted to work with people who are different to them (Questions 18, Category 3).

After the complete discussion with the blind and derived consequences, we are in a better position to propose a solution to the problem.

Blind Co-Authoring Platform (BCAP) is a synchronous and multi-user shared word document. Each user joins the platform after providing the login credentials. Users can get an audio alert to know which part of the document, a user has edited and updated, when he/she has left the session. Each user can edit different parts of the shared document at the same time. Each user is able to hear who other is online and working on the document. All members of the group can join anytime and the unauthorized users cannot access the document. Users work remotely and are present on separate places. They contact with each other via a chat messenger and make discussion, when it is required. Our platform is based on a shared document, a chat messenger and a technique to get the notifications of messenger for the blind users separately. The availability of authors, tools, Internet, and protocols is also ensured. To achieve the requirements, a network for sharing resources, a mechanism for automatically saved changes and a text-to-speech converter are deployed into the system. The architecture of our platform contains three layers: main, synchronous interface, and asynchronous (see Fig. 1).

Main Layer where the entities are authors sharing Internet resources like a document. Users work jointly on the document. To cooperate and be in touch with collaborators, a chat messenger is embedded in the system. 'Time in and Time out' are the modules of the session. When the session starts, other modules of this layer are launched: 'Combine Work', audible 'Notifications', and 'Save Changes'. Amaya library [18] assures the edit and update of the shared document. In Amaya, the content of the document, structure and the presentation remain separate. The internal structure is in the form of an abstract tree that contains headings, sub-headings, paragraphs, and lists. Other elements include DTD (containing rules of the document), Presentation Schema (image views), Box Tree (view presenter) and APIs (for addressing outer environ of Amaya).

Synchronous Interface Layer (SIL) includes the text-to-speech converter as well as tools and protocol to be used. Both are synced to a specific session in which it is must for all authors to be available. It acts as a bridge between the other two layers. The Text-to-Speech Converter enables authors to be aware of the notifications. The protocol module specifies the social rules follows by members, i.e. all the members agree to the terms and conditions of the use of document, privacy, authorized access, the deadline of completing the work, mutual cooperation, quality of work, etc. There is an ordered list of all occurred events. The session activities like, opening, closing the document and the modules of time in, and time out are handled by the session manager. The event manager is responsible to display the timing of all events. For each activity and change

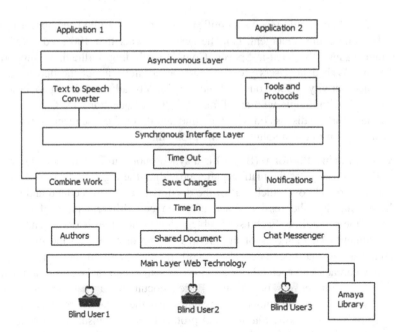

Fig. 1. Architecture of BCAP

made in the document, there is a specific beep. On recognizing the type of beep, they can easily guess which action notification is this about. If someone is busy or wants to check the notification later, he may at least come to know the priority of the action done by some other member and notified by the beep. For joining the platform, signing in, editing, writing, deleting, and adding something, there is a particular beep. On clicking the notification, the text converts into speech and members are able to hear it conveniently.

Asynchronous Layer in which App1 and App2 applications are running asynchronously. These applications are not depending upon the session. They work in the background without any timing restriction. Thus, without using other applications in the background, all tools and technologies have been considered in the proposed scheme as a part of a single co-authoring platform, i.e., users do not need to open separately the document, chat messenger, and contact with other group members on cell or via email.

4 Implementation and Main Features of BCAP

The active participation of each group member is managed by assigning roles that are changed from time to time. Due to the dynamic roles, the participants learn a lot by sharing their skills, i.e., once a member can be a writer, while the other time, he/she has the responsibility of an editor. In this way, co-authors not only contribute willingly in group activities.

Group Awareness by Speech Alerts. No other platform for the blind gives speech alerts about signing in, editing, writing or signing out. Whenever, a group member joins, edits, or updates the document, all others receive a notification alert as an audio beep appearing on one side of the document. On clicking the notification, the text converts to speech and notifies the user about the updates. They are aware of who is working on the document and the role played. The user knowledge is increased, helping them in new learning, they never had a chance to do before.

This editing rule of the figure can be explained as Author X is working on the first section of the document. The role of the author Y is as an editor. The session of the author X has started. Author Y is editing the figure. Speech alert is sent to X notifying that Y has edited that Figure (see Fig. 2). The rule of figure editing speech alert triggers as:

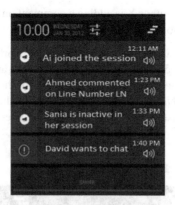

Fig. 2. BCAP speech alerts

```
StartRule "Figure Editing Speech Alert"
      If Author(First_Section) = X
         Role(X) = "Writer"
  Session_Start(X) = True
         Author(First_Section) = Y
         Role(Y) = "Editor"
         Action(Y) = "Edit_Figure"
      Then SendSpeechAlert(X) <- "Y edited the Figure just now"
EndRule
```

Interested Users Activity. When a user leaves a comment on a particular line in the document; the interested users get a comment speech alert containing the new and other unchecked comments on the right side of the document. The rule about 'adding a comment speech alert' fires as:

```
StartRule "Adding a Comment Speech Alert"
        If Author(Second_Section) = X
            Role(X) = "Writer"
            Session_Start(X) = True
            Author(Second_Section) = Y
            Role(Y) = "Reviewer"
            Action(X) = "Add a Comment on Line No. LN"
        Then SendSpeechAlert(Y)<-"X added a comment on Line No"
EndRule
```

This rule defines that an author X is adding a comment on the line number (LN) and a speech alert notifies Y about this fact.

Virtual Proximity works when authors are going to work on the same task. The notification of adding some content, editing, or deleting by any of them is received by that particular group of authors while the other authors of the shared document simply get a general notification. No other application provides this feature to maintain the virtual proximity without disturbing the other group members. The triggered rule is as follows (see Fig. 3).

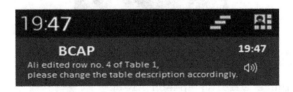

Fig. 3. Virtual proximity speech alert

```
StartRule "Virtual Proximity Speech Alert between X and Y"
        If Author(Third_Section) = X
            Role(X) = "Writer"
            Session_Start(X) = True
            Author(Third_Section) = Y
            Role(Y) = "Writer"
        Action(X)= Edit(Row-RN,table), Delete(Column-CN,table)
        Then
SpeechAlert(Y)<- Edit(Row-RN,table) & Deleted(Column-CN,table)
EndRule
```

Inactive Member Speech Alert. When a threshold time are passed testing the inactivity of a user, a different beep alert (automatic audible) goes to all active members (if any) to report the absent co-author production (i.e., inactivity in session). The rule testing inactive member and speech alert is as follows.

```
StartRule "Inactive Member Speech Alert"
        If Author(First_Section) = X
           Role(X) = "Writer"
        Author(First_Section) = Y
           Role(Y) = "Reviewer"
         Author(First_Section) = Z
           Role(Z) = "Writer"
           Session_Start(Z) = False
           Session_Start(X) = True
           Session_Start(Y) = True
           Action(X) = "Active"
           Action(Y) = "Active"
      Then  SendSpeechAlert(X) <- Inactive_session(Z)
            SendSpeechAlert(Y) <- Inactive_session(Z)
  EndRule
```

Communication among Co-authors in group work, a person may want to discuss a point, one may need permission of his co-author to quit for some time, one may have to contact the other author for guidance, etc. Till now, the blind community has no such system to use by which they can communicate, chat, or call during the work on the same platform. They contact each other via cell phones, Skype, Yahoo Messenger or Google Talk, etc. BCAP offers a way of communication: send and receive messages, and also do voice chat with all or some particular authors as per need while the work is going on. The rule for voice chat is as follows.

```
StartRule "Voice Chat between X and Y authors"
        If Author(Third_Section) = X
           Role(X) = "Writer"
           Session_Start(X) = True
           Author(Third_Section) = Y
           Role(Y) = "Writer"
           Action(X) = Call(Y)    /* discussion about Figure
        Then SendSpeechAlert(Y) <- Call(X)
  EndRule
```

Performance Evaluation of BCAP. An experiment has been performed to evaluate the performance of the developed system with the performance of one of the existing system "Google Docs UI for the Blind" [10] used for collaborative writing. For the performance evaluation experiments, two groups of 10, 10 authors have been created. All of the authors selected for these groups are going to use BCAP first time and none of them is expert in using it.

Group-A used Google Docs for working on a shared document and Group B used BCAP (Fig. 4).

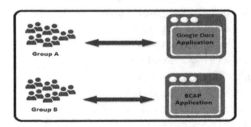

Fig. 4. Performance evaluation experiment

After 10 days, Group A was asked about their experience with the Google Docs application, they told that they found it very good. They could work anywhere remotely, but they had to contact each other using some other application or via email/phone and they were not aware of each other activities unless they asked from each other. If an author was not working on the document, they did not know and at what time, someone joined was hard to check. On the other hand, Group B that used BCAP first time, remarked that they were fully aware of each author's activities because of the timely speech alerts and in case of any problem in learning or wherever they needed to discuss some point, they used the communication functionality of BCAP and they did not have to use any other application for that. Besides, they had complete information about the inactive status of the absent authors and they got speech alerts with exact timing as well. This experiment shows the success of BCAP application.

5   Conclusion and Future Work

Within computer supported cooperative writing and editing, there is no particular application able to provide an environment for the blind in which they have minimum external assistance and the management of different roles on the production of the cooperative writing. A Web co-authoring platform for the blind can open the doors of enthusiasm and quality of life for them. The reward incentive can boost up their interest towards the project. BCAP has been tested successfully, however, in future, the limitations will be overcome, such as the blind people face problems of the recognition of colors, tabular format and image reading, especially, because the text to speech converter does not read it the way we sighted people see. The idea can be enhanced and we will also work on a group of the deaf, slow learners and other disabled people.

References

1. Dasgupta, T., Basu, A.: A speech enabled Indian language text to Braille transliteration system. In: Information and Communication Technologies and Development (ICTD), pp. 201–211 (2009)
2. http://www.thenews.com.pk/Todays-News-4-173929-Two-million-blind-people-in-Pakistan (2015)
3. http://www.worldometers.info/world-population/. Accessed 19 Feb 2015
4. http://www.who.int/mediacentre/factsheets/fs282/en/. Accessed 19 Feb 2015
5. Kalra, N., Lauwers, T., et al.: Iterative design of a Braille writing tutor to combat illiteracy. In: Proceedings of the 2nd IEEE/ACM International Conference on Information and Communication Technologies and Development, December 2007
6. Martínez-Enríquez, A.M., Muhammad, A., Decouchant, D., Favela, J.: An inference engine for web adaptive cooperative work. In: Coello Coello, C.A., Albornoz, A., Sucar, L.E., Battistutti, O.C. (eds.) MICAI 2002. LNCS, vol. 2313, pp. 526–535. Springer, Heidelberg (2002). doi:10.1007/3-540-46016-0_55
7. Stephanidis, C. (ed.): UAHCI 2011. LNCS, vol. 6765. Springer, Heidelberg (2011). doi:10.1007/978-3-642-21672-5
8. Bruder, I., Jaworek, G.: Blind and visually impaired people: human-computer interaction and access to graphics. In: Miesenberger, K., Klaus, J., Zagler, W., Karshmer, A. (eds.) ICCHP 2008. LNCS, vol. 5105, pp. 767–769. Springer, Heidelberg (2008). doi:10.1007/978-3-540-70540-6_113
9. Kobayashi, M.: Voice browser for groupware systems: VoBG - a simple groupware client for visually impaired students. In: Miesenberger, K., Klaus, J., Zagler, W., Karshmer, A. (eds.) ICCHP 2008. LNCS, vol. 5105, pp. 777–780. Springer, Heidelberg (2008). doi:10.1007/978-3-540-70540-6_115
10. Mori, G., Buzzi, M.C., Buzzi, M., Leporini, B., Penichet, Victor M.R.: Making "Google Docs" user interface more accessible for blind people. In: Cipolla Ficarra, F.V., Castro Lozano, C., Pérez Jiménez, M., Nicol, E., Kratky, A., Cipolla-Ficarra, M. (eds.) ADNTIIC 2010. LNCS, vol. 6616, pp. 20–29. Springer, Heidelberg (2011). doi:10.1007/978-3-642-20810-2_4
11. Isewon, I., Oyelade, O.J.: Design and Implementation of Text To Speech Conversion for Visually Impaired People (2014)
12. Robertson, P., Laddaga, R.: An agent architecture for information fusion and its application to robust face identification. In: Conference on Applied Informatics – AI, Massachusetts Institute of Technology AI Laboratory, pp. 132–139 (2003)
13. Shoval, S., Ulrich, I., Borenstein, J.: Computerized obstacle avoidance systems for the blind and visually impaired. In: Invited Chapter, Intelligent Systems and Technologies in Rehabilitation Engineering, pp. 414–448, 26 December 2000
14. Gharieb, W.: Intelligent robotic walker design. In: 6th International Congress for Global Science and Technology, EE Department, College of Engineering, King Saud University Riyadh, 7–12 June 2006
15. Mills, K.L.: Computer-Supported Cooperative Work. National Institute of Standards and Technology, Gaithersburg, Maryland, USA (2003)
16. Rizzi, C.B., Alonso, C.M.C., Hassan, E., et al.: EquiText: a helping tool in the elaboration of collaborative texts. In: The 11th International Conference, San Diego, CA, USA, 2000
17. Yang, Y., et al.: Real-time cooperative editing on the internet. IEEE Internet Comput. **4**(3), 18–25 (2000)

18. Guetari, R., Quint, V., Vatton, I.: Amaya: an Authoring Tool for the Web. WWW Consortium (1998)
19. Schoeberlein, J.G.: Accessible Collaborative Writing For Persons Who Are Blind, December 2013
20. Schoeberlein, J.G., Wang, Y.: Providing an Accessible Track Changes Feature for Persons Who Are Blind (2013)
21. Buzzi, M.C., Buzzi, M., Leporini, B., Mori, G., Penichet, V.M.R.: Collaborative editing: collaboration, awareness and accessibility issues for the blind. In: Meersman, R., et al. (eds.) OTM 2014. LNCS, vol. 8842, pp. 567–573. Springer, Heidelberg (2014). doi:10.1007/978-3-662-45550-0_58

Social Networks and Opinion Mining

Friends and Enemies of Clinton and Trump: Using Context for Detecting Stance in Political Tweets

Mirko Lai[1,2]([⊠]), Delia Irazú Hernández Farías[1,2], Viviana Patti[1], and Paolo Rosso[2]

[1] Dipartimento di Informatica, Università degli Studi di Torino, Turin, Italy
milai@unito.it
[2] Pattern Recognition and Human Language Technologies Research Center, Universitat Politécnica de Valéncia, Valencia, Spain

Abstract. Stance detection, the task of identifying the speaker's opinion towards a particular target, has attracted the attention of researchers. This paper describes a novel approach for detecting stance in Twitter. We define a set of features in order to consider the context surrounding a target of interest with the final aim of training a model for predicting the stance towards the mentioned targets. In particular, we are interested in investigating political debates in social media. For this reason we evaluated our approach focusing on two targets of the SemEval-2016 Task 6 on Detecting stance in tweets, which are related to the political campaign for the 2016 U.S. presidential elections: Hillary Clinton vs. Donald Trump. For the sake of comparison with the state of the art, we evaluated our model against the dataset released in the SemEval-2016 Task 6 shared task competition. Our results outperform the best ones obtained by participating teams, and show that information about enemies and friends of politicians help in detecting stance towards them.

1 Introduction

Social media provide a way for expressing opinions about different topics. From this kind of user-generated content it is possible to discover relevant information under several perspectives. A wide range of research has been carried out in order to exploit the vast amount of data generated in social media. One of the most interesting research areas concerns to investigate how people expose their feelings, evaluations, attitudes and emotions. These kinds of aspects are the subject of interest of Sentiment Analysis (SA) [1].

Determining the subjective value of a piece of text is the most general task of SA. Recently, the interest on studying finer-grained and different facets of sentiment in texts has derived in areas such as *Aspect based sentiment analysis* [2] and *Stance Detection* (SD) [3], which is the focus of our work. Identifying the speaker's opinion towards a particular target is the main goal of SD. It is not enough to recognize whether or not a text is positive/negative/neutral but it is necessary to infer the point of view of the tweeter towards a particular target.

© Springer International Publishing AG 2017
G. Sidorov and O. Herrera-Alcántara (Eds.): MICAI 2016, Part I, LNAI 10061, pp. 155–168, 2017.
DOI: 10.1007/978-3-319-62434-1_13

Stance detection could not only provide useful information for improving the performance of SA but it could also help to better understand the way in which people communicate ideas in order to highlight their point of view towards a particular target entity. This is particularly interesting when the target entity is controversial issue (e.g., political reforms [4,5]) or a polarizing person (e.g., candidates in political elections). Therefore, detecting stance in social media could become a helpful tool for various sectors of society, such as journalism, companies and government, having politics as an especially good application domain. Several efforts have been made in order to investigate different aspects related to social media and politics [6]. We are interested in political debates in social media, particularly in the interaction between polarized communities. We consider that being able to detect stance in user-generated content could provide useful insights to discover novel information about social network structures. Political debate texts coming from social media where people discuss their different points of view offer an attractive information source.

This year, for the first time a shared task on stance detection in tweets was organized [3]. Two of the targets considered in order to evaluate stance detection systems were: Hillary Clinton and Donald Trump[1]. Both targets have been the focus of different research, for instance in [7] the authors studied their speeches during the 2016 political campaign. In such way, studying these targets is an attracting topic of research due to the impact of the use of social media during the political campaign for the 2016 U.S. Presidential elections.

Our approach to detect stance in tweets relies mainly on the context of the targets of interest: Hillary Clinton and Donald Trump. Besides, we also took advantage of widely used features in SA.

The paper is organized as follows. Section 2 introduces the first shared task on Twitter stance detection. Section 3 describes our method to detect stance by exploiting different features. Section 4 describes the evaluation and results. Finally, Sect. 5 draws some conclusions.

2   Detecting Stance on Tweets

The SemEval-2016 Task 6: Detecting Stance in Tweets[2] was the first shared task on detecting stance from tweets. Mohammad et al. in [3] describe the task as: *Given a tweet text and a target entity (person, organization, movement, policy, etc.), automatic natural language systems must determine whether the tweeter is in favor of the target, against the given target, or whether inference is likely.*
    Let us to introduce the following example[3]:
Support #independent #BernieSanders because he's not a liar. #POTUS #libcrib #democrats #tlot #republicans #WakeUpAmerica #SemST

---

[1] They are the candidates who won the Party Presidential Primaries for the Democratic and Republican parties, respectively.

[2] http://alt.qcri.org/semeval2016/task6/.

[3] This tweet was extracted from the training set of SemEval-2016 Task 6.

The target of interest is "Hillary Clinton". Here, the tweeter expresses a positive opinion towards an adversary of the target. Consequently the annotator inferred that the tweeter expresses a negative opinion towards the target. As can be noticed, this tweet does not contain any explicit clue to find the target.

For evaluating the task, the organizers annotated near to 5,000 English tweets for stance towards six commonly known targets in the United States: "Atheism", "Climate Change is a Real Concern", "Feminism Movement", "Hillary Clinton", "Legalization of Abortion", and "Donald Trump" (Stance Dataset, henceforth). A set of hashtags widely used by people when tweeting about these targets was compiled; then it was used to retrieve tweets according three categories: in-favor hashtags, against hashtags and stance-ambiguous hashtags. The tweets were manually annotated by crowdsourcing. More details about the Stance Dataset can be found in [3].

The participants in the SemEval-2016 Task 6 were required to classify tweet-target pairs into exactly one of three classes: *Favor*: It can be inferred from the tweet that the tweeter supports the target (e.g., directly or indirectly by supporting someone/something, by opposing or criticizing someone/something opposed to the target, or by echoing the stance of somebody else); *Against*: It can be inferred from the tweet that the tweeter is against the target (e.g., directly or indirectly by opposing or criticizing someone/something, by supporting someone/something opposed to the target, or by echoing the stance of somebody else); and *Neither*: None of the above.

The SemEval-2016 Task 6 was divided into two subtasks:

- Task A. Supervised Framework. The participating systems were asked to perform stance detection towards the following targets: "Atheism", "Climate Change is a Real Concern", "Feminism Movement", "Hillary Clinton", and "Legalization of Abortion". For evaluation the organizer provided a training (2,914 tweets) and test (1,249 tweets) sets.
- Task B. Weakly Supervised Framework. The task was detecting stance towards one target "Donald Trump" in 707 tweets. For this task the participants were not provided with any training data about this target.

Nineteen teams participated in Task A while only nine competed in Task B. It is important to highlight that only two systems were evaluated specifically on Task B. Figure 1 shows a brief summary of the systems. Further information about the systems in the task can be found in [8][4].

Both tasks were addressed in similar ways. Most teams exploited standard text classification features such as n-grams and word embedding vectors. Besides, some SA features from well-known lexical resources, such as *EmoLex* [9], *MPQA* [10], *Hu and Liu* [11] and *NRC Hashtag* [12], were used to detect stance in tweets. Furthermore, some teams decided to take advantage of additional data by harvesting Twitter using stance-bearing hashtags in order to have more stance tweets. It is important to highlight that the best system in Task A (MITRE) did

---

[4] Notice that not all the reports describing systems and approaches of teams participating at SemEval-2016 Task 6 are available in [8].

Table 1. Brief description of the participating systems at SemEval-2016 Task 6

System	Description
MITRE [13]	**Overall approach:** Recurrent neural networks
Task A	**External resources:** Words embeddings with the word2vect skip-gram method. Near to 300,000 tweets containing hashtags related to the targets
pkudblab [14]	**Overall approach:** Convolutional neural network
Tasks A and B	**External resources:** Words embeddings using the Google News dataset
TakeLab [15]	**Overall approach:** An ensemble of learning algorithms (such as SVM, random forest) fine-tuned using a genetic algorithm
Task A	**External resources:** Word features, word embeddings, frequency of emoticons, uppercase characters, among others
ECNU [16]	**Overall approach:** A pipeline-based procedure involving relevance and orientation detection
Tasks A and B	**External resources:** N-grams, topic features and sentiment lexicon features (such as Hu & Liu and MPQA, among others)
CU-GWU [17]	**Overall approach:** Classification using SVM
Task A	**External resources:** N-grams, Stanford's SA system and LIWC
IUCL-RF [18]	**Overall approach:** Classification algorithms (SVM, random forest, gradient boosting decision trees) and an ensemble classifier (TiMBL)
Task A	**External resources:** Bag-of-Words and word vectors
DeepStance [19]	**Overall approach:** A set of naive bayes classifiers using deep learning
Task A	**External resources:** More than 1.5 million of tweets were added by using representative hashtag for target-stance pairs
UWB [20]	**Overall approach:** Maximum entropy classifier
Tasks A and B	**External resources:** N-grams, PoS labels, General Inquirer. Additional tweets were gathered based on frequent hashtags in the training set
IDI@NTNU [21]	**Overall approach:** A soft voting classifier approach (naive bayes and logistic regression)
Task A	**External resources:** Word vectors, n-grams, char-grams, negation, punctuation marks, elongated words, among others
Tohoku [22]	**Overall approach:** Two methods: a feature based approach and a neural network based approach
Task A	**External resources:** Bag-of-Words, PoS labels, SentiWordNet. Additional Twitter data was gathered from target words
ltl.uni-due [23]	**Overall approach:** Multidimensional classification problem
Tasks A and B	**External resources:** N-grams, punctuation marks, negation, nouns
JU_NLP [24]	**Overall approach:** Classification using SVM
Task A	**External resources:** N-Gram and sentiment analysis resources such as: SentiWordNet, EmoLex and NRC Hashtag Emotion Lexicon
nldsucsc [25]	**Overall approach:** Classification using SVM, J48 and naive bayes
Task A	**External resources:** N-grams, PoS labels, LIWC. Additional tweets were gathered based on frequent hashtags in the training set
INF_UFRGS [26]	**Overall approach:** Set of rules together with SVM
Task B	**External resources:** N-grams
USFD [27]	**Overall approach:** Classification using logistic regression
Task B	**External resources:** Bag-of-words autoencoder. Additional tweets were gathered by using two keywords per target

use this alternative. A similar approach was adopted by the three best ranked systems on Task B (pkudblab, LitisMind, and INF-UFRGS). For what concerns to Task B, in order to deal with the lack of training data, some systems attempted to generalize the supervised data from task A in different ways such as defining rules or by exploiting multi-stage classifiers (Table 1).

3   Our Approach

We are proposing a supervised approach for stance detection[5]. Our work is focused on detecting stance towards Hillary Clinton and Donald Trump that are currently contesting the political campaign for the 2016 U.S. Presidential election. An important aspect to mention concerns to the fact that when the Stance Dataset was built the two targets were still participating to the Party Presidential Primaries for the Democratic and Republican parties, respectively. We address the stance detection in tweets, casting it as a classification task. A set of features that comprises different aspects was exploited. The most novel one refers to the extraction of context-related information regarding to the target of interest. Our hypothesis is that domain knowledge could provide useful information to improve the performance of SD systems. For instance, in order to correctly identify stance in a tweet as the one mentioned in Sect. 2, it is needed to recognize that *Bernie Sander* was an adversary of Hillary Clinton during the Party Presidential Primaries of the Democratic party. Attempting to capture information related to domain knowledge, we define two concepts: "enemies" and "friends". These concepts are used for denoting the entities related to the target. By using the terms "enemies" and "friends", we are trying to infer that when a tweeter is against an "enemy"/"friend" of the target, then the tweeter is in favor/against towards the target and, on the other hand, when a tweeter is in favor towards an "enemy"/"friend" of the target, then the tweeter is against/in favor towards the target. Figure 1 shows an example of the relationships between the "friends" and "enemies" according to their political party, in this case the target of interest is Hillary Clinton.

Three groups of features were considered: sentiment, structural, and context-based.

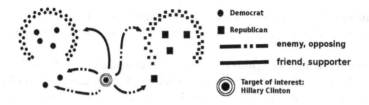

Fig. 1. Diagram of relationships between friends and enemies of Hillary Clinton

---

[5] https://github.com/mirkolai/Friends-and-Enemies-of-Clinton-and-Trump.

3.1 Sentiment-Based Features

We shared the idea that stance detection is strongly related to sentiment analysis [3,16]. As far as we know, there are not sentiment analysis lexica retrieved specifically in the political domain[6]; thus, in order to take advantage of sentiment features it is possible to exploit the wide range of resources available for English. We used a set of four lexica to cover different facets of affect ranging from prior polarity of words to fine-grained emotional information:

- **AFINN**. It is an affective lexicon of 2,477 English words manually labeled with a polarity value between −5 to +5. AFINN was collected by Finn Årup Nielsen [28]. We consider one feature from AFINN: the sum of the polarity of the words present in each tweet.
- **Hu & Liu (HL)**. It includes about 6,800 positive and negative words. We calculate the difference between the positive and negative words in a tweet as a feature.
- **LIWC**. The Linguistic Inquiry and Word Counts (LIWC) [29] is a dictionary that contains about 4,500 entries distributed in 64 categories that can be further used to analyse psycholinguistic features in texts. We calculate the difference between PosEmo (with 405 entries) and NegEmo (with 500 entries) categories in a tweet as a feature.
- **DAL**. The Dictionary of Affect in Language (DAL) contains 8,742 English words; it was developed by Whissell [30]. Each word is rated in a three-point scale into three dimensions: Pleasantness (It refers to the degree of pleasure produced by words), Activation (It refers the degree of response that humans have under an emotional state) and Imagery (It refers to how difficult to form a mental picture of a given word is). We consider six features, i.e. the sum and the mean of the rates of the words present in the tweet for each one of the three dimensions.

3.2 Structural Features

We also explore structural characteristics of tweets because we believe that could be useful to detect stance. We experimented with several kinds of structural features, however only the most relevant ones were included in the final approach:

- **Hashtags**. The frequency of hashtags present in each tweet.
- **Mentions**. The frequency of screen names (often called mentions) in each tweet.
- **Punctuation marks (punct_marks)**. We consider a set of 6 different features: the frequency of exclamation marks, question marks, periods, commas, semicolons, and finally the sum of all the punctuation marks mentioned before.

---

[6] For example, the term *vote* is strongly related to politics, but it is not present in commonly used SA lexica such as: AFINN, Hu & Liu, and LIWC.

3.3   Context-Based Features

Our hypothesis is that the context-based features should capture some domain-related information. An overall perspective of the context surrounding a target can be acquired by the relationships that exist between the target and other entities in its domain. As mentioned before we are interested in investigating Political debates: for this reason we selected as targets of interest politicians such as Hillary Clinton and Donald Trump. We manually created a list of entities related to the Party Presidential Primaries for the Democratic and Republican parties from Wikipedia[7]. We exploited 6 types of context-based features considering different kinds of relationships between the target and the entities around the target:

- **Target of interest mentioned by name (targetByName)**: This feature captures the presence of the target of interest in the tweet in hand. *#StopHillary2016 HillaryClinton if there was a woman with integrity and honesty I would vote for such as woman president, NO.* The list of tokens used to check the presence of the target of interest are: *hillaryclinton, hillary, clinton,* and *hill* for Hillary Clinton; while for Donald Trump are *realdonaldtrump, donald,* and *trump.*
- **Target of interest mentioned by pronoun (targetByPronoun)**: This feature allows to identify those cases when the target of interest is mentioned by using a pronoun. In the following example, knowing that the target of the tweet is Hillary Clinton, it is possible to exploit the pronoun "she" to capture the presence of the target in hand. *HomeOfUncleSam ScotsFyre RWNutjob1 SA_Hartdegen She's too old to understand the internet...that she can be fact checked.*
  Two pronouns were considered for each one of the targets of interest: *she* and *her* for Hillary Clinton, while *he* and *his* for Donald Trump.
- **Target's party (targetParty)**: As people involved in politics, our targets belong to a political party. Using this feature we identify if the stance against (or in favor) towards the target of interest was expressed mentioning the name of the party instead of the target. In the following example the tweeter expresses a negative opinion toward Hillary Clinton party.
  It's a miracle, suddenly #Democrats don't mind having someone who voted for war.
  In this case we consider the tokens *dem, democratic, democrat, democrats, progressive* in order to check the entity party for Hillary Clinton, while we consider the tokens *republican, republicans,* and *conservative* for Donald Trump.
- **Party colleague opposite (targetPartyColleagues)**: We also considered the case where the party colleagues of the target of interest are mentioned to express an opinion towards it. We use the name and the surnames of the candidates for the Party Presidential Primaries for both Democratic and Republican parties. In the example, Hillary Clinton's party colleagues are mentioned.

---

[7] Articles: *Democratic Party presidential primaries, 2016* and *Republican Party presidential candidates, 2016.*

*msnbc **Lawrence** JoeBiden Sen**Sanders** we love Joe and **Bernie**–but they ARE too OLD–they would end up a #OneTerm President #SemST.*

The list of names used for Hillary Clinton is: *bernie, sanders, martin, o'malley, lincoln, chafee, webb, lawrence,* and *lessig*; while for Donald Trump is: *ted, cruz, marco, rubio, john, kasich, ben, carson, jeb, bush, rand, paul, mike, huckabee, carly, fiorina, chris, christie, rick, santorum, gilmore, rick, perry, scott, walker, bobby, jindal, lindsey, graham, george, pataki.*

- **Target's oppositors party (targetsOppositors):** This feature captures the presence of oppositors belonging to the rival party of target of interest's. In the following example a positive opinion is expressed towards two candidates from the Republican party. Thus, the tweet is against Hillary Clinton. *PhilGlutting megadreamin Thank you so much for RT and FAV!!! #WakeUpAmerica #Rubio2016 #Cruz2016 #SemST.*
  We use the Donald Trump's tokens lists targetParty and targetPartyColleagues in order to create Hillary Clinton's targetsOppositors tokens list, while we use Hillary Clinton's tokens lists targetParty and targetPartyColleagues in order to create Donald Trump's targetsOppositors tokens list.

- **Nobody (nobody):** This feature allows to catch those cases where any of the above described entities are mentioned in a tweet. In the following example the term *Ambassador* refers to Chris Stevens, who served as the U.S. Ambassador to Libya and who was killed at Bengasi in 2012. The diplomat is related to Hillary Clinton in a situation not related with the election campaign[8].
  I don't want to be appointed to an Ambassador post.
  The example also shows how difficult is to infer the stance without a deep knowledge of the context.

After the evaluation of participating systems, the organizers of Semeval-2016 Task 6 annotated the Stance Datataset for sentiment and target in order to explore the relationship between sentiment and stance [3,31][9]. In particular, tweets were manually annotated by using two additional labels: *Sentiment* and *Opinion Towards*, used to mark the overall sentiment polarity of the tweet and information about the fact that opinion is expressed directly towards the target, respectively:

- **Sentiment.** It can be positive, negative, neutral or none.
- **Opinion_target.** It can take three different values: (1) if a tweet expresses an opinion about the target; (2) if a tweet expresses an opinion related to an aspect of the target or related to something that is not the target; and (3) if there is not opinion expressed.

We decided to exploit such new labels, by enriching our model with corresponding **labeled-based features**, with the aim to experiment with both context and sentiment information provided by human annotators.

---

[8] https://en.wikipedia.org/wiki/J._Christopher_Stevens.

[9] Notice that this is the first publicly available Twitter dataset annotated with both stance and sentiment.

4   Evaluation

We experimented with a set of tweets belonging to Hillary Clinton and Donald Trump from the Stance Dataset, the Table 2 shows the distribution of tweets annotated with stance in the training and the test set for our targets of interest.

Table 2. Distribution of stance in training and test set

Targets	% Instances in training				% Instances in test			
	Total	Against	Favor	None	Total	Against	Favor	None
Hillary Clinton	689	57.1	17.1	25.8	295	58.3	15.3	26.4
Donald Trump	-	-	-	-	707	42.3	20.9	36.8

We evaluated our approach by using the same measure defined in [3] in order to compare our results with those participating in the task. We trained a Gaussian Naive Bayes classifier [32] implemented in Scikit-learn Python library[10] to built a model for identifying stance in tweets.

We adopted two experimental setting: (a) **experiment1**. It means to the use of the Sentiment-based, Structural and Context-based features; (b) **experiment2**. It refers to the use of all the features described in Sect. 3 including the labeled-based ones. Besides, we experimented using different feature combinations in order to identify which kinds of features could be more relevant for stance detection.

Table 3. Best features combination for Hillary Clinton, and the respective results for Donald Trump with experiment1 setting

Feature set	Hillary Clinton			Donald Trump		
	F_{avg}	$F_{against}$	F_{favor}	F_{avg}	$F_{against}$	F_{favor}
Mention punct_marks AFINN LIWC HL context_based	63.75	71.95	55.56	53.46	50.29	56.63
Punct_marks AFINN LIWC HL context_based	62.70	71.47	53.93	52.76	49.61	55.91
Hashtag punct_marks AFINN LIWC HL DAL context_based	62.3	70.43	54.17	50.44	47.69	53.19

Tables 3 and 4 present the best results obtained for Hillary Clinton in the experiment1 and experiment2, respectively. Moreover, those obtained by using the same set of features for Donald Trump are shown. From the results can be noted that the F1-score in "against" class is higher than in "favor". Interestingly,

---

[10] http://scikit-learn.org/.

Table 4. Feature set for Hillary Clinton and the respective results for Donald Trump with experiment2

Feature set	Hillary Clinton			Donald Trump		
	F_{avg}	$F_{against}$	F_{favor}	F_{avg}	$F_{against}$	F_{favor}
Hashtag mention context-based labeled-based	71.21	77.17	65.26	69.59	61.99	77.19
Hashtag context-based labeled-based	71.02	76.77	65.26	70.40	62.77	78.48
Hashtag mention LIWC context-based labeled-based	70.98	78.23	63.73	70.20	63.06	77.35

the opposite happens for Donald Trump. The results in Table 4 are higher than those from Table 3. Table 5 shows the best results for Donald Trump using for both experiment1 and experiment2.

Table 5. Best feature set for Donald Trump using experiment2 and experiment1 setting

Feature set	Donald Trump		
	F_{avg}	$F_{against}$	F_{favor}
* LIWC HL context_based labeld_based	74.49	69.26	79.72
Mention punc_marks HL context_based	55.51	50	61.02

The * indicate the use of features belonging exclusively to experiment2

As can be noted the context-based features seem to be so relevant for both targets. Besides, it is important to highlight that the best result for each target was not achieved by the same set of features. This is maybe not surprising, if we consider the different political campaign marketing strategies of the two candidates, which can influence also the communication of candidates' oppositors and supporters, both in terms of language register used and addressed topics. For the sake of comparison with the state of the art, we present the results obtained by the three best ranked systems at SemEval-2016 Task 6. We only include the results concerning to Hillary Clinton and Donald Trump. Both the F-measure average and the rank position of each system are included in the Table 6. We also show our best results for the two targets using both experimental settings as well as the position in the official ranking in the shared task.

Our approach achieves strongly competitive results. We ranked in the first position for both Task A and Task B using the experiment2 setting considering Hillary Clinton and Donald Trump results. For what concerns to the experiment1 we ranked in the third position for Task A and the second one for Task B. The obtained results outperform the baselines proposed in [3][11]. Besides, our

---

[11] The authors experimented with n-grams, char-grams and majority class to establish the baselines for the task.

Table 6. Results of task A and B

	Task A: Hillary Clinton		Task B: Donald Trump	
	F_{avg}	Ranking	F_{avg}	Ranking
Experiment1 for Hillary Clinton	**63.75**	3	53.46	2
Experiment1 for Donald Trump	61.25	4	**55.51**	2
Experiment2 for Hillary Clinton	**71.21**	1	69.59	1
Experiment2 for Donald Trump	68.29	1	**74.49**	1
Systems in the official competition				
INF-UFRGS	-	-	42.32	3
LitisMind	42.08	17	44.66	2
pkudblab	64.41	2	**56.28**	1
PKULCWM	62.26	3	-	-
TakeLab	**67.12**	1	-	-

outcomes outrank those obtained by submissions from all teams participating in the shared task (both task A and B). Overall, the results for Hillary Clinton are higher than those for Donald Trump. This was in someway expected, due to the lack of a training set of tweets concerning the target *Donald Trump*.

5   Conclusions

In this paper we have shown that including context-related information is crucial in order to improve the performance of stance detection systems. Experiments confirms that stance detection is highly dependent on the domain knowledge of the target in hand. Our approach relies on the presence of entities related to a target in order to try to extract the opinion expressed towards it. Besides, our proposal allows to infer the stance in both cases when the target is explicitly mentioned and also when it is not. The results obtained by exploiting context-related features outperforms those from the best ranked systems in the SemEval-2016 Task 6.

Let us highlight that we are not using either n-grams or any word-based representation, but our approach mainly relies on the context of the target in hand. We plan to investigate the performance of our approach in different domains. Exploiting semantic resources in order to catch additional context information is also an interesting line for future research. Also user's information and her social network structure could be useful. For what concerns to the sentiment-related features, overall results confirm that these kinds of features help in identifying the stance towards a particular target. We exploited different sentiment-related features, ranging from those extracted from affective resources to manually assigned polarity labels.

A further interesting matter of future work could be explore also the stance w.r.t. different aspects of a political target entity. This means to perform a sort of aspect-based sentiment analysis in a political domain, e.g., a tweeter can be in favor of Hillary for aspects related to "Health", but not for other aspects.

Finally, we think that it could be also interesting to investigate how to fruitfully combine information about stance and information about the presence of figurative devices in tweets, such as irony and sarcasm [33,34], since the use of such devices is very frequent in political debates also in social media and detecting irony and sarcasm have been considered as one of the biggest challenges for sentiment analysis.

Acknowledgments. The National Council for Science and Technology (CONA-CyT Mexico) has funded the research work of Delia Irazú Hernández Farías (218109/313683). The work of Paolo Rosso has been partially funded by the SomEM-BED TIN2015-71147-C2-1-P MINECO research project and by the Generalitat Valenciana under the grant ALMAMATER (PrometeoII/2014/030). The work of Viviana Patti was partially carried out at the Universitat Politècnica de València within the framework of a fellowship of the University of Turin co-funded by Fondazione CRT (World Wide Style Program 2).

References

1. Liu, B.: Sentiment Analysis and Opinion Mining. Synthesis Lectures on Human Language Technologies vol. 5, pp. 1–167. Morgan & Claypool Publishers, San Rafael (2012)
2. Pontiki, M., Galanis, D., Papageorgiou, H., Androutsopoulos, I., Manandhar, S., AL-Smadi, M., Al-Ayyoub, M., Zhao, Y., Qin, B., De Clercq, O., Hoste, V., Apidianaki, M., Tannier, X., Loukachevitch, N., Kotelnikov, E., Bel, N., Jiménez-Zafra, S.M., Eryiğit, G.: Semeval-2016 task 5: aspect based sentiment analysis. In: Proceedings of the 10th International Workshop on Semantic Evaluation (SemEval-2016), pp. 19–30. ACL (2016)
3. Mohammad, S., Kiritchenko, S., Sobhani, P., Zhu, X., Cherry, C.: SemEval-2016 task 6: detecting stance in tweets. In: Bethard et al. [8], pp. 31–41 (2016)
4. Bosco, C., Lai, M., Patti, V., Virone, D.: Tweeting and being ironic in the debate about a political reform: the French annotated corpus twitter-mariagepourtous. In: Proceedings of the Tenth International Conference on Language Resources and Evaluation (LREC 2016), pp. 1619–1626. ELRA (2016)
5. Stranisci, M., Bosco, C., Hernández Farías, D.I., Patti, V.: Annotating sentiment and irony in the online Italian political debate on #labuonascuola. In: Proceedings of the Tenth International Conference on Language Resources and Evaluation (LREC 2016), pp. 2892–2899. ELRA (2016)
6. Maldonado, M., Sierra, V.: Twitter predicting the 2012 US presidential election? Lessons learned from an unconscious value co-creation platform. J. Organ. End User Comput. (JOEUC) **28**, 10–30 (2016)
7. Schumacher, E., Eskenazi, M.: A readability analysis of campaign speeches from the 2016 US presidential campaign. CoRR abs/1603.05739 (2016)
8. Bethard, S., Carpuat, M., Cer, D., Jurgens, D., Nakov, P., Zesch, T. (eds.): Proceedings of the 10th International Workshop on Semantic Evaluation (SemEval-2016). Association for Computational Linguistics, San Diego (2016)
9. Mohammad, S.M., Turney, P.D.: Crowdsourcing a word-emotion association lexicon. Computat. Intell. **29**, 436–465 (2013)

10. Wilson, T., Wiebe, J., Hoffmann, P.: Recognizing contextual polarity in phrase-level sentiment analysis. In: Proceedings of the Conference on HLT and Empirical Methods in Natural Language Processing, pp. 347–354. ACL (2005)

11. Hu, M., Liu, B.: Mining and summarizing customer reviews. In: Proceedings of the Tenth ACM SIGKDD International Conference on Knowledge Discovery and Data Mining, KDD 2004, Seattle, WA, USA, pp. 168–177. ACM (2004)

12. Mohammad, S., Kiritchenko, S., Zhu, X.: NRC-Canada: building the state-of-the-art in sentiment analysis of tweets. In: Proceedings of the Seventh International Workshop on Semantic Evaluation Exercises (SemEval-2013), Atlanta, Georgia, USA (2013)

13. Zarrella, G., Marsh, A.: MITRE at SemEval-2016 task 6: transfer learning for stance detection. In: Bethard et al. [8], pp. 470–475 (2016)

14. Wei, W., Zhang, X., Liu, X., Chen, W., Wang, T.: pkudblab at SemEval-2016 task 6: a specific convolutional neural network system for effective stance detection. In: Bethard et al. [8], pp. 396–400 (2016)

15. Tutek, M., Sekulic, I., Gombar, P., Paljak, I., Culinovic, F., Boltuzic, F., Karan, M., Alagić, D., Šnajder, J.: TakeLab at SemEval-2016 task 6: stance classification in tweets using a genetic algorithm based ensemble. In: Bethard et al. [8], pp. 476–480 (2016)

16. Zhang, Z., Lan, M.: ECNU at SemEval 2016 task 6: relevant or not? Supportive or not? A two-step learning system for automatic detecting stance in tweets. In: Bethard et al. [8], pp. 463–469 (2016)

17. Elfardy, H., Diab, M.: CU-GWU perspective at SemEval-2016 task 6: ideological stance detection in informal text. In: Bethard et al. [8], pp. 446–451 (2016)

18. Liu, C., Li, W., Demarest, B., Chen, Y., Couture, S., Dakota, D., Haduong, N., Kaufman, N., Lamont, A., Pancholi, M., Steimel, K., Kübler, S.: IUCL at SemEval-2016 task 6: an ensemble model for stance detection in twitter. In: Bethard et al. [8], pp. 406–412 (2016)

19. Vijayaraghavan, P., Sysoev, I., Vosoughi, S., Roy, D.: Deepstance at SemEval-2016 task 6: detecting stance in tweets using character and word-level CNNs. In: Bethard et al. [8], pp. 425–431 (2016)

20. Krejzl, P., Steinberger, J.: UWB at SemEval-2016 task 6: stance detection. In: Bethard et al. [8], pp. 420–424 (2016)

21. Bøhler, H., Asla, P., Marsi, E., Sætre, R.: IDI@NTNU at SemEval-2016 task 6: detecting stance in tweets using shallow features and glove vectors for word representation. In: Bethard et al. [8], pp. 457–462 (2016)

22. Igarashi, Y., Komatsu, H., Kobayashi, S., Okazaki, N., Inui, K.: Tohoku at SemEval-2016 task 6: feature-based model versus convolutional neural network for stance detection. In: Bethard et al. [8], pp. 413–419 (2016)

23. Wojatzki, M., Zesch, T.: ltl.uni-due at SemEval-2016 task 6: stance detection in social media using stacked classifiers. In: Bethard et al. [8], pp. 440–445 (2016)

24. Patra, B.G., Das, D., Bandyopadhyay, S.: JU_NLP at SemEval-2016 task 6: detecting stance in tweets using support vector machines. In: Bethard et al. [8], pp. 452–456 (2016)

25. Misra, A., Ecker, B., Handleman, T., Hahn, N., Walker, M.: NLDS-UCSC at SemEval-2016 task 6: a semi-supervised approach to detecting stance in tweets. In: Bethard et al. [8], pp. 432–439 (2016)

26. Dias, M., Becker, K.: INF-UFRGS-OPINION-MINING at SemEval-2016 task 6: automatic generation of a training corpus for unsupervised identification of stance in tweets. In: Bethard et al. [8], pp. 390–395 (2016)

27. Augenstein, I., Vlachos, A., Bontcheva, K.: USFD at SemEval-2016 task 6: any-target stance detection on twitter with autoencoders. In: Bethard et al. [8], pp. 401–405 (2016)
28. Nielsen, F.Å.: A new ANEW: evaluation of a word list for sentiment analysis in microblogs. CoRR abs/1103.2903 (2011)
29. Pennebaker, J.W., Francis, M.E., Booth, R.J.: Linguistic Inquiry and Word Count: LIWC 2001. Lawrence Erlbaum Associates, Mahwah (2001)
30. Whissell, C.: Using the revised dictionary of affect in language to quantify the emotional undertones of samples of natural language. Psychol. Rep. **105**, 509–521 (2009)
31. Mohammad, S., Kiritchenko, S., Sobhani, P., Zhu, X., Cherry, C.: A dataset for detecting stance in tweets. In: Proceedings of the Tenth International Conference on Language Resources and Evaluation (LREC 2016). ELRA (2016)
32. Chan, T.F., Golub, G.H., LeVeque, R.J.: Updating formulae and a pairwise algorithm for computing sample variances. Technical report, Stanford University, Stanford (1979)
33. Hernández Farías, D.I., Patti, V., Rosso, P.: Irony detection in twitter: the role of affective content. ACM Trans. Internet Technol. **16**, 19:1–19:24 (2016)
34. Sulis, E., Hernández Farías, D.I., Rosso, P., Patti, V., Ruffo, G.: Figurative messages and affect in twitter: differences between #irony, #sarcasm and #not. knowledge-based systems. New Ave. Knowl. Bases Nat. Lang. Process. **108**, 132–143 (2016)

Additive Regularization for Topic Modeling in Sociological Studies of User-Generated Texts

Murat Apishev[2,4], Sergei Koltcov[1], Olessia Koltsova[1], Sergey Nikolenko[1,3(✉)], and Konstantin Vorontsov[4,5]

[1] National Research University Higher School of Economics, St. Petersburg, Russia
sergey@logic.pdmi.ras.ru
[2] Moscow State University, Moscow, Russia
[3] Steklov Institute of Mathematics, St. Petersburg, Russia
[4] Yandex, Moscow, Russia
[5] Moscow Institute of Physics and Technology, Moscow, Russia

Abstract. Social studies of the Internet have adopted large-scale text mining for unsupervised discovery of topics related to specific subjects. A recently developed approach to topic modeling, additive regularization of topic models (ARTM), provides fast inference and more control over the topics with a wide variety of possible regularizers than developing LDA extensions. We apply ARTM to mining ethnic-related content from Russian-language blogosphere, introduce a new combined regularizer, and compare models derived from ARTM with LDA. We show with human evaluations that ARTM is better for mining topics on specific subjects, finding more relevant topics of higher or comparable quality. We also include a detailed analysis of how to tune regularization coefficients in ARTM models.

1 Introduction

Topic models have become a common tool for unsupervised analysis of large text corpora. In essence, a topic model decomposes the sparse word-document matrix into a product of word-topic and topic-document matrices; this idea was first fleshed out in probabilistic latent semantic analysis (PLSA) [8], and now the topic model of choice is latent Dirichlet allocation (LDA), which is a Bayesian version of PLSA with Dirichlet priors assigned to word-topic and topic-document distributions [4,7]. Over the years, many extensions have been developed for LDA, but each of them has been a separate research project, with a new version of one of the two basic inference algorithms for LDA: either a variational approximation for the new posterior distribution or a new Gibbs sampling scheme. Hence, it is hardly practical to expect a researcher, especially in social sciences, to develop new LDA extensions for each new problem.

We use a recently developed approach called *additive regularization for topic modeling* (ARTM) [18,20] and the corresponding open-source implementation BigARTM [19]. ARTM extends the basic PLSA model with a general regularization mechanism that can directly express desired properties in the objective

© Springer International Publishing AG 2017
G. Sidorov and O. Herrera-Alcántara (Eds.): MICAI 2016, Part I, LNAI 10061, pp. 169–184, 2017.
DOI: 10.1007/978-3-319-62434-1_14

function, and the inference algorithm results automatically. Flexibility is a big advantage of ARTM in practice, especially for digital humanities where one often has but a feeling of what one is looking for. Having trained a trial model in the form of regular LDA or ARTM without regularizers, a researcher can formulate what is lacking and what is desired of the resulting topic model. In most cases, BigARTM lets a researcher combine regularizers from a built-in library in order to meet a set of requirements to the model quickly and efficiently.

In this work, we show one such application of the ARTM approach for the problem of mining a large corpus/stream of user-generated texts (in our case, blog posts) for specific topics of discourse (in our case, ethnic-related topics) defined with a fixed dictionary of subject terms (ethnonyms). To achieve a good topic model, we split the entire set of topics into subject-related and background topics, develop a new regularizer that deals with this predefined dictionary of subject terms, and build a combination of regularizers to make topics more interpretable, sparse, and diversified. The ARTM framework lets us do all of these things seamlessly, without complicated inference and developing new algorithms.

We present an extensive evaluation of our results, including an evaluation of topic interpretability produced by a team of human assessors, a gold standard for the quality of a topic model. Experimental results suggest that while the basic (unregularized or weakly regularized) ARTM model is no better than regular LDA, new regularizers significantly improve both number and quality of relevant topics. We also perform a separate study of a problem that plagues many probabilistic models when they are applied in practice: how to tune the hyperparameters (regularization coefficients) in ARTM models.

The paper is organized as follows. In Sect. 2, we introduce the basic PLSA model, its Bayesian counterpart LDA, and the general setting of the ARTM approach. In Sect. 3, we review regularizers used in this work and comment on their effect on the resulting topic model. Section 4 lists the specific models we have trained and covers the results of our case study in finding ethnic-related texts in a large dataset of blog posts. Section 5 contains a study on how to tune regularization parameters for ARTM models, and Sect. 6 concludes the paper.

2   Topic Modeling

Let D denote a finite set (collection) of documents (texts) and let W denote a finite set (vocabulary) of all terms from these documents. Each term can represent a single word or a key phrase. Following the "bag of words" model, we represent each document d from D as a subset of terms from the vocabulary W. Assume that each term occurrence in each document refers to some latent topic from a finite set of topics T. A text collection is considered as a sequence of triples (d_i, w_i, t_i), $i = 1, \ldots, n$, drawn independently from a discrete distribution $p(d, w, t)$ over the finite probability space $D \times W \times T$. Terms w_i and documents d_i are observable variables, while topics t_i are latent variables.

A *probabilistic topic model* represents the probabilities $p(w \mid d)$ of terms occurring in documents as mixtures of term distributions in topics $\phi_{wt} = p(w \mid t)$ and topic distributions in documents $\theta_{td} = p(t \,|\, d)$: $p(w \,|\, d) = \sum_{t \in T} p(w \,|\, t)\, p(t \,|\, d) = \sum_{t \in T} \phi_{wt} \theta_{td}$. This mixture also directly corresponds to the generative process for a document d: for each term position i, sample topic index t_i from distribution $p(t \,|\, d)$ and then sample the word w_i from distribution $p(w \,|\, t_i)$. Parameters of a probabilistic topic model are usually represented as matrices $\Phi = (\phi_{wt})_{W \times T}$ and $\Theta = (\theta_{td})_{T \times D}$ with non-negative and normalized columns ϕ_t and θ_d representing multinomial word-topic and topic-document distributions respectively.

In *Probabilistic Latent Semantic Analysis* (PLSA) [8], the topic model is trained by log-likelihood maximization with linear constraints of nonnegativity and normalization: $L(\Phi, \Theta) = \sum_{d \in D} \sum_{w \in d} n_{dw} \ln \sum_{t \in T} \phi_{wt} \theta_{td} \rightarrow \max_{\Phi, \Theta}$ under constraints $\sum_{w \in W} \phi_{wt} = 1$, $\phi_{wt} \geq 0$, $\sum_{t \in T} \theta_{td} = 1$, $\theta_{td} \geq 0$, where n_{dw} is the number of occurrences of term w in document d. The solution of this optimization problem satisfies the following Karush–Kuhn–Tucker conditions with auxiliary variables p_{tdw}, n_{wt}, n_{td}: E-step $p_{tdw} = \underset{t \in T}{\mathrm{norm}}(\phi_{wt} \theta_{td})$ and M-step $\phi_{wt} = \underset{w \in W}{\mathrm{norm}}(n_{wt})$, $\theta_{td} = \underset{t \in T}{\mathrm{norm}}(n_{td})$, where $n_{wt} = \sum_{d \in D} n_{dw} p_{tdw}$, $n_{td} = \sum_{w \in d} n_{dw} p_{tdw}$, and the "norm" operator transforms a vector $(x_t)_{t \in T}$ into $(\tilde{x}_t)_{t \in T}$ representing a discrete distribution: $\tilde{x}_t = \underset{t \in T}{\mathrm{norm}}(x_t) = \frac{\max\{x_t, 0\}}{\sum_{s \in T} \max\{x_s, 0\}}$. The simple-iteration method for this system of equations is equivalent to the EM algorithm and is typically used in practice. The E-step can be understood as the Bayes rule for the probability distribution of topics $p_{tdw} = p(t \,|\, d, w)$ for each term w in each document d. The M-step can be interpreted as frequency estimation for conditional probabilities ϕ_{wt} and θ_{td}. The iterative process begins with a random initialization of Φ and Θ.

The latent Dirichlet allocation (LDA) model [4,7] introduces prior Dirichlet distributions for the vectors of term probabilities in topics $\phi_t \sim \mathrm{Dir}(\beta)$ as well as for the vectors of topic probabilities in documents $\theta_d \sim \mathrm{Dir}(\alpha)$ with vector parameters $\beta = (\beta_w)_{w \in W}$ and $\alpha = (\alpha_t)_{t \in T}$ correspondingly. Inference in LDA is usually done via either variational approximations or Gibbs sampling, with the latter reducing to the so-called *collapsed Gibbs sampling*, where topic t_i for each word position (d_i, w_i) is iteratively resampled from $p(t \,|\, d, w)$ distribution similar to PLSA, but with smoothed Bayesian estimates of conditional probabilities: $\phi_{wt} = \underset{w \in W}{\mathrm{norm}}(n_{wt} + \beta_w)$, $\theta_{td} = \underset{t \in T}{\mathrm{norm}}(n_{td} + \alpha_t)$, where n_{wt} is the number of times term w has been generated from topic t and n_{td} is the number of terms in document d generated from topic t except the current triple (d_i, w_i, t_i). Over the recent years, the basic LDA model has been subject to many extensions, each presenting either a variational of a Gibbs sampling algorithm for a model that extends LDA to incorporate some additional information or presumed dependencies. For our present purpose of mining and analyzing documents related to a specific user-defined topic (in our case, ethnicity), the LDA extensions that appear to be most relevant are the *Topic-in-Set knowledge* model and its extension with Dirichlet forest priors [1,2], where words are assigned with "z-labels"; a z-label represents the topic this specific word should fall into, and the Interval Semi-Supervised LDA (ISLDA) model [5,12] where specific words are assigned to specific topics, and sampling distributions are projected onto that subset.

Topic modeling can be viewed as a special case of matrix factorization, where the problem is to find a low-rank approximation $\Phi\Theta$ of a given sparse matrix of term-document occurrences. Note, however, that the product $\Phi\Theta$ is defined only up to a linear transformation since $\Phi\Theta = (\Phi S)(S^{-1}\Theta)$. Therefore, our problem is ill-posed and generally has an infinite set of solutions. Previous experiments on simulated data [18] and real social media data [5] show that neither PLSA nor LDA can ensure a stable solution. To make the solution more appropriate one must introduce additional optimization criteria, usually called *regularizers* [16].

In *Additive Regularization of Topic Models* (ARTM) [20] a topic model is trained by maximizing a linear combination of the log-likelihood $L(\Phi,\Theta)$ and r regularizers $R_i(\Phi,\Theta)$, $i = 1,\ldots,r$ with *regularization coefficients* τ_i:

$$R(\Phi,\Theta) = \sum_{i=1}^{r} \tau_i R_i(\Phi,\Theta), \quad L(\Phi,\Theta) + R(\Phi,\Theta) \to \max_{\Phi,\Theta}.$$

Karush–Kuhn–Tucker conditions for this non-linear problem yield (under some technical restrictions) necessary conditions for the local maximum [18]:

$$p_{tdw} = \operatorname*{norm}_{t\in T} \phi_{wt}\theta_{td}, \; \phi_{wt} = \operatorname*{norm}_{w\in W}\left[n_{wt} + \phi_{wt}\frac{\partial R}{\partial \phi_{wt}}\right], \; \theta_{td} = \operatorname*{norm}_{t\in T}\left[n_{td} + \theta_{td}\frac{\partial R}{\partial \theta_{td}}\right],$$

where $n_{wt} = \sum_{d\in D} n_{dw}p_{tdw}$, $n_{td} = \sum_{w\in d} n_{dw}p_{tdw}$. Again, this system of equations can be solved with the EM algorithm. The strength of ARTM is that each additive regularization term R_i yields a simple additive modification of the M-step. Many models previously developed within the Bayesian framework can be easier reinterpreted, trained, and combined in the ARTM framework [17,18]; e.g., PLSA does not use regularization at all, $R = 0$, and LDA with Dirichlet priors $\phi_t \sim \text{Dir}(\beta)$ and $\theta_d \sim \text{Dir}(\alpha)$ and maximum a posteriori estimation of Φ,Θ corresponds to the smoothing regularizer interpreted as a minimizer of KL-divergences between the columns of Φ,Θ and fixed distributions β,α respectively.

3   Additive Regularization

3.1   General Approach

In this section, we consider an exploratory search problem of discovering all ethnic-related topics in a large corpus of blog posts. Given a set of ethnonyms as a query $Q \subset W$, we would like to get a list of ethnically relevant topics. We use a semi-supervised topic model with lexical prior to solve this problem; similar models have appeared for news clustering tasks [9], discovering health topics in social media [13] and ethnic-related topics in blog posts [5,12]. In all these studies, researchers specify for each predefined topic a certain set of *seed words*, usually very small, e.g., a news category or ethnicity. This means that we must know in advance how many topics we would like to find and what each topic should be generally about. The *interval semi-supervised LDA* model (ISLDA) allows to specify more than one topic per ethnicity [5], but it is difficult to guess how many topics are associated with each ethnicity, and in [5,12], where the case study was similar to our present work, seed words related to different ethnicities were separated into different topics, so no multi-ethnic topics could appear.

We address the above problems by providing a lexical prior determined by a set of ethnonyms Q common for all ethnically relevant topics. The model itself determines which ethnicity or combination of ethnicities make up each relevant topic. First of all, we split the entire set of topics T into two subsets: domain-specific *subject* topics S and *background* topics B. Regularizers will treat S and B differently. The relative size of S and B depends on the domain and has to be set in advance by the user. The idea of background topics that gather uninteresting words goes back to the *special words with background* (SWB) topic model [6], but unlike SWB, we define not one but many background topics in order to model irrelevant non-ethnic-related topics better.

3.2 Smoothing and Sparsing

A straightforward way to integrate lexical priors is to use smoothing and sparsing regularizers with uniform β distribution restricted to a set of ethnonyms Q: $\beta_w = \frac{1}{|Q|}[w \in Q]$. We introduce a smoothing regularizer that encourages ethnonyms $w \in Q$ to appear in ethnic-related topics S together with a sparsing regularizer that prevents ethnonyms from appearing in background topics B:

$$R(\Phi) = \tau_1 \sum_{t \in S} \sum_{w \in Q} \ln \phi_{wt} - \tau_2 \sum_{t \in B} \sum_{w \in Q} \ln \phi_{wt}.$$

In the exploratory search task, relevant content usually constitutes a very small part of the collection. In our case, the entire ethnicity discourse in a large dataset of blog posts is unlikely to add up to more than one percent of the total volume. Our goal is to mine fine-grained thematic structure of relevant content with many small but diverse and interpretable subject topics S, but also to describe a much larger volume of content with a smaller number of background topics B. Formally, we introduce a smoothing regularizer for background topics B in Θ and a sparsing regularizer that uniformly supresses ethnic-related topics S:

$$R(\Theta) = \tau_3 \sum_{d \in D} \sum_{t \in B} \ln \theta_{td} - \tau_4 \sum_{d \in D} \sum_{t \in S} \ln \theta_{td}.$$

The idea is to make background topics B smooth, so that they will contain irrelevant words, and subject topics S sparse, so that they will be as distinct as possible, with each topic concentrating on a different and meaningful subject.

3.3 Decorrelation

Diversifying the term distributions of topics is known to make the resulting topics more interpretable [15]. In order to make the topics as different as possible, we introduce a regularizer that minimizes the sum of covariances between ϕ_t vectors over all specific topics t:

$$R(\Phi) = -\tau_5 \sum_{t \in S} \sum_{s \in S \setminus t} \sum_{w \in W} \phi_{wt} \phi_{ws} + \tau_6 \sum_{t \in B} \sum_{w \in W} \ln \phi_{wt}.$$

The decorrelation regularizer also stimulates sparsity and tends to group stop-words and common words into separate topics [15]. To move these topics from S to B, we add a second regularizer that uniformly smoothes background topics.

3.4 Modality of Seed Words (Ethnonyms)

Another possible way to use lexical priors is to distinguish ethnonyms into a separate modality, i.e., a separate class of tokens (sample modalities include named entities, tags, foreign words, n-grams, authors, categories, time stamps, references, user names etc.). Each modality has its own vocabulary and its own Φ matrix normalized independently. A multimodal extension of ARTM has been proposed in [19] and implemented in BigARTM. We introduce two modalities: words and ethnonyms. The latter is defined by a seed vocabulary Q and matrix $\tilde{\Phi}$ of size $|Q| \times |T|$. In ARTM, the log-likelihood of a modality is treated as a regularizer:

$$R(\tilde{\Phi}, \Theta) = \tau_7 \sum_{d \in D} \sum_{w \in Q} n_{dw} \ln \sum_{t \in T} \tilde{\phi}_{wt} \theta_{td},$$

where regularization coefficient τ_7 is in fact a multiplier for word-document counters n_{dw} of the second modality.

In order to make ethnic-related topics more diverse in their ethnonyms, we introduce an additional decorrelation regularizer for the modality of ethnonyms:

$$R(\tilde{\Phi}) = -\tau_8 \sum_{t \in S} \sum_{s \in S \setminus t} \sum_{w \in Q} \tilde{\phi}_{wt} \tilde{\phi}_{ws}.$$

Note that we introduce decorrelation for subject topics S separately for words modality with Φ matrix and for ethnonyms modality with $\tilde{\Phi}$ matrix.

4   Evaluation

4.1 Datasets and Settings

From the sociological point of view, the goal of our project is to mine and monitor ethnic-related discourse in social networks, e.g., find how popular topics are related to various ethnic groups, perhaps in specific regions, and identify worrying rising trends that might lead to ethnic-related outbursts or violence. While multimodal analysis that would account for topic evolution in time and their geospatial distribution remains a subject for further work, we evaluate our models on a real life dataset mined from the most popular Russian blog platform *LiveJournal*. The dataset contains ≈ 1.58 million lemmatized posts from the top

2000 *LiveJournal* bloggers embracing an entire year from mid-2013 to mid-2014. Data were mined weekly according to the *LiveJournal*'s rating that was quite volatile, which is why the number of bloggers in the collection comprized several dozens of thousands. The complete vocabulary amounted to 860K words, but after preprocessing (leaving only words that contain only Cyrillic symbols and perhaps a hyphen, are at least 3 letters long, and occur ≥ 20 times in the corpus) it was reduced to 90K words in ≈ 1.38 million nonempty documents.

To choose the number of topics, we have trained PLSA models with 100, 300, and 400 topics, evaluated (by a consensus of a team of human assessors) that the best result was at 400 topics, and hence chose to use 400 topics in all experiments. This corresponds to our earlier experiments with the number of topics in relation to mining ethnic discourse [5,12].

The collection was divided into batches of 10000 documents each. All ARTM-based models were trained by an online algorithm with a single pass over the collection and 25 passes over each document; updates are made after processing every batch. For the semi-supervised regularizer, we have composed a set of several hundreds ethnonyms—nouns denoting various ethnic groups, based on literature review, Russian census and UN data, expert advice and other sources; 249 of those words occurred in the collection. More details on how and why the ethnonyms have been selected are given in a companion journal paper [3].

4.2   Models

In BigARTM experiments, we have trained a series of topic models. In all models with hyperparameters, we have chosen regularization coefficients manually based on the results of several test experiments. In all additively regularized models with lexical priors, we divided topics into $|S| = 250$ subject topics and $|B| = 150$ background topics. Next we list the different models compared in the experiments below and provide the motivation behind introducing and comparing these specific topics:

(1) plsa: reference PLSA model with no regularizers;
(2) lda: LDA model implemented in BigARTM with smoothness regularizers on Φ and Θ with uniform α and β and hyperparameters $\alpha_0 = \beta_0 = 10^{-4}$;
(3) smooth: ARTM-based model with smoothing and sparsing by the lexical prior, with regularization coefficients $\tau_1 = 10^{-5}$ and $\tau_2 = 100$ (tuned by hand); besides, in this and all subsequent regularized models we used the smoothing regularizer for the Θ matrix with coefficients $\tau_3 = 0.05$ and $\tau_4 = 1$;
(4) decorrelated: ARTM-based model that extends (3) with decorrelation with coefficients $\tau_5 = 5 \times 10^4$ and $\tau_6 = 10^{-8}$; the smoothing coefficient for ethnically relevant subject topics was $\tau_1 = 10^{-6}$;
(5) restricted dictionary: ARTM-based model that extends (4) by adding a modality of ethnonyms with coefficients $\tau_7 = 100$ and $\tau_8 = 2 \times 10^4$; the decorrelation coefficients was $\tau_5 = 1.5 \times 10^6$ and $\tau_6 = 10^{-7}$; subject words were smoothed with coefficient $\tau_1 = 1.1 \times 10^{-4}$; for this model we used a dictionary with $|Q| = 249$ ethnonyms;

Model	Sample topic
(1)	Muslim, religious, Islam, extrasensoric, sect, Christian, alley, radical, labyrinth, Uzbekistan, Christian^{adj}, Islam^{adj}, Tajikistan, religion, extremist
(2)	republic, Caucasus, sometimes, Chechen, Caucasian^{adj}, Dagestan, nationality, Checnya, region, power, Ingushetia, Kazan, inhabitant, frighteningly, prose, Russian
(3)	Armenia, Azerbaijan, Armenia^{adj}, Armenian, caravan, Yerevan, Tajik, Azeri, Azeri^{adj}, Uzbek, Alice, SSR, Tatar, survey, republic, Turk, Ildar, Ataturk, Tajik^{adj}, Turkmen^{adj}
(5)	Uzbek, Russian, Russia, migrant, Uzbekistan, work^{adj}, Moscow, country, Tajik, janitor, place, work, citizen, home, Asia, live, police
(6)	Russian, Uzbek, Tajik, migrant, Russia, work, janitor, border, work, Uzbekistan, guest worker, place, town, Asia, sometimes, work^{adj}, live, people
	Kazakhstan, Asia, region, central, Kyrgizia, Tajikistan, Afganistan, country, republic, Middle, Uzbekistan, territory, Russia, Kyrgiz^{adj}, Kazakh^{adj}
(7)	migrant, country, Russia, migration, Asia, illegal, migrant^{adj}, Tajikistan, guest worker, citizen, work^{adj}, work, Middle, Uzbekistan, Tajik, problem, Russian
	Kazakhstan, region, country, Asia, republic, Kyrgizia, Russia, state, military, central, territory, defense, collaboration, Russian, Kyrgiz^{adj}, Afganistan, cider

Fig. 1. Sample ethnic-related topics from several models.

(6) **extended dictionary:** same as (5) but with dictionary extended by adjectives and country names if respective ethnonyms did not occur; the positive outcome here would be that more relevant topics can be found with an extended dictionary, while the negative outcome is that ethnic topics could instead get lost within topics on international relations;

(7) **recursive:** the basic PLSA model trained on a special subset of documents, namely documents retrieved from topics that were considered ethnic-relevant by assessors in model 5 with a threshold of 10^{-6} in the Θ matrix for all subject topics; here, the hypothesis was that a collection with a higher concentration of relevant documents could yield better topics;

(8) **keyword documents:** PLSA model identical to (7) but trained on a subset of only those documents that contained at least one word from the dictionary.

Models 7 and 8 were introduced to test two different ways of enriching the initial collection: through a preliminary cycle of topic modeling or via a simple keyword search. Figure 1 shows several sample topics from some of the models (translated to English; superscript ^{adj} denotes an adjectival form of the word, usually a different word in Russian). It appears that models 6 and 7 yield topics better suited for the ethnic purpose of our study; in what follows, we will expand and quantify this observation.

4.3   Results

In this section, we briefly discuss some of the qualitative and quantitative results of our study. We provide a much more thorough analysis of the qualitative assessment part of our study in a companion journal paper [3], which also discusses an additional setting of two-stage topic modeling, when a smaller dataset is selected at the first stage and then a second-level topic model is used to get the final interpretable topics. On the quantitative side, results coming from the assessors were

Table 1. Average coherence and tf-idf coherence for all models in the study.

Model	T	coh_{10}	tfidf_{10}	coh_{20}	tfidf_{20}
1 (plsa)	400	−325.3	−212.0	−1447.0	−1011.6
2 (lda)	400	−344.2	−230.9	−1539.8	−1121.2
3 (smooth)	400	−367.1	−261.2	−1583.9	−1210.2
4 (decorr)	400	−378.9	−274.0	−1651.2	−1296.1
5 (restricted dictionary)	400	−310.0	−196.4	−1341.9	−908.4
6 (extended dictionary)	400	−321.7	−209.6	−1409.1	−995.3
7 (recursive)	400	−326.5	−212.1	−1415.6	−982.5
8 (keyword)	400	−328.8	−214.4	−1463.6	−1014.5

supplemented with values of the tf-idf coherence quality metric introduced earlier in [5,12]. It has been shown that tf-idf coherence better matches the human judgment of topic quality than the traditional coherence metric [11].

Results on average coherence and tf-idf coherence for all topics in every model are shown in Table 1; we show two versions of coherence-based metrics, computed with top 10 words in a topic and computed with top 20 words. For all models except 3 and 4 (judged to produce significantly worse topics), assessors were asked to interpret the topics based on 20 most probable words in every topic of each model. For each topic, two assessors answered six questions related both to the overall quality and to the ethnic nature of our study; the answers were further used to divide the topics into three classes: highly interpretable, partially interpretable, and uninterpretable. A detailed description of the assessment procedure and results of individual questions can be found in [3].

Since the models we test here all attempt to extract a certain number of high-quality topics while filtering out "trash" topics into a specially created "ghetto", it makes little sense to compare the models by the overall quality of all topics. It is much more important to look at the coherence of those topics that were found either good or relevant by the assessors. Table 2 summarizes the most important results on quality understood as interpretability and its relation to tf-idf coherence. It shows that model 6 (extended dictionary) outperforms all the rest by coherence and tf-idf coherence calculated over all topics. Model 5 (restricted dictionary) does produce higher values of coherences and tf-idf coherences in the groups of interpretable topics, but note that the number of interpretable topics is lower, so model 5 finds fewer but on average better topics.

Table 3 summarizes our most important findings regarding how relevant the topics are to our goal. Here we again see the same two leaders, models 5 and 6, and the former outperforms the latter in terms of tf-idf coherence of relevant topics, while the latter outperforms the former in terms of the number of topics considered relevant by the assessors, both for ethnic and international relations topics and for both levels of relevance. This means that our extension of the seed dictionary brings more generally interpretable and relevant topics to both

Table 2. Experimental results: general interpretability and coherence for partially, highly, and generally interpretable models.

	#	coh_{10}	$tfidf_{10}$	coh_{20}	$tfidf_{20}$
Partially interpretable topics					
1 (plsa)	139	−258.7	−145.3	−1145.9	−696.9
2 (lda)	192	−274.9	−163.3	−1224.1	−777.5
5 (restricted dictionary)	237	−284.6	−163.0	−1247.9	−768.8
6 (extended dictionary)	146	−258.6	−141.2	−1156.0	−686.1
7 (recursive)	239	−281.9	−166.3	−1235.7	−788.1
8 (keyword)	114	−256.3	−140.2	−1141.4	−682.8
Highly interpretable topics					
1 (plsa)	119	−318.0	−206.6	−1414.7	−982.5
2 (lda)	120	−389.5	−273.1	−1743.7	−1324.6
5 (restricted dictionary)	87	−330.7	−227.0	−1410.7	−1028.2
6 (extended dictionary)	103	−313.8	−199.9	−1372.6	−936.4
7 (recursive)	58	−349.2	−241.1	−1498.1	−1086.1
8 (keyword)	106	−310.0	−198.9	−1354.3	−914.8
Both partially and highly					
1 (plsa)	258	−286.0	−173.6	−1269.9	−828.7
2 (lda)	312	−319.0	−205.5	−1424.0	−988.0
5 (restricted dictionary)	324	−297.0	−180.2	−1291.6	−838.5
6 (extended dictionary)	249	−281.5	−165.5	−1245.6	−789.6
7 (recursive)	297	−295.1	−180.9	−1287.0	−846.3
8 (keyword)	220	−282.2	−168.5	−1244.0	−794.6

international relations and ethnicity, although average coherence of these topics becomes somewhat lower. Ethnic topics, thus, do not get substituted by or lost among topics on international relations. A more detailed investigation of the assessment [3] also shows that model 6 is preferable at this stage.

Models 7 (recursive) and 8 (keyword texts) yield interesting results: by the data shown in Table 3 the recursive model looks similar to model 5 with restricted dictionary in terms of our evaluation metrics (fewer, but more coherent topics of interest), and the keyword-based model is similar to model 6 (more numerous and a little less coherent topics of interest). It means that repeated topic modeling on a subset of texts extracted in the first iteration does not bring improvement, or even brings deterioration, and therefore is excessive and useless. Single-iteration modeling on a collection selected by keyword produces the results on par with or not much worse than model 6, but the sets of ethnicity-related topics found by these two approaches are significantly different, so to get the best possible coverage we recommend a combination of these techniques.

Table 3. Topics' relevance and coherence

Topics	Relevant topics														
	partially					highly					both				
	#	coh_{10}	$tfidf_{10}$	coh_{20}	$tfidf_{20}$	#	coh_{10}	$tfidf_{10}$	coh_{20}	$tfidf_{20}$	#	coh_{10}	$tfidf_{10}$	coh_{20}	$tfidf_{20}$
1 (plsa)															
ethnic	5	-313.2	-190.2	-1399.2	-904.8	12	-334.0	-207.1	-1480.9	-996.1	17	-327.9	-202.1	-1456.9	-969.4
IR	20	-279.1	-150.7	-1227.0	-733.8	19	-315.3	-194.0	-1410.7	-946.8	39	-296.8	-171.8	-1316.5	-837.6
all relev.	20	-289.6	-163.0	-1271.2	-784.9	25	-315.9	-194.3	-1408.0	-938.7	45	-304.2	-180.4	-1347.2	-870.3
2 (lda)															
ethnic	2	-239.7	-124.4	-1158.5	-646.0	13	-306.8	-190.0	-1369.1	-927.9	15	-297.9	-181.3	-1341.0	-890.3
IR	21	-285.1	-158.9	-1266.2	-763.1	29	-353.3	-225.7	-1580.6	-1097.5	50	-324.7	-197.7	-1448.6	-957.1
all relev.	18	-289.4	-162.3	-1287.3	-777.7	37	-336.3	-212.2	-1496.3	-1023.0	55	-320.9	-195.9	-1427.9	-942.7
5 (restricted dictionary)															
ethnic	18	-288.7	-164.7	-1264.2	-798.5	30	-331.6	-222.3	-1419.0	-1015.8	48	-315.5	-200.7	-1360.9	-934.3
IR	33	-269.1	-142.5	-1190.8	-707.7	26	-323.1	-207.4	-1358.1	-917.3	59	-292.9	-171.1	-1264.5	-800.1
all relev.	36	-267.2	-142.0	-1177.6	-695.1	47	-322.7	-211.1	-1374.5	-958.4	83	-298.7	-181.1	-1289.1	-844.2
6 (extended dictionary)															
ethnic	8	-288.4	-160.5	-1315.2	-805.1	22	-280.7	-150.0	-1226.8	-713.8	30	-282.8	-152.8	-1250.4	-738.2
IR	18	-250.0	-126.3	-1130.6	-641.1	29	-287.4	-156.3	-1240.9	-740.8	47	-273.1	-144.8	-1198.7	-702.6
all relev.	22	-261.2	-136.5	-1199.9	-707.7	37	-285.5	-158.3	-1234.6	-741.8	59	-276.4	-150.2	-1221.7	-729.1
7 (recursive)															
ethnic	18	-308.2	-181.3	-1418.7	-952.6	22	-320.1	-201.8	-1431.0	-971.4	40	-314.7	-192.6	-1425.5	-962.9
IR	30	-283.3	-161.6	-1236.8	-780.4	30	-291.4	-171.4	-1292.9	-827.3	60	-287.4	-166.5	-1264.9	-803.9
all relev.	34	-285.4	-161.3	-1269.0	-810.6	47	-299.0	-180.1	-1331.3	-869.8	81	-293.3	-172.2	-1305.1	-844.9
8 (keyword)															
ethnic	5	-289.7	-161.1	-1315.9	-805.0	37	-297.9	-175.6	-1318.9	-834.7	42	-297.0	-173.9	-1318.6	-831.1
IR	18	-264.7	-138.4	-1168.7	-670.7	32	-278.5	-164.3	-1240.7	-782.9	50	-273.5	-155.0	-1214.8	-742.5
all relev.	17	-279.5	-154.3	-1230.7	-741.3	52	-282.5	-165.5	-1260.1	-793.1	69	-281.8	-162.8	-1252.8	-780.4

4.4 Perplexity

Perplexity is a common evaluation metric for topic models. The idea is rather general and natural for probabilistic models as a whole: we characterize the quality of a model with the likelihood of a held-out test dataset. Formally speaking, fr a topic model perplexity is defined as the likelihood of the documents in the test set normalized at the log scale by the lengths of these documents: $perplexity(D_{test}) = \exp\left(-\frac{\sum_{w \in D_{test}} \log p(\mathbf{w})}{\sum_{w \in D_{test}} N_d}\right)$. Figure 2 shows how the perplexities of our topic models changed during their training. In our study, perplexity is useful since it demonstrates that all models converge and can serve as a convenient characterization of how they have converged and be used in a stopping criterion for the training. At the same time, note the effect on Fig. 2: additional regularization increases perplexity, that is, decreases the likelihood of test data. This is, of course, expected, as new regularizers decrease the overall likelihood, and the total likelihood value has absolutely no correlation with either the number of ethnic-related topics or their interpretability by human assessors. We would like to warn against using perplexity to compare different topic models: perplexity is a useful tool but it is not the final goal in and of itself.

5 Tuning Regularizers in Topic Models

As we have seen in Sect. 3, the ARTM approach offers a very expressive framework for constructing any kind of topic models with various regularizers and a unified algorithm to efficiently train these models. However, this comes at a cost; from the practical point of view the most important disadvantage lies in the new parameters for numerous regularizers that ARTM models employ. Our full ARTM model includes eight different hyperparameters, τ_1 to τ_8. In this section, we provide insights on how to tune hyperparameters in ARTM models.

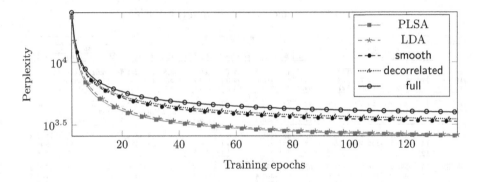

Fig. 2. Perplexities of topic models during their training.

The problem of tuning optimal regularization parameters does not have a final satisfactory solution. In practice, one often has to resort to various kinds of enumerations of all possible hyperparameters, perhaps with some heuristics to help in the process. In our experiments, we have constructed a large number of different variations for the topic models, specifically enumerating many versions of the models in every class of regularizers, and have performed preliminary human evaluation by a single assessor. This has let us find several good models that have been evaluated with the above techniques and shown in our result tables. However, the process of tuning regularizing coefficients itself has led to several interesting conclusions. In this section we present certain insights that we have noted as a result of tuning regularizers.

LDA. In the LDA model, we used symmetric Dirichlet priors for both matrices of parameters, which means that we have to tune two hyperparameters, α and β. The value of 10^{-4} has been chosen for both coefficients and has proven to be suitable for both α and β; the range of admissible values was approximately from 10^{-4} to 10^{-3}. Smaller values would have no influence on the model at all compared to unregularized pLSA, while larger values cause overregularization, leading to very general, highly overlapping, and generally useless topics like the ones shown in Fig. 3a.

Smoothing regularizer. The main parameter for the smooth model is the smoothing regularizer τ_1 for subject topics with ethnonyms. Again, we have tried a wide range of values, and the range of reasonable models was about an order of magnitude in size, and in our preliminary assessment we have chosen $\tau_1 = 10^{-5}$ as producing the best values. If we decrease the value of this coefficient, the smoothing does not work and we get fewer subject topics, and if we increase it too much, we get topics that consist completely of ethnonyms with no real relation to each other, as shown in Fig. 3b.

Regularizing Θ. Regularizing coefficients for the Θ matrix did not undergo such a strict optimization process since they have a rather wide range of admissible values, so they are hard to get wrong. Nevertheless, it is possible to overregularize the Θ matrix as well. If we increase the sparsing regularizer τ_4 by a factor

(a) Oversmoothed LDA, α and β larger than 10^{-3}
1 good, house, time, rouble, old, sweet, cost, Russian, voice, work, day, hour, October, word, speak, group, server, love, truth
2 time, good, life, day, child, case, Russia, old, hour, full, faucet, history, different, red, Moscow, movie, woman, Soviet, tell
3 good, place, old, day, Russia, word, sweet, different, cost, full, case, arm, leg, money, time, history, question, tell
(b) smooth model with too large τ_1
1 Mongoloid, Italian, Irish, Judean, German, Bedouin, Sorbian, Somalian, infidel, Dargin, Bosnian, Singaporean, dark-skinned, Peruan, Russian, Manchu, Sicilian
2 Montenegrin, New Zealander, Swahili, Mari, Algerian, Japanese, Cuban, Somalian, Serbian, Singaporean, Kenigsbergian, Hungarian, German, Nogai, Alan, English, Ethiopian, Venezuelan, Greek, American
3 New Zealander, Hungarian, Negro, Ingush, Austrian, Tuvinian, Ukrainian, Yakut, Maroccan, Papua, Canadian, Belorussian, Sicilian, Kurdish, Swahili, Scandinavian, Latin American, Gagauz, Uzbek
(c) Models with too large τ_4
1 Russian, Nenets, New Zealander, Latinos, Osman, Mongoloid, Apache, Caucasian, Chilean, Indian, Judean, Magyar, Venezuelan, Sudanese, Komi–Permyak, American, Kygryz, Ingrian, Nigerian, German
2 Kurdish, Eskimo, Khmer, Vietnamese, Montenegrin, Bosnian, Maroccan, Lezgin, Bashkir, Finno-Ugric, Peruan, Mexican, Crimean, Qatari, Kenigsbergian, Show, Aztec, Azerbaijani, Baltic, Siberian
3 Syrian, Karelian, Kabardian, Veps, Mongol, Khanty, Berberian, Israeli, New Zealander, Abkhazian, Brazilean, Bohemian, Nenets, Italian, Dominican, Afroamerican, Tungissian, Algerian, Konigswinter, Mansi
(d) Over-decorrelated models with too large τ_5
1 break in, Nyenschantz, misanthrope, Erzurum, inferior, redeem, cocky, calmly, approximately, chapiteau, Messiah, around, lull, revolution, Osman
2 Sverdlosvk, federal, palmchrist, thermal protection, uncultured, formally, EDS, Uralpolit, Innopolis, Expo, American, Altaic, supercapacitor, Russian, formal, Chinese
3 Reichstag, Dimitrov, TV studio, Zhigulevsk, frogs, shut up, Cassandra, Sebastian, American, Velikanov, Plekhanov, three-day, Jew

Fig. 3. Sample topics for several models with bad values of various regularizers.

of five, the model degenerates as shown in Fig. 3c: all word counts were basically set to zero by the large Θ sparsing, and the only words left were ethnonyms supported by the smoothing of Φ. As a result, the initial weights for every model with overregularized Θ remained fixed and did not change regardless of the other parameters.

Subject decorrelation and background smoothing in the decorrelated model. For the decorrelated model, we add two new regularizing coefficients: decorrelation of subject topics τ_5 and smoothing background topics τ_6. The latter did not have to be significantly tuned, the main requirement for τ_6 is that it is significantly smaller than τ_2: background smoothing should be negligible compared to sparsing background topics with respect to ethnonyms and should not lead to overregularization. As a result, we have found several suitable ranges of values and chosen one of them for the model.

The key parameters that should be tuned in this model are τ_5 and τ_1. These regularizers have, strictly speaking, virtually the opposite effect: the decorrelator is a sparsing regularizer that can significantly reduce large count values, while smoothing is needed to increase the weights of counts corresponding to ethnonyms in subject topics. The latter regularizer is problem-oriented, and the former works to make the topics more distinct and easier to interpret. As a result, we have a problem of parallel tuning for two parameters so that we could get a model both smoothed with respect to ethnonyms and possessing a variety of subject topics. We have enumerated a wide range of possible values and solved this problem in a satisfactory (albeit perhaps not optimal) way. There is a complex and strong dependence between these two regularizers, so significant variation in regularization parameters can lead to deterioration in the model. If we increase the decorrelator τ_5 by a factor of 3-4, it leads to non-interpretable topics, sometimes filled with ethnonyms, like the ones shown in Fig. 3d; if we increase τ_1 by an order of magnitude it leads to low interpretability, and then to the same topics oversmoothed with respect to ethnonyms as shown in Fig. 3b.

Full model. Accumulating all previous results, the final model is further complicated with a new regularizer of ethnonym modality. This regularizer, with coefficient $\tau_7 = 100$, has the strongest influence on the model as a whole; it has let us obtain a significant improvement in modeling quality in terms of increasing the number of interpretable topics. Mutual relations between regularizers are far from obvious here, so jointly tuning all hyperparameters for this model required a lot of work. The Θ matrix regularizers were fixed for their previous values since they yield satisfactory results and we do not need to increase the search space dimension with them. Important regularizers included in this case also the regularizer of subject topics in the modality of ethnonyms.

We tuned the parameters jointly, first to get roughly adequate models and then with more refined steps to find the optimal configuration of parameters. As a result, we have seen that the key, most important parameter for the model was regularization with the modality of ethnonyms: varying τ_7 led to significant changes in the model. For instance, if τ_7 was too small, influence of the other regularizers became excessive, and we obtained topics over-smoothed with respect to ethnonyms, as in Fig. 3b. The range of admissible values for other regularizers is rather wide, which indicates a relatively weak influence as compared to the modality regularizer. At the same time, when we switched these regularizers off completely, we obtained a model which was assessed to be worse than the model with all regularizers in place.

6   Conclusion

In this work, we have shown that *additive regularization of topic models* (ARTM) can provide social scientists with an effective tool for mining specific topics in large collections of user-generated content. Our best model has outperformed basic LDA both in terms of the number of relevant topics found and in terms of their quality, as it was found in experiments with topics related to ethnicity.

What is especially important for digital humanities, additive regularization allows one to easily construct nontrivial extensions of topic models without mathematical research or software development. By combining built-in regularizers from the BigARTM library, one can get topic models with desired properties. In this work, we have combined eight regularizers and constructed a topic model for exploratory search that can take a long list of keywords (in our case, ethnonyms) as a query and output a set of topics that encompass the entire relevant content. This model can be used to explore narrow subject domains in large text collections. In general, this study shows that ARTM provides unprecedented flexibility in constructing topic models with given properties, outperforms existing LDA implementations in terms of training speed, and provides more control over the resulting topics. Both specific regularizers introduced here and the general ARTM approach can be used in further topical studies of text corpora concentrating on different subjects and/or desired properties of the topics.

Acknowledgments. This work was supported by the Russian Science Foundation grant no. 15-18-00091.

References

1. Andrzejewski, D., Zhu, X.: Latent Dirichlet allocation with topic-in-set knowledge. In: Proceedings of NAACL HLT 2009 Workshop on Semi-Supervised Learning for Natural Language Processing, SemiSupLearn 2009, pp. 43–48. Association for Computational Linguistics, Stroudsburg (2009)
2. Andrzejewski, D., Zhu, X., Craven, M.: Incorporating domain knowledge into topic modeling via Dirichlet forest priors. In: Proceedings of 26th Annual International Conference on Machine Learning, ICML 2009, pp. 25–32. ACM, New York (2009)
3. Apishev, M., Koltcov, S., Koltsova, O., Nikolenko, S., Vorontsov, K.: Mining ethnic content online with additively regularized topic models. Computacion y Sistemas **20**(3), 387–403 (2016)
4. Blei, D.M., Ng, A.Y., Jordan, M.I.: Latent Dirichlet allocation. J. Mach. Learn. Res. **3**(4–5), 993–1022 (2003)
5. Bodrunova, S., Koltsov, S., Koltsova, O., Nikolenko, S., Shimorina, A.: Interval semi-supervised LDA: classifying needles in a haystack. In: Castro, F., Gelbukh, A., González, M. (eds.) MICAI 2013. LNCS (LNAI), vol. 8265, pp. 265–274. Springer, Heidelberg (2013). doi:10.1007/978-3-642-45114-0_21
6. Chemudugunta, C., Smyth, P., Steyvers, M.: Modeling general and specific aspects of documents with a probabilistic topic model. In: Advances in Neural Information Processing Systems, vol. 19, pp. 241–248. MIT Press (2007)
7. Griffiths, T., Steyvers, M.: Finding scientific topics. Proc. Nat. Acad. Sci. **101**(Suppl. 1), 5228–5335 (2004)
8. Hoffmann, T.: Unsupervised learning by probabilistic latent semantic analysis. Mach. Learn. **42**(1), 177–196 (2001)
9. Jagarlamudi, J., Daumé III., H., Udupa, R.: Incorporating lexical priors into topic models. In: Proceedings of EACL 2012, pp. 204–213 (2012)
10. Koltcov, S., Koltsova, O., Nikolenko, S.I.: Latent Dirichlet allocation: stability and applications to studies of user-generated content. In: Proceedings of WebSci 2014, pp. 161–165 (2014)
11. Mimno, D., Wallach, H.M., Talley, E., Leenders, M., McCallum, A.: Optimizing semantic coherence in topic models. In: Proceedings of EMNLP 2011, pp. 262–272 (2011)
12. Nikolenko, S.I., Koltsova, O., Koltsov, S.: Topic modelling for qualitative studies. J. Inf. Sci. **43**, 88–102 (2015)

13. Paul, M.J., Dredze, M.: Discovering health topics in social media using topic models. PLoS ONE **9**(8), e103408 (2014)
14. Sociopolitical processes in the internet. Laboratory for Internet Studies. Internal report, National Research University Higher School of Economics, reg. no. 01201362573, Moscow (2013)
15. Tan, Y., Ou, Z.: Topic-weak-correlated latent Dirichlet allocation. In: 7th International Symposium Chinese Spoken Language Processing (ISCSLP), pp. 224–228 (2010)
16. Tikhonov, A.N., Arsenin, V.Y.: Solution of Ill-Posed Problems. W.H. Winston, Washington, D.C. (1977)
17. Vorontsov, K.V., Potapenko, A.A.: Tutorial on probabilistic topic modeling: additive regularization for stochastic matrix factorization. In: Ignatov, D.I., Khachay, M.Y., Panchenko, A., Konstantinova, N., Yavorskiy, R.E. (eds.) AIST 2014. CCIS, vol. 436, pp. 29–46. Springer, Cham (2014). doi:10.1007/978-3-319-12580-0_3
18. Vorontsov, K.V., Potapenko, A.A.: Additive regularization of topic models. Mach. Learn. **101**(1), 303–323 (2015). Special Issue on Data Analysis and Intelligent Optimization with Applications
19. Vorontsov, K., Frei, O., Apishev, M., Romov, P., Suvorova, M., Yanina, A.: Non-bayesian additive regularization for multimodal topic modeling of large collections. In: Proceedings of TM 2015, pp. 29–37. ACM, New York (2015)
20. Vorontsov, K.: Additive regularization for topic models of text collections. Dokl. Math. **89**(3), 301–304 (2014)

Effects of the Inclusion of Non-newsworthy Messages in Credibility Assessment

Chaluemwut Noyunsan[1], Tatpong Katanyukul[1(✉)], Carson K. Leung[2], and Kanda Runapongsa Saikaew[1]

[1] Department of Computer Engineering, Faculty of Engineering,
Khon Kaen University, Khon Kaen 40002, Thailand
chaluemwut@kkumail.com, {tatpong,krunapon}@kku.ac.th
[2] Department of Computer Science, Faculty of Science,
University of Manitoba, Winnipeg, MB R3T 2N2, Canada
kleung@cs.umanitoba.ca

Abstract. Social media has become influential and affects large public perception. Anyone can post and share messages on social networking sites. However, not all posts are trustworthy. Many online messages contain misleading or false information. There has been an extensive research to assess the credibility of social media data. Previous studies evaluate all online messages, which may be inappropriate due to a large amount of such data that can result in ineffectiveness of the system. This paper studies and presents the effects of the inclusion of such data—namely, non-newsworthy messages—in credibility assessment. Our findings affirm a negative effect of training a model with non-newsworthy data. The degree of performance degradation is also shown to have a strong connection to a degree of non-newsworthiness in training data.

Keywords: Social media · Social network analysis · Social networks · Credibility measurement · Newsworthiness · Data mining · Decision trees

1 Introduction

Social media has become a popular mass media channel, influencing great social perception. There are various kinds of social media, including the following:

- Facebook[1] provides various kinds of contents. Users can post messages with texts, photos, videos, and URLs;
- Instagram[2] is social media targeting photographic posts; and
- Twitter[3] is a message service. Users can post messages with length limited to 140 characters.

---

[1] https://www.facebook.com/.
[2] https://www.instagram.com/?hl=en or https://www.instagram.com/?hl=th.
[3] https://twitter.com/?lang=en or https://twitter.com/?lang=th.

© Springer International Publishing AG 2017
G. Sidorov and O. Herrera-Alcántara (Eds.): MICAI 2016, Part I, LNAI 10061, pp. 185–195, 2017.
DOI: 10.1007/978-3-319-62434-1_15

There is an increasing number of users, who use social media around the world. For instance, at the end of June 2016, there were

- 1.71 billion monthly active Facebook users[4],
- more than 500 million Instagram users[5], and
- 313 million monthly active Twitter users[6],

respectively.

Accessibility of social media brings its popularity. With ease, social media users can post news, opinions, and pictures. However, that also has a downside: Impersonation and fake news are common. It is often difficult to identify fake news or gauge credibility of contents in social media. To abate the issues, many studies [2,5,6,10] assign credibility score to social media posts. The credibility score indicates how much trustworthy the post is.

Previous studies assess every online post. It would be beneficial to exclude online data that are unimportant or uninteresting to the general public. In this study, we view *non-newsworthy* data as personal opinions, personal matters that do not affect the well-being of others, or spammers [1]. Such messages are, for example, selfie or grumble posts. The notion of such messages often refers to as non-newsworthiness [8].

In this paper, we study an effect of non-newsworthy messages. The inclusion of non-newsworthy messages may confuse users with a credibility score. Also, our assumption is that since such messages do not contain information related to credibility, exclusion of such messages would enable a more efficient machine learning model.

Our *key contributions* of this paper is the studies on the effects of the inclusion these non-newsworthy messages in credibility assessment.

In terms of organization, the reminder of this paper is organized as follows. The next section describes related works. Section 3 describes our studies on the effects of the inclusion of non-newsworthy messages in credibility assessment. Section 4 presents our experimental results. Finally, discussion and conclusions are given in Sect. 5.

2   Related Works

Early automatic credibility assessment studies targeted posts on Twitter via offline evaluation. These studies [4,5] collected data using Twitter API and randomly selected posts for labeling. The labeled posts were separated into training and test data sets. Then a machine learning model was built based on the training data set and evaluated on the test data set. Recent systems [2,6,10] evaluated credibility assessment online. Rather than using offline test data set, these recent systems were deployed on a Google Chrome extension to generate real-time assessment and collect users' feedbacks.

---

[4] http://newsroom.fb.com/company-info/.

[5] https://www.instagram.com/press/?hl=en.

[6] https://about.twitter.com/company.

As one of the earliest works, Castillo et al. [4] developed automatic credibility assessment on Twitter posts. In particular, they collected social media posts and employed human via crowdsourcing by first separating news posts from "chat" posts and then labeling each news post no matter whether it is trustworthy or not. Chat posts are discarded because they are messages based on only personal messages or subjective opinions or conversations among friends. Hence, they are of no interest to general public outside a personal's circle. Their notion of chat posts is similar to our non-newsworthiness. Given collected data, they characterized each post by features, such as the number of re-tweets, text length in a tweet, and the number of URLs. Then, J48 decision tree model was built to predict a credibility score of a given post with accuracy in the range of 70% to 80%, on the offline evaluation.

Gupta et al. [5] worked on credibility assessment of high impact topics, such as "Hurricane Irene", "Google acquires Motorola Mobility", and "New Facebook Messenger". They used Pseudo Relevance Feedback to improve upon Castillo et al. [4]'s approach, which resulted in the increase of the prediction performance about 5–10 %.

Aggarwal et al. [2] intended to identify tweets having phishing contents. For data preparation, they obtained labels, whether phishing or safe, of posts by cross-checking URLs in posts on the online blacklist services, PhishTank[7] and Google Safebrowsing[8]. Given the training data, they compared naive Bayes, decision trees and random forest. It turned out that random forest delivered the best performance. Therefore, they used the random forest model for phishing classification.

Gupta et al. [6] developed a real-time credibility assessment, called Tweed-Cred. SVM-rank model was used to predict a credibility score of a Twitter post on a scale from 1 to 7 (where 1 indicates the lowest credibility and 7 indicates the highest credibility). The model was trained on data collected via Twitter API. They employed crowdsourcing to label data. Regarding newsworthiness, they selected only informative news posts to train the model. However, the concept of newsworthiness was not distinguished in their evaluation process which they later realized and commented in their discussion.

Although newsworthiness was studied in many previous research works, its effect has not been formally studied. For instance, Castillo et al. [4] simply employed human to cull out non-newsworthy posts. Aggarwal et al. [2] intended to identify phishing content, instead of credibility. The nature of their system did not need awareness of newsworthiness. Gupta et al. [6] used only newsworthy posts to build their credibility prediction system, but overlooked the issue in their evaluation. In contrast, our work in this paper emphasizes the issue of newsworthiness and formally studies its effect in building a credibility prediction model.

---

[7] http://www.phishtank.com/.
[8] https://developers.google.com/safebrowsing/.

3   Methodology

After describing some related works—especially, on credibility assessment, let us describe our methodology in this section. In particular, we describe our studies on the effects of the inclusion of non-newsworthy messages in credibility assessment.

Here, we intend to quantify how much the inclusion of non-newsworthy posts would affect the building of a supervised learning model. We conducted the performance comparison of the following models:

- the supervised model trained with only newsworthy data, and
- the ones trained with various degrees of the mixture of both newsworthy and non-newsworthy data.

The focused studied data was Facebook posts collected through our developed Google Chrome extension. Our Chrome extension recorded the following information:

- post contents,
- their related features, and
- the corresponding labels from our human annotators.

Note that a human annotator was hired to assess a Facebook post and assign the post with certainty by using one of the following two labels:

- "trustworthy", or
- "non-trustworthy".

The human annotator was also informed to skip any post that is uncertain to assign a label. This removes uncertainty. There was the total of 1,500 records of well-labeled posts acquired between January 20, 2015 and September 8, 2015 inclusive. Out of the collected data, we chose 100 non-newsworthy records and 100 newsworthy records for the training data set. The remaining data containing 1,300 records was put into the test data set. Each record contained the features shown in Table 1.

In general, a *non-newsworthy post* is media post conveying information that is of no effect and of no interest to general public. The flow chart in Fig. 1 illustrates the process to determine non-newsworthiness.

To elaborate, given an input social media post (e.g., Facebook post), a human annotator determines whether or not such a social media post has any effect on many people. If such a social media post has some effect on many people, then the post is labeled as "trustworthy"—one of the two labels. On the contrary, if such a social media post does not have any effect on many people, then the human annotator needs to consider the post further. Specifically, the human annotator needs to determine whether the post involves any public figure and irregular events. If so (i.e., although the post does not have any effect on many people but it involves some public figure and irregular events), then the post is labeled as "trustworthy". Otherwise (i.e., labeled as "trustworthy") If not (i.e., the post does not have any effect on many people nor does it involve any public figure or irregular events), then the post is labeled as "non-trustworthy". See the pseudocode in Fig. 2.

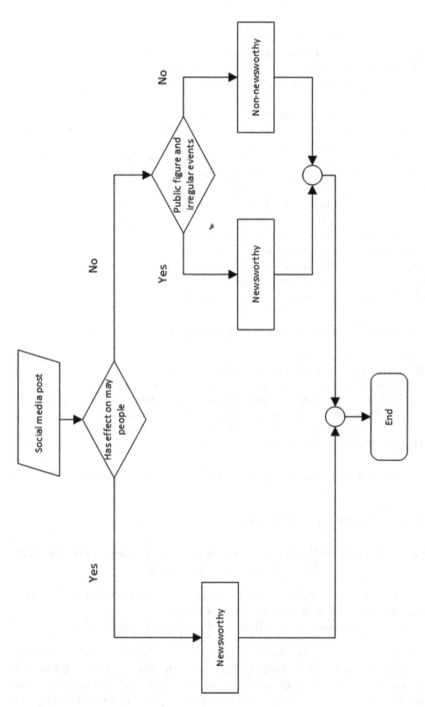

Fig. 1. Flow chart to determine non-newsworthiness.

Table 1. Features (including social media features and word features) used in a decision tree

Social media feature	Description
Comments	Number of comments responded to each post
Feeling status	True-false logic whether a post has feeling status
Hashtags	Number of hashtags presented in each post
Images	Number of images presented in each post
Likes	Number of likes responded to each post
Public post	True-false logic whether a post each public (Any person can see the post)
Shares	Number of shares responded to each post
Shares with location	True-false logic whether a post has a location share
Tags with friends	Number of tags to other users in each post
Urls	Number of URLs presented in each post
Video	Number of videos presented in post
Word feature	Description
Exclamation marks	Number of exclamation marks in a post
Length characters	Number of characters in a post
Question marks	Number of question marks in a post
Words	Number of words in a post
Words in dictionary	Number of words found in dictionary

Algorithm 1. Determination of non-newsworthiness

1. **Input:** A social media post P
2. **if** the social media post P has effects on many people
   3. **then** label of the social media post $P \leftarrow$ "newsworthy"
   4. **else if** the social media post P involves public figure or irregular events
      5. **then** label of the social media post $P \leftarrow$ "newsworthy"
      6. **else** label of the social media post $P \leftarrow$ "non-newsworthy"
7. **Output:** Label of the social media post P

Fig. 2. A pseudocode for determining non-newsworthiness.

4   Experiments and Results

To evaluate the effects of the inclusion of non-newsworthy messages in credibility assessment, we conducted the following two experiments:

1. The first experiment was to quantify performance degradation with respect to various proportions of non-newsworthy posts.
2. The second experiment was to illustrate the effect of additional data.

Both experiments used the decision tree method—specifically, Classification and Regression Trees algorithm (CART) [3,7,11]—as our prediction model. Decision tree was a simple and fast method that seemed suitable for classification of low dimensional data, which was fitted with the characteristics of social media posts. The trained decision trees were evaluated on 1,300 social posts. F1-Score was used as a performance index. A higher value of F1-Score means better performance.

Our experiments were conducted on Python 2.7 platform with scikit-learn 0.16.0 as a machine learning library. Note that Python scikit-learn[9] is one of the most comprehensive and widely-used machine learning environments [9]. The experiments were run on Mac OSX 10.11.5 processor Intel Core i5 2.3 GHz memory 8 GB.

The first experiment examined five decision trees trained with 0%, 25%, 50%, 75% and 100% of non-newsworthy posts out of 100 social posts. Figure 3 describes how the first experiment was conducted. The source code was published on github[10].

Algorithm 2. Procedure for the first experiment

1. **Input:** 200 trials
2. **for each** of the 200 trials **do**
   3. choose 1,300 posts to be in a test data set
   4. evaluate Treatment 11 (i.e., training on 100% newsworthy posts)
   5. evaluate Treatment 12 (i.e., training on 75% newsworthy and 25% non-newsworthy posts)
   6. evaluate Treatment 13 (i.e., training on 50% newsworthy and 50% non-newsworthy posts)
   7. evaluate Treatment 14 (i.e., training on 25% newsworthy and 75% non-newsworthy posts)
   8. evaluate Treatment 15 (i.e., training on 100% non-newsworthy posts)
9. **Output:** Percentage of degradation

Fig. 3. Procedure of how the first experiment was conducted.

Figure 4 shows the result of this first experiment. The x-axis shows the percentage of non-newsworthiness in training data. The y-axis shows the percentage of performance degradation. Round marks display the percentage of decreasing performance at specified degree of non-newsworthiness. For example, the second mark from the left is located roughly on (25, 5), indicating that 25% of non-newsworthy posts in training data led to 5% performance drop. The percentage of performance degradation quantifies the decreasing performance from the best performing model, which is trained without non-newsworthy posts. Given f_i as the F1-score of Treatment i (for $i = 11, \ldots, 15$), the percentage of performance degradation is computed as follows:

$$p = \frac{f_i - f_{11}}{f_{11}} \times 100\%, \qquad (1)$$

where f_{11} is a F1-score of Treatment 11 (with 0% non-newsworthiness). Dash line shows the estimated relation between non-newsworthiness and a degree of

[9] https://pypi.python.org/pypi/scikit-learn/0.16.0.
[10] https://github.com/chaluemwut/FBFilterCML.git.

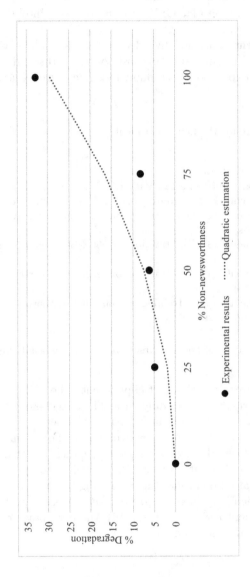

Fig. 4. Percentages of performance degradation from various degrees of non-newsworthiness in training data.

credibility prediction performance degradation. It is deduced from the following quadratic function:

$$y = ax^2 + bx + c, \tag{2}$$

where y is the estimated percentage of performance degradation, x is the percentage of non-newsworthiness, whereas a, b and c are function parameters with values determined by using the Least Squared Method.

The second experiment examined the effects of additional data through the following three decision tree models:

1. a model trained with 50 newsworthy posts (i.e., *base case*),
2. a model trained with 50 base posts and 50 additional news-worthy posts (i.e., *additional good case*), and
3. a model trained with 50 base posts and 50 additional non-newsworthy posts (i.e., *additional bad case*).

The procedure in Fig. 5 describes how the second experiment was conducted. Each experiment was repeated 200 times and average F1-Scores were used to indicate performances of the treatments.

Algorithm 2. Procedure for the second experiment

1. **Input:** 200 trials
2. **for each** of the 200 trials **do**
   3. choose 1,300 posts to be in a test data set
   4. evaluate Treatment 21 (i.e., training on 50 newsworthy posts)
   5. evaluate Treatment 22 (i.e., training on 100 newsworthy posts)
   6. evaluate Treatment 23 (i.e., training on 50 newsworthy and 50 non-newsworthy posts)
9. **Output:** F1-score and %difference

Fig. 5. Procedure of how the second experiment was conducted.

Table 2 shows the second experimental results. Column 3 (i.e., %difference) shows the difference percentage of F1-Score from the base case. The second row shows the performance of Treatment 22 in which additional data are all

Table 2. Effects of additional training data. With good additional data (all additional records are newsworthy), accuracy of credibility prediction increases slightly. However additional bad data (all additional records are non-newsworthy) jeopardizes the performance by almost 3%.

	Training data	F1-score	%difference
Treatment 21:	Base data	0.9058	0.000
Treatment 22:	Base and additional newsworthy data	0.9064	0.057
Treatment 23:	Base and additional non-newsworthy data	0.8789	−2.977

newsworthy; The third row shows the performance of Treatment 23 in which additional data are mixed with non-newsworthy data. When compared with the base data (i.e., Treatment 21), the additional good set (i.e., Treatment 22) resulted in a slightly better F1-Score. However, when compared with the base data (i.e., Treatment 1), the additional bad set (i.e., Treatment 23) affirms a negative impact on non-newsworthiness in training data: Despite that Treatment 3 involved more training data than Treatment 21, its performance was worse with non-newsworthy data.

5   Discussion and Conclusion

Our experimental result shows that prediction performance decreases when there is an increasing degree of non-newsworthiness in training data. This performance degradation due to a degree of non-newsworthiness can be estimated as a quadratic curve. The negative effect of non-newsworthiness on training data is also apparent such that a large training data set with a very high degree of non-newsworthiness may lead to a worse performance than a smaller set with a low degree of non-newsworthiness. This affirms and supports our speculation of the importance of removing non-newsworthy posts from training data set. Our findings reveal viability of a notion of newsworthiness in building a credibility assessment system. This insight leads to a practical structure of a credibility assessment that requires two distinct processes. One is to select newsworthy posts deserved to be in a training data set or to be assessed. Another one is to assess the worthy posts for credibility. A reliable credibility assessment would hopefully help online society to be aware of false information widely spread on social media and to be safe from being deceived and possibly loss of time, money, and even personal welfare.

Acknowledgements. This project is partially supported by Natural Sciences and Engineering Research Council of Canada (NSERC).

References

1. Cerón-Guzmán, J.A., León, E.: Detecting social spammers in colombia 2014 presidential election. In: Lagunas, O.P., Alcántara, O.H., Figueroa, G.A. (eds.) MICAI 2015. LNCS (LNAI), vol. 9414, pp. 121–141. Springer, Cham (2015). doi:10.1007/978-3-319-27101-9_9
2. Aggarwal, A., Rajadesingan, A., Kumaraguru, P.: PhishAri: Automatic realtime phishing detection on Twitter. In: Proceedings of the 2012 eCrime Researchers Summit (eCrime 2012), Las Croabas, PR, USA, 23–24 October 2012, pp. 1–12. IEEE, Piscataway, NJ, USA (2012)
3. Breiman, L., Friedman, J., Olshen, R., Stone, C.: Classification and Regression Trees. Chapman and Hall/CRC, Boca Raton, FL, USA (1984)
4. Castillo, C., Mendoza, M., Poblete, B.: Information credibility on twitter. Proceedings of the 20th International Conference on World Wide Web (WWW 2011), Hyderabad, India, 28 March–1 April 2011, pp. 675–684. ACM, New York, NY, USA (2011)

5. Gupta, A., Kumaraguru, P.: Credibility ranking of tweets during high impact events. In: Proceedings of the 1st Workshop on Privacy and Security in Online Social Media (PSOSM 2012), Lyon, France, 17 April 2012, no. 2. ACM, New York, NY, USA (2012)
6. Gupta, A., Kumaraguru, P., Castillo, C., Meier, P.: TweetCred: Real-time credibility assessment of content on twitter. In: Aiello, L.M., McFarland, D. (eds.) SocInfo 2014. LNCS, vol. 8851, pp. 228–243. Springer, Cham (2014). doi:10.1007/978-3-319-13734-6_16
7. Han, J., Kamber, M., Pei, J.: Data Mining: Concepts and Techniques, 3rd edn. Morgan Kaufmann, Burlington, MA, USA (2011)
8. Noyunsan, C., Katanyukul, T., Wu, Y., Runapongsa Saikaew, K.: Social network newsworthiness filter based on topic analysis. In: Proceedings of the 6th KKU International Engineering Conference (KKU-IENC 2016) (2016)
9. Pedregosa, F., Varoquaux, G., Gramfort, A., Michel, V., Thirion, B., Grisel, O., Blondel, M., Prettenhofer, P., Weiss, R., Dubourg, V., Vanderplas, J., Passos, A., Cournapeau, D., Brucher, M., Perrot, M., Duchesnay, É.: Scikit-learn: machine learning in Python. J. Mach. Learn. Res. 12, 2825–2830 (2011)
10. Runapongsa Saikaew, K., Noyunsan, C.: Features for measuring credibility on Facebook information. Int. Sch. Sci. Res. Innov. 9(1), 174–177 (2015)
11. Tan, P.N., Steinbach, M., Kumar, V.: Introduction to Data Mining. Addison-Wesley, Boston, MA, USA (2006)

On the Impact of Neighborhood Selection Strategies for Recommender Systems in LBSNs

Carlos Ríos, Silvia Schiaffino$^{(\boxtimes)}$, and Daniela Godoy

ISISTAN (CONICET-UNCPBA), Campus Universitario, Tandil, Argentina
{carlos.rios,silvia.schiaffino,daniela.godoy}@isistan.unicen.edu.ar

Abstract. Location-based social networks (LBSNs) have emerged as a new concept in online social media, due to the widespread adoption of mobile devices and location-based services. LBSNs leverage technologies such as GPS, Web 2.0 and smartphones to allow users to share their locations (check-ins), search for places of interest or POIs (Point of Interest), look for discounts, comment about specific places, connect with friends and find the ones who are near a specific location. To take advantage of the information that users share in these networks, Location-based Recommender Systems (LBRSs) generate suggestions based on the application of different recommendation techniques, being collaborative filtering (CF) one of the most traditional ones. In this article we analyze different strategies for selecting neighbors in the classic CF approach, considering information contained in the users' social network, common visits, and place of residence as influential factors. The proposed approaches were evaluated using data from a popular location based social network, showing improvements over the classic collaborative filtering approach.

1 Introduction

The great explosion of cell phone use, the easiness to acquire the geographical location of people, and the development of wireless communications, has allowed the creation of social services whose main feature is the geographical location of users. Foursquare[1] is the most popular social network among these services, allowing users to easily share their geographical location as well as contents related to that location in an online way. The user location is a new dimension in social networks that narrows the gap between the physical world and online social networking services, creating new opportunities and challenges for traditional recommendation systems. These systems are an alternative to deal with the problem of information overload that users face while seeking information about items of interest in vast amounts of knowledge. Traditional methods such as collaborative filtering (CF), content-based recommendation (CB) and hybrid methods [14] process information derived from the ratings provided by users and the characteristics of the items involved to generate a list of recommendations.

---

[1] http://es.foursquare.com/.

© Springer International Publishing AG 2017
G. Sidorov and O. Herrera-Alcántara (Eds.): MICAI 2016, Part I, LNAI 10061, pp. 196–207, 2017.
DOI: 10.1007/978-3-319-62434-1_16

However, in social networks there is additional information that recommendation methods should take into account, such as users' behavior and relations of friendship between them [20].

Regarding location based social networks (LBSNs), geo-localized data is a physical dimension that traditional social networks do not possess. In this new era, users can benefit from obtaining a pervasive and ubiquitous access to location-based services from anywhere through mobile devices. In a LBSN, there are relationships of various types, such as the User-User relationship, showing the friendship between two users or coincidence in places visited by these users; the User-Place relationship showing that a user visited a given place; the Place-Place relationship, which shows distance relationships or categorical membership. In addition to these relationships, users generate content-based relations, such as comments after visiting a place.

In this context, location based recommender systems have emerged [16] as a means to exploit geographical properties as an auxiliary source for recommending friends [11,15], places [10], activities [5,21] and events [9,12]. The heterogeneity of the data produced by location-based social networks creates the need for new approaches in recommendation systems, using different data sources and methodologies for enhancing recommendation. The Collaborative Filtering (CF) approach, for example, relates users to items through ratings or opinions, so that it can be straightforwardly applied to the construction of LBRSs. However, traditional CF approach lacks of the geo-localization dimension.

In this work, we propose different strategies for including the additional dimensions available in LBSNs in the context of user-based collaborative filtering for recommending locations. User-based approaches recommend items (e.g. places) based on an aggregation of the preferences of similar users or neighbors, i.e. users with similar tastes. As user-based CF trusts neighbors as information sources, the quality of recommendations are a direct consequence of the selected neighborhood. Our main hypothesis is that location-based social networks provide rich information for establishing relations beyond similarity, which can improve the selection of potential neighbors and, therefore, improve the estimation of preferences during the recommendation process.

The rest of the article is organized as follows. In Sect. 2 we describe related works. In Sect. 3, we present the different neighborhood selection strategies proposed and evaluated in this work. In Sect. 4, we describe the experimental results we carried out to analyze these strategies. Finally in Sect. 5 we present our conclusions and outline some future works.

2   Related Work

Location-based social networks (LBSNs) allow users to build connections with their friends, share their locations via check-ins for points of interests (POIs) (e.g., restaurants, tourist spots, and stores) as well as location-related contents (e.g., geo-tagged photos and comments). In addition to provide users a social interaction platform, LBSNs are a rich source of information (containing social relationships, check-in history and tips) to mine users' preferences.

Thus, location-based social networks open new possibilities for recommender systems [3], which can suggest different types of items such as: friends, places or points of interest (POI), activities and events.

Location-based recommender systems use the geographical property of LBSNs as an auxiliary source to improve recommendations of places or activities in which a target user may be interested in. Recent studies show the importance of location in generating new friendship relations. For example, in [15] the problem of friend recommendation was studied and it was concluded that about 30% of new links are chosen from users who visited the same places. In [7] the authors propose an approach for recommending friends who have similar interests as well as real-life location and dwell time with the target user. Geographic-Textual-Social Based Followee Recommendation (GTS-FR) approach is proposed in [18] for followee recommendation in LBSNs by exploring geographic, textual and social properties simultaneously.

Point-of-Interest (POI) recommender systems play an important role in LBSNs as they can help users explore attractive locations. Traditional CF relies on explicit ratings for items for generating recommendations. Although ratings are not available in LBSNs, the frequencies of check-ins recorded by LBSNs implicitly reflect the users' preferences for a given POI. Hence, several works [5,6,17] applied user-based CF approaches starting from mining the check-in patterns of users. In [17], the authors argue that geographical influence between POIs plays an important role in the behavior of users' check-ins and propose a framework for POI recommendation that merges user preferences as well as social and geographical influence. In [5], the authors propose an approach for detecting the current user context, inferring possible leisure activities and recommend appropriate content on the site (shops, parks, movies). Berjani et al. [6] applied a Regularized Matrix Factorization (RMF) technique for CF-based personalized recommendation of potentially interesting spots. Within the CF framework, [8] uses highly available GPS trajectories to enhance visitors with context-aware POI recommendations, [23] extract the user travel experience in the target region to reduce the range of candidate POIs. [19] introduce the temporal behavior of users into a time-aware POI recommendation and [22] propose an opinion-based POI recommendation framework taking advantage of the user opinions on POIs expressed as text-based tips. Differently from these works, the strategies presented in this paper aim to explore how to better select neighbors in CF-based POI recommendation by introducing the different elements available in LBSNs, such as friend relationships and geo-located checkins.

3   Neighborhood Selection Strategies

In a traditional CF scenario, there are m users $U = u_1, u_2, ..., u_m$, and a list of n items $I = i_1, i, ..., i_n$, that can be recommended to users. Each user has expressed her opinion about a set of items $I_{u_i} \subseteq I$, generally in an explicit way with a rating or value in a given numerical scale. This information is stored in a user-item matrix M of size $m \times n$, such that the value of each cell in M represents the preference score (rating) given by user i to item j. Memory-based CF approaches make predictions based on the user-item matrix in two ways, based on users or based on items [1]. Given an active user who requires a prediction for an item without rating, CF algorithms measure the similarities between the active user and other users (user-based approach), or between the item and the remaining items (item-based approach). Therefore, a rating is predicted by an aggregation of the ratings that the item received from similar users in the first case, or ratings given by the active user to similar items in the second case.

The classic user-based CF model is then defined as in Eq. 1 [13]:

$$\tilde{r}(u,i) = \bar{r}(u) + C_o \sum_{v \in N_k(u,i)} sim(u,v)(r(v,i) - \bar{r}(v)) \tag{1}$$

where $r(v,i)$ is the rating given by user v to item i, $\tilde{r}$ is the rating prediction (different from the observed rating r), $N_k(u,i)$ is the set of k most similar users to u and $sim(u,v)$ is the function that determines the similarity between users u and v. C_o is a normalizing factor. The preference of user u for an item i is predicted according to the average rating $\bar{r}(u)$, the sum of deviations of the ratings given by the neighbors v to item i and the average ratings $\bar{r}(v)$, weighting by the similarity with neighbors.

User-based approaches assume that not all users are equally useful in the prediction for a given user, thus two main problems emerge: (1) selecting neighbors for a user to generate recommendations; (2) how to use properly the information provided by those neighbors in the generation of recommendations. Usually, the selection of neighbors is based on their similarity to the active user, while a common practice is to define a maximum number of users to narrow the neighborhood. Once the neighborhood is defined, the contribution of each neighbor to the prediction is weighted based on their distance from the active user. For example, a widely used alternative is a linear combination of the ratings weighted by the similarity with the neighbors. However, there are other factors that may be valuable for selecting neighbors. For example, in the case of this work the users' history of visits can be considered relevant beyond the ratings similarity.

To properly separate the two problems, the selection of neighbors on one hand and the weighting of their opinions on the other, [4] propose a modification the classic formula. This new formula considered an allocation score function (scoring) depending on the active user u, a neighbor v and an item i, or some combination thereof. This function gives a higher value when the triplet of user-neighbor-item is more valuable or expected to work better in predicting a rating according to the available information. Equation 1 is then generalized as Eq. 2:

$$\tilde{r}(u,i) = \bar{r}(u) + C_o \sum_{v \in g(u,i;k;s)} f(s(u,i,v), sim(u,v)) * (r(v,i) - \bar{r}(v)) \tag{2}$$

where g is the function that selects neighbors and f is an aggregation function that combines the outcomes of the scoring function s and $sim(u,v)$ the similarity between users.

The selection of neighbors involves the determination of the similarity of users to the target user, by making a comparison with all the users in the database. So any user that is similar to the target user may contribute to the preference estimation. The function g (selection of neighbors) may be influenced by relations present in a LBSN. Thus, restricting with some criteria the potential neighborhood of a target user by exploiting the information generated in LBSN, we can reduce the number of comparisons and, at the same time, improve the preference estimation. In this context, we present different approaches to the selection of potential neighbors.

In this paper we propose four different strategies for selecting neighbors in a user-based CF approach for recommendation based on the following information extracted from the LBSN: (1) friend relationships established by users, (2) common places visited by users, (3) area of residence, and (4) visiting area of users. These four strategies are used for defining the function g in Eq. 2, i.e. the way in which neighbors are selected, whereas the rest of the formula remains unchanged. Then, once neighbors are selected based on a given strategy, the similarity of their preferences is assessed.

The first approach consists in using information from the actual social network created by users in the system. In this strategy, the set of neighbors that can contribute to the preference estimation of a target user is restricted to those that relate socially with this user (see Fig. 1(a)). These relationships can be direct relationships (direct friends) or indirect relationships (friends of friends). In other words, this strategy searches for the k users most socially similar/related to predict the preferences of the target user by exploring the ego-centric social network of the target user up to a certain level.

In addition to the social relationship mentioned above, users can be related by common visited places. These may be represented in a network as in Fig. 1(b), where users are nodes and the edges represent the number of times that users coincided in one place, producing a geo-located relationship. With the same idea as in the social network approach, you can limit the set of users who may be potential neighbors of the target user up to a certain level in the network. Therefore, this strategy seeks for the k most similar users to the target user in the set of users with a geo-localized relation with the target user.

Another way to select potential users to form a given user neighborhood is using the users' demographic information provided by the LBSN. The simplest strategy is grouping users according to the area where they live (see Fig. 1(c)), with the hypothesis that users of the same district, state, or country are the most appropriate for comparing preferences with, as they have the same customs. So potential neighbors that will contribute to the estimated preference for the target user may be those that have the same place of residence. This strategy looks for the k most similar users in the set of users who live in the same area that the target users, where area can be defined at different granularity levels, such as country, state, city and county.

Finally, the last strategy is based on the idea that users visiting places in same area are alike (see Fig. 1(d)). Then, the strategy requires first to identify the area

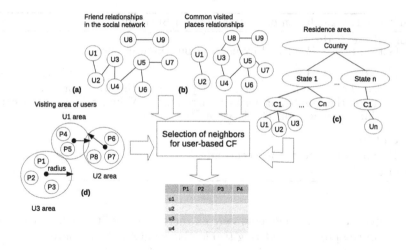

Fig. 1. Overview of the proposed neighbor selection strategies.

delimiting the places a user visited and, then, to calculate the intersection with the visiting area of other users. It is assumed that the greater the intersection with the target user, the more useful the preferences of the user for predicting the rating of a given item are. Algorithm 1 describes the steps followed to calculate the visiting area of users, with $X=1$.

4   Experimental Results

This section describes the experiments conducted to evaluate the different approaches for neighborhood selection under the user-based CF approach, and the results obtained.

4.1   Experimental Design

In order to evaluate the proposed strategies for selecting neighbors in the collaborating filtering method within LBSNs, several experiments were run and compared in their performance at recommending places. For these experiments different neighborhood sizes were considered (5, 10, 20, 30, and 50 users), whereas the similarity of preferences is calculated using the standard cosine similarity. For each of the defined strategies several parameters can be configured, the reported experiments were set as follows:

- Strategy 1: Potential neighbors were extracted from the social network considering different levels of friendship relationships (levels 1, 2, 3, 4, 5).
- Strategy 2: Potential neighbors were extracted from the network of visits considering different levels of geo-location relationships (levels 1, 2, 3, 4, 5).

Algorithm 1. Calculation of visiting area for Strategy 4.

1: **for all** $u \in U$ **do**
2:    Get all places P_u visited by user u from the user checkins

3:    **for all** $p \in P_u$ **do**
4:       Use $\langle Latitude, Longitude \rangle$ of the place p as the area centroid
5:       Count the number of visits in a radius of X km, taking into account taking into account all places in P_u

6:    **end for**
7:    Calculate the most dense centroid
8: **end for**

- Strategy 3: Potential neighbors were extracted considering their place of residence in the profile considering two levels, county and state level.
- Strategy 4: Potential neighbors were extracted analyzing common patterns in geo-localized behavior.

The defined strategies were compared against the baseline, the traditional user-based CF approach in which the k most similar users are selected by calculating the cosine similarity of preferences between the target user and all users in the system. For the different experiments, we carried out some data processing on the selected dataset, which is detailed in Sect. 4.2. The performance of the different strategies at predicting the preferences of a user was evaluated using the standard MAE (Mean Absolute Error) metric given by Eq. 3, which measures the error in the estimation for the set of user-item pairs T.

$$MAE = \frac{1}{|T|} \sum_{(u,i) \in T} | \bar{r}_{ui} - r_{ui} | \tag{3}$$

4.2 Dataset

For the experiments the dataset from [2] was used, containing data collected from one of the most widely used LBSN, *Foursquare*. The dataset contains the following information: *Places*, information about the places visited, *Users*, data of the users using the system, *Tips*, information about check-ins made by users, *Friendship*, information on the social relationship between users and *Categories*; information of the categories of *Foursquare* places. In the dataset there are users from all over the world, but for our experiments only users belonging to the state of New York were considered, as they are greater in quantity. Out of the 47,220 users in the dataset, the 27,000 users from New York were used.

For Strategy 1, we used the social network among users in *Foursquare*, which is an undirected network and it has no weights in the edges. The dataset has a total of 47,220 nodes and 1,192,758 edges. For Strategy 2, the dataset was processed to generate the network of common places visited. In this network a node is a user and the relationship between two users is given by the number of common visits. Relationships based on a single visit in common were eliminated, because they can be just a coincidence. The resulting network of common visits can be categorized as an undirected network, with weighted edges (number of common visits between users).

For Strategy 3, the variable "Home city" from the user profiles was considered to group users from New York in counties (e.g. Manhattan, Brooklyn, Queens). We used the service from Google maps[2] to obtain more information about the place of residence. For Strategy 4, two steps were required. First we obtained the places visited for each user according to the checkins made and calculated the visiting area according to Algorithm 1. Then, the distance between the area visited by two users was calculated using the cosine measure regarding their centroids and considering the earth radius of 6378.1 km.

Finally, visits or checkins were used as as a means to assess the user preferences in the user-item matrix M, because if a person often visits a place we can deduce that he/she liked it. In this context, for generating the preference matrix, we considered a 5 stars scale, where 1 represents "bad", 2 represents "regular", 3 represents "good", 4 indicates "very good", and 5 indicates "excellent". These were mapped to the scale of values as follows, 1 visit is mapped to the value 2, 2 visits to a value of 3, 3 visits to a value 4 and 4 or more visits to a value 5.

4.3   Results

Figure 2 shows the experimental results obtained for the different strategies. In Fig. 2(a) it is possible to observe the results considering different levels of friend relationships according to Strategy 1. The Baseline is the traditional collaborative filtering approach that selects the k most similar users based con the cosine similarity of their preferences exclusively. Considering a single level of relationships, i.e., only the direct friends of the target user, the results obtained are worst than the baseline. However, friend-of-a-friend relationships (the level 2) are the best performing, reducing the MAE considerably with respect to the baseline. If the social graph is further explored, after the second level (level 3 ahead) the error increases, but it is still better than the baseline.

Figure 2(b) shows the results considering the network formed by common visited places defined in Strategy 2. This strategy outperformed the baseline in all its variations. The best performing option was using the direct edges, i.e. users that visit the same places than the target user. Exploring further this network the MAE values grow, even though they are still better than the baseline.

Figure 2(c) reports the results of the strategies concerning with geolocalization. Selecting neighbors from the same state reaches comparable results to the baseline. Specializing more the region, i.e., using New York counties, the prediction error is reduced. In addition, Strategy 4 attains an important improvement, reducing the MAE scores significantly. Then, if the influence or visiting area of users is taken into account, those users hanging around the same places than the target user seem to be the most useful for interest prediction.

---

[2] https://developers.google.com/maps/web-services/overview?hl=es.

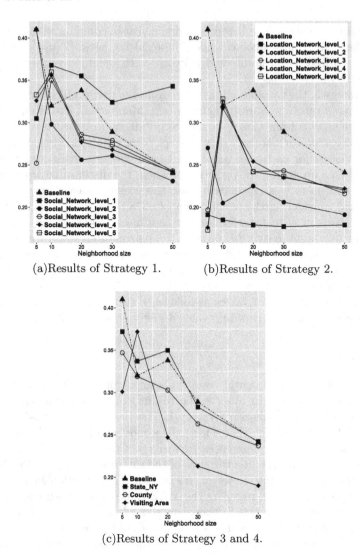

(a)Results of Strategy 1.   (b)Results of Strategy 2.

(c)Results of Strategy 3 and 4.

Fig. 2. Experimental results for all the strategies

In general terms, the proposed strategies for selecting neighbors based on the different elements available in LBSNs achieve better results than the traditional CF approach. An additional advantage of these strategies is the number of users involved in the computation of predictions. User-based CF is based on the similarity computations of the target user with every other user in the dataset, for choosing the k most similar ones. In the proposed strategies, this number of users is reduced. Figure 3 reports the average number each target user needs for determining the neighborhood for each strategy, in decreasing order. The baseline uses all of the 47240 users. If the friend relationships are used, the number increases as more levels of the network are explored. The best performing option, that was friend-of-a-friend (level 2) involves 10649 users (22%). The best performing variation using the network of common visited places (level 1) is based in only 19 users. Also, using the visiting area of users involves 3111 users (6.5%). Naturally, in the case of Strategies 2 and 4, the visiting graph and the visiting area requires previous data calculation and their updating with its consequent computational cost. This effort, however, can be done off-line. Strategies 1 and 3, instead, use data accessible from the profiles in the LBSN (friends and residence).

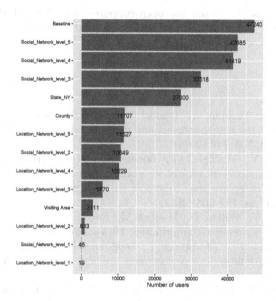

Fig. 3. Number of users compared for selecting the neighborhood.

5   Conclusions

In this article we have proposed different strategies for selecting neighbors in the context of collaborative filtering for the recommendation of places of interest (POI) in LBSNs. The different elements available in these networks, such as the relationships among users and the geo-localization of data, allows us to select users that are potentially more useful for prediction. In this direction, we proposed four strategies, two based on relationships such as friendship and co-located visits, and two using geographical information, such as the place where users live and walk around. The experimental results showed that all of these strategies are capable of improving the baseline, which is the traditional user-based CF approach. Moreover, most of them require less computation in the selection of the neighborhood. The selection based on the friend-of-a-friend network, the users that visit more than a common place, the users in the same county and those visiting places in an intersecting area, were the best alternatives for each of the strategies. All in all, the best performing strategy was to select the neighbors from those that have visited some places in common with the target users. Notably, this strategy not only reduced the error in prediction significantly, but also was the one involving less users in this step of the CF approach. As regards future work, we plan to integrate other elements of LSBNs, such as the text-based tips to estimate the preferences as well as to evaluate functions to weight the selected neighbors for improving prediction.

Acknowledgements. This work has been supported by ANPCyT PICT No. 2011-0366, CONICET PIP No. 11220150100030CO (2015–2017) and PIP 112-201101-00078 (2012–2015).

References

1. Adomavicius, G., Tuzhilin, A.: Toward the next generation of recommender systems: a survey of the state-of-the-art and possible extensions. IEEE Trans. Knowl. Data Eng. **17**(6), 734–749 (2005)
2. Bao, J., Zheng, Y., Mokbel, M.F.: Location-based and preference-aware recommendation using sparse geo-social networking data. In: Proceedings of the 20th International Conference on Advances in Geographic Information Systems (SIGSPATIAL), pp. 199–208 (2012)
3. Bao, J., Zheng, Y., Wilkie, D., Mokbel, M.: Recommendations in location-based social networks: a survey. Geoinformatica **19**(3), 525–565 (2015)
4. Bellogín, A., Castells, P., Cantador, I.: Neighbor selection and weighting in user-based collaborative filtering: a performance prediction approach. ACM Trans. Web **8**(2), 12:1–12:30 (2014)
5. Bellotti, V., Begole, B., Chi, E.H., Ducheneaut, N., Fang, J., Isaacs, E., King, T., Newman, M.W., Partridge, K., Price, B., Rasmussen, P., Roberts, M., Schiano, D.J., Walendowski, A.: Activity-based serendipitous recommendations with the Magitti mobile leisure guide. In: Proceedings of the SIGCHI Conference on Human Factors in Computing Systems (CHI 2008), Florence, Italy, pp. 1157–1166 (2008)
6. Berjani, B., Strufe, T.: A recommendation system for spots in location-based online social networks. In: Procedings of the 4th Workshop on Social Network Systems (SNS 2011), Salzburg, Austria, pp. 4:1–4:6 (2011)
7. Chu, C.-H., Wu, W.-C., Wang, C.-C., Chen, T.-S., Chen, J.-J.: Friend recommendation for location-based mobile social networks. In: Proceedings of the 17th International Conference on Innovative Mobile and Internet Services in Ubiquitous Computing (IMIS 2013), Taichung, China, pp. 365–370 (2013)
8. Huang, H., Gartner, G.: Using context-aware collaborative filtering for POI recommendations in mobile guides. In: 8th International Symposium on Location-Based Services (LBS 2011), Vienna, Austria, pp. 131–147 (2011)
9. Lee, R., Wakamiya, S., Sumiya, K.: Discovery of unusual regional social activities using geo-tagged microblogs. World Wide Web **14**(4), 321–349 (2011)
10. Long, X., Joshi, J.: A HITS-based POI recommendation algorithm for location-based social networks. In: IEEE/ACM International Conference on Advances in Social Networks Analysis and Mining (ASONAM 2013), Niagara, Canada, pp. 642–647 (2013)

11. Papadimitriou, A., Symeonidis, P., Manolopoulos, Y.: Friendlink: link prediction in social networks via bounded local path traversal. In: International Conference on Computational Aspects of Social Networks (CASoN 2011), Salamanca, Spain, pp. 66–71 (2011)

12. Quercia, D., Lathia, N., Calabrese, F., Di Lorenzo, G., Crowcroft, J.: Recommending social events from mobile phone location data. In: IEEE 10th International Conference on Data Mining (ICDM 2010), Sydney, Australia, pp. 971–976 (2010)

13. Resnick, P., Iacovou, N., Suchak, M., Bergstrom, P., Riedl, J.: GroupLens: an open architecture for collaborative filtering of netnews. In: Proceedings 1994 ACM Conference on Computer Supported Cooperative Work (CSCW 1994), pp. 175–186 (1994)

14. Ricci, F., Rokach, L., Shapira, B.: Introduction to recommender systems handbook. In: Ricci, F., Rokach, L., Shapira, B., Kantor, P.B. (eds.) Recommender Systems Handbook, pp. 1–35. Springer, New York (2011). doi:10.1007/978-0-387-85820-3_1

15. Scellato, S., Noulas, A., Mascolo, C.: Exploiting place features in link prediction on location-based social networks. In: Proceedings of the 17th ACM SIGKDD International Conference on Knowledge Discovery and Data Mining (KDD 2011), pp. 1046–1054 (2011)

16. Symeonidis, P., Papadimitriou, A., Manolopoulos, Y., Senkul, P., Toroslu, I.: Geosocial recommendations based on incremental tensor reduction and local path traversal. In: Proceedings of the 3rd ACM SIGSPATIAL International Workshop on Location-Based Social Networks (LBSN 2011), Chicago, USA, pp. 89–96 (2011)

17. Ye, M., Yin, P., Lee, W.-C., Lee, D.-L.: Exploiting geographical influence for collaborative point-of-interest recommendation. In: Proceedings of the 34th International ACM SIGIR Conference on Research and Development in Information Retrieval, pp. 325–334 (2011)

18. Ying, J.J.-C., Lu, E.H.-C., Tseng, V.S.: Followee recommendation in asymmetrical location-based social networks. In: Proceedings of the 2012 ACM Conference on Ubiquitous Computing (UbiComp 2012), Pittsburgh, USA, pp. 988–995 (2012)

19. Yuan, Q., Cong, G., Ma, Z., Sun, A., Thalmann, N.M.: Time-aware point-of-interest recommendation. In: Proceedings 36th Int. ACM SIGIR Conference on Research and Development in Information Retrieval (SIGIR 2013), pp. 363–372 (2013)

20. Zafarani, R., Abbasi, M., Liu, H.: Social Media Mining: An Introduction. Cambridge University Press, Cambridge (2014)

21. Zanda, A., Menasalvas, E., Eibe, S.: A social network activity recommender system for ubiquitous devices. In: Proceedings of the 11th International Conference on Intelligent Systems Design and Applications (ISDA 2011), Cordoba, Spain, pp. 493–497 (2011)

22. Zhang, J.-D., Chow, C.-Y., Zheng, Y.: ORec: an opinion-based point-of-interest recommendation framework. In: Proceedings of the 24th ACM International Conference on Information and Knowledge Management (CIKM 2015), pp. 1641–1650 (2015)

23. Zhou, E., Huang, J., Xu, X.: A point-of-interest recommendation method based on user check-in behaviors in online social networks. In: Thai, M.T., Nguyen, N.P., Shen, H. (eds.) CSoNet 2015. LNCS, vol. 9197, pp. 160–171. Springer, Cham (2015). doi:10.1007/978-3-319-21786-4_14

Fuzzy Logic

For Multi-interval-valued Fuzzy Sets, Centroid Defuzzification Is Equivalent to Defuzzifying Its Interval Hull: A Theorem

Vladik Kreinovich[1($\boxtimes$)] and Songsak Sriboonchitta[2]

[1] Department of Computer Science, University of Texas at El Paso,
El Paso, TX 79968, USA
vladik@utep.edu
[2] Faculty of Economics, Chiang Mai University, Chiang Mai, Thailand
songsakecon@gmail.com

Abstract. In the traditional fuzzy logic, the expert's degree of certainty in a statement is described either by a number from the interval $[0,1]$ or by a subinterval of such an interval. To adequately describe the opinion of several experts, researchers proposed to use a union of the corresponding sets – which is, in general, more complex than an interval. In this paper, we prove that for such set-valued fuzzy sets, centroid defuzzification is equivalent to defuzzifying its interval hull.

As a consequence of this result, we prove that the centroid defuzzification of a *general* type-2 fuzzy set can be reduced to the easier-to-compute case when for each x, the corresponding fuzzy degree of membership is *convex*.

1 Formulation of the Problem

Outline of this section. Our main objective is to come up with a centroid defuzzification formula for multi-interval-valued fuzzy sets. Before we start describing our results and algorithms, let us briefly recall why we need centroid defuzzification and why we need multi-interval-valued fuzzy sets. To explain this need:

- we will start with the regular fuzzy sets,
- then we explain the need for interval-valued fuzzy sets, and
- the need for multi-interval-valued fuzzy sets;
- finally, we explain the need for centroid defuzzification for all these types of fuzzy sets.

Need for interval-valued fuzzy sets: a brief reminder. In the traditional fuzzy logic, an expert describes his or her degree of confidence in different statements by a number from the interval $[0,1]$. In particular, for statements like "x is small" corresponding to different values x, the corresponding degree $\mu(x)$ form a *membership function* describing the imprecise (fuzzy) concept like "small"; see, e.g., [1,6].

In many practical situations, experts are not comfortable describing their degree of confidence by an exact number; they feel more comfortable describing

© Springer International Publishing AG 2017
G. Sidorov and O. Herrera-Alcántara (Eds.): MICAI 2016, Part I, LNAI 10061, pp. 211–218, 2017.
DOI: 10.1007/978-3-319-62434-1_17

their degree of confidence by an interval – e.g., by an interval $[0.7, 0.8]$. In particular, for statements like "x is small", the corresponding interval-valued degrees of confidence $\left[\underline{\mu}(x), \overline{\mu}(x)\right]$ form an *interval-valued* membership function.

The intuitive meaning of this membership function is that in principle, we can have many different number-valued membership functions $\mu(x)$ as long as $\mu(x) \in \left[\underline{\mu}(x), \overline{\mu}(x)\right]$ for every x.

Another case when an interval-valued membership function naturally appears is when we ask several experts. For the same value x, different experts give, in general, different degrees of confidence $\mu_1(x)$, ..., $\mu_n(x)$. When experts are equally good, there is no reason to select one of these values, it make more sense to consider the interval $\left[\min_i \mu_i(x), \max_i \mu_i(x)\right]$ spanned by these values. This smallest interval containing the values $\mu_1(x), \dots, \mu_n(x)$ is also known as the *interval hull* of the corresponding finite set $\{\mu_1(x), \dots, \mu_n(x)\}$.

Need for multi-interval-valued fuzzy sets. Once each expert provides his or her degree $\mu_i(x)$ or interval-valued degree $\left[\underline{\mu}_i(x), \overline{\mu}_i(x)\right]$, then, instead of taking the interval hull of all these degrees, we can get a more adequate description of the experts' opinions if we simply take the *union* of these values and intervals. Such unions are known as *multi-intervals*. If for each x, the experts' degrees of confidence in the corresponding statement "x is small" is described by a multi-interval $M(x)$, then we get a multi-interval-valued membership function $M(x)$; see, e.g., [7].

Centroid defuzzification for regular fuzzy sets. In control (or, more generally, decision) applications, when for each possible value x of control, we know the degree $\mu(x)$ to which this value is reasonable, we then need to decide which control value c to apply.

In fuzzy applications, we usually select the value c for which the weighted mean square deviation from this value is the smallest possible:

$$\int_{\underline{L}}^{\overline{L}} \mu(x) \cdot (x - c)^2 \, dx \to \min_c,$$

where $\left[\underline{L}, \overline{L}\right]$ is the range of possible values of x. Differentiating this objective function with respect to the unknown c and equating the derivative to 0, we conclude that

$$c(\mu) = \frac{\displaystyle\int_{\underline{L}}^{\overline{L}} x \cdot \mu(x) \, dx}{\displaystyle\int_{\underline{L}}^{\overline{L}} \mu(x) \, dx}.$$

This formula is known as *centroid defuzzification*.

Centroid defuzzification for interval-valued fuzzy sets. As we have mentioned, an interval-valued fuzzy set $\left[\underline{\mu}(x), \overline{\mu}(x)\right]$ means that many different membership functions $\mu(x) \in \left[\underline{\mu}(x), \overline{\mu}(x)\right]$ are possible. For different possible membership functions $\mu(x)$, in general, we have different defuzzification results $c(\mu(x))$. It is therefore reasonable to find the set of all possible value of these results:

$$\{c(\mu) : \underline{\mu}(x) \leq \mu(x) \leq \overline{\mu}(x) \text{ for all } x\}.$$

It is known (see, e.g., [3–5]) that this range is always an interval $[\underline{c}, \overline{c}]$, where

$$\underline{c} = \frac{\displaystyle\int_{\underline{L}}^{x_-} x \cdot \overline{\mu}(x)\, dx + \int_{x_-}^{\overline{L}} x \cdot \underline{\mu}(x)\, dx}{\displaystyle\int_{\underline{L}}^{x_-} \overline{\mu}(x)\, dx + \int_{x_-}^{\overline{L}} \underline{\mu}(x)\, dx}$$

and

$$\overline{c} = \frac{\displaystyle\int_{\underline{L}}^{x_+} x \cdot \underline{\mu}(x)\, dx + \int_{x_+}^{\overline{L}} x \cdot \overline{\mu}(x)\, dx}{\displaystyle\int_{\underline{L}}^{x_+} \underline{\mu}(x)\, dx + \int_{x_+}^{\overline{L}} \overline{\mu}(x)\, dx}$$

for appropriate values x^- and x^+. These formulas underlie the known algorithms for computing the range $[\underline{c}, \overline{c}]$.

Formulation of the problem. Now, we are ready to formulate our problem. What if instead of an interval-values fuzzy set, we have a multi-interval-valued fuzzy set $M(x)$? What will then be the set

$$\{c(\mu) : \mu(x) \in M(x) \text{ for all } x\}?$$

2   Analysis of the Problem and the Main Result

Discussion. A multi-set is a union of finitely many one-points sets and (closed) intervals. Each of the united sets is closed, thus their union $M(x)$ is closed. In general, we will consider functions that assign, to each value x, a closed set $M(x) \subseteq [0, 1]$; see, e.g., [7].

Each such closed set contains its own infimum $\underline{M}(x) \stackrel{\text{def}}{=} \inf M(x)$ and supremum $\overline{M}(x) \stackrel{\text{def}}{=} \sup M(x)$. The interval hall of the set $M(x)$ is the interval $[\underline{M}(x), \overline{M}(x)]$.

We assume that this function $M(x)$ is defined for all the values x from some interval $[\underline{L}, \overline{L}]$. We also assume that the lower and upper bounds $\underline{M}(x)$ and $\overline{M}(x)$

are measurable functions. It turns out that under these conditions, the centroid defuzzification of the set-valued membership function $M(x)$ is equivalent to the centroid defuzzification of its interval hull $[\underline{M}(x), \overline{M}(x)]$. Let us formulate this result in precise terms.

Definition. *By a set-valued membership function, we mean a function M that assigns, to each real number from some interval $[\underline{L}, \overline{L}]$, a closed set $M(x) \subseteq [0, 1]$ for which the functions*

$$\underline{M}(x) = \inf M(x) \, and \, \overline{M}(x) = \sup M(x)$$

are measurable.

Proposition. *For the centroid defuzzification functional $c(\mu)$, we have*

$$\{c(\mu) : \mu(x) \in M(x) \, for \, all \, x\} = \{c(\mu) : \mu(x) \in [\inf M(x), \sup M(x)] \, for \, all \, x\}.$$

Comment. Thus, the result of applying centroid defuzzification to the original set-valued fuzzy set $M(x)$ is equivalent to applying the same centroid defuzzification to its interval hull $[\underline{M}(x), \overline{M}(x)]$.

Proof

$1°$. Let us first prove that out of all possible functions $\mu(x) \in M(x)$, the smallest and the largest possible values of $\mu(x)$ are attained when for each x, the value $\mu(x)$ is equal to either $\underline{M}(x)$ or to $\overline{M}(x)$.

It is sufficient to prove this result in the discrete case, when instead of the whole interval $[\underline{L}, \overline{L}]$, we have finitely many value $x_1, \ldots, x_n$: e.g., the values $x_i = \underline{L} + h \cdot (i - 1)$, where $h = \dfrac{\overline{L} - \underline{L}}{n - 1}$; the general case can be obtained when we take $n \to \infty$. In this discrete cases, instead of the whole membership function $\mu(x)$, we have n values $\mu(x_n)$, and the centroid defuzzification takes the form

$$c = \frac{\sum\limits_{i=1}^{n} x_i \cdot \mu(x_i) \cdot h}{\sum\limits_{i=1}^{n} \mu(x_i) \cdot h}.$$

Dividing both the numerator and the denominator of this expression by the common factor h, we get a simplified expression

$$c = \frac{\sum\limits_{i=1}^{n} x_i \cdot \mu(x_i)}{\sum\limits_{i=1}^{n} \mu(x_i)}.$$

Let us show that for each j, this expression is either monotonically increasing or monotonically decreasing as a function of $\mu(x_j)$. A monotonic function attains its maximum and its minimum on an interval on the endpoints of this interval, thus, the minimum and maximum are attained when either $\mu(x_j) = \underline{M}(x_j)$ or $\mu(x_j) = \overline{M}(x_j)$.

Let us prove the desired monotonicity. Indeed, the above expression for c can be described in the following equivalent form:

$$c = \frac{\sum_{i \neq j} x_i \cdot \mu(x_i) + x_j \cdot \mu(x_j)}{\sum_{i \neq j} \mu(x_i) + \mu(x_j)}.$$

If we subtract x_j from the right-hand side (and bring the difference to the common denominator) and then add x_j to the result, we get the following equivalent expression:

$$c = x_j + \frac{\sum_{i \neq j}(x_i - x_j) \cdot \mu(x_i)}{\sum_{i \neq j} \mu(x_i) + \mu(x_j)}.$$

The denominator is an increasing function of $\mu(x_i)$, and the numerator does not depend on $\mu(x_i)$ at all. Thus:

- if the numerator is positive, the expression is a decreasing function of $\mu(x_i)$, and
- if the numerator is negative, then the expression is an increasing function of $\mu(x_i)$.

The statement is proven.

2°. We have shown that the maximum and minimum of $c(\mu)$ – when for each x, we have $\mu(x) \in M(x)$ – is equal either to the smallest possible value $\underline{M}(x)$ or to the largest possible value $\overline{M}(x)$. Thus, the maximum and minimum of $c(\mu)$ over all $\mu(x) \in M(x)$ are equal to, correspondingly, the maximum and the minimum of $c(\mu)$ over all $\mu(x) \in \{\underline{M}(x), \overline{M}(x)\}$:

$$\overline{c} = \max\{c(\mu) : \mu(x) \in M(x) \text{ for all } x\} =$$
$$\max\left\{c(\mu) : \mu(x) \in \{\underline{M}(x), \overline{M}(x)\} \text{ for all } x\right\}$$

and

$$\underline{c} = \min\{c(\mu) : \mu(x) \in M(x) \text{ for all } x\} =$$
$$\min\left\{c(\mu) : \mu(x) \in \{\underline{M}(x), \overline{M}(x)\} \text{ for all } x\right\}.$$

As we have mentioned earlier, a similar property holds for interval-valued fuzzy sets, when instead of the restriction $\mu(x) \in M(x)$, we impose an interval restriction $\mu(x) \in [\underline{M}(x), \overline{M}(x)]$: here also,

$$\max\left\{c(\mu) : \mu(x) \in \left[\underline{M}(x), \overline{M}(x)\right] \text{ for all } x\right\} =$$
$$\max\left\{c(\mu) : \mu(x) \in \left\{\underline{M}(x), \overline{M}(x)\right\} \text{ for all } x\right\}$$

and

$$\min\left\{c(\mu) : \mu(x) \in \left[\underline{M}(x), \overline{M}(x)\right] \text{ for all } x\right\} =$$
$$\min\left\{c(\mu) : \mu(x) \in \left\{\underline{M}(x), \overline{M}(x)\right\} \text{ for all } x\right\}.$$

Thus, the maximum and minimum of $c(\mu)$ under the *set* condition $\mu(x) \in M(x)$ are equal to the maximum and minimum of $c(\mu)$ under the *interval* condition $\mu(x) \in \left[\underline{M}(x), \overline{M}(x)\right]$.

So, to complete our proof, we need to show that in both cases, every real number in between $\underline{c}$ and $\overline{c}$ belongs to the desired range, i.e., has the form $c(\mu)$ for an appropriate membership function $\mu(x)$, i.e., a membership function for which we have either $\mu(x) \in M(x)$ (in the set case) or $\mu(x) \in \left[\underline{M}(x), \overline{M}(x)\right]$ (in the interval case).

We will show that for every $c \in [\underline{c}, \overline{c}]$, we can select a function $\mu(x)$ for which $\mu(x) \in \left\{\underline{M}(x), \overline{M}(x)\right\}$ – this would guarantee both that $\mu(x) \in M(x)$ and that $\mu(x) \in \left[\underline{M}(x), \overline{M}(x)\right]$.

To prove the existence of such a function, let us start with the functions $\mu_-(x) \in \left\{\underline{M}(x), \overline{M}(x)\right\}$ and $\mu_+(x) \in \left\{\underline{M}(x), \overline{M}(x)\right\}$ for which $c(\mu_-) = \underline{c}$ and $c(\mu_+) = \overline{c}$. For each value $\ell \in [\underline{L}, \overline{L}]$, we can now consider an auxiliary function $\mu_\ell(x)$ which is:

- equal to $\mu_+(x)$ for $x \leq \ell$ and
- equal to $\mu_-(x)$ for $x > \ell$.

For each x, the value of $\mu_\ell(x)$ is equal to either the value $\mu_-(x)$ or to the value $\mu_+(x)$. Since both of these values are from the set $\left\{\underline{M}(x), \overline{M}(x)\right\}$, the value $\mu_\ell(x)$ also belongs to this set for all x.

Since we assumed that the functions $\underline{M}(x)$ and $\overline{M}(x)$ are measurable, we can conclude that the value $c(\mu_\ell)$ is a continuous function of ℓ.

When $\ell = \underline{L}$, the function $\mu_\ell(x)$ coincides with $\mu_-(x)$, and for $\ell = \overline{L}$, it coincides with $\mu_+(x)$. Thus, as ℓ changes from $\underline{L}$ to $\overline{L}$, the value of $c(\mu_\ell)$ continuously changes from $c(\mu_-) = \underline{c}$ to $c(\mu_+) = \overline{c}$. A continuous function attains all intermediate values, so for each $c \in [\underline{c}, \overline{c}]$, there indeed exists a value ℓ for which $c(\mu_\ell) = c$, for the corresponding function $\mu_\ell(x) \in \left\{\underline{M}(x), \overline{M}(x)\right\}$.

The statement is proven, and so is the proposition.

3 From Set-Valued to General Type-2 Fuzzy Sets

Type-2 fuzzy sets: reminder. Instead of considering, for each x, a crisp set $M(x)$ of possible values of the degree of confidence $\mu(x)$, it makes sense to consider a more general case, when this set of possible values of the degree is fuzzy. Such situations are known as *type-2 fuzzy sets*; see, e.g., [4,5].

In precise terms, for each x and for each real number $\mu \in [0,1]$, instead of deciding whether this number is a possible value of the degree or not, we now have a *degree* $d(\mu, x)$ describing to what extent the number μ is a possible expert's degree of confidence that x satisfies the given property (e.g., "is small").

Centroid defuzzification: general type-2 case. We have a functional $c(\mu)$ defined for crisp function $\mu(x)$. In fuzzy techniques, a natural way to extend this functional to fuzzy-valued membership functions – i.e., to type-2 fuzzy sets – is to use Zadeh's extension principle.

It is known that this principle can be equivalently described in terms of α-cut: for any function $y = f(x_1, \ldots)$ and for fuzzy sets $X_1, \ldots$, the α-cut $Y(\alpha) \stackrel{\text{def}}{=} \{y : \mu_Y(y) \geq \alpha\}$ of the result $Y = f(X_1, \ldots)$ of applying the function f to fuzzy sets $X_1, \ldots$ is equal to the range of the function on the alpha-cuts $X_i(\alpha) = \{x_i : \mu_i(x_i) \geq \alpha\}$ of the inputs X_i:

$$Y(\alpha) = f(X_1(\alpha), \ldots) = \{f(x_1, \ldots) : x_1 \in X_1(\alpha), \ldots\}.$$

In particular, for the centroid defuzzification, we start with a function $c(\mu)$ that depends on infinitely many real-valued inputs $\mu(x)$. For type-2 fuzzy sets, the inputs $\mu(x)$ are also fuzzy. Thus, the result of a centroid defuzzification is also a fuzzy set C. the α-cut $C(\alpha)$ of this fuzzy set C of defuzzification results is equal to the range of the values $c(\mu)$ under the condition that for all x, we have $\mu(x) \in M_x(\alpha) = \{\mu : d(\mu, x) \geq \alpha\}$.

Consequence of our main result: centroid defuzzification of a general type-2 fuzzy set can be reduced to the convex case. Our main result states that for each set-valued function $M(x)$, the range of the centroid defuzzification is equal to the range of its interval hull $\left[\underline{M}(x), \overline{M}(x)\right]$.

Thus, for each type-2 membership function $d(\mu, x)$, the range $C(\alpha)$ is equal to the range computed based on the interval hull $[\inf M_x(\alpha), \sup M_x(\alpha)]$ of the set $M_x(\alpha)$.

In other words, the result C of applying the centroid defuzzification $c(\mu)$ to the general type-2 fuzzy set is equal to the result of applying $c(\alpha)$ to an auxiliary fuzzy set in which each α-cut is a (convex) interval $[\inf M_x(\alpha), \sup M_x(\alpha)]$. Thus, *centroid defuzzification of a general type-2 fuzzy set can indeed be reduced to the convex case* – the case for which there exist efficient algorithms; see, e.g., [2].

Acknowledgments. We acknowledge the partial support of the Center of Excellence in Econometrics, Faculty of Economics, Chiang Mai University, Thailand. This work was also supported in part by the National Science Foundation grants HRD-0734825 and HRD-1242122 (Cyber-ShARE Center of Excellence) and DUE-0926721, and by an award "UTEP and Prudential Actuarial Science Academy and Pipeline Initiative" from Prudential Foundation.

The authors are thankful to all the participants of the 2016 IEEE World Congress on Computational Intelligence WCCI'2016 (Vancouver, Canada, July 24–29, 2016) for valuable discussions.

References

1. Klir, G., Yuan, B.: Fuzzy Sets and Fuzzy Logic. Prentice Hall, Upper Saddle River (1995)
2. Kreinovich, V.: From processing interval-valued fuzzy data to general type-2: towards fast algorithms. In: Proceedings of the IEEE Symposium on Advances in Type-2 Fuzzy Logic Systems, T2FUZZ 2011, Part of the IEEE Symposium Series on Computational Intelligence, Paris, France, pp. ix–xii, 11–15 April 2011
3. Lea, R., Kreinovich, V., Trejo, R.: Optimal interval enclosures for fractionally-linear functions, and their application to intelligent control. Reliable Comput. **2**(3), 265–286 (1996)
4. Mendel, J.M.: Uncertain Rule-Based Fuzzy Logic Systems: Introduction and New Directions. Prentice-Hall, Upper Saddle River (2001)
5. Mendel, J.M., Wu, D.: Perceptual Computing: Aiding People in Making Subjective Judgments. IEEE Press and Wiley, New York (2010)
6. Nguyen, H.T., Walker, E.A.: A First Course in Fuzzy Logic. Chapman and Hall/CRC, Boca Raton (2006)
7. Ruiz, G., Pomares, H., Rojas, I., Hagras, H.: Towards general forms of interval type-2 fuzzy logic systems. In: Proceedings of the 2016 IEEE World Congress on Computational Intelligence, Vancouver, Canada, 24–29 July 2016

Metric Spaces Under Interval Uncertainty: Towards an Adequate Definition

Mahdokht Afravi[1], Vladik Kreinovich[1(✉)],
and Thongchai Dumrongpokaphoan[2]

[1] Department of Computer Science, University of Texas at El Paso,
El Paso, TX 79968, USA
`mafravi@miners.utep.edu`, `vladik@utep.edu`
[2] Department of Mathematics, Faculty of Science,
Chiang Mai University, Chiang Mai, Thailand
`tcd43@hotmail.com`

Abstract. In many practical situations, we only know the bounds on the distances. A natural question is: knowing these bounds, can we check whether there exists a metric whose distance always lies within these bounds – or such a metric is not possible and thus, the bounds are inconsistent. In this paper, we provide an answer to this question. We also describe possible applications of this result to a description of opposite notions in commonsense reasoning.

1 An AI Problem and the Resulting Mathematical Problem

Starting point: commonsense negation vs. formal negation. Negation and opposites are an important part of our reasoning. Thus, to better understand human reasoning, it is desirable to analyze how we use negation.

The standard way to describe negation is to use mathematical logic. In mathematical logic, negation has a very precise meaning: a negation $\neg S$ of a statement S is true if and only if the statement S is false. This formal logical notion of a negation corresponds to the notion of a complement to a set: a complement $-S$ is the set of all the objects that do not belong to the original set S.

Similarly, in fuzzy logic (see, e.g., [7,8,10]):

– once we have a fuzzy set, i.e., a function μ_P that assigns, to each object x, a degree $\mu(x)$ to which this object satisfies a given imprecise property P (e.g., is small),
– then the negation is usually defined as a membership function

$$\mu_{\neg P}x = 1 - \mu_P(x).$$

The logical notion of negation corresponds to the intuitive idea of an opposite. However, in contrast to the formal negation – which is uniquely determined by the original concept – there can be many different opposite to a given notion,

© Springer International Publishing AG 2017
G. Sidorov and O. Herrera-Alcántara (Eds.): MICAI 2016, Part I, LNAI 10061, pp. 219–227, 2017.
DOI: 10.1007/978-3-319-62434-1_18

depending on a context. For example, depending on a context, the opposite to a man is either a boy or a woman (see, e.g., [9], where an interesting formalism is developed for describing opposites).

Why there may be several different opposites to the same notion: a natural explanation. In our opinion, the existence of several different opposites has a simple explanation: when we reason, we try our best to use simple, basic concepts. A formal negation of the notion of a man is *not* an intuitively simple concept. So, instead of using this complicated concept, we select one of the basic concepts: namely, the one which is the closest to the original negation.

Depending on the context, we may have different metrics, and thus, different concepts are the closest to the original negation.

Beyond negation. A similar idea can be applied to other logical connectives such as "and" and "or": instead of the original formal intersection or union, we the basic notion which is the closest to the corresponding formal result.

Comment. The very fact that, depending on the context, "and" and "or" may have different meanings, is well known. For example, one of the main motivations behind linear logic (see, e.g., [5,6]) was to formally explain the difference between different commonsense meanings of "and".

Let us formalize this idea. Let us describe this idea in precise terms. The distance is usually described as a *metric*, i.e., as a function $d : X \times X \to [0, \infty)$ that assigns, to every two objects a and b from the universal set X, a non-negative number $d(a, b)$ with the following properties:

– first, $d(a, b) = 0$ if and only if $a = b$;
– second, $d(a, b) = d(b, a)$, and
– finally, we must have the triangle inequality $d(a, c) \leq d(a, b) + d(b, c)$.

In the case of negation, we have a list of basic notions $A_1, \ldots, A_n$, and we have their negations $\neg A_1, \ldots, \neg A_n$. For each concept A_i, we need to select the concept A_j which is, in a given metric d, the closest to $\neg A_i$, i.e., for which

$$d(A_j, \neg A_i) = \min_k d(A_k, \neg A_i).$$

Similarly, to describe the concept corresponding to $A_i \& A_j$, we need to select a concept A_k which is the closest to the conjunction $A_i \& A_j$:

$$d(A_k, A_i \& A_j) = \min_\ell d(A_\ell, A_i \& A_j).$$

The resulting mathematical problem: first approximation. In principle, in the case of n concepts and their negations, we have $2n$ objects, thus, we can have distances $d(A_i, A_j)$, $d(A_i, \neg A_j)$, and $d(\neg A_i, \neg A_j)$. To make the above selection of the opposite A_j to A_i (or of the corresponding disjunction), we do not need to know the distances $d(A_i, A_j)$ and $d(\neg A_i, \neg A_j)$, we only need to know the distances $d(A_i, \neg A_j)$.

While we *do not need* to know the values $d(A_i, A_j)$ and $d(\neg A_i, \neg A_j)$, to analyze all possible situations, we *do need* to make sure that the distances $d(A_i, \neg A_j)$ are such that for *some* values $d(A_i, A_j)$ and $d(\neg A_i, \neg A_j)$, we get the triangle inequality and all the properties of the metric.

Similarly, to describe a commonsense "and", we may not need to know the distances $d(A_i, A_j)$ and $d(A_i \& A_j, A_k \& A_\ell)$, but we must make sure that there exist some values that, combined with the known values $d(A_i, A_j \& A_k)$, form a metric.

The mathematical problem: towards a final formulation. The above description assumes that a person can give us the exact number $d(A_i, \neg A_j)$ describing the similarity between the basic concept A_i and the negation $\neg A_j$. In reality, people can usually only make approximate judgments about their opinions. Thus, at best, a person will provide us with some *bounds* $\underline{d}(A_i, \neg A_j)$ and $\overline{d}(A_i, \neg A_j)$ so that the actual (unknown) distance lies somewhere in the interval

$$[\underline{d}(A_i, \neg A_j), \overline{d}(A_i, \neg A_j)].$$

Thus, to each pair $(a, b) = (A_i, \neg A_j)$, instead of a real number $d(a, b)$, we assign an interval $[\underline{d}(a, b), \overline{d}(a, b)]$ of possible values. We are then facing the same problem: when does there exist a metric $d(a, b)$ for which, for all these pairs (a, b), we have $d(a, b) \in [\underline{d}(a, b), \overline{d}(a, b)]$?

Since we allow intervals anyway, we can describe the fact that we know nothing about the distances such $d(A_i, A_j)$ by assigning to each such pair $(a, b) = (A_i, A_j)$, an infinite interval $[0, \infty)$. Thus, we arrive at the following problem.

Resulting mathematical problem. We have a final set X. For every two elements a and b from this set, we have an interval $[\underline{d}(a, b), \overline{d}(a, b)]$, where the upper bound $\overline{d}(a, b)$ may be infinite.

We would like to find the conditions on these intervals which are equivalent to the existence of a metric $d(a, b)$ for which $d(a, b) \in [\underline{d}(a, b), \overline{d}(a, b)]$ for all a and b.

An important particular case. An important particular case of this problem is when – like in case of negation or disjunction – the set X consists of two disjoint subsets X^+ and X^-, so that we only know the distances between the elements of X^+ and X^-.

In the negation example, X^+ is the set of all basic notions A_i, and X^- is the set of all negations $\neg A_i$. In the disjunction example, X^+ is the set of all basic notions, while X^- is the set of all possible formal disjunctions $A_i \& A_j$, etc.

2   Towards Solving the Mathematical Problem: How are Interval-Valued Metric Spaces Defined Now

Current definition: motivations. The need to extend metric spaces to the case of interval uncertainty has been recognized for a few decades already. There exist natural interval-valued extensions of metric spaces; see, e.g., [1–4]. Before we give the corresponding definition, let us first explain the motivations behind this definition.

The main property of a metric $d(a, b)$ is that it must satisfy the triangle inequality $d(a, c) \leq d(a, b) + d(b, c)$ for all a, b, and c.

In the case of interval uncertainty, we do not know the exact values $d(a, b)$, $d(b, c)$, and $d(a, c)$, we only know the intervals $[\underline{d}(a, b), \overline{d}(a, b)]$, $[\underline{d}(b, c), \overline{d}(b, c)]$, and $[\underline{d}(a, c), \overline{d}(a, c)]$ that contain these values. It is therefore reasonable to require that for all a, b, and c, the corresponding three intervals are selected in such a way that the triangle inequality is satisfied for some values from the corresponding intervals.

This condition is easy to describe. When $d(a, b) \in [\underline{d}(a, b), \overline{d}(a, b)]$ and $d(b, c) \in [\underline{d}(b, c), \overline{d}(b, c)]$, then the possible values of the sum $d(a, b) + d(b, c)$ form the interval $[\underline{d}(a, b) + \underline{d}(b, c), \overline{d}(a, b) + \overline{d}(b, c)]$. A value can be smaller than one of the values from this interval if it is smaller than its upper bound $\overline{d}(a, b) + \overline{d}(b, c)$.

Thus, the triangle inequality is satisfied if at least one value $d(a, c)$ from the interval $[\underline{d}(a, c), \overline{d}(a, c)]$ is smaller than or equal to the sum $\overline{d}(a, b) + \overline{d}(b, c)$. Of course:

- if a value $d(a, c)$ from the interval $[\underline{d}(a, c), \overline{d}(a, c)]$ is smaller than equal that the sum, then the lower endpoint $\underline{d}(a, c) \leq d(a, c)$ is also smaller than or equal to the sum;
- vice versa, if the lower endpoint $\underline{d}(a, c)$ is smaller than or equal to the sum, then, since this endpoint belongs to the interval $[\underline{d}(a, c), \overline{d}(a, c)]$, we have a value $d(a, c) \in [\underline{d}(a, c), \overline{d}(a, c)]$ which is smaller than or equal to the sum.

Thus, the existence of the values $d(a, b) \in [\underline{d}(a, b), \overline{d}(a, b)]$, $d(b, c) \in [\underline{d}(b, c), \overline{d}(b, c)]$, and $d(a, c) \in [\underline{d}(a, c), \overline{d}(a, c)]$ for which the triangle inequality is satisfied is equivalent to the following inequality

$$\underline{d}(a, c) \leq \overline{d}(a, b) + \overline{d}(b, c).$$

And this is how interval-valued metric spaces are defined now: that the above inequality holds for all possible a, b, and c.

Problem with the current definition. While every interval-valued metric that contains the actual metric $d(a, b)$ must satisfy the above inequality, it turns out that this inequality is not sufficient to guarantee that there is a metric inside the corresponding intervals.

Indeed, let us consider the case when $d(A_i, \neg A_j) = 1$ for all i and j except for $d(A_1, \neg A_1) = 4$, and when for $d(A_i, A_j)$ and $d(\neg A_i, \neg A_j)$ we only know that these values are in the infinite interval $[0, \infty)$.

In this case, the above inequality is trivially satisfied, since there are no a, b, and c for which for all three distances $d(a, b)$, $d(b, c)$, and $d(a, c)$, there will be non-trivial interval. Indeed:

- If we have a finite intervals for $d(a, b)$, this means that a and b belong to different subsets X^+ and X^-.
- Similarly, if $d(b, c)$ is finite, this means that b and c belong to different subsets.

– Thus, a and c belong to the same subset – and thus, we only have an infinite bound for $d(a, c)$.

On the other hand, if we have a metric $d(a, b) \in [\underline{d}(a, b), \overline{d}(a, b)]$, then from the triangle inequality, we would be able to conclude that

$$d(A_1, \neg A_1) \leq d(A_1, \neg A_2) + d(A_2, \neg A_2) + d(A_2, \neg A_1).$$

Here, the right-hand side is 3, but $d(A_1, \neg A_1) = 4 > 3$.

So, the usual definition of an interval-valued metric space is satisfied, but still no metric is possible. Thus, to solve our problem, we need to come up with a more adequate definition.

3   Solving the Mathematical Problem: Definition and the Main Result

Definition 1. *By an* interval-valued metric *on a set X, we mean a mapping that assigns, to each pair of elements a, b from the set X, an interval $[\underline{d}(a, b), \overline{d}(a, b)]$ with $\underline{d}(a, b)$ that satisfies the following properties:*

– *first, $d(a, a) = [0, 0]$ and $\overline{d}(a, b) > 0$ for $a \neq b$;*
– *second, $\underline{d}(a, b) = \underline{d}(b, a)$ and $\overline{d}(a, b) = \overline{d}(a, b)$, and*
– *finally, for every finite chain $a_1, a_2, \ldots, a_m$, we have*

$$\underline{d}(a_1, a_m) \leq \overline{d}(a_1, a_2) + \overline{d}(a_2, a_3) + \ldots + \overline{d}(a_{m-1}, a_m).$$

Discussion. It is easy to check that if we have an interval-valued metric that contains the actual metric, then the above version of triangle inequality must be satisfied. It turns our that, vice versa, once this inequality is satisfied, there exists a metric contained in all these intervals.

Proposition 1. *For every interval-valued metric space X with an interval metric $[\underline{d}(a, b), \overline{d}(a, b)]$, there exists a metric $d(a, b)$ for which $d(a, b) \in [\underline{d}(a, b), \overline{d}(a, b)]$ for all a and b.*

Proof
1°. Let us first consider the case when every two elements $a, b \in X$ can be connected by a chain $a = a_1, a_2, \ldots, a_{m-1}, a_m = b$ for which $\overline{d}(a_i, a_{i+1}) < +\infty$ for every i.

In this case, let us take

$$d(a, b) = \inf \left\{ \sum_{i=1}^{m-1} \overline{d}(a_i, a_{i+1}) \right\},$$

where the infimum is taken over all the chains connecting a and b.

2°. Let us prove that $\underline{d}(a, b) \leq d(a, b) \leq \overline{d}(a, b)$ for all a and b.

Indeed, by our version of the triangle inequality, $\underline{d}(a,b)$ is smaller than or equal than each of the sums $\sum\limits_{i=1}^{m-1} \overline{d}(a_i, a_{i+1})$. Thus, it is smaller than or equal to the smallest of these sums, i.e., indeed, $\underline{d}(a,b) \leq d(a,b)$.

On the other hand, the chain $a_1 = a$, $a_2 = b$ is one of the possible chains connecting a ad b. For this chain, the sum $\sum\limits_{i=1}^{m-1} \overline{d}(a_i, a_{i+1})$ is simply equal to $\overline{d}(a,b)$. Since $d(a,b)$ is the smallest of these sums, we thus conclude that

$$d(a,b) \leq \overline{d}(a,b).$$

3°. Let us now prove that the function $d(a,b)$ satisfies the triangle inequality, i.e., that $d(a,c) \leq d(a,b) + d(b,c)$. Indeed, let $a = a_1, a_2, \ldots, a_m = b$ be a chain connecting a and b for which the sum is the smallest (and is equal to $d(a,b)$). Let $b = b_1, \ldots, b_p = c$ be the chain connecting b and c for which the sum is the smallest – and is equal to $d(b,c)$. Then, for the combined chain $a_1, a_2, \ldots, a_m = b_1, b_2, \ldots, b_p$ the sum is equal to the sum of the sums corresponding to the two chains, i.e., to $d(a,b) + d(b,c)$. Since $d(a,v)$ is the smallest over all possible chains – not necessarily passing through b – we thus have $d(a,c) \leq d(a,b) + d(b,c)$.

4°. Let us now consider the general case, when the relation

"a and b can be connected by a chain in which $d(a_i, a_{i+1}) < +\infty$"

divides the original finite set X into several equivalence classes.

Within each equivalence class, the above formula for $d(a,b)$ describes a metric. Let us select a point within each equivalent class. For each element $a \in X$, let us describe the point selected for the corresponding equivalent class by a_0.

For elements a and b that belong to different equivalent classes, let us defined the distance $d(a,b)$ as $d(a,b) \stackrel{\text{def}}{=} d(a, a_0) + d(b, b_0) + 1$. Let us show that thus extended distance satisfies the triangle inequality $d(a,c) \leq d(a,b) + d(b,c)$ for every triple (a,b,c).

To prove this inequality, let us list all possible cases.

- First, we need to consider the case when all three elements a, b, and c belong to the same equivalence class. In this case, the triangle inequality follows from the fact that on each equivalence class, $d(a,b)$ is a metric.
- The next case when two of the elements belong to the same equivalence class, while the third element belongs to a different equivalence class. We have to consider two subcases of this case:
  - the subcase when a and c belong to the same equivalence class, and
  - the subcase when a and b belong to the same equivalence class (the subcase when b and c belong to the same equivalence class is similar).
- Finally, we need to consider the case when all three elements a, b, and c belong to different equivalence classes.

Let us consider these cases one by one.

4.1°. Let us first consider the case when a and c belong to the same equivalence class (so $a_0 = c_0$), and b belongs to a different equivalent class.

In this case, the desired inequality has the form

$$d(a, c) \leq d(a, a_0) + d(b, b_0) + 1 + d(b, b_0) + d(c, a_0) + 1.$$

This is indeed true: from the triangle inequality for the equivalence class containing a and c, we get $d(a, c) \leq d(a, a_0) + d(c, a_0)$. Since $d(b, b_0) \geq 0$, we get the desired inequality

$$d(a, c) \leq d(a, a_0) + d(c, a_0) \leq d(a, a_0) + d(b, b_0) + 1 + d(b, b_0) + d(c, a_0) + 1.$$

4.2°. Let us now consider the case when a and b belong to the same equivalence class (so $a_0 = b_0$), and c belongs to a different equivalence class.

In this case, the desired inequality takes the form

$$d(a, a_0) + d(c, c_0) + 1 \leq d(a, b) + d(b, a_0) + d(c, c_0) + 1.$$

Indeed, for a, c and a_0, we have the triangle inequality $d(a, a_0) \leq d(a, b) + d(b, a_0)$. By adding $d(c, c_0) + 1$ to both sides, we get the desired inequality.

4.3°. Finally, let us consider the case when all three elements a, b, and c belong to different equivalence classes. In this case, the desired inequality has the form

$$d(a, a_0) + d(c, c_0) + 1 \leq d(a, a_0) + d(b, b_0) + 1 + d(b, b_0) + d(c, c_0) + 1.$$

Indeed, the right-hand side of this inequality is obtained from the left-hand side by adding the sum $2d(b, b_0) + 1$. Since $d(b, b_0) \geq 0$, the added sum is always positive, so the inequality is indeed always true.

We have considered all possible cases, so the proposition is proven.

4 Auxiliary Result: What About the Original Case When We Have Two Disjoint Subsets

Now that we have proven a general result, let us consider the case when the set X is divided into two disjoint sets.

Proposition 2. *Let a set X be a union of two disjoint subsets X^+ and X^-. Assume that we know the values $d(a, b) \geq 0$ for every pair (a, b) in which $a \in X^+$ and $b \in X^-$. Then, the following two conditions are equivalent to each other:*

– there exist a metric $d(a, b)$ whose restriction to pairs $(a \in X^+, b \in X^-)$ coincides withe the given values, and
– for every $a, a' \in X^+$ and $b, b' \in X^-$, we have

$$d(a, b') \leq d(a, a') + d(b, a') + d(b, b').$$

Proof. If there is a metric extending given values, then the above inequality follows from the triangle inequality: $d(a, b') \leq d(a, a') + d(b, b')$ and $d(b, b') \leq d(b, a') + d(b, b')$, hence indeed $d(a, b') \leq d(a, a') + d(b, a') + d(b, b')$.

Vice versa, let us assume that the above equality is always satisfied. Let us then show that the given values $a(a, b)$ satisfy the inequality from Proposition 1. This case is a particular case of the general interval-valued metric space, when we have $\underline{d}(a, b) = \overline{d}(a, b) = d(a, b)$ when a and b belong to different subsets and $\underline{d}(a, b) = 0$ and $\overline{d}(a, b)$ when a and b belong to different subsets.

If a and b belong to the same subset, then $\underline{d}(a, b) = 0$ and the condition from Proposition 1 is trivially satisfied.

If a and b belong to different subsets, this means that $a = a_1$ and a_2 belong to different subsets, a_2 and a_3 belong to different subsets, etc. In other words, $a_1, a_3, \ldots$ belong to one subset, while a_2, a_4, etc. belong to the opposite subset. The above inequality implies that

$$d(a, b) = \underline{d}(a, b) \leq \overline{d}(a, a_2) + \overline{d}(a_2, a_3) + \overline{d}(a_3, b) = d(a, a_2) + d(a_2, a_3) + d(a_3, b).$$

Similarly, $d(a_3, b) \leq d(a_3, a_4) + d(a_4, a_5) + d(a_5, b)$, hence

$$d(a, b) \leq d(a_1, a_2) + \ldots + d(a_5, b),$$

etc., so we get the desired inequality for chains for arbitrary length.

Since all the inequalities from Proposition 1 are satisfied, by Proposition 1, there exists the desired metric. The proposition is proven.

Acknowledgments. We acknowledge the partial support of the Center of Excellence in Econometrics, Faculty of Economics, Chiang Mai University, Thailand. This work was also supported in part by the National Science Foundation grants HRD-0734825 and HRD-1242122 (Cyber-ShARE Center of Excellence) and DUE-0926721, and by an award "UTEP and Prudential Actuarial Science Academy and Pipeline Initiative" from Prudential Foundation.

The authors are thankful to all the participants of the 2016 IEEE World Congress on Computational Intelligence WCCI'2016 (Vancouver, Canada, July 24–29, 2016), especially to Javier Montero, for valuable discussions.

References

1. Coppola, C., Pacelli, T.: Interval semimetric spaces for approximate distances. In: Proceedings of the 2005 Conference of the European Society for Fuzzy Logic and Technology, EUSFLAT 2015, pp. 1263–1268 (2015)
2. Coppola, C., Pacelli, T.: Approximate distances, pointless geometry, and incomplete information. Fuzzy Sets Syst. **157**, 2371–2383 (2006)
3. Gerla, G.: Poinless metric spaces. J. Symb. Logic **55**, 207–219 (1990)
4. Gerla, G.: Pointless geometries. In: Bueckenhout, F. (ed.) Handbook of Incidence Geometry, pp. 1015–1031. Elsevier, Amsterdam (1994)
5. Di Cosmo, R., Miller, D.: Linear logic. In: Zalta, E.N. (ed.) The Stanford Encyclopedia of Philosophy. Spring (2016). http://plato.stanford.edu/archives/spr2016/entries/logic-linear/

6. Girard, J.-Y.: Linear logic. Theor. Comput. Sci. **50**, 1–102 (1987)
7. Klir, G., Yuan, B.: Fuzzy Sets and Fuzzy Logic. Prentice Hall, Upper Saddle River (1995)
8. Nguyen, H.T., Walker, E.A.: A First Course in Fuzzy Logic. Chapman and Hall/CRC, Boca Raton (2006)
9. Tinguaro Rodríguez, J., Franco, C., Gómez, D., Montero, J.: Paired structures, imprecision types and two-level knowledge representation by means of opposites. In: Atanassov, K.T., et al. (eds.) Novel Developments in Uncertainty Representation and Processing. AISC, vol. 401, pp. 3–15. Springer, Cham (2016). doi:10.1007/978-3-319-26211-6_1
10. Zadeh, L.A.: Fuzzy sets. Inf. Control **8**, 338–353 (1965)

A Study of Parameter Dynamic Adaptation with Fuzzy Logic for the Grey Wolf Optimizer Algorithm

Luis Rodríguez, Oscar Castillo[(✉)], and José Soria

Tijuana Institute of Technology, Tijuana, Mexico
ocastillo@tectijuana.mx

Abstract. The main goal of this paper is to present a general study of the Grey Wolf Optimizer algorithm. We perform tests to determine in the first part which parameters are candidates to be dynamically adjusted and in the second stage to determine which are the parameters that have the greatest effect in the performance of the algorithm. We also present a justification and results of experiments as well as the benchmark functions that were used for the tests that are presented. In addition we are presenting a simple fuzzy system with the results obtained based on this general study.

Keywords: Grey Wolf Optimizer · Fuzzy logic · Dynamic parameter adaptation

1 Introduction

Nowadays computer science is solving problems through their different areas, depending on the complexity of the problem and the expected results comes the idea to optimize (minimize or maximize) the solution to a problem.

Researchers lately have turned to meta-heuristics because they can have superior abilities than conventional optimization techniques, and this is mainly due to their ability to avoid a local optimum result.

Optimization techniques based on meta-heuristics have become very popular over the past two decades, for example the Genetic Algorithm (GA) [1], Particle Swarm Optimization (PSO) [2], Ant Colony Optimization (ACO) [3] and the Artificial Bee Colony (ABC) algorithm [4]. In addition to the huge amount of theoretical work, these optimization techniques have been used in various areas of application. The answer to why they have become so popular can be summarized into four main reasons: simplicity, flexibility, derivative free mechanism, and because they have more ability to avoid local optima.

This paper is organized as follows: Sect. 2 describes the original Grey Wolf Optimizer algorithm. Section 3 describes the Benchmark Functions, Sect. 4 shows the experiments and results and Sect. 5 offers the Conclusions.

G. Sidorov and O. Herrera-Alcántara (Eds.): MICAI 2016, Part I, LNAI 10061, pp. 228–238, 2017.
DOI: 10.1007/978-3-319-62434-1_19

2 Grey Wolf Optimizer

The Grey Wolf Optimizer algorithm (GWO) [5] is a meta-heuristic that was originated in 2014 created by Seyedali Mirjalili, inspired basically because in the literature there was not a Swarm Intelligence (SI) [6] technique based on the Grey Wolf hunting features. Meta-heuristic techniques nowadays can be classified as follows:

- Evolutionary (based on the concepts of evolution in nature) [7]: Genetic Algorithms (GA), Evolutionary Programming (EP), and Genetic Programming (GP).
- Based on Physics (imitate the physical rules) [8]: Big-Bang Big Crunch (BBBC), Gravitational Search Algorithm (GSA), and Artificial Chemical Reactions Optimization Algorithm (ACROA).
- Swarm Intelligence (Social Behavior of swarms, herds, flocks or schools of creatures in nature) [9]: Particle Swarm Optimization (PSO), Ant Colony Optimization (ACO), and the Bat-inspired Algorithm (BA).

The NFL Theorem [10] (No Free Lunch) has logically proved that there is no meta-heuristic appropriately suited for solving all optimization problems (Wolpert and Macready in 1997).

For example, a particular meta-heuristic can give very promising results for a set of problems, but the same algorithm can show poor performance on a set of different problems. Therefore exists a diversity of techniques and new meta-heuristic are proposed for solving optimization problems.

2.1 Grey Wolf Optimizer

The hierarchy of leaders and the mechanism of the grey wolf hunting are illustrated in the next pyramid (Fig. 1).

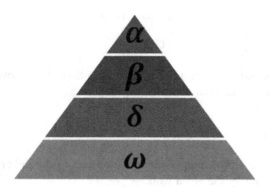

Fig. 1. Hierarchy pyramid.

In addition we can say that the social hierarchy of the grey wolf in the group of hunters has a very interesting social behavior.

According to C. Muro [11] the main phases of the grey wolf hunting are:

- Tracking, chasing, and approaching the prey.
- Pursuing, encircling, and harassing the prey until it stops moving.
- Attack towards the prey.

2.2 Social Hierarchy

In order to mathematically model the social hierarchy of wolves when designing the GWO, we consider the fittest solutions as the alpha (α) wolves. Consequently, the second and third best solutions are called beta (β) and delta (δ) respectively. The rest of the candidate solutions are assumed to be omega (ω). In the GWO algorithm the hunting (optimization) is guided by α, β, and δ. The ω wolves follow these three wolves.

2.3 Encircling Prey

As mentioned above, grey wolves encircle prey during the hunt. In order to mathematically model encircling behavior the following equations are proposed:

$$D = \left\| C \cdot X_p(t) - X(t) \right\| \qquad (1)$$

$$X(t + 1) = X_p(t) - AD \qquad (2)$$

Where t indicates the current iteration, A and C are coefficients, X_p is the position vector of the prey, and X indicates the position vector of a grey wolf.

The A and C coefficients are calculated as follows:

$$A = 2a \cdot r_1 - a \qquad (3)$$

$$C = 2 \cdot r_2 \qquad (4)$$

Where the components of a are linearly decreased from 2 to 0 over the course of iterations and r_1, r_2 are random numbers in [0, 1].

2.4 Hunting

Grey wolves have the ability to recognize the location of prey and encircle them. The hunt is usually guided by the alpha wolf.

In order to mathematically simulate the hunting behavior of grey wolves, we assume that the alpha (best candidate solution), beta and delta have better knowledge about the potential location of prey. Therefore, we save the first three best solutions obtained so far and force the other search agents (including the omegas) to update their positions according to the position of the best search agents. The following equations have been proposed in this regard.

$$\mathbf{D}_\alpha = \|\mathbf{C}_1 \cdot \mathbf{X}_\alpha - \mathbf{X}\|, \mathbf{D}_\beta = \|\mathbf{C}_2 \cdot \mathbf{X}_\beta - \mathbf{X}\|, \mathbf{D}_\delta = \|\mathbf{C}_3 \cdot \mathbf{X}_\delta - \mathbf{X}\| \tag{5}$$

$$\mathbf{X}_1 = \mathbf{X}_\alpha - \mathbf{A}_1 \cdot (\mathbf{D}_\alpha), \mathbf{X}_2 = \mathbf{X}_\beta - \mathbf{A}_2 \cdot (\mathbf{D}_\beta), \mathbf{X}_3 = \mathbf{X}_\delta - \mathbf{A}_3 \cdot (\mathbf{D}_\delta) \tag{6}$$

$$\mathbf{X}(t + 1) = \frac{\mathbf{X}_1 + \mathbf{X}_2 + \mathbf{X}_3}{3} \tag{7}$$

Equation 7 represents the updating of the positions based on the best three wolves, where X_1, X_2 and X_3, represent the alpha, beta and delta wolves respectively, and X $(t + 1)$ represents an omega wolf that should move where the leaders of the pack (center) indicate.

2.5   Attacking and Searching the Prey

Based on the main equations we can conclude interesting behaviors in the algorithm for example regarding the exploration and exploitation.

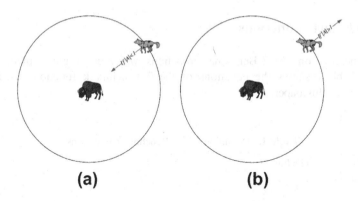

Fig. 2. Attacking prey versus searching for prey

When random values of A are in $[-1, 1]$, the next position of a search agent can be in any place between its current position and the position of the prey. Figure 2(a) shows that $|A| < 1$ forces the wolves to attack towards the prey.

(a) If $|A| < 1$ then attacking prey (exploitation)
(b) If $|A| > 1$ then searching for prey (exploration)

In addition it is important to say that the "C" coefficient also represents the exploration in the algorithm because it represents a random movement of a grey wolf in searching for the prey, and indirectly the exploitation, if, in the next position is near to the prey. Figure 3 shows the pseudocode of the algorithm.

```
Initialize the grey wolf population Xᵢ(i = 1, 2, ..., n)
Initialize a, A and C
Calculate the fitness of each search agent
Xα = the best search agent
Xβ = the second best agent
Xδ = the third best search agent
while (t < Max number of iterations)
        for each search agent
                    Update the position of the current
                    search agent by equation (7)
        end for
        Update a, A and C
        Calculate the fitness of all search agents
        Update Xα, Xβ and Xδ
        t = t+ 1
end while
return Xα
```

Fig. 3. Pseudocode of the algorithm

3 Benchmark Functions

In this paper we consider 7 Benchmark functions, which are briefly explained below
[12–15]. Table 1 shows the equations of the 7 benchmark functions used in the
experiments of this paper.

Table 1. Definition of the Benchmark Functions

Name	Definition
Sphere	$f(x) = \sum\limits_{i=1}^{n} x_i^2$
Rosenbrock	$f(x) = \sum\limits_{i=1}^{n-1} \left[100\left(x_{i+1} - x_i^2\right)^2 + (x_1 - 1)^2 \right]$.
Quartic	$f(x) = \sum\limits_{i=1}^{n} i x_i^4 + random[0, 1]$
Schwefel	$f(x) = \sum\limits_{i=1}^{n} -x_i \sin\left(\sqrt{|x_i|}\right)$
Rastrigin	$f(x) = \sum\limits_{i=1}^{n} \left[x_i^2 - 10\cos(2\pi x_i) + 10 \right]$
Ackley	$f(x) = 20\,exp\left(-0.2\sqrt{\frac{1}{n}\sum\limits_{i=1}^{n} x_i^2}\right) - exp\left(\frac{1}{n}\sum\limits_{i=1}^{n} \cos(2\pi x_i)\right) + 20 + e$
Griewank	$f(x) = \frac{1}{4000}\sum\limits_{i=1}^{n} x_1^2 - \prod\limits_{i=1}^{n} \cos\left(\frac{x_i}{\sqrt{i}}\right) + 1$

In the following experiments we present two classes for the benchmark functions

- Unimodal
- Multimodal

Also it is important to say that we analyze with the two classifications of the benchmark functions because the objective is that this algorithm can solve general problems and analyze its performance with different problems.

In this paper we analyze three unimodal benchmark functions (Sphere, Rosenbrock and Quartic respectively) and four multimodal benchmark functions (Schwefel, Rastrigin, Ackley and Griewank respectively).

4   Experiments and Results

The parameters that we can consider in the area of optimization are the coefficients of the algorithm, which are the values of A and C. The parameters for the experiments are presented by "a", and "C" respectively.

4.1   Results, Experiments and Analysis of the "a" and "C" Parameters

In the original paper the author does not justify the range for the "a" and "C" parameters, so we decided to analyze the performance of the parameters with other ranges. The original ranges in both parameters are [0, 2], so we manually perform tests with values from 0 to 3, with an increase of 0.1 for each parameter and we perform the experiments of 30 runs for each benchmark function in order to support the results by a hypothesis test. Figure 4 shows an example of the averages obtained by these experiments for the sphere and quartic functions respectively.

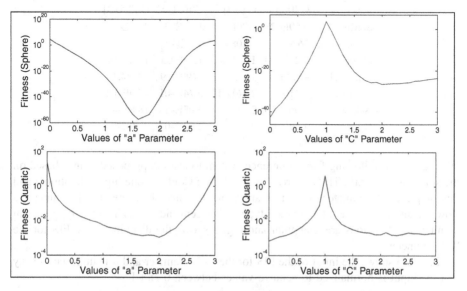

Fig. 4. Example of plots of the results of the general study

The conclusion that we have obtained with the study is a new range for the "a" and "C" parameters which are: for the "a" parameter the new range is [0.5, 2.5] which was the range where this parameter obtained better performance in the analyzed benchmark functions. In the "C" parameter we can note that there are two possible ranges for the optimization algorithm. When the function has one optimal solution (for example 0) the values that work best for that problem are in a range of [0, 0.5] and when the function has more than one optimal point, it can be observed in the experiments that the best values for "C" parameter, can also be higher values, in this case the explored range was [2.5, 3].

4.2   Summary of the Results

Tables 2 and 3 contain general information on the results with the three analyzed ranges (original, explored and proposed)

Table 2. Summary of results with the "a" parameter

Function	a [0,2]	a [0,3]	a [0.5,2.5]
Sphere	6.59E–28	7.16E–23	**1.15E–30**
Rosenbrock	26.8126	**26.7090**	27.0824
Quartic	2.21E–03	2.08E–03	**1.64E–03**
Schwefel	–6123.10	–5453.34	**–3972.06**
Rastrigin	0.3105	2.6729	**1.44E–12**
Ackley	**1.06E–13**	3.3964	6.1064
Griewank	4.49E–03	3.61E–03	**1.38E–03**

Table 3. Summary of results with the "C" parameter

Function	C [0,2]	C [0,3]	C [0, 0.5]	C [2.5, 3]
Sphere	6.59E–28	1.90E–32	**1.17E–35**	2.03E–25
Rosenbrock	**26.81**	27.0841	27.4340	27.2901
Quartic	2.21E–03	**1.43E–03**	1.53E–03	1.58E–03
Schwefel	–6123.10	–5270.75	–4997.29	**–4274.15**
Rastrigin	0.3105	**2.46E–14**	6.74E–01	4.79E–01
Ackley	1.06E–13	3.61E–14	**3.05E–14**	18.8594
Griewank	4.49E–03	**0**	2.03E–03	4.79E–04

We present the following fuzzy inference system to test the proposed ranges based on the study in this work. The features are as follows: Contains one input (iterations) and one output ("a" parameter) and these are granulated into three membership functions (low, medium, high), is of Mamdani type, it has centroid defuzzification type and all membership functions are triangular and Fig. 5 shows the diagram of the FIS for the "a" parameter.

Figure 6 shows the input of the FIS for the "a" parameter and it is important to say that the input is normalized to achieve values between 0 and 1.

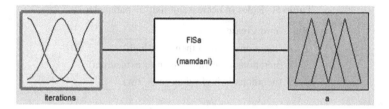

Fig. 5. FIS of the "a" parameter

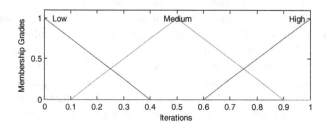

Fig. 6. FIS of the "a" parameter

Figure 7 shows the output of the FIS for the "a" parameter, which is the value of "a" and it is important to remember that we have three different ranges for this output.

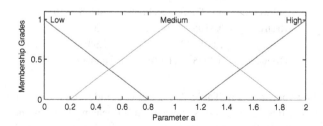

Fig. 7. Output of FIS of "a" parameter

The Fuzzy system rules are shown in Tables 4 and 5. It is important to say that the same specifications and rules of the fuzzy system were implemented also for the "C" parameter.

Table 4. Rules in increase of the "a" parameter

Rules in increase
1.- if (iterations is low) then (a is low)
2.- if (iterations is medium) then (a is medium)
3.- if (iterations is high) then (a is high)

Table 5. Rules in decrease of the "a" parameter

Rules in decrease
1.- if (iterations is low) then (a is high)
2.- if (iterations is medium) then (a is medium)
3.- if (iterations is high) then (a is low)

Finally we present a comparison between the original results and the results of the proposed ranges for "a" and "C" parameters with fuzzy logic. For these experiments the GWO algorithm was executed 30 times on each benchmark function with 30 dimensions and the results are the averages of the 30 executions and the letters at one side of the range refers to "I" for rules in increment and "D" for rules in decrease.

Analyzing each of the experiments and with the help of Table 6, we can say that the best characteristics for the dynamically adaptation of the "a" parameter are in the range of [0.5, 2.5] and the rules in decrease because this range has better performance in 4 of the 7 analyzed functions. In addition it is important to say that in general the best performance of the algorithm is when we use fuzzy logic in the algorithm.

Table 6. Results for the "a" parameter with fuzzy logic

Function	Original	a[0.5, 2.5] I	a[0.5, 2.5] D
Sphere	6,59E–28	3,79E–42	**5,61E–43**
Rosenbrock	**26,8126**	28,0622	27,2738
Quartic	0.0022	0,0037	**0,0015**
Schwefel	–6123,10	**–3896,68**	–4258,2816
Rastrigin	**0,3105**	142,2852	0,3837
Ackley	1,06E–13	9,65E–01	**1,50E–14**
Griewank	0,0045	0,0057	**0,0034**

Based on the experiments in Table 7, we can conclude that the best performance is obtained when the rules of the fuzzy system are in increasing fashion and the range for the "C" parameter is [0, 0.5] which performs better in the analyzed benchmark functions and also we can conclude that in general the best performance of the algorithm is when we use fuzzy logic in the algorithm because it has better performance in 6 of the 7 analyzed functions.

Table 7. Results of "C" parameter with fuzzy logic

Function	Original	C[0, 0.5] I	C[0, 0.5] D	C[2.5, 3] I	C[2.5, 3] D
Sphere	6.59E–28	**8.17E–36**	5.40E–34	1.06E–25	5.17E–25
Rosenbrock	**26.8126**	27.5013	27.338	27.4048	27.5036
Quartic	0.0022	**0.0012**	0.0016	0.0019	0.0019
Schwefel	–6123.10	–4696.76	–5272.45	**–4030.64**	–4119.06
Rastrigin	0.3105	0.2524	11.8879	6.27E–13	**6.25E–13**
Ackley	1.06E–13	**2.92E–14**	3.74E–14	18.22	19.47
Griewank	0.0045	0.0011	0.0067	**0.0004**	**0.0004**

5 Conclusions

We conclude that in a study of the algorithm we can find the parameters, which can be optimized using a dynamic method through an exhaustive search of the "a" and "C" parameters respectively in which we can determine the best ranges to optimize the analyzed benchmark functions. Based on the experiments we proposed the following ranges: the "a" parameter with a range of [0.5, 2.5] and the "C" parameter with a range of [0, 0.5].

Also we proposed a fuzzy system with ranges based on the best obtained results in these experiments, that we can conclude that the "a" parameter has better performance when its rules are in decrease and for the "C" parameter is otherwise, the better performance is when the its rules are in increase.

It's important to say that in both studies the algorithm has better performance when we use fuzzy logic so we can show that fuzzy logic improves significantly the performance of the algorithm, no matter what parameter is adjusted dynamically.

In addition and as a future work it is important to test the performance of the fuzzy logic approach with the three different proposed ranges (original, explored and proposed), make a study of the performance with a hypothesis test to demonstrate the significance of the results. Finally, design a fuzzy system for dynamic simultaneous adaptation of parameters in the algorithm.

References

1. Bonabeau, E., Dorigo, M., Theraulaz, G.: Swarm Intelligence: From Natural to Artificial Systems. OUP, Oxford (1999)
2. Kennedy, J., Eberhart, R.: Particle swarm optimization. In: IEEE International Conference on Neural Networks, 1995 Proceedings, pp. 1942–1948 (1995)
3. Dorigo, M., Birattari, M., Stutzle, T.: Ant colony optimization. Comput. Intell. Mag. **1**, 28–39 (2006). IEEE
4. Basturk, B., Karaboga, D.: An artificial bee colony (ABC) algorithm for numeric function optimization. In: IEEE Swarm Intelligence Symposium, pp. 687–697 (2006)
5. Mirjalili, S., Mirjalili, M., Lewis, A.: Grey wolf optimizer. Adv. Eng. Softw. **69**, 46–61 (2014)
6. Beni, G., Wang, J.: Swarm intelligence in cellular robotic systems. In: Dario, P., Dario, P., Sandini, G., Aebischer, P. (eds.) Robots and biological systems: towards a new bionics?. NATO ASI Series, pp. 703–712. Springer, Heidelberg (1993)
7. Maier, H.R., Kapelan, Z.: Evolutionary algorithms and other metaheuristics in water resources: Current status, research challenges and future directions. Environ. Model Softw. **62**, 271–299 (2014)
8. Can, U., Alatas, B.: Physics based metaheuristic algorithms for global optimization. Am. J. Inf. Sci. Comput. Eng. **1**, 94–106 (2015)
9. Yang, X., Karamanoglu, M: Swarm intelligence and bio-inspired computation: an overview. Swarm Intell. Bio-Inspired Comput. **1**, 3–23 (2013)
10. Wolpert, D.H., Macready, W.G.: No free lunch theorems for optimization. IEEE Trans. Evol. Comput. **1**, 67–82 (1997)

11. Muro, C., Escobedo, R., Spector, L., Coppinger, R.: Wolfpack (canis lupus) hunting strategies emerge from simple rules in computational simulations. Behav. Process. **88**, 192–197 (2011)
12. Yao, X., Liu, Y., Lin, G.: Evolutionary programming made faster. IEEE Trans. Evol. Comput. **3**, 82–102 (1999)
13. Digalakis, J., Margaritis, K.: On benchmarking functions for genetic algorithms. Int. J. Comput. Math. **77**, 481–506 (2001)
14. Molga, M., Smutnicki, C.: Test functions for optimization needs (2005)
15. Yang, X-S.: Test problems in optimization. arXiv, preprint arXiv:1008.0549 (2010)

Interval Type-2 Fuzzy Logic for Parameter Adaptation in the Gravitational Search Algorithm

Beatriz González, Fevrier Valdez, and Patricia Melin[✉]

Tijuana Institute of Technology, Calzada Tecnologico s/n, Tijuana, Mexico
betygm8@hotmail.com, {fevrier,pmelin}@tectijuana.mx

Abstract. In this paper we are presenting a modification of the Gravitational Search Algorithm (GSA) using type-2 fuzzy logic to dynamically change the alpha parameter and provide a different gravitation and acceleration values to each agent in order to improve its performance. We test this approach with benchmark mathematical functions. Simulation results show the advantages of the proposed approach.

Keywords: Type-2 · Fuzzy · Logic · GSA · Optimization · Parameter · Search

1 Introduction

In recent years, it has been shown by many researchers that metaheuristic algorithms are well suited to solve complex problems. For example genetic algorithms (GAs) are inspired on Darwinian evolutionary theory [7], ant colony optimization (ACO) mimics the behavior of ants foraging for food [9], and particle swarm optimization (PSO) simulates the behavior of flocks of birds [5, 6]. On the other hand, the bat algorithm (BA) is inspired by the echolocation behavior of microbats [13], etc. In this paper we consider the gravitational search algorithm (GSA), which is a metaheuristic optimization method based on the laws of gravity and mass interactions [4].

There exists different works concerning the gravitational search algorithm, but only the most important and relevant for this paper will be reviewed [3, 10–12]. There also exists a previous proposal of a fuzzy gravitational search algorithm (FGSA), and its application to the optimal design of multimachine power system stabilizers (PSSs). The FGSA based-PSS design is validated for two multimachine systems: a 3-machine 9-bus system and a 10-machine 39-bus. In this case, fuzzy logic is used to speed up the end stages of the process and find the accurate results in a shorter time, even for very large problems. In this proposed GSA the fuzzy based mechanism and fitness sharing are applied to aid the decision maker to choose the best compromise solution from the Pareto front [2]. However, we are now proposing in this work, the use of type-2 fuzzy logic in the gravitational search algorithm (FGSA) to dynamically change the alpha parameter values and provide a different gravitation and acceleration values to each agent in order to improve its performance, which was originally presented in a similar fashion with type-1 fuzzy logic in [1].

G. Sidorov and O. Herrera-Alcántara (Eds.): MICAI 2016, Part I, LNAI 10061, pp. 239–249, 2017.
DOI: 10.1007/978-3-319-62434-1_20

The meaning of optimization in this case is finding the parameter values in a function that produces a better solution. All appropriate values are possible solutions and the best value is the optimal solution [8].

The rest of the paper describes this approach in detail and is organized as follows. In Sect. 2, we show some of the previous works and basic concepts. In Sect. 3 experimental results are presented and in Sect. 4 the conclusions are offered.

2 Background and Basic Concepts

2.1 Previous Work

In the work of Rashedi et al. a Gravitational Search Algorithm as a new optimization algorithm based on the law of gravity and mass interactions was proposed [4]. In the proposed algorithm, the search agents are a collection of masses, which interact with each other based on the Newtonian gravity and the laws of motion.

In the work Sombra et al. the authors proposed a new gravitational search algorithm using fuzzy logic for parameter adaptation. In this case they proposed a new Gravitational Search Algorithm (GSA) using type-1 fuzzy logic to change the alpha parameter and give a different gravitation and acceleration to each agent in order to improve its performance, and this new approach was used for mathematical functions and a comparison with the original approach was presented [1].

2.2 The Law of Gravity and Second Motion Law

Isaac Newton proposed the law of gravity stating that "The gravitational force between two particles is directly proportional to the product of their masses and inversely proportional to the square of the distance between them" [4]. The gravity force is present in each object in the universe and its behavior is called "action at a distance", and this means gravity acts between separated particles without any intermediary and without any delay. The gravity law is represented by the following equation:

$$F = G\frac{M_1 M_2}{R^2} \tag{1}$$

where:

F   = is the magnitude of the gravitational force,
G   = is gravitational constant,
M_1 and M_2 = are the mass of the first and second particles respectively and,
R   = is the distance between the two particles.

The Gravitational search algorithm furthermore to be based on the Newtonian gravity law it is also based on Newton's second motion law, which says "The acceleration of an object is directly proportional to the net force acting on it and inversely proportional to its mass" [4]. The second motion law is represented by the following equation:

$$\alpha = \frac{F}{M} \tag{2}$$

Where:
A = is the magnitude of acceleration,
F = is the magnitude of the gravitational force and,
M = is the mass of the object.

2.3 Gravitational Search Algorithm

The approach was proposed by E. Rashedi et al. where they introduce a new algorithm for finding the best solution in problem search spaces using physical rules. Based on populations and the same time it takes as fundamental principles the law of gravity and second motion law, its principal features are that agents are considered as objects and their performance is measured by their masses. All these objects are attracted to each other by the gravity force, and this force causes a global movement of all objects, the masses cooperate using a direct form of communication, through gravitational force, an agent with heavy mass corresponds to a good solution therefore it moves more slowly than lighter ones, finally its gravitational and inertial masses are determined using a fitness function [4].

In addition, due to the effect of decreasing gravity, the actual value of the "gravitational constant" depends on the actual age of the universe. Equation (3) gives the decrease of the gravitational constant, G, with the age [15].

We can notice that in Eq. (1) the gravitational constant G appears, this is a physic constant, which determines the intensity of the gravitational force between the objects and it is defined as a very small value. The equation by which G is defined is given as follows:

$$G(t) = (G(t_0)) \left(\frac{t_0}{t} \right)^{\beta}, \beta < 1 \tag{3}$$

where:
$G(t)$ = is the value of the gravitational constant at time t and,
$G_0(t)$ = is the value of the gravitational constant at the first cosmic quantum-interval of time t_0.

Now, consider a system with N agents (masses). We define the position of the ith agent by:

$$X_i = \left(X_i^1, \ldots, X_i^d, \ldots, X_i^n \right) \quad for \quad i = 1, 2, \ldots, N, \tag{4}$$

Where X_i^d presents the position of the ith agent in the dth dimension.

At a specific time 't', we define the force acting on mass 'i' from mass 'f' as follows:

$$F_{ij}^d(t) = G(t) \frac{M_{pi}(t) \times M_{aj}(t)}{R_{ij}(t) + \varepsilon} \left(x_j^d(t) - x_i^d(t) \right). \tag{5}$$

Where M_{aj} is the active gravitational mass related to agent j, M_{pi} is the passive gravitational mass related to agent i, G(t) is the gravitational constant at time t, ε is a small constant, and $R_{ij}(t)$ is the Euclidian distance between two agents i and j:

$$R_{ij}(t) = \| X_i(t), X_j(t) \|_2 \tag{6}$$

To provide a stochastic characteristic to this algorithm can be based on the idea that the total force that acts on agent i in a dimension d be a randomly weighted sum of dth components of the forces exerted from other agents:

$$F_i^d(t) = \sum_{j=i, j \neq i}^{N} rand_j F_{ij}^d(t) \tag{7}$$

Where $rand_j$ is a random number in the interval [0, 1]. The acceleration now is expressed as,

$$a_i^d(t) = \frac{F_i^d(t)}{M_{ii}(t)} \tag{8}$$

Where M_{ii} is the inertial mass of ith agent. To determine the velocity of an agent we consider that is as a fraction of its current velocity added to its acceleration.

$$V_i^d(t+1) = rand_i x V_i^d(t) + a_i^d(t) \tag{9}$$

The position of the agents could be calculated as the position in a specific time t added to its velocity in a time t + 1 as follows,

$$X_i^d(t+1) = X_i^d(t) + V_i^d(t+1) \tag{10}$$

In this case the gravitational constant G is initialized at the beginning and will be reduced with time to control the search accuracy. Its Equation is:

$$G(t) = G(G_0, t) \tag{11}$$

This is because G is a function of the initial value G_0 and time t. As mentioned previously the gravitational and inertia masses are simply calculated by the fitness evaluation and a heavier mass means a more efficient agent. The update of the gravitational and inertial masses is performed with the following equations,

$$M_{ai} = M_{pi} = M_{ii} = M_i, \ i = 1, 2, \ldots, N, \tag{12}$$

$$m_i(t) = \frac{fit_i(t) - worst(t)}{best(t) - worst(t)} \tag{13}$$

$$M_i(t) = \frac{m_i(t)}{\sum_{j=1}^{N} m_j(t)} \tag{14}$$

Where $fit_i(t)$ represents the fitness value of the agent i at time t, and worst(t) and best(t) are defined as follows (for a minimization problem):

$$best(t) = \min_{j \in \{1,\ldots,N\}} fit_j(t) \tag{15}$$

$$worst(t) = \max_{j \in \{1,\ldots,N\}} fit_j(t) \tag{16}$$

It is to be noted that for a maximization problem, Eqs. (15) and (16) are changed to Eqs. (17) and (18), respectively:

$$best(t) = \max_{j \in \{1,\ldots,N\}} fit_j(t) \tag{17}$$

$$worst(t) = \min_{j \in \{1,\ldots,N\}} fit_j(t) \tag{18}$$

The gravitational search algorithm has a kind of elitism in order that only a set of agents with the bigger mass apply their force to the others. This is with the objective to have a balance between exploration and exploitation with lapse of time that is achieved by only the Kbest agents that will attract the other Kbest as a function of time, with the initial value K_0 at the beginning and decreasing with time. In such a way, at the beginning, all agents apply the force, and as time passes, Kbest is decreased linearly and at the end there will be just one agent applying force to the others. For this reason Eq. (7), can be modified as follows,

$$F_i^d(t) = \sum_{j \in Kbest, j \neq i} rand_j F_{ij}^d(t) \tag{19}$$

Where *Kbest* is the set of first K agents with the best fitness value and largest mass. A better representation of the GSA process is shown in Fig. 1, and is the principle of this algorithm.

First, an initial population is generated, next the fitness of each agent is evaluated, thereafter we update the gravitational constant G, best and worst of the population; the next step is calculating the mass and acceleration of each agent, until meeting the end of the iterations, in this case the maximum of iterations then returns the best solution, else execute the same steps starting from the fitness evaluation. It is in the third step, where we apply the modification in this algorithm, in this case we propose changing the alpha parameter to update G and help the GSA achieve a better performance.

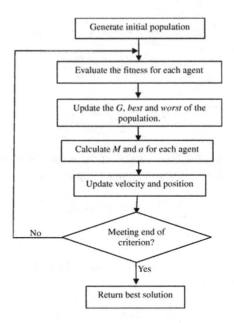

Fig. 1. General principle of GSA. Based on [4]

Now we have focused on the third block, particularly the update of G, Fig. 2 is a representation of our idea, where we use a fuzzy system to obtain the values of alpha and thus updating the value of G.

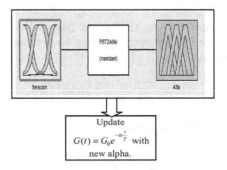

Fig. 2. Proposal to change alpha using type-2 fuzzy logic

If we change the alpha values along the iterations, we can make the algorithm apply a different G value, at the same time influence the gravitational force for to each of the agents and finally change its acceleration providing an opportunity to agents explore other good solutions in the search space and improve the final result.

But otherwise, the variables that determine the gravitational constant G (alpha and G_0) affect significantly the performance of the algorithm because they work jointly, since once G is established we can use it to determine the magnitude of the gravity force and at the same time determines the agent acceleration. We have chosen the alpha parameter to be modified throughout the execution of the algorithm because Eq. (11) in this case is defined as follows:

$$G(t) = G_0 e^{-\alpha t/T} \tag{20}$$

and alpha as a very small negative exponent impacts greatly the result of G for being just an exponent. Meanwhile G_0 is considered an initial value of G, so that, effectively has an impact in the final result, but it is not as drastic change as it if we make a change in the alpha value.

We have as input variable the elapsed number of iterations and it is granulated as follows (Fig. 3):

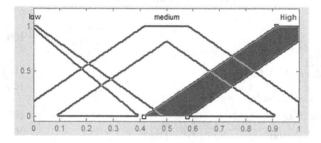

Fig. 3. Fuzzy system input for increase alpha value

Otherwise the output is the alpha value, and it is granulated as follows (Fig. 4):

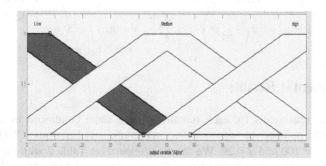

Fig. 4. Fuzzy system output for increase alpha value

The rules are:

1. If (Iteration is Low) then (Alpha is Low)
2. If (Iteration is Medium) then (Alpha is Medium)
3. If (Iteration is High) then (Alpha is High)

With this new approach, the rules were designed based on if, iterations are low then the alpha value should be low, because we need more gravity and acceleration for better search space exploration. Moreover, in high iterations we need a large alpha value to reduce the gravitation and acceleration of the agents, in order to exploit the search space.

2.4   Benchmark Functions

In the field of evolutionary computation, it is common to compare different algorithms using a large test set, especially when the test set involves function optimization. We have made a previous study of the functions to be optimized for constructing a test set with a benchmark function selection [14] (Table 1).

Table 1. Benchmark functions

Expresión	s
$F_1(x) = \sum_{i=1}^{n} x_i^2$	$[-100, 100]^n$
$F_2(x) = \sum_{1=1}^{n} \lvert x_i \rvert + \prod_{i=1}^{n} \lvert x_i \rvert$	$[-10, 10]^n$
$F_3(x) = \sum_{i=1}^{n} \left(\sum_{j=1}^{i} x_j \right)^2$	$[-100, 100]^n$
$F_4(x) = max\{ \lvert x_i \rvert, 1 \leq i \leq n \}$	$[-100, 100]^n$
$F_5(x) = \sum_{i=1}^{n-1} \left[100(x_{x+1} - x_i^2)^2 + (x_i - 1)^2 \right]$	$[-30, 30]^n$
$F_6(X) = \sum_{i=1}^{n} ([x_i + 0.5])^2$	$[-100, 100]^n$
$F_7(x) = \sum_{i=1}^{n} i x_i^4 + random[0, 1]$	$[-1.28, 1.28]^n$
$F_8(x) = \sum_{i=1}^{n} -x_i sin\left(\sqrt{\lvert x_i \rvert} \right)$	$[-500, 500]^n$
$F_9(x) = \sum_{i=1}^{n} \left[x_i^2 - 10\cos(2\pi x_i) + 10 \right]$	$[-5.12, 5.12]^n$
$F_{10}(x) = -20exp\left(-0.2 \sqrt{\frac{1}{n} \sum_{i=1}^{n} x_i^2} \right) - exp\left(\frac{1}{n} \sum_{i=1}^{n} \cos(2\pi x_i) \right) + 20 + e$	$[-32, 32]^n$

3   Experimental Results

We made 30 experiments for each function on the same conditions as the original proposal, with number of agents = 50, maximum of iterations = 1000, dimensions = 30, $G_0 = 100$ and a = 20. We show a comparative Table 2 with the average of the best-so-far solution for original GSA, FGSA with type-1 fuzzy logic, FGSA with type-2 fuzzy logic and PSO.

We show a comparative Table 3 with the average of the best-so-far solution of the FGSA with type-2 fuzzy logic with triangular MF (increase), FGSA with type-2 fuzzy logic with triangular MF (Decrement), and FGSA with type-2 fuzzy logic with Gauss MF (increase).

Table 2. Comparative table with the average of the best-so-far solution for the original GSA, FGSA with type-1 fuzzy logic, FGSA with type-2 fuzzy logic. and PSO.

Function	GSA [4]	FGSA_T1_I [1]	FGSA_T2_I	PSO [4]
F1	7.3×10^{-11}	$\mathbf{8.85 \times 10^{-34}}$	2.4×10^{-17}	1.8×10^{-3}
F2	4.03×10^{-5}	$\mathbf{1.15 \times 10^{-10}}$	2.41×10^{-08}	2
F3	$\mathbf{0.16 \times 10^{+3}}$	$4.68 \times 10^{+2}$	$2.008 \times 10^{+02}$	$4.1 \times 10^{+3}$
F4	3.7×10^{-6}	0.0912	$\mathbf{3.3 \times 10^{-09}}$	8.1
F5	**25.16**	61.2473	26.66	$3.6 \times 10^{+4}$
F6	8.3×10^{-11}	0.1	**0**	1.0×10^{-3}
F7	0.018	0.0262	**0.017**	0.04
F8	$-2.8 \times 10^{+3}$	$\mathbf{-2.6 \times 10^{3}}$	$-2.7 \times 10^{+03}$	$-9.8 \times 10^{+3}$
F9	15.32	17.1796	**14.59**	55.1
F10	6.9×10^{-6}	$\mathbf{6.33 \times 10^{-15}}$	3.7×10^{-09}	9.0×10^{-3}

Table 3. Rastrigin function

Dimensions	FGSA_Inc_Triang	FGSA_Dec_Triang	FGSA__Inc_Gauss
30	14.5	**12.93**	14.59
100	**71.31**	72	75.5

We show a comparative Table 4 with the average of the best-so-far solution of the FGSA with type-2 fuzzy logic with triangular MF (increase), FGSA with type-2 fuzzy logic with triangular MF (Decrement), and FGSA with type-2 fuzzy logic with Gauss MF (increase).

Table 4. Rosenbrock function

Dimensions	FGSA_Inc_Triang	FGSA_Dec_Triang	FGSA__Inc_Gauss
30	26.6	**26.09**	26.10
100	$7.84 \times 10^{+02}$	**26.10**	$1.758 \times 10^{+3}$

We show a comparative Table 5 with the average of the best-so-far solution of the FGSA with type-2 fuzzy logic with triangular MF (increase), FGSA with type-2 fuzzy logic with triangular MF (Decrement), and FGSA with type-2 fuzzy logic with Gauss MF (increase).

Table 5. Ackley function

Dimensions	FGSA_Inc_Triang	FGSA_Dec_Triang	FGSA__Inc_Gauss
30	3.7×10^{-09}	3.6×10^{-09}	$\mathbf{3.52 \times 10^{-09}}$
100	$\mathbf{5.9 \times 10^{-01}}$	1.2	9.76×10^{-01}

We show a comparative Table 6 with the average of the best-so-far solution of the FGSA with type-2 fuzzy logic with triangular MF (increase), FGSA with type-2 fuzzy logic with triangular MF (Decrement), and FGSA with type-2 fuzzy logic with Gauss MF (increase).

Table 6. Sum squared function

Dimensions	FGSA_Inc_Triang	FGSA_Dec_ Triang	FGSA_Inc_Gauss
30	2.41×10^{-08}	2.46×10^{-08}	$\mathbf{2.38 \times 10^{-08}}$
100	$\mathbf{4.74 \times 10^{-01}}$	1.20	1.08

4 Conclusions

As can be noted in our experiments with different gravitational search algorithm modifications, we can improve the results in the mathematical functions; therefore we verify that a change in the alpha value along the algorithm iterations helps in a better convergence. We realize that the idea of changing the alpha value and specifically with a fuzzy system to increase its value is a good concept because in some cases the FGSA with type-2 fuzzy provides a better solution than the traditional algorithm. This is because when we make a change in the alpha value, recalculates the value of the gravitational constant G, which in turn changes the force of gravity between agents and thereafter changes its acceleration. Once we do the above, we achieved to give more opportunity for agents to accelerate in another direction and could be able to be attracted by another agent with a heavy mass and reach a better solution. A Comparison with the average of the best-so-far solution for original GSA, FGSA with type-1 fuzzy logic, FGSA with type-2 fuzzy logic and PSO applied to Benchmark mathematical functions using 30 dimensions. The numerical results indicated that FGSA with type-2 fuzzy logic method offers much higher performance than the existing methods on optimization problems. A comparison with the average of the best-so-far solution FGSA with type-2 fuzzy logic with triangular MFs (increase), FGSA with type-2 fuzzy logic with triangular MFs (Decrement), and FGSA with type-2 fuzzy logic with Gaussian MFs (increase) applied to Benchmark mathematical functions using 30 and 100 dimensions is present.

Acknowledgements. We would like to express our gratitude to CONACYT, Tijuana Institute of Technology for the facilities and resources granted for the development of this research.

References

1. Sombra, A., Valdez, F., Melin, P.: A new gravitational search algorithm using fuzzy logic to parameter adaptation. In: Proceedings of IEEE Congress on Evolutionary Computation, Cancun, México, pp. 1068–1074 (2013)
2. Ghasemi, A., Shayeghi, H., Alkhatib, H.: Robust design of multimachine power system stabilizers using fuzzy gravitational search algorithm. Int. J. Electr. Power Energy Syst. **51**, 190–200 (2013)

3. Dowlatshahi, M., Nezamabadi-Pour, H.: GGSA: a grouping gravitational search algorithm for data clustering. Eng. Appl. Artif. Intell. **36**, 114–121 (2014)
4. Rashedi, E., Nezamabadi-pour, H., Saryazdi, S.: GSA: a gravitational search algorithm. Inf. Sci. **179**(13), 2232–2248 (2009)
5. Bergh, F.V.D., Engelbrecht, A.P.: A study of particle swarm optimization particle trajectories. Inf. Sci. **176**, 937–971 (2006)
6. Kennedy, J., Eberhart, R.C.: Particle swarm optimization. In: Proceedings of IEEE International Conference on Neural Networks, vol. 4, pp. 1942–1948 (1995)
7. Tang, K.S., Man, K.F., Kwong, S., He, Q.: Genetic algorithms and their applications. IEEE Signal Process. Mag. **13**(6), 22–37 (1996)
8. Liu, Y., Passino, K.M.: Swarm intelligence: a survey. In: International Conference of Swarm Intelligence (2005)
9. Dorigo, M., Maniezzo, V., Colorni, A.: The ant system: optimization by a colony of cooperating agents. IEEE Trans. Syst. Man Cybern. B **26**(1), 29–41 (1996)
10. Dowlatshahi, M., Nezamabadi, H., Mashinchi, M.: A discrete gravitational search algorithm for solving combinatorial optimization problems. Inf. Sci. **258**, 94–107 (2014)
11. Mirjalili, S., Mohd, S., Moradian, H.: Training feedforward neural networks using hybrid particle swarm optimization and gravitational search algorithm. Appl. Math. Comput. **218** (22), 11125–11137 (2012)
12. Yazdani, S., Nezamabadi, H., Kamyab, S.: A gravitational search algorithm for multimodal optimization. Swarm Evol. Comput. **14**, 1–14 (2014)
13. Yang, X.: Bat algorithm: a novel approach for global engineering optimization. Eng. Comput. Int. J. Comput. Aided Eng. Softw. **29**(5), 464–483 (2012)
14. Yao, X., Liu, Y., Lin, G.: Evolutionary programming made faster. IEEE Trans. Evol. Comput. **3**, 82–102 (1999)
15. Mansouri, R., Nasseri, F., Khorrami, M.: Effective time variation of G in a model universe with variable space dimension. Phys. Lett. **259**, 194–200 (1999)

Water Cycle Algorithm with Fuzzy Logic for Dynamic Adaptation of Parameters

Eduardo Méndez[1], Oscar Castillo[1], José Soria[1], Patricia Melin[1(✉)], and Ali Sadollah[2]

[1] Tijuana Institute of Technology, Calzada Tecnologico s/n, Tijuana, Mexico
{ocastillo,pmelin}@tectijuana.mx
[2] Nanyang Technological University, Singapore, Singapore

Abstract. This paper describes the enhancement of the Water Cycle Algorithm (WCA) using a fuzzy inference system to adapt its parameters dynamically. The original WCA is compared regarding performance with the proposed method called Water Cycle Algorithm with Dynamic Parameter Adaptation (WCA-DPA). Simulation results on a set of well-known test functions show that the WCA can be improved with a fuzzy dynamic adaptation of the parameters.

Keywords: WCA · Fuzzy logic · Optimization

1 Introduction

Dynamic parameter adaptation can be done in many ways, the most common being linearly increasing or decreasing a parameter, other approaches include nonlinear or stochastic functions. In this paper, a different approach was taken which is using a fuzzy inference system to replace a function or to change its behavior, with the final purpose of improving the performance of the Water Cycle Algorithm (WCA). The water cycle algorithm (WCA) is a population-based and nature-inspired meta- heuristic, which is inspired by a simplified form of the water cycle process [2, 12].

Using a fuzzy inference system to enhance global optimization algorithms is an active area of research, some works of enhancing particle swarm optimization are PSO-DPA [9], APSO [17] and FAPSO [13]. Since the WCA has some similarities with PSO, a fuzzy inference system (FIS) similar to the one in [9] was developed.

A comparative study was conducted which highlights the similarities and differences with other hierarchy based meta-heuristics. And a performance study between the proposed Water Cycle Algorithm with Fuzzy Parameter Adaptation (WCA-FPA), the original WCA, and the Gravitational Search Algorithm with Fuzzy Parameter Adaptation (GSA-FPA) [16] was also conducted, using ten well-known test functions frequently used in tin the literature.

This paper is organized as follows. In Sect. 2 the Water Cycle Algorithm (WCA) is described. In Sect. 3, some similarities with other meta-heuristics are highlighted. Section 4 it's about how to improve the WCA with fuzzy parameter adaptation. A comparative study is presented in Sect. 5 and, finally in Sect. 6 some conclusions and future work are given.

© Springer International Publishing AG 2017
G. Sidorov and O. Herrera-Alcántara (Eds.): MICAI 2016, Part I, LNAI 10061, pp. 250–260, 2017.
DOI: 10.1007/978-3-319-62434-1_21

2 The Water Cycle Algorithm

The water cycle algorithm is a population-based and nature-inspired meta-heuristic, where a population of streams is formed from rain water drops. This population of streams follows a behavior inspired by the hydrological cycle. In which streams and rivers flow downhill towards the sea. This process of flowing downhill is a simplified form of the runoff process of the hydrologic cycle. After the runoff, some of the streams are evaporated, and some new streams are created from rain as part of the hydrologic cycle.

2.1 The Landscape

There are some landforms involved in the hydrologic cycle, but in the WCA only three of them are considered, which are streams, rivers, and the sea. In this subsection, the structure, preprocessing and initialization of the algorithm are described.

In the WCA an individual (a.k.a. stream), it's an object which consists of n variables grouped as a n-dimensional column vector:

$$\mathbf{x}_k = [x_{k1}, \ldots x_{kn}]^\mathrm{T} \in \mathbb{R}^n. \tag{1}$$

The number of streams and rivers are defined by the equations:

$$N_{sr} = \text{Number of Rivers} + \underbrace{1}_{sea}, \tag{2}$$

$$N_{streams} = N - N_{sr}, \tag{3}$$

Where N is the size of the population of streams, N_{sr} is a value established as a parameter of the algorithm and N streams is the number of remaining streams.

The whole population of N streams is represented as a $N \times n$ matrix:

$$\mathbf{X} = \begin{matrix} sea \left\{ \vphantom{\begin{bmatrix}a\end{bmatrix}} \right. \\ rivers \left\{ \vphantom{\begin{bmatrix}a\\a\end{bmatrix}} \right. \\ \\ streams \left\{ \vphantom{\begin{bmatrix}a\\a\\a\end{bmatrix}} \right. \end{matrix} \begin{bmatrix} \mathbf{x}_1^\mathrm{T} \\ \mathbf{x}_2^\mathrm{T} \\ \mathbf{x}_3^\mathrm{T} \\ \vdots \\ \mathbf{x}_{N_{sr}}^\mathrm{T} \\ \mathbf{x}_{N_{sr}+1}^\mathrm{T} \\ \mathbf{x}_{N_{sr}+2}^\mathrm{T} \\ \vdots \\ \mathbf{x}_{N_{sr}+N_{streams}}^\mathrm{T} \end{bmatrix} = \begin{bmatrix} x_{11} & x_{12} & \cdots & x_{1n} \\ x_{21} & x_{22} & \cdots & x_{2n} \\ \vdots & \vdots & \vdots & \vdots \\ x_{N1} & x_{N2} & \cdots & x_{Nn} \end{bmatrix}. \tag{4}$$

In matrix (4) the individuals are ordered by their fitness, and the fitness of each stream is obtained by:

$$\mathbf{f}_i = f(\mathbf{x}_i) = f(x_{i1}, x_{i2}, \dots, x_{in}), \quad \text{for} \quad i = 1, 2, 3, \dots, N, \tag{5}$$

where $f(\cdot)$ is a problem dependent function to estimate the fitness of a given stream. This fitness function it's what the algorithm tries to optimize.

Each of the $N_{streams}$ is assigned to a river or sea; this assignation can be done randomly. But the stream order [14, 15], which is the number of streams assigned to each river/sea is calculated by:

$$\mathbf{so}_i = \left\lfloor \left| \frac{\mathbf{f}_i}{\sum_{j=1}^{N_{sr}} \mathbf{f}_j + \varepsilon} \right| \cdot N_{streams} \right\rfloor, \quad n = 1, 2, \dots, N_{sr}, \tag{6}$$

$$\mathbf{so}_1 \leftarrow \mathbf{so}_1 + \left(N_{streams} - \sum_{i=1}^{N_{sr}} \mathbf{so}_i \right), \tag{7}$$

where $\varepsilon \approx 0$. The idea behind the Eq. (6) is that the amount of water (streams) entering a river or sea varies, so when a river is more abundant (has a better fitness) than another, it means that more streams flow into the river. Hence the discharge (stream-flow) is mayor; therefore, the stream-flow magnitude of rivers is inversely proportional to its fitness in the case of minimization problems.

The Eq. (6) has been changed from the original proposed in [2], a floor function replaced the round function, a value of ε was added to the divisor, and the Eq. (7) was also add to handle the remaining streams. These changes are for implementation purposes and an alternative to the method proposed in [12].

After obtaining the stream order of each river and sea, the streams are randomly distributed among them.

2.2   The Run-Off Process

The runoff process is one of the three processes considered in the WCA, which handles the way water flows in the form of streams and rivers towards the sea. The following equations describe how the flow of streams and rivers is simulated at a given instant (iteration):

$$\mathbf{x}_{stream}^{i+1} = \mathbf{x}_{stream}^{i} + \mathbf{r} \cdot C \cdot \left(\mathbf{x}_{sea}^{i} - \mathbf{x}_{stream}^{i} \right), \tag{8}$$

$$\mathbf{x}_{stream}^{i+1} = \mathbf{x}_{stream}^{i} + \mathbf{r} \cdot C \cdot \left(\mathbf{x}_{river}^{i} - \mathbf{x}_{stream}^{i} \right), \tag{9}$$

$$\mathbf{x}_{river}^{i+1} = \mathbf{x}_{river}^{i} + \mathbf{r} \cdot C \cdot \left(\mathbf{x}_{sea}^{i} - \mathbf{x}_{river}^{i} \right), \tag{10}$$

for $i = 1, 2, \dots, N_{it}$, where N_{it} and C are parameters of the algorithm, and $\mathbf{r}$ is an n-dimensional vector of independent and identically distributed (i.i.d) values, that follow a uniform distribution:

$$\mathbf{r} \sim U(0, 1)^n. \tag{11}$$

The Eq. (8) defines the movement of streams which flow directly to the sea, Eq. (9) is for streams which flow towards the rivers, and Eq. (10) is for the rivers flow toward the sea. A value of $C > 1$ enables streams to flow in different directions towards the rivers or sea. Typically, the value of C is chosen from the range $[1, 2]$ being two the most common.

2.3 Evaporation and Precipitation Process

The run-off process of the WCA consists of moving indirectly towards the global best (sea). Algorithms focused on following the global best although they are fast, tend to premature convergence or stagnation. The way in which WCA deals with exploration and convergence is with the evaporation and precipitation processes. So when streams and rivers are close enough to the sea, some of those streams are evaporated (discarded) and then new streams are created as part of the precipitation process. This type of re-initialization is similar to the cooling down and heating up re-initialization process of the simulated annealing algorithm [3].

The evaporation criterion is: if a river is close enough to the sea, then the streams assigned to that river are evaporated (discarded), and new streams are created by raining around the search space. To evaporate the streams of a given river the following condition must be satisfied:

$$\underbrace{\left| \mathbf{x}_{sea} - \mathbf{x}_{river} \right| < d_{\max}}_{\text{evaporation criterion}}, \tag{12}$$

where $d_{max} \approx 0$ is a parameter of the algorithm. This condition must be applied to every river, and if it's satisfied each stream who flow towards this river must be replaced as:

$$\underbrace{\mathbf{x}_{stream} = \mathbf{b}_{lower} + \mathbf{r} \cdot \left(\mathbf{b}_{lower} - \mathbf{b}_{upper} \right)}_{\text{raining around the search space}}, \tag{13}$$

a high value of d_{max} will favor the exploration, and a low one will favor the exploitation.

3   Similarities and Differences with Other Meta-Heuristics

The WCA has some similarities with other meta-heuristics but yet is different from those. Some of the similarities and differences have already been studied, for example: In [2], differences and similarities with Particle Swarm Optimization (PSO) [7] and Genetic Algorithms (GA) [4] are explained. In [11], WCA is compared with the Imperialist Competitive Algorithm (ICA) [1] and PSO [7]. And in [12], WCA is compared with two nature-inspired meta-heuristics: the Intelligent Water Drops (IWD) [5] and Water Wave Optimization (WWO) [18]. So far similarities and differences with population-based and nature-inspired meta-heuristics have been studied, in this subsection, WCA is compared with two meta-heuristics who use a hierarchy.

3.1 Hierarchical Particle Swarm Optimization

In Hierarchical Particle Swarm Optimization (H-PSO), particles are arranged in a regular tree hierarchy that defines the neighborhoods structure [6]. This hierarchy is defined by a height h and a branching degree d; this is similar to the landscape (hierarchy) of the WCA. In fact, the WCA would be like a tree of height $h = 3$ (sea, rivers, streams), but with varying branching degrees, since the level-2 consist of N_{sr} branches (rivers), and the level-3 depends on the stream order. Therefore, WCA hierarchy it's not a nearly regular tree.

Another difference is that H-PSO uses velocities to update the positions of the particles just like in standard PSO. But a similarity is that instead of moving towards the global best like in PSO they move towards their parent node, just like streams flow to rivers and rivers flow to the sea. As in WCA, in H-PSO particles move up and down the hierarchy, and if a particle at a child node has found a solution that is better than the best so far solution of the particle at the parent node, the two particles are exchanged. This is similar yet different to the run-off process of the WCA, the difference being that WCA uses only the social component to update the positions, and H-PSO uses both the social and cognitive components, and also the velocity with inertia weight. The cognitive component and the inertia weight are the ways in which H-PSO deals with exploration and exploitation. The WCA uses the evaporation and precipitation processes for those phases.

3.2 Grey Wolf Optimizer

The Grey Wolf Optimizer (GWO) algorithm mimics the leadership hierarchy and hunting mechanism of gray wolves in nature. Four types of gray wolves are simulated: alpha, beta, delta, and omega, which are employed for simulating the leadership hierarchy [10]. This social hierarchy is similar to the WCA hierarchy with a $N_{sr} = 3$, where the alpha could be seen as the sea, the beta and delta as the rivers and the omegas as the streams. Although the hierarchy is similar, the way in which the GWO algorithm updates the positions of the individuals is different. GWO positions update depends on the hunting phases: searching for prey, encircling prey, and attacking prey. Those hunting phases are the way in which the GWO deals with exploration and exploitation. As mentioned before, the WCA uses the evaporation and precipitation process which are very different to the hunting phases.

4 Fuzzy Parameter Adaptation

The objective of dynamic parameter adaptation is to improve the performance of an algorithm by adapting its parameters. Dynamic parameter adaptation can be done in many ways, the most common being linearly increasing or decreasing a parameter, usually the acceleration coefficients. Other approaches include using nonlinear or stochastic functions. In this paper, a different approach is taken which is using a fuzzy system to replace a function or to change its behavior.

In the WCA there are two parameters which can be adapted dynamically, that is while the algorithm is running. One is the parameter C which is used in Eqs. (13) to (14) for updating the positions of the streams. The other one is the parameter d_{max} used in Eq. (12) as a threshold for the evaporation criterion. In [12] the parameter d_{max} is linearly decreased, and a stochastic evaporation rate for every river is introduced, together those changes improve the performance of the WCA.

Since there are already improvements with the parameter d_{max}, the subject of study in this paper is the parameter C.

A single-input and multiple-output (SIMO) Mamdani's Fuzzy Inference System [8] was developed. The system consists of the input Iteration and the outputs Cstream and Criver. In Fig. 1, the layout of the fuzzy inference system is shown. The idea is to use different values of the parameter C, one for Eqs. (13) and (14) which are for the flow of streams and another one (Criver) for Eq. (15) which is for the flow of rivers.

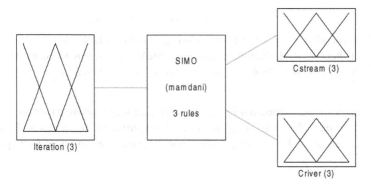

Fig. 1. Single-input and multiple-output Mamdani's Fuzzy Inference System

The input Iteration is calculated by the equation:

$$Iteration = \frac{i}{N_{it}}, \quad \text{for} \quad i = 1, 2, \ldots, N_{it}. \tag{14}$$

The range of the first output Cstream had been chosen as the interval $[1, 2.2]$, and for the output Criver the interval $[1.6, 4]$, the details of the membership functions are shown in Fig. 2. The idea of using higher values for these parameters is to favor the

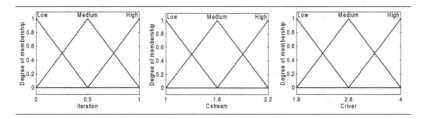

Fig. 2. Membership functions

exploration in the run-off process at an early stage, since having a greater value than two means that there is a higher probability of moving beyond the rivers or the sea. For the special case of Criver, it also helps to prevent the evaporation and precipitation processes.

The fuzzy rules are simple, the algorithm begins with higher values of C favoring exploration and slowly decreases to favor exploitation.

5 Experimental Setting

To test the performance of WCA-FPA and for comparison, we used a diverse subset of 10 unconstrained test functions, shown in Table 1 and Fig. 3. All the functions are well-known minimization problems previously used as benchmarks in the literature.

Table 1. Rules of the fuzzy inference system

1.	If (Iteration is Low) then (Cstream is High) (Criver is High) (1)
2.	If (Iteration is Medium) then (Cstream is Medium) (Criver is Medium) (1)
3.	If (Iteration is High) then (Cstream is Low) (Criver is Low) (1)

Experiments were carried out in 10 and 30 dimensions (variables), using a sample size of 50 for each function. As a measure of performance, the mean and standard deviation fitness of the best-obtained solution were considered and used for hypothesis testing.

Table 2. Set of 10 unconstrained test functions

No.	Function		Range
f_1	Egg Holder	$f(x) = \sum\limits_{i=1}^{n-1} \left[-(x_{i+1}+47)\sin\sqrt{\left\vert x_{i+1}+\frac{x_i}{2}+47\right\vert} - x_i \sin\sqrt{\left\vert x_i-(x_{i+1}+47)\right\vert} \right]$	$-512 \le x_i \le 512$
f_2	Rana	$f(x) = \sum\limits_{i=1}^{n-1} x_i \sin\left([\sqrt{\vert x_{i+1}-x_i+1\vert}] \right) \cos\left(\sqrt{\vert x_{i+1}+x_i+1\vert} \right)$ $\quad + (x_{i+1}+1)\sin\left(\sqrt{\vert x_{i+1}+x_i+1\vert}\right)\cos\left(\sqrt{\vert x_{i+1}-x_i+1\vert}\right)]$	$-500 \le x_i \le 500$
f_3	Michalewicz	$f(x) = -\sum\limits_{i=1}^{n} \sin(x_i) \cdot \left[\sin\left(\frac{ix_i^2}{\pi}\right)\right]^{2m}, \quad m=0$	$0 \le x_i \le \pi$
f_4	Rosenbrock	$f(x) = \sum\limits_{i=1}^{n-1} \left[(x_i-1)^2 + 100(x_{i+1}-x_i^2)^2 \right]$	$-5 \le x_i \le 5$
f_5	De Jong	$f(x) = \sum\limits_{i=1}^{n} x_i^2$	$-5.12 \le x_i \le 5.12$
f_6	Schewefel	$f(x) = -\sum\limits_{i=1}^{n} x_i \sin(\sqrt{\vert x_i\vert})$	$-500 \le x_i \le 500$
f_7	Ackley	$f(x) = -20\exp\left(-\frac{1}{5}\sqrt{\frac{1}{n}\sum\limits_{i=1}^{n} x_i^2}\right) - \exp\left(\frac{1}{n}\sum\limits_{i=1}^{n}\cos(2\pi x_i)\right) + 20 + \exp(1)$	$-32.768 \le x_i \le 32.768$
f_8	Rastrigin	$f(x) = -10n + \sum\limits_{i=1}^{n} \left[x_i^2 - 10\cos(2\pi x_i)\right]$	$-5.12 \le x_i \le 5.12$
f_9	Griewank	$f(x) = \frac{1}{4000}\sum\limits_{i=1}^{n} x_i^2 - \prod\limits_{i=1}^{n}\cos\left(\frac{x_i}{\sqrt{i}}\right) + 1$	$-600 \le x_i \le 600$
f_{10}	Yang	$f(x) = \left(\sum\limits_{i=1}^{n} x_i\right)\exp\left[-\sum\limits_{i=1}^{n}\sin(x_i^2)\right]$	$-2\pi \le x_i \le 2\pi$

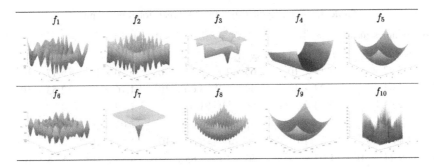

Fig. 3. Test functions surface plots for 2-dimensions

The comparisons are against the original WCA and the Gravitational Search Algorithm with Fuzzy Parameter Adaptation (GSA-FPA).

For a fair comparison, a black-box optimization approach is adopted, using the same fixed parameter settings for all the problems, although the algorithms are allowed to adapt some of its parameters at running time (Table 2).

The fixed parameters are: population size $N = 25$ and number of iterations $N_{it} = n \cdot 10^4/N$; for the water cycle algorithms $N_{sr} = 4$ and $d_{max} = 0.01$; and for the GSA-FPA an initial $G_0 = 100$.

All experiments were performed using MATLAB with 64 bits' double precision.

Tables 3 and 4 summarize the statistics results for 10-dimensional and 30-dimensional problems respectively.

Table 3. Summary statistics for 10-dimensional problems

No.	Samples means			Samples deviations		
	μ_{WCA}	$\mu_{WCA-FPA}$	$\mu_{GSA-FPA}$	σ_{WCA}	$\sigma_{WCA-FPA}$	$\sigma_{GSA-FPA}$
f_1	-3.54×10^3	-4.02×10^3	-1.38×10^3	2.97×10^2	2.07×10^2	2.41×10^2
f_2	-1.87×10^3	-1.97×10^3	-8.26×10^2	9.92×10^1	3.67×10^1	1.60×10^2
f_3	-7.73	-9.24	-2.73	7.44×10^{-1}	3.64×10^{-1}	4.11×10^{-1}
f_4	1.67	1.18	2.27	3.27	1.78	3.62
f_5	2.64×10^{-10}	7.76×10^{-10}	2.02×10^{-39}	2.38×10^{-10}	4.68×10^{-10}	9.03×10^{-39}
f_6	-3.54×10^3	-3.70×10^3	-1.45×10^3	2.66×10^2	1.72×10^2	2.70×10^2
f_7	2.15×10^{-5}	3.12×10^{-5}	4.44×10^{-15}	9.24×10^{-6}	1.07×10^{-5}	0
f_8	5.37	5.57×10^{-1}	6.71	2.63	7.56×10^{-1}	5.08
f_9	1.25×10^{-1}	8.93×10^{-2}	1.05×10^{-2}	9.40×10^{-2}	5.28×10^{-2}	9.22×10^{-3}
f_{10}	1.45×10^{-3}	8.64×10^{-4}	8.50×10^{-4}	3.49×10^{-4}	3.44×10^{-4}	2.67×10^{-4}

Samples size: 50 Parameters: $N = 25$ n = 10 $N_{it} = 4000$

Table 4. Summary statistics for 30-dimensional problems

No.	Samples means			Samples deviations		
	μ_{WCA}	$\mu_{\text{WCA-FPA}}$	$\mu_{\text{GSA-FPA}}$	σ_{WCA}	$\sigma_{\text{WCA-FPA}}$	$\sigma_{\text{GSA-FPA}}$
f_1	-8.97×10^3	-1.15×10^4	-2.65×10^3	8.76×10^2	5.90×10^2	5.17×10^2
f_2	-4.84×10^3	-5.77×10^3	-1.44×10^3	3.00×10^2	1.76×10^2	2.53×10^2
f_3	-1.94×10^1	-2.44×10^1	-1.66×10^1	1.67	1.29	2.03
f_4	8.48	1.75×10^1	6.10×10^1	8.53	1.02×10^1	3.53×10^2
f_5	1.44×10^{-9}	2.69×10^{-9}	5.24×10^{-1}	8.16×10^{-10}	1.41×10^{-9}	3.71
f_6	-9.24×10^3	-1.07×10^4	-2.50×10^3	5.85×10^2	4.58×10^2	5.08×10^2
f_7	6.82	4.29×10^{-5}	8.42×10^{-15}	8.73	1.17×10^{-5}	1.37×10^{-15}
f_8	1.33×10^2	9.41	9.77×10^1	3.16×10^1	3.14	4.08×10^1
f_9	1.08×10^{-1}	7.40×10^{-2}	1.33×10^{-3}	1.15×10^{-1}	6.94×10^{-2}	5.20×10^{-3}
f_{10}	1.08×10^{-11}	1.36×10^{-11}	7.90×10^{-12}	1.07×10^{-12}	1.92×10^{-12}	1.00×10^{-12}

Samples size: 50 Parameters: $N = 25$ n $= 30$ $N_{it} = 12000$

Table 5 shows the two-sample Z-test results, which are interpreted as follows:

Table 5. Two-sample Z-test results

No.	10-dimensional				30-dimensional			
	z_{WSA}		$z_{\text{GSA-FPA}}$		z_{WSA}		$z_{\text{GSA-FPA}}$	
f_1	9.33	$+^{99\%}$	58.82	$+^{99\%}$	16.87	$+^{99\%}$	79.65	$+^{99\%}$
f_2	6.40	$+^{99\%}$	49.08	$+^{99\%}$	18.77	$+^{99\%}$	99.26	$+^{99\%}$
f_3	12.89	$+^{99\%}$	83.90	$+^{99\%}$	16.83	$+^{99\%}$	22.79	$+^{99\%}$
f_4	0.93	$\approx$	1.91	$+^{95\%}$	-4.81	$-^{99\%}$	0.87	$\approx$
f_5	-6.91	$-^{99\%}$	-11.74	$-^{99\%}$	-5.43	$-^{99\%}$	1.00	$\approx$
f_6	3.58	$+^{99\%}$	49.84	$+^{99\%}$	14.18	$+^{99\%}$	85.01	$+^{99\%}$
f_7	-4.85	$-^{99\%}$	-20.59	$+^{99\%}$	5.53	$+^{99\%}$	-25.82	$-^{99\%}$
f_8	12.45	$+^{99\%}$	8.46	$+^{99\%}$	27.49	$+^{99\%}$	15.26	$+^{99\%}$
f_9	2.36	$+^{99\%}$	-10.39	$+^{99\%}$	1.79	$+^{95\%}$	-7.39	$-^{99\%}$
f_{10}	8.48	$+^{99\%}$	-0.23	$\approx$	-8.95	$-^{99\%}$	-18.60	$-^{99\%}$

Sample size $= 50$ $z_{99\%} = \pm 2.33$ $z_{95\%} = \pm 1.645$

For example, for the function 4 (i.e. Rosenbrok's) as a 10-dimensional problem the z-score against the WCA is 0.93 which means there is not enough evidence to reject the null hypothesis of a right tailed test, hence the results are similar (i.e. $\approx$).

Same problem but against the GSA-FPA is a z-score of 1.91 which means there is enough evidence with a 95% of confidence to accept the alternative hypothesis that the WCA-FPA is significantly better (i.e. $+^{95\%}$).

Now the same function but as a 30-dimensional problem with a z-score of -4.81 in a left-tailed test the original WCA is significantly better than our proposal with a 99% of confidence (i.e. $-^{99\%}$).

6 Conclusions

From the hypothesis test results can be concluded that dynamically adapting the parameter "C" can significantly improve the performance of the water cycle algorithm. Although for most of the tests problems our proposal is significantly better with a 99% of confidence it seems to be something in common with functions in which it did worse. Those functions are either unimodal or have a predominant valley, which could mean that our proposal has some exploitation problems. This problem could be solved by setting a smaller value for d_{max}, or by extending the fuzzy adaptive algorithm to also adapt the parameter "d" in a non-linear manner.

References

1. Atashpaz-Gargari, E., Lucas, C.: Imperialist competitive algorithm: an algorithm for optimization inspired by imperialistic competition. In: IEEE Congress on Evolutionary Computation, pp. 4661–4667. IEEE (2007)
2. Eskandar, H., et al.: Water Cycle Algorithm - A Novel Metaheuristic Optimization Method for Solving Constrained Engineering Optimization Problems. Comput. Struct. **110–111**, 151–166 (2012)
3. Gelatt, C.D., Vecchi, M.P.: Optimization by simulated annealing. Science **220**(4598), 671–680 (1983)
4. Goldberg, D.E.: Genetic Algorithms in Search. Optimization and Machine Learning. Addison-Wesley Longman Publishing Co. Inc., Boston (1989)
5. Hosseini, H.S.: Problem solving by intelligent water drops. In: IEEE Congress on Evolutionary Computation, CEC 2007, pp. 3226–3231 (2007)
6. Janson, S., Middendorf, M.: A hierarchical particle swarm optimizer and its adaptive variant. IEEE Trans. Syst. Man, Cybern. Part B **35**(6), 1272–1282 (2005)
7. Kennedy, J., Eberhart, R.C.: Particle swarm optimization. In: Proceedings of the IEEE International Conference on Neural Networks, pp. 1942–1948 (1995)
8. Mamdani, E.H., Assilian, S.: An experiment in linguistic synthesis with a fuzzy logic controller. Int. J. Mach. Stud. **7**(1), 1–13 (1975)
9. Melin, P., et al.: Optimal design of fuzzy classification systems using PSO with dynamic parameter adaptation through fuzzy logic. Expert Syst. Appl. **40**(8), 3196–3206 (2013)
10. Mirjalili, S., et al.: Grey wolf optimizer. Adv. Eng. Softw. **69**, 46–61 (2014)
11. Sadollah, A., et al.: Water cycle algorithm for solving multi-objective optimization problems. Soft. Comput. **19**(9), 2587–2603 (2015)
12. Sadollah, A., et al.: Water cycle algorithm with evaporation rate for solving constrained and unconstrained optimization problems. Appl. Soft Comput. **30**, 58–71 (2015)
13. Shi, Y., Eberhart, R.C.: Fuzzy adaptive particle swarm optimization. In: Proceedings of the 2001 Congress on Evolutionary Computation, vol. 1, pp. 101–106 (2001)
14. Shreve, R.L.: Infinite topologically random channel networks. J. Geol. **75**(2), 178–186 (1967)
15. Shreve, R.L.: Statistical law of stream numbers. J. Geol. **74**(1), 17–37 (1966)

16. Sombra, A., et al.: A new gravitational search algorithm using fuzzy logic to parameter adaptation. In: 2013 IEEE Congress on Evolutionary Computation, pp. 1068–1074 (2013)
17. Zhan, Z.H., et al.: Adaptive particle swarm optimization. IEEE Trans. Syst. Man Cybern. Part B **39**(6), 1362–1381 (2009)
18. Zheng, Y.-J.: Water wave optimization: {A} new nature-inspired metaheuristic. Comput. {&} {OR} **55**, 1–11 (2015)

Off-line Tuning of a PID Controller Using Type-2 Fuzzy Logic

Heberi R. Tello-Rdz, Luis M. Torres-Treviño[(⊠)], and Angel Rodríguez-Liñan

CIIDIT - FIME, Universidad Autónoma de Nuevo León,
San Nicolás de los Garza, Mexico
luis.torres.ciidit@gmail.com

Abstract. Tuning of PID controllers is a hard task, sometimes that's almost an art. Different paradigms have been proposed to optimize the tuning of these controllers, some of them have given acceptable results, others have not done it. From heuristics to artificial intelligence have been used, but in this paper we used Type-2 Fuzzy Logic to tuning a PID controller applied in three transfer functions, and we obtained their step responses, then we compared them with the Type-1 Fuzzy Logic's results.

Keywords: Tuning PID · Type II fuzzy systems · Intelligent tuning

1 Introduction

The control strategy most commonly used in the industry is the PID controller, because it does not need a mathematical model of the system to be controlled. It consists of three gains Proportional-Integral-Derivative, they are the parameters of which depends the effect of the controller on the system response. And they can be tuning by heuristic (try and failure) or using some method, probably the most used in the literature is the Ziegler-Nichols method [1], in this paper we used Type-2 Fuzzy Logic [2] to tuning the gains, but before we have to attend the Type-1 Fuzzy Logic [3], these systems generate a degree of membership from linguistic values (partitions) in our case they are five (Very Low, Low, Medium, High and Very High) referring to the values of the input variables, for this is necessary a Data Base that contains rules, which will guide the Fuzzy system's behavior depending on the values of the inputs. The number of rules is given for the number of combinations of the inputs (combinations = partitions^{inputs}) Type-2 Fuzzy Logic have a similar structure than Type-1, these systems admit some uncertainty in the linguistic input values, so they should show a better performance than Type-1, because of this a uncertainty band is generated and we will obtain two degrees of membership: upper and lower.

In Fig. 1 is shown the general structure of the Type-2 Fuzzy Logic Systems, where T2FL is Type-2 Fuzzy Logic and COS is Center of Set (Method of the Defuzifier). Many paradigms have been used to tune in PID controller [4,5], for example PSO and Genetics Algorithms, also Type-1 Fuzzy Logic has been

© Springer International Publishing AG 2017
G. Sidorov and O. Herrera-Alcántara (Eds.): MICAI 2016, Part I, LNAI 10061, pp. 261–269, 2017.
DOI: 10.1007/978-3-319-62434-1_22

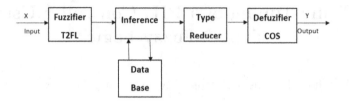

Fig. 1. Type-2 Fuzzy Logic System's structure.

used [6]. We are proposing to use T2FL to do this task. The Data Base was made by an expert in PID controllers and we took like inputs overshoot, setting time and steady state error to generate the outputs, in this case the outputs are the changes of the gains Proportional (K_p), Integral (K_i) and Derivative (K_d).

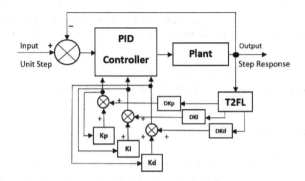

Fig. 2. Tuning of a PID controller using Type-2 Fuzzy Logic.

A simple diagram of the work that was made in this paper is shown in Fig. 2, where the gains (K_p, K_i and K_d) must to have initial conditions, DKp, DKi and DKd are the changes of the gains and have to be multiplied by a proportion. The algorithm should to improve overshoot, steady state error and setting time, changing the gains in each cycle.

2   Experiments and Discussion

We have three Transfer Functions to carry out the experiment:

$$G(s) = \frac{1}{s(s+1)(s+5)} \tag{1}$$

$$G(s) = \frac{0.01s^2 - 0.6s + 12}{s(0.5s+1)(0.25s+1)(0.01s^2 + 0.6s + 12)} \tag{2}$$

$$G(s) = \frac{1}{(s+1)(\alpha s + 1)(\alpha^2 s + 1)(\alpha^3 s + 1)} \tag{3}$$

where $\alpha = [0.1, 0.2, 0.5, 1]$. It is necessary to run the algorithm to each value of α for the third Transfer Function. Then we will do a comparison between the step response of T1FL and T2FL. We will have the number of cycles (NC), overshoot (Mp), steady state error (errorss) and setting time (ts) in seconds. The pseudo-code below shown is the main function of the program implemented:

```
for i=1 to NC
      y           = respPID(Kp,Ki,Kd)
  errorss,ts,Mp = EvalControl(y,YD)
      dKp         = FuzzySysKp(Mp,errorss,ts)
      dKi         = FuzzySysKi(Mp,errorss,ts)
      dKd         = FuzzySysKd(Mp,errorss,ts)
      Kp          = Kp + pkp * dKp
      Ki          = Ki + pki * dKi
      Kd          = Kd + pkd * dKd
  end of cycle
```

NC is the number of cycles. Times to run the program, respPID is the function that obtains the response of the system with the PID controller. EvalControl computes the characteristics of the transitory. FuzzySysKp calculates the change (dKp) for the proportional gain (Kp). $Kp = Kp + pkp * dKp$, Updating the Kp, and pkp is a proportion that multiplies to the change dKp. Responses of both systems are presented for every transfer function. Final tuning result considering first transfer function is presented in Table 1. Performance are shown in Figs. 3 and 4. Final tuning result considering second transfer function is presented in Table 2 and performance of both fuzzy systems are shown in Figs. 5 and 6. Final tuning result considering third transfer function with $\alpha = 0.1$ is presented in Table 3. Performance are shown with a zoom in Figs. 7 and 8 to appreciate its performance. Final tuning result considering third transfer function with $\alpha = 0.5$ is presented in Table 4. Performance are shown with a zoom in Figs. 9 and 10 to appreciate its performance. Finally, final tuning result considering third transfer function with $\alpha = 1$ is presented in Table 5 and performance of both fuzzy systems are shown in Figs. 11 and 12.

Table 1. Number of tuning cycles for each type fuzzy Logic first transfer function.

Method	NC	Mp	errorss	ts	K_p	K_i	K_d
T1FL	2	0.007	0.007	1.82	7.067	0.098	6.667
T2FL	5	0.019	0.017	6.725	3.399	0.1	10.999

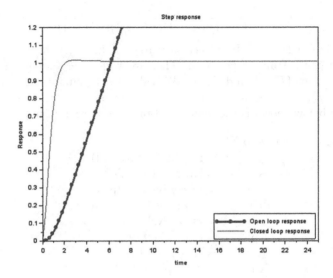

Fig. 3. Response using T1FL of the first transfer function.

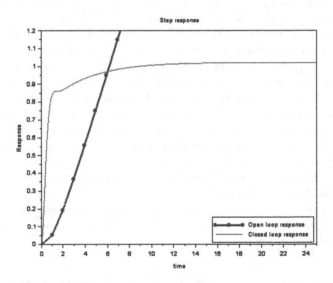

Fig. 4. Response using T2FL of the first transfer function.

Table 2. Number of tuning cycles for each type fuzzy logic second transfer function.

Method	NC	Mp	errorss	ts	K_p	K_i	K_d
T1FL	2	0.402	0.007	3.48	5.556	0.099	8.713
T2FL	2	0.158	0.011	4.115	2.399	0.1	5.999

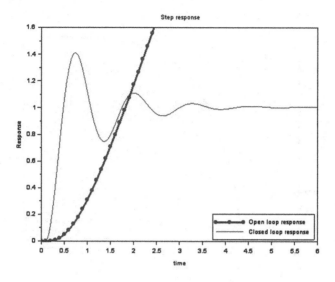

Fig. 5. Response using T1FL of second transfer function.

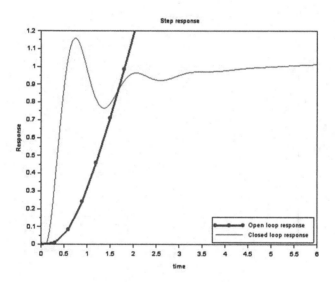

Fig. 6. Response using T2FL of second transfer function.

Table 3. Number of tuning cycles for each type fuzzy logic for third transfer function with $\alpha = 0.1$.

Method	NC	Mp	errorss	ts	K_p	K_i	K_d
T1FL	2	0	0.00001	10.545	5.018	1.072	5.151
T2FL	2	0	0.00008	16.705	0.972	0.1	4.879

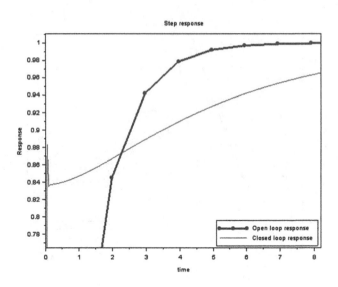

Fig. 7. Response using T1FL of third transfer function with $\alpha = 0.1$ with zoom.

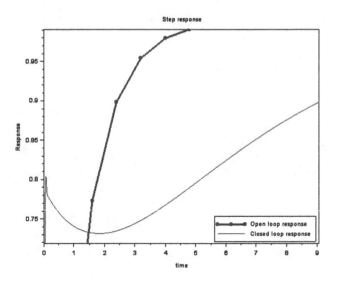

Fig. 8. Response using T2FL of third transfer function with $\alpha = 0.1$ with zoom.

Table 4. Number of tuning cycles for each type fuzzy logic for third transfer function with $\alpha = 0.5$.

Method	NC	Mp	errorss ,	ts	K_p	K_i	K_d
T1FL	2	0.278	0.00001	9.675	7.051	1.072	7.184
T2FL	2	0.009	0.000006	15.605	0.972	0.1	4.219

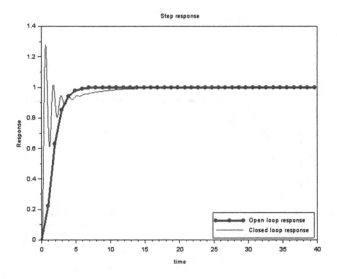

Fig. 9. Response using T1FL of third transfer function with $\alpha = 0.5$.

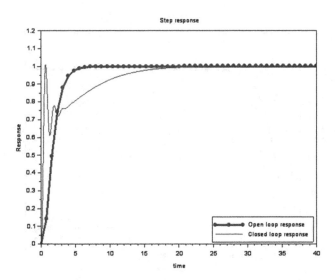

Fig. 10. Response using T2FL of third transfer function with $\alpha = 0.5$.

Table 5. Number of tuning cycles for each type fuzzy logic for third transfer function with $\alpha = 1$.

Method	NC	Mp	errorss	ts	K_p	K_i	K_d
T1FL	2	0.496	0.001	24.525	5.120	1.072	11.295
T2FL	2	0.001	0.000003	11.585	0.972	0.1	2.855

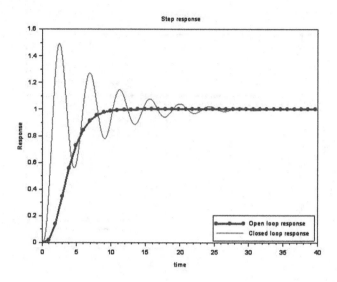

Fig. 11. Response using T1FL of third transfer function with $\alpha = 1$.

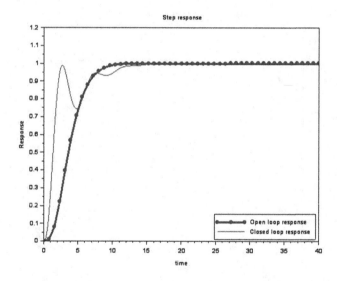

Fig. 12. Response using T2FL of third transfer function with $\alpha = 1$.

3   Conclusions

Type 2 fuzzy logic systems have a better performance than Type 1 fuzzy logic systems in the third transfer function, it is the most difficult of the three, in the others it has a similar performance, only with a longer setting time. We suppose the problem with the T2FL is its difficulty to work in the ends of the rank of the normalized values of the inputs $[0, 1]$, in this paper was necessary to change this rank to $(0, 1)$, excluding the ends. Maybe the T2FL could be used in cases where there are disturbances in the system, as these will allow some uncertainty. Future work includes a comparison of tuning in processes with a grade of disturbances, dynamic parameters and multivariable systems.

References

1. Meshram, P.M., Kanojiya, R.G.: Tuning of PID controller using Ziegler-Nichols method for speed control of DC motor. In: 2012 International Conference on Advances in Engineering, Science and Management (ICAESM), pp. 117–122 (2012)
2. Mendel, J.M., John, R.I., Liu, F.: Interval type-2 fuzzy logic systems made simple. IEEE Trans. Fuzzy Syst. **14**, 808–821 (2006)
3. Mendel, J.M.: Fuzzy logic systems for engineering: a tutorial. Proc. IEEE **83**, 345–377 (1995)
4. Geetha, M., Balajee, K.A., Jerome, J.: Optimal tuning of virtual feedback PID controller for a continuous stirred tank reactor (CSTR) using particle swarm optimization (PSO) algorithm. In: 2012 International Conference on Advances in Engineering, Science and Management (ICAESM), pp. 94–99 (2012)
5. Pareek, S., Kishnani, M., Gupta, R.: Optimal tuning of PID controller using meta heuristic algorithms. In: 2014 International Conference on Advances in Engineering and Technology Research (ICAETR), pp. 1–5 (2014)
6. Hong, H.P., Park, S.J., Han, S.J., Cho, K.Y., Lim, Y.C., Park, J.K., Kim, T.G.: A design of auto-tuning PID controller using fuzzy logic. In: Proceedings of the 1992 International Conference on Industrial Electronics, Control, Instrumentation, and Automation, 1992. Power Electronics and Motion Control, vol. 2, pp. 971–976 (1992)

Detection of Faults in Induction Motors Using Texture-Based Features and Fuzzy Inference

Uriel Calderon-Uribe, Rocio A. Lizarraga-Morales[✉],
Carlos Rodriguez-Donate, and Eduardo Cabal-Yepez

Division de Ingenierias, Departamento de Estudios Multidisciplinarios,
Universidad de Guanajauto, Yuriria, Guanajuato, Mexico
{u.calderonuribe,ra.lizarragamorales,c.rodriguezdonate,educabal}@ugto.mx

Abstract. The most popular rotating machine in the industry is the induction motor, and the harmful states on such motors may have consequences in costs, product quality, and safety. In this paper, a methodology that allows to detect faults in induction motors is proposed. Such methodology is based on the use of texture-inspired features in a fuzzy inference system. The features are extracted from the start-up current signal using the histograms of sum and differences, which have not been used for this kind of applications. The detected states in a given motor are: misalignment, motor with one broken bar and motor in good condition. The proposed methodology shows satisfactory results, using real signals of faulty motors, providing a new approach to detect faults in an automatic manner using only the current signals from the start-up stage.

Keywords: Fault detection · Induction motor · Texture analysis · Fuzzy inference

1 Introduction

Nowadays, it is of utmost importance the development of new monitoring systems for rotating machines. Such importance is due to the need of detecting more accurately various defects at an early stage. The earlier the defect is detected, the easier is the repairing process, benefiting the industry in cost and maintenance time. Squirrel-cage induction motors are the most popular motors used in industry due to their robust structure and easy design. Such popularity is also reflected with the fact that they consume around 85% of the electric power in the world [16]. A fault in induction motors, could produce unexpected production line interruptions, with consequences on costs, product quality, and others. For this reason, early detection of faults in induction motors has been of great interest for researchers in recent years.

A number of conventional vibration and current analysis techniques exist by which certain faults in rotating machinery can be identified. Unfortunately, most of them focus on detecting a single specific fault, such as broken rotor bars [17], bearing faults [9,13], unbalance [5,6], or rotors faults [1]. Broken rotor bars

© Springer International Publishing AG 2017
G. Sidorov and O. Herrera-Alcántara (Eds.): MICAI 2016, Part I, LNAI 10061, pp. 270–278, 2017.
DOI: 10.1007/978-3-319-62434-1_23

are one of the most difficult to detect faulty conditions because the induction motor keeps working without any perceivable change. One of the most recent works shows, with entropy properties, a detection of multiple faults in induction motors including outer race damage, unbalance, one broken bar and healthy conditions [15]. In spite of this, the problem is that the number of faults detected are very few compared to the vast amount of failures that may have an induction motor. The identification of multiple faults in induction motors remains a major challenge for researchers [3,4].

In this paper, texture features extracted from the current signals provide a quantitative reference for a fault detection. Texture is commonly used in image processing, however, as far as the authors know, texture has never been used for the analysis of one-dimensional signals. Moreover, the main contribution of this research is the combination of texture in a fuzzy inference system for this application. In this approach, a fuzzy system is structured according to the texture properties proposed and tested on real healthy and faulty motors. The importance of this approach is the development of a system which helps to detect states such as motor with misalignment (M), motor with one broken bar (BRB) and motor in good condition (G).

The content of this paper is composed as follows: in Sect. 2, the development of a fuzzy inference system comprising texture characteristics is described. Results and experiments are presented in Sect. 3 and conclusions are shown in Sect. 4.

2 Fuzzy Inference for Faults Detection in Induction Motors

The system of fuzzy inference developed in this study consists of four phases: signal acquisition, texture features extraction, fuzzy inference system and motor diagnosis (See Fig. 1). In the phase of the input signal, we received a current signal of the transient state of the motor. In the texture features phase, the signal is taken and the corresponding texture features are extracted. In the fuzzy inference system phase, the extracted features are analyzed and evaluated with the knowledge base for a decision, which is the label to be assigned. In the motor diagnosis, the result of our fuzzy system inference is used to determine the motor diagnosis.

The fuzzy inference system proposed in this paper consists of two stages: the training and recognition phases. The training phase consists mainly in the definition of the fuzzy if-then rules. This process is detailed in Sect. 2.1. The set

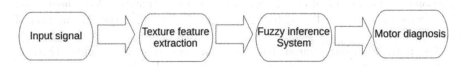

Fig. 1. Overall process for obtaining state diagnosis motor.

of rules obtained are used in the recognition phase for obtaining a class label. Through a fuzzy inference process, the label assignation is achieved (See Fig. 2) as described in Sect. 2.2.

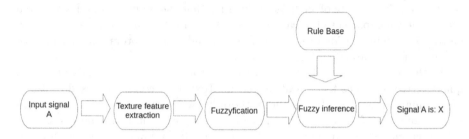

Fig. 2. Process for classifying a signal entry through the fuzzy inference system.

In this study, the start up-transient current signal is used to detect the faults and classify the condition. This is because this signal describes the dynamic characteristics of the induction motor. Figure 3(a) shows the experimental setup used in our experiments, where different 1-hp three-phase induction motors (model WEG 00136APE48T) are used to test the performance of the proposed methodology for identifying and classifying the fault conditions treated in this paper. The tested motors have 2 poles and 28 bars and receive a power supply of 220 V ac at 60 Hz. The applied mechanical load is that of an ordinary alternator, which represents a quarter of load for the motor. The start of the motor is controlled by a relay in order to synchronize the data acquisition with the motor switch on. One phase of the current signal is acquired using an ac current clamp model i200s from Fluke, as shown in Fig. 3(b). In this figure, an example of the signal of a motor with one broken rotor bar is shown. A 16-bit serial-output analog-to-digital converter ADS7809 from Texas Instruments Incorporated is used in the data acquisition system (DAS). The instrumentation system uses a sampling frequency f0 of 1.5 kHz, obtaining 4096 samples during the induction motor startup transient and acquiring up to the tenth harmonic of the fundamental frequency. In this study, the faults were artificially produced and 20 signals of each class were taken.

2.1 Training of the Fuzzy Inference System

The first step in the formulation of our inference system is the definition of the functional and operational characteristics. It is important to select classes and characteristics to be used to define the linguistic terms for the formulation of the rules base.

The purpose of our approach is a system consisting of 4 inputs (textural features) and one output (corresponding to the class label) in a Mamdani type inference (MA) model. In this model, the inputs and outputs are defined in

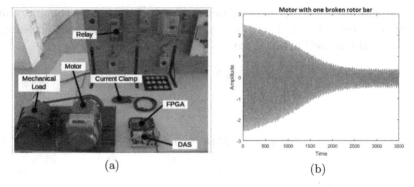

Fig. 3. (a)Test bench used for experimentation and (b) a sample of the signals used for experiments.

linguistic terms, interrelated through rules known as if-then rules. Thus, we consider the entries as $X = \{x_1, x_2, x_3, ..., x_i\}$, the vector corresponding to one-dimensional characteristics with i elements, where each element belongs to a specified texture feature. The output of our system, $\Omega = \{w_1, w_2, w_3, ..., w_n\}$ takes values of the set corresponding of n labels of known classes. In our system $n = 3$, where:

$$w_1 = misalignment,$$
$$w_2 = motor\ with\ one\ broken\ bar,$$
$$w_3 = motor\ in\ good\ condition.$$

In the following section, the feature extraction, the linguistic terms definition and the if-then rules formulation are described.

2.2 Feature Extraction

As textural features, we use a subset from the statistical features proposed by Unser [7]. These features are computed from the Sum and Differences Histograms (SDH), which are a quick alternative proposed to the co-occurrence matrix by Harlick [11]. According to the definition given by Unser, considering a digital signal $I(r)$ with R samples such that $r \in 0, 1, 2, ..., R - 1$, and assuming that there are at most J different quantized values in $I(s)$, that is $I(r) \in \{0, 1, 2, ..., J-1\}$; taking two points in a relative position fixed by v, $I(r)$ and $I(r + v)$, the sums and differences between these two points are defined as:

$$D_{r,v} = I(r) - I(r + v),\tag{1}$$
$$S_{r,v} = I(r) + I(r + v).\tag{2}$$

The sum and difference histograms $h_{s,v}(k)$ and $h_{d,v}(l)$ registers the occurrences of $S_{m,v}$ and $D_{m,v}$, respectively. When the histograms are normalized with the total number of occurrences, we obtain the discrete joint probability functions of differences $P_d(l)$ and sums $P_s(k)$. From these distributions, four features are computed and used in our study:

$$mean = \frac{1}{2}\sum_k k \cdot P_s(k) = \mu, \tag{3}$$

$$energy \simeq \sum_k P_s(k)^2 \cdot \sum_l P_d(l)^2, \tag{4}$$

$$contrast = \sum_l l^2 \cdot P_d(l), \tag{5}$$

$$homogenity = \sum_l \frac{1}{1+l^2} \cdot P_d(l), \tag{6}$$

$$Cluster Prominence = \sum_k (k - 2\mu)^3 \cdot P_s(k). \tag{7}$$

In this study, four elements compose the feature vector $\mathbf{X}$: Energy (x_1), Contrast (x_2), Homogeneity(x_3) and Cluster prominence (x_4).

Linguistic Term Definition. After defining the classes and features to be used, the second step of the learning process is the definition of linguistic terms and fuzzy sets. From the vector of features X, each input x_i is a value that enters the domain of linguistic terms, partitioned into any number of fuzzy sets.

The definition of fuzzy sets is one of the most important steps in designing the system, so the performance of our system depends on it. To achieve the resolution of our system, the linguistic terms were separated into three fuzzy sets. This number was chosen arbitrarily. To determine the parameters of each fuzzy set in each linguistic term, 10 samples of each class were used. These samples were analyzed for the extraction of the features vector and the parameters of fuzzy sets are determined following the methodology proposed in [10] using the K-means algorithm [11]. Samples of the corresponding fuzzy sets of the Contrast and Homogeneity features are depicted in Fig. 4. The trapezoidal and triangular functions were chosen after testing with 3 membership functions (Gaussian, triangular and trapezoidal) and observe that these are better suited to our need.

If-then Rules Formulation. The third step in our training process is the formulation of the rules base. In the proposed approach, each input and output is represented linguistically and related by means of rules called if-then rules. Such rules are expressions that represent the status of inference such that if a factor,

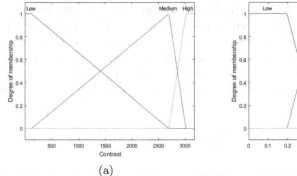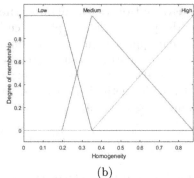

(a)   (b)

Fig. 4. Samples of linguistic terms for the texture features: (a) Contrast and (b) Homogeneity.

or combination of factors, are known (antecedent), a consequence (consequent) can be inferred. The generic form of the nth of these rules is:

$$R^n : \text{IF } x_1 \text{ IS } A_{(1,m_1)} \text{ AND } x_2 \text{ IS } A_{(2,m_2)} \text{ AND } \dots \text{ AND}$$
$$x_i \text{ IS } A_{(i,m_i)}, \text{ THEN } \Omega \text{ is } \omega^n,$$

where, $A(i, m)$ is the m_i^{th} fuzzy set in the ith texture feature for the nth rule, and ω^n represents the nth fuzzy set in Ω. R^n is the nth rule that belong to the set of rules $\mathbf{R}$ where n is the motor diagnosis. The definition of the antecedent $A_{(i,m)}$ is given by the maximum membership value of each feature in each corresponding fuzzy set, as it is depicted in Eq. 8.

$$A_{(i,m)} = max_m(\mu_{(i,1)}(x_i), \mu_{(i,2)}(x_i), \mu_{(i,3)}(x_i), \mu_{(i,4)}(x_i)), \tag{8}$$

where $\mu_{(i,1)}(x_i)$ is the degree of the membership of x_i in the fuzzy set $A_{(i,m)}$. The consequent of the nth rule is ω^n.

The rules formulated for each class are stated as follows:

R^1 : IF *Energy* IS *Mediume* AND *Contrast* IS *Medium* AND *Homogeneity* IS *Low* AND *Cluster Prominence* IS *Low*, THEN Ω IS *Missalignment*.

R^2 : IF *Energy* IS *High* AND *Contrast* IS *Medium* AND *Homogeneity* IS *Low* AND *Cluster Prominence* IS *Low*, THEN Ω IS *Motor with one broken rotor bar.*

R^3 : IF *Energy* IS *Mediume* AND *Contrast* IS *Medium* AND *Homogeneity* IS *High* AND *Cluster Prominence* IS *High*, THEN Ω IS *Motor in good condition.*

In our case, we assign the linguistic labels of low, medium and high to the sets $A(i,1)$, $A(i,2)$ and $A(i,3)$ respectively.

Rule Evaluation to Determine the Motor Diagnosis. For the motor diagnosis, the process was mapping a current signal within a known class. In this part of our approach, different samples from the training process of each current signals are submitted to the system for computing the feature vector. The feature vector determines the best output through an inference process. Based on the MA model method of inference, the degree of the membership to a nth class is computed as in Eq. 9

$$\mu_\omega^n(X) = \prod_i \mu_{(i,m)}^n(x_i), \tag{9}$$

and the assigned label Ω, correspond to the maximum level of activation from all the 3 rules as it is shown in Eq. 10.

$$\Omega = max\left[\mu_\omega^1(X), \mu_\omega^2(X), \mu_\omega^3(X), \mu_\omega^4(X)\right]. \tag{10}$$

3   Experimental Results

In this study, 60 samples of the current signals were used. From this set, 30 samples were taken for training and 30 samples are taken for evaluate the performance of our system. We have evaluated the performance of our system in terms of the classification accuracy. The performance of our approach was measured as the amount of current signals correctly assigned to the source class. In Table 1 the results of our approach by using a confusion matrix, are shown. As it can be seen in this table, all the current signals used in our system were assigned correctly. A 100% of classification is reached by using only half of the current signals for training and the other half for testing.

Table 1. Confusion matrix of our system. Class 1, Class 2 and Class 3 are for Misalignment, Motor in good condition and Motor with one broken rotor bar, respectively.

Test\Class	Class 1	Class 2	Class 3	Total
Class 1	100%			100%
Class 2		100%		100%
Class 3			100%	100%

In order to evaluate the position of our methodology in terms of the state-of-the-art, we compare our method with other approaches proposed to the same task. In Table 2, we present the method in the state-of-the-art, the features proposed by the given approach, the number of defects that each system is able to detect and the classification accuracy in a percentage. As it can be seen in this table, our method proposes a novel methodology using texture features and it is able to detect 3 different states (2 faults and regular state) with an accuracy of 100%.

Table **2.** Comparison of our methodology with the state of the art.

Method	Features	No. of defects	Accuracy (%)
M. Pineda-Sanchez [14]	Frequency	1	100%
J. Rafiee [13]	Wavelets	1	100%
M. Karakse [12]	Current signals	2	97.2%
Ilhan Aydin [8]	Current signal	2	98.14%
Abdenour Soualhi [2]	Stator current	3	90.62%
Our proposal	Texture	3	100%

4   Conclusion

A fuzzy method for classification of states in induction motor has been discussed. The method is a system with multiple inputs and one output, where the inputs are based in statistical textural features extracted from a current signal and the output is a label (class) assignation. A set of if-then type rules has been built (one for each class) from known current signals from each class and the recognition is evaluated using unknown current signals from each class. The given signal is assigned to the rule whose activation level is the highest.

A fuzzy classifier is an alternative to the traditional systems, because of their tolerance to imprecision and uncertainty. In addition, we can highlight benefits by using fuzzy rules, since they can describe a signal using linguistic terms. In this sense, we can see that our system is an appropriate option for the industry to detect different conditions in induction motors. Moreover, as it was shown, it presents a methodology based in texture features that have never been used before in the literature.

Acknowledgments. Calderon-Uribe would like to acknowledge for the grant provided by the Mexican National Council of Science and Technology (CONACyT). This research was supported by the University of Guanajuato and the PRODEP through the NPTC project with number DSA/103.5/15/7007.

References

1. Patel, R.A., Bhalja, B.R.: Induction motor rotor fault detection using artificial neural network. In: 2015 International Conference on Energy Systems and Applications, pp. 45–50 (2015)
2. Soualhi, A., Clerc, G., Razik, H.: Detection and diagnosis of faults in induction motor using an improved artificial ant clustering technique. IEEE Trans. Industr. Electron. **60**, 4053–4062 (2013)
3. Antonino-Daviu, J., Rodriguez, P.J., RieraGuasp, M., Pineda-Sanchez, M., Arkkio, A.: Detection of combined faults in induction machines with stator parallel branches through the DWT of the startup current. Mech. Syst. Signal Process. **23**, 2336–2351 (2009)

4. Ballal, M.S., Khan, Z.J., Suryawanshi, H.M., Sonolikar, R.L.: Adaptive neural fuzzy inference system for the detection of inter-turn insulation and bearing wear faults in induction motor. IEEE Trans. Ind. Electron. **54**, 250–258 (2007)

5. Contreras-Medina, L.M., Romero-Troncoso, R.J., Cabal-Yepez, E., Rangel-Magdaleno, J.J., Millan-Almaraz, R.: FPGA-based multiple-channel vibration analyzer for industrial applications in induction motor failure detection. IEEE Trans. Instrum. Meas. **59**, 63–72 (2010)

6. Frosini, L., Bassi, E.: Stator current and motor efficiency as indicators for different types of bearing faults in induction motors. IEEE Trans. Ind. Electron. **57**, 244–251 (2010)

7. Haralick, R., Shanmugan, K., Dinstein, I.: Textural features for image classification. IEEE Trans. Syst. Man Cybern. **3**, 610–621 (1973)

8. Aydin, I., Karakose, M., Akin, E.: Visual texture classification using fuzzy inference. J. Intell. Manuf. **23**, 1489–1499 (2012)

9. Zarei, J.: Induction motors bearing fault detection using pattern recognition techniques. Expert Syst. Appl. **39**, 68–73 (2012)

10. Lizarraga-Morales, R.A., Sanchez-Yanez, R.E., Ayala-Ramirez, V.: Visual texture classification using fuzzy inference. In: 2011 10th Mexican International Conference on Artificial Intelligence (MICAI), Puebla, pp. 150–154 (2011)

11. Lloyd, S.: Least squares quantization in PCM. IEEE Trans. Inf. Theory **28**, 129–137 (1982)

12. Karakse, M., Aydin, I., Akin, E.: The intelligent fault diagnosis frameworks based on fuzzy integral. In: SPEEDAM, pp. 1634–1639 (2010)

13. Jayaswal, P., Verma, S.N., Wadhwani, A.K.: Development of EBP-artificial neural network expert system for rolling element bearing fault diagnosis. J. Vib. Control **17**, 1131–1148 (2011)

14. Pineda-Sanchez, M., Riera-Guasp, M., Antonio-Daviu, J.A., Roger-Folch, J., Perez-Cruz, J., Puche-Panadero, R.: Instantaneous frequency of the left sideband harmonic during the start-up transient: a new method for diagnosis of broken bars. IEEE Trans. Ind. Electron. **56**, 4557–4570 (2009)

15. Romero-Troncoso, R.J., Cabal-Yepez, E., Osornio-Rios, R.A., Huber, N.: FPGA-based online detection of multiple combined faults in induction motors through information entropy and fuzzy inference. IEEE Trans. Ind. Electron. **58**, 5263–5270 (2011)

16. Siyambalapitiya, D.J., Mclaren, P.G.: Reliability improvement and economic benefits of on-line monitoring systems for large induction machines. IEEE Trans. Ind. Appl. **26**, 1018–1025 (1990)

17. Godoy, W.F., da Silva, I.N., Goedtel, A., Palacios, R.H.C., Lopes, T.D.: Application of intelligent tools to detect and classify broken rotor bars in three-phase induction motors fed by an inverter. IET Electr. Power Appl. **10**, 430–439 (2016)

Time Series Analysis and Forecasting

Trend Detection in Gold Worth
Using Regression

Seyedeh Foroozan Rashidi[1], Hamid Parvin[2,3(✉)],
and Samad Nejatian[4,5]

[1] Department of Computer Engineering, College of Technical and Engineering,
Omidiyeh Branch, Islamic Azad University, Omidiyeh, Iran
[2] Department of Computer Engineering,
Yasooj Branch, Islamic Azad University, Yasooj, Iran
parvin@iust.ac.ir
[3] Young Researchers and Elite Club, Nourabad Mamasani Branch,
Islamic Azad University, Nourabad Mamasani, Iran
[4] Department of Electrical Engineering,
Yasooj Branch, Islamic Azad University, Yasooj, Iran
[5] Young Researchers and Elite Club, Yasooj Branch,
Islamic Azad University, Yasooj, Iran

Abstract. A mapping chase autoregression shape is applied to predict gold worth here. Previous works centered on prediction of the instability of gold worth to reveal the characteristics of gold market. By the way, due to the fact that the data of gold worth have high dimensionality, MCAF is suitable and able to predict gold worth more accurately rather than other mechanisms. In this paper, the MCAF is used to the everyday worth of gold. The experimental results indicate MCAF outperforms BPNN technique, especially on stability, which reveals the advantage of MCAF technique in dealing with huge amounts of data.

Keywords: Gold worth · Mapping chase autoregression · Predict shape

1 Introduction

Artificial intelligence has been used in many applications [1–15]. Data mining is one of the branches of artificial intelligence. Extraction of knowledge from a large amount of data is named data mining [16–34]. Based on our different expectations, different data mining tasks emerged. The most important category of tasks in data mining is supervised learning tasks [34–36].

The understanding and prediction of the overall trend of the gold market is a hot topic considering its monetary and financial significance. In earlier studies, the instability of gold worth has been explained with many techniques. Many regression methods have been advised recently [37–41]. There is always a problem in which it is desired to predict the next value in a series that is named time series forecasting [42]. This series can be stock value records, where we want to know the next value of the stock. ANFIS-Based Multi-Factor Time Series (ABMFTS) model has been advised in [42]. ARCH shape has been advised to investigate the law of the variation of the price

G. Sidorov and O. Herrera-Alcántara (Eds.): MICAI 2016, Part I, LNAI 10061, pp. 281–289, 2017.
DOI: 10.1007/978-3-319-62434-1_24

rises' series in the UK [43]. GARCH shape has been advised then and it has been applied to express the characteristics of the economic time sequence [43]. After that, the GARCH forms turned out to be one of the major methods in the field of gold worth instability.

GARCH-M shape has been used to fit the trend of gold worth, and analyzed the relationship between risk and return of China's gold market [43]. Authors also conclude that risk and return are positively correlated [43]. A hybrid ANN-GARCH shape has been advised to predict the gold worth instability and decide the main financial features that can affect the gold worth instability [44].

All these studies focused on fitting and predicting the instability of gold worth. However, the ability to predict the gold worth in a short term is more important for depositors to make investment decisions in the gold market. In this regard, GARCH forms make great resultant errors. Therefore, the neural network techniques have been used to build more accurate forms to fit and predict gold worth. Yuan [45] and Chen [46] advised a hybrid mapping chase BP neural network shape to predict 20 days gold worth. Nonetheless, the limitation of this technique lies in its weak stability. They studied a short term gold worth within 100 days, which realized a high accuracy in predicting. But, when the sample size expands, the algorithm collapses fast and over fitting appears.

Mapping chase technique was advised by Kruskal [47] and generalized by Friedman and Tukey [48]. It projects high-dimensional data to low-dimensional space and preserve the necessary information at the same time. In this study, a mapping chase autoregression shape is applied to predict gold worth for the first time. Compared with other forms, the sample size has been expanded and the accuracy of predicting has been raised. Therefore, the conclusion of this study is important for depositors to diminish risk and to get a better asset allocation.

In continuation of this work is divided into three parts. First, the realization of MCAF performance evaluation index has been described. Second, the empirical analysis was conducted to test the effectiveness and accuracy of MCAF and the results were compared with other forms. Finally, the last section summarizes the work and put the perspective of future research.

2 Technology

2.1 Procedure of MCAF

MCAF bases on the form of the mapping chase, and combined with time series autoregression technique. Through linear mapping, high-dimensional data can be low-dimensionally projected. At this time, the necessary information is still preserved. Then, using the ridge regression and polynomial approximation, the function is finally realized. This method has advantages in convergence rate and accuracy of forecasts. The process is as follows:

(1) Determine the mapping value z_i:

$$z_i = \sum_{e=1}^{p} \alpha_e x_{i-e} \ (i = p+1, p+2, \cdots, n) \tag{1}$$

Where, $\alpha_e = (\alpha_1, \alpha_2, \cdots, \alpha_p)$ is the mapping direction. p is the number of prediction factor, x_{i-e} is the sample values.

(2) Based on orthogonal Hermit polynomial, the MCAF shape is built as:

$$\hat{x} = \sum_{i=1}^{M} \sum_{j=1}^{r} v_{ij} h_{ij}(z) \ (i = 1, 2, \cdots, M; j = 1, 2, \cdots, r) \tag{2}$$

where $\hat{x}$ is the prediction value, M is the number of ridge function, and r is the polynomial order. v are the coefficients of the polynomial, and can be obtained by least square technique. h is the orthogonal Hermit polynomial.

(3) Optimize performance indicators mapping. Based on real coded accelerating genetic algorithm to solve this problem is to minimize the performance indicators mapping the best way to show a character with high dimensional data structure as much as possible. Therefore, the best estimate for mapping is estimated by

$$\min F(\alpha, v) = \frac{1}{n-p} \sum_{i=p+1}^{n} (x_i - \hat{x}_i)^2$$

$$s.t. \sum_{j=1}^{p} \alpha_j^2 = 1 \tag{3}$$

(4) Calculating and fitting residual error $r_i = x_i - \hat{x}_i$. If the results meet the condition, the shape parameter will be returned. Otherwise, x_i will be replaced by r_i. And the calculating will go back to step (1) for the next optimization until the condition is meet and return the final results.

2.2 Performance Evaluation Index

The accuracy and stability performance will be assessed. NMSE (normalized mean square error) and MRE (mean relative error) can accurately predict the mapping performance. Lens EF (Error Fluctuation) [49] the range of fluctuation is generally used to indicate that a stable shape. The index is calculated:

$$NMSE = \frac{1}{NS^2} \sum_{i=1}^{N} (x_{Oi} - x_{Ti})^2 \tag{4}$$

$$MRE = \frac{1}{M} \sum_{j=1}^{M} \left| \frac{x_{Oj} - x_{Fj}}{x_{Oj}} \right| \tag{5}$$

$$EF = \frac{\sum\limits_{t=1}^{N+M-1} \sum\limits_{p=t}^{N+M} \sqrt{|\sigma_t - \sigma_p|}}{\sum\limits_{t=1}^{N+M} t} \tag{6}$$

Where N is the number of training period sample, S^2 is the sample variance of training period sample. x_{Oi} is the target value of sample i and x_{Ti} is the training value of sample i within training period. M is the number of predicting period sample. x_{Oj} is the target value of sample j and x_{Fj} is the training value of sample j within predicting period. σ_t and σ_p are the relative errors of sample t and sample p. The shape has higher accuracy when the values of NMSE and MSE are lower, and the value of EF is also the smaller the better, which means the shape is more stable in predicting.

3 Empirical Results and Analysis

3.1 Results of MCAF Shape

The value of gold (T + D) on the Shanghai Gold Exchange has been chosen to test the performance of the MCAF. Au (T + D) is one of the gold trade for the future, and in this study, the daily closing value of Jan in 2008 to July in 2013 (data from the RESSET http://www.resset.com) it is divided into two parts: the period of training (1200 forward), and sample the forecast period (rare 256 data). The data are shown in Fig. 1.

Data of training period sample are normalized and the best mapping direction is returned as:

$$\alpha = [0.098 \quad 0.060 \quad -0.034 \quad -0.027 \quad 0.046 \quad -0.025 \quad 0.014 \quad 0.006 \quad 0.092$$
$$0.021 \quad -0.083 \quad 0.033 \quad 0.013],$$

When the training period sample is input and one ridge function is used to fit. Within the procedure, the polynomial order is selected as 15. Using R language program, the fitted value of training period are gained, and the actual value and fitted value are shown in Fig. 2.

It can be installed from Fig. 2 that values are approximate, and the actual value can be seen, and MCAF a great advantage in connections. Thus, the MCAF can be used to predict the short-term the value of gold. In this way, the order is predictable 1. After calculating the predictive value of the test period, output, and thus predict that shown in Fig. 3.

It can be seen from Fig. 3 that MCAF shape has permitted error in predicting. Furthermore, the MCAF shape takes one step predicting, which means within testing period, all the data are predictions except the first one. However, it shows that MCAF shape is stable for making a short term predicting, and even after 200 days, the error is still small. Altogether, the MCAF shape is effective and feasible.

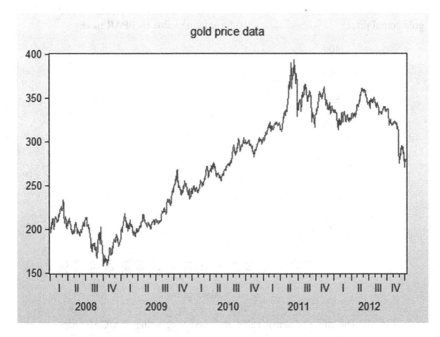

Fig. 1. Gold worth data from Jan 2th in 2008 to July 31th in 2013

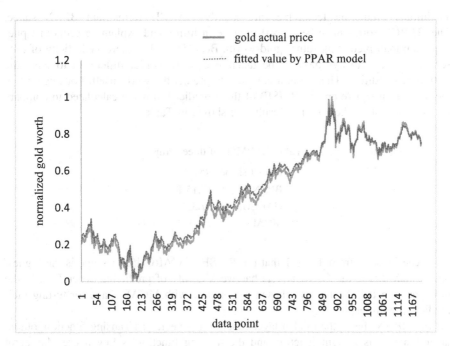

Fig. 2. The curve of actual value and fitted value of MCAF shape

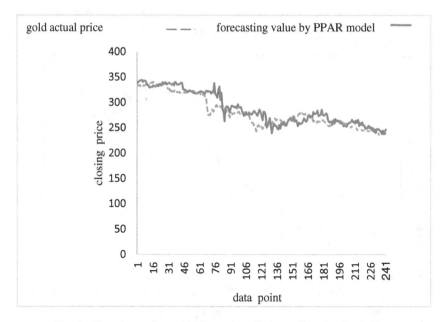

Fig. 3. The curve of actual value and predicting value of MCAF shape

3.2   Compare with Results of Other Forms

Traditional predicting techniques are mainly GARCH forms and BPNN shape. The GARCH forms have better performance in fitting and explaining economic phenomenon than predicting future gold worth. Because of the heteroskedasticity of time series, the data always have to be taken one or two-order difference to meet the stationary condition. Therefore, it is hardly to predict the worth itself. For this reason, the root mean square errors (RMSE) of three predict forms are calculated to compare the accuracy of predicting. The results are shown in Table 1.

Table 1.   RMSE of three forms

Predict shape	RMSE
BPNN	17.15%
GARCH(1,1)	57.33%
MCAF	12.79%

It can be seen from Table 1 that the RMSE of GARCH(1,1) shape is the highest one, which means the GARCH(1,1) has weak ability of predicting. Therefore, in the next part, the BPNN shape is chosen to compare with MCAF shape for testing their predicting abilities.

For BPNN shape, the hidden layer function is selected as Tansing function, output layer function is Purelin function and the training function is Levenberg-Marquardt function. The results of performance evaluation index are shown in Table 2.

Table 2. Performance indicators of different prediction forms

Shape	NMSE	MRE	EF
MCAF	3.82%	3.60%	20.71%
BPNN	1.02%	6.35%	54%

It is shown in Table 2 that in the predicting period, all the performance indicators of MCAF shape are smaller. The NMSE of MCAF shape is higher than that of BPNN shape, but the MRE of MCAF shape is lower than that of BPNN shape which means these two forms have similar performance in accuracy ability. However, the EF of MCAF shape is much lower than that of BPNN shape, which means MCAF shape is much more stable than BPNN shape in predicting. And the stability of shape can be tested by enhance the size of sample. In that case, BPNN shape loses efficiency faster than MCAF shape.

4   Conclusion

In order to fitting the high nonlinear and mutable data of the gold daily closing worth and predicting precisely the future worth, the MCAF shape is applied to solve the problem for the first time. And by comparing with other forms, it shows that the high-dimensional data approximate capability of MCAF shape can better realize the purpose of predicting the future worth from the inherent mechanism of financial data. The MCAF algorithm shows robust computing power for large data, so the future research may want to analyze new hybrid forms to predict future data when the sample size is bigger than that in this study. And the results will help the depositors making decisions and get a better asset allocation and portfolio diversification.

References

1. Ding, J., Liu, Y., Zhang, L., Wang, J., Liu, Y.: An anomaly detection approach for multiple monitoring data series based on latent correlation probabilistic model. Appl. Intell. **44**(2), 340–361 (2016)
2. Cerrada, M., Sanchez, R.-V., Pacheco, F., Cabrera, D., Zurita, G., Li, C.: Hierarchical feature selection based on relative dependency for gear fault diagnosis. Appl. Intell. **44**(3), 687–703 (2016)
3. Novoa-Hernández, P., Corona, C.C., Pelta, D.A.: Self-adaptation in dynamic environments - a survey and open issues. IJBIC **8**(1), 1–13 (2016)
4. Adewumi, A.O., Arasomwan, A.M.: On the performance of particle swarm optimisation with(out) some control parameters for global optimisation. IJBIC **8**(1), 14–32 (2016)
5. Wang, H., Wang, W., Sun, H., Rahnamayan, S.: Firefly algorithm with random attraction. IJBIC **8**(1), 33–41 (2016)
6. Castelli, M., Vanneschi, L., Popovic, A.: Parameter evaluation of geometric semantic genetic programming in pharmacokinetics. IJBIC **8**(1), 42–50 (2016)

7. Srinivasa Rao, B., Vaisakh, K.: Multi-objective adaptive clonal selection algorithm for solving optimal power flow problem with load uncertainty. IJBIC **8**(2), 67–83 (2016)

8. Cai, Q., Ma, L., Gong, M., Tian, D.: A survey on network community detection based on evolutionary computation. IJBIC **8**(2), 84–98 (2016)

9. Junior, L.D.R.S.S., Nedjah, N.: Distributed strategy for robots recruitment in swarm-based systems. IJBIC **8**(2), 99–108 (2016)

10. Jia, Z., Duan, H., Shi, Y.: Hybrid brain storm optimisation and simulated annealing algorithm for continuous optimisation problems. IJBIC **8**(2), 109–121 (2016)

11. Srivastava, P.R.: Test case optimisation a nature inspired approach using bacteriologic algorithm. IJBIC **8**(2), 122–131 (2016)

12. Xu, Z., Ünveren, A., Acan, A.: Probability collectives hybridised with differential evolution for global optimisation. IJBIC **8**(3), 133–153 (2016)

13. Osuna-Enciso, V., Cuevas, E., Oliva, D., Sossa, H., Pérez Cisneros, M.A.: A bio-inspired evolutionary algorithm: allostatic optimisation. IJBIC **8**(3), 154–169 (2016)

14. Ahirwal, M.K., Kumar, A., Singh, G.K.: Study of ABC and PSO algorithms as optimised adaptive noise canceller for EEG/ERP. IJBIC **8**(3), 170–183 (2016)

15. Niknam, T., Kavousi-Fard, A.: Optimal energy management of smart renewable micro-grids in the reconfigurable systems using adaptive harmony search algorithm. IJBIC **8**(3), 184–194 (2016)

16. Alishavandi, H., Gouraki, G.H., Parvin, H.: An enhanced dynamic detection of possible invariants based on best permutation of test cases. Comput. Syst. Sci. Eng. **31**(1), 156–164 (2016)

17. Parvin, H., Minaei-Bidgoli, B., Alinejad-Rokny, H.: A new imbalanced learning and dictions tree method for breast cancer diagnosis. J. Bionanoscience **7**(6), 673–678 (2013)

18. Parvin, H., Alinejad-Rokny, H., Minaei-Bidgoli, B., Parvin, S.: A new classifier ensemble methodology based on subspace learning. J. Exp. Theor. Artif. Intell. **25**(2), 227–250 (2013)

19. Parvin, H., Minaei-Bidgoli, B., Alinejad-Rokny, H., Punch, W.F.: Data weighing mechanisms for clustering ensembles. Comput. Electr. Eng. **39**(5), 1433–1450 (2013)

20. Parvin, H., Alizadeh, H., Minaei-Bidgoli, B.: A new method for constructing classifier ensembles. JDCTA **3**(2), 62–66 (2009)

21. Parvin, H., Alinejad-Rokny, H., Asadi, M.: An ensemble based approach for feature selection. J. Appl. Sci. Res. **7**(9), 33–43 (2011)

22. Parvin, H., Alizadeh, H., Minaei-Bidgoli, B., Analoui, M.: CCHR: combination of classifiers using heuristic retraining. In: International Conference on Networked Computing and Advanced Information Management, NCM 2008, pp. 302–305 (2008)

23. Parvin, H., Alizadeh, H., Fathy, M., Minaei-Bidgoli, B.: Improved face detection using spatial histogram features. In: IPCV 2008, pp. 381–386 (2008)

24. Parvin, H., Alinejad-Rokny, H., Parvin, S.: A classifier ensemble of binary classifier ensembles. Int. J. Learn. Manag. Syst. **1**(2), 37–47 (2013)

25. Parvin, H., Minaei-Bidgoli, B.: A clustering ensemble framework based on elite selection of weighted clusters. Adv. Data Anal. Classif. **7**(2), 181–208 (2013)

26. Alizadeh, H., Minaei-Bidgoli, B., Parvin, H.: Optimizing fuzzy cluster ensemble in string representation. IJPRAI **27**(2), 1793–6381 (2013)

27. Parvin, H., Beigi, A., Mozayani, N.: A clustering ensemble learning method based on the ant colony clustering algorithm. Int. J. Appl. Comput. Math. **11**(2), 286–302 (2012)

28. Alizadeh, H., Minaei-Bidgoli, B., Parvin, H.: To improve the quality of cluster ensembles by selecting a subset of base clusters. J. Exp. Theor. Artif. Intell. **26**(1), 127–150 (2014)

29. Alizadeh, H., Minaei-Bidgoli, B., Parvin, H.: Cluster ensemble selection based on a new cluster stability measure. Intell. Data Anal. **18**(3), 389–408 (2014)

30. Minaei-Bidgoli, B., Parvin, H., Alinejad-Rokny, H., Alizadeh, H., Punch, W.F.: Effects of resampling method and adaptation on clustering ensemble efficacy. Artif. Intell. Rev. **41**(1), 27–48 (2014)
31. Parvin, H., Minaei-Bidgoli, B.: A clustering ensemble framework based on selection of fuzzy weighted clusters in a locally adaptive clustering algorithm. Pattern Anal. Appl. **18**(1), 87–112 (2015)
32. Parvin, H., Mirnabibaboli, M., Alinejad-Rokny, H.: Proposing a classifier ensemble framework based on classifier selection and decision tree. Eng. Appl. AI **37**, 34–42 (2015)
33. Parvin, H., Mohammadi, M., Rezaei, Z.: Face identification based on Gabor-wavelet features. Int. J. Digital Content Technol. Appl. **6**(1), 247–255 (2012)
34. Khan, M.A., Shahzad, W., Baig, A.R.: Protein classification via an ant-inspired association rules-based classifier. IJBIC **8**(1), 51–65 (2016)
35. Lee, C.-P., Lin, W.-S.: Using the two-population genetic algorithm with distance-based k-nearest neighbour voting classifier for high-dimensional data. IJDMB **14**(4), 315–331 (2016)
36. Zhu, M., Liu, S., Jiang, J.: A hybrid method for learning multi-dimensional Bayesian network classifiers based on an optimization model. Appl. Intell. **44**(1), 123–148 (2016)
37. Kim, M.: Sparse inverse covariance learning of conditional Gaussian mixtures for multiple-output regression. Appl. Intell. **44**(1), 17–29 (2016)
38. Tanveer, M., Shubham, K., Aldhaifallah, M., Nisar, K.S.: An efficient implicit regularized Lagrangian twin support vector regression. Appl. Intell. **44**(4), 831–848 (2016)
39. Balasundaram, S., Meena, Y.: Training primal twin support vector regression via unconstrained convex minimization. Appl. Intell. **44**(4), 931–955 (2016)
40. Yang, L., Qian, Y.: A sparse logistic regression framework by difference of convex functions programming. Appl. Intell. **45**(2), 241–254 (2016)
41. Bang, S., Cho, H.J., Jhun, M.: Adaptive lasso penalised censored composite quantile regression. IJDMB **15**(1), 22–46 (2016)
42. Chen, Y.-S., Cheng, C.-H., Chiu, C.-L., Huang, S.-T.: A study of ANFIS-based multi-factor time series models for forecasting stock index. Appl. Intell. **45**(2), 277–292 (2016)
43. Efimova, O., Serletis, A.: Energy markets instability forming using GARCH. Energy Econ. **43**, 264–273 (2014)
44. Werner, K., Marcel, C.M.: Gold worth instability: a predicting approach using the artificial neural network-GARCH shape. Expert Syst. Appl. **42**, 7245–7251 (2015)
45. Yuan, G.: Study on gold worth predicting technique based on neural network optimized by GA with mapping chase algorithm. JCIT **7**, 558–565 (2012)
46. Chen, Li: Gold worth predicting shape based on mapping chase and neural network. Comput. Simul. **30**, 354–363 (2012)
47. Kruskal, J.B.: Linear Transformation of Multivariate Data: Theory and Application in the Behavioral Science. London Semimar Press, New York (1972)
48. Friedman, J.H., Tukey, J.W.: A mapping chase algorithm for exploratory data analysis. Trans. Comput. IEEE **23**, 881–889 (1974)
49. Ran, D., Li, M., Sheng, W., et al.: Research on multi-shape predicts in mid-long term runoff in DanjiangKou reservoir. JHE **9**, 1069–1073 (2010)

Internet Queries as a Tool for Analysis of Regional Police Work and Forecast of Crimes in Regions

Anna Boldyreva[1,2(✉)], Mikhail Alexandrov[2,3], Olexiy Koshulko[4], and Oleg Sobolevskiy[1]

[1] Moscow Institute of Physics and Technologies, National Research University,
Dolgoprudny, Russia
anna.boldyreva@phystech.edu,
oleg.sobolevskiy.mipt@gmail.com
[2] Russian Presidential Academy of National Economy and Public
Administration, Moscow, Russia
[3] Autonomous University of Barcelona, Barcelona, Spain
malexandrov@mail.ru
[4] Glushkov Institute of Cybernetics, Kiev, Ukraine
koshulko@gmail.com

Abstract. In the paper we propose two technologies for processing web search queries related to criminal activity. The first one is based on the comparison of the relative number of crimes and the corresponding queries in different regions. Such analysis allows to evaluate the work of the regional police. The second technology uses the correlation between the dynamics of crimes and the dynamics of queries for the Group Method of Data Handling (GMDH) application. It allows to forecast crimes in regions. The source data is taken from Internet depositories of the Yandex company and the Office of the Prosecutor General of Russia. The results of analysis coincide with the official governmental statistics. The results of forecast prove to be very high (2% – 6% of errors). This circumstance gives us the possibility to recommend the proposed technologies for the police departments.

Keywords: Internet queries · Regional crimes · Regional police · GMDH

1 Introduction

1.1 Problem Setting

There is a stable statistical dependency between the intensity of search queries and the manifestation of various events or development of various processes related to the activities of the information society. In this paper we use this dependency for analysis

---

Work done under partial support of the Institute of Applied Economic Research under Russian Presidential Academy of National Economy and Public Administration (RANEPA).

G. Sidorov and O. Herrera-Alcántara (Eds.): MICAI 2016, Part I, LNAI 10061, pp. 290–302, 2017.
DOI: 10.1007/978-3-319-62434-1_25

and forecast of crimes in regions of Russia. The basic hypothesis here consists in the following. Let there be a person, who has some plan to complete a crime or has already completed this crime. He/she tries to find in the Internet any similar cases such as any concomitant circumstances of the crime, punishment for the crime, and various ways to avoid it. Dynamics of such queries, the crimes registered in the Office of the Prosecutor General of Russia, and the data about the population in regions can be used both for the evaluation of the criminal situation in regions and for the forecast of crimes in these regions.

1.2   Related Works

By the moment the number of publications in the area under consideration is limited and the majority of publications refer to the problem of forecasting crimes but not to the problem of analysis of criminal situations. The presented paper is our attempt to attract the attention of professionals to possibilities of processing web search queries for the solution of the mentioned problems.

1. Examples of applications

In [1] the authors consider general questions of validity and reliability related to processing queries to Internet search engines and calls to mobile communication services. Among the examples presented in this paper there are dynamics of crimes concerning stealing and robbery. Here, the principal method the authors used for the forecast was the traditional regression.

The paper [2] describes a research using data from Twitter. The authors consider spatial-temporal data related to 25 types of crimes. The proposed method for processing queries in Twitter allowed to improve the performance of crime prediction for 19 types of crimes from the given 25.

The authors of [3] describe the spatial-temporal generalized additive model for the forecast of crimes. They combine queries to Internet search engines and posts in Twitter to outperform the quality of their previous model.

The technique of Hotspot Mapping for forecasting spatial patterns of crime is presented in [4]. The authors consider 4 types of crimes: burglary, street crimes, theft from vehicles and theft of vehicles. The authors show how to attune the mentioned technique for different types of crimes.

2. Our contribution

Our first paper refers to the forecast of economic crimes using 2 methods: the traditional regression analysis (RA) and the Group Method of Data Handling (GMDH) [5]. The dependent variable was the total number of crimes belonging to the category of economic crimes with respect to all the territories of Russia. The independent variables were Internet search queries. We selected the search queries reflecting the contents of crimes and having significant correlation with the dynamics of the mentioned crimes. Experiments demonstrated the significant advantage of GMDH over RA. For this reason in our further studies we use only this method to forecast. In particularly, we use the platform GMDH Shell containing modified algorithms of GMDH [6].

In our next paper [7] we studied different GMDH-algorithms and different procedures of data preprocessing to forecast economic crimes. In this work we used so-called
'barometers' being a composition of 10 time series of search queries having the
strongest correlation with the dynamics of the mentioned crimes. These barometers
were the modification of barometers that Google had used in one of its early applications [8]. Here the term 'GMDH-algorithms' means various variants of combinatorial
and neuro-similar algorithms from GMDH Shell, and the term 'preprocessing' means
various data transformations as logarithm, square root, and so on. The results proved to
be very promising. Namely, the reached level of MAPE was equal 2% – 6%, where
MAPE stands for the well-known Mean Absolute Percentage Error.

The difference of this paper from our previous studies consists in:

- carrying out the data analysis with respect to the work of regional police, it is our
  first study;
- carrying out the forecast with respect to certain crimes in concrete regions unlike the
  previous study;
- using 153 descriptors instead of 10 – 20, with which we dealt in our experiments
  from our previous paper.

The rest of the paper is organized as follows. Section 2 contains the description of
data used in our research. In Sect. 3 we consider the work of regional police departments. In Sect. 4 we present the results of the forecast for given types of crimes in
regions. Section 5 concludes the paper.

2 Data

2.1 Indicators and Descriptors

Hereinafter we use the following notations:

- SQ, search queries to Internet
- RC, registered crimes in the Office of the Prosecutor General of Russia
- CC, Criminal Code of Russia
- FD, federal districts of Russia

SQ in relative terms are SQ normalized on all search queries in a given region. RC
in relative terms are RC normalized on the population of a given region.

Statistics of crimes in the regions of Russia are in open access on the site of the
Office of the Prosecutor [9]. In the paper we consider crimes reflected in the following
3 articles from the CC:

- Article 111 (CC). Intended infliction of grievous bodily harm;
- Article 222 (CC). Illegal purchase, transfer, selling, keeping, transportation of
  weapons;
- Article 291 (CC). Bribery.

Time span under consideration covers October 2013 – December 2015, which is 2
years. Such a restriction is defined by the conditions of the Yandex company [10].

We prefer to use the query statistics of Yandex because its data is presented both in absolute and relative terms. Google presents its data only in absolute form [11].

We created a data base (DB) of descriptors, which covered all the articles from the CC. The names of these descriptors are very simple: 'article 111', 'article 112', 'article 113', etc. Additionally, we included in the DB a set of word combinations, which will be useful for forecasting, such as: 'unlawful entry', 'purchase of gun', 'restraint of liberty', 'punishment', 'especially big', 'especially grave', 'aggravating', 'offense", 'use of weapons', etc.

2.2 Hypothesis

In the beginning of the paper we made an assumption that a person, who plans to complete a crime or has already completed this crime, searches the Internet to find any useful information concerning the crime. Moreover, at first this person is interested in his/her punishment for the crime and he/she uses SQ with the direct mention of the corresponding article(s). With these assumptions we can fix the following concrete hypotheses:

1. The number of people having completed a given crime during a given period in a given region is a certain share of all SQ reflecting this crime
2. The number of SQ with the direct mention of article(s) related to a given crime is a certain share of all SQ reflecting this crime

Therefore in the framework of these hypotheses, behind the SQ 'article X' there is a certain number of real people. With this assumption we can interpret the results presented in Sects. 3 and 4.

However, some simple conclusions can be done without any additional processing. For example, let the dynamics of indicator 'bribe' have a strong correlation with the dynamics of the descriptors 'article 191' (illicit trafficking of precious metals, natural precious stones or pearls) and 'article 269' (violation of safety regulations during construction, operation and maintenance of main pipelines). In this case one could make an assumption about certain abuses with materials related to construction.

3   Analysis of Regional Police Operations

3.1   Trend Analysis of SQ and RC

We can formulate the following statements related to the analysis of the criminal situation in regions:

- According to the hypotheses presented in Sect. 2.2 the bigger the difference between SQ and RC – the worse is the situation in a given region with respect to a given article;
- In order to exclude the dependence on population in each region, RC should be presented in relative terms;

– In order to take into account the general Internet activity in a given region, SQ should be presented in relative terms;

Our approach to evaluating the work of the regional police in a given region with a given type of crime consists in two positions: (1) the comparison of SQ and RC in the region under consideration, and (2) the comparison of situations in all other regions.

To interpret correctly the results of such comparisons we needed to make sure in the positive relation of the number of SQ and the number of RC. For this, in our initial experiment we considered the coherence between SQ 'article 111', 'article 291' and 'article 222' and the official crime statistics concerning these articles [9]. The crime statistics took into account the regional population. The results are presented on Fig. 1, where each region (it is the federal districts) is reflected by one point. The time span was October 2013 – December 2015, which is 27 months. Therefore each chart contains $27 \times 8 = 216$ points.

For the visual presentation, the numbers of RC were rescaled per 100000, 100000 and 1000000 population for the articles 111, 222 and 291 respectively. Additionally, the numbers of SQ were divided on 1000, 1000 and 100 for the articles 111, 222 and 291 respectively. The results are presented on the Fig. 1.

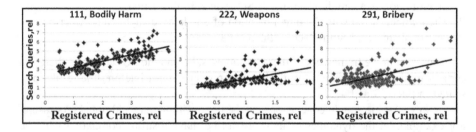

Fig. 1. Dependence (RC, SQ) for 8 FD and 3 articles

The trend analysis demonstrates that the number of search queries in regions increases with the growth of recorded crimes. Besides it is easy to see that the ascending trend is much more expressed for the article 111 (intended infliction of grievous bodily harm) in comparison with the articles 222 (illegal operations with weapons) and 291 (bribery). Such a situation can be easily explained by the following: unlike the article 111 there are no people interested in the detection of crimes related to the articles 222 and 291. For these reason, many crimes related to these articles are unregistered.

3.2   Method Based on Comparison of Scaled (RC, SQ)

1. Data preparation

We conducted the analysis of RC and SQ concerning 3 articles under consideration in 8 FD. For this we completed the following procedures of preprocessing:

- RC data of each region was normalized on the total population of this region. Then these values were normalized on their sum.
- SQ data of each region were normalized on their sum.

The results are presented on Fig. 2 in the form of percentages. Here: FE, NW and NC stand for the Far-Eastern and North-Western regions and the North Caucasus respectively. To evaluate the activity of a regional police one needs to consider the difference between the calculated relative RC and SQ. These results are presented on the Fig. 3. The regions are ordered here according this difference.

2. Results of comparative analysis

The left parts of the histograms show the regions, where the level of RC exceeds the level of SQ. So, here we can suppose the good work of regional police. And vice

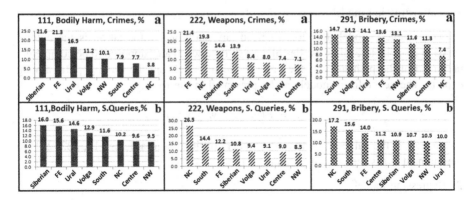

Fig. 2. (a) Registered Crimes in relative terms for FD as a percentage of their total number; (b) Search Queries in relative terms for FD as a percentage of their total number

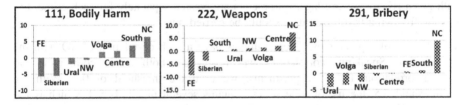

Fig. 3. The difference between Registered Crimes (%) and Search Queries (%)

versa, the right parts of the histograms show the regions, where the level of RC is less than the level of SQ. So, now we can say about the bad police work. Obviously, the terms 'good' and 'bad' have the relative sense.

To confirm the results of our analysis we need the official information from the Russian Ministry of Internal Affairs. However this information is closed and the site of the Ministry says nothing about the regional police work [12]. The only source of information is the Russian Mass Media. These publications say that the Far-Eastern, Siberian and North-Western regions demonstrate the best crime situations. The worst region is the North Caucasus. The latter concerns all types of crimes. In total these observations correspond to our results.

4   Forecast of Crimes

4.1   Types of Models

We aim to build 3 models for forecasting crimes related to the articles 111, 222, and 291 mentioned above. The horizon of forecast is 1 month. According the opinion of the police investigation officers the time between crime planning and crime completing usually doesn't exceed 3 months. So, we consider 3 months as a restriction of possible lags in the models and use the built models to forecast crimes for 1,2 and 3 months.

1. Autoregression model

The simplest model that doesn't need any additional information is the autoregression model. Here all properties of a given time series are supposed to be completely presented in the prehistory of the process. Such models are the most popular among experts. The generalized model can be presented in the form

$$y_{t+1} = F(y_t, y_{t-1}, y_{t-2}, y_{t-3})$$

Here: y_i is the value of the indicator under consideration (articles 111, 222, 291) in the moment i, t is the current moment of time.

2. Regression model

The next type of models is the regression of search queries and these models are the most interesting for us. The principal problem we met here was the huge number of SQ being regressors in regression model. To avoid this difficulty we used so-called barometers. Barometers are averaged time series of SQ having the strongest correlation with given RC for several lags. Barometers are created separately for each crime. For this the following two procedures should be carried out:

1. Selection of top samples. These samples have a high correlation of SQ with the indicator. Speaking 'correlation' we mean here both direct correlation and anti-correlation. In our experiments, we used the threshold of 0.7. With the threshold 0.5, the list of time series contains several hundreds SQ, which is too large. With the threshold 0.9, this list gets reduced to a dozen or two samples, therefore, we lose information. The threshold 0.7 is taken as a compromise. The

correlation is tested using the Pearson criterion for the current moment and for the lags 1, 2, and 3 months. Totally we had 153 SQ.

2. Creation of 8 barometers. 4 barometers contain the average value of time series from the top samples having high correlation with the indicator for lags = 0, 1, 2, 3 months respectively. The other 4 barometers contain the average value of time series from the top samples having high anti-correlation with the indicator for the same lags.

The resulting generalized model can be presented in the form:

$$y_{t+1} = F\left(b_{1,t}, \ldots b_{1,t-3}, b_{2,t}, \ldots b_{2,t-3} \ldots b_{8,t}, \ldots b_{8,t-3}\right)$$

Here: $b_{i,j}$ are barometers, i is the number of the barometer, j is the moment of time.

3. Combined model

This type of model includes both autoregression and regressors:

$$y_{t+1} = F\left(b_{1,t}, \ldots b_{1,t-3}, b_{2,t}, b_{2,t-3}, \ldots b_{8,t}, \ldots b_{8,t-3}, y_t, y_{t-1}, y_{t-2}, y_{t-3}\right)$$

All denotations here have been described above.

4.2 Method of Modeling

1. Group Method of Data Handling

To build the concrete model we use the Group Method of Data Handling (GMDH). This method was proposed by the Ukrainian scientist O. Ivakhnenko at the 70s of the previous century and now GMDH is being developed by his pupils and followers. The review of the traditional GMDH algorithms and the new algorithms are described in detail in [13]. The theoretical base of GMDH is presented in [14]. The list of algorithms reflecting the GMDH approach contains dozens of modifications. Both algorithms and their applications are regularly presented on the annual International conferences and seminars in Ukraine and European countries. As an example we can mention here the well-known conference ICIM-2013 dedicated to the memory of O. Ivakhnenko [15].

GMDH is a method (or rather a 'technology'), which allows to build a model of optimal complexity from a given class of models. GMDH demonstrates its advantages when: (a) a volume of experimental data is very limited, and (b) a priori information about the model to be built is absent or almost absent. The general scheme of the method consists of the following steps:

1. An expert defines a class of models, from the simplest to more complex ones.
2.. Experimental data are divided into two data sets: training data and control data, either manually or using an automatic procedure.
3. For a given kind of model, the best parameters are determines using the training data. Here any internal criteria of concordance between the model and the data may be used, e.g., the least squares criterion.

4. This model is tested using the control data on the basis of any external criteria. For example, it can be the square root deviation of the model data from the control data.
5. The external criteria (or the most important one) are checked on having reached a stable optimum. In this case the search is finished. Otherwise, more complex model is considered and the process is repeated from the step 3.

Here is why the external criteria reach an optimum (minimum). The experimental data is supposed to contain: (a) a regular component defined by the model structure, and (b) a random component—noise. Obviously, the model is to be capable to reflect the changes of the regular component. When the model is too simple, it is weakly sensible to this regular component and insensible to the noise. When the model is too complex, it reflects well the regular component but also the changing of the random component. In both cases the values of the penalty function (external criterion) are large. So, we expect to find a point where the criterion reaches its minimum.

2. GMDH Shell as a platform for GMDH

GMDH Shell is a platform for modeling using various GMDH-based algorithms [6]. Just this platform was used in our experiments. GMDH Shell includes: (a) initial data transformations (logarithms, squares, etc.) with lags and fictive variables; (b) the basic combinatorial algorithm (COMBI) and the basic neuro-similar algorithm (MIA) with modifications; (c) various ways to control model quality as k-fold cross validation etc. Both algorithms mentioned above are described in detail in [13].

COMBI is the name of the group of algorithms that take into account all combinations of model parameters in the framework of a given class. Here are the examples of such classes of models:

A. The class of model is lineal functions of n-variables

Level 1: $y_i = a_0 + a_i x_i$ $i = 1, 2, \ldots n$
Level 2: $y_k = a_0 + a_i x_i + a_j x_j$ $i, j = 1, 2, \ldots n;$
etc.

B. The class of models is polynomial functions of n-variables with the limited degree (e.g. 2)

Level 1: $y_k = a_0 + a_i x_i^p$ $i = 1, 2, \ldots n;$ $p = 1, 2$
Level 2: $y_k = a_0 + a_i x_i^p + a_j x_j^q$ $i, j = 1, 2, \ldots n;$ $p, q = 1, 2$
Level 3: $y_k = a_0 + a_i x_i^p + a_j x_j^q + b_{ij} x_i x_j$ $i, j = 1, 2, \ldots n;$ $p, q = 1, 2$
etc.

MIA is the name of the group of algorithms based on the inheritance of the best parameter combinations. Here, the fix number of the best models on a current layer form new variables on the next layer using a given function of transformation:

Layer 1: $y_i = a_0 + a_i x_i$ $i = 1, 2, \ldots n$
Layer 2: $z_k = a_0 + f(y_i, y_j)$ $i, j = 1, 2, \ldots n;$ $(i, j$ refer to selected models$)$
Layer 3: $g_k = a_0 + f(z_i, z_j)$ $i, j = 1, 2, \ldots n;$ $(i, j$ refer to selected models$)$
etc.

The typical transformations of f are:

Lineal: $f(s,t) = a_0 + a_1 s + a_2 t$

Quadratic: $f(s,t) = a_0 + a_1 s + a_2 t + a_3 st + a_4 s^2 + a_5 t^2$

3. Results of modeling

We studied 10 models using GMDH Shell. The models differed on the following characteristics: (a) algorithms are COMBI or MIA; (b) variables are autoregression, barometers, or both autoregression and barometers; (c) degrees of polynomial or neuron function are lineal (1) or quadratic (2).

We used 2-fold cross validation for checking model quality. The last 3 months were excluded from the consideration and were used for testing the accuracy of the forecast. Table 1 contains model descriptions and absolute percentage errors of forecast for 1, 2, 3 months (with their mean value) for the article 111. Here '1', '2' and '3' are the notations for months. The best model with respect to the mean value of the forecast is built with COMBI. It is marked in the Table 1.

Table 1. Models and errors of the forecast for the article 111

Algorithms	Autoreg	Barom.	Degree	1,%	2,%	3,%	Mean,%
COMBI	+		1	5,0	3,3	0,9	3,1
COMBI		+	1	1,0	2,8	3,9	2,6
COMBI		+	2	1,0	6,2	3,2	3,5
COMBI	+	+	1	5,0	3,3	2,0	3,4
COMBI	+	+	*2*	*2,0*	*0,2*	*0,3*	*0,8*
MIA	+		1	7,9	1,3	9,5	6,2
MIA		+	1	1,0	2,8	0,8	1,5
MIA		+	2	2,4	4,8	0,8	2,7
MIA	+	+	1	1,8	8,7	1,7	4,1
MIA	+	+	2	2,0	2,2	3,7	2,6

As for the articles 222 and 291, their errors of the forecast for 1 month for the best 3 models are equal 15% and 10%. All these models include barometers.

To demonstrate the real dynamics of RC for the articles 111, 222 and 291 we show 3 screenshots. They also reflect the work of the GMDH Shell. Figure 4 refers to the article 111, the forecast was completed here with the MIA algorithm. Figures 5 and 6 refer to the articles 222 and 291 respectively, the forecast was completed with the COMBI algorithm. Both MIA and COMBI used autoregression and barometers.

The general results of modeling are the following:

- Barometers allow to improve the quality of the forecast for all models and all articles. Only in one case for the article 111 the results remained the same.
- The forecast for article 111 is significantly better than the forecast for the other articles. The reason lies in the fact, that the data on registration of crimes under articles 222 and 291 is distorted. In crimes concerning article 111 there is a victim, who is interested in the registration and disclosure of the crime. In crimes concerning articles 222 and 291 are no such victims.

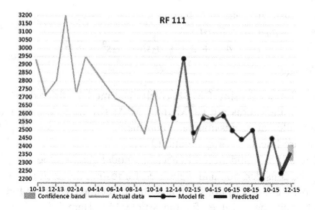

Fig. 4. Forecast for the article 111 using the MIA algorithm

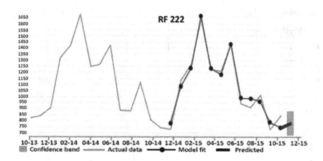

Fig. 5. Forecast for the article 222 using the COMBI algorithm

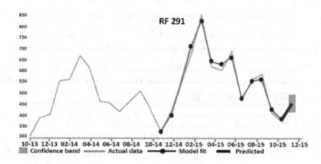

Fig. 6. Forecast for the article 291 using the COMBI algorithm

5 Conclusions

In this paper, we proposed a method for evaluation of the operation of regional police. The method consists in the comparison of the number of registered crimes and search queries after special procedures of scaling. In the experiments we considered the police work in 8 Federal Districts of Russia with respect to 3 given type of crimes. The obtained results in total correspond to the information reflected in the Russian Mass Media.

We also studied the possibilities to forecast the mentioned crimes using different models on the GMDH Shell platform and selected the best models for each type of crime. The accuracy of forecast proves to be very high for crimes with victims and lower for victimless crimes.

We suppose that the proposed technologies will be useful for the regional police departments.

References

1. Zhu, J., Wu, L.: Assessing public opinion trends based on user search queries: validity, reliability, and practicality. In: Web Mining Lab, Department of Media and Communication, City University of Hong Kong, School of Communication, Shenzhen University, China (2016)
2. Gerber, M.S.: Predicting Crime using Twitter and Kernel Density Estimation, USA (2014). www.sciencedirect.com/science/article/pii/S0167923614000268
3. Wang, X., Brown, D.E., Gerber, M.S.: Spatio-temporal modeling of criminal incidents using geographic, demographic, and twitter-derived information. In: Proceedings of International Conference on Intelligence and Security Informatics (ISI-2012), pp. 36–41 (2012). http://ptl. sys.virginia.edu/ptl/sites/default/files/ISI2012_WBG.pdf
4. Chaineya, S., Tompson, L., Uhlig, S.: The utility of hotspot mapping for predicting spatial patterns of crime. Secur. J. **21**, 4–28 (2008). doi:10.1057/palgrave.sj.8350066. http://www. palgrave-journals.com/sj/journal/v21/n1/full/8350066a.html
5. Boldyreva, A., Koshulko, O.: Forecasting models of economic crimes based on queries to internet: regression vs GMDH. In: Mathematical Modeling of Social Processes', Proceedings of Sociology, Faculty of MSU (Lomonosov Moscow State University), vol. 17, pp. 34–42 [rus]. House MSU (2015)
6. GMDH Shell: platform for inductive modeling. http://www.gmdhshell.com/
7. Boldyreva, A., Koshulko, O.: GMDH helps to build models based on queries to yandex for the forecast of economic crimes. In: Proceedings of 5-th International Workshop on Inductive Modeling, pp. 9–11. NAS of Ukraine, Kyev (2015). http://www.mgua.irtc.org.ua/attach/ICIM-IWIM/2015/index2015.html
8. Ginsberg, J., et al.: Detecting influenza epidemics using search engine query data. Nature **457**, 1012–1014 (2009)
9. Russian resources: General office of the Russian public prosecutor, Legal Statistics. http://crimestat.ru/offenses_map
10. Russian resources: Yandex statistics. http://wordstat.yandex.com
11. Russian resources: Google Trends. http://www.google.ru/trends
12. Russian resources: Ministry of Internal Affairs. http://xn–b1aew.xn–p1ai

13. Stepashko, V.: Ideas of academician O. Ivakhnenko in inductive modeling field from historical perspective. In: Proceedings of 4-th International Conference on Inductive Modeling (ICIM-2013), pp. 31–37. House NAS of Ukraine, Prague Technical University, Kyev (2013)
14. Stepashko, V.: Method of critical variances as an analytical tool of the Inductive Modeling Theory. J. Inf. Autom. Sci. **40**(3), 47–58 (2008). Begell House Inc.
15. Stepashko, V. (ed.): Proceedings of the 4-th International Conference on Inductive Modeling (ICIM-2013). House NAS of Ukraine, Prague Technical University, Kyev (2013). http://www.mgua.irtc.org.ua/attach/ICIM-IWIM/2013/index2013.html

Creating Collections of Descriptors of Events and Processes Based on Internet Queries

Anna Boldyreva[1,2(✉)], Oleg Sobolevskiy[1], Mikhail Alexandrov[2,3],
and Vera Danilova[2]

[1] Moscow Institute of Physics and Technologies,
National Research University, Moscow, Russia
anna.boldyreva@phystech.edu,
oleg.sobolevskiy.mipt@gmail.com
[2] Russian Presidential Academy of National Economy
and Public Administration, Moscow, Russia
malexandrov@mail.ru, maolve@gmail.com
[3] Autonomous University of Barcelona, Barcelona, Spain

Abstract. Search queries to Internet are a real reflection of events and processes that happen in the informative society. Moreover, the recent research shows that search queries can be an effective tool for the analysis and forecast of these events and processes. In the paper, we present our experience in creating databases of descriptors (queries and their combinations) to be used in real problems. An example related to the analysis and forecast of regional economy illustrates an application of the mentioned descriptors. The paper is intended for those who use or plan to use Internet queries in their applied research and practical applications.

Keywords: Internet queries · Situation descriptors · Barometers · Regional economy

1 Introduction

1.1 Terminology and Problem Settings

There is a stable statistical dependence between the intensity of search queries and real-world events and social processes. For example, Fig. 1 shows the dynamics of the query 'swimsuit' in USA from the statistical service Google-Trends [18]. One can see the jumps in February and May-June. The dynamics reflects holiday preparations of Americans. However, special efforts are needed to form a set of descriptors based on queries when one deals with real applications.

Work done under partial support of the Institute of Applied Economic Research under Russian Presidential Academy of national economy and public administration (RANEPA).

G. Sidorov and O. Herrera-Alcántara (Eds.): MICAI 2016, Part I, LNAI 10061, pp. 303–314, 2017.
DOI: 10.1007/978-3-319-62434-1_26

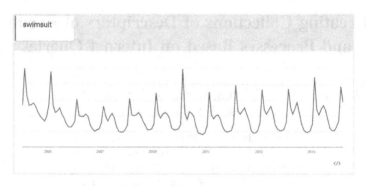

Fig. 1. The dynamics of the descriptor 'swimsuit'

To set the problem we introduce the following terminology:

- *Search query* is a request made by an Internet user to obtain information from a search engine;
- *Search engine* is a specialized service for information retrieval;
- *Descriptor* is a word or a phrase that forms part of search queries introduced by users;
- *Indicators* are economic, social, demographic and other indicators that are analyzed or forecasted by analysts and researchers;
- *Top-rated lists of descriptors* are search queries that are the most highly correlated with selected indicators;
- *Barometer* is the mean value of the normalized dynamics of the top-rated selection.

In the paper we propose a technology for selecting descriptors and constructing barometers, which can be used by applied researchers in the problems of analysis and forecast of the indicators. Our approach is based on:

1. the correlation between the dynamics of indicators and that of descriptors;
2. the restrictions for the length of lags;
3. the possible (probable) process development in case of data absence.

Unlike our previous publications concerning collections of descriptors in this paper we give a more clear and complete description of tonality-based descriptors, so-called technical databases with n-grams of symbols, and barometers. Also we introduce domain-oriented graphical databases. Taken together with our previous results all the presented databases show the technology that could be useful for users.

We demonstrate an example, already described in a previous paper, where tonality-based descriptors and barometers based on these descriptors are used for the analysis of the average per capita income in various regions and for the forecast of this income in a given region. The continuation of this experiment (using inductive modeling to study the possibilities of forecasting per capita income on the basis of negative sentiments intensity in a given region) is presented for the first time in this paper.

1.2 Related Works

At the moment, there is a significant number of publications, where search queries to Internet are the basis for the analysis and forecast of various indicators. For example, we can mention some of the frequently cited works. The authors [10] analyze relations between search queries and economical indexes in autobusiness. The lag 4–5 weeks showed good correlation for the dynamics of the queries and sales. Search service of Google is used in [3] for studing problems of unemployment. The forecast of news based on search queries is described in [28]. The needs of users of search machines are studied in [15, 35]. The research of search queries and exchange dynamics of DJIA show that the growth of intensity of 'financial search queries' as market, debt, stocs, etc. leads to the fall of the market [25, 26]. The relations between search queries and the sickness rate of cancer are demonstrated in [11]. Another interesting application of search queries is the forecast of epidemy development [22].

However, the application of tools mentioned above proves not to be effective, when we deal with more complex problems. Here, one should apply: (a) descriptors being elementary regressors without a clear relation to a domain (i.e., n-grams of symbols); (b) descriptors, which reflect tonality of a query and have a specific statistical distribution (i.e., shifted center); (c) descriptors from a given domain, which are related to a given indicator with a certain time dependence (i.e., lags); (d) combinations of descriptors (i.e., barometers) that are highly correlated with given indicators.

These descriptors allowed to solve problems related to demography [5], analysis of the population's mood in various regions of Russia [4, 8], forecast of economic crimes [6, 7]. By the moment, we are unaware of any overviews where the formation of collections of search queries would have been considered. This circumstance is the main reason why we decided to write this paper.

2 Online Services for the Analysis of Search Queries

Here, we compare the functionalities of two popular search machines Yandex and Google to provide researchers with accessible information. The former is the largest Russian Internet service [38]. The latter is a well-known US service with its branch in Russia [18].

Their comparative properties are the following:

- Yandex indexes significantly less pages than Google;
- Yandex provides data coverage
  - for the last 2 years with the minimum step of 1 month;
  - for the last year with the minimum step of 1 week.
  Google presents
  - monthly data since 2004;
  - each minute for the last hour;
- Yandex presents data both in the absolute scale and in the relative scale. Google publishes data only in the relative scale with respect to a given time period. Namely, value 100 corresponds to the maximum value of the descriptor under consideration

in the mentioned time period. To obtain data in the absolute scale in Google one should use Google Adwords [19].

As for the tools:

- Yandex has a tool for publishing comparative values of the descriptor under consideration with respect to the total number of search queries in a given region. Google has no such tool and, therefore, users should select these values themselves;
- Google has a special service, Google Correlate, to reveal descriptors having correlation with a given indicator [20]. The drawback of this service is a large number of false correlations that have no relation to the indicator. Yandex has no such tool, therefore, users should select these descriptors themselves.

The archives of descriptors from the mentioned search engines contain millions of words and word combinations. For example, Yandex archive contains approximately 5 millions of entries. In order to collect data and process the dynamic series of the database, one needs several years. So, the first and the most important phase in studying search queries is the creation of individual bases of descriptors being relevant for each indicator under consideration. These local bases usually contain from several hundreds to several thousands of search queries.

In this paper, we classify databases as: domain-oriented, domain-oriented graphical, emotional and technical. This classification may help researchers select necessary sets of descriptors being relevant to the indicators under consideration. These databases are presented in the subsequent sections.

3 Domain-Oriented Databases

3.1 Domain-Oriented Databases and Their Applications

Domain-oriented databases contain the maximum number of search queries on the topic under consideration. To create them one usually uses free-share domain-oriented vocabularies. Terms are selected if they:

- occur in the list of Internet queries;
- have significant correlation with a given indicator(s) with any lag.

The correlation of a given descriptor and a given indicator with a given lag is calculated using the well-known formula:

$$R(D, I, \tau) = \sum_i [D(t_i) \times I(t_i - \tau)] / [\sqrt{\sum_i D^2(t_i)} \times \sqrt{\sum_i I^2(t_i)}],$$

where R is the correlation coefficient, $D(t_i)$ is the time series of a descriptor, $I(t_i)$ is the time series of an indicator, τ is the lag and t_i is the moment of time.

To set the preferable level of correlation we tested three values: 0.5, 0.7, and 0.9 on several practical examples. It has been proved that 0.7 provides the best collections of descriptors both for the problems of analysis and forecast.

For our applied research, we created the following domain-oriented databases in Russian:

1. database of economic terms [29];
2. database of juridical terms [30];
3. database of crimes [31];
4. database of medical terms, described in the paper [9];
5. database of the well-known brands and goods titles downloaded from different sites;
6. database of exchange terms [32];
7. database of slang used in finance, computers and other domains, and young people's slang downloaded from various sources;
   Besides, we created two databases in English:
8. database of exchange terms [33];
9. database of economic terms [34].

We present here some examples of applications for the Russian databases (1)–(4).

Databases of economic and juridical terms were used for the analysis of the indicators 'retail trade', 'per capita income', 'unemployment', 'price index for food and industrial goods', etc. in different Russian regions [4, 8, 9].

Database of crimes is used for the forecast of economic crimes [6, 7, 9]. The fact is that before the crime a criminal tries to find in Internet any correspondent laws to determine his/her responsibility. This circumstance can be taken into account to forecast rise/fall of crimes for the following period and it can be used for the additional control of published reports related to crimes.

Database of medical terms is specially created to reveal the causes of increased mortality in different regions of Russia [9]. It includes specific medical terms, an alphabetical list of symptoms, an alphabetical list of medicines and a set of descriptions related to the activity of hospitals, such as 'phone number of the doctor on duty', 'emergency call', and so on.

Usually we study the relation between one indicator and a set of descriptors taken from one or several domain-oriented databases. However, sometimes we can reveal new information by considering several indicators simultaneously. For this, it is necessary:

- to select descriptors having high correlation with these indicators;
- to compare relative frequencies of these descriptors.

For example, in our experiment in [9] we considered the indicators 'registered marriages' and 'registered newborns' together with the database of brands. The lower correlation threshold was equal to 0.7. It was proved that the relative frequency of descriptors highly correlated with the first indicator is equal to 15.7% and with the second indicator - 0.4%. It means that newly married couples are more interested in buying something than young parents. This information can be of use for sellers.

3.2   Enriched Top Databases

The correction of a domain-oriented database under consideration makes it possible to extract more information about a given indicator and region. For this, it is necessary

- to form a top-rated list of descriptors from the mentioned database, named as 'domain-oriented top database';
- to add new elements to the created top database using special online services.
  The last step can be completed on the Yandex platform using the procedures:
- descriptors from the top database are introduced to the central page of the Yandex search machine then we download words and word combinations in the mode 'searched together with this word';
- descriptors from the top database are introduced to the statistical service of Yandex then we download words and word combinations from the section 'using words'.

When one deals with the Google search machine it is necessary to use specialized Google services [18, 19].

Note that domain-oriented top databases can be constructed independently on the regions or to be associated with a given region. The latter is preferable, when we study specific regional problems.

4 Special Databases

4.1 Domain-Oriented Graphical Databases and Their Applications

In order to create domain-oriented databases we need

- free-share domain-oriented vocabularies;
- data on the dynamics of indicator(s) under consideration.

What can we do if we have no dynamic data? There is an approach that allows to avoid this difficulty: forming an artificial graph that illustrates the probable dynamics of a given process and use this graph for term selection. The corresponding database is named "domain-oriented graphical database".

As an example, we consider the creation of a database of social activity-related terms. The process takes several steps. First, the type of social activity (for example, protests) in a region is set and then its start and end dates are determined. Then, we construct an artificial graph reflecting the mentioned activity. The start and end dates of the graph are described by small values of a given variable, and the middle part is described by large values of a given variable presenting the intensity of actions (for example, the amount of participants). Next, one selects the so-called basic descriptors: queries that clearly reflect the types of selected activity (for example, demonstrations, strikes, etc.). Then, their dynamics in a given region and during a given time period is downloaded. For example, the following words (marche, rassemblement, police, lutte) have been selected to study social activity in France. Figure 2 shows the artificial graph and dynamics of the relative frequencies of these descriptors. The data is taken from [20]. If the graphs of basic descriptors have high correlation with the artificial graph, we construct a list of lemmas (see Sect. 4.3) that refer to a given region and period of time. Finally, we select all descriptors from this list that have high correlation with the artificial graph.

By this way we obtain a database that can be useful for the analysis of causes related to social activity. In our research we use materials from the publications [12, 13].

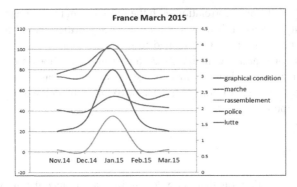

Fig. 2. Basic descriptors reflecting social activity in Paris in January 2015

4.2 Databases of Emotional Words and Their Applications

Two databases of words and word combinations have been created: a database of descriptors with negative tonality and a database of descriptors with positive tonality.

Each database includes approximately 800 entries. To form these databases we initially used limited vocabularies (about two hundred words) prepared by a professional Spanish linguist for the opinion mining of Peruvian Facebook and Twitter [1]. We also used data from SentiWordNet (about thousand words), a large lexical resource that forms part of the well-known WordNet [2].

These databases can be used for the study of an event, politician, brand, macroeconomic parameter or other. In our studies, we obtain new knowledge when

- comparing one region with the other ones;
- analyzing the dynamics of the mentioned indicators for a given region.

For example, we revealed a clear correspondence between the intensity of negative descriptors use and the economic situation in several Russian regions [4, 8]. On the other hand, we revealed nothing when we tried to find relations (correlations) between the use of negative descriptors and statistics of crimes or socio-political situation in Russia. It means that Russians are totally indifferent to these processes.

4.3 Technical Databases and Their Applications

By 'technical databases' we mean vocabularies of lemmas and vocabularies of n-grams of letters (symbols).

To form the database of lemmas, a well-known vocabulary of lemmas [23] is used. We only eliminate repeated words referring to different parts of speech from this vocabulary. The database of lemmas is an auxiliary tool being a good addition to domain-oriented databases. Lemmas help the analyst see where he/she should look for new relevant descriptors. For example, when we were studying the causes of an increase in mortality in the Petersburg region we found the descriptor 'reservoir' [9].

This descriptor had stronger correlation with the mortality in the Petersburg region than with the mortality in Russia. It means that regional authorities should pay much more attention to the problem of security related to rest areas near rivers or lakes.

The database of n-grams contains 2-, 3- and 4-grams. It does not include rare or repeating combinations of letters and it is used mainly to deal with forecast-related problems, where we need to construct an approximate model without a qualitative analysis of descriptors.

5 Barometers

Barometers are linguistic tools that allow to significantly reduce the amount of data in the problem of forecast. Domain-oriented and special databases described above are used to form a set of time series of descriptors with a given time step on a given time period. However, the amount of data here results too large for processing. To reduce it, we create the so-called top samples of descriptors and barometers based on these top samples. Top samples and barometers are formed separately for each indicator under consideration.

Here is the description of the top-samples formation procedure:

- Time series of a given indicator is downloaded from its depository;
- Time series of search queries taken from the corresponding domain-oriented databases and the database of n-grams are downloaded from the mentioned Internet resource;
- The correlation threshold is set and all descriptors having higher correlation with the indicator are selected;
- The preceding procedure is repeated with several lags;
- The resulting set of descriptors constitutes the top-sample.

Speaking 'correlation' we mean here both direct correlation and anti-correlation. To test the correlation, the Pearson criterion is applied. In our experiments, we used the threshold of 0.7 and lags of 1, 2, and 3 months. The selection of these values is justified by the following. With the threshold 0.5, the list of time series contains several hundreds samples, which is too large. With the threshold 0.9, this list gets reduced to a dozen or two samples, therefore, we lose information. The threshold 0.7 is taken as a compromise. As for the lags, in most of our experiments the correlation sharply decreases when the lags exceed 2–5 months. So, the maximum lag of 3 months is taken a compromise.

The authors of [10, 25] also use such lagging. Unlike them, we do not limit the number of lags by taking into account the behaviour of the correlation coefficient for various lags.

Top samples can be transformed into the so-called barometers. Each barometer is one averaged time series based on 10–20 time series taken from the created top sample. All time series are preliminarily normalized to the interval [0, 1]. Some information is lost in the averaging process, however, this procedure allows to filter false tendencies. In our experiments we use up to 8 barometers. Each barometer is calculated using the simple formula:

$$B(t_i) = \sum S_k(t_i) / N,$$

where $B(t_i)$ is the time series of a barometer, $S_k(t_i)$, k = 1,2,...N are time series of top samples, N is the number of top samples, t_i is the moment of time.

Google also uses barometers. This process is described in detail in [14]. Unlike Google we use 8 barometers instead of 1. Each of them is tuned to different lags. It has allowed us to complete several forecasts related to these lags and to compare them.

6 Application Examples

In this section, we consider an application of the considered databases of descriptors: *Negative words in search queries to Internet as an indicator of average per capita incomes in the Federal regions of Russia*. This material is a short version of the paper [4]. We use the following notation: PCI is per capita income, NS are words that express negative sentiments, (μSQ, NS, rel, norm) is averaged normalized value of NS-descriptor dynamics in relative terms.

The database of NS words is created. It contains 575 descriptors. We use official PCI and calculate (μSQ, NS, rel, norm) for all Federal regions of Russia (except Crimea). The data covers the period between September 2013 – August 2015. Our results clearly show that the higher the value of PCI the lower the value of (μSQ, NS, rel, norm). This conclusion has been supported by the Spearman coefficient of rang correlation (approximately 0.85). This result is obviously expected, but our purpose is to illustrate the potential of the applications of NS after the necessary pre-processing. Figure 3 shows the distribution of the averaged normalized value of NS-descriptors between 8 regions. The leaders are Far East, North Caucasus, South Federal region and Siberia. It is a good signal for the regional authorities of these regions.

We also studied the possibility to forecast PCI using the intensity of NS in a given region. For this, we used the package GMDH Shell [16] that includes the algorithms of inductive modeling based on the Group Method of Data Handling (GMDH) [24, 37].

Fig. 3. Distribution of averaged normalized value of NS-descriptors between Russian Federal regions

In the experiments, we use the GMDH-type neural network algorithm. Cross-validation is performed on two samples. External criterion is defined by the Mean Absolute Percentage Error (MAPE). We calculate 1 month forecast and evaluate its accuracy using relative deviation from the real value (P). In total, we have constructed 8 models for all Federal regions. Figure 4 shows real and forecasted data for the Far East. The results are quite promising: MAPE = 1.6%, P = 1%.

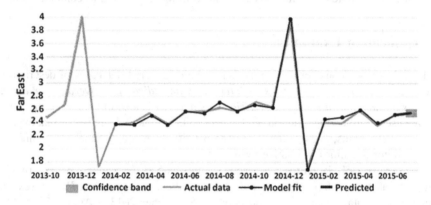

Fig. 4. Real data and forecast for the far east federal region

7   Conclusions and Future Work

In this paper, we propose a technology for the creation of databases of descriptors related to search queries and present several practical applications of these databases.
Descriptors and barometers can be used

- to monitor the economic situation in regions in real time avoiding difficulties related to the lack of data, as explained above;
- for parallel control of official information, which allows to reveal distortions introduced by official institutions;
- for forecasting economic, demographic and social parameters during a crisis period;
- for forecasting dynamics of various socio-economic and socio-political processes in other countries. Here we do not need official data that is published with delay.
  As the future work we consider
- proposing a technology to use the mentions of descriptors in social media;
- developing a procedure for processing queries including outliers related to force major circumstances;
- developing models for fuzzy forecasting taking into account qualitative dynamics of queries.

References

1. Alexandrov, M., Danilova, V., Koshulko, A, Tejada, J.: Models for opinion classication of blogs taken from Peruvian Facebook. In: Proceedings of 4th International Conference on Inductive Modeling (ICIM-2013), pp. 241–246. Publication House ITRC-NASU, Kyev (2013)
2. Baccinella, S., Esuli, A., Sebastiani, F.: SentiWordNet 3.0: an enhanced lexical resources for sentiment analysis and opinion mining. In: LREC10, pp. 2200–2204 (2010). http://nmis.isti.cnr.it/sebastiani/Publications/LREC10.pdf
3. Baker, S.: What drives job search. Evidence from Google search data. [Electronic resource], Technical report, Stanford University (2011)
4. Boldyreva, A., Alexandrov, M., Surkova, D.: Negative words in search queries to internet as an indicator of average per capita incomes in Federal regions of Russia. In: Inductive Modeling of Complex Systems, NASU (Ukraine), vol. 7, pp. 77–92 [rus] (2015)
5. Boldyreva, A.: Demographic forecasts based on queries to Yandex search machine. In: Proceeding of International Workshop on Inductive Modeling, pp. 7–8. Publication House ITRC-NASU (Ukraine) and Czech Technical University, Kyev (2015)
6. Boldyreva, A., Koshulko, O.: Forecasting models of economic crimes based on queries to internet: Regression vs. GMDH. In: Proceeding of Sociological Faculty on Mathematical Modeling of Social Processes, vol. 17, pp. 34–42. Lomonosov Moscow State University [rus] (2015)
7. Boldyreva, A., Koshulko, O.: GMDH helps to build models based on queries to Yandex for forecast of economic crimes. In: Proceeding of International Workshop on Inductive Modeling, pp. 9–11. Publication House ITRC-NASU (Ukraine) and Czech Technical University, Kyev (2015)
8. Boldyreva, A.: Method for assessing moods of Internet users with search queries (pilot study of Russian regions). In: Proceeding of Sociological Faculty on Mathematical Modeling of Social Processes, vol. 18, pp. 26–34. Lomonosov Moscow State University [rus] (2016)
9. Boldyreva, A.: Building models for analysis and forecast of economic and social conjuncture using intensity of search queries to Internet. In: Modern Economy: Theory, Politics, Innovation, vol. 21, pp. 36–61, RANEPA, Moscow [rus] (2016)
10. Choi, H.: Predicting the present with google trends, [Electronic resource] (2011). http://people.ischool.berkeley.edu/ ~ hal/Papers/2011/ptp.pdf
11. Cooper, C.: Cancer internet search activity on a major search engine [Electronic resource]. J. Med. Internet Res. **7**, e36 (2005). http://www.ncbi.nlm.nih.gov/pmc/articles/PMC1550657/
12. Danilova, V.: A pipeline for multilingual protest event selection and annotation. In: Proceeding of TIR-2015 Workshop (Text-based Information Retrieval), pp. 309–314. IEEE (2015)
13. Danilova, V.: Linguistic support for protest event data collection. Ph.D. thesis, Autonomous University of Barcelona (2015)
14. Ginsberg, J., et al.: Detecting influenza epidemics using search engine query data. Nature **457**, 1012–1014 (2009)
15. Huang, H.: Constructing consumer sentiment index for U.S using Google searches. [Electronic resource], Technical report, University of Alberta (2009) http://econpapers.repec.org/paper/risalbaec/2009_5f026.htm
16. GMDH Shell: Algorithms of inductive modeling www.gmdhshell.com/
17. Goel, S., et al.: Predicting consumer behavior with Web search Proc. USA Acad. Sci. **107**(41), 17486–17490 (2010). www.pnas.org/content/107/41/17486.full

18. Google Resource: Google trends. www.google.ru/trends
19. Google Resource: AdWords. www.google.com/adwords/
20. Google Resource: Search patterns. www.google.com/trends/correlate/
21. Google Resource: Protests in France. www.google.ru/trends/explore#q=marche%2C% 20rassemblement%2C%20police%2C%20lutte&geo=FR&cmpt=q&tz=Etc%2FGMT-6
22. Kang, M., et al.: Using google trends for influenza surveillance in South China. PLoS ONE **8** (1), e55205 (2013). doi:10.1371/journal.pone.005520
23. Lyashevskaya, O.: Frequent vocabulary of modern Russian. Publication House Azbukovnik [rus] (2009). dict.ruslang.ru/freq.php
24. Madala, H., Ivakhnenko, A.: Inductive Learning Algorithms for Complex Systems Modeling. CRC Press, Boca Raton (1994)
25. Preis, T.: Complex dynamics of our economic life on different scales: insights from search engine query data [Electronic Resource]. Phil. Trans. R. Soc. A **368**, 5707–5719 (2010)
26. Preis, T.: Quantifying the semantics of search behavior before stock market moves Proc. Nat. Acad. Sci. USA **111**, 11600–11605 (2013). http://www.ncbi.nlm.nih.gov/pubmed/23619126
27. Program platform GMDH Shell. www.gmdhshell.com
28. Radinsky, K.: Predicting the news of tomorrow using patterns in web search queries [Electronic resource]. In: Proceeding of IEEE/WIC/ACM International Conference on Web Intelligence (WI2008) (2009). http://portal.acm.org/citation.cfm?id=1487070
29. Russian Resource: Economical vocabulary of terms. www.economicportal.ru/terms.html
30. Russian Resource: Large juridical vocabulary (terms, notions). www.petrograd.biz/ dictionaries/dict_big_law.php
31. Russian Resource: General office of Russian public prosecutor, legal statistics. crimestat.ru/ offenses_map
32. Russian Resource: Data base of exchange terms. www.multitran.ru/c/m.exe?a=110&s=% E0&sc=67&dict=
33. Terms (English): Money in motion, key terms vocabulary. www.cnbc.com/id/100001502
34. Terms (English): Economics A-Z terms. www.economist.com/economics-a-to-z/a
35. Schmidt, T.: Forecasting private consumption: survey-based indicators vs. Google trends, [Electronic resource] (2009). http://ideas.repec.org/p/rwi/repape/0155.html
36. Stepashko, V.: Ideas of academician O. Ivakhnenko in Inductive Modeling field from historical perspective. In: Proceeding of 4th International Conference on Inductive Modeling (ICIM-2013), pp. 31–37. Publication House NAS of Ukraine, Prague Technical University, Kyev (2013)
37. Stepashko, V.: Method of critical variances as an analytical tool of the Inductive Modeling Theory. J. Inform. Automat. Sci. **40**(3), 47–58 (2008). Begell House Inc.
38. Yandex statistics. wordstat.yandex.com

Planning and Scheduling

Using a Grammar Checker to Validate Compliance of Processes with Workflow Models

Roman Barták$^{(\boxtimes)}$ and Vladislav Kuboň

Faculty of Mathematics and Physics, Charles University,
Malostranské nám. 25, 118 00 Prague 1, Czech Republic
bartak@ktiml.mff.cuni.cz, vk@ufal.mff.cuni.cz

Abstract. Grammar checking has been used for a long time to validate if a given sentence - a sequence of words - complies with grammar rules. Recently attribute grammars have been proposed as a formal model to describe workflows. A workflow specifies valid processes, which are sequences of actions. In this paper we show how a grammar checker developed for natural languages can be used to validate whether or not a given process complies with the workflow model expressed using an attribute grammar. The checker can also suggest possible corrections of the process to become a valid process.

1 Introduction

Although the description of workflows and the syntactic analysis of natural languages seem to constitute very distant research topics, the closer look at the nature of the tasks being solved reveals interesting similarities. If we look at them from a more abstract point of view, we may notice that they both deal with large units which may be decomposed into smaller units (the workflows into individual tasks and activities, the natural language sentences into clauses and individual words) and which have certain inner structure.

Workflows are used to formally describe processes of various types such as business and manufacturing processes. There exist many formal models to describe workflows [1] that include decision points and conditions for process splitting as well as loops to describe repetition of activities. Hierarchical structure of workflows is in particular interesting for real-life workflows [2] as many workflows are obtained by decompositions of tasks. Barták and Čepek [6] proposed a hierarchical workflow model called Nested Temporal Networks with Alternatives that was later extended with extra constraints to model a wider range of workflows [4]. Later on, it has been shown that nested workflows with extra constraints can be represented by attribute grammars [3], which constitute grounds to exploiting grammar-related techniques in workflow processing. For example, the problem of verifying whether a given word belongs to the language of a given grammar seems intrinsically similar to verify whether a specific process complies with the description of a workflow using an attribute grammar.

This paper shows how a certain type of a grammar developed originally for the purpose of grammar checking of natural languages (see [8]) might be

© Springer International Publishing AG 2017
G. Sidorov and O. Herrera-Alcántara (Eds.): MICAI 2016, Part I, LNAI 10061, pp. 317–331, 2017.
DOI: 10.1007/978-3-319-62434-1_27

used for validation of a compliance of processes with the workflow models. More concretely, we are going to show how certain special properties exploited in grammar checking may be used also for error detection in project plans and what kind of modifications of the original grammar are required in order to fulfill this task.

2   Nested Workflows

In this work we use nested workflows from the FlowOpt system [4]. The nested workflows were formally introduced in [5] and for completeness, we will recapitulate the formal definitions here.

The *nested workflow* is obtained from a root task by applying decomposition operations that split the task into subtasks until primitive tasks, corresponding to activities, are obtained. Three decomposition operations are supported, namely parallel, serial, and alternative decompositions. Figure 1 gives an example of a nested workflow that shows how the tasks are decomposed. The root task *Chair* is decomposed serially to two tasks, where the second task is a primitive task filled by activity *Assembly*. The first task *Create Parts* decomposes further to three parallel tasks *Legs*, *Seat*, and *Back Support*. *Back Support* is the only example here of alternative decomposition to two primitive tasks with *Buy* and *Welding* activities (*Welding* is treated as an alternative to *Buy*). Hence the workflow describes two alternative processes. Naturally, the nested workflow can be described as a tree of tasks (Fig. 1 bottom right).

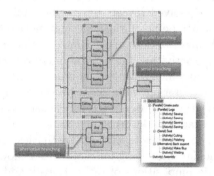

Fig. 1. Example of a nested workflow as it is visualized in the FlowOpt Workflow Editor (from top to down there are parallel, serial, and alternative decompositions).

Formally, the nested workflow is a set *Tasks* of tasks that is a union of three disjoint sets: *Parallel*, *Alternative*, and *Primitive*. Serial decomposition is modeled as a parallel decomposition with extra precedence constraints. For each task T (with the exception of the *root* task), function $parent(T)$ denotes the parent task in the hierarchical structure. Similarly for each task T we can define the set $subtasks(T)$ of its child nodes ($subtasks(T) = \{C \in Tasks | parent(C) = T\}$).

The tasks from sets Parallel and Alternative are called *compound tasks* and they must decompose to some subtasks:

$$\forall T \in (Parallel \cup Alternative) : subtasks(T) \neq \emptyset, \tag{1}$$

while the *primitive tasks* do not decompose:

$$\forall T \in Primitive : subtasks(T) = \emptyset. \tag{2}$$

The workflow defines one or more processes in the following way. *Process* selected from the workflow is defined as a subset $P \subseteq Tasks$ in the workflow satisfying the following constraints:

$$\forall T \in P, T \neq root : \qquad\qquad parent(T) \in P \tag{3}$$
$$\forall T \in P \cap Parallel : \qquad\qquad subtasks(T) \subseteq P \tag{4}$$
$$\forall T \in P \cap Alternative : \qquad |subtasks(T) \cap P| = 1 \tag{5}$$

Formula (3) says that for each task in the process (except the root) its parent task is also in the process. Formula (4) says that all subtasks of a parallel task in the process must also be in the process. Finally, Formula (5) says that exactly one subtask is in the process for each alternative task in the process.

In addition to the hierarchical structure of the nested workflow, the nested structure also defines certain implicit temporal (ordering) constraints (the arcs in Fig. 1). These temporal relations must hold for all tasks in a single process. Assume that S_i is the start time and E_i is the end time of task T_i. The primitive tasks T_i are filled with activities and each activity has certain duration D_i. Then for tasks in the process P the following relations hold:

$$\forall T_i \in P \cap Primitive : S_i + D_i = E_i \tag{6}$$
$$\forall T_i \in P \cap (Parallel \cup Alternative) :$$
$$S_i = min\{S_j | T_j \in P \cap subtasks(T_i)\}$$
$$E_i = max\{E_j | T_j \in P \cap subtasks(T_i)\}. \tag{7}$$

Notice that the duration of a compound task is defined by the time allocation of its subtasks while the duration of a primitive task is defined by the activity.

A *feasible process* is a process where the time variables S_i and E_i of tasks in the process can be instantiated in such a way that they satisfy the above temporal constraints. It is easy to realize that if there are no additional constraints then any process is feasible. The process defines a partial order of tasks so their start and end times can be set in the left-to-right order while satisfying the constraints (6) and (7).

The nested structure may not be flexible enough to describe naturally some additional relations in real-life processes, for example when an alternative for one task influences the selection of alternatives in other tasks. The following constraints can be added to the nested structure to simplify description of these additional relations between any two tasks T_i and T_j [4]:

precedence $(i \rightarrow j)$:	$T_i, T_j \in P \Rightarrow E_i \le S_j$	(8)
start-start sync. $(i \; ss \; j)$:	$T_i, T_j \in P \Rightarrow S_i = S_j$	(9)
start-end sync. $(i \; se \; j)$:	$T_i, T_j \in P \Rightarrow S_i = E_j$	(10)
end-start sync. $(i \; es \; j)$:	$T_i, T_j \in P \Rightarrow E_i = S_j$	(11)
end-end sync. $(i \; ee \; j)$:	$T_i, T_j \in P \Rightarrow E_i = E_j$	(12)
mutual excl. $(i \; mutex \; j)$:	$T_i \notin P \vee T_j \notin P$	(13)
equivalence $(i \Leftrightarrow j)$:	$T_i \in P \Leftrightarrow T_j \in P$	(14)
implication $(i \Rightarrow j)$:	$T_i \in P \Rightarrow T_j \in P$	(15)

Note that if extra constraints are used then the existence of a feasible process is no longer guaranteed. For example an equivalence constraint between the tasks *Buy* and *Welding* in Fig. 1 causes no feasible process to exist.

In summary, we can model the nested workflow with extra constraints as a tuple $W = (Parallel, Alternative, Primitive, root, parent, D, \mathcal{C})$, where the *parent* relation defines a tree rooted at the node *root* with leaves *Primitive* and internal nodes $Parallel \cup Alternative$. The set $\mathcal{C}$ defines the extra constraints (8)–(15) and D maps the tasks in *Primitive* to non-negative integers defining durations of primitive tasks. The process is a subtree of this tree satisfying constraints (3)–(5) and (13)–(15), where each node T_i has assigned two integers S_i and E_i satisfying the constraints (6)–(12).

3   Robust Free Order Dependency Grammar

The paper [3] shows that attribute grammars [9] might serve as an alternative tool for the description of hierarchical workflows. In this paper we would like to present how a concrete type of an attribute grammar with certain special properties originally implemented for the purpose of grammar checking of natural languages may also be exploited for a validation of compliance of a concrete process with the workflow model. We will not address the second important type of validation, namely the validation of the model itself.

The attribute grammar called Robust Free Order Dependency Grammar (RFODG) has been used for a pivot implementation of a grammar checker for Czech, see [8]. Further extensions and modifications have been thoroughly described in [7]. Let us now mention those properties of its implementation which are relevant for our purpose.

3.1   Concepts Used in RFODG

The input data for RFODG have the form of a sequence of data items representing individual word forms and punctuation marks from the input sentence. Each data item has a general form of a list of attributes and their values. Some attributes are obligatory (the attributes describing the original word form, its lemma, Part–of–speech information and syntactic properties), the rest of attributes is optional. The application of individual grammar rules might be restricted by certain keywords, as, e.g. the keyword NEGATIVE which indicates an error anticipation rule, i.e. the rule describing a possible grammatical error. Such rule was then applied only in case that the grammar fails to analyze the input sentence by means of grammar rules describing correct constructions only.

The grammar rules of RFODG have a common general form $AB \Rightarrow X$ (RFODG had been used as an analytical grammar) where the letters A and B represent two data items from the input sentence and A stands (immediately) to the left from B (i.e., the order of those two items in the input sentence is relevant). In case that some rule is successfully applied to items A and B, a new item X is created (X inherits all attributes and their values from a dominant item – the dominance of either A or B is explicitly expressed by assignments $X := B$ or $X := A$. Each grammar rule is interpreted as a sequence of tests or assignments, it actually expresses a procedural description of the process of checking the applicability of a given rule to a particular pair of items A and B.

The grammar uses also the following concepts relevant for our purpose:

- Hard (A.x = B.y) and soft (A.x ? B.y ERR) constraints. The concept of soft constraints allows to capture grammatical errors. If a soft constraint is violated, the processing continues, but the rule inserts an error flag ERR into the syntactic tree of the input sentence. If a hard constraint is violated, the processing of the rule immediately stops for the given pair of A and B.
- Branching in a form of a simple IF THEN ELSE ENDIF command.
- Constants OK and FAIL marking a successful and unsuccessful end of application of a particular grammar rule to a given pair of data items.
- Comments (any text following a semicolon located at the beginning a row of a text)

Let us now present a sample grammar rule in RFODG. It processes the incongruous attribute standing to the right of a governing noun.

```
IF A.SYNTCL = noun THEN ELSE
   IF A.SYNTCL = prephr THEN ELSE
      FAIL
   ENDIF
ENDIF
B.SYNTCL = noun
B.CASE = gen
A.RIGHTGEN ? yes   Second_genitive
X:=A
X.RIGHTGEN := no
OK
END_P
```

The rule works in the following way:

The symbol A must represent either a noun or a prepositional group. If not, the application of the rule immediately fails. The symbol B must represent a noun in the genitive case. The soft constraint checks whether this is the first incongruous attribute in genitive case being attached to the same noun. If not, it inserts an error flag. Then A is selected as the governing word and X inherits all its attributes. The subsequent assignment($X.RIGHTGEN := no$) marks the fact that the incongruous attribute in genitive case is being attached and thus no other such attribute may be attached in the future. The keyword OK confirms a successful application of the rule on the given pair of symbols A and B.

4 Decomposition in RFODG

RFODG has been developed as an analytical grammar, therefore the validation of a concrete process is the most natural task which we may use it for. Let us start with the basic concepts first.

As it was already mentioned above, each workflow may be decomposed into the primitive tasks by three decomposition operations, namely parallel, serial and alternative decompositions. Let us now look at the possible ways how these three operations may be described in the RFODG.

4.1 Serial Decomposition

Serial decomposition seems to be the most natural one for RFODG. Two primitive tasks in a sequence actually correspond to two word forms of a natural language, one preceding the other in a sentence. RFODG distinguishes the mutual position of items A and B (A standing always to the left of B), therefore in the rule describing the sequence *Create parts* and *Assembly* from our workflow example, A will represent the task *Create parts* and B will correspond to *Assembly*. The first two commands of a grammar rule describing this sequence may then look like this:

```
A.task = Create_parts
B.task = Assembly
```

Unlike in the analysis of a natural language, in the workflow validation it is not necessary to distinguish between the governing (dominant) and dependent item, therefore the assignment of A or B to X is practically arbitrary. We only must make sure that all relevant attributes are transferred from both tasks to X. For example, if both A and B have attributes marking the start and end time of each task, the rest of our grammar rule might look like this:

```
X := A
X.task := Chair
X.end := B.end
OK
END_P
```

It is not necessary to transfer explicitly the value of A.start because all attributes and their values from A are inherited by X.

4.2   Alternative Decomposition

Alternative decomposition can also be handled relatively easily. RFODG makes it possible to handle alternatives by means of a conditional statement IF, as we can see in the following example of a grammar rule for the alternative tasks of Buying and Welding.

```
IF A.task = Buy THEN ELSE
   IF A.task = Welding THEN ELSE
     FAIL
   ENDIF
ENDIF
X := A
X.task := Back_support
OK
END_P
```

This grammar rule has two possible outcomes, the resulting item *Back support* will consists either from the task *Buy* or from the task *Welding*, but it cannot include both primitive tasks. If the input sequence of primitive tasks will contain both alternatives, the grammar interpreter will apply this rule twice, once for each primitive task, but because the grammar will not contain a grammar rule combining together *Back support* with any of the two primitive tasks, the grammar will fail and thus it will indicate that the input sequence is incorrect.

4.3   Parallel Decomposition

Unlike in the theoretical model described in the paper [5] where the parallel decomposition served even as a possible model for serial decomposition, it constitutes a serious issue for verification. Just recall that parallel decomposition means that child tasks can be used in any order. A specific order is used in the grammar rule, but this order can be arbitrary and does not correspond to actual temporal allocation of tasks [3].

This actually means that the information which tasks are parallel has to be incorporated into the grammar. Instead of having a single grammar rule for each decomposition, we have to combine n-1 grammar rules together in a way which will guarantee that all primitive parallel tasks are present in the input sequence. For this purpose we might exploit some technical items which whose only role will be to bind the set of grammar rules together. The solution for the complex task *Legs* which has been parallely decomposed into four primitive tasks *Saw1*, *Saw2*, *Saw3* and *Saw4* might then look for example like this (It is of course necessary to make sure that all necessary attributes from *Saw2*, *Saw3* and *Saw4* are properly inherited, this is not contained in the sample grammar rules.):

```
A.task = Saw1
B.task = Saw2
```

```
X := A
X.task := Saw12
OK
END_P

A.task = Saw12
B.task = Saw3
X := A
X.task := Saw123
OK
END_P

A.task = Saw123
B.task = Saw4
X := A
X.task := Legs
OK
END_P
```

There is one more issue which might require certain modifications of RFODG. The above mentioned grammar rules would work only in the case that the parallely decomposed primitive tasks are ordered (we suppose that although they are parallel, they will constitute a part of a input sequence of tasks) in the same way as it is expected by the grammar rules, i.e. *Saw1* will stand to the left from *Saw2* and so on. This ordering of the input represents the application of certain additional input constraints, different from the the actual order of individual tasks in time. Let us note that these constraints are not going to contradict the time constraints because the latter ones are going to be explicitly written in the attributes and thus they don't have to be repeated in the input. Possible modification of the RFODG formalism so that it will be able to ignore the general requirement for an item A being to the left from item B for a specified set of grammar rules the constitutes a second option how to solve this issue.

5   Additional Constraints in RFODG

Let us now look at the constraints which might be used in nested workflows. The case of constraints (1)–(5) from the section Nested Workflows has been described in the previous section because these constraints actually describe the natural properties of the three kinds of decomposition. The temporal constraints (6) and (7) require the first modification of RFODG. The constraints used in RFODG are able to compare the values of individual attributes on equality only. This is caused by the expectation that values of attributes always have the form of text, using any other data type does not make sense in natural language analysis. For the smooth transformation of constraints from nested workflows into RFODG constraints it will be necessary to enrich the set of applicable data types and comparison operators. For the constraint (6) it will also require to include an arithmetic operation of adding. This should be merely a technical issue.

Let us now show how the constraint (7) can be handled for a compound task consisting of only two subtasks:

```
...
X := A
IF A.Start >= B.Start THEN X := B.Start ELSE ENDIF
IF A.End <= B.End THEN X:= B.End ELSE ENDIF
....
```

This set of commands exploits the fact that all attributes of an A subtask are being inherited and thus it is necessary to modify the attributes of the compound task X only in case that either the subtask B starts sooner than A or ends later. Let us notice that this mechanism will work also in the case of synchronization of more than two subtasks. In such a case it will only be necessary to split the synchronization of n tasks into n-1 grammar rules in a similar way as it is done in the process of transformation of a context free grammar into Chomsky normal form.

The constraints of types (8)–(15) require more detailed investigation. In their case we will also subsume that the numerical values describing starting and ending time and the duration of each process will be contained in attributes *Start, End* and *Duration*, respectively. The precedence constraint (8) may then be described in RFODG in thee following way (provided that we extend the syntax so that it will allow to use also other operators than equality):

```
A.End <= B.Start
```

A similar mechanism may also be used for the synchronization constraints (9)–(12). It will not even require any syntax extension because it uses only equality in all cases. The following rules will be able to desribe those constraints:

```
A.Start = B.Start
A.Start = B.End
A.End = B.Start
A.End = B.End
```

The mutual exclusion constraint constitutes much bigger challenge. The constraint may be handled in RFODG in the similar way as we have handled certain phenomena in a natural language. For example, certain types of words are also mutually exclusive in case that they both modify the same governing noun. This issue can be solved by introducing a special attribute whose initial value will be *Nil*. When the first word (or subtask, in our case) is processed by the grammar rule, the value of this special attribute is set to *Yes* and it would thus block the processing of the second mutually exclusive word (or subtask). Let us note that if the process description contains more pairs of mutually exclusive subtasks, it is necessary to use a corresponding number of these special attributes.

The grammar rules may then look for example like this (with *Mutex* being the special attribute and A being the subtask which is mutually exclusive with some other subtask):

```
IF A.Mutex = Yes THEN FAIL ELSE
  X:= A
  X.Mutex := Yes
ENDIF
```

Such grammar rule will be used exactly once for each mutually exclusive subtask, the attempt to add a second subtask will be blocked by the IF command.

The last two constraints are to a certain extent similar to the mutual exclusivity constraint. The equivalence (14) guarantees that if any of the two equivalent tasks is a part of a compound task, the other task must be a part of it as well. The compound task containing among its subtasks a pair of equivalent ones will not be complete until both of them are contained in the compound task. The treatment of equivalence is in fact similar to the treatment of mutual exclusivity constraint, but it is technically harder to describe because it is necessary to guarantee that a compound task lacking one of the two equivalent subtasks will not be processed further. On top of that, it is not guaranteed that the equivalent tasks are located next to each other in the project plan, neither it is known which of the two subtasks A and B belongs to the equivalent pair; and also, as in the previous case, if there are more equivalent pairs among the subtasks, it is necessary to introduce a special attribute for each pair separately. If two subtasks are equivalent, the value of the corresponding *Eq1* attribute will be *Yes* for both of them. This value actually means that the equivalence is not complete. When the two equivalent subtasks will be processed by a particular grammar rule, the value of the corresponding *Eq1* attribute will be changed back to *No*. In this way it will be possible to handle uniformly the tasks which do not contain any equivalent subtasks as well as the tasks which contain all of them, with no unsatisfied equivalence, and which may then be processed further. For the sake of simplicity, let us suppose that in the following example we have only a single equivalent pair. The corresponding part of the grammar rule may then look like this:

```
...
X := A
IF A.Eq1 = B.Eq1 THEN  X.Eq1  := No
   ELSE IF B.Eq1 = Yes  THEN X.Eq1 := Yes
   ELSE ENDIF
ENDIF
...
```

The first IF statement inserts *No* into the *Eq1* attribute of the compound task X in case that both subtasks contain either *No* or *Yes*. In both cases it means that the equivalence is complete. Due to the fact that X inherits the value of *Eq1* from A, it is only necessary to explicitly handle the combination *A.Eq1* = *No* and *B.Eq1* = *Yes* by the second IF statement.

The implication can be handled in a similar way as equivalence. We will also use special attributes *ImpI*, but unlike in the case of equivalence, it will be necessary to use the value of these attributes in order to distinguish which side of the implication is the subtask on. Let us use the values *Left* and *Right* for this purpose. The corresponding part of a grammar rule may look for example like this:

```
...
X := A
IF B.Imp1 = Right THEN   IF A.Imp1 = Left THEN X.Imp1 := No
     ELSE X.Imp1 := Right ENDIF
   ELSE   IF B.Imp1 = Left THEN IF A.Imp1 = Right THEN X.Imp1 := No
     ELSE X.Imp1 := Left ENDIF
ELSE   ENDIF
ENDIF
...
```

This complex IF statement guarantees that regardless of the mutual position of the subtasks A and B (it is not guaranteed that the subtask on the left-hand side of the implication also actually stands to the left from the subtask from the right-hand side of the implication!), the compound task X either inherits the *Left* or *Right* value from any of the two subtasks, or it is assigned the value *No* in case that the implication is fulfilled.

6   Compliance Validation

The previous sections have shown how it is possible to transform the description of a nested workflow into a special kind of an attribute grammar, including all kinds of constraints. Let us now show how we can exploit some properties of that particular grammar in order to validate the compliance of a concrete process with a workflow model. For this we are going to exploit two special features of the RFODG which had originally been developed for grammar checking of natural languages.

One of those features is the ability of RFODG to capture certain types of errors by means of constraint relaxation technique. The syntax of RFODG distinguishes between two types of conditions - hard ones and soft ones. Hard conditions (those using equation sign for comparison of two values) are never relaxed, they must be true in all circumstances if the processing of a particular grammar rule should be successful. Soft conditions (using a question mark instead of =) are not being applied so strictly. If the grammar is interpreted in error searching mode, the soft conditions may be violated. If this happens, the processing of the affected grammar rule still continues, but an error mark is inserted into the data structure (a tree) describing the process. These error marks may later be evaluated and provide an information about the nature of the problem which actually made the process plan invalid (or a natural language sentence incorrect, in the original application area of grammar checking).

The second error-detecting feature are so called error anticipating rules. These are special grammar rules which describe certain expected error configurations of the input, as, e.g. a missing subtask etc. They are typically used for those types of errors where the simple constraint relaxation is not sufficient.

Let us now demonstrate the use of RFODG for the validation of a compliance of a concrete process description with workflow model. For this purpose we are going to use the workflow from Fig. 1. The RFODG grammar describing the process may look for example like this:

```
Rule 1
A.task = Parts
B.task = Assembly
A.End <? B.Start
X := A
X.task := Chair
X.End := B.End
OK
END_P

Rule 2a
A.task ? Legs Missing_Legs
B.task = Seat
X := A
X.task := LS
IF B.Start < A.Start THEN X.Start := B.Start ELSE ENDIF
IF A.End < B.End THEN X.End := B.End ELSE ENDIF
OK
END_P

Rule 2b
A.task = LS
B.task ? Back Missing_Back
X := A
X.task := Parts
IF B.Start < A.Start THEN X.Start := B.Start ELSE ENDIF
IF A.End < B.End THEN X.End := B.End ELSE ENDIF
OK
END_P

Rule 3a
A.task = Saw1
B.task = Saw2
X := A
X.task := Saw12
```

```
IF B.Start < A.Start THEN X.Start := B.Start ELSE ENDIF
IF A.End < B.End THEN X.End := B.End ELSE ENDIF
OK
END_P


Rule 3b
A.task = Saw12
B.task = Saw3
X := A
X.task := Saw123
IF B.Start < A.Start THEN X.Start := B.Start ELSE ENDIF
IF A.End < B.End THEN X.End := B.End ELSE ENDIF
OK
END_P


Rule 3c
A.task = Saw123
B.task = Saw4
X := A
X.task := Legs
IF B.Start < A.Start THEN X.Start := B.Start ELSE ENDIF
IF A.End < B.End THEN X.End := B.End ELSE ENDIF
OK
END_P


Rule 4
A.task = Cutting
B.task = Polishing
A.End <? B.Start
X := A
X.task := Seat
X.End := B.End
OK
END_P


Rule 5
IF A.task = Buy THEN ELSE
  IF A.task = Welding THEN ELSE
    FAIL
  ENDIF
ENDIF
X := A
X.task := Back
OK
END_P
```

```
Rule 6
Negative
A.task = Legs
IF B.task = Back   THEN A.task ? Seat Missing_Seat ELSE FAIL ENDIF
X := A
X.task := Parts
IF B.Start < A.Start THEN X.Start := B.Start ELSE ENDIF
IF A.End < B.End THEN X.End := B.End ELSE ENDIF
OK
END_P
```

The grammar contains some features which would help us to detect errors in a concrete workflow. The soft conditions $A.End <?$ $B.Start$ applied to attributes carrying the starting and ending times of particular subtasks will detect possible inconsistencies in these times of subtasks in a sequence. The soft conditions in rules 2a and 2b (for example $A.task <?$ $Legs$ $Missing\_Legs$) together with the error anticipation rule 6 detect the possible error consisting in a missing part (one of the three, Legs, Seat or Back support). If the grammar is applied in an error detecting mode, these conditions and rules will not only make it possible to continue the checking of the workflow even when some of the subtasks are missing, they will also insert an error mark (the text following the soft condition, in our case $Missing\_Legs$, $Missing\_Back$ and $Missing\_Seat$ indicating which subtask is missing.

We may notice a small difference in the use of error anticipation rules between the two application areas we are interested in. In grammar checking, it is very often the case that certain types of grammatical errors are much more frequent than others simply because people tend to make certain errors relatively regularly. These errors may then be expected on the basis of linguistic investigations based on large volumes of data. In the area of workflow validation it is different because in principle any subtask may be forgotten and thus it is necessary to create substantially larger set of error anticipation rules than in the case of grammar checking. Also in our sample grammar, if we would aim at its practical exploitation, we would need many more rules. The Rule 6 serves only as a kind of a template for such rules.

7   Conclusions

The work described in this paper shows that the nested workflows may be described by attribute grammars not only theoretically, as it has been already shown in several papers, but also practically, by means of a concrete grammar formalism originally developed for seemingly very distant application area. RFODG represents a grammar formalism with several special properties, some of which may be directly exploited for a validation of the compliance of a concrete process with its model. The paper explains how constraint relaxation and error anticipation techniques of RFODG may be applied to workflow validation in a similar way as they had been originally applied to grammar checking of natural languages. It also indicates the modifications of RFODG which are necessary for a complete transformation of a description of nested workflows into corresponding RFODG grammars.

The next natural step in our research will be the investigation whether the RFODG may also serve for an inverse task, the generation of processes and what kind of additional modifications it would require.

Acknowledgments. The research reported in this paper has been supported by the Czech Science Foundation GACR, grant No. P103-15-19877S.

References

1. van der Aalst, W., t. Hofstede, A.H.M.: Yawl: yet another workow language. Inf. Syst. **30**, 245–275 (2005)
2. Bae, J., Bae, H., Kang, S.H., Kim, Z.: Automatic control of workflow processes using eca rules. IEEE Trans. Knowl. Data Eng. **16**, 1010–1023 (2004)
3. Barták, R.: Using attribute grammars to model nested workflows with extra constraints. In: Freivalds, R.M., Engels, G., Catania, B. (eds.) SOFSEM 2016. LNCS, vol. 9587, pp. 171–182. Springer, Heidelberg (2016). doi:10.1007/978-3-662-49192-8_14
4. Barták, R., Cully, M., Jaška, M., Novák, L., Rovenský, V., Sheahan, C., Skalický, T.: Workflow optimization with flowopt, on modelling, optimizing, visualizing, and analysing production workflows. In: Proceedings of Conference on Technologies and Applications of Artificial Intelligence (TAAI 2011), pp. 167–172. IEEE Conference Publishing Services (2011)
5. Barták, R., Rovenský, V.: On verification of nested workflows with extra constraints: from theory to practice. Expert Syst. Appl. **41**, 904–918 (2014)
6. Barták, R., Čepek, O.: Nested precedence networks with alternatives: recognition, tractability, and models. In: Dochev, D., Pistore, M., Traverso, P. (eds.) AIMSA 2008. LNCS, vol. 5253, pp. 235–246. Springer, Heidelberg (2008). doi:10.1007/978-3-540-85776-1_20
7. Holan, T.: Nástroje pro vývoj závislostních analyzátorů přirozených jazyků s volným slovosledem. MFF UK, Prague (2001). (in Czech)
8. Holan, T., Kuboň, V., Plátek, M.: A prototype of a grammar checker for czech. In: Proceedings of the Fifth Conference on Applied Natural Language Processing, pp. 147–154. ACL, Washington, DC (1997)
9. Knuth, D.E.: Semantics of context-free languages. Math. Syst. Theory **2**, 127–145 (1968)

On Verification of Workflow and Planning Domain Models Using Attribute Grammars

Roman Barták$^{(\boxtimes)}$ and Tomáš Dvořák

Faculty of Mathematics and Physics, Charles University,
Malostranské nám. 25, Praha 1, Czech Republic
bartak@ktiml.mff.cuni.cz

Abstract. Recently, attribute grammars have been suggested as a unifying framework to describe workflow and planning domains models. One of the critical aspects of the domain model is its soundness, that is, the model should not contain any dead-ends and should describe at least one plan. In this paper we describe how the domain model can be verified by using the concept of reduction of attribute grammars. Two verification methods are suggested, one based on transformation to context-free grammars and one direct method exploiting constraint satisfaction.

Keywords: Modeling · Workflows · Planning domains · Verification · Attribute grammars

1 Introduction

Despite the recent rise of so called model-free methods in artificial intelligence, formal models are still important for problem modeling and solving. One of important aspects of formal models is possibility of model verification that ensures that the model is internally consistent and satisfies some desirable properties. Generally speaking consistency means that a solution based on the formal model exists. For example, if we have a formal model of a workflow, we need to be sure that a real process exists based on this workflow and that the workflow does not contain any branches that can never be used due to violation of constraints.

Workflow verification has been studied for some time. Various methods of verification have been proposed, e.g., using Petri Nets [10], graph reductions [9], and logic-based verification [4]. These methods deal with complex workflow structures that are used for example to model business processes. The focus of verification methods for such workflows is on structural properties of the workflows but these methods are not applicable to extra constraints that go beyond the core workflow structure. A method to verify nested workflows with extra constraints has been suggested in [3]. This method covers all aspects of the workflow model. Recently, attribute grammars have been suggested to model nested workflows with extra constraints [1]. Attribute grammars bring recursion to the workflow model and hence support modeling of planning problems. The hope

© Springer International Publishing AG 2017
G. Sidorov and O. Herrera-Alcántara (Eds.): MICAI 2016, Part I, LNAI 10061, pp. 332–345, 2017.
DOI: 10.1007/978-3-319-62434-1_28

is that other formalism for modeling workflows and planning domains can be transformed to attribute grammars. Hence, it would be useful, if a method for verification of attribute grammars exists as then any formal model, that can be transformed to an attribute grammar, can be verified without additional effort.

This paper presents novel methods, how to verify attribute grammars. We will first formalize the verification problem as the problem of finding whether or not an attribute grammar is in a reduced form. Then we propose two methods to transform any attribute grammar with finite-domain attributes to its reduced form. These methods can identify invalid non-terminal symbols as well as invalid rewriting rules so these verification methods can point at particular mistakes in the grammar. This is important for practical applicability as explanation of mistakes is the first step to repair them.

2   Background

In this section, we recall some basic notions and techniques used in the paper, namely constraint satisfaction, attribute grammars, and nested workflows.

2.1   Constraint Satisfaction

Constraint satisfaction technology originated in Artificial Intelligence as a technique for declarative modeling and solving of combinatorial optimization problems. A *constraint satisfaction problem* (CSP) is a triple (X, D, C), where X is a finite set of decision variables, for each $x_i \in X$, $D_i \in D$ is a finite set of possible values for the variable x_i (the domain), and C is a finite set of constraints [5]. A *constraint* is a relation over a subset of variables (its scope) that restricts the possible combinations of values to be assigned to the variables in its scope. Constraints can be expressed in extension using a set of compatible value tuples or as a formula. We will be using constraints expressed as arithmetic and logical formulas, such as $S + D = E$. A *solution* to a CSP is a complete instantiation of variables such that the values are taken from respective domains and all constraints are satisfied. We say that a CSP is *consistent* if it has a solution.

2.2   Attribute Grammars

Attribute grammars were introduced by Knuth [7] to add semantics to context-free grammars in a syntax-directed fashion. The primary application area was the design of compilers. Briefly speaking an attribute grammar is a context-free grammar where symbols are associated with sets of attributes and rewriting (production) rules are associated with sets of attribute computation (semantic) rules defining values of certain attributes based on values of other attributes. We will slightly modify the original definition here by using constraints rather than the semantic rules with synthesized attributes and inherited attributes.

We define an *attribute grammar* as a tuple $G = (\Sigma, N, \mathcal{P}, S, A, \mathcal{C})$, where Σ is an alphabet – a finite set of terminal symbols, N is a finite set of non-terminal symbols with S as the start symbol, $\mathcal{P}$ is a set of rewriting (production) rules (see below), A associates each grammar symbol $X \in \Sigma \cup N$ with a set of attributes (variables in terms of a CSP), and $\mathcal{C}$ associates each production $R \in \mathcal{P}$ with a set of constraints over the attributes of symbols used in the rule. $G = (\Sigma, N, \mathcal{P}, S)$ is a classical context-free grammar with the production rules in the form $X \rightarrow w$, where $X \in N$ is a non-terminal symbol and $w \in (\Sigma \cup N)^*$ is a finite sequence of terminal and non-terminal symbols. If A are the attributes for symbol X, we will write $X(A)$ in the production rule. To separate grammar symbols in a string (a word) we will use the dot (.) notation. We will also include the constraints associated with the rule directly in the rule inside the brackets $[c_1, \ldots]$. This is an example of a production rule:

$$Seat(S_S, E_S) \rightarrow Cutting(S_C, E_C).Polishing(S_P, E_P)$$
$$[S_S = S_C, E_C \leq S_P, E_P = E_S]$$

Let (w, C) denote a state of the rewriting system, where w is a string of grammar symbols with their attributes and C is a set of constraints over these attributes. We say that (w, C) directly rewrites to (w', C') using the production rule $X(A) \rightarrow u[c]$ if and only if $w = u_1.X(B).u_2$, $C' = C \cup \{A = B\} \cup c$, and C' is a consistent CSP over the variables from attributes of w', where $w' = u_1.u.u_2$. We denote this rewriting as $(w, C) \Rightarrow (w', C')$. Briefly speaking, a non-terminal symbol X is substituted by u in the string w and constraints from the production rule are added to the constraints in the state. Note that we assume classical standardization apart of the production rules, that is, each production rule is used with fresh variables/attributes. For a sequence of direct rewritings, called a *derivation*, $(w_1, C_1) \Rightarrow (w_2, C_2) \Rightarrow \cdots \Rightarrow (w_n, C_n)$ we will use classical notation $(w_1, C_1) \Rightarrow^* (w_n, C_n)$. The language generated by an attribute grammar $G = (\Sigma, N, \mathcal{P}, S, A, \mathcal{C})$ is:

$$L(G) = \{w\sigma | (S, \emptyset) \Rightarrow^* (w, C), w \in \Sigma^*, \sigma \text{ is a solution to a CSP } C\}.$$

σ is an instantiation of attributes (substitution of values to variables) and $w\sigma$ means applying substitution σ to w, i.e., a word w, where the attributes are substituted by values defined in σ.

2.3   Nested Workflows

In [1] the author suggested using attribute grammars for modeling nested workflows with extra constraints used in the FlowOpt system [2]. The nested workflows were formally introduced in [3], where also an ad-hoc verification technique was proposed. For completeness, we will recapitulate the notion of nested workflows together with its translation to attribute grammars.

The *nested workflow* is obtained from a root task by applying decomposition operations that split the task into subtasks until primitive tasks, corresponding to activities, are obtained. Three decomposition operations are supported, namely parallel, serial, and alternative decompositions. Figure 1 gives an example of a nested workflow that shows how the tasks are decomposed. The root task

Chair is decomposed serially to two tasks, where the second task is a primitive task filled by activity *Assembly*. The first task *Create Parts* decomposes further to three parallel tasks *Legs*, *Seat*, and *Back Support*. *Back Support* is the only example here of alternative decomposition to two primitive tasks with *Buy* and *Welding* activities (*Welding* is treated as an alternative to *Buy*). Hence the workflow describes two alternative processes. Naturally, the nested workflow can be described as a tree of tasks (Fig. 1 bottom right).

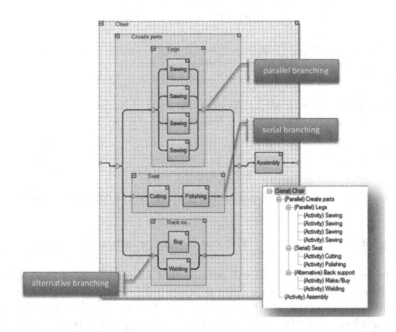

Fig. 1. Example of a nested workflow as it is visualized in the FlowOpt Workflow Editor (from top to down there are parallel, serial, and alternative decompositions).

The nested structured resembles a tree structure so it is natural to model nested workflows using attribute grammars. The author in [1] showed that even the extra binary constraints beyond the nested structure can be included in this translation. Hence nested workflows with extra constraints can be fully modeled as attribute grammars. Figure 2 shows a complete attribute grammar modeling the nested workflow from Fig. 1 (extra constraints are not included there).

Attribute grammars provide one significant extension over the nested workflows and this is recursion. The task can be decomposed to itself so we can model repetition of tasks which brings even more planning capabilities to the formal model. In fact, as classical planning can be seen as finding a path in a finite state transition space, and hence we can model it using finite state automaton, it is obvious that an attribute grammar, which is an extension of a context-free grammar, can model any classical planning problem. Hierarchical structures were already used in planning, for example Hierarchical Task Networks (HTN)

$Chair(S_{chair}, E_{chair}) \rightarrow Parts(S_{parts}, E_{parts}).Assembly(S_{assembly}, E_{assembly})$
$[S_{chair} = min\{S_{parts}, S_{assembly}\}, E_{chair} = max\{E_{parts}, E_{assembly}\},$
$\quad E_{parts} \leq S_{assembly}, S_{assembly} + D_{assembly} = E_{assembly}]$

$Parts(S_{parts}, E_{parts}) \rightarrow Legs(S_{legs}, E_{legs}).Seat(S_{seat}, E_{seat}).Back(S_{back}, E_{back})$
$[S_{parts} = min\{S_{legs}, S_{seat}, S_{back}\}, E_{parts} = max\{E_{legs}, E_{seat}, E_{back}\}]$

$Legs(S_{legs}, E_{legs}) \rightarrow Saw(S_1, E_1), Saw(S_2, E_2), Saw(S_3, E_3), Saw(S_4, E_4)$
$[S_{legs} = min\{S_1, S_2, S_3, S_4\}, E_{legs} = max\{E_1, E_2, E_3, E_4\},$
$\quad S_1 + D_1 = E_1, S_2 + D_2 = E_2, S_3 + D_3 = E_3, S_4 + D_4 = E_4]$

$Seat(S_{seat}, E_{seat}) \rightarrow Cutting(S_{cut}, E_{cut}).Polishing(S_{polish}, E_{polish})$
$[S_{seat} = min\{S_{cut}, S_{polish}\}, E_{seat} = max\{E_{cut}, E_{polish}\},$
$\quad E_{cut} \leq S_{polish}, S_{cut} + D_{cut} = E_{cut}, S_{polish} + D_{polish} = E_{polish}]$

$Back(S_{back}, E_{back}) \rightarrow Buy(S_{buy}, E_{buy})$
$[S_{back} = S_{buy}, E_{back} = E_{buy}, S_{buy} + D_{buy} = E_{buy}]$

$Back(S_{back}, E_{back}) \rightarrow Weld(S_{weld}, E_{weld})$
$[S_{back} = S_{weld}, E_{back} = E_{weld}, S_{weld} + D_{weld} = E_{weld}]$

Fig. 2. An attribute grammar modeling the nested workflow from Fig. 1.

[8] though it is not obvious if HTNs can be fully translated to attribute grammars.

In the rest of the paper we will assume that all attributes of the attribute grammar take their values from finite domains only. Theoretically, this reduces the expressive power of attribute grammars. Nevertheless, in practice, this restriction is less significant as planning and scheduling problems frequently deal with finite domains only. For example, the attribute grammars generated from nested workflows with extra constraints [1] as well as the grammars modeling classical planning problems satisfy this assumption.

3   Attribute Grammar Verification Problem

In the rest of the paper we will abstract from a particular workflow and planning domain model and we will focus solely on attribute grammars. The goal is to provide a verification mechanism for any attribute grammar. The major advantage is that by having a mechanism to verify attribute grammars, we naturally have a mechanism to verify any other model that translates to an attribute grammar.

The first question is what it means to verify an attribute grammar. The definition of the workflow verification problem from [3] says that the *workflow verification problem* is the problem of checking that for each task there exists a feasible process. In terms of attribute grammars it means that it is possible to generate some terminal word from the non-terminal symbol corresponding to any task. Formally, we can define a language $L(G, X)$ of words that can be generated from X using the rules of grammar G as:

$$L(G, X) = \{w\sigma | (X, \emptyset) \Rightarrow^* (w, C), w \in \Sigma^*, \sigma \text{ is a solution to a CSP } C\}.$$

So the workflow verification problem from [3] can be formulated as checking of the following condition:

$$\forall X \in N : L(G, X) \neq \emptyset, \tag{1}$$

where $G = (\Sigma, N, \mathcal{P}, S, A, \mathcal{C})$ is an attribute grammar describing the workflow.

The reader may immediately notice that this condition is similar to one condition for a context-free grammar to be so called *reduced* [11], namely that any non-terminal symbol should generate a terminal word. The other condition of a reduced context-free grammar says that any non-terminal symbol should be reachable from the start non-terminal symbol. In terms of workflow verification it means that any given task can be generated from the root task, which was assumed to always hold in [3]. In case of attribute grammars, we must formalize this condition more carefully as these grammars do not preserve the property of being context-free. In particular, attributes of a non-terminal symbol A may by connected to attributes of another non-terminal symbol B and this way the word generated from A may restrict possible words generated from B and vice versa. The following simple attribute grammar nicely demonstrates this property:

$$S(N_S) \rightarrow A(N_A).B(N_B) \qquad\qquad [N_S = N_A, N_S = N_B]$$
$$A(N) \rightarrow a \qquad\qquad\qquad\qquad\qquad [N = 1]$$
$$A(N) \rightarrow a.a \qquad\qquad\qquad\qquad\quad [N = 2]$$
$$B(N) \rightarrow b.b \qquad\qquad\qquad\qquad\quad [N = 2]$$

This grammar generates a language $\{aabb\}$, while its context-free counterpart (without the constraints) would generate a language $\{abb, aabb\}$. The first rule for symbol A cannot be applied in any derivation starting at S and leading to a terminal word. In terms of workflow verification it means that even if a task can be decomposed to subtasks locally, this decomposition might not be applicable in the context of neighboring tasks, which indicates a serious problem in the workflow model.

Based on above observations, we suggest to formalize the *attribute grammar verification problem* as the problem of verifying whether or not the grammar is in its reduced form.

Definition 1. *The attribute grammar* $G = (\Sigma, N, \mathcal{P}, S, A, \mathcal{C})$ *is in the* reduced form, *if and only if the following condition holds:*

$$\forall X \in N, \forall p = (X(A) \rightarrow u[c]) \in \mathcal{P} \; \exists u_1, u_2 \in (\Sigma \cup N)^*, w \in \Sigma^* :$$
$$(S, \emptyset) \Rightarrow^* (u_1.X(B).u_2, C_1) \Rightarrow^p (u_1.u.u_2, C_1 \cup \{A = B\} \cup c) \Rightarrow^* \ldots$$
$$\Rightarrow^* (w, C) \wedge C \text{ is consistent}$$

The definition basically says that each non-terminal symbol and each rewriting rule can be used in some derivation (starting at S) leading to a terminal word. This formulation covers both the reachability property as well as the property of generating terminal words. Obviously, if a non-terminal X violates the property (1) then it does not satisfy the condition in the Definition 1. Moreover, the definition also deals with non-applicable rewriting rules, which is important in the context of workflow verification as such a rule indicates that a given task decomposition cannot be applied.

We will now present techniques to reduce a given attribute grammar, i.e., to transform any attribute grammar G to an attribute grammar G_R in the reduced form such that $L(G) = L(G_R)$. Such a technique will detect if an attribute grammar is in the reduced form, $G = G_R$ (the underlying workflow model is correct), and in case of not being reduced, $G_R \subsetneq G$, it will also provide "wrong" non-terminal symbols and rewriting rules. This is important in the context of workflow verification as it will provide the modeler information about which task is modeled incorrectly.

4   Verification via Translation to CFG

In this section we will show how to reduce an attribute grammar by transforming it to a context-free grammar, reducing that grammar, and transforming the reduced context-free grammar back to an attribute grammar.

Let us recall first the two conditions for a context-free grammar $G = (\Sigma, N, \mathcal{P}, S)$ to be reduced:

$$\forall X \in N (\exists w \in \Sigma^* : X \Rightarrow^* w) \wedge (\exists u, v \in (\Sigma \cup N)^* : S \Rightarrow^* uXv).$$

There exists a classical technique to find non-terminal symbols satisfying the above property [11]. This technique works in two steps. First, non-terminal symbols violating the condition $X \Rightarrow^* w$ of generating a terminal word are eliminated. This is done in an iterative way by constructing sets U_i containing symbols that can be rewritten to a terminal word in i (or fewer) steps. Formally:

$$U_0 = \Sigma, \ U_{i+1} = U_i \cup \{X \mid X \in N, \exists (X \to u) \in \mathcal{P}, u \in U_i^*\}$$

Obviously $U_i \subseteq U_{i+1} \subseteq (\Sigma \cup N)$ and therefore there exists some k such that $U_{k+1} = U_k$. Any non-terminal symbol $X \notin U_k$ can be removed from the grammar as this symbol does not generate a terminal word and similarly, any rewriting rule containing such a symbol can be discarded. If S is removed then the grammar does not generate any terminal word.

In the second step, the non-terminal symbols that are not reachable from S are removed while preserving the property of generating terminal words. Again, this is done in an iterative way by finding sets V_i of non-terminal symbols reachable from the start symbol S in i (or fewer) steps as follows:

$$V_0 = \{S\}, \ V_{i+1} = V_i \cup \{X \mid X \in N, \exists Y \in V_i, (Y \to u.X.v) \in \mathcal{P}\}.$$

Again, as $V_i \subseteq V_{i+1} \subseteq N$ there exists some l such that $V_{l+1} = V_l$. Any non-terminal symbol $X \notin V_l$ can be removed from the grammar as it is not reachable and similarly, any rewriting rule containing such a symbol can be discarded. The property of generating terminal words remains untouched for the non-terminal symbols in V_l (any symbol used to get a terminal word from $X \in V_l$ is reachable if X is reachable).

The open question is how to transform an attribute grammar to a context-free grammar. We will use the process known as *grounding*. Let $A(X)$ be a vector of attributes of a symbol X and $a(X)$ be a vector of possible values for these attributes. Then for each symbol X of an attribute grammar, we introduce a set of symbols $X^{a(X)}$ of a context-free grammar. Let us denote this set $Ground(X)$. Now let $X \to Y_1.Y_2 \ldots Y_k$ be a rewriting rule of an attribute grammar with an attached set of constraints c. We generate rewriting rules $X^{a(X)} \to Y_1^{a(Y_1)}.Y_2^{a(Y_2)} \ldots Y_k^{a(Y_k)}$ such that the value tuples $a(X), a(Y_1), \ldots, a(Y_k)$ satisfy the constraints c. This way we a get a context-free grammar that can be seen as grounding of the original attribute grammar.

The following table shows the verification process for the attribute grammar from the previous section, where we assume the domains of all attributes to be $\{1, 2\}$. First, the grammar is grounded (the left column). Formally, this grounded context-free grammar may have more starting non-terminal symbols (S^1, S^2 in the example), but this is not a problem as we can start the second stage of the reduction process with $V_0 = Ground(S)$. Next, (the middle column) in the first stage the non-terminals, that do not generate a terminal word, are eliminated (S^1 in this example). Finally (the right column), in the second stage the non-terminals, that are not reachable, are eliminated (A^1 in this example).

Grounded	1st stage	2nd stage
$S^1 \to A^1.B^1$		
$S^2 \to A^2.B^2$	$S^2 \to A^2.B^2$	$S^2 \to A^2.B^2$
$A^1 \to a$	$A^1 \to a$	
$A^2 \to a.a$	$A^2 \to a.a$	$A^2 \to a.a$
$B^2 \to b.b$	$B^2 \to b.b$	$B^2 \to b.b$

Now, let N' be a set of non-terminal symbols from the reduced context-free grammar. We will keep a non-terminal symbol X in the attribute grammar if and only if $Ground(X) \cap N' \neq \emptyset$. In the above example, all non-terminal symbols $\{S, A, B\}$ are kept in the grammar. Similarly, we will only keep those rewriting rules such that at least one of their grounded counterparts is in the reduced context-free grammar. This way we will get the following reduced attribute grammar:

$$S(N_S) \rightarrow A(N_A).B(N_B) \qquad\qquad [N_S = N_A, N_S = N_B]$$
$$A(N) \rightarrow a.a \qquad\qquad\qquad\qquad\qquad [N = 2]$$
$$B(N) \rightarrow b.b \qquad\qquad\qquad\qquad\qquad [N = 2]$$

This example demonstrates why we need to assume rewriting rules in the Definition 1 explicitly and not just via non-terminal symbols as for the context-free grammars. As a side effect, we also know that the only allowed value for attributes in the above grammar is 2. This reduced domain can be obtained by projecting the grounded non-terminal symbols to individual attributes.

It should be clear that any symbol X in the reduced attribute grammar satisfies the property $(S, \emptyset) \Rightarrow^* (u.X.v, C_1) \Rightarrow^* (w, C_2)$. First, as X is kept in the grammar then in the reduced context-free grammar there exists $X^{a(X)}$ such that $S^{a(S)} \Rightarrow^* u'.X^{a(X)}.v'$, where u' and v' are groundings of u and v. The rules used in this derivation are such that the attribute values from indexes of symbols satisfy the constraints (this is how the grounded rules were generated) and therefore C_1 is consistent. Next, it also holds that $X^{a(X)} \Rightarrow^* w'$ and $u' \Rightarrow^* u'', v' \Rightarrow^* v''$, where $u''.w'.v''$ is a grounding of w. Again, the rules used in these derivations satisfy the constraints and hence C_2 is consistent. Actually, the indexes of the grounded symbols used in these derivations describe one possible solution of constraints C_2. Finally, if the rewriting rule is kept in the reduced attribute grammar then there is some grounded version of that rule in the reduced context-free grammar. This grounded rule has been used in some derivation of the reduced context-free grammar so the lifted version of that derivation is a derivation in the attribute grammar.

5   Direct Verification with CSP Solving

The workflow verification problem in [3] was formulated as a constraint satisfaction problem. Unfortunately, due to possibility of using recursion in the attribute grammars, this approach cannot be directly applied for verification of attribute grammars – there could be an infinite number of possible derivations and hence an infinite number of corresponding CSPs. Nevertheless, we can do the following observation. Assume a non-terminal symbol $X(A)$ of the attribute grammar G. Even if the language $L(G, X)$ can be infinite, the number of projections of solutions of corresponding CSPs to the attributes A is finite (recall, that we assume finite-domain attributes only). Hence, if $X(A)$ appears in some derivation, we can represent all words generated from X as a new constraint over the attributes A. This constraint defines valid value tuples for attributes A. There is the following relation between these constraints and non-terminal symbols in the reduced context-free grammar. If a is such a valid value tuple then X^a is the grounded symbol from the reduced context-free grammar.

We will show now, how to find out the above attribute constraints by mimicking the two stage approach of reduction of context-free grammars. At the first stage, we will find the value tuples $a(X)$ such that $X^{a(X)} \Rightarrow^* u$ for some terminal word u in the transformed context-free grammar. In other words, we will find the set U^k used in the reduction of context-free grammars. The idea is as follows. We will start with an empty set $G(X)$ of attribute value tuples for each non-terminal symbol X. Then we take the rewriting rules having only terminal symbols on their right side and find all solutions of CSPs defined by rule constraints. This way we get attribute value tuples corresponding to non-terminal symbols in U_1. Then, we repeat this process with rules having on their right side only terminals or non-terminals X with non-empty sets $D(X)$ of attribute value tuples. These sets $D(X)$ are used as additional constraints in the rewriting rules. For example, if we have sets $G(A) = \{1,2\}, G(B) = \{2\}$ and a rewriting rule $S(N_S) \rightarrow A(N_A).B(N_B)\ [N_S = N_A, N_S = N_B]$ then we are solving the CSP with constraints: $N_S = N_A, N_S = N_B, N_A \in \{1,2\}, N_B \in \{2\}$, which gives a single solution $N_S = 2, N_A = 2, N_B = 2$. Each such solution defines a (new) value tuple for the non-terminal symbol on the left side of the rule, in our example we get $D(S) = \{2\}$. We repeat the process while the sets G are changing. As these sets can only enlarge, the algorithm must finish sometime.

This method corresponds to the first stage of reduction of context-free grammars. The major difference is that we introduce the non-terminal symbols $X^{a(X)}$ incrementally by finding only those value tuples $a(X)$ such that $X^{a(X)} \Rightarrow^* u$ for some terminal word u. Moreover, instead of introducing all possible grounded rules at once, we solve the CSPs defined by constraints in the rules. Note, that a constraint satisfaction algorithm that finds all solutions is necessary. We also explicitly mark each rewriting rule as useful if it is used in some successful derivation (the corresponding CSP has a solution). The Algorithm 1 describes this method formally.

In our example grammar, each non-terminal symbol has one attribute. The Algorithm 1 generates the following attribute value sets: $G(A) = \{1,2\}, G(B) = \{2\}, G(S) = \{2\}$ and marks all rules as useful. Notice the relation between these attribute value sets and grounded non-terminal symbols passing the first stage of reduction of the corresponding context-free grammar $\{S^2, A^1, A^2, B^2\}$.

Similarly to reduction of context-free grammars, we need to filter out attribute value tuples that are not "reachable" from the start non-terminal. Actually, we will rather select those attribute value tuples from sets G that are reachable. We will use sets $G'(X)$ to collect these reachable value tuples. Initially, these sets will be empty except the set $G'(S) = G(S)$ for the start non-terminal S. Each time, we extend the set $G'(X)$ we explore all rewriting rules having X on their left side. Obviously, we start with rules having S on their left side. Again, processing the rule means solving a CSP defined by its constraints. For each such a CSP we also assume constraints defined by sets $G(Y)$ for each non-terminal symbol Y on the right side of the rule and the constraint defined by the set $G'(X)$ for the non-terminal symbol X on the left side of the rule. All obtained solutions are then projected to non-terminals on the right side of the rule to update their sets G'. For our example grammar, we start this stage with $G(A) = \{1,2\}, G(B) = \{2\}, G(S) = \{2\}$ from the first stage

Algorithm 1. First stage

```
 1: for all X ∈ N do
 2:     G(X) ← ∅
 3: end for
 4: for all p : (X → Y₁.....Yₙ) ∈ P do
 5:     useful(p) ← false
 6:     if Y₁ ∈ Σ & ... & Yₙ ∈ Σ then
 7:         RULE_QUEUE.PUSH
 8:     end if
 9: end for
10: while !RULE_QUEUE.EMPTY do
11:     p : (X → X₁.....Xₙ) ← RULE_QUEUE.POP
12:     solutions ← CSP(p)[A(X)]   ▷ all solutions of a CSP defined by constraints of
                                     rule p projected to attributes of X
13:     if solutions = ∅ then
14:         continue
15:     end if
16:     useful(p) ← true
17:     if solutions ⊈ G(X) then              ▷ some new value tuples for X found
18:         G(X) ← G(X) ∪ solutions
19:         for all q : (Y₀ → Y₁.....Yₙ) ∈ P do
20:             if X ∈ {Y₁, ..., Yₙ} & G(Y₁) ≠ ∅ & ... & G(Yₙ) ≠ ∅ then
21:                 RULE_QUEUE.PUSH
22:             end if
23:         end for
24:     end if
25: end while
```

and $G'(A) = \{\}, G'(B) = \{\}, G'(S) = \{2\}$ as the initial G' sets. The first rule to be processed is $S(N_S) \rightarrow A(N_A).B(N_B)\ [N_S = N_A, N_S = N_B]$ with additional constraints $N_A \in G(A) = \{1, 2\}, N_B \in G(B) = \{2\}, N_S \in G'(S) = \{2\}$. There is only one solution $N_S = 2, N_A = 2, N_B = 2$, which defines new sets $G'(A) = \{2\}, G'(B) = \{2\}$. Hence rules with A or B on the left side will be processed next. Notice for example the rule $A(N) \rightarrow a\ [N = 1]$ that will be augmented by the constraint $N \in G(A) = \{2\}$. Hence there is no solution to this CSP and the rule will not be marked as useful. The other two rules $A(N) \rightarrow a.a\ [N = 2]$ and $B(N) \rightarrow b.b\ [N = 2]$ with augmented constraints will have solutions so they remain in the grammar (marked as useful), but they do not extend sets G' so the algorithm stops there as there is no other rule to explore. The above method is formally described by the Algorithm 2.

The soundness of the Algorithm 2 goes from its correspondence to the second stage of reduction of context-free grammars. Briefly speaking, the grounded rules used in constructions of sets V_i are generated on demand from the original non-grounded rules augmented by constraints defined by sets G and set G'. The detailed formal proofs are available in thesis [6].

We have implemented an experimental attribute grammar editor with the direct verification method using a CSP solver from the Microsoft Solver

Algorithm 2. Second stage

1: **for all** $x \in N$ **do**
2:     $G'(X) \leftarrow \emptyset$
3: **end for**
4: $G'(S) \leftarrow G(S)$
5: **for all** $p : (Y_0 \rightarrow Y_1.....Y_n) \in P$ **do**
6:     $useful(p) \leftarrow false$
7:     **if** $Y_0 = S$ **then**
8:         $RULE\_QUEUE.PUSH$
9:     **end if**
10: **end for**
11: **while** $!RULE\_QUEUE.EMPTY$ **do**
12:     $p : (X \rightarrow X_1.....X_n) \leftarrow RULE\_QUEUE.POP$
13:     $solutions \leftarrow CSP(p)$
14:     **if** $solutions = \emptyset$ **then**
15:         **continue**
16:     **end if**
17:     $useful(p) \leftarrow true$
18:     **for all** $x \in \{X_1, ..., X_n\}$ **do**
19:         $solution \leftarrow solutions[A(x)]$
20:         **if** $solution \nsubseteq G'(x)$ **then**
21:             $G'(x) \leftarrow G'(x) \cup solution$
22:             **for all** $q : (x \rightarrow Y_1.....Y_n) \in P$ **do**
23:                 $RULE\_QUEUE.PUSH$
24:             **end for**
25:         **end if**
26:     **end for**
27: **end while**

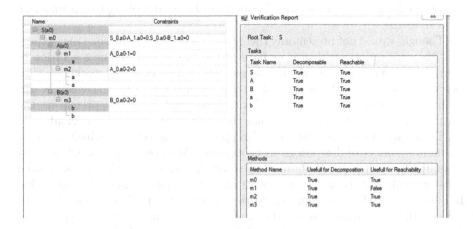

Fig. 3. Experimental editor with the verification function (the left part shows the grammar tree for the example grammar from this paper; the right part shows the result of verification).

Foundation. The editor supports editing of rewriting rules (called decomposition methods) and constraints and visualization of the grammar tree (the left part of Fig. 3). The result of verification is displayed to the user (the right part of Fig. 3) and the found bugs are also highlighted in the editor.

6   Conclusions

Verification of workflow and planning domain models is an important step in the design of formal models. Though there exists some ad-hod approaches for workflow verification (we are not aware about any approach for verification of planning domain models), we believe that a more useful method is having a verification algorithm for some general concept, such as attribute grammars, to which other modeling frameworks can be translated.

In this paper, we formulated the problem of verification of attribute grammars as their reduction, we gave a definition of a reduced attribute grammar, and we proposed two approaches to do the reduction, one based on translation to a context-free grammar via grounding and one direct approach with CSP solving. These two approaches do the reduction from opposite sides. The translation approach generates all assignments of attribute values via grounding and then eliminates those assignments that are not applicable (either do not lead to a terminal word or are not reachable). The direct approach first incrementally generates assignments leading to terminal words and in the second stage it generates assignments reachable from the start non-terminal, but only assuming assignments from the first stage. These approaches are quite computationally expensive as they involve finding all solutions to CSPs. Moreover, the direct approach repeatedly solves CSPs corresponding to the same rule (but with extended sets G or G', that corresponds to relaxing some constraints). Hence, it would be useful to exploit an incremental CSP solver rather that looking for all solutions from scratch.

Though, we did not present any theoretical complexity result, one may expect that the verification problem is as hard as the problem of finding a solution (a plan) for a given model. As the problem of verification of nested workflows with extra constraints is NP-complete [3] and using attribute grammars covers this problem, the theoretical time complexity is at least NP-c. By presenting the verification algorithms, we proved that the verification problem is decidable.

The major difficulty of the verification problem was recursion which may lead to infinite number of derivations to be explored. We overcame this difficulty by assuming finite-domain attributes only so all the derivations starting at a given non-terminal symbol collapse to a constraint with a finite number of value tuples. In our direct method, we represented this constraint explicitly as a set of value tuples. An open problem is whether the constraint can be represented implicitly, for example, using a formula, which would immediately give a verification method even for attributes with infinite domains.

In summary, the following three research directions are useful for exploration. First, there is still missing translation of the HTN formalism [8] to attribute grammars. Second, incremental constraint solving or intelligent grammar grounding would improve practical efficiency of the proposed verification technique. Third, an intentional representation of constraints would remove the restriction of using finite-domain attributes and may also contribute to better efficiency of verification.

Acknowledgements. Research is supported by the Czech Science Foundation under the project P103-15-19877S.

References

1. Barták, R.: Using attribute grammars to model nested workflows with extra constraints. In: Freivalds, R.M., Engels, G., Catania, B. (eds.) SOFSEM 2016. LNCS, vol. 9587, pp. 171–182. Springer, Heidelberg (2016). doi:10.1007/978-3-662-49192-8_14
2. Barták, R., Cully, M., Jaška, M., Novák, L., Rovenský, V., Sheahan, C., Skalický, T., Thanh-Tung, D.: Workflow optimization with flowopt, on modelling, optimizing, visualizing, and analysing production workflows. In: Proceedings of Conference on Technologies and Applications of Artificial Intelligence (TAAI 2011), pp. 167–172. IEEE Conference Publishing Services (2011)
3. Barták, R., Rovenský, V.: On verification of nested workflows with extra constraints: from theory to practice. Expert Syst. Appl. **41**(3), 904–918 (2014). Elsevier
4. Bi, H.H., Zhao, J.L.: Applying propositional logic to workflow verification. Inf. Technol. Manag. **5**(3–4), 293–318 (2004)
5. Dechter, R.: Constraint Processing. Morgan Kaufmann, San Francisco (2003)
6. Dvořák, T.: Hierarchické modelování plánovacích problémů. Master Thesis (in Czech), Charles University (2016)
7. Knuth, D.E.: Semantics of context-free languages. Math. Syst. Theor. **2**(2), 127–145 (1968)
8. Nau, D.S., Au, T.-C., Ilghami, O., Kuter, U., Murdock, J.W., Wu, D., Yaman, F.: SHOP2: an HTN planning system. J. Artif. Intell. Res. (JAIR) **20**, 379–404 (2003)
9. Sadiq, W., Orlowska, M.E.: Analyzing process models using graph reduction techniques. Inf. Syst. **25**(2), 117–134 (2000)
10. van der Aalst, W., ter Hofstede, A.H.M.: Verification of workflow task structures: a petri-net-based approach. Inf. Syst. **25**(1), 43–69 (2000)
11. Taniguchi, K., Kasami, T.: Reduction of context-free grammars. Inf. Control **17**(1), 92–108 (1970)

Tramp Ship Scheduling Problem with Berth Allocation Considerations and Time-Dependent Constraints

Francisco López-Ramos[1]([⊠]), Armando Guarnaschelli[2],
José-Fernando Camacho-Vallejo[3], Laura Hervert-Escobar[1],
and Rosa G. González-Ramírez[4]

[1] Centre for Innovation in Design and Technology, Instituto Tecnológico y de Estudios Superiores de Monterrey. Campus Monterrey, Monterrey, Mexico
{francisco.lopez.r,laura.hervert}@itesm.mx
[2] School of Transportation Engineering, Pontificia Universidad Católica de Valparaíso, Valparaíso, Chile
armando.guarnaschelli@pucv.cl
[3] Faculty of Physical and Mathematical Sciences, Universidad Autónoma de Nuevo León, San Nicolás de los Garza, Mexico
jose.camachovl@uanl.edu.mx
[4] Faculty of Engineering and Applied Sciencies, Universidad de Los Andes, Santiago de Chile, Chile
rgonzalez@uandes.cl

Abstract. This work presents a model for the Tramp Ship Scheduling problem including berth allocation considerations, motivated by a real case of a shipping company. The aim is to determine the travel schedule for each vessel considering multiple docking and multiple time windows at the berths. This work is innovative due to the consideration of both spatial and temporal attributes during the scheduling process. The resulting model is formulated as a mixed-integer linear programming problem, and a heuristic method to deal with multiple vessel schedules is also presented. Numerical experimentation is performed to highlight the benefits of the proposed approach and the applicability of the heuristic. Conclusions and recommendations for further research are provided.

Keywords: Tramp ship scheduling · Berth allocation · Multiple docking · Time-dependent constraints

1 Introduction

Maritime shipping accounts for more than 80% of foreign trade, positioning this mode of transport as the most relevant in world trade. The world fleet has experienced a continuous growth with an annual increase of 4.1% in 2013, reaching a total of 1.69 billion dwt (deadweight tonnages) in January 2014 [11]. Shipping companies are constantly seeking to achieve economies of scale in order

© Springer International Publishing AG 2017
G. Sidorov and O. Herrera-Alcántara (Eds.): MICAI 2016, Part I, LNAI 10061, pp. 346–361, 2017.
DOI: 10.1007/978-3-319-62434-1_29

to reduce transportation costs. These costs are highly influenced by fuel cost. Because of this, the planning and scheduling of routes is critical.

The ship scheduling problem considering berth assignment has been pointed out as a promising area of research in both operational and economic terms [1,2]. These issues have practical implications especially for the shipping companies that do not have control of berth assignment decisions at public port terminals.

In this paper, we address a tramp ship scheduling problem (TSSP) with berth allocation considerations and time-dependent constraints. The problem is motivated by a tramp shipping company that provides transport services to export palletized fruit. The aim of the decision problem is to determine the route for each vessel, the operations and travel schedule whilst satisfying berth access limitations which are explicitly modeled. Due to the access limitations to berths (availability and draft restrictions), the shipping company is allowed to assign a vessel to the same berth several times to overcome capacity and operational limitations. A mixed-integer linear programming model using an expanded berth-node network representation is proposed, as well as a heuristic decomposition method to deal with large-sized instances.

The remainder of the paper is organized as follows. Section 2 discusses the related works on TSSP and Berth allocation problems. Section 3 describes the problem under study. Section 4 presents the underlying network structure. Section 4 introduces the notation and the mathematical formulation of the optimization model. Section 6 provides the solution approach. Section 7 presents the numerical results. Finally, the conclusions and recommendations for further research are provided in Sect. 8.

2 Related Works

This work is related to two well-known problems, the Ship Scheduling Problem and the Berth Allocation Problem (BAP). The integration of these two intertwined problems has recently been pointed out as a promising area of research in both operational and economic terms [1,2].

In this regard, the work in [9] proposes an integrated model for ship scheduling and berth allocation, motivated by the case of shipping lines with self-owned terminals. In a follow-up work [10], the authors incorporate transshipment. Both works present a case study of a feeder service company operating around the Pearl River Delta region. A discrete layout of each port terminal with time window constraints is considered. However, a vessel cannot visit the same terminal more than once during the planning horizon.

The problem addressed in this work is concerned with the transportation of palletized perishable cargo (fruits) during the fruit season. There is a wide variety of industrial applications (e.g. [5,6]) related to the bulk size and break-bulk cargo. However, this work differs from other approaches by considering operational features such as decisions related to the number of contracts to be fulfilled, load splitting at berths instead of ships [4,7,8]. It also includes features from the BAP, such as spatial, temporal, handling time, and performance [1]. The spatial attribute describes the berth layout and water depth restrictions. Temporal attribute are constraints for providing the service at berths. The handling time attribute applies for vessel and berths. Finally, the performance attribute is associated with the objective function.

Under these considerations, this work contributes to the state-of-art on TSSP by considering specific characteristics originated by a practical case study. Therefore, filling a gap in the literature taking into account real-world features of the problem [4].

3   Problem Definition

Consider a set of contracts C with due date, destination and cargo to be fulfilled by the shipping company. There exists a number of port terminals for loading the cargo in the vessels. Each port terminal has a number of berths with different draft capacities limiting the amount of cargo that can be loaded in the vessels. Also, berths have a variety of time windows in which vessels can be moored.

A consideration in the problem is that cargoes may not be fully loaded in a vessel if not profitable. If a cargo is not fully loaded, a compensation expense is paid to its customer. Also, the draft of the vessel should be evaluated during the definition of the schedule. The draft of a vessel is equivalent to the maximum displacement when fully loaded. A vessel-displacement takes place whenever there is a change in the vertical distance between the waterline and the bottom of the hull when loading pallets in the vessel. In this way, it is desired to find:

- A route for each vessel, composed of the ordered set of berths to be visited.
- A schedule for each route, considering the arrival and departure times at time windows associated with the berths contained in the route and avoiding time clashes among vessels operating in the same time window.
- Amount of pallets to be loaded in each vessel in each berth time window in which the vessel operates.

The problem is modeled as a mixed-integer linear programming model, with the following assumptions:

- Cargoes are pre-assigned to one or more vessels.
- Cargoes are loaded in vessels at a constant average rate.
- Vessels origins are known beforehand.
- Vessels destinations are associated with the destination ports of their pre-assigned cargoes.
- Vessels have enough capacity to carry all their assigned cargoes.
- Vessels sail with a specific constant speed on each leg.
- Vessels have enough fuel in order to reach their destination.

4   Network Flow Representation

Cargoes are divided into pallets that are represented as variable flows going through a directed graph $G = (N, A)$. Nodes $i \in N$ contain the vessel origins, the berth time windows in which pallets can be loaded in the vessels, and the vessel destinations according to the pre-assigned cargoes; whereas, links $(i,j) \in A$ model possible sailing legs.

An illustrative example consisting of two vessels, two contracts (one per vessel) and two berths, having each one two time windows (w_i, w_j), is shown on Fig. 1. In that example, vessels start their routes at the blue nodes representing the vessel origins, and sail to some yellow nodes reproducing the available time windows of berths where pallets from cargoes C1 and C2 can be loaded in vessels V1 and V2, respectively. Vessels may dock at the same berth twice (one in each time window) if necessary. Time windows of different berths can also be used by the same vessel. This practice is frequently used by the shipping company as it allows reducing operation costs significantly. Loaded pallets from cargoes are finally carried to the green nodes, representing their destinations established in the contract.

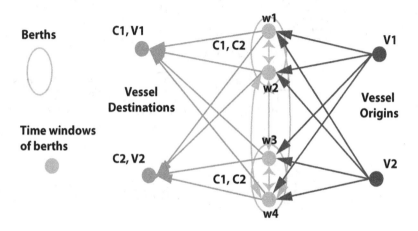

Fig. 1. The network flow representation for a case consisting of two vessels, two contracts (one per vessel), and two berths, having each one two time windows (w_i, w_j). (Color figure online)

5   Model Formulation

This section presents the mathematical formulation of the optimization model for the tramp ship scheduling problem with berth allocation issues.

Decision Variables

d_{ij}^v Continuous non-negative variable denoting the draft variation of vessel $v \in V$ when sailing through link $(i,j) \in \tilde{A}(v)$.

p_w^c Continuous non-negative variable denoting the number of pallets loaded in vessel $v \in V$ from contract $c \in C^v$ in berth time window $w \in W^v$.

s^c Continuous non-negative variable denoting the number of pallets from contract $c \in C$ which are not transported by any vessel.

t_i^v Continuous non-negative variable denoting the arrival time of vessel $v \in V$ at node $i \in N(v)$.

x_{ij}^v Binary variable with value 1 when vessel $v \in V$ sails through link $(i, j) \in A(v)$, value 0 otherwise.

$y_w^{v_1, v_2}$ Binary variable with value 1 when vessel $v_1 \in V$ docks before vessel $v_2 \in V$ in time window $w \in W^{v_1, v_2}$, value 0 otherwise.

Optimization Model

$$
\max_{d,p,s,t,x,y} f = \sum_{\substack{v \in V \\ c \in C^v \\ w \in W^v}} \psi_w^c p_w^c - \sum_{\substack{v \in V \\ w \in W^v \\ i \in N^w \\ j \in N_i^+(v)}} \theta_w^v x_{ji}^v - \sum_{\substack{v \in V \\ j \in D(v) \\ i \in O(v)}} \rho^v \left(t_j^v - t_i^v \right)
$$

$$
- \sum_{\substack{v \in V \\ (i,j) \in A(v)}} \phi^v \pi_{ij}^v x_{ij}^v - \sum_{\substack{v \in V \\ (i,j) \in \tilde{A}(v)}} \phi^v \pi_{ij}^v \frac{d_{ij}^v}{d_0^v} - \sum_{\substack{v \in V \\ c \in C^v}} \sigma_c^v s^c
$$

$$
\tag{1}
$$

s.t.:

$$
\sum_{w \in W^v} p_w^c + s^c = g^c, \quad \forall v \in V, \, c \in C^v
\tag{2}
$$

$$
\sum_{j \in N_i^+(v)} x_{ji}^v - \sum_{j \in N_i^-(v)} x_{ij}^v = \begin{cases} 1 & \text{if } i \in O(v) \\ -1 & \text{if } i \in D(v) \\ 0 & \text{otherwise} \end{cases}, \, \forall v \in V, \, i \in N(v)
\tag{3}
$$

$$
\sum_{j \in \tilde{N}_i^+(v)} d_{ji}^v - \sum_{j \in \tilde{N}_i^-(v)} d_{ij}^v = \begin{cases} -\Delta^p \sum_{c \in C_w^v} p_w^c & \text{if } w \in W_i^v \\ \Delta^p \sum_{c \in C^v} (g^c - s^c) & \text{otherwise} \end{cases} \quad \forall v \in V, \, i \in \tilde{N}(v)
\tag{4}
$$

$$
d_{ij}^v \leq M_1 \, x_{ij}^v, \quad \forall v \in V, \, (i, j) \in \tilde{A}(v)
\tag{5}
$$

$$
p_w^c \leq M_2 \sum_{j \in N_i^-(v)} x_{ji}^v, \quad \forall v \in V, \, c \in C^v, \, w \in W^v, \, i \in N^w
\tag{6}
$$

$$t_j^v \geq t_i^v + \pi_{ij}^v - M_3(1 - x_{ij}^v), \quad \forall v \in V, \ (i,j) \in A(v) : i \in O(v) \tag{7}$$

$$t_j^v \geq t_i^v + \sum_{c \in C_w^v} \gamma_w^p \, p_w^c + \pi_{ij}^v - M_4(1 - x_{ij}^v), \quad \forall v \in V, \ (i,j) \in A(v), \ w \in W_i^v \tag{8}$$

$$t_i^{v_2} \geq t_i^{v_1} + \sum_{c \in C_w^{v_1}} \gamma_w^p \, p_w^c - M_5(1 - y_w^{v_1,v_2}), \quad \forall v_1, v_2 \in V, \ w \in W^{v_1,v_2}, \ i \in N^w \tag{9}$$

$$\sum_{j \in N_i^+(v_1)} x_{ji}^{v_1} + \sum_{j \in N_i^+(v_2)} x_{ji}^{v_2} \leq y_w^{v_1,v_2} + y_w^{v_2,v_1} + 1, \quad \forall v_1, v_2 \in V, \ w \in W^{v_1,v_2}, \ i \in N^w \tag{10}$$

$$\sum_{j \in \tilde{N}_i^+(v)} d_{ji}^v + \Delta^p \sum_{c \in C_w^v} p_w^c \leq \Delta_w^v, \quad \forall v \in V, \ w \in W^v, \ i \in N^w \tag{11}$$

$$t_i^v \geq l_w \sum_{j \in N_i^-(v)} x_{ji}^v, \quad \forall v \in V, \ w \in W^v, \ i \in N^w \tag{12}$$

$$t_i^v + \sum_{c \in C_w^v} \gamma_w^p \, p_w^c \leq u_w, \quad \forall v \in V, \ w \in W^v, \ i \in N^w \tag{13}$$

$$t_i^v \leq \xi^c, \quad \forall v \in V, \ c \in C^v, \ i \in D(v) \tag{14}$$

The objective function (1) maximizes the benefit of the tramp shipping company given the total income ψ_w^c from the pallets transported p_c^v (first term) and the costs incurred given by the fixed fares θ_w^v associated with the berth time windows where vessels operate x_{ji}^v (second term), the vessel renting cost ρ^v (third term), the fuel consumption ϕ_v throughout the vessel route (fourth and fifth terms), and the compensation expenses σ_w^c incurred due to pallets not carried (six term). The fourth term captures the minimum fuel consumption cost according to the light draft of vessels (without load) on each sailing leg ($x_{ij}^v = 1$); whereas the fifth term considers the extra fuel cost when carrying some load according to the ratio between the vessel draft variation and the light draft of the vessel ($\frac{d_{ij}^v}{d_0^v}$). Constraints (2) perform the balance of loaded pallets in each contract. This constraint allows partially fulfilling a contract, i.e., some pallets may not be loaded in any vessel s^c. Constraints (3) represent the ship flow balance where the source node is associated with the origin of the vessel $O(v)$

and the sink node corresponds to the destination of the vessel $D(v)$. Thus, the rest of nodes are intermediate nodes $N(v)$ where flow conservation is guaranteed. Constraints (4) perform the balance of the draft variation of vessels throughout a subnetwork where only links connecting pairs of expanded berth nodes, as well as those links connecting the expanded berth nodes with the destination nodes of the contracts are considered. When balancing the flow in a node, two situations may arise. If it is a berth time window ($w \in W_i^v$), a draft increment is done. This increment is proportional to the number of loaded pallets in the vessel at the time window, and is calculated using parameter Δ^p. Otherwise, it is a destination of some contracts and a draft decrement is performed. This decrement is also proportional to the number of transported pallets from the contracts having this destination. Constraints (5) and (6) link the ship routing variables (x_{ij}^v) to draft variation flows (d_{ij}^v), and to the amounts of loaded pallets in each berth time windows (p_w^c), respectively. Large constants M_1 and M_2 limit the maximum values that decision variables d_{ij}^v and p_w^c can take. The former takes into account the maximum allowable draft of the berth associated with the time windows; whereas the latter considers the total amount of pallets to be loaded according to the established contract. Constraints (7) and (8) establish the schedule of two nodes $(i, j) \in A(v)$ when visited consecutively by the same vessel (i.e., $x_{ij}^v = 1$). In both sets of constraints, the sailing time between these pair of nodes (π_{ij}^v) is considered. In (8), the time spent for loading pallets in the vessel in node i is also considered if this node is related to a berth time windows $w \in W_i^v$. Large constants M_3–M_4 disables these constraints when vessel v does not sail between nodes i, j (i.e., $x_{ij}^v = 0$). Constraints (9) and (10) coordinate the scheduling of two vessels $v_1, v_2 \in V$ when operating in the same time window $w \in W^{v_1, v_2}$. If vessel v_1 docks first ($y_w^{v_1, v_2} = 1$) then (9) ensures that vessel v_2 docks after all pallets of v_1 have been loaded. Otherwise, $y_w^{v_1, v_2} = 0$, and large constant M_5 disables this constraint. The value of $y_w^{v_1, v_2}$ is set by (10). Constraints (11) ensure that the vessels draft variation does not exceed the allowable maximum variation for each berth time window in which the vessel operates. The vessel's draft variation is measured according to the current transit draft variation through the incoming link plus the draft increment due to pallet loading in the berth time window. Constraints (12) and (13) guarantee that vessels operate within the available time windows of berths. Constraints (12) verify that vessels do not operate before than the lower bound of the time windows, whereas (13) do not allow vessels to stay longer than the upper bound of this time window. The latter also considers loading pallet time. Finally, constraints (14) make sure that vessels arrive at the destination ports of the cargoes not later than the due date established in their contracts.

Time Windows Reduction Rules

Information of berth time windows can be used to reduce problem size, thus enhancing solution efficiency. The narrower the time window the larger the number of binary variables and sequencing constraints that can be removed from the problem formulation. The time window-based elimination rules that consider the time windows as hard constraints are inspired on [3]. In this way, a vessel is prevented from using a time window if there is not enough time in for arriving and loading pallets. In this case, binary variable x_{ij}^v and constraints (5)–(8) can all be dropped from the problem formulation. Also, a time window is prevented from being used if the service time remaining at the berth when a vessel arrives from its origin node is not enough to load a minimum amount of pallets. Therefore, binary variable x_{ij}^v and constraints (7) can be eliminated from the model.

6 Solution Approach

The MILP model in this work becomes harder to solve as the number of vessels increases. All the decision variables and constraints of the model are indexed over the set of vessels. Moreover, constraints (9) and (10) link decisions between pairs of vessels and, thus, the schedules of the vessels cannot be determined separately. Therefore, a heuristic decomposition method has been developed for solving efficiently instances with several vessels. As shown in Fig. 2, the method is divided into two phases. Phase 1 determines quickly an initial schedule for each vessel, whereas phase 2 tries to improve/verify that these schedules are (near-)optimal while not spending too much time.

The algorithm for the first phase is described in Table 1 and works as follows. Initially, constraints (9) and (10) are dropped from the model, and tentative schedules for each vessel are computed separately. Then, the schedule of the vessel with the highest benefit is fixed and constraints (9) and (10) related to this vessel are released. Next, the rest of schedules are again computed and the following vessel schedule with the highest benefit is fixed. This procedure is repeated as long as two or more vessel schedules have not been fixed. Finally, the schedule of the vessel with the lowest benefit is determined. The time spent in this phase can be dramatically decreased if the procedure is implemented in parallel, i.e., in each iteration (IT), the computation of each vessel schedule can be done in a different CPU, so that the whole iteration time would be the highest time spent in solving one single vessel schedule.

An illustrative application of this phase is shown on the top of Fig. 2. In that application, the initial schedules of three vessels labeled as V1, V2 and V3 are determined. In the first iteration (IT 1.1), the schedules of each vessel are computed in parallel, having benefits ($f_1(Vi)$) of 2000, 3000 and 2500, respectively. As $f_1(V2)$ is the highest one, then the schedule of V2 is fixed in iteration 2 (IT1.2), so the schedules of V1 and V3 are re-optimized, having new benefits of 2000 and 1800, respectively. $f_1(V1)$ is now the highest benefit of the remaining vessels, so the schedule of V1 is fixed in iteration 3 (IT1.3), where only the new schedule of V3 is determined.

Phase 2 tries to improve the initial vessel schedules determined in phase 1. In this phase, the schedules of pair of vessels are re-optimized in the hope that the two new schedules may lead to a better global solution, although the solution for the schedule of one vessel in the pair may be worse. The total number of pair evaluations increases dramatically with the number of vessels, therefore a

Phase 1. Find an initial feasible schedule for each vessel

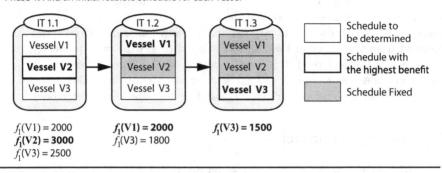

$f_1(V1) = 2000$ $f_1(V1) = 2000$ $f_1(V3) = 1500$
$f_1(V2) = 3000$ $f_1(V3) = 1800$
$f_1(V3) = 2500$

Phase 2. Improve vessel schedules by pairs

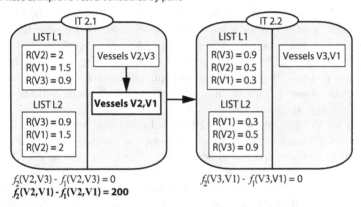

$f_2(V2,V3) - f_1(V2,V3) = 0$ $f_2(V3,V1) - f_1(V3,V1) = 0$
$f_2(V2,V1) - f_1(V2,V1) = 200$

Fig. 2. An illustrative example for the 2-phase heuristic consisting of three vessels.

mechanism for evaluating a reduced number of these has been developed. By comparing the solutions provided by the first phase and the resolution of the full model, a suitable selection of pair of vessels can be determined by using a ratio measure. This ratio evaluates the relationship between the remaining capacity of the vessel (ΔQ) and the average remaining bandwidth of the berth time windows ($\Delta \overline{B}$). ΔQ is computed by reducing the vessel capacity (Q) according to the number of pallets loaded in the vessel in each time window; whereas $\Delta \overline{B}$ is obtained in three steps. First, the bandwidth of each time window $w \in W$ (B_w) is calculated as the difference between its upper and lower bounds (u_w and l_w, respectively). Then, each B_w in which the vessel has operated is reduced according to the time spent in loading pallets in the vessel in that time window. Finally, all B_w are averaged yielding to $\Delta \overline{B}$. Experimentation practice on small-sized instances, where optimal schedules are achieved by solving directly the model (1) and (14), shows that re-optimizing schedules of vessel pairs where one vessel has a high ratio and another a low one leads also to the optimal schedules.

Table 1. Algorithm for the phase 1 of the heuristic.

1. **Set** $\tilde{V} \leftarrow V$;
2. **Drop** constraints (9) & (10) from the model;
3. **Compute** schedules $\forall v \in \tilde{V}$;
4. **If** $\|\tilde{V}\| = 1$ **then return** Initial Schedules;
5. **Fix** schedule of $\tilde{v} \in \tilde{V} : f(\tilde{v}) = \max_{v \in \tilde{V}} f(v)$;
6. **Update** $\tilde{V} \leftarrow \tilde{V} \backslash \{\tilde{v}\}$;
7. **Release** constraints (9) & (10) in which v is involved **and goto 3**;

The procedure of this phase is shown in Table 2 and works as follows. Initially, the ratio measure of each vessel $(R(v))$ is first computed, and then two lists (L1 and L2) are built. In list L1, vessels are sorted in descending ratio, whereas in L2 vessels are ordered in an increasing fashion. Next, the algorithm goes into an iteration process working as follows. A vessel is picked up from each list conforming a pair that has not been previously evaluated $(\tau(L1(p_1), L2(p_2)) = 0)$, and that the ratio of the vessel from L1 is greater than the one from L2 $(R(L1(p_1)) > R(L2(p_2)))$. The schedules of each pair of vessels meeting these requirements are re-optimized as long as no improvements are found, and all valid pairs are not evaluated. Once the benefit of a pair $(f(L1(p_1), L2(p_2)))$ is improved, the iteration process is terminated, and another iteration process is started by updating the ratios of the vessels associated with that pair as well as lists L1 and L2. The procedure is terminated when all pairs of valid vessels have been evaluated.

An illustrative application of phase 2 is shown on the bottom of Fig. 2. On this figure, improved schedules for the initial schedules obtained in the application example of phase 1 are sought after. Initially, the ratio measures of vessels $V1$, $V2$ and $V3$ ($R(V1)$, $R(V2)$ and $R(V3)$, respectively) are computed. Then, lists $L1$ and $L2$ are built and valid pairs of vessels are evaluated in the first iteration process (IT 2.1.). Vessels V2 and V3 are in the top of each list and $R(V2) > R(V3)$, so the schedules for this pair are re-optimized. As the benefit of the pair is not improved (i.e., $f_2(V2, V3) = f_1(V2, V3)$), the following pair is evaluated. This corresponds to $(V2, V1)$ since $V1$ is next to $V3$ in $L2$ and $R(V2) > R(V1)$. Having re-optimized pair $(V2, V1)$, an improved benefit of 200 is obtained. Therefore, ratios of $R(V2)$ and $R(V1)$ are updated, as well as lists L1 and L2, and the second iteration process(IT 2.2) is started. Now, the pair $(V3, V1)$ is evaluated as vessels $V3$ and $V1$ are in the top of lists L1 and L2, and $R(V3) > R(V1)$. The re-optimization of this pair does not improve the benefit (i.e., $f_2(V3, V1) = f_1(V3, V1)$), and as no further valid pairs are found (i.e., pairs $(V3, V2)$ and $(V2, V1)$ have already been evaluated in IT 2.1.), phase is terminated.

Table 2. Algorithm for the phase 2 of the heuristic.

1. **Set** $\tilde{f}(v) \leftarrow f(v) \; \forall v \in V$, **and** $\tau(v_i, v_j) \leftarrow 0 \; \forall v_i, v_j \in V$;
2. **Compute** $R(v) \; \forall v \in V$;
3. **Set** L1 $\leftarrow v \in V$ **sorted by** $R(v)$ **in decreasing** fashion;
L2 $\leftarrow v \in V$ **sorted by** $R(v)$ **in ascending** fashion;
4. **Set** $p_1 \leftarrow 1, \quad p_2 \leftarrow 1$;
5. **If** $\tau(L1(p_1), L2(p_2)) = 1$ **or** $R(L1(p_1)) < R(L2(p_2))$ **then jump to** 10;
6. **Compute** schedules for pair $(L1(p_1), L2(p_2))$;
7. **If** $f(L1(p_1), L2(p_2)) > \tilde{f}(L1(p_1), L2(p_2))$ **then jump to** 10;
8. **Set** $\tilde{f}(L1(p_1)) \leftarrow f(L1(p_1)), \quad \tilde{f}(L2(p_2)) \leftarrow f(L2(p_2))$ **and** $\tau(L1(p_1), L2(p_2)) \leftarrow 0$;
9. **Update** $R(L1(p_1)), R(L2(p_2))$ **and goto** 3;
10. **If** $p_2 < \lvert L2 \rvert$ **then** $p_2 \leftarrow p_2 + 1$, **and goto** 5;
11. **If** $p_1 < \lvert L1 \rvert$ **then** $p_1 \leftarrow p_1 + 1$, **and goto** 5;
12. **Return** Improved schedules;

7 Results

To evaluate the model as well as the performance of the heuristic, several experiments based on a real case have been conducted. The model and the heuristic have been coded in AMPL, and the Branch and Bound of CPLEX v12.5.0.0 is used for solving the model, as well as the reduced models constructed during the heuristic execution, under a workstation R5500 with processor Intel(R) Xeon(R) CPU E5645 2.40 GHz and 48 GBytes of RAM. 30 min of time limit for the full model and for the heuristic has been set since the availability of time windows may change afterwards, and thus the provided solution would be unrealistic.

The main components of each instance includes the number of vessels that can be used, the number of contracts willing to be carried, the number of berths where vessels can operate, the number of available time windows per berth, and the total number of pallets that can be loaded in the vessels. Observe that, the instance identifier contains all this information except for the amount of pallets provided in Table 3. For example, the group of instances containing the string $S4B5W2C18$ are made up of 4 vessels, 18 contracts, 5 berths and 2 time windows per berth. Detailed information on the planning process currently being used is not shown due to confidentiality issues.

Table 4 shows the performance results for the tested experiments. From left to right of the table, it is given the best objective functions (f), the relative gaps in percentage (GAP (%)), and the computational times in seconds (T_{CPU}) for the direct resolution of the model (FM), and each phase of the heuristic. H1 stands for the first phase of the heuristic, which is implemented in parallel, whereas H2 denotes the second phase. Finally, HT represents the whole time spent by the heuristic.

Table 3. Characterization of the performed experiments

Instance	# Pallets			
	A	B	C	D
S4B5W2C18	22189	21703	23758	22741
S8B7W3C36	45132	43381	45472	45462
S12B10W3C54	67141	68910	66995	68027
S16B24W3C72	89759	90291	92184	91359
S20B30W3C90	111755	111292	112816	109642

Table 4. Summary results for the performed experiments.

Instance	f(USD × 10³)			GAP (%)		T_{CPU} (s)			
	FM	H1	H2	H1	H2	FM	H1	H2	HT
S4B5W2C18A	1414	1397	1414	1.2%	0%	10	1	5	6
S4B5W2C18B	1630	1630	1630	0%	0%	44	2	13	15
S4B5W2C18C	1404	1271	1404	9.5%	0%	21	1	8	9
S4B5W2C18D	1611	1599	1611	0.8%	0%	3	1	3	4
S8B7W3C36A	2081	2078	2081	0.2%	0%	1800	3	44	47
S8B7W3C36B	1729	1640	1729	5%	0%	1800	5	186	191
S8B7W3C36C	1704	1704	1704	0%	0%	1800	3	65	68
S8B7W3C36D	2739	2539	2779	7%	−1.5%	1800	6	222	228
S12B10W3C54A	3052	3052	3052	0%	0%	1800	200	1600	1800
S12B10W3C54B	2725	2725	2725	0%	0%	1800	89	1711	1800
S12B10W3C54C	2700	2700	2703	0%	−0.1%	1800	64	1736	1800
S12B10W3C54D	2634	2890	2894	−9.8%	−9.9%	1800	99	1701	1800
S16B24W3C72A	3829	4122	4129	−7.6%	−7.8%	1800	303	1697	1800
S16B24W3C72B	3745	3788	3791	−1.1%	−1.2%	1800	255	1745	1800
S16B24W3C72C	3748	3937	3938	−5%	−5%	1800	256	1744	1800
S16B24W3C72D	3848	3911	3914	−1.6%	−1.7%	1800	265	1735	1800
S20B30W3C90A	4467	4467	4562	0%	−2%	1800	554	1246	1800
S20B30W3C90B	4855	5027	5034	−3.5%	−3.7%	1800	299	1501	1800
S20B30W3C90C	4519	4529	4529	−0.2%	−0.2%	1800	591	1209	1800
S20B30W3C90D	4300	4369	4376	−1.6%	−1.8%	1800	477	1323	1800

Results show that the heuristic outperforms the resolution of the full model. For small-sized instances (4 vessels), the heuristic finds always the optimum having improved the initial solution. For medium-sized instances (8 vessels), the heuristic finds at least the same feasible solution (this solution is not guaranteed to be optimal since the resolution of the full model have been earlier stopped,

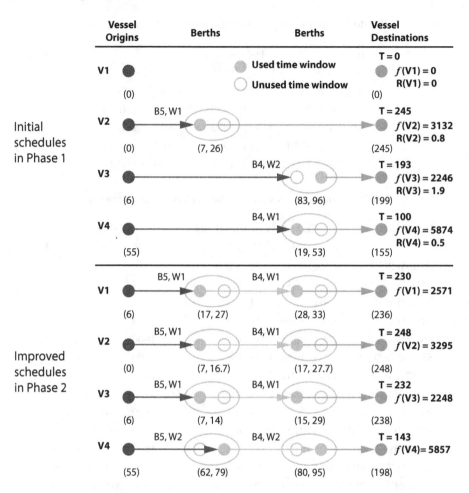

Fig. 3. Schedules determined in phases 1 and 2 of the heuristic for instance S4B5W2C18C.

having reached the time limit of 30 min). Moreover, the heuristic only spends a few minutes. Finally, for larger instances (12–20 vessels), the heuristic provides better solutions, and quite frequently in early phase 1. In some cases, phase 2 improves the initial solution but not substantially. This is because solving times reach the time limit and, thus, phase 2 is terminated earlier.

Next Fig. 3 shows the workings of the heuristic for instance S4B5W2C18C, the instance with the highest improvement obtained in phase 2. It can be observed that in phase 1, there is no schedule determined for vessel 1 and that the rest of vessels only dock once and in a different time window. However, by coordinating arrivals at the same time window and by docking twice, phase 2 obtains better schedules (i.e., benefits are higher) and allows vessel 1 to operate.

Table 5. Some features of the solution results for the performed experiments.

Instance	# Docks (Av-Max)			Av. Used Cap.			Cargo Satisfied		
	FM	H1	H2	FM	H1	H2	FM	H1	H2
S4B5W2C18A	1.6–3	1.6–2	1.6–3	41%	40%	41%	57%	56%	57%
S4B5W2C18B	1.6–2	1.6–2	1.6–2	45%	45%	45%	57%	57%	57%
S4B5W2C18C	2–2	1–1	2–2	51%	46%	51%	50%	47%	50%
S4B5W2C18D	2–2	1.6–2	2–2	45%	44%	45%	58%	57%	58%
S8B7W3C36A	1.5–2	1.5–2	1.5–2	48%	48%	48%	58%	58%	58%
S8B7W3C36B	1–1	1–1	1–1	27%	25%	27%	60%	57%	60%
S8B7W3C36C	1.2–2	1.2–2	1.2–2	31%	31%	31%	53%	53%	53%
S8B7W3C36D	1.8–2	1.3–2	2–3	41%	38%	42%	35%	32%	35%
S12B10W3C54A	1.3–2	1.3–2	1.3–2	46%	46%	46%	46%	46%	46%
S12B10W3C54B	1–1	1–1	1–1	41%	41%	41%	54%	54%	54%
S12B10W3C54C	1–1	1–1	1–1	31%	31%	31%	57%	57%	57%
S12B10W3C54D	1.3–3	1.3–2	1.3–2	39%	45%	45%	33%	40%	40%
S16B24W3C72A	1.3–2	1.3–2	1.3–2	39%	70%	70%	26%	64%	64%
S16B24W3C72B	1.8–3	1.4–3	1.4–3	46%	48%	48%	46%	48%	48%
S16B24W3C72C	1–2	1.2–2	1.3–2	35%	43%	43%	36%	43%	44%
S16B24W3C72D	1–2	1.3–2	1.2–2	48%	51%	51%	46%	49%	40%
S20B30W3C90A	1.4–3	1.3–3	1.5–3	40%	43%	43%	45%	48%	48%
S20B30W3C90B	1.3–3	1.3–3	1.3–3	46%	48%	48%	47%	48%	48%
S20B30W3C90C	1.3–2	1.2–2	1.2–2	52%	53%	53%	56%	57%	57%
S20B30W3C90D	1.4–2	1.4–2	1.2–2	25%	25%	27%	37%	37%	38%

Finally, Table 5 provides some details of the solution results. From left to right of the table, it is provided the average and maximum values for the number of docks (# Docks), the average used capacity of the vessels (Av. Used Cap.), and the percentage of cargo satisfaction (Cargo Satisfied (%)) for the direct resolution of the model and each phase of the heuristic.

Results show that vessel capacities are underused, around 50% on average, and with minimum and maximum values of 26% and 64%, respectively. Another important aspect to highlight is that vessels do not dock more than 3 times, an issue that also happens in real practice. However, the average number of docks is around 1.5, meaning that in the schedule solution one half of the vessels docks once and the other half twice. Regarding to the amounts of carried pallets, they are low but the company has benefit as shown in the previous table. In reality, the company would have important losses during the fruit season if all cargoes were carried, so lower benefits are obtained since the time windows at berths are narrower and operational costs are difficult to absorb.

8   Conclusions and Further Research

This work introduces an optimisation model that deals with the tramp ship scheduling problem considering berth allocation issues. The model is formulated as a mixed-integer linear problem and carries out the assignment of berth time windows to vessels where cargoes are loaded, the itineraries of the vessels with the possibility of docking several times at the same or different berth, and the coordination of vessels operating at the same berth time window. Moreover, the model takes into account berth limitations regarding to water depth or draft capacity. These limitations have not been previously addressed on the scant literature integrating the berth allocation to the tramp ship scheduling problem.

From a business practice perspective, the proposed approach provides a decision-support tool for the tramp shipping company. Current planning activities are done manually by operations planners, who find themselves with several difficulties in the search of a feasible plan. These difficulties arise when trying to match temporal availability, draft capacities and scheduling issues at the same time. These aspects need a precise coordination for a schedule to be feasible, and this is the cause for the success of this modeling approach when dealing with the tramp ship scheduling with berth allocation issues. Furthermore, this optimization approach allows operation planners to perform scenario analysis by varying different problem aspects such as cargo size, loading times, time window fare or draft, among others.

For further research, several extensions can be considered for the tramp ship scheduling problem. In this regard, we propose to incorporate as a decision variable the assignment of cargo to vessels, which is currently not considered in the mathematical model motivated by the fact that the shipping company assumes that this is a decision taken by the commercial department of the company. However, integrating this decision variable could lead to better solutions and reduce overall costs. Another potential extension is related to speed optimization, which currently is assumed as a fixed value. This can be done by incorporating an emission estimation model in order to account for environmental concerns. Another research avenue to extend the proposed model is to deal with risk and uncertainty as modelling elements and provide an optimization framework to deal with disruption events in the day-to-day operations. Finally, because of the interaction between berth allocation decisions of the stevedores and the shipping company, we propose to formulate the problem as a bilevel optimization model in which the port terminal managers can be the leader that determines the berth assignment and schedules, and the shipping company the follower that receives this information as berth availability time windows. Other integration approaches can be also considered such as a pre-processing or a feedback loop can be also explored.

Acknowledgements. This work was supported by the Mexican National Council for Science and Technology (CONACYT), through research grant SEP-CONACYTCB-2014-01-240814 (third author); and by the Vice Presidency of Research and Graduate Studies of Pontificia Universidad Católica de Valparaíso, through research project

037.499/2015 (second author). Additionally, we acknowledge the determination and effort performed by the Mexican Logistics and Supply Chain Association (AML) and the Mexican Institute of Transportation (IMT) for providing us an internationally recognized collaboration platform. Last, but not least, special thanks to the undergraduate students, David Hirmas and Marco Sanhueza from the Pontificia Universidad Católica de Valparaíso, for their help in developing computational experiments, and an anonymous planner of the shipping company who allowed us to fully understand the complex planning process of the company.

References

1. Bierwirth, C., Meisel, F.: A follow-up survey of berth allocation and quay crane scheduling problems in container terminals. Eur. J. Oper. Res. **244**, 675–689 (2015)
2. Christiansen, M., Fagerholt, K., Nygreen, B., Ronen, D.: Ship routing and scheduling in the new milenium. Eur. J. Oper. Res. **228**, 467–483 (2013)
3. Dondo, R., Cerdá, J.: A cluster-based optimization approach for the multi-depot heterogeneous fleet vehicle routing problem with time windows. Eur. J. Oper. Res. **176**, 1478–1507 (2007)
4. Fagerholt, K., Ronen, D.: Bulk ship routing and scheduling: solving practical problems may provide better results. Mari. Policy Manage. **40**, 48–64 (2013)
5. Hennig, F., Nygreen, B., Christiansen, M., Fagerholt, K., Furman, K.C., Song, J., Kocis, G.R., Warrick, P.H.: Maritime crude oil transportation - a split pickup and split delivery problem. Eur. J. Oper. Res. **218**, 764–774 (2012)
6. Jetlund, A.S., Karimi, I.A.: Improving the logistics of multi-compartment chemical tankers. Comput. Chem. Eng. **28**, 1267–1283 (2004)
7. Korsvik, J.E., Fagerholt, K.: A tabu search heuristic for ship routing and scheduling with flexible cargo quantities. J. Heuristics **16**, 117–137 (2010)
8. Korsvik, J.E., Fagerholt, K., Laporte, G.: A large neighbourhood search heuristic for ship routing and scheduling with split loads. Comput. Oper. Res. **38**, 474–483 (2011)
9. Li, C.L., Pang, K.W.: An integrated model for ship routing and berth allocation. Int. J. Shipp. Transp. Logist **3**, 245–260 (2011)
10. Pang, K.W., Liu, J.: An integrated model for ship routing with transshipment and berth allocation. IIE Trans. **46**, 1357–1370 (2014)
11. UNCTAD Secretariat: Review of Maritime Transport. United Nation Publications, Geneva (2014)

Hierarchical Task Model for Resource Failure Recovery in Production Scheduling

Roman Barták and Marek Vlk[✉]

Faculty of Mathematics and Physics, Charles University,
Malostranské nám. 25, 118 00 Praha 1, Czech Republic
{bartak,vlk}@ktiml.mff.cuni.cz

Abstract. Attaining optimal results in real-life scheduling is hindered by a number of problems. One such problem is dynamics of manufacturing environments with breaking-down resources and hot orders coming during the schedule execution. A traditional approach to react to unexpected events occurring on the shop floor is generating a new schedule from scratch. Complete rescheduling, however, may require excessive computation time. Moreover, the recovered schedule may deviate a lot from the ongoing schedule. Some works have focused on tackling these shortcomings, but none of the existing approaches tries to substitute jobs that cannot be executed with a set of alternative jobs. This paper describes the scheduling model suitable for dealing with unforeseen events using the possibility of alternative processes and proposes an efficient heuristic-based approach to recover an ongoing schedule from a resource failure.

Keywords: Predictive-reactive scheduling · Rescheduling · Schedule updates · Alternative processes · Constraint satisfaction

1 Introduction

Scheduling, the aim of which is to allocate scarce resources to activities in order to optimize certain objectives, has been frequently addressed in the past decades. Developing a detailed schedule in manufacturing environment helps maintain efficiency and control of operations.

In the real world, however, manufacturing systems face uncertainty owing to unforeseen events occurring on the shop floor. Machines break down, operations take longer than anticipated, personnel do not perform as expected, urgent orders arrive, others are canceled, etc. These disturbances may bring inconsistencies into the ongoing schedule. If the ongoing schedule becomes infeasible, the simple approach is to collect the data from the shop floor when the disruption occurs and to generate a new schedule from scratch. Because most of the scheduling problems are NP-hard, complete rescheduling usually involves prohibitive computation time and an excessive deviation of the recovered schedule from the original schedule.

© Springer International Publishing AG 2017
G. Sidorov and O. Herrera-Alcántara (Eds.): MICAI 2016, Part I, LNAI 10061, pp. 362–378, 2017.
DOI: 10.1007/978-3-319-62434-1_30

To avoid the problems of rescheduling from scratch, reactive scheduling, which may be conceived as the continuous correction of precomputed predictive schedules, is becoming more and more important. Reactive scheduling is con-tradistinguished from predictive scheduling mainly by its on-line nature and asso-ciated real-time execution requirements. The schedule update must be accom-plished before the running schedule becomes invalid, and this time window may be very short in a complex environment.

Several novel sophisticated methods attempt to cope with the shortcomings of complete rescheduling, e.g., by rescheduling only the activities somehow affected by the disturbance. To the best of our knowledge, however, none of the existing approaches tries to replace some activities by a set of alternative activities (using other available resources) to achieve the same goal.

In this paper we propose the model with the hierarchical structure of tasks that we deem suitable also for the field of predictive-reactive scheduling. Further, we suggest an effective technique for recovering a schedule from a resource failure, exploiting the possibility of alternative processes, i.e., to re-plan the influenced part of the schedule.

We first survey briefly the closely related works on which our approach is based. Section 3 then describes the problem tackled in this paper and the hierar-chical task model used. The suggested algorithm for a resource failure recovery is described in Sect. 4. The experimental results are given in Sect. 5, and the final part points out possible future work.

2 Related Work

The approaches how to tackle dynamics of the scheduling environment can be divided basically into two branches according to whether or not the predictive schedule is computed before the execution starts [14]. If the predictive schedule is not computed beforehand and individual activities are assigned to resources pursuant to some so called dispatching rules during the execution, we talk about *completely reactive scheduling* or on-line scheduling. This strategy is suitable for very dynamic environments, where it is not known in advance which activities it will be necessary to process. On the other hand, it is obvious that this approach seldom leads to an optimal or near-optimal schedule.

If the schedule is crafted beforehand and then updated during its execution, it is referred to as *predictive-reactive scheduling*. When correcting the ongoing schedule in response to changes within the environment, the aim is usually to minimize the schedule modification. The motivation for minimizing the modifi-cation of the schedule is that every deviation may lead to deterioration in the performance of the manufacturing system because of affecting other planned activities based upon the original schedule. Similarity of two schedules may be formally defined for example as a *minimal perturbation problem* [3].

There is an extensive literature on rescheduling [9,11]. First, the *heuristic-based* approaches do not guarantee finding an optimal solution, but they respond in a short time. The simplest schedule-repair technique is the *right shift rescheduling* [1], which shifts the operations globally to the right on the time axis in order to cope with disruptions. This may lead to schedules of very bad quality.

Another simple heuristic is *affected operation rescheduling* [13], also referred to as partial schedule repair, the essence of which is to reschedule only the operations directly and indirectly affected by the disruption in order to minimize the deviation from the initial schedule.

Better schedules to the detriment of computational efficiency may be attained by using *meta-heuristics* such as simulated annealing, genetic algorithms, tabu search, and iterative flattening search [8]. These high level heuristics guide local search methods to escape from local optima by occasional accepting worse solutions or by generating better initial solutions for local probing in some sophisticated way.

The attempts to absorb certain amount of uncertainty based on the past executions of schedules is considered in another strategy, usually referred to as *robust proactive scheduling*. One such example is a model and an algorithm generating a predictive schedule of production workflows that is (proactively) robust with regard to so called immediate events, which include breakdown of a workstation and faulty termination of a workflow execution [5]. The shortcoming of the algorithm is the assumption that every resource failure is only temporary, and the time for how long the resource is unavailable in case of its failure is known in advance.

While there is a great amount of work devoted to planning with time and resources and to integrating planning and scheduling techniques, to the best of our knowledge, there is no research carried out aiming at the possibility of re-planning in the field of predictive-reactive scheduling.

In our work we employ mainly techniques from the field of constraint programming, namely *Conflict-directed Backjumping with Backmarking* [6]. We also need *Simple Temporal Networks* (STN) [4] and *Incremental Full Path Consistency* (IFPC) algorithm [10], which incrementally maintains the *All Pairs Shortest Path* (APSP) property.

3   Scheduling Model

We work with the scheduling model that is based on the notion of *manufacturing workflows*. Workflow in general may be understood as a scheme of performing some complex process, itemized into simpler processes and relationships among them. Manufacturing workflow is then an outline how to obtain a desired product.

In order to make editing of workflows easier, the workflows in our model match up the structure of Nested Temporal Networks with Alternatives [2], where the nodes of a network correspond to the tasks of a workflow. The tasks decompose into other tasks, referred to as their subtasks. There are two types of decomposition: parallel and alternative. The tasks that do not decompose further (i.e., leaves) are called *primitive tasks*. The primitive tasks correspond to activities and are associated with some additional parameters, namely start, duration, and resource. From now on we will use the terms primitive tasks and activities interchangeably.

An example of a workflow and its decomposition tree are depicted in Figs. 1 and 2. It contains eight activities, three parallel tasks, and two alternative tasks.

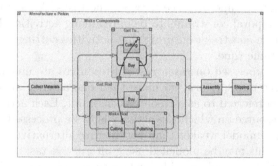

Fig. 1. An example of a workflow [12].

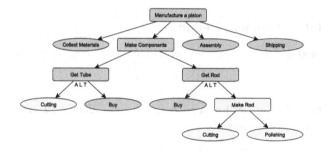

Fig. 2. A decomposition tree for the workflow. The label "ALT" beneath tasks stands for alternative decomposition; the other decompositions are parallel. Activities are ellipse-shaped. The highlighted tasks form an example of a selected process.

The workflows as described define a number of feasible processes. A *process* is a subset of tasks selected to be processed. While a *parallel task* requires all its children to be processed, an *alternative task* requires exactly one of its children to be processed. If an arbitrary task is not in a process, none of its offspring is in the process either. Hence, to ensure that an instance of a workflow is actually processed, its root task has to be in the selected process. An example of a process is depicted in Fig. 2.

To introduce some restrictions in terms of occurrences of tasks in the process and their time data, a pair of tasks can be bound by a *logical constraint*. Logical constraints include *implications* (if one task is in the process, the other task must be in the process too), *equivalences* (either both tasks must be in the process or neither of them can be in the process), and *mutual exclusions* (at most one of the tasks can be in the process).

In Fig. 1, there is one equivalence constraint enforcing that a tube and a rod are both either bought or made.

Further, there are simple temporal constraints [4] to determine the maximum (as well as minimum) time distance between the tasks. At this time being, we assume simple temporal constraints to be only among activities. In Fig. 1, there is a synchronization constraint ensuring that activities cutting tube and cutting rod start at the same time.

Activities are processed on *resources*. All resources are unary, which means that each resource may perform no more than one activity at any time. This limitation is often referred to as a resource constraint. Each activity is specified by exactly one resource on which the activity is to be processed. Note that this does not make the model weaker than considering alternative resources for an activity, because this may be modelled using alternative tasks.

Note that workflow is only a guideline how to manufacture a particular product. If a user wants n such products, n instances of the corresponding workflow are inserted into the model. An instance of a workflow is referred to as an *order*. It may contain some additional data, such as due date and lateness penalty.

Finally, a resulting schedule is *feasible* if all constraints are satisfied.

3.1   Scheduling Problem Definition

Formally, schedule S is a triplet of three sets: *Tasks*, *Constraints*, and *Resources*.

Tasks. Every task T either has a parent, i.e., $\exists P \in Tasks : Parent(T) = P$, or is a root, i.e., $Parent(T) = null$.

- $Subtasks(T) = \{C \in Tasks \mid Parent(C) = T\}$
- $Roots = \{R \in Tasks \mid Parent(R) = null\}$

There are three types of tasks: *parallel*, *alternative*, and *primitive* tasks.

- $Tasks = Parallel \cup Alternative \cup Primitive$
- $\forall T \in Parallel \cup Alternative : Subtasks(T) \neq \emptyset$
- $\forall T \in Primitive : Subtasks(T) = \emptyset$

Let process $P \subseteq Tasks$ be the set of tasks selected to be processed. Making the process feasible introduces the following constraints:

- $T \in P \cap Parallel : Subtasks(T) \subseteq P$
- $T \in P \cap Alternative : |Subtasks(T) \cap P| = 1$
- $T \notin P : Subtasks(T) \cap P = \emptyset$

Let S_i and E_i denote the start time and end time, respectively, of task T_i. Each activity corresponding to the primitive task T_i is specified by the duration D_i. As we consider only non-interruptible activities, the equality $E_i = S_i + D_i$ holds for all the activities.

Constraints. There are two basic types of constraints: logical, and temporal.

Logical constraints are of three types: implications, equivalences, and mutexes. The semantics of the constraints is as follows:

- $(i \Rightarrow j) : T_i \in P \Rightarrow T_j \in P$
- $(i \Leftrightarrow j) : T_i \in P \Leftrightarrow T_j \in P$
- $(i \ mutex \ j) : T_i \notin P \vee T_j \notin P$

The time distance between two distinct activities may be restricted by a *simple temporal constraint* [4]. This constraint can be written as a triplet (T_i, T_j, w_{ij}), determining that $S_j - S_i \leq w_{ij}$, where $w_{ij} \in \mathbb{Z}$.

Resources. Each activity is specified by exactly one resource where it can be processed. Let $T_i \in Primitive$, then the resource that can process the activity T_i is denoted R_i.

All resources in a schedule are unary, which means that they cannot execute more tasks simultaneously. Therefore, in a feasible schedule for all selected primitive tasks $T_i \neq T_j$ the following holds:

- $R_i = R_j \Rightarrow E_i \leq S_j \vee E_j \leq S_i$

3.2   Schedule

A schedule S (sometimes referred to as a resulting schedule or a solution) is acquired by determining the set P, and allocating the primitive tasks from P in time, that is, assigning particular values to the variables S_i and E_i for each $T_i \in P$.

To make a schedule *feasible*, the process selection and the allocation must be conducted in such a way that all the mentioned constraints in the problem are satisfied.

3.3   Rescheduling Problem

The problem we actually deal with is that we are given a particular instance of the scheduling problem along with a feasible schedule, and also with a change in the problem specification. The aim is to find another schedule that is feasible in terms of the new problem definition. The feasible schedule we are given is referred to as an original schedule or an ongoing schedule.

The resource failure, which is also referred to as a machine breakdown, may happen in the manufacturing system at any point in time, say t_f, and means that a particular resource cannot be used anymore, i.e., for all $t \geq t_f$. For the sake of simplicity, let us now assume that a resource fails at the beginning of the time horizon (at time point $t = 0$), i.e., right before the schedule execution begins. How to get rid of this assumption is described in Sect. 4.4.

Formally, let Sch_0 be the schedule to be executed and R be the failed resource; the aim is to find a feasible schedule Sch_1, such that R is not used at any point in time $t \geq 0$. Sch_1 is referred to as a recovered schedule. The intention is to find Sch_1 as fast as possible and, regardless of the initial objectives, as similar to Sch_0 as possible. For this purpose we need to evaluate the modification distance.

Let P_0 denote the selected process P in the original schedule Sch_0 and P_1 denote the selected process P in the recovered schedule Sch_1 Then, apart from computation time, we take into account the following distance function:

$$f = |\{T \in P_1 \cap Primitive \setminus P_0\}| + |\{T \in P_0 \cap Primitive \setminus P_1\}|$$

In words, function f is the number of activities that were removed from the original schedule plus the number of activities that were added to the recovered schedule.

4   Resource Failure Recovery Algorithm

The method that handles a resource failure consists of two main steps that are iterated: finding another process and scheduling the process. The alternative process found may be unschedulable because of the simple temporal constraints, and there may be even no alternative feasible process. If there is no alternative process with feasible allocation of activities in time, the schedule is said to be unrecoverable.

On the other hand, there may be exponential number of feasible processes in a workflow, so that trying all processes is impermissible. That is why we designed an algorithm in such a way that finding another process is heuristically "guided" by the scheduling routine.

The main ingredient of the algorithm is the conflict-directed backjumping algorithm (CBJ) [6], which is an improved version of simple backtracking. In CBJ, a conflict set for each of variables is maintained. When a value of the current variable x_i conflicts with an assigned value of some past variable x_j, the variable x_j is added to the conflict set of x_i. When all values of the current variable x_i have been tried, the algorithm jumps back to the most recently assigned variable x_j in the conflict set of x_i, and, also, the variables in the conflict set of x_i (except for x_j) are added to the conflict set of x_j, thus all information about conflicts is kept.

In our case, the variables x_i correspond to whether or not task T_i is selected in the process P. The crucial idea of our approach is that during scheduling the process, the conflict set is also determined and used for finding another process. Except for these two main steps that are iterated, the algorithm starts with preprocessing, which bans and removes tasks from the process that provably cannot be in the process, and returns the index where the finding alternative process will backjump. More details follow.

4.1   Banning the Tasks

Banning the tasks is based on the constraints that follow from the hierarchical structure of tasks. Recall that if task T_q cannot be in the selected process, and $Parent(T_q) \in Parallel$, then $Parent(T_q)$ cannot be in the process either. That is why it is necessary to seek the alternative task that is the predecessor of T_q. Similarly, if task T_q cannot be in the selected process, none of its subtasks can be in the process either.

We assume that the tasks are pre-order indexed, that is, the index of any task is lower than the indices of its subtasks (the index of root is 1). The following methods are used (Fig. 3). $AltAnc(q)$ returns the index of the highest-indexed (= deepest) ancestor of task T_q that is of alternative decomposition, or 0 if there is no such task. $AltAncSon(q)$ returns the index of the son of $T_{AltAnc(q)}$ that is on the path from $T_{AltAnc(q)}$ to T_q. Finally, $Subtree(T_k)$ returns the set of tasks in the subtree rooted at T_k, including T_k.

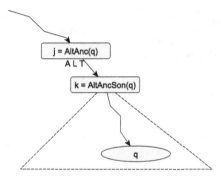

Fig. 3. An illustration for banning the tasks. Task with index q is popped from queue Q, then all the tasks in the tree rooted at the task with index k are banned and removed from the process.

The routine for banning the tasks works as follows (Algorithm 1). If first acquires all the activities that are executable on the failed resource and stores them to a queue Q. Then it keeps processing the tasks from Q until it is empty. If the task T_q that is dequeued from Q is already banned, nothing needs to be done. Otherwise it hinges on index j, which is $AltAnc(q)$. If j is 0, it follows that there is no alternative process and hence the workflow is unalterable. Otherwise, if $T_j \in P$, then the returning value Ret retains the minimum of its current value and j, because this is where the routine $FindProcess$ will "backjump". Note that the condition $T_j \in P$ may not be met because the queue Q may contain also activities that were not in the original process.

Further, the entire subtree rooted at T_k, which is $T_{AltAncSon(q)}$, is banned and removed from the process P. This is done in the outer for-all cycle. During this, all implications and equivalences emanating to the tasks being banned are propagated, that is, each task, from which the implication or equivalence emanates, is added to the queue Q, unless it has already been banned. This is carried out in the inner for-all cycle. Finally, the routine returns the value Ret, which is the lowest-indexed task whose son has been unselected from the process.

Algorithm 1. Banning the tasks

```
function BanUnusable(Resource R)
    Ret ← ∞
    Q ← {T_q | T_q ∈ Primitive & R_q = R}
    while Q ≠ ∅ do
        T_q ← Q.Dequeue()
        if ¬Banned(T_q) then
            j ← AltAnc(q)
            if j = 0 then
                FAIL                                   ▷ Schedule is unrecoverable
            else
                if T_j ∈ P then
                    Ret ← min(Ret, j)
                end if
                k ← AltAncSon(q)
                for all T_i ∈ Subtree(T_k) do
                    P ← P \ {T_i}
                    Banned(T_i) ← True
                    for all (p ⇒ i) ∈ Implications, (p ⇔ i) ∈ Equivalences do
                        if ¬Banned(T_p) then
                            Q ← Q ∪ {T_p}
                        end if
                    end for
                end for
            end if
        end if
    end while
    Return Ret
end function
```

4.2   Finding Another Process

The aim of the following algorithm is to find an alternative process P (Algorithm 2). Recall that the underlying coat of the algorithm is CBJ. The variable i then contains the index of the current task T_i that is tried to be added to the process P. To ease the description, we first describe finding alternative process as if the original process was discarded so that the search starts from the root task in a depth-first-search manner. Hence the algorithm first assigns variable i to 1.

Every time the main loop is entered, the algorithm checks wether the task T_i is already in the process P. The task T_i may be in P because of propagation of some constraints. If T_i is not in P, it is added there and the function $CheckAndPropagate$ is called. If T_i cannot be added to the process, $CheckAndPropagate$ returns the index of an alternative task, whereof reselection of its subtask is promising to make it possible to consistently add T_i to P. If T_i may stay in P, $CheckAndPropagate$ returns ∞. Details of $CheckAndPropagate$ will be given further.

If T_i has been successfully added to P, it may have enforced some other tasks to be added to P. To keep this information, the set $Forced(i)$ stores indices of tasks that have been added to P because of adding T_i, and oppositely for each $j \in Forced(i)$, $ForcedBy(j) = i$. If task T_j is not forced, then $ForcedBy(j) = \infty$.

Next steps, provided that T_i has been added to P, depend on the type of task T_i. If $T_i \in Parallel$, then variable j is set to $i + 1$, because all the subtasks of T_i must also be added to P.

If $T_i \in Alternative$, we need to select its subtask T where to proceed. It may happen that T_i has already one subtask forced in P (because of constraint propagation), in which case that task is set to be the task T, otherwise $T_i.NextChild()$ is called. This returns the subtask that should be tried next (so that all subtasks except the banned tasks are tried if we backjump to task T_i sufficient number of times). If no task has been tried yet, $T_i.NextChild()$ returns the subtask that was in the original process (if T_i was in the original process). If all tasks have been tried, then $T_i.NextChild()$ returns $null$, and in this case (line 20), $AltAnc(i)$ is added to the conflict set of task T_i, i.e., $cs[i]$, and the maximum index in this set is stored as variable j, which is where to backjump.

Special case must be handled when we have just backjumped to parallel task T_i that has forced subtask T (line 23). In this case, $AltAnc$ of the task that is forcing T is added to $cs[i]$.

Last option, if $T_i \in Primitive$, then j is set to $Next(i)$, which is where to jump (forward) to. Recall that all subtasks of selected parallel task must be also selected, whereas only one subtask of selected alternative task must be selected. So, $Next(i)$ is computed (beforehand) as follows. It passes from T_i towards the root until it reaches a parallel task, say T_p, and then returns the index of the subtask of T_p that has the smallest index but greater than that of the task from which it reached T_p. If there is no such greater index, it proceeds further to the root and repeats. If the root has passed without finding the index where to jump to, it returns ∞, that is, no more tasks need to be added to P after T_i has been added.

Now, if $j = \infty$ (line 31), it means that the process P is feasible and it is time to schedule the activities from P. It will be described in the next subsection, but important thing is that it returns the conflict set cs, which is merged to $cs[i]$, and the search proceeds to find another process. If cs is empty, then the algorithm terminates and outputs the best schedule found.

If the task T_i could not be added to P, then the values err returned by $CheckAndPropagate$ as well as $AltAnc(i)$ are added to $cs[i]$ (line 38).

Finally, if j was set smaller than i, then backjump is carried out (starting from line 41). If j is 0, it means no alternative process can be found, so that the algorithm terminates and returns the best schedule found. Otherwise, the conflict set $cs[i]$ is merged into $cs[j]$, excluding j itself. Next, all the tasks that are jumped over are removed from P, unless they are forced by some task with index smaller or equal to j (condition at line 47). In addition, all the (future) tasks forced by some task that is being removed from P, are also removed from

P (line 49). Calling $ResetNextChild()$ (line 56) on an alternative task removed from P ensures that the method $NextChild()$ will consecutively try all subtasks again, first trying the subtask from the original process (if any).

In any case, i is set to j (line 62) and the main while loop is to be entered again.

As we said, we described the routine as if the original process was discarded. But in fact, instead of setting i to 1, the method $BanUnused$ from the previous subsection is called, and j is set to its returned value, which is where to backjump. This backjump is conducted in pretty much the same way as at lines 41–62. Note that it requires only $Forced$ and $ForcedBy$ to be precomputed, which may be done in linear time.

Checking the Constraints. It remains to describe how $CheckAndPropagate$ (Algorithm 3) works. It is passed two parameters: $iorig$, which is the original index of task that was added to P, and hence $FindProcess$ calls this method; and i, which is the index of task that causes calling this method recursively.

It first sets err to ∞, and throughout the method, err is the smallest-indexed alternative task that will have to change selection of its subtask so as to enable the task T_i to be (possibly) added to P.

First, mutex constraints are handled. Suppose T_j is the second task in a mutex. Then T_i cannot be added to P if $T_j \in P$. If $T_j \in P$ (line 4), then it must be distinguished whether or not T_j is forced, and err is updated accordingly.

Next, the implications and equivalences are handled. Suppose T_j is the second task in an implication or an equivalence. First case is when $j < iorig$. Then $T_j \notin P$ implies that T_i cannot be added to P, so that err is updated. It is necessary to use $AltAnc$ repeatedly until a task from P is reached.

Second case is when $j > iorig$. Then $T_j \notin P$ implies (unlike in the previous case) that we need to propagate the constraint. This is done in the while cycle (line 21). The task T_j is added to P, and so are the tasks on the path from T_j towards the root, until it reaches a task, say T, that is already in P (condition at line 33). If the task T is alternative, then it is necessary to check whether there is more than one selected subtask (starting from line 35), which is prohibited.

After all constraints are checked, then if err is smaller than ∞ (condition at line 51), all newly forced tasks are removed from P. Note that the condition $i = iorig$ ensures that this "rollback" is conducted only once (in the outermost call). In any case, the value err is returned.

Algorithm 2. Search for alternative process

```
 1 function FINDPROCESS
 2    i ← 1
 3    iprev ← i
 4    while i ≤ NumberOfTasks do
 5        err ← ∞
 6        if Tᵢ ∉ P then
 7            P ← P ∪ {Tᵢ}
 8            err ← CHECKANDPROPAGATE(i, i)
 9        end if
10        if err = ∞ then
11            if Tᵢ ∈ Parallel then
12                j ← i + 1
13            else if Tᵢ ∈ Alternative then
14                S ← Subtasks(Tᵢ) ∩ P
15                if S ≠ ∅ then
16                    T ← the only member of S
17                else
18                    T ← Tᵢ.NextChild()
19                end if
20                if T = null then
21                    cs[i] ← cs[i] ∪ AltAnc(i)
22                    j ← max(cs(i))
23                else if ForcedBy(IndexOf(T)) < ∞ ∧ iprev > i then
24                    cs[i] ← cs[i] ∪ AltAnc(ForcedBy(IndexOf(T)))
25                    j ← max(cs(i))
26                else
27                    j ← IndexOf(T)
28                end if
29            else                                          ▷ Tᵢ ∈ Primitive
30                j ← Next(i)
31                if j = ∞ then                             ▷ P is now feasible
32                    cs ← FindSchedule(P)
33                    cs[i] ← cs[i] ∪ cs
34                    j ← max(cs(i))
35                end if
36            end if
37        else
38            cs[i] ← cs[i] ∪ {err} ∪ {AltAnc(i)}
39            j ← max(cs(i))
40        end if
41        if j < i then                                     ▷ jumping back to j
42            if j = 0 then
43                STOP                                      ▷ no process found
44            end if
45            cs[j] ← cs[j] ∪ cs[i] \ {j}
46            for k ← j + 1 to i do
47                if ForcedBy(k) > j then
48                    P ← P \ Tₖ
49                    for all l ∈ Forced(k) do
50                        P ← P \ Tₗ
51                        ForcedBy(l) ← ∞
52                    end for
53                    Forced(k) ← ∅
54                end if
55                if Tₖ ∈ Alternative then
56                    Tₖ.ResetNextChild()
57                end if
58                cs[k] ← ∅
59            end for
60        end if
61        iprev ← i
62        i ← j
63    end while
64 end function
```

Algorithm 3. Checking constraints and propagation

```
 1 function CHECKANDPROPAGATE(iorig, i)
 2     err ← ∞
 3     for all (i, j), (j, i) ∈ Mutexes do
 4         if T_j ∈ P then
 5             if ForcedBy(j) < ∞ then
 6                 err ← min{err, AltAnc(ForcedBy(j))}
 7             else
 8                 err ← min{err, AltAnc(j)}
 9             end if
10         end if
11     end for
12     for all (i, j) ∈ Implications, (i, j), (j, i) ∈ Equivalences do
13         if j < iorig ∧ T_j ∉ P then
14             newerr ← AltAnc(j)
15             while newerr ≥ 1 ∧ T_newerr ∉ P do
16                 newerr ← AltAnc(newerr)
17             end while
18             err ← min{err, newerr}
19         else if j > iorig ∧ T_j ∉ P then
20             T ← T_j
21             while T ≠ null do
22                 k ← IndexOf(T)
23                 P ← P ∪ {T}
24                 Forced(iorig) ← Forced(iorig) ∪ {k}
25                 ForcedBy(k) ← iorig
26                 newerr ← CHECKANDPROPAGATE(iorig, k)
27                 if newerr = ∞ then
28                     T ← Parent(T)
29                 else
30                     err ← min{err, newerr}
31                     Break
32                 end if
33                 if T ∈ P then
34                     if T ∈ Alternative then
35                         for all T_l ∈ Subtasks(T) do
36                             if T_l ∈ P ∧ l ≠ k then
37                                 if ForcedBy(l) < ∞ then
38                                     err ← min{err, AltAnc(ForcedBy(l))}
39                                 else
40                                     err ← min{err, AltAnc(l)}
41                                 end if
42                                 Break
43                             end if
44                         end for
45                     end if
46                     Break
47                 end if
48             end while
49         end if
50     end for
51     if err < ∞ ∧ i = iorig then
52         for all l ∈ Forced(i) do
53             P ← P \ {T_l}
54             ForcedBy(l) ← ∞
55         end for
56         Forced(i) ← ∅
57     end if
58     Return err
59 end function
```

4.3   Scheduling the Activities

Similarly, the routine for scheduling the set of activities from the new process is based on conflict-directed backjumping with backmarking. The simple temporal network (STN) with the all-pairs-shortest-path property is assumed to have been computed beforehand. Due to space restrictions, we omit the pseudocode.

The activities from the new process are first ordered increasingly in their earliest possible start times that are obtained from the STN. Then the algorithm conducts an object-level search, that is, it takes one activity after another and allocates them in time on the associated resources. If the activity is successfully assigned its start time, it proceeds to another activity, otherwise it backjumps to some previously allocated activity and increments its start time (if possible, otherwise backjumps further).

The question is how to determine the conflict set cs that is to be returned and then used for finding another process. Note that we might also want to try some more processes even if a schedule of good quality is found. Our "backjumping heuristic" works as follows.

Before the search for start times begins, we may easily detect infeasibility if there is a pair of activities that are to be executed on the same resource and that necessarily overlap. More precisely, we go over all pairs of activities, say T_i and T_j, such that $i \neq j$ and $R_i = R_j$, and check whether the following condition holds:

$$w_{i,j} < D_i \wedge w_{j,i} < D_j$$

If the condition holds, the indices $AltAnc(i)$ and $AltAnc(j)$ are added to the conflict set cs. If cs is non-empty after examining all the pairs of activities, the algorithm concludes that the set of activities is unschedulable and returns cs. Otherwise the algorithm proceeds to the search stage itself. Note that there still may be no solution. During the search, the algorithm counts for each activity the number of times the activity was being set its start time, that is, every time an activity is being instantiated, the counter for the activity is incremented.

After the search terminates, the conflict set cs is constructed as follows. Assume the activity on the i-th position in the order of instantiation is the activity $T_{Index(i)}$. Then if i-th activity was instantiated at least 4 times more than $(i-1)$-th activity (the number 4 was found empirically to give the best results), add $AltAnc(Index(i))$ to the conflict set cs. If a feasible schedule for the set of activities has not been found, add also the activities that were instantiated more times than average.

In fact, any implementation of this scheduling routine is possible. The only requirement is that it returns the conflict set containing tasks whose reconsideration is promising to yield a better schedule.

4.4   Failure at Arbitrary Time

Section 3.3 set the assumption that the resource fails at time $t_f = 0$. To allow the time of a failure to be arbitrary $t_f \in \mathbb{N}$, banning the tasks must be adjusted such that the already executed activities $(E_i \leq t_f)$ are fixed to stay in the process P, which may be propagated up to the root task, and the already executed activities are not included in the scheduling part. Since the already executed activities are actually fixed in time, the chance that the schedule is not recoverable may thus significantly increase due to the temporal constraints between the already executed activities and the not-yet-executed activities.

The only technical issue is whether the activities that were being processed at time t_f are devastated and thus must be performed for the original duration or only for the remaining number of time units.

Another option might be not fixing the already executed activities to stay in the process. Thus the already executed activities that are not in the recovered process are considered to have been processed in vain, hence minimization of the wasted work might be another objective function of interest, though somewhat amalgamating with the modification distance minimization.

5   Experimental Results

The number of feasible processes in a workflow is expected to grow exponentially in the size of the workflow. That is why our heuristic-based approach is designed to be somewhat greedy, that is, it should examine only constant (independent of the problem size) number of processes. To verify our hypotheses, we compare our backjumping heuristic algorithm (BH), as described in the previous section, against exhaustive search (ES), which tries all feasible processes in the workflow and thus attains the best schedule.

We performed experiments with randomly generated problems composed of 5 resources; duration of activities is at most 15, each task has at most 5 children, the number of simple temporal constraints in a workflow is equal to the number of activities in the workflow (some may be redundant). The following figures depict functions of the number of activities in a workflow. For each size of the workflow we generated 100 instances, so that the number of logical constraints increases from 0 up to the number of activities in the workflow (or to 99).

The algorithms run on Intel(R) Core(TM) i7-2600K CPU @ 3.40 GHz, 3701 Mhz, kernels: 4, logical processors: 8; RAM: 8,00 GB.

The experimental results confirmed the hypotheses. While the number of processes in a workflow grows exponentially, BH examines only constant number of processes (Fig. 4). The reason why the average number of examined processes over all instances is below 1 is that most instances have no alternative process (roughly 38 % of instances were recoverable). The average runtime (Fig. 5a) corresponds to the number of tried processes, that is, prohibitive for ES while very small for BH. Although the average runtime in the figure is approximately 10 seconds, for 113 activities and no logical constraints in a workflow ES did not finish in a reasonable time and the experiments were terminated. On the other hand, the schedules found by BS are almost as good as those found by ES (Fig. 5b) w.r.t. the distance function f, i.e., the number of activities removed from the original process plus the number of activities added to the new process.

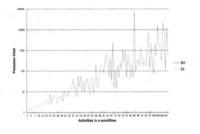
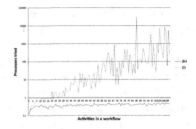

(a) Average over recoverable instances only.

(b) Average over all 100 instances.

Fig. 4. The number of examined processes as the function of the number of activities in a workflow, comparing backjumping heuristic algorithm (BH) to exhaustive search (ES).

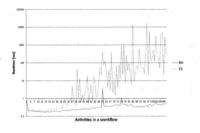
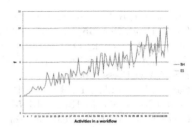

(a) The runtime in milliseconds as the function of the number of activities in a workflow. Average over all 100 instances.

(b) The modification distance function f as the function of the number of activities in a workflow.

Fig. 5. Comparison for backjumping heuristic algorithm (BH) and exhaustive search (ES).

Most importantly, although there is no guarantee that BH finds a solution every time a solution exists, we did not manage to contrive a problem that would prove the opposite.

6   Conclusions

This paper proposes using the hierarchical model with alternatives in the field of predictive-reactive scheduling. In response to unexpected events occurring during the schedule execution, existing approaches only modify the allocation of already selected activities. The model we described makes it possible to replace tasks in the process by other tasks that are not in the process, i.e., to re-plan some (ideally the smallest necessary) subset of the schedule.

We focused on the resource failure recovery problem and suggested a back-jumping heuristic algorithm that examines only a constant number of processes but gives near-optimal solution.

Our future target is to extend the model by recursion, that is, tasks will be able to decompose to themselves, and to suggest algorithms for this enhanced model. The recursion will bring the full power of planning, i.e., the possibility to generate tasks according to a given target. The main inspiration comes from the Hierarchical Task Networks Planning [7].

Acknowledgments. This research is partially supported by the Charles University in Prague, project GA UK No. 158216, by SVV project number 260 333, and by the Czech Science Foundation under the project P103-15-19877S.

References

1. Abumaizar, R.J., Svestka, J.A.: Rescheduling job shops under random disruptions. Int. J. Prod. Res. **35**(7), 2065–2082 (1997)
2. Barták, R., Čepek, O.: Nested temporal networks with alternatives. In: AAAI Workshop on Spatial and Temporal Reasoning, Technical Report WS-07-12, pp. 1–8. AAAI Press (2007)
3. Barták, R., Muller, T., Rudová, H.: Minimal perturbation problem-a formal view. Neural Netw. World **13**(5), 501–512 (2003)
4. Dechter, R., Meiri, I., Pearl, J.: Temporal constraint networks. Artif. Intell. **49**(1), 61–95 (1991)
5. Dulai, T., Werner-Stark, Á.: A database-oriented workflow scheduler with historical data and resource substitution possibilities. In: Proceedings of the International Conference on Operations Research and Enterprise Systems, pp. 325–330. SciTePress (2015)
6. Kondrak, G., Van Beek, P.: A theoretical evaluation of selected backtracking algorithms. Artif. Intell. **89**(1), 365–387 (1997)
7. Nau, D.S., Au, T.C., Ilghami, O., Kuter, U., Murdock, J.W., Wu, D., Yaman, F.: Shop2: an HTN planning system. J. Artif. Intell. Res. (JAIR) **20**, 379–404 (2003)
8. Oddi, A., Policella, N., Cesta, A., Smith, S.F.: Boosting the performance of iterative flattening search. In: Basili, R., Pazienza, M.T. (eds.) AI*IA 2007. LNCS, vol. 4733, pp. 447–458. Springer, Heidelberg (2007). doi:10.1007/978-3-540-74782-6_39
9. Ouelhadj, D., Petrovic, S.: A survey of dynamic scheduling in manufacturing systems. J. Schedul. **12**(4), 417–431 (2009)
10. Planken, L.R.: New algorithms for the simple temporal problem. Ph.D. thesis, TU Delft, Delft University of Technology (2008)
11. Raheja, A.S., Subramaniam, V.: Reactive recovery of job shop schedules - a review. Int. J. Adv. Manuf. Technol. **19**, 756–763 (2002)
12. Skalický, T.: Interactive Scheduling and Visualisation. Master's thesis, Charles University in Prague (2011)
13. Smith, S.F.: Reactive scheduling systems. In: Brown, D., Scherer, W. (eds.) Intelligent scheduling systems, pp. 155–192. Springer US, Boston (1995)
14. Vieira, G., Herrmann, J., Lin, E.: Rescheduling manufacturing systems: a framework of strategies, policies, and methods. J. Schedul. **6**, 39–62 (2003)

A Multi-objective Hospital Operating Room Planning and Scheduling Problem Using Compromise Programming

Alejandra Duenas[1(✉)], Christine Di Martinelly[1], G. Yazgı Tütüncü[1,2],
and Joaquin Aguado[3]

[1] IESEG, School of Management (LEM-CNRS),
3 rue de la Digue, 59000 Lille, France
{a.duenas,c.dimartinelly,y.tutuncu}@ieseg.fr
[2] Department of Mathematics, İzmir University of Economics,
Sakarya cad. No: 156 Balçova, İzmir, Turkey
[3] University of Bamberg, Bamberg, Germany
joaquin.aguado@uni-bamberg.de

Abstract. This paper proposes a hybrid compromise programming local search approach with two main characteristics: a capacity to generate non-dominated solutions and the ability to interact with the decision maker. Compromise programming is an approach where it is not necessary to determine the entire set of Pareto-optimal solutions but only some of them. These solutions are called compromise solutions and represent a good tradeoff between conflicting objectives. Another advantage of this type of method is that it allows the inclusion of the decision maker's preferences through the definition of weights included in the different metrics used by the method. This approach is tested on an operating room planning process. This process incorporates the operating rooms and the nurse planning simultaneously. Three different objectives were considered: to minimize operating room costs, to minimize the maximum number of nurses needed to participate in surgeries and to minimize the number of open operating rooms. The results show that it is a powerful decision tool that enables the decision makers to apply compromise alongside optimal solutions during an operating room planning process.

Keywords: Multi-objective optimization · Compromise programming · Mixed integer programming · Local search · Operating room scheduling

1 Introduction

Governments in industrialized countries are trying to rationalize the funding allotted to hospitals. Therefore, the hospital operating room planning and scheduling problem has been of interest to management science researchers for a number of years as it represents a critical and complex problem. Indeed, operating rooms amount to a significant part of the hospital budget [1], and generate a core part of the hospital activity and impact on the resources consumption in other departments [2]. The operating room manager plans and schedules the surgical interventions over a specified time horizon

© Springer International Publishing AG 2017
G. Sidorov and O. Herrera-Alcántara (Eds.): MICAI 2016, Part I, LNAI 10061, pp. 379–390, 2017.
DOI: 10.1007/978-3-319-62434-1_31

(usually one or two weeks), taking into account the availabilities and preferences of the personnel (surgeons, anesthesiologists, nurses), and the availability of high cost equipment.

Due to the number of constraints and variables that have to be taken into account, traditional approaches have focused on a decomposition approach and have considered a single objective [3, 4]. First, a patient is assigned to a surgical day and operating room, considering the number of available nurses. Then, the scheduling phase determines the starting time of each surgery. The economical objective usually maximizes utility or minimizes costs [5, 6].

This kind of approach leads to two problems. Firstly, the surgical schedule obtained by a decomposition approach might be infeasible due to the unavailability of resources [7, 8]. Secondly, the use of a single economic objective function does not reflect the complexity of developing an operating room surgical planning procedure. Other elements such as surgeons' preferences, patient age, emergency criteria, overtime, might be taken into account by the operating room manager while building the surgical planning.

Some researchers have partially addressed these problems. Roland et al. [9] considered the planning and scheduling of the elective surgeries over one week while considering the constraints on the various resources (availability of surgeons, requirements in nurses and materials). They modeled the problem as a Resource Constrained Project Scheduling Problem (RCPSP) and suggested a genetic algorithm to obtain good solutions within a reasonable computation time. The objective function is the economic cost of using the operating rooms. Papers developing a multi-objective approach focused either on the planning or on the scheduling phase. Sier et al. [10] proposed a multi-objective approach based on simulated annealing, where different goals with different units were aggregated into one objective function. Exponential functions were then defined to make the goals comparable. The solution found showed to be sensitive to the weights given to the different goals. A similar problem was faced by Cardoen et al. [11] who developed a mixed integer programming approach based on heuristics in order to get feasible planning. To make the goals comparable and be independent of the measurement units, they "normalized" each objective function value. The objective function value was expressed as a fraction of the difference between the best and worse values obtained in the case of a single objective optimization. Meskens et al. [12] proposed a multi-objective decision tool system based on constraint programming to solve the scheduling of surgical interventions taking into account nurses' and surgeons' preferences.

The objective of our research is to build the planning and schedule of the surgical interventions while taking into account human and materials constraints. We complement the research done by Roland et al. [9] by using a multi-objective approach in order to consider the complexity of conflicting decisions related to the operating rooms.

Multi-objective optimization seeks to optimize the decision maker's (DM) utility or preference function [13]. Usually, objectives involved are conflicting. As a result, the aim of multi-objective optimization techniques is to identify the non-dominated solutions or efficient solutions [14].

Research done in planning and scheduling the operating rooms transformed the different objectives into a single objective function, together with preference information expressed as weights. The main drawback of those techniques is that a strong assumption is made about the ability of the DM to give a-priori very precise information [15].

A-posteriori methods are concerned with finding all or most of the efficient solutions to a problem without first asking the decision-maker about his preferences. The objective of these methods is to generate the Pareto set of optimal solutions. However, generating the entire set of Pareto optimal solutions can be time consuming [16]. To overcome this problem, compromise programming was developed by Zeleny [17] to speed up the solution process by selecting only a subset of the Pareto optimal solutions.

This paper is organized as follows. Section 2 contains the proposed multi-objective optimization method. A case study based on the assignment and scheduling of surgical interventions under resource constraints in a hospital in Belgium is solved in Sect. 3. The results are presented and discussed in Subsect. 3.2. Finally, conclusions and directions for future work are outlined in Sect. 4.

2 Methodology

2.1 Multi-objective Optimization

A multi-objective problem (MOP) can be defined as:

$$\text{Minimize} f(x) = (f_1(x), \ldots, f_n(x))^T \tag{1}$$

Subject to $x \in V$, where x is a vector of decision variables and V represents the set of candidate solutions which meets all the constraints m. The number of objective functions is represented by n. In most cases the objective functions are in conflict and this causes that no single solution minimizes all objectives at the same time. Therefore, the concept of non-dominated solutions appears in the literature as Pareto optimum or efficient solution. A non-dominated solution (Pareto-optimal solution) of the MOP is the solution in which it is not possible to improve one objective without increasing the other objectives. In a formal way x^* is a non-dominated solution if and only if there is not any $x \in V$ such that $f_i(x) \le f_i(x^*)$ for all i, where $i = 1, \ldots, n$, and $f_j(x) < f_j(x^*)$ for at least one j, $j = 1, \ldots, n$ [18]. Therefore, a non-dominated solution represents a trade-off between conflicting objectives. Several methods to generate the set of non-dominated solutions have been developed such as the weighting method [19], and the ε-constraint method [20].

2.2 Compromise Programming

The compromise programming technique, developed by Zeleny [17], is an approach where it is not necessary to determine the entire set of Pareto-optimal solutions but only some of them. These are called compromise solutions and represent a good tradeoff between conflicting objectives. In order to measure the quality of the compromise solutions a scalarizing function is used. This technique is based on the idea of obtaining an optimal solution for each single-objective under consideration and then finding a compromise solution which is as close to the optimal/ideal value as possible. Therefore, mathematical programming problems can be solved using commercial solvers (Xpress IVE, CPLEX, GAMS etc.) for each single objective without considering the other objectives. These commercial solvers allow finding an optimal value for each objective in a feasible amount of time. These optimal values are used to generate a set u used to measure the deviation between these (ideal) values and the candidate solutions $x \in V$. The ideal objective values vector f_{id} is defined as follows:

$$f_{id} = (f_1(u_1), f_2(u_2), \cdots f_n(u_n)) \tag{2}$$

The compromise programming method introduces a family of L_p – metrics used to measure the fitness of a solution x. The L_p – metrics $(p = 1, 2, \infty)$ are defined as the weighted distances between u and x [21].

$$L_p(x) = \left\{ \sum_{i=1}^{n} [w_i(f_i(x) - f_i(u_i))]^p \right\}^{1/p} \tag{3}$$

In the metric L_1 $(p = 1)$, all distances from the ideal point are equally weighted (Manhattan metric); in L_2 $(p = 2)$, each deviation is weighted in proportion to its magnitude (Euclidian metric); in L_∞ $(p = \infty)$ the problem becomes min-max and the metric is called Tchebycheff [22].

$$L_\infty = \min_{x \in X} \max_{i=1,\ldots,n} [w_i(f_i(x) - f_i(u_i))], \ 0 \le w_i \le 1, \ \sum_{i=1}^{n} w_i = 1 \tag{4}$$

Other metrics can be also used to measure these distances and are generally known as "degrees of closeness". The ideal objective values vector f_{id} is obtained by solving the mathematical programming for each individual objective. The parameters w_i represent the DM's preferences. There are many methods to determine the criterion weights. SMART and SWING are known weight ratio estimation methods where the DM assigns points to denote the relative importance of other attributes compared to the most important. These two methods are algebraic and use a simple equation system [23]. There are other methods for the DM's preference elicitation, such as the analytic hierarchy process (AHP) [24] which is based on a pair-wise comparisons matrix and the eigenvalue procedure.

Then, a local search is combined with the compromise programming method where the L_p – metric works as the cost function of the local search. In this approach, the search space should be defined in a way that only represents feasible solutions. Additionally, an elitist strategy is added to the local search in such a way so that the best solutions found by the compromise programming technique are kept in the population and stored. At the end, the DM is given a list of the best solutions and can select the one that reflects his or her preferences. Figure 1 illustrates the compromise programming local search hybrid approach developed in this paper.

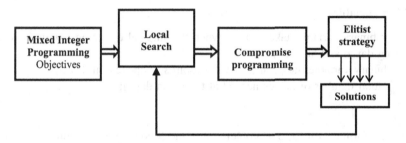

Fig. 1. Hybrid multi-objective approach

3   Case Study

3.1   Problem Description

A problem of assignment and scheduling of surgical interventions under constraint of resources in a hospital in Belgium solved by Roland et al. [9] is used in this paper to show the advantages of the compromise programming approach. This problem was solved using a mixed integer programming (MIP) model.

Indices

- j: number of surgical interventions to schedule; $j = 1, \ldots, J$;
- s: number of operating rooms; $s = 1, \ldots, S$;
- d: number of opening days; $d = 1, \ldots, D$;
- t: number of periods in a day; $t = 1, \ldots, T$;
- c: number of surgeons; $c = 1, \ldots, C$.
- k: type of personnel required for an intervention; $k = 1, \ldots, K$.

Parameters

- p_j: operating duration of surgical intervention j;
- ES_j: earliest starting day for surgical intervention j;
- LS_j: latest starting day for surgical intervention j;
- $r_{j,k}$: number of personnel of type $k \in K$ required for intervention j;
- $R_{k,d}$: availability of personnel of type k for day d;
- $O_{j,s}$: OR s where the surgical intervention j can take place;
- $R^C_{j,d,t}$: when the surgical operation j can take place, considering the day d and period t availabilities of the surgeon c;
- n_j: number of nurses required to undertake surgery j;
- $D^N_{s,d}$: availability of room s for day d, in normal hours;
- $D^M_{s,d}$: the total amount of periods available for room s on day d (normal and overtime hours);
- C^{open}: opening cost of a room;
- C^{over}: cost of opening a room in overtime, per period;
- P: maximum number of nurses allowed to work simultaneously over a week.

Decision variables

- $x_{j,s,d,t}$: binary variable; take value 1 when the surgical operation j starts in room s during day d and at time period t;
- $z_{s,d}$: binary variable; take value 1 when room s is opened on day d;
- $nr_{t,d}$: total number of nurses needed at time t on day d;

Model

The model formulation for our problem takes the following expression:

$$\min_{z,nr} \sum_s \sum_d \left(C^{open} * z_{s,d}\right) + \sum_{t=v}^{T} \sum_d \left(C^{over} * nr_{t,d}\right) \tag{5}$$

Subject to

$$ES_j \leq \sum_s \sum_d \sum_t d * x_{j,s,d,t} \leq LS_j \quad \forall j \tag{6}$$

$$\sum_s \sum_d \sum_t x_{j,s,d,t} = 1 \quad \forall j \tag{7}$$

$$\sum_j \sum_s r_{j,k} \sum_{r=t-p_j+1,r\geq 0}^{t} x_{j,s,d,r} \leq R_{k,d} \quad \forall d, \forall t, \forall k \tag{8}$$

$$\sum_j \sum_s n_j \sum_{r=t-p_j+1,r\geq 0}^{t} x_{j,s,d,r} \leq nr_{t,d} \quad \forall d, \forall t \tag{9}$$

$$x_{j,s,d,t} \leq R_{j,d,t}^{C} \quad \forall d, \forall t, \forall j, \forall s \tag{10}$$

$$(p_j + t) * x_{j,s,d,t} \leq D_{s,d}^{M} * z_{s,d} \quad \forall s, \forall d, \forall t \tag{11}$$

$$\sum_j \sum_{r=t-p_j+1}^{t} x_{j,s,d,r} \leq 1 \quad \forall s, \forall d, \forall t \tag{12}$$

$$\sum_d \sum_t x_{j,s,d,t} \leq O_{j,s} \quad \forall j, \forall s \tag{13}$$

$$x_{j,s,d,t} \leq D_{s,d}^{N} \quad \forall j, \forall s, \forall d, \forall t \tag{14}$$

$$x_{j,s,d,t} = 0 \quad \forall j, \forall s, \forall d, \forall t \notin [ES_j, LS_j] \tag{15}$$

$$x_{j,s,d,t} = 0 \quad \forall j, \forall s, \forall d, \forall t \quad \text{when } t + p_j > D_{s,d}^{M} \tag{16}$$

$$x_{j,s,d,t}, z_{s,d} \in \{0,1\} \quad \forall j, \forall s, \forall d, \forall t \tag{17}$$

where the binary variables (17) $x_{j,s,d,t}$ take value 1 when the surgical operation j starts in room s during day d and at time period t while $z_{s,d}$ take value 1 when room s is opened on day d.

The problem considered is the planning and scheduling of J surgical elective procedures over a one week time period. Each performed intervention requires specific resources to be available. The amount of resources may vary. Personnel resources include: anesthetists, nurses and scrub nurses. The daily availability of anesthetists and scrub nurses is constant but can vary over the week. The availability of nurses is subject to daily and weekly variations therefore a pool of nurses must be available.

Each day is divided into T periods of 15 min. Each surgical intervention j has a deterministic processing time p_j. Each operation j has to be carried out between an earliest and a latest starting day, ES_j and LS_j respectively. An operation cannot start before the admission day of the patient and has to be carried out within an acceptable delay to maximize patient satisfaction. Each surgical treatment is assigned to a particular surgeon c, who is available in half day time slots.

There are S operating rooms managed according to a block scheduling management policy. Each of these rooms has a regular availability for day d, representing the normal opening hours of the room defined by a number of 32 periods ($N = 32$ periods). Since we allow an elective operation to occur after the normal working hours (in overtime) $t = v = 33$ an operating room also has a maximal availability for day d that depicts the total amount of periods available that day for that room (opening hours and overtime); there are 8 periods of overtime. An imposed constraint is that surgery cannot start during the overtime period.

Three different objective functions are considered in this paper. These objectives are derived from the model presented above. Solving this mathematical model considering these three objectives simultaneously can result in a large MIP that might become computationally intractable.

The first objective is to minimize the costs. In which case, each time an operating room is opened, the hospital spends C^{open}€, and pays a fixed amount for each time unit an operating room is open in overtime, C^{over}€ per time unit. Hence, the objective is to minimize the costs associated with room openings. This is similar to minimize the makespan in every operating room and overtime pay.

$$Objective\ 1: \quad \min_{z,nr} \sum_s \sum_d \left(C^{open} * z_{s,d} \right) + \sum_{t=v}^{T} \sum_d \left(C^{over} * nr_{t,d} \right) \quad (18)$$

The second objective function to be used is to minimize the maximum number of nurses needed to do the surgeries. The third objective is to minimize the number of operating room open over the week.

$$Objective\ 2: \quad \min P; \ with \quad nr_{t,d} \le P \quad \forall d, \forall t \quad (19)$$

$$Objective\ 3: \quad \min \sum_s \sum_d \left(z_{s,d} \right) \quad (20)$$

The three objective functions are tested while keeping the same constraints to allow for comparisons between the different scenarios.

3.2 Compromise Programming Results

In this case study, the three metrics outlined above ($p = 1, 2, \infty$) to ensure the generation of a good approximation in the Pareto set of the OR planning process problem are used.

The values obtained solving the MIP for each individual objective in a specific week, are presented in Table 1 together with the results from the compromise programming method using the L_p – metrics ($p = 1, 2$), considering the same priority for all objectives (equal weights).

Table 1. Results of compromise programming with equal weights

10 best solutions after 100 runs p = 1			10 best solutions after 100 runs p = 2		
Objective 1	Objective 2	Objective 3	Objective 1	Objective 2	Objective 3
50640	7	21	50640	7	21
46590	6	21	46590	6	21
47130	7	21	47130	7	21
44520	8	21	44520	8	21
43680	9	21	48630	6	22
43680	10	21	49170	7	22
43770	11	21	46560	8	22
48630	6	22	50700	6	23
49170	7	22	51210	7	23
50700	6	23	52740	6	24

Optimal solutions when objectives are run separately for a specific week (week 6): Objective 1 Min Cost = 43080; Objective 2 Min Nurses = 6; Objective 3 Min OR = 20

Figure 2 shows some solutions graphically displayed so the DM can better visualized the solutions found as well as their non-dominance. To generate this chart, the objective values were normalized using the minimum value found for each objective $f_{i_{min}}$ and each objective optimal/ideal value $f_{i_{optimal}}$ where $i = 1, \ldots, n$, and n is the number of objectives.

$$f_{i_{normalized}} = \frac{f_{non-dominated} - f_{i_{min}}}{f_{i_{max}} - f_{i_{min}}} \tag{21}$$

The problem solved in this case study is a minimization problem. Therefore, $f_{i_{normalized}}$ can take values between 0 and 1 where value of 0 means that the ideal value for that specific objective was achieved and 1 means that the objective value achieved is equal to the maximum value that objective can take.

From the results it is possible to see that, while an optimal solution was achieved for objective 2 (min nurses), the solutions found for objectives 1 and 3 were only near-optimal. When using the Tchebycheff metric ($p = \infty$) the best solution found was

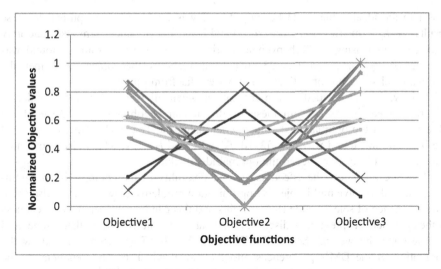

Fig. 2. Parallel objectives to identify dominance

$f_1 = 46590$, $f_2 = 6$, and $f_3 = 21$, which also shows that objective 2 met the optimal/ideal value while objectives 1 and 3 were only near-optimal.

In order to analyze the impact that objectives 1 and 3 may have on the solution, it was decided to obtain the results when higher priority was given to objective 1 (min cost). The model was run for a different week so the optimal/ideal values for the three objectives changed; the objectives are presented in Table 2. From this table, it can be seen that although objective 1 achieved an optimal solution (52640), objective 3 was

Table 2. Results of compromise programming

10 best solutions after 100 runs p = 1, p = 2, $w_1 = 0.6$, w_2 and w_3 are randomly generated			10 best solutions after 100 runs p = 1, p = 2 and randomly generated w_i		
Objective 1	Objective 2	Objective 3	Objective 1	Objective 2	Objective 3
52740	15	24	52740	15	24
52640	15	25	53910	15	26
53010	14	24	53010	14	24
52710	13	24	52650	14	25
52920	13	25	54900	14	26
53280	12	24	52710	13	25
52950	12	25	52920	13	24
52680	11	24	53280	12	25
53730	11	25	52950	12	24
52920	10	24	55380	10	25

Optimal solutions when objectives are run separately:
Objective 1 Min Cost = 52640; Objective 2 Min Nurses = 8; Objective 3 Min OR = 23

closer to the ideal value of 23 but objective 2 was far from being optimal. In these results the L_p – metrics used were $p = 1$ and 2 and the p values were also randomly selected. When using the Tchebycheff metric ($p = \infty$) the best solution found was $f_1 = 52640$, $f_2 = 15$, and $f_3 = 25$, which also shows that objective 2 met the optimal/ideal value but objectives 1 and 3 were far from optimal.

Finally, it was decided to run the model when all weights w_i were randomly generated (see Table 2). From these results, it can be observed that none of the objectives met the optimal/ideal value. When using the Tchebycheff metric ($p = \infty$) the best solution found was $f_1 = 52710, f_2 = 13$, and $f_3 = 24$, which also shows that none of the objectives achieved the optimal/ideal value.

These results show the effectiveness and flexibility of the compromise programming method to solve multi-objective optimization problems. However, they also show the importance of selecting the right weights and this can be considered as a weakness in the approach. As previously discussed, there are different techniques that can be used to determine the weights SMART, SWING and AHP. These techniques allow the integration of the DM's preferences into the model which can be beneficial to the decision making process.

4   Conclusion

A hybrid compromise programming local search approach was developed in this paper with two main characteristics: the capacity to generate non-dominated solutions and the ability to interact with the DM.

This approach was successfully applied to a real-world operating room and nurse planning problem in a hospital in Belgium. This problem involved the optimization of three objectives simultaneously: to minimize operating rooms opening costs, to minimize the makespan and overtime pay in every operating room and to minimize the total number of nurses needed to participate in surgeries. The results obtained showed that the proposed approach can be used as an effective decision making tool for a hospital manager who supervises the planning process of operation rooms using state of the art optimization approaches. Moreover, it can be concluded that it is possible to simplify a complex and large MIP problem through the use of a hybrid multi-objective optimization technique.

For future research, it would be interesting to incorporate the DM's (operating room manager) judgment through multi-criteria decision making methods (SMART, SWING, AHP etc.) or interactive compromise programming [21]. There is also the possibility of improving the model by also taking into account the nurses' preferences and other staffing constraints [25] while considering the minimization of the makespan and overtime costs.

References

1. Macario, A.: Are your hospital operating rooms "efficient"? A scoring system with eight performance indicators. Anesthesiology **105**(2), 237–240 (2006)
2. Beliën, J., Demeulemeester, E.: Building cyclic master surgery schedules with leveled resulting bed occupancy. Eur. J. Oper. Res. **176**(2), 1185–1204 (2007)
3. Jebali, A., Alouane, A.B.H., Ladet, P.: Operating rooms scheduling. Int. J. Prod. Econ. **99**(1–2), 52–62 (2006)
4. Guinet, A., Chaabane, S.: Operating theatre planning. Int. J. Prod. Econ. **85**, 69–81 (2003)
5. Fei, H., Chu, C., Meskens, N.: Solving a tactical operating room planning problem by a column-generation-based heuristic procedure with four criteria. Ann. Oper. Res. **166**(1), 91–108 (2009)
6. Lamiri, M., et al.: A stochastic model for operating room planning with elective and emergency demand for surgery. Eur. J. Oper. Res. **185**(3), 1026–1037 (2008)
7. Beliën, J., Demeulemeester, E., Cardoen, B.: Visualizing the demand for various resources as a function of the master surgery schedule: a case study. J. Med. Syst. **30**(5), 343–350 (2006)
8. Di Martinelly, C., Baptiste, P., Maknoon, Y.: Evaluation de l'impact de l'intégration de la conception d'horaires infirmiers sur la programmation opératoire in 9e Congrès International de Génie Industriel. Saint-Sauveur, Canada (2011)
9. Roland, B., et al.: Scheduling an operating theatre under human resource constraints. Comput. Ind. Eng. **58**(2), 212–220 (2010)
10. Sier, D., Tobin, P., McGurk, C.: Scheduling surgical procedures. J. Oper. Res. Soc. **48**(9), 884–891 (1997)
11. Cardoen, B., Demeulemeester, E., Beliën, J.: Optimizing a multiple objective surgical case sequencing problem. Int. J. Prod. Econ. **119**(2), 354–366 (2009)
12. Meskens, N., Duvivier, D., Hanset, A.: Multi-objective operating room scheduling considering desiderata of the surgical team. Decis. Support Syst. **55**, 650–659 (2012)
13. Shin, W.-S., Ravindran, A.: An interactive method for multiple-objective mathematical programming problems. J. Optim. Theory Appl. **68**(3), 539–561 (1991)
14. Ehrgott, M.: Multicriteria Optimization, 2nd edn. Springer, Heidelberg (2005). doi:10.1007/3-540-27659-9
15. Mavrotas, G., Diakoulaki, D.: Multi-criteria branch and bound: a vector maximization algorithm for mixed 0-1 multiple objective linear programming. Appl. Math. Comput. **171**(1), 53–71 (2005)
16. Miettinen, K., Mäkelä, M.M.: Synchronous approach in interactive multiobjective optimization. Eur. J. Oper. Res. **170**(3), 909–922 (2006)
17. Zeleny, M.: Compromise programming. In: Cochrane, J., Zeleny, M. (eds.) Multiple Criteria Decision Making, pp. 262–301. University of South Carolina Press, Columbia (1973)
18. Hwang, C.L., Masud, A.S.M., Paidy, S.R.: Multiple Objective Decision Making, Methods and Applications: A State-of-the-Art Survey. Springer, Heidelberg (1979). doi:10.1007/978-3-642-45511-7
19. Zadeh, L.: Optimality and non-scalar-valued performance criteria. IEEE Trans. Autom. Control **AC-8**, 59–60 (1963)
20. Cohon, J.L.: Multiobjective Programming and Planning. Academic Press, New York (1978)
21. Ramazan, E.: Interactive compromise programming. J. Oper. Res. Soc. **38**(2), 163–172 (1987)

22. Shiau, J.T., Wu, F.C.: Compromise programming methodology for determining instream flow under muliobjective water allocation criteria. J. Am. Water Resour. Assoc. **42**(5), 1179–1191 (2006)
23. Weber, M., Borcherding, K.: Behavioral influences on weight judgments in multiattribute decision making. Eur. J. Oper. Res. **67**, 1–12 (1993)
24. Saaty, T.L.: Fundamentals of Decision Making and Priority Theory with the Analytic Hierarchy Process. RWS Publications, Pittsburgh (1994)
25. Duenas, A., Tutuncu, G.Y., Chilcott, J.B.: A genetic algorithm approach to the nurse scheduling problem with fuzzy preferences. IMA J. Manage. Math. **20**(4), 369–383 (2009)

Solving Manufacturing Cell Design Problems Using the Black Hole Algorithm

Ricardo Soto[1], Broderick Crawford[1], Nicolás Fernandez[1], Víctor Reyes[1(✉)], Stefanie Niklander[2], and Ignacio Araya[1]

[1] Pontificia Universidad Católica de Valparaíso, Valparaíso, Chile
{ricardo.soto,broderick.crawford,ignacio.araya}@ucv.cl,
{nicolas.fernandez.a01,victor.reyes.r}@mail.pucv.cl
[2] Universidad Autónoma de Chile, Santiago, Chile
stefanie.niklander@uai.cl

Abstract. In this paper we solve the Manufacturing Cell Design Problem. This problem considers the grouping of different machines into sets or cells with the objective of minimizing the movement of material. To solve this problem we use the Black Hole algorithm, a modern population-based metaheuristic that is inspired by the phenomenon of the same name. At each iteration of the search, the best candidate solution is selected to be the black hole and other candidate solutions, known as stars, are attracted by the black hole. If one of these stars get too close to the black hole it disappears, generating a new random star (solution). Our approach has been tested by using a well-known set of benchmark instances, reaching optimal values in all of them.

Keywords: Black Hole algorithm · Metaheuristics · Manufacturing Cell Design Problems

1 Introduction

The Manufacturing Cell Design Problem (MCDP) consist in grouping components under the statement: "Similar things should be manufactured in the same way". In order to increase the efficiency and productivity, machines that create products with similar requirements must be close to each other. This machine-grouping, known as cell, allow the production to be dedicated and organized. Then, the goal of the MCDP is to minimize the movement and exchange of material, by finding the best machine-grouping combination.

The research that has been done to solve the cell formation problem has followed two complementary lines, which can be classified in two different groups: approximate and complete methods. Most approximate methods focus on the search for an optimal solution in a limited time, however, a global optimal is not guaranteed. On the other hand, complete methods aims to analyze the whole search space to guarantee a global optima but this require a higher cost in both memory and time.

Within the approximate methods, different metaheuristics have been used for cell formation. Aljaber et al. [1] made use of Tabu Search. Wu et al. [9] presented

© Springer International Publishing AG 2017
G. Sidorov and O. Herrera-Alcántara (Eds.): MICAI 2016, Part I, LNAI 10061, pp. 391–398, 2017.
DOI: 10.1007/978-3-319-62434-1_32

a Simulated Annealing (SA) approach. Durán et al. [4] combined Particle Swarm Optimization (PSO), which consists of particles that move through a space of solutions and that are accelerated in time, with a data mining technique. Venugopal and Narendran [17] proposed using the Genetic Algorithms (GA), which are based on the genetic process of living organisms. Gupta et al. [5] also used GA, but focusing on a different multi-objective optimization, consisting in the simultaneous minimization of the total number of movements between cells and load variation between them. It is also possible to find hybrid techniques in the problem resolution. Such is the case of Wu et al. [18], who combined SA with GA. James et al. [7] introduced a hybrid solution that combines local search and GA. Nsakanda et al. [10] proposed a solution methodology based on a combination of GA and large-scale optimization techniques. Soto et al. [16], utilized Constraint Programming (CP) and Boolean Satisfiability (SAT) for the resolution of the problem, developing the problem by applying five different solvers, two of which are CP solvers, two SAT solvers and a CP and SAT hybrid.

With regard to the complete methods, preliminary cell formation experiments were developed through the use of linear programming, such as the work of Purcheck [12], and Olivia-López and Purcheck [11].

Kusiak and Chow [8] and Boctor [2] proposed the use of linear-quadratic models. Sankaran [14] and, Shafer and Rogers [15] proposed the use of Goal Programming (GP). This technique can be seen as a generalization of linear programming for the manipulation of multiple objective functions.

Lastly, some research has been done combining both approximate and complete methods. Such is the case of Boulif and Atif [3], who combined branch-and-bound techniques with GA.

In this work, we solve the MCDP by using the Black Hole algorithm. Black Hole is a modern metaheuristic that starts with an initial population of candidate solutions, evaluating each of them using the fitness. At each iteration, the best candidate solution is selected to be the black hole and the rest are defined as stars. After, the black hole starts pulling the stars around it. Stars close to the black hole are swallowed, creating a new random star.

The rest of this paper is organized as follows. In Sect. 2 the mathematical model of the MCDP is described and explained in detail. The Black Hole Algorithm is presented in Sect. 3. Finally, Sect. 4 illustrates the experimental results that we obtained by using a well-known set of benchmarks instances, followed by conclusions and future work.

2   Manufacturing Cell Design Problem

The MCDP consists in organizing a manufacturing plant or facility into a set of cells, each of them made up of different machines meant to process different parts of a product, that share similar characteristics. We represent the processing requirements of machine parts by an incidence zero-one matrix A, known as the *machine-part matrix*. Table 1 shows an example of this matrix.

The main objective, is to minimize movements and exchange of material between cells, in order to reduce production costs and increase productivity.

Table 1. Initial machine-part matrix

Machine	Part									
	1	2	3	4	5	6	7	8	9	10
A						1				1
B		1				1	1			
C		1						1		1
D		1				1				
E	1						1			
F	1		1							
G	1						1			
H					1				1	
I				1					1	
J					1				1	

Table 2 shows the solution obtained after the initial machine-part matrix is processed.

Table 2. Final machine-part matrix

Machine	Pieza									
	1	3	7	2	6	8	10	4	5	9
E	1		1							
F	1	1								
G	1		1							
A					1		1			
B				1	1	1				
C				1		1	1			
D				1	1					
H									1	1
I								1		1
J									1	1

2.1   MCDP Representation

The optimization model is stated as follows. Let:

- M: the number of machines.
- P: the number of parts.
- C: the number of cells.
- i: the index of machines ($i = 1, ..., M$).
- j: the index of parts ($j = 1, ..., P$).
- k: the index of cells ($k = 1, ..., C$),
- M_{max}: the maximum number of machines per cell.
- $A = [a_{ij}]$: the binary machine-part incidence matrix, where:

$$a_{ij} = \begin{cases} 1 \text{ if machine } i \text{ process the part } j \\ 0 \text{ otherwise} \end{cases}$$

- $B = [y_{ik}]$: the binary machine-cell incidence matrix, where:

$$y_{ik} = \begin{cases} 1 \text{ if machine } i \text{ belongs to cell } k \\ 0 \text{ otherwise} \end{cases}$$

- $C = [z_{jk}]$: the binary part-cell incidence matrix, where:

$$z_{jk} = \begin{cases} 1 \text{ if part } j \text{ belongs to cell } k \\ 0 \text{ otherwise} \end{cases}$$

Then, the MCDP is represented by the following mathematical model [2]:

$$\min \sum_{k=1}^{C} \sum_{i=1}^{M} \sum_{j=1}^{P} a_{ij} z_{jk} (1 - y_{i_k}) \tag{1}$$

Subject to the following constraints:

$$\sum_{k=1}^{C} y_{ik} = 1 \quad \forall i \tag{2}$$

$$\sum_{k=1}^{C} z_{jk} = 1 \quad \forall j \tag{3}$$

$$\sum_{i=1}^{M} y_{ik} \leq M_{max} \quad \forall k \tag{4}$$

Constraint 2 defines that each machine belongs to one and only cell. Constraint 3 guarantee that each part is assigned to only one cell. Finally Constraint 4 determines the maximum number of machines that a cell could have.

3   Black Hole Algorithm

To solve the MCDP we propose the Black Hole algorithm [6], a modern population-based metaheuristic based on the black hole phenomenon. *What is a black hole?* A black hole is a high mass space region, such that any object, even light, close to it can not escape from its gravitational pull [13].

Like other population-based algorithms, a set of feasible candidate solutions or stars are randomly generated. After this, each star is evaluated and the one with the better fitness is considered as the black hole, leaving the other solutions as stars. Each star stars moving around towards the black hole. Stars close to the black hole are absorbed. The absorption of the stars is formulated as follows in the Eq. 5:

$$x_i(t+1) = x_i(t) + rand(x_{bh} - x_i(t)) \geq 1, \quad \forall i = 1, 2, 3...N \tag{5}$$

where $x_i(t+1)$ is the location of the i-th star for the $(t+1)$ iteration, rand is a random number between 0 and 1, x_{bh} is the location of the black hole in space search and N represents the number of solutions (stars). In addition, there is a distance between stars and the black hole, stars getting to close to the black hole (known as event horizon) will be absorbed by it, generating a new candidate solution and distributed randomly in the space search. The radius of the event horizon of the black hole algorithm is calculated using the following Eq. 6:

$$E = \frac{f_{bh}}{\sum_{i=1}^{N} f_i} \tag{6}$$

Where f_{bh} is the fitness value of the black hole, f_i is the fitness value of the i-th star and N is the number of candidate solutions. When the distance from the

Table 3. Experimental results using two cells.

P	$M_{max} = 8$		$M_{max} = 9$		$M_{max} = 10$		$M_{max} = 11$		$M_{max} = 12$	
	Boctor	BH	Boctor	BH	Boctor	BH	Boctor	BH	Boctor	BH
1	11	11	11	11	11	11	11	11	11	11
2	7	7	6	6	4	4	3	3	3	3
3	4	4	4	4	4	4	3	3	1	1
4	14	14	13	13	13	13	13	13	13	13
5	9	9	6	6	6	6	5	5	4	4
6	5	5	3	3	3	3	3	3	2	2
7	7	7	4	4	4	4	4	4	4	4
8	13	13	10	10	8	8	5	5	5	5
9	8	8	8	8	8	8	5	5	5	5
10	8	8	5	5	5	5	5	5	5	5

Table 4. Experimental results using three cells

P	$M_{max} = 6$		$M_{max} = 7$		$M_{max} = 8$		$M_{max} = 9$	
	Boctor	BH	Boctor	BH	Boctor	BH	Boctor	BH
1	27	27	18	18	11	11	11	11
2	7	7	6	6	6	6	6	6
3	9	9	4	4	4	4	4	4
4	27	27	18	18	14	14	13	13
5	11	11	8	8	8	8	6	6
6	6	6	4	4	4	4	3	3
7	11	11	5	5	5	5	4	4
8	14	14	11	11	11	11	10	10
9	12	12	12	12	8	8	8	8
10	10	10	8	8	8	8	5	5

(Column header: C = 3)

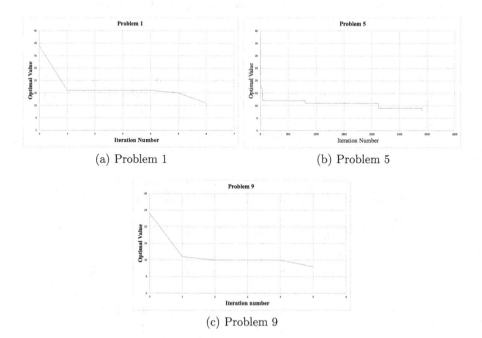

(a) Problem 1   (b) Problem 5

(c) Problem 9

Fig. 1. Convergence plots for benchmarks 1, 5 and 9, with 2 cells and a M_{max} of 8, 7 and 10 respectively

black hole with the star is smaller than the radius, that is, when the difference in fitness between the black hole and the star is smaller than the radius, that star is swallowed by the black hole.

4   Experimental Results

Our approach has been implemented in Java, using a CPU Intel Core i5-4210U with 6GB RAM computer with Windows 8.1 and tested out by using a set of 10 incidence matrices [2]. Tests were carried out based on these 10 test problems (each of them executed 20 times), using 2 cells with a M_{max} value between 8 and 12, and using 3 cells with a M_{max} value between 6 and 9. For our approach, we considerer a number of stars of 5.

Tables 3 and 4 show detailed information about the results obtained by using our approach with the previous configuration. We compare our results with the optimum values reported in [2]. Convergence charts can be seen in Fig. 1.

Experimental results show that the proposed algorithm provides high quality solutions and good performance using two and three cells, where all the expected optima were achieved.

5   Conclusions and Future Work

Manufacturing cell design is a well-known problem within manufacturing factories, as they seek to increase productivity by reducing times and costs. For this reason we have proposed the Black Hole Algorithm, a novel method to tackle this type of problem reporting optimum values for all the tested instances. The proposed algorithm has shown excellent results and high convergence rates in early stages of the search for most of the tested instances. One of the most important features of the Black Hole Algorithm is that is free from parameter tunning issues, making the experiments easy to perform.

As a future work, we plan to implement new modern metaheuristics for solving the MCDP. An hibridization with other metaheuristics could be another direction for research as well.

Acknowledgements. Ricardo Soto is supported by Grant CONICYT/FONDECYT/ REGULAR/1160455, Broderick Crawford is supported by Grant CONICYT/ FONDECYT/REGULAR/1171243, Victor Reyes is supported by Grant INF-PUCV and Ignacio Araya is supported by Grant CONICYT/FONDECYT/REGULAR/ 1160224.

References

1. Aljaber, N., Baek, W., Chen, C.-L.: A tabu search approach to the cell formation problem. Comput. Ind. Eng. **32**(1), 169–185 (1997)
2. Boctor, F.F.: A linear formulation of the machine-part cell formation problem. Int. J. Prod. Res. **29**(2), 343–356 (1991)

3. Boulif, M., Atif, K.: A new branch-&-bound-enhanced genetic algorithm for the manufacturing cell formation problem. Comput. Oper. Res. **33**(8), 2219–2245 (2006)
4. Durán, O., Rodriguez, N., Consalter, L.A.: Collaborative particle swarm optimization with a data mining technique for manufacturing cell design. Expert Syst. Appl. **37**(2), 1563–1567 (2010)
5. Gupta, Y., Gupta, M., Kumar, A., Sundaram, C.: A genetic algorithm-based approach to cell composition and layout design problems. Int. J. Prod. Res. **34**(2), 447–482 (1996)
6. Hatamlou, A.: Black hole: a new heuristic optimization approach for data clustering. Inf. Sci. **222**, 175–184 (2013)
7. James, T.L., Brown, E.C., Keeling, K.B.: A hybrid grouping genetic algorithm for the cell formation problem. Comput. Oper. Res. **34**(7), 2059–2079 (2007)
8. Kusiak, A., Chow, W.S.: Efficient solving of the group technology problem. J. Manuf. Syst. **6**(2), 117–124 (1987)
9. Lozano, S., Adenso-Diaz, B., Eguia, I., Onieva, L., et al.: A one-step tabu search algorithm for manufacturing cell design. J. Oper. Res. Soc. **50**(5), 509–516 (1999)
10. Nsakanda, A.L., Diaby, M., Price, W.L.: Hybrid genetic approach for solving large-scale capacitated cell formation problems with multiple routings. Eur. J. Oper. Res. **171**(3), 1051–1070 (2006)
11. Oliva-Lopez, E., Purcheck, G.F.: Load balancing for group technology planning and control. Int. J. Mach. Tool Des. Res. **19**(4), 259–274 (1979)
12. Purcheck, G.F.K.: A linear-programming method for the combinatorial grouping of an incomplete power set. J. Cybern. **5**(4), 51–76 (1975)
13. Ruffini, R., Wheeler, J.A.: Introducing the black hole. Phys. Today **24**(1), 30 (1971)
14. Sankaran, S., Rodin, E.Y.: Multiple objective decision making approach to cell formation: a goal programming model. Math. Comput. Model. **13**(9), 71–81 (1990)
15. Shafer, S.M., Rogers, D.F.: A goal programming approach to the cell formation problem. J. Oper. Manag. **10**(1), 28–43 (1991)
16. Soto, R., Kjellerstrand, H., Orlando, D., Crawford, B., Monfroy, E., Paredes, F.: Cell formation in group technology using constraint programming and boolean satisfiability. Expert Syst. Appl. **39**(13), 11423–11427 (2012)
17. Venugopal, V., Narendran, T.T.: A genetic algorithm approach to the machine-component grouping problem with multiple objectives. Comput. Ind. Eng. **22**(4), 469–480 (1992)
18. Wu, T.-H., Chang, C.-C., Chung, S.-H.: A simulated annealing algorithm for manufacturing cell formation problems. Expert Syst. Appl. **34**(3), 1609–1617 (2008)

Image Processing and Computer Vision

Efficient Computation of the Euler Number of a 2-D Binary Image

Juan Humberto Sossa-Azuela[1](✉), Ángel A. Carreón-Torres[1],
Raúl Santiago-Montero[2], Ernesto Bribiesca-Correa[3],
and Alberto Petrilli-Barceló[4]

[1] Instituto Politécnico Nacional (CIC),
Av. Juan de Dios Bátiz S/N, Gustavo A. Madero, 07738 Mexico City, Mexico
humbertosossa@gmail.com, angelcarreon01@hotmail.com
[2] Instituto Tecnológico de León,
Av. Tecnológico S/N, Frac. Julián de Obregón, León, Guanajuato, Mexico
rsantiago66@gmail.com
[3] Universidad Nacional Autónoma de México (IIMAS),
Apdo. 20-726, Mexico City, Mexico
bribiesca@iimas.unam.mx
[4] Universidad Tecnológica de la Mixteca (División de Estudios de Posgrado),
Ciudad de Huajuapan de León, Oaxaca, Mexico
petrilliae@gmail.com

Abstract. A new method to compute the Euler number of a 2-D binary image is described in this paper. The method employs three comparisons unlike other proposals that utilize more comparisons. We present two variations, one useful for the case of images containing only 4-connected objects and one useful in the case of 8-connected objects. To numerically validate our method, we firstly apply it to a set of very simple examples; to demonstrate its applicability, we test it next with a set of images of different sizes and object complexities. To show competitiveness of our method against other proposals, we compare it in terms of processing times with some of the state-of-the-art-formulations reported in literature.

1 Introduction

The Euler number is one of the topological features that can be used to characterize an image or an object. It has been used in multiple applications, for example: industrial part recognition [1], real-time thresholding [2], object number calculation [3], and real-time Malayan license plate recognition [4]. Mathematically speaking, the Euler number: e of a digital binary image can be estimated as:

$$e = o - h \tag{1}$$

with o the number of objects or (binary regions) in the image and h the number of holes (i.e., isolated regions of the image's background).

© Springer International Publishing AG 2017
G. Sidorov and O. Herrera-Alcántara (Eds.): MICAI 2016, Part I, LNAI 10061, pp. 401–413, 2017.
DOI: 10.1007/978-3-319-62434-1_33

Many methods have been developed to obtain the Euler number of a digital binary image $I(x, y)$. Refer, for example, to [5–9, 13–20, 24, 25]. For instance, the algorithm outlined in [5] was most probably one of the first reported in literature. The most popular algorithm of this method is used by the image processing tool of MATLAB. It calculates the Euler number of a binary image as follows:

$$e = \frac{s1 - s3 - 2 \cdot x}{4}. \tag{2}$$

where $s1$ is the number of times the four bit quad patterns shown in row Q_1 of Fig. 1 are found in $I(x, y)$ when it is scanned, $s3$ is the number of times the four bit quad patterns shown in row Q_3 of Fig. 1 are found in $I(x, y)$ and x is the number of times the two bit quad patterns of row Q_D of Fig. 1 are found in $I(x, y)$. As we can see, before using (2), the MATLAB algorithm needs to perform up to 10 comparisons on each image pixel. Time complexity for this method is of $O(N^2)$ for a $N \times N$ image, which is linearly dependent on the number of pixels. For image processing tasks, where the data could be huge the constant term that is so often hidden in the *big-Oh* notation becomes important [19].

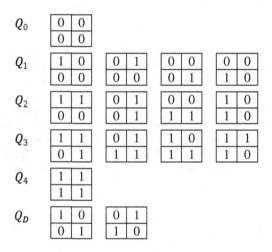

Fig. 1. 16 bit quad patterns according to [5].

In this note we introduce a very simple but efficient method to compute the Euler number of a 2-D binary image; it employs a limited number of comparisons (three) unlike other proposals that utilize more comparisons. We describe two variations of the method, one useful for the case of images containing only 4-connected objects and one useful in the case of 8-connected objects. To numerically validate our proposed methods we firstly apply them to a set of very simple examples; secondly, to demonstrate their applicability we test them with a set of images of different sizes and object complexities. To show that our methods are competitive, we compare them (in terms of processing times) with some of the state-of-the-art-formulations reported in literature.

The rest of the paper is organized as follows. In Sect. 2 we give a set of definitions useful to easily follow the lecture of the remainder of the paper. Section 3 is focused to describe our proposed method; illustrative results to demonstrate its functioning are also provided in this section. Experimental results to show the applicability and advantages of our method as well as a short discussion are given in Sect. 4. Finally, Sect. 5 is devoted to present the conclusions and directions for further work.

2 Background

In this section we present the set of definitions that will help the interested reader to easily follow the lecture of the remaining material presented in this note. Whenever necessary we provide examples to better understand the idea of the definitions.

Definition 1. A digital binary image is a two-dimensional array $I(x, y)$ composed of $M \times N$ elements with grey levels 0 or 1.

Example 1. Figure 2(a) shows a binary image of 4×4 elements where half of its elements have value 1 (grey squares) and the remaining have value 0 (white squares).

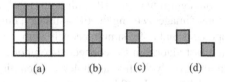

(a)   (b)   (c)   (d)

Fig. 2. (a) Instance of a binary image of 4×4 pixels. (b) Two side connected pixels. (c) Two pixels connected by a corner. (d) Two not connected pixels.

As usual, from now on, an element of image $I(x, y)$ will be called *pixel* (picture element). All pixels in an image are supposed to be squared.

Definition 2. Let p_1 and p_2 be two pixels of an image. If p_1 and p_2 share a side, then it is said that both pixels are *side connected*; otherwise, if p_1 and p_2 are connected by one of their corners, then they are *connected by a corner*; else, p_1 and p_2 are not connected at all.

Example 2. Figure 2(b), (c) and (d) show the prior three cases given in Definition 2 as follows: In Fig. 2(b) the two pixels are *side connected*; in Fig. 2(c) the two pixels are corner connected, in Fig. 2(d) the two pixels are not connected.

Definition 3. A binary object or binary shape S_c composed of c pixels in a binary image $I(x, y)$ is any region whose elements are connected by their sides, their corners or a combination of both. If all the pixels of shape S_c are connected only by sides, then S_c is said to be *side connected* or *4-connected*, if all the pixels of S_c are connected by their sides and/or by their corners then S_c is said to be *8-connected*. In short if all pixels of S_c are connected only by their corners then S_c is said to be *strictly 8-connected*.

Example 3. Figure 3 shows three shapes with the same number of pixels ($c = 9$), the first shape is 4-connected, the second one is 8-connected while the third one is strictly 8-connected.

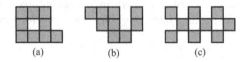

(a)   (b)   (c)

Fig. 3. (a) A 4-connected shape. (b) An 8-connected shape. (c) A strictly 8-connected shape.

Definition 4. A 2×2 binary pixel pattern with values 0 or 1 is called *bit quad*. According to [5], the 16 bit quads patterns illustrated in Fig. 1 can be defined.

According to what we have discussed, the formulation proposed in [5] and used by MATLAB to compute the Euler number of a 2-D binary image make use of bit quads sets: Q_1, Q_3 and Q_D.

Related works in this direction can be summarized as follows. In [20], the authors present an improvement to the method used by MATLAB that allows reducing the processing time by using the information obtained during checking the previous pixel. In [22], the authors present an algorithm called HCS algorithm that allows calculating the Euler number of a 2-D binary image by using the ELS-strategy, initially proposed in [21] to label connected components and holes simultaneously with the same data structures. In [23], authors present a fast algorithm for connected-component labelling and Euler number computation simultaneously. In this case holes are identified during the first scan of connected component labelling. In [24], authors present another algorithm that combines graph theory and bit quad patterns; by using the information obtained during processing the previous bit quad, the average number of pixels to be checked for processing a bit quad is of 1.75. In short, a very similar work is reported in [25].

In the following section we will introduce our method that utilizes only three bit quads as shown in Fig. 1 to obtain the Euler number of a 2-D binary image.

3   Our Proposed Formulation

In this section we introduce our formulation that allows obtaining the Euler number of a 2-D binary image in terms of just three bit quads. In Sect. 3.1 we will first derive the formulation of the 4-connected case. We will do the same for the 8-connected case in Sect. 3.2. In both cases, we will suppose that the corresponding formulation to compute the Euler number of a 2-D binary image is a combination of some of the 16 bit quad shown in Fig. 1. We want to obtain the smallest combination of bit quads that exactly allows determining the Euler number of a 2-D binary image as stated in (1).

3.1   Formulation for the 4-Connected Case

To derive the formulation to compute the Euler number of a 2-D image for the 4-connected case, let us take the set of eight 6×6 images shown in Fig. 4. As can be seen, each image in the first row of Fig. 4 contains one 4-connected region while each image of the second row of Fig. 4 contains two 4-connected regions. Let us choose the first bit quad of set $Q_1 \left(\begin{bmatrix} 1 & 0 \\ 0 & 0 \end{bmatrix} = Q_{11} \right)$ as our first guess to be used to compute e for a 2-D binary image. Let $\# Q_{11}$ represent the number of times this bit quad outputs a "1" as it is found along the image. Let thus $e = \# Q_{11}$ be our first proposal to compute the Euler number of a 2-D binary image.

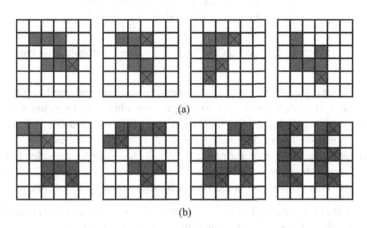

(a)

(b)

Fig. 4. (a) Images with one 4-connected shape. (b) Images with two 4-connected shapes.

Figure 4(a) shows the positions, marked with an "×", where $Q_{11} = 1$. We can see that for the first and the fourth images, $\# Q_{11} = 1$, for the second image $\# Q_{11} = 2$ while for the third image $\# Q_{11} = 3$. Because all of these images have only one shape, we would expect $e = \# Q_{11} = 1$ in all four cases. Something is certainly wrong in the case of the second and third images. The application of this bit quad is not enough to obtain the desired e of an image. We hypothesize that adding a new bit quad will contribute to have a better approximation of e.

Let us go further, let us hypothesize that the fourth bit quad of set $Q_3 \left(\begin{bmatrix} 1 & 1 \\ 1 & 0 \end{bmatrix} = Q_{34} \right)$ can be combined with bit quad Q_{11} to have a better approximation of e for this set of images. How? By subtracting the number of times Q_{34} is detected in the image. Let thus state $e = \# Q_{11} - \# Q_{34}$ as our refined proposal to compute e of 2-D binary image. If we apply this new formulation to these same four images, we obtain in all four cases: $e = 1$! This happens because bit quad Q_{34} appears zero times in the first and the four image, once in second image and twice in third image. To verify if this new approximation is useful, let us test it with the set of four images shown in second row of Fig. 4(b). These four images have now two

4-connected shapes. By applying our new proposal the reader can easily verify that for these new four images, we obtain: $e = 2$ as desired. We would like to know verify if our new approximation is valid for 4-connected shapes having holes. For this let us take the two images 8×8 images of Fig. 5.

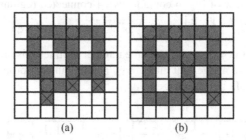

(a)   (b)

Fig. 5. (a) 4-connected shape with two holes. (b) 4-connected shape with four holes.

As can be seen the first shape has two holes while the second one has four holes. If we apply our formulation to these two images, we obtain as expected $e = -1$ and $e = -3$, respectively. In both figures, the positions where bit quad $Q_{11} = 1$ are marked as "×"; the positions where bit quad $Q_{34} = 1$ are marked by circles.

The reader can verify that formulation $e = \# Q_{11} - \# Q_{34}$ provides the desired value of e for any image w n here their shapes are exactly 4-connected, with holes or without holes. This proposition could be established formally as follows:

Lemma 1. Let $I(x, y)$ be any 2-D binary image with o 4-connected objects and h holes. The Euler number of $I(x, y)$ as stipulated by (1) can be computed as:

$$e = \# \begin{bmatrix} 1 & 0 \\ 0 & 0 \end{bmatrix} - \# \begin{bmatrix} 1 & 1 \\ 1 & 0 \end{bmatrix} \tag{3}$$

Proof. By mathematical induction on the number of pixels n of the image I_n, for the base case of and image I_1 consisting of a single pixel, $\#Q_{34} = 0$, value satisfying Eq. (3).

Induction step: let us assume that Eq. (3) holds for the case of image I_n consisting now of pixels. Let $n1'$ and $n3'$, be the number of times bit-quads: Q_{11} and Q_{34}, respectively are found over image I_{n+1} that is obtained by adding one pixel to the image I_n. Let $N1$ and $N3$ be the number of times bit-quads Q_{11} and Q_{34} are found over this new image. We have that:

$$n1' = \# Q_{11} + N1 \tag{4}$$

$$n3' = \# Q_{34} + N3 \tag{5}$$

We have to show that Eq. (3) holds for I_{n+1}, i.e.

$$e' = \#Q_{11} + N1 - \#Q_{34} - N3. \tag{6}$$

But this equation can be rewritten as follows:

$$e' = \#Q_{11} - \#Q_{34} + N1 - N3. \tag{7}$$

This equation simplifies to:

$$e' = e + N1 - N3. \tag{8}$$

which we know is true.   ∎

Until now the reader can see that the proposal works. What is left to verify is that if (3) works also with images as depicted in Fig. 6(a) and (b). In both cases the pixels appear connected by corners but because we are working with 4-connected shapes, then in both cases all the pixels are disconnected. In both cases, (3) should output $e = 4$. When applying it to these two images we can verify that in the first case, effectively, $e = 4$, as desired. Figure 6(a) shows the positions where bit quad $Q_{11} = 1$, producing the desired result. However when applying it to the shape depicted in Fig. 6(b), $e = 1$, which is wrong! Again, something is missing. By observing this figure we can that the first bit quad of set $Q_D \left(\begin{bmatrix} 1 & 0 \\ 0 & 1 \end{bmatrix} = Q_{D1} \right)$ appears three times in the image. Let us hypothesize that this bit quad can be used to produce the desired result of e when pixels appear as stairs as shown in Fig. 6(b).

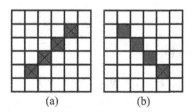

(a)   (b)

Fig. 6. (a) Image with four pixels as a stair from down-left to up-right. (b) Image with four pixels as a stair from up-right to down-left.

To produce the desired result, at least in this case, let us add the number of times Q_{D1} is detected in the image. We thus have $e = \#Q_{11} - \#Q_{34} + \#Q_{D1}$ as our new guess to compute e of an image. If we apply this new formulation to the image shown in Fig. 6(b), we can effectively see that, $e = 4$, as desired. Again, the reader can verify that the formulation $e = \#Q_{11} - \#Q_{34} + \#Q_{D1}$ provides the desired value of e for any image where their shapes are 4-connected, with holes or without holes. This new proposition can be established formally as:

Theorem 1. Let $I(x,y)$ be any 2-D binary image with o 4-connected objects and h holes. The Euler number of $I(x,y)$ as stipulated by (1) can be computed as:

$$e = \# \begin{bmatrix} 1 & 0 \\ 0 & 0 \end{bmatrix} - \# \begin{bmatrix} 1 & 1 \\ 1 & 0 \end{bmatrix} + \# \begin{bmatrix} 1 & 0 \\ 0 & 1 \end{bmatrix} \tag{9}$$

Proof. Again, by mathematical induction on the number of pixels n of the image I_n, for the base case of and image I_1 consisting of a single pixel, $\# Q_{34} = \# Q_{D1} = 0$, value satisfying Eq. (9).

Induction step: let us assume that Eq. (9) holds for the case of image I_n consisting now of n pixels. Let $n1'$, $n3'$, and nD' be the number of times bit-quads: Q_{11}, Q_{34}, and Q_{D1}, respectively are found over image I_{n+1} that is obtained by adding one pixel to the image I_n. Let $N1$, $N3$, and ND be the number of times bit-quads Q_{11}, Q_{34}, and Q_{D1} are found over this new image. We have that:

$$n1' = \# Q_{11} + N1 \tag{10}$$

$$n3' = \# Q_{34} + N3 \tag{11}$$

$$nD' = \# Q_{D1} + ND \tag{12}$$

We have to show that Eq. (9) holds for I_{n+1}, i.e.

$$e' = \# Q_{11} + N1 - \# Q_{34} - N3 + \# Q_{D1} + ND \tag{13}$$

But this equation can be rewritten as follows:

$$e' = \# Q_{11} - \# Q_{34} + \# Q_{D1} + N1 - N3 + ND. \tag{14}$$

This equation simplifies to:

$$e' = e + N1 - N3 + ND. \tag{15}$$

which we know is true.   ∎

3.2   Formulation for the 8-Connected Case

By reasoning the same way, we can introduce our second proposition to compute the Euler number of a 2-D binary image containing now 8-connected shapes:

Theorem 2. Let $I(x,y)$ be any 2-D binary image with o 8-connected objects and h holes. The Euler number of $I(x,y)$ as stipulated by (1) can be computed as:

$$e = \# \begin{bmatrix} 1 & 0 \\ 0 & 0 \end{bmatrix} - \# \begin{bmatrix} 1 & 1 \\ 1 & 0 \end{bmatrix} - \# \begin{bmatrix} 0 & 1 \\ 1 & 0 \end{bmatrix} \tag{16}$$

Proof. As for Theorem 1.

4 Experimental Results and Discussion

In this section we present several experiments to demonstrate the characteristics and advantages of our proposed formulations. In the first experiment we show the validity of Eq. (9) in the case of images containing only 4-connected shapes. We do the same for the case of 8-connected shapes in the second experiment. In short, in the third experiment, we compare our proposal against several state-of-the-art methods in terms of processing times.

4.1 Experiment 1

Here we demonstrate the validity of (9) with 100 images of different sizes and 4-connected shapes. Due to space limitations, we present the results with eight 256×256 images, these eight images are shown, as depicted in Fig. 7.

Table 1 resumes the results. Second row of this Table depicts the true values of e for these eight images, while third row shows the computed values. As predicted by

Fig. 7. Eight of the 100 4-connected images used to experimentally validate Eq. (9).

Table 1. Numerical validation of Eqs. (9) and (16).

	Image number							
	1	2	3	4	5	6	7	8
True values of e for the eight test images (4-connected case)	1	−5	−2	−6	−3	−2	−1	3
Computed values of e by means of (9)	1	−5	−2	−6	−3	−2	−1	3
True values of e for the eight test images (8-connected case)	1	−2	3	0	−1	6	−5	1
Computed values of e by means of (16)	1	−2	3	0	−1	6	−5	1

Theorem 1, in all cases the computed values coincide with the true values. The average time over 100 images was of 0.1068 s.

All the experiments were run on a desktop computer with an Intel Xeon (R) CPU 2.00 GHZ × 12 cores and 16 GB of RAM; operating system: Linux Ubuntu 14.04.3 LTS (x86_64) and kernel Linux 3.19.0-43-generic.

4.2   Experiment 2

Now we demonstrate the validity of Eq. (16) with a set of 100 images containing 8-connected shapes. Again, we present results with only eight 256 × 256 images as shown in Fig. 8.

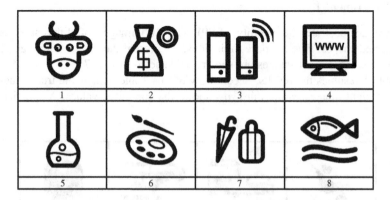

Fig. 8. Eight of the 8-connected binary images use to test Eq. (16).

Fifth row of Table 1 shows the true values of e for these eight images, while sixth row shows the computed values. As expected, again, in all cases the computed values coincide with the true values. The average time over 100 images was of 0.1048 s.

4.3   Experiment 3

As a complementary outcome to the results presented in Sects. 4.1 and 4.2, in this third sub-section we show the applicability of Eqs. (9) and (16) to 680 × 480 binary images. Three of these images are shown in Figs. 9(a), (b), and (c), respectively. They come from photos of blood cells.

Table 2 shows the computed values for e by Eqs. (9) and (16) for the three images as well as the invested processing times.

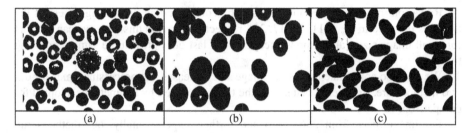

Fig. 9. Three of the 680 × 480 binary images used to test Eqs. (9) and (16).

Table 2. Numerical validation of Eqs. (9) and (16) with the three binary images of 680 × 480 pixels of Fig. 9.

	Image number		
	(j)	(b)	(c)
Computed values of e by means of Eq. (9)	−46	38	38
Invested time in seconds	0.58	0.58	0.57
Computed values of e by means of Eq. (16)	−59	38	24
Invested time in seconds	0.56	0.55	0.56

4.4 Experiment 4

In this part we compared the running times of our proposals with some of the state-of-the-art methods reported in literature. For this, we took six sets of 100 images each. Size of first set of images was of 16 × 16 pixels, size of second set was of 32 × 32 pixels, and so on until 512 × 512 pixels for sixth image set.

Average times to process the 100 images by means of the selected methods are shown in Table 3. Second and third rows of this table show the average times for processing the 100 images by means of our proposed formulations (Eqs. (9) and (16)).

Table 3. Running times in seconds of our proposed Eqs. (9) and (16) against some other state-of-the-art methods for each subset of images.

Method	16 × 16	32 × 32	64 × 64	128 × 128	256 × 256	512 × 512
Equation (9)	0.002	0.005	0.018	0.053	0.107	0.500
Equation (16)	0.002	0.005	0.018	0.052	0.105	0.479
Reference [14]	0.002	0.005	0.018	0.053	0.120	0.610
Reference [22]	0.002	0.005	0.019	0.056	0.160	0.630
Reference [5]	0.002	0.006	0.020	0.060	0.164	0.665
Reference [17]	0.008	0.022	0.090	0.252	0.700	2.790
Reference [9]	0.016	0.044	0.160	0.530	1.400	5.880
Reference [11]	0.300	0.700	1.200	7.100	15.300	74.000

Rows fourth to ninth of Table 3 show the corresponding processing times for the methods reported in [5, 9, 11, 14, 17, 22], respectively. From this table we can see that for small image sizes, all methods except for the last ones present the same processing times.

We can also appreciate that as the image size increases, the processing times for our two methods are, in general, better than the times provided by the methods adopted for comparison.

For image sizes from 256×256 and further, experimentally, our methods run faster.

5 Conclusions and Further Work

We have introduced two formulations to efficiently compute the Euler number of a 2-D binary image, one useful for the case of 4-connected regions and one useful in the case of 8-connected shapes.

Both formulations employs three comparisons unlike other proposals that utilize more comparisons. We numerically validate both formulations with very simple examples and applied them to realistic images. As shown our method is competitive compared to several state-of-the-art methods reported in literature.

Nowadays we are working through the extension of the proposed formulation to the case of 3-D binary images composed of voxels.

Acknowledgements. Humberto Sossa would like to thank IPN-CIC and CONACYT (projects SIP 20161126, and CONACYT under projects 155014 and 65 within the framework of call: Frontiers of Science 2015) for the economic support to carry out this research. Ángel Carreón thanks CONACYT for the economic support to carry out his Master studies.

References

1. Yang, H.S., Sengupta, S.: Intelligent shape recognition for complex industrial tasks. IEEE Control Syst. Mag. **8**(3), 23–30 (1988)
2. Snidaro, L., Foresti, G.L.: Real-time thresholding with Euler numbers. Pattern Recogn. Lett. **24**, 1533–1544 (2003)
3. Lin, X., Ji, J., Gu, G.: The Euler number study of image and its application. In: Proceedings of 2nd IEEE Conference on Industrial Electronics and Applications (ICIEA 2007), pp. 910–912 (2007)
4. Al Faqheri, W., Mashohor, S.: A real-time Malaysian automatic license plate recognition (M-ALPR) using hybrid fuzzy. Int. J. Comput. Sci. Netw. Secur. **9**(2), 333–340 (2009)
5. Gray, S.B.: Local properties of binary images in two dimensions. IEEE Trans. Comput. **20** (5), 551–561 (1971)
6. Dyer, C.: Computing the Euler number of an image from its quadtree. Comput. Vis. Graph. Image Process. **13**, 270–276 (1980)
7. Bieri, H., Nef, W.: Algorithms for the Euler characteristic and related additive functionals of digital objects. Comput. Vis. Graph. Image Process. **28**, 166–175 (1984)

8. Bieri, H.: Computing the Euler characteristic and related additive functionals of digital objects from their bintree representation. Comput. Vis. Graph. Image Process. **40**, 115–126 (1987)
9. Chen, M.H., Yan, P.F.: A fast algorithm to calculate the Euler number for binary images. Pattern Recogn. Lett. **8**(12), 295–297 (1988)
10. Chiavetta, F.: Parallel computation of the Euler number via connectivity graph. Pattern Recogn. Lett. **14**(11), 849–859 (1993)
11. Díaz de León, J.L., Sossa-Azuela, J.H.: On the computation of the Euler number of a binary object. Pattern Recogn. **29**(3), 471–476 (1996)
12. Bribiesca, E.: Computation of the Euler number using the contact perimeter. Comput. Math Appl. **60**, 136–137 (2010)
13. Sossa, H., Cuevas, E., Zaldivar, D.: Computation of the Euler Number of a binary image composed of hexagonal cells. J. Appl. Res. Technol. **8**(3), 340–351 (2010)
14. Sossa, H., Cuevas, E., Zaldivar, D.: Alternative way to compute the Euler Number of a binary image. J. Appl. Res. Technol. **9**(3), 335–341 (2011)
15. Imiya, A., Eckhardt, U.: The Euler characteristics of discrete objects and discrete quasi-objects. Comput. Vis. Image Underst. **75**(3), 307–318 (1999)
16. Kiderlen, M.: Estimating the Euler characteristic of a planar set from a digital image. J. Vis. Commun. Image Represent. **17**(6), 1237–1255 (2006)
17. Di Zenzo, S., Cinque, L., Levialdi, S.: Run-based algorithms for binary image analysis and processing. IEEE Trans. Pattern Anal. Mach. Intell. **18**(1), 83–89 (1996)
18. Sossa, H., Cuevas, E., Zaldivar, D.: Computation of the Euler number of a binary image composed of hexagonal cells. JART **8**(3), 340–351 (2010)
19. Sossa, H., Rubio, E., Peña, A., Cuevas, E., Santiago, R.: Alternative formulations to compute the binary shape euler number. IET-Comput. Vis. **8**(3), 171–181 (2014)
20. Yao, B., Wu, H., Yang, Y., Chao, Y., He, L.: An improvement on the euler number computing algorithm used in MATLAB. In: TECNON 2013, 2013 IEEE Region 10 Conference, 22–25 October 2013, Xi'an, China (2013)
21. He, L., Chao, Y., Suzuki, K.: A linear-time two-scan labelling algorithm. In: Proceedings of IEEE International Conference on Image Processing (ICIP 2007), San Antonio, TX, USA, September 2007, pp. V-241–V-244 (2007)
22. Feng He, L., Yan Chao, Y., Susuki, K.: An Algorithm for connected-component labeling, hole labeling and Euler number computing. J. Comput. Sci. Technol. **28**(3), 468–478 (2013)
23. He, L., Chao, Y.: A very fast algorithm for simultaneously performing connected-component labeling and Euler number computing. IEEE Trans. Image Process. **24**(9), 2725–2735 (2015)
24. Yao, B., He, L., Kang, S., Chao, Y., Zhao, X.: A novel bit–quad–based Euler number computing algorithm. SpringerPlus **4**(735), 1–16 (2015)
25. Yao, B., Kang, S., Zhao, X., Chao, Y., He, L.: A graph-theory-based Euler number computing algorithm. In: Proceedings of the 2015 IEEE International Conference on Information and Automation, Lijiang, China, pp. 1206–1209, August 2015

Image Filter Based on Block Matching, Discrete Cosine Transform and Principal Component Analysis

Alejandro I. Callejas Ramos, Edgardo M. Felipe-Riveron,
Pablo Manrique Ramirez, and Oleksiy Pogrebnyak[✉]

Instituto Politecnico Nacional, Centro de Investigacion en Computacion,
Ave. Miguel Othón de Mendizábal S/N, 07738 Mexico D.F, Mexico
ivan_grin22@hotmail.com,
{edgardo,pmanriq,olek}@cic.ipn.mx

Abstract. An algorithm for filtering the images contaminated by additive white Gaussian noise is proposed. The algorithm uses the groups of Hadamard transformed patches of discrete cosine coefficients to reject noisy components according to Wiener filtering approach. The groups of patches are found by the proposed block similarity search algorithm of reduced complexity performed on block patches in transform domain. When the noise variance is small, the proposed filter uses an additional stage based on principal component analysis; otherwise the experimental Wiener filtering is performed. The obtained filtering results are compared to the state of the art filters in terms of peak signal-to-noise ratio and structure similarity index. It is shown that the proposed algorithm is competitive in terms of signal to noise ratio and almost in all cases is superior to the state of the art filters in terms of structure similarity.

Keywords: Image filtering · Principal component analysis · Block matching

1 Introduction

Noise is one of the main factors that degrades image quality [1, 2] and often it is additive white Gaussian noise (AWGN). Despite various methods for image denoising are currently presented [2–8], researchers continue their attempts to design new, more efficient techniques. The reason is that the obtained denoising results are still not completely satisfactory for the final users.

The image denoising techniques of state of the art fall into two families [5]: (1) non-local filters [2] based on searching for similar patches and their joint processing, such as BM3D [3] and SA-DCT [4]; (2) those based on image clustering, kernel regression, singular value decomposition or principal component analysis for dictionary learning and image sparse representation [5–8].

Among the family of non-local filters, nowadays the BM3D filter [3] has been shown to be the most efficient for processing most grayscale test images [5, 9] and component-wise denoising of color test images [10] corrupted by AWGN. On the other hand, the filters based on sparse representation show good results, which in some cases

© Springer International Publishing AG 2017
G. Sidorov and O. Herrera-Alcántara (Eds.): MICAI 2016, Part I, LNAI 10061, pp. 414–424, 2017.
DOI: 10.1007/978-3-319-62434-1_34

are superior to BM3D technique [7], but this type of filters has a tremendous computational complexity due to clustering stage, dictionary learning, localized histogram and other feature calculation, and an iterative search for more sparse data representation. Besides, the iterative sparse minimization not always leads to better denoising but there is no other criterion to stop the iterations.

Another aspect is denoising filter efficiency. Usually, a mean square criterion in the form of peak signal-to-noise ratio (PSNR) is used to estimate the quality of the filtered images. Unfortunately, such an approach not always means a better visual quality nor provides a more appropriate image data for the posterior treatment and classification [12]. On the other hand there are some relatively novel image quality criterions, such as based on the properties of human visual system (PSNR-HVSM) [13, 14], feature similarity index (FSIM) [15], structure similarity index (SSIM) [16] or multiscale structure similarity index (MSSIM) [17].

In this paper, we take the advantages of both filter families. The presented filtering technique uses discrete cosine transform (DCT), the proposed block matching algorithm in the transform domain of reduced computational complexity, Hadamard transform for patch group hard thresholding [11] and Karunen-Loeve transform (KLT) hard thresholding (for a small noise variance) or Wiener filtering at the final stage. The obtained results with the proposed filter in terms of PSNR are similar to those obtained with BM3D, K-SVD [6] and NCSR [7], but are better in terms of SSIM.

The paper is organized as follows: image Wiener filtering principle is considered; a way how it reduces to a hard thresholding filter is shown in Sect. 1. Details of the proposed filtering technique are presented in Sect. 2. Numerical simulation results for the proposed filter in comparison to the best known filters of both mentioned above families are presented in Sect. 3. Finally, the conclusions follow.

2 Wiener Filtering and Thresholding in DCT Domain

Let us consider an additive observation equation (model)

$$u(x, y) = s(x, y) + n(x, y) \tag{1}$$

where $u(x, y)$ is an observed noisy image, x, y are Cartesian coordinates, $s(x, y)$ denotes a noise-free image, and $n(x, y)$ is a white Gaussian noise not correlated with $s(x, y)$. The problem is to find an estimate of the noise-free image $\hat{s}(x, y)$ such that it minimizes mean square error (MSE) $E\left\{[s(x, y) - \hat{s}(x, y)]^2\right\}$, where $E\{\cdot\}$ denotes the expectation operator.

The optimal linear filter that minimizes the MSE is the well-known Wiener filter that in the spectral domain can be formulated as [9]:

$$H_W(\omega_x, \omega_y) = \frac{P_s(\omega_x, \omega_y)}{P_s(\omega_x, \omega_y) + P_n(\omega_x, \omega_y)}, \tag{2}$$

where $P_s(\omega_x, \omega_y), P_n(\omega_x, \omega_y)$ are power spectral densities of the signal and noise, respectively. In practice, the exact power spectra densities $P_s(\omega_x, \omega_y), P_n(\omega_x, \omega_y)$ are unavailable and substituted by their estimates $\hat{P}_s(\omega_x, \omega_y), \hat{P}_n(\omega_x, \omega_y)$ that allow obtaining an estimate of the frequency response of the Wiener filter $\hat{H}_W(\omega_x, \omega_y)$. In the considered case of additive white Gaussian noise, the model for noise power spectral density is $\hat{P}_n(\omega_x, \omega_y) = \sigma^2$ where σ^2 is noise $n(x, y)$ variance, and the estimated Wiener filter transforms to

$$\hat{H}_W(\omega_x, \omega_y) = \frac{\hat{P}_s(\omega_x, \omega_y)}{\hat{P}_s(\omega_x, \omega_y) + \sigma^2}. \tag{3}$$

Let us assume the pass band cut point of -3 dB gain:

$$\hat{H}_W^{-3dB}(\omega_x, \omega_y) = \frac{\hat{P}_s^{-3dB}(\omega_x, \omega_y)}{\hat{P}_s^{-3dB}(\omega_x, \omega_y) + \sigma^2} = \frac{1}{\sqrt{2}}. \tag{4}$$

At this point, one can find the pure signal power spectrum threshold value is

$$\hat{P}_s^{-3dB}(\omega_x, \omega_y) = \frac{1}{\sqrt{2} - 1}\sigma^2 \approx 2.414\sigma^2 \tag{5}$$

On the other hand, according to the observation model (1), the power spectral density of the noisy signal can be expressed at the point of -3 dB gain as

$$P_u(\omega_x, \omega_y) = \tilde{P}_s^{-3dB}(\omega_x, \omega_y) + 2\sigma\sqrt{\tilde{P}_s^{-3dB}(\omega_x, \omega_y)} + \sigma^2. \tag{6}$$

where $\tilde{P}_s^{-3dB}(\omega_x, \omega_y)$ denotes the estimate of true signal power density at the point of -3 dB that can be derived from the periodogramm $P_u(\omega_x, \omega_y)$. Using (5), we rewrite (6) and derive the estimate $\tilde{P}_s^{-3dB}(\omega_x, \omega_y)$ in terms of $P_u(\omega_x, \omega_y)$:

$$\tilde{P}_s^{-3dB}(\omega_x, \omega_y) = P_u(\omega_x, \omega_y) - 2\sigma^2\left(\sqrt{\frac{1}{\sqrt{2} - 1}} + 1\right). \tag{7}$$

Now, consider again the frequency response of the Wiener filter but in terms of the estimate (7) at the point of -3 dB:

$$\tilde{H}_W^{-3dB}(\omega_x, \omega_y) = \frac{P_u(\omega_x, \omega_y) - 2\sigma^2\left(\sqrt{\frac{1}{\sqrt{2}-1}} + 1\right)}{P_u(\omega_x, \omega_y) - 2\sigma^2\left(\sqrt{\frac{1}{\sqrt{2}-1}} + 1\right) + \sigma^2} = \frac{1}{\sqrt{2}}. \tag{8}$$

From (8), it is possible to find the condition for the pass band cut frequency at -3 dB level of the Wiener filter:

$$P_u(\omega_x, \omega_y) = \sigma^2 \frac{2\left(\sqrt{\frac{1}{\sqrt{2}-1}}+1\right)\left(\sqrt{2}-1\right)+1}{\sqrt{2}-1} \approx 6.5217615 \cdot \sigma^2. \tag{9}$$

According to (9), the estimated Wiener filtering leads to the hard thresholding of spectral coefficients with $\beta = \sqrt{6.5217615} = 2.55377397$:

$$H_T(\omega_x, \omega_y) = \begin{cases} 1, & \text{if } |U(\omega_x, \omega_y)| \geq 2.55377397 \cdot \sigma \\ 0 & \text{otherwise} \end{cases}, \tag{10}$$

where $U(\omega_x, \omega_y)$ is the voltage spectrum of the observed noisy image $u(x, y)$, $U(\omega_x, \omega_y) = \mathscr{F}\{u(x, y)\}$, $\mathscr{F}\{\cdot\}$ denotes Fourier transform operator. The proposed hard thresholding Wiener filter (8) is an adaptive filter that can adapt its characteristics to the local spectrum properties. We propose to perform the processing in the spectral domain using the discrete cosine transform instead of Fourier transform, within the overlapped image blocks. The transform is performed using matrix multiplication

$$\mathbf{U}^{(m)} = \mathbf{T}_{DCT}^{(m)} \mathbf{u}^{(m)} \left(\mathbf{T}_{DCT}^{(m)}\right)^T \tag{11}$$

where $m \times m$ is the block size; for comparison purposes, it was chosen $m = 8$. The filtered image block then can be obtained taking the inverse transform as:

$$\mathbf{u}^{(m)} = \left(\mathbf{T}_{DCT}^{(m)}\right)^T \left(H_T(\mathbf{U}^{(m)})\right) \mathbf{T}_{DCT}^{(m)}.$$

3 Proposed Filtering Technique

In this paper, we present the advanced filtering technique based on the BM3D [11] filtering strategy that assumes the search of the similar blocks in the vicinity of the current image block, forming the lists of the patches of DCT coefficients, their processing using Hadamard transform, hard thresholding and aggregation of the processed patches to form the filtered image.

The proposed filtering technique starts with the pre-processing stage forming the DCT patches for each image pixel in the range of $(M - m) \times (N - m)$ pixels, $M \times N$ is the image size, $m = 8$. Then, at this step the search of similar image blocks using the DCT transformed data is performed. After the pre-processing, the first filtering pass performed forming the pre-filtered image for the final filtering, where the noisy image is treated using the pre-filtered one; for a small noise variance, sparse filtering using KLT is performed, and in the case when the noise level is high, empirical Wiener filtering is performed according to (3).

3.1   Similar Block Searching Algorithm

When the DCT block patches are calculated according to (11), the proposed algorithm starts searching for similar patches within a defined range. It is a kind of hierarchical search that starts from calculating the distances from the mean value of the current i,j-th image block and the mean values of the block patches within the search range; these values correspond to the direct current (DC) component $\omega_x = \omega_y = 0$ of the spectrum:

$$\mathbf{d}^1(i,j) = \left\{ \left(U_{1,1}(i,j) - U_{1,1}(i \pm shift, j \pm shift) \right)^2 \right\}, \tag{12}$$

where $U_{1,1}(i,j)$ is the DC component, the parameter *shift* defines the range of the searching area. Then, the distances are sorted, and the half of the found blocks is considered for the more precise searching using DCT coefficients of the found blocks at the next step:

$$\mathbf{d}^2(i,j) = \left\{ \left(U_{p,q}(i,j) - d_k^1 \left(i,j, U_{p,q}^{\mathbf{d}^1(i,j)} \right) \right)^2 \middle| p,q \in \overline{1,5}; k \in \overline{1(shift+1)^2/2} \right\}, \tag{13}$$

where $d_k^1(\cdot)$ denotes the k-th patch of DCT coefficients found at the first step. Note, that p,q varies from 1 to $5 < m^2$ excluding at this step the DC component, $U_{1,1}$. The computational complexity of the proposed search technique is lower than in the case of the calculation of all distances between pixels of the current block $\mathbf{u}^{(m)}$ and the pixels of all blocks within the $(shift+1)^2$ range.

At the final stage of the block searching, the list of the patch coordinates, $\mathbf{l}_U(i,j) = \{l_1(i,j)...l_{b_{max}}(i,j)\}$, where $l_1(i,j)...l_{b_{max}}(i,j)$, b_{max} is the maximal number of similar patches, and the distances $\mathbf{d}(i,j)$ are recorded for their usage in the filtering process.

3.2   Sparse Filtering Using Hadamard Transform of the DCT Patches

At the second stage, a preliminary filtering is performed forming the image estimate for the third stage. Before the filtering, the estimate of the current i,j-th image block data spectrum $\hat{P}_s$ is calculated using the list of patches $\mathbf{l}_U(i,j)$:

$$\hat{P}_s(i,j) = \sum_{k=1}^{b_{max}/2} U_k(l_k(i,j)) \cdot w_k^P(i,j), \tag{14}$$

where $w_k^P(i,j)$ is a normalized weighting coefficient calculated on the patch distances as

$$w_k^P(i,j) = \frac{\exp\{-d_k(i,j)/200\}}{\|\mathbf{w}^P(i,j)\|}, \tag{15}$$

where $\|\mathbf{w}^P(i,j)\|$ denotes the sum of the non-normalized coefficients $w_k^P(i,j)$.

With the estimate $\hat{P}_s$, the provisional Wiener filter frequency response at i,j-th block position $\hat{H}_{i,j}(\omega_x, \omega_y)$ is formed according to (3). Next, Hadamard transform in the third dimension is applied to the group of patches $\mathbf{U}(i,j) = \{\mathbf{U}_k(l_k(i,j)), k = \overline{1, b_{\max}}\}$

$$\mathbf{U}_{Hadamard} = Hadamard\{\mathbf{U}(i,j)\}. \tag{16}$$

Then, we propose to apply the following thresholding procedure:

$$\tilde{\mathbf{U}}_{Hadamard} = \begin{cases} \mathbf{U}_{Hadamard}(\omega_x, \omega_y) & if\ \omega_x = \omega_y = 0 \\ else\ \mathbf{U}_{Hadamard}(\omega_x, \omega_y) & if\ |\mathbf{U}_{Hadamard}(\omega_x, \omega_y)| \geq T(\omega_x, \omega_y), \\ 0 & otherwise \end{cases} \tag{17}$$

where the fuzzy thresholds are formed according to $\hat{H}_{i,j}(\omega_x, \omega_y)$ as

$$T(\omega_x, \omega_y) = \begin{cases} \beta_{\min} \cdot \sigma & if\ \hat{H}_{i,j}(\omega_x, \omega_y) > 0.87 \\ \beta_{\max} \cdot \sigma & f\ \hat{H}_{i,j}(\omega_x, \omega_y) < 0.3 \\ \beta \cdot \sigma & otherwise \end{cases}, \tag{18}$$

and $\beta_{\min} = 1$, $\beta_{\max} = 2.9$; $\beta = 2.55377397$ according to Eq. (10).

After the thresholding and the inverse Hadamard transform, $\tilde{\mathbf{U}}(i,j) = Hadamard^{-1}\{\tilde{\mathbf{U}}_{Hadamard}\}$ the aggregation is performed. Note that, opposite to scanning window filtering, the filtered values are obtained simultaneously for all pixels of a given block and for all patches in the group $\mathbf{l}(i,j)$. The averaged aggregation is performed as

$$\hat{\mathbf{s}}_\Sigma(\mathbf{l}_U(i,j)) = \sum_{k=1}^{b_{\max}} (\hat{\mathbf{U}}_k(l_k(i,j))) \cdot w_k^A(i,j), R_\Sigma(\mathbf{l}_U(i,j)) = \sum_{k=1}^{b_{\max}} w_k^A(i,j),$$
$$w_k^A,(i,j) = \exp\{-d_k(i,j)/500\}, (\tilde{\mathbf{s}})_* = \frac{(\hat{\mathbf{s}}_\Sigma)_*}{(\mathbf{R}_\Sigma)_*} \tag{19}$$

where $\hat{\mathbf{s}}_\Sigma(\mathbf{l}(i,j))$ are the sum of the blocks defined by the list $\mathbf{l}(i,j)$, $R_\Sigma(\mathbf{l}(i,j))$ is the sum of weighting coefficients $w_k^A(i,j)$, $\tilde{\mathbf{s}}$ is the estimated image obtained from the pre-filtering stage, $()_*$ denotes element-wise operations.

3.3   Final Filtering Using Sparse Representation Minimization

At the third stage, if the noise variance is greater than or equal to 100, $\sigma^{2|} \geq 100$, the empirical Wiener filtering is applied to the groups of blocks found at the first stage, $\mathbf{l}(i,j)$:

$$\mathbf{U}_{Hadamard} = Hadamard\{\mathbf{U}(i,j)\},$$

$$\tilde{\mathbf{S}}_{Hadamard} = Hadamard\{\tilde{\mathbf{S}}(i,j)\}, \ \tilde{\mathbf{S}}(i,j) = \{\tilde{\mathbf{S}}_k(l_k(i,j)), \ k = \overline{1, b_{\max}}\}$$

$$\hat{\mathbf{U}}(i,j) = Hadamard^{-1}\left\{(\mathbf{U}_{Hadamard})_* \frac{(\tilde{\mathbf{S}})_*}{(\tilde{\mathbf{S}} + \sigma^2)_*}\right\}, \tag{20}$$

where $\tilde{\mathbf{S}} = \mathbf{T}_{DCT}\tilde{\mathbf{s}}(\mathbf{T}_{DCT})^T$ is DCT transform of the prefiltered image block $\tilde{\mathbf{s}}$.

And for small noise variances, $\sigma^{2|} < 100$, we propose to use the following treatment: if the block local variance is small, i.e., less than $2\sigma^{2|}$, the block estimation is $\hat{\mathbf{s}} = \tilde{\mathbf{s}}$, otherwise, sparse representation minimization is performed. To this end, firstly the covariance matrix of the (i,j) image block is formed as follows:

$$\mathbf{C}(i,j) = \frac{(\mathbf{s}(i,j) - \tilde{\mathbf{s}}(i,j)) \cdot (\mathbf{s}(i,j) - \tilde{\mathbf{s}}(i,j))^T}{m \times m - 1}. \tag{21}$$

Note that the prefiltered data $\tilde{\mathbf{s}}$ are used here as an estimate of the mean pixel values to produce better filtering results.

Then, eigenvectors $\mathbf{Q}$ of $\mathbf{C}(i,j)$ are determined and KLT of the first two blocks in the list $\mathbf{l}(i,j)$ is calculated: $\mathbf{S} = \mathbf{Q}(\mathbf{s}(i,j) - \tilde{\mathbf{s}}(i,j))$. Next, hard thresholding is performed

$$\left(\hat{\mathbf{S}}\right)_* = \begin{cases} (\mathbf{S})_* & if (\mathbf{S})_* < 2.7\sigma \\ 0 & otherwise \end{cases}, \tag{22}$$

the block data estimate is obtained

$$\hat{\mathbf{s}} = \mathbf{Q}^T\hat{\mathbf{S}} + \tilde{\mathbf{s}}. \tag{23}$$

Finally, the aggregation of the processed two blocks similar to (19) is calculated using the weights $w_k(i,j) = \exp\{-d_k(i,j)/40\}$.

4 Results

The numerical simulations using standard test images with plain regions "Lena", "F-16", "peppers" and textural images "aerial", "baboon", "bridge" are performed. For the comparison purposes, three best state-of-the-art filters, K-SVD, BM3D (with the same search area defined by the parameter *shift* = 21) and NCSR were used.

The filtering results are illustrated in Fig. 1, and the obtained values of PSNR and SSIM are presented in Tables 1 and 2, respectively. The visual quality of the images processed by the considered filters is very similar, although NCSR presents some over smoothing and BM3D sometime introduces visible artifacts.

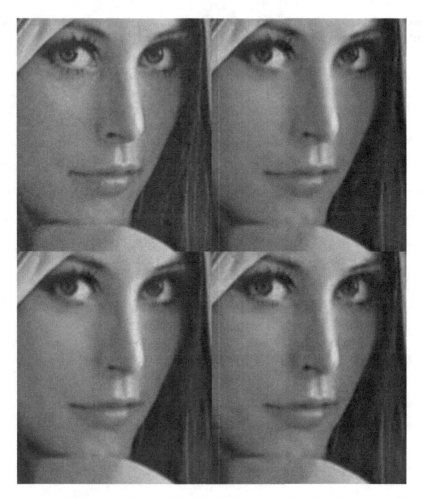

Fig. 1. Augmented fragments of image "Lena" distorted with $\sigma^{2|} = 225$ AWGN and processed by different filters (from left to right and top to bottom): original, NCSR, BM3D, proposed.

From the data presented in Tables 1 and 2 it follows that the proposed filtering technique is competitive with the state-of-the-art filters in PSNR sense, but almost in all cases is superior in term of SSIM.

Table 1. Results of the filtering of the standard test images with different techniques in terms of PSNR. The best results are marked as bold.

Image	σ^2	Noisy	K-SVD	BM3D	NCSR	Proposed
Lena	25	34.14	38.554	38.686	38.674	**38.801**
	100	28.132	35.428	**35.906**	35.866	35.888
	225	24.616	33.544	**34.263**	34.175	34.169
	400	22.137	32.21	**33.056**	32.867	32.895
F-16	25	34.14	39.067	39.258	39.232	**39.286**
	100	28.132	35.479	**35.854**	35.849	35.837
	225	24.627	33.4	33.886	**33.887**	33.855
	400	22.191	31.928	**32.508**	32.443	32.468
peppers	25	34.146	37.657	37.609	**37.866**	37.774
	100	28.167	34.766	35.024	**35.081**	35.009
	225	24.681	33.239	**33.732**	33.69	33.621
	400	22.22	32.073	**32.723**	32.613	32.564
aerial	25	34.145	36.673	**37.08**	37.04	36.98
	100	28.142	32.289	**32.792**	32.789	32.637
	225	24.644	29.879	30.438	**30.481**	30.329
	400	22.199	28.187	**28.835**	28.812	28.765
baboon	25	34.141	35.177	35.247	35.264	**35.277**
	100	28.135	30.451	30.61	30.598	**30.696**
	225	24.618	*27.960*	28.217	28.232	**28.318**
	400	22.129	*26.307*	26.642	26.64	**26.772**
bridge	25	34.159	35.578	**35.765**	35.695	35.698
	100	28.169	30.94	**31.207**	31.143	31.157
	225	24.682	28.544	28.822	28.824	**28.842**
	400	22.23	26.98	27.284	27.259	**27.377**

Table 2. Results of the filtering of the standard test images with different techniques in terms of SSIM. The best results are marked as bold.

Image	σ^2	Noisy	KSVD	BM3D	NCSR	Proposed
Lena	25	0.650071	0.729343	0.706594	0.702052	**0.729986**
	100	0.434195	0.612688	0.620161	0.616173	**0.635876**
	225	0.321075	0.54803	0.570386	0.564288	**0.582004**
	400	0.250943	0.503566	0.532345	0.516749	**0.538954**
F-16	25	0.573694	0.677342	0.67417	0.664878	**0.687661**
	100	0.407647	0.571205	0.583485	0.574901	**0.595023**
	225	0.322104	0.516994	0.531316	0.520495	**0.540428**
	400	0.266426	0.477619	0.493573	0.470992	**0.500174**
peppers	25	0.698161	0.742456	0.704669	**0.736183**	0.735144
	100	0.460156	0.588543	0.579873	0.588272	**0.60069**
	225	0.334244	0.526644	0.534485	0.527292	**0.548582**
	400	0.259053	0.490874	0.503144	0.487441	**0.514074**

(*continued*)

Table 2. (*continued*)

Image	σ^2	Noisy	KSVD	BM3D	NCSR	Proposed
aerial	25	0.84257	0.899446	**0.907226**	0.900802	0.906303
	100	0.697669	0.81245	0.832167	0.826998	**0.832912**
	225	0.587101	0.740628	0.771846	0.768144	**0.772791**
	400	0.500772	0.671283	0.71822	0.707465	**0.720075**
baboon	25	0.91839	**0.929301**	0.926673	0.924035	0.927581
	100	0.790511	0.824671	0.828144	0.81302	**0.841045**
	225	0.678611	0.733180	0.751595	0.734304	**0.76799**
	400	0.585645	0.654664	0.685388	0.65984	**0.706898**
bridge	25	0.913643	0.938448	**0.941021**	0.937837	0.939819
	100	0.780924	0.849257	0.859999	0.854613	**0.863266**
	225	0.658758	0.755813	0.777584	0.774548	**0.787016**
	400	0.556196	0.666819	0.701251	0.691471	**0.718897**

5 Conclusions

A filtering technique to process the images contaminated by additive white Gaussian noise has been presented. The algorithm uses discrete cosine transform and the groups of patches similar to the current image block, which are found using the proposed search algorithm of reduced complexity. The noisy components are rejected according to Wiener filtering approach using Hadamard transform for thresholding and weighted aggregation. An additional stage based on principal component analysis or experimental Wiener filtering is performed to form the final image. The obtained filtering results in comparison to the state-of-the-art filters, such as K-SVD, BM3D, NCSR show that the proposed algorithm is competitive in terms of signal to noise ratio and almost in all cases is superior in terms of structure similarity; meanwhile, the visual quality of the considered filters is very similar although the proposed filter does not over smooth the image details nor introduce visible artifacts.

Acknowledgment. This work partially was supported by Instituto Politecnico Nacional as a part of research project SIP#20161173.

References

1. Pratt, W.K.: Digital Image Processing, 4th edn. Wiley-Interscience, New York (2007)
2. Buades, A., Coll, B., Morel, J.M.: A review of image denoising algorithms, with a new one. J. SIAM **2**(4), 490–530 (2005)
3. Dabov, K., Foi, A., Katkovnik, V., Egiazarian, K.: Image denoising by sparse 3D transform-domain collaborative filtering. IEEE Trans. Image Process. **16**(8), 2080–2095 (2007)
4. Foi, A., Katkovnik, V., Egiazarian, K.: Pointwise shape-adaptive DCT for high-quality denoising and deblocking of grayscale and color images. IEEE Trans. Image Process. **16**(5), 1395–1411 (2007)

5. Chatterjee, P., Milanfar, P.: Is denoising dead? IEEE Trans. Image Process. **19**(4), 895–911 (2010)

6. Aharon, M., Elad, M., Bruckstein, A.M.: K-SVD: an algorithm for designing overcomplete dictionaries for sparse representation. IEEE Trans. Signal Process. **54**(11), 4311–4322 (2006)

7. Dong, W., Zhang, L., Shi, G., Li, X.: Nonlocally centralized sparse representation for image restoration. IEEE Trans. Image Process. **22**(4), 1620–1630 (2013)

8. He, N., Wang, J.-B., Zhang, L.-L., Xu, G.-M., Lu, K.: Non-local sparse regularization model with application to image denoising. Multimed. Tools Appl. **75**(5), 2579–2594 (2016)

9. Pogrebnyak, O., Lukin, V.V.: Wiener discrete cosine transform-based image filtering. J. Electron. Imaging **21**(4), 043020-1–043020-1 (2012). doi:10.1117/1.JEI.21.4.043020. USA, ISSN 1017-9909

10. Fevralev, D., Lukin, V., Ponomarenko, N., Abramov, S., Egiazarian, K., Astola, J.: Efficiency analysis of color image filtering. EURASIP J. Adv. Signal Process. **2011**, 41 (2011). doi:10.1186/1687-6180-2011-41

11. Lebrun, M.: An analysis and implementation of the BM3D image denoising method http://dx.doi.org/. Image Process. Line **2**, 175–213 (2012). http://dx.doi.org/10.5201/ipol.2012.l-bm3d

12. Lukin, V., Abramov, S., Krivenko, S., Kurekin, A., Pogrebnyak, O.: Analysis of classification accuracy for pre-filtered multichannel remote sensing data. Expert Syst. Appl. **40**(16), 6400–6411 (2013). doi:10.1016/j.eswa.2013.05.061. ISSN 0957-4174

13. Egiazarian, K., Astola, J., Ponomarenko, N., Lukin, V., Battisti, F., Carli, M.: New full-reference quality metrics based on HVS. In: CD-ROM Proceedings of the Second International Workshop on Video Processing and Quality Metrics, Scottsdale, USA (2006), 4 p

14. Ponomarenko, N., Silvestri, F., Egiazarian, K., Carli, M., Lukin, V.: On between-coefficient contrast masking of DCT basis functions. In: CD-ROM Proceedings of Third International Workshop on Video Processing and Quality Metrics for Consumer Electronics VPQM-07 (2007), 4 p

15. Zhang, L., Zhang, L., Mou, X., Zhang, D.: FSIM: a feature similarity index for image quality assessment. IEEE Trans. Image Process. **20**(8), 2378–2386 (2011)

16. Wang, Z., Bovik, A.C., Sheikh, H.R., Simoncelli, E.P.: Image quality assessment: from error visibility to structural similarity. IEEE Trans. Image Process. **13**(4), 600–612 (2004). doi:10.1109/TIP.2003.819861. ISSN 1057-7149

17. Wang, Z., Simoncelli, E.P., Bovik, A.C.: Multiscale structural similarity for image quality assessment. In: Conference Record of the Thirty-Seventh Asilomar Conference on Signals, Systems and Computers, 1 November 2003, vol. 2, pp. 1398–1402 (2004). doi:10.1109/ACSSC.2003.1292216

Support to the Diagnosis of the Pap Test, Using Computer Algorithms of Digital Image Processing

Solangel Rodríguez-Vázquez[✉]

Centro de Geoinformática y Señales Digitales (GEYSED),
Universidad de las Ciencias Informáticas, Havana, Cuba
svazquez@uci.cu

Abstract. 40 years ago, uterine cervix cancer represented one of the greatest threats of cancer death among women. With continued advances in medicine and technology, deaths from this disease have declined significantly. The investigations concerning this issue have been determined key symptoms to detect the disease in time to give timely treatment. Conventional cytology is one of the most commonly used techniques being widely accepted because it´s inexpensive, and provide many control mechanisms. In order to alleviate the workload to specialists, some researchers have proposed the development of computer vision tools to detect and classify the changes in the cells of the cervix region. This research aims to provide researchers with an automatic classification tool applicable to the conditions in medical and research centers in the country. This tool classifies the cells of the cervix, based solely on the features extracted from the nucleus region and reduces the rate of false negative Pap test. From the study, a tool using the technique k-nearest neighbors with distance Manhattan, which showed high performance while maintaining AUC values greater than 91% and reaching 97.1% with a sensitivity of 96% and 88% of obtained specificity.

Keywords: Uterine cervical cancer · Cervical cells · Cell classification · kNN · Cell nucleus · Pap test

1 Introduction

Cytological test, also called Pap smear or Pap test is a screening gynecological that allows to appreciate changes in the morphology of cells of the cervix [1]. In these samples, cells from inside and surrounding the cervix area are taken. The cells are extended on a slide or sheet glass, and sent to a lab for processing. The observation and analysis of tissues let you check the status of the cells. This test allows an early warn about even asymptomatic anomalies in the female genital tract, contributing to improve the quality of life of women. This study diagnoses infections, disorders and morphological changes in cells of the uterus neck and body. It can warn of such a common condition in women and cancer of the cervix, which facilitates early detection and treatment increases the chances of healing.

© Springer International Publishing AG 2017
G. Sidorov and O. Herrera-Alcántara (Eds.): MICAI 2016, Part I, LNAI 10061, pp. 425–436, 2017.
DOI: 10.1007/978-3-319-62434-1_35

The Pap test, due to the massive nature of its application in the female population, generates considerable workload for laboratories that analyze cytological smears resulting from this technique under the microscope. In a typical smear can be found up to 300,000 cells, limiting productivity to no more than a 60–80 Pap smears per working day and observer [2]. From the experience of the application of this test for many years, it has been determined that there are different factors that affect the quality of the results. These are mainly errors taking the samples, processing, reading and interpretation [2]. About the latter case, the need to analyze a large number of samples with very low rate of positive cases tends to skew the outcome of the evaluation. Also it causes errors due to fatigue routine and analysts.

As a result of the different mentioned errors, a certain rate of false negatives can affect the final result. These imply that a precursor lesion to progress, or carcinoma *in situ* (curable) can become an invasive cancer, without the patient being subjected to any treatment [2].

Traditional methods used in the detection of premalignant cells in the female uterus are based on microscopic analysis, molecular methods or transmission electron microscopy tests and polymerase chain reaction (PCR techniques called) [3]. Now it is more common to use data capture systems, which have robust tools or image processing modules. These tools allow full recognition and treatment of the particles or microorganisms in the sampled images [4].

The analysis of microscopy images is increasingly important for both, the generation of diagnostics and for research carried out in the Computer Science and Health. Therefore, the development of new techniques that made a practical analysis of samples is necessary. Among these is the cell vaginal epithelium level [4], which provides information for detecting cell strains and diseases, leading to early diagnosis or prevent treatments.

This research aims to provide specialists with a tool to support them in the classification of cervical cells at the time of evaluating them. It will reduce the effort of technical personnel as well as decrease the rate of false negatives in the final result. This tool also decreases the costs of spending on purchase equipment for carrying out this task.

2   Related Works

Despite the proven effectiveness of Pap smears in reducing the incidence of cervical cancer, many have worried about the accuracy of this diagnostic test [5], which depends on its specificity and sensitivity to detect.

Because of the concern of doctors to the occurrence of false negative finding methods who match effectively on the evidence and the interpretation thereof it has been necessary. Added to this is the need to increase the productivity of laboratories and reduce the rate of false negatives.

Several methods have been proposed for the classification of cells in images of the Pap test and refer to techniques such as Bayesian classifiers [6], artificial neural networks [7], support vector machines (SVM) [8] and k-nearest neighbors algorithm (kNN) [9]. It should be noted that most of these methods use pre-segmented images that contain only one cell, so that the correct segmentation of the nucleus and cyto-plasm is feasible (Fig. 1 (a)).

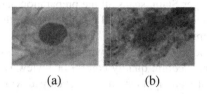

(a)   (b)

Fig. 1. (a) Image of a single cell, (b) image overlapping cells

Methods using digital image processing and computer vision, have begun to play an important role in recent years. In [10] systems are exposed as *AutoPap systems Primary Screening System (Tri-Path Imaging), BD FocalPointTM Slide Profiler, ThinPrep Imaging System, AutoPap Primary Screening System (Tri-Path Imaging).* Mas et al. [10] presents an assessment of the state of the art and states that brings together the technologies that preceded Autocyte SCREEN (Roche), Auto-Pap (Neo-Path) and PAPNET (Neuromedical Systems). These technologies are used to maintain by a new analysis of negative cases, control of the quality of work done by human analysts. The cases are suspect, undergo further analysis. It is designed for primary screening to detect squamous carcinoma, adenocarcinoma and precursor forms. Scans sheets of conventional Pap smear and classified samples according to the abnormality level. This system was designed to look for anomalies sheet by sheet, and to exclude 25% of the sheets with the lowest risk.

These sheets were automatically excluded from the list that require manual microscopic review and reduce the work of examiners 25% [11]. It also carries out the analysis of samples in two forms: primary and secondary screening. In the primary screening is diagnosed with high reliability pursues a certain percentage of cases as negative, thereby reducing the workload of analysts. An evaluation of this technique reveals that while its negative predictive value is very high, a small rate of false negatives [12] still appears.

During the early years of the century, has been adopted as a method for preparing samples the liquid-based cytology (CBL) because it resolves five fundamental prob-lems [3]: (1) lack of capturing the entire sample, (2) poor fixation, (3) random distri-bution of abnormal cells, (4) existence of disturbing elements and (5) poor quality of the smear. This technique increases the sensitivity of high-grade intraepithelial lesions and carcinomas, without variation in specificity.

BD FocalPoint Slide Profiler TM: is a tool for automated evaluation of pap smear tests currently available. It is designed for use in the initial screening for cervical cytology sheets. The FocalPoint identifies up to 25% successfully processed sheets that do not need further review. It also identifies at least 15% of the processed sheets Successfully for a second manual review. It can be used with conventional preparations and cervical cytology sheets SurePath (formerly AutoCyte®PREP). In both preparation methods, this tool detects sheets with evidence of squamous cell carcinoma and ade-nocarcinoma and their usual precursor cells conditions [11].

Another tool that increases the productivity of human analyst to over 300 sheets per day is ThinPrep Imaging System. This allows a significant increase in sensitivity, but also somewhat reduced specificity. It is designed for liquid-based cytology and to be stained with Hologic Imager Stain, scans all the preparation and selected 22 fields that are displayed by the reader doing revision. If a fault in one of the 22 fields is suspected, a full screening of the preparation is done. This system does not assign categories to preparations and are able to select those without abnormalities and do not require review or select those that require quality control or review [13].

In 2015, in Peru a software application was developed with remote access through the Web [14], aiming to increase productivity and improve the results achieved in conducting such tests in polyclinics public health in that country. This research, like this, have in common lower costs of buying computers that perform this type of image processing as the above.

This research unlike other do not need many hardware features for performance only ensure that the processing is flexible as possible. It uses only text files with the features of each of the cells so it does not need a database storage, or much disk space for its persistence over time. Next, the operation mode and the specifications of the tool developed is explained.

3   Proposed Methodology

The need to streamline and increase the quality of cytological tests, serves as motivation for building a support tool for early detection of possible diseases in the cervix. Using classification algorithms, and comparing a training base with an array of features extracted from the images to evaluate, can get a classification of cells obtained through cytological test.

A cytological test sample contains several cells itself. These cells overlap interfering with the delimitation of the region of the cytoplasm of ones and others. Conversely, if the nucleus is possible to identify, as shown in Fig. 2 (a) and (b). The region of the cell nucleus is more feasible to be accurately segmented by digital image processing. Answering previous investigations [15, 16] and to the above, the tests and samples used in the validation of the tool are the features extracted from the nucleus region.

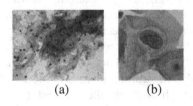

(a)   (b)

Fig. 2. Overlapping cells with identification of the nucleus

3.1   Characterization of Process Stages

In Fig. 3 the flow diagram shown the tool developed. This solution consists of two phases: validation and classification. Matrices traits (training base (m × n)) and (test (m × n)) are first validated (structurally) so they can be used by the classifier, where m is the case y n traits associated with cases. After validating the internal structure of these matrices of traits, qualifying provides results in a matrix result (m × 1) containing the classification of cells in diseased or healthy in the same order they appear in the matrix proof.

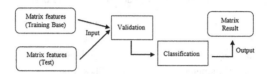

Fig. 3. Flow diagram of the proposed solution

In the validation phase is proposed that input matrices features (training base and test) possess an internal structure as follows, because it is the structure that recognizes the implemented tool (Fig. 4):

```
1 1:1410 2:139.882251 3:38.49138889 4:46.8209946 5:0.905531895
1 1:1948 2:166.6101731 3:42.96818515 4:57.88582281 5:0.881852165
1 1:1487 2:143.882251 3:39.32615747 4:48.27557167 5:0.902622978
1 1:1623 2:148.1248917 3:42.35424047 4:48.86739614 5:0.929549009
-1 1:4524 2:269.8650071 3:58.63828838 4:98.82672345 5:0.78061935
-1 1:3078 2:275.6639969 3:58.97125237 4:68.24491694 5:0.509000703
-1 1:2267 2:206.7523087 3:43.91737894 4:66.93235594 5:0.666439375
-1 1:3499 2:231.8650071 3:60.70398481 4:74.32903026 5:0.81786832
```

Fig. 4. Matrix structure features (Base training)

The first value represents the case classification (1 for normal cases and −1 for abnormal cases), then a structure is observed n r, where n represents the trait that can vary from feature 1 … feature k always ascending, the (:) separator act as r represents the value of the extracted cell trait. The test files, have the same structure with the difference that the value of the classification of the case always take the value 0.

To carry out the qualifying round must have obtained prior matrices features (knowledge base) and (test file) to classify. Subsequently sorting functionality is used and the tool returns a file containing the classification (sick or well) cells in the same order found in the test file.

3.2   Description and Methodology of Using the Proposed Algorithms

In images containing groups of cells (Fig. 1 (b)), cytoplasm border detection is a difficult problem. So far, don't exist any technique in the consulted literature that mentions studied algorithms with good results in the delimitation of the borders of the region of the cytoplasm. However, detection and segmentation of nucleus containing images overlapping cells and cell clusters has been successfully addressed in several studies [17, 18].

Methods relating to image classification based on Pap calculating the features extracted from both the nucleus region and the cytoplasm (Table 1). For this investigation, this analysis is important because the input to the classifier is a matrix [cases × features].

Table 1. Features extracted of each image in the database [19]

Features of cytoplasm	Features of the nucleus
1. Area	1. Area
2. Brightness	2. Brightness
3. Short diameter	3. Short diameter
4. Longer diameter	4. Longer diameter
5. Elongation	5. Elongation
6. Roundness	6. Roundness
7. Perimeter	7. Perimeter
8. Maxim[1]	8. Maxim[1]
9. Minimum[1]	9. Minimum[1]
10. The Nucleus Position	
11. Size Nucleus / Cytoplasm	

[1]The number of pixels with the value of maximum / minimum intensity in an area of 3 × 3 of the specific region.

In [15] use of the nine nucleus features proposed in [19], set as spectral clustering techniques and fuzzy c-means with dimensionality reduction it is made. Unlike the present research is directed towards the selection of an unreduced classifier, only five of the nine features are used: area, perimeter, short diameter, longest diameter and roundness. This selection seeks to demonstrate that, from a simplified set of basic geometric data, it is possible to effectively binary classification of images on the Pap test [20].

Feature extraction is one of the fundamental steps in image processing because with better selection of the attributes, more successful will be the final classification of cells. This makes the proper selection of features one of the limitations in research for image classification. Without the appropriate features, the results obtained by the classifier will not have the quality needed. In this research the feature matrices used were extracted from the previously segmented images (Fig. 5 (b)) belonging to the Herlev database [19].

(a)   (b)

Fig. 5. Abnormal cells. (A) RGB image, (b) Segmented image in which the region corresponding to the nucleus is highlighted in light blue and at which he performs the calculation of the proposed features

4   Results and Discussion

To comply with the proposed in this research objective was defined the use of three classification algorithms for comparison and subsequent selection: the support vector machines (SVM) [8], k-nearest neighbors algorithm (kNN) [9] and artificial neural networks (ANN) [7]. In order to estimate the capacity of discrimination of internal parameters for the operation of these algorithms a series of experiments using the kernels (RBF [8], Linear [8]) in SVM case, distances (Euclidean [9], Manhattan [9], Mahalanobis [9]) for kNN and two RNA (Multilayer Perceptron [7], RBF Network [7]). For this experimental scheme, cross-validation of k partitions (k-fold cross validation) was used. The same data sets were tested for each classifier, both internal comparisons of these algorithms and subsequent comparison there between. For comparisons of the results in each algorithm, the three partitions that best results showed as to the Pn measures, area under the ROC curve (AUC) and the harmonic mean H and F were used.

In this research were used to evaluate the effectiveness of different classifications used, rates of effectiveness, known as sensitivity, specificity, positive and negative predictability and correct classification rate. Other indices of effectiveness used in this research to assess distances in the classifier were the area under the ROC curve and measures F and H, given by:

$$F - \text{measure} = 2 \times (\text{Precision} \times S_e)\text{Precision} + S_e \tag{1}$$

$$H - \text{mean} = (2 \times (S_p \times S_e))/(S_p + S_e) \tag{2}$$

Through a comparison made by the author of the internal characteristics with which algorithms show the best results in the classification of these cells were obtained. The SVM algorithm with the kernel RBF showed results in the classification behave between 78% and 86% negative predictivity (Pn) as well as its low computational cost than the linear kernel which showed Pn between 79% and 85% with a high computational cost. In the case of neural networks compared evidenced that RBF Network is more efficient at the time of classification behaving between 81 and 91% of Pn compared to the neural network MLP that maintained behavior between 81% and 86%. Using the algorithm kNN, the distance Manhattan get results showed in qualifying that behave between 84 and 93% of Pn with respect to the Mahalanobis distance was 84 and 90% of Pn. For the selection of these characteristics were taken into account also the values obtained in terms of effectiveness rates below are also used in this investigation. These algorithms yielded results that demonstrate the efficiency of each in the classification of the cervical cells.

To determine the relative quality of the results a comparison between the above classifiers was performed using own application written in Java and were also the package WEKA Data mining was used.

4.1   Comparative Analysis of Classifiers

For the selection of the classifier used in the developed application it was necessary to assess the existence of any significant difference to demonstrate the superiority of a classifier over others. To this end the recommendations made by Demšar [21] and extensions made by Garcia and Herrera [22] were followed. Was perform a statistical analysis by nonparametric tests for unrelated samples k by Friedman test [21] in order to test the null hypothesis that all classifiers achieve the same results on average. As post-hoc test it was first applied the Bonferroni-Dunn test [21] to define significant differences between the top-ranked classifier and the next. To compare the results Holm test [21] was applied.

Tables 2, 3 and 4 show the experimental results of the three classifiers (SVM with kernel RBF, kNN with RNA Manhattan distance and RBF Network) for each of the partitions made in the dataset. The last two rows show the ranking of each of the classifiers and position. After statistically analyzing the results to test for significant differences between classifiers for each of the measures used, it was found that the Friedman test rejected the null hypothesis for AUC with a value of $p = 0.01$ and for measuring F with $p = 0.04$, while for Pn no significant differences were found. For this reason, only post-hoc test for measurement and measurement AUC F. For both measures were applied the Bonferroni-Dunn and Holm test rejected the null hypothesis for $p \leq 0.025$ values of $p \leq 0.05$ respectively, with a confidence value $\alpha = 0.05$ (Tables 5 and 6). The results presented in Table 5 show that the kNN classifier has better performance than SVM and equivalent RNA made for partitioning data. In the case of Table 6, the results presented show that the classifier RNA has a better performance than SVM and kNN equivalent for partitioning made of the data.

Table 2. Results for AUC for the classifiers

Partitions	SVM	kNN	RNA
1	0.82	0.913	0.865
2	0.814	0.948	0.928
3	0.894	0.952	0.94
4	0.901	0.945	0.94
5	0.90	0.971	0.971
6	0.856	0.925	0.92
7	0.888	0.951	0.939
Ranking	2.99	1.07	1.92
Position	3	1	2

Table 3. Results obtained for Pn by classifiers

Partitions	SVM	kNN	RNA
1	0.74	0.77	0.73
2	0.79	0.79	0.80
3	0.87	0.85	0.89
4	0.85	0.8	0.84
5	0.81	0.88	0.86
6	0.82	0.83	0.81
7	0.89	0.93	0.91
Ranking	2.21	1.78	2.0
Position	3	1	2

Table 4. F for measuring results by classifiers.

Partitions	SVM	kNN	RNA
1	0.863	0.88	0.909
2	0.866	0.872	0.884
3	0.923	0.918	0.928
4	0.923	0.897	0.918
5	0.914	0.934	0.929
6	0.895	0.901	0.902
7	0.922	0.927	0.933
Ranking	2.57	2.14	1.28
Position	3	2	1

Table 5. Order of classifiers for the value of p and adjusting the value of α for the Holm procedure with $\alpha = 0.05$ for the AUC measure

i	Classifier	$z = (R_0 - R_i)/SE$	p	α/i
2	SVM	3.60	3.08×10^{-4}	0.025
1	RNA	1.60	0.10	0.05

Table 6. Order of classifiers for the value of p and adjusting the value of α for the Holm procedure with $\alpha = 0.05$ for the measurement F

i	Classifier	$z = (R_0 - R_i)/SE$	p	α/i
2	SVM	2.40	0.01	0.025
1	RNA	1.60	0.10	0.05

According to the analysis, it is evident that there are significant differences between RNA kNN and SVM classifiers with respect to AUC according to the measure and the measure F, not between kNN and RNA. Therefore, it is necessary to analyze the behavior of kNN and RNA classifiers according to the values obtained in both measures in Tables 7 and 8. It is evident that the highest value obtained in both measures between the two classifiers was obtained by kNN with a 93.4% value of the extent and 97.1% F for the AUC measured. After assessed the measures in each classifier, it is evident that the best performing classifier in the classification of cervical cells to the studied data set is kNN using Manhattan distance. Said classifier presents the best results for the measures assessed, with mean values of 90.4% as F, Pn of 83% and 94.3% AUC. Furthermore, this high performance classifier maintaining showed AUC values greater than 91% and up to 97.1% arriving (Table 7). For these reasons we recommend using the kNN classifier with Manhattan distance in the classification tool developed.

Table 7. Behavior evaluation measure AUC iterations tests by classifier

	Datasets						
	1	2	3	4	5	6	7
SVM	0.82	0.81	0.89	0.90	0.90	0.85	0.88
kNN	0.91	0.94	0.95	0.94	0.97	0.92	0.95
RNA	0.86	0.92	0.94	0.94	0.97	0.92	0.93

Table 8. Measure F behavior in iterations of tests performed by classifier

	Datasets						
	1	2	3	4	5	6	7
SVM	0.86	0.86	0.92	0.92	0.91	0.89	0.92
kNN	0.88	0.87	0.91	0.89	0.93	0.90	0.92
RNA	0.90	0.88	0.92	0.91	0.92	0.90	0.93

4.2   Other Approaches to Literature Studied

Table 9 shows the results of the statistical evaluation obtained depending on the effectiveness indexes sensitivity and specificity. These results were obtained using (as mentioned above) based Herlev kNN algorithm data and the Manhattan distance. The result obtained by this research demonstrates that achieved good results in terms of sensitivity, because the probability of correctly classifying a sick individual, i.e., the probability that an individual patient is obtained in the test a score positive was 96%. So the ability of the test is improved to detect disease. As specificity is considered that a good result is because a probability of 88% that for a healthy subject a negative result is obtained is achieved.

Table 9. Classification results in terms of sensitivity and specificity

Classifiers	Sensitivity	Specificity
Proposed tool	0.96	0.88

For Table 10 the statistical evaluation of the results obtained in the application performed in [14] based on sensitivity and specificity shown. These results were obtained using a database created by the authors of [14].

Table 10. Classification results in terms of sensitivity and specificity

Classifiers	Sensitivity	Specificity
Julio Alberto Oscanoa Aida y Marcelo Mena Moretti [14]	0.51	0.96

A comparison between the two tools cannot be made because they do not have access to the database used in [14] or the algorithms used for the development of this tool so we can only show the results obtained by each tools according to the results shown in [14].

5 Conclusions

In this paper, the binary classification of the cells was performed in the Pap test in order to reduce the rate of false negatives in the final result. A study of the possibilities to detect anomalies from the information contained in its nucleus cells was performed. A comparison between the classification algorithms kNN, SVM and RNA was performed to obtain the proper function of the results for the classification of cervical cells. Pre segmented images Herlev base data were used. The results obtained showed the tool developed more accurate in terms of AUC higher than 91% and up to 97.1% arriving with a sensitivity of 96% and specificity of 88% classification. The results showed advantages of using ranking only features the nucleus. This suggests a number of alternatives to be evaluated in future studies, for example: the search for new methods to extract features and selecting them for classification using methods of dimensionality reduction, and try other classification algorithms.

References

1. Maisanava, J.M.L., Soriano, J.Á.M., Murcia, A.P.: Citología Exfoliativa Cervicovaginal (Método de Papanicolaou). Servicio de Anatomía Patológica del Hospital Obispo Polanco de Truel. Boletín Oncológico, vol. 8, pp. 46–54 (1998)
2. Lorenzo-Ginori, J.V., Rodríguez-Santos, I.: Aplicación de técnicas de visión computacional en la prueba de Papanicolaou. Medicentro Electrónica 16(3), 196–198 (2012)
3. Campo, P., Bonilla, L.J., Calderon, A.: Cáncer cervical: Citología en base líquida, convencional y otras pruebas de tamizaje. Revista Repertorio de Medicina y Cirugía 21(3), 155–164 (2012)
4. Ramos, C.M.Á.: Sistema de reconocimento y clasificación de agentes patógenos de nosemosis. In: Departamento de Ingeniería del Software e Inteligencia Artificial, Universidad Complutense de Madrid: Madrid, España (2010)

5. Lorenzo-Ginori, J.V., Curbelo-Jardines, W., López-Cabrera, J.D., Huergo-Suárez, Sergio B.: Cervical cell classification using features related to morphometry and texture of nuclei. In: Ruiz-Shulcloper, J., Sanniti di Baja, G. (eds.) CIARP 2013. LNCS, vol. 8259, pp. 222–229. Springer, Heidelberg (2013). doi:10.1007/978-3-642-41827-3_28

6. Riana, D., Murni, A.: Performance evaluation of Pap smear cell image classification using quantitative and qualitative features based on multiple classifiers. In: International Conference on Advanced Computer Science and Information Systems, ACSIS (2009)

7. Mat-Isa, N.A., Mashor, M.Y., Othman, N.H.: An automated cervical pre-cancerous diagnostic system. Artif. Intell. Med. 42(1), 1–11 (2008)

8. Huang, P.-C., Chan, Y.-K., Chan, P.-C., Chen, Y.-F., Chen, R.-C., Huang, Y.-R.: Quantitative assessment of pap smear cells by pc-based cytopathologic image analysis system and support vector machine. In: Zhang, D. (ed.) ICMB 2008. LNCS, vol. 4901, pp. 192–199. Springer, Heidelberg (2007). doi:10.1007/978-3-540-77413-6_25

9. Marinakis, Y., Dounias, G., Jantzen, J.: Pap smear diagnosis using a hybrid intelligent scheme focusing on genetic algorithm based feature selection and nearest neighbor classification. Comput. Biol. Med. 39(1), 69–78 (2009)

10. Mas, J.A.G., et al.: Evaluación de dispositivos automatizados para diagnóstico citológico en la prevención del cáncer de cérvix. Revista Española de Patología 35(3), 301–314 (2002)

11. Patten, S.F., et al.: The AutoPap 300 QC system multicenter clinical trials for use in quality control rescreening of cervical smears. Cancer Cytopathol. 81(6), 337–342 (1997)

12. Troni, G.M., et al.: Quality control of the autopap screening system employed as a primary screening device: rapid review of smears coded as no further review. Tumori J. Exp. Clin. Oncol. 92(4), 276 (2006)

13. Soler Font, I., et al.: Aplicación de la lectura automatizada de citología ginecológica. el punto de vista de los citotécnicos. Revista Española de Patología 43(2), 69–72 (2010)

14. Aida, J.A.O., Moretti, M.M.: Desarrollo de un aplicativo de software, con acceso remoto vía web, orientado a mejorar la calidad del diagnóstico de las pruebas de Papanicolau, utilizando algoritmos computacionales de procesamiento digital de imágenes, in Facultad de Ingeniería, Universidad Peruana de Ciencias Aplicadas, Lima, Perú (2015)

15. Plissiti, M.E., Nikou, C.: Cervical cell classification based exclusively on nucleus features. In: Campilho, A., Kamel, M. (eds.) ICIAR 2012. LNCS, vol. 7325, pp. 483–490. Springer, Heidelberg (2012). doi:10.1007/978-3-642-31298-4_57

16. Plissiti, M.E., Nikou, C.: On the importance of nucleus features in the classification of cervical cells in Pap smear images. University of Ioannina (2012)

17. Plissiti, M.E., Nikou, C., Charchanti, A.: Combining shape, texture and intensity features for cell nuclei extraction in Pap smear images. Pattern Recogn. Lett. 32(6), 838–853 (2011)

18. Plissiti, M.E., et al.: Automated detection of cell nuclei in pap smear images using morphological reconstruction and clustering. IEEE Trans. Inf Technol. Biomed. 15(2), 233–241 (2011)

19. Jantzen, J., et al.: Pap-smear benchmark data for pattern classification. In: Proceedings of NiSIS 2005, pp. 1–9. Nature inspired Smart Information Systems (NiSIS), Albufeira (2005)

20. Velezmoro, G.A.B., Villafuerte, D.F.: Factores de riesgo que pronóstican el hallazgo de citologías cervicales anormales en dos poblaciones: mujeres de obreros de construcción civil vs. mujeres control en la posta médica "Construcción Civil" ESSALUD, de junio a septiembre del 2000, in Facultad de Medicina Humanap, p. 67. Universidad Nacional Mayor de San Marcos, Lima (2001)

21. Demšar, J.: Statistical comparisons of classifiers over multiple data sets. J. Mach. Learn. Res. 7, 1–30 (2006)

22. García, S., Herrera, F.: An extension on "statistical comparisons of classifiers over multiple data sets" for all pairwise comparisons. J. Mach. Learn. Res. 9, 2677–2694 (2008)

Implementation of Computer Vision Guided Peg-Hole Insertion Task Performed by Robot Through LabVIEW

Andres Sauceda Cienfuegos[1(✉)], Enrique Rodriguez[1], Jesus Romero[2],
David Ortega Aranda[2], and Baidya Nath Saha[3]

[1] Universidad Autónoma de Nuevo León, San Nicolás de los Garza, Mexico
`andres_sau.cien@hotmail.com, luis_e@outlook.com`
[2] Centro de Ingeniería y Desarrollo Industrial (CIDESI), Monterrey, Mexico
`{jaromero,ortega.a}@posgrado.cidesi.edu.mx`
[3] Centro de Investigación en Matemáticas (CIMAT), Monterrey, Mexico
`baidya.saha@cimat.mx`
`http://www.uanl.mx/en, http://www.cidesi.com,`
`http://www.cimat.mx/~baidya.saha`

Abstract. This paper presents a computer vision guided peg hole insertion task conducted by a robot. We mounted two cameras: one capturing top view and the other capturing side view to calibrate the three dimensional co-ordinates of the center position of the peg and hole found in the image to the actual world co-ordinates so that the robot can grab and insert the peg into the hole automatically. We exploit normalized cross correlation based template matching and distortion model (grid) calibration algorithm for our experiment. We exploit a linear equation for the linear and rotational displacement of the arm and gripper of the robot respectively for computing the pulse required for the encoder. We utilize gantry robot to conduct the experiment. The implementation was carried out in LabVIEW environment. We achieved significant amount of accuracy with an experimental error of 5% for template matching and ± 2.5 mm for calibration algorithm.

1 Introduction

Peg-in-hole insertion is a topic largely addressed in robotic research, not only due to its clear relevance in many industrial assembly tasks, but also for its complexity as a control problem that requires both position and force regulation. Peg in hole assembly is the most basic and benchmark problem in which a peg is placed into a hole which has a bigger dimension [1]. This can be apparently an easy task for humans, because we have the ability to perceive naturally all the factors that this process involves, nevertheless for a robot this task can be very complex. On the other hand, automate this process has several advantages such as increased productivity, costs reductions, and manual repetitive task reduction. Computer vision can automate the realization of this assembly process.

© Springer International Publishing AG 2017
G. Sidorov and O. Herrera-Alcántara (Eds.): MICAI 2016, Part I, LNAI 10061, pp. 437–458, 2017.
DOI: 10.1007/978-3-319-62434-1_36

In this research, we presented an automated computer vision guided peg-hole insertion task performed by the gantry robot. Gantry is a widely used industrial robot that provides the advantage of large work areas, ability to reach at different angles and better positioning accuracy. Towards achieving this goal, we mounted two cameras: one capturing top view and other capturing side view to find the three dimensional world coordinate of the peg, hole and gripper. We first implemented a template matching algorithm to identify the peg and hole pair based on their shape. We exploited **Normalized Cross Correlation (NCC)** technique as a template matching algorithm which is invariant to brightness. Then we executed a calibration algorithm which takes the pixel coordinate of the peg, hole and gripeer and returns their three dimensional world coordinates. We exploited the **distortion model (grid) calibration algorithm** for this experiment because the distortion model can incorporate lens distortion as well as angular view of the objects of interest, peg, hole and gripper in this experiment. Then we utilized a linear equation based on pulse and ball screw pitch constants of the servomotor of the gantry robot to compute the pulse required for the encoder to provide the linear and rotational displacement of the arm and gripper of the robot respectively so that the robot can perform the peg-hole insertion task respectively. The peg-hole insertion task performed by the robot kinematic controller involves four sequential steps: (i) linear displacement of the gripper from its initial position to the center position of the peg; (ii) adjust the gripper by rotating its arm based on the rotation of the peg and grab the peg; (iii) carry and bring the peg to the hole; (iv) adjust the peg by rotating the gripper arm based on the rotation of the hole and insert the peg into the hole; (v) release the peg and return the gripper into its initial position (return home). Step (i) and (iii) involves the rotation of the encoder of the arm servomotor, (ii) and (iv) involves the rotation of the encoder of the gripper servomotor, and (v) involves the rotation of the encoder of both the gripper and arm servomotor. We executed the robot vision and kinematic computer program in LabVIEW [10] environment. LabVIEW supports relevant libraries for data transmission and acquisition from external hardware and both the robot vision and kinematics can be accommodated in a single integrated system. A decent amount of accuracy was achieved with an error of 5% for template matching and a ±2.5 mm error for calibration algorithm.

The organization of the paper is as follows. Section 2 presents literature review. Section 3 discusses different algorithms of two computer vision algorithms: template matching and calibration method used in this study. Computer vision based proposed methodology for peg hole insertion task are presented in Sect. 4. Results and discussions are demonstrated in Sect. 5. Section 6 concludes this work. Relevant references are listed at the end of the paper.

2   Literature Review

Existing automatic "peg-hole" insertion task algorithms can be categorized into three groups: dynamic and static models, machine learning and computer vision sensors. Dynamic and static models use mechanical contact model, machine learning based algorithm exploits force sensor torques whereas vision sensor uses camera to automate "peg-hole" insertion task. Details of these three groups are given below.

First Group: Dynamic and Static Models

Automated assembly has a lot of problems with uncertainties in the environment. Dietrich et al. [6] analyzed the implementation of static contact models in assembly situations using parallel robots.

Navarro et al. [18] introduced a multimodal assembly controller approach to effectively increase the knowledge of industrial robots in multimodal robots working in manufacturing. The performance of the operation increases with time, as the robot learns more efficient ways of completing the task.

Because of the uncertainties in a robot assembly process, problems with collision and small positional alignments often occur. To solve this, Xia et al. [27] developed a compliant contact dynamic model to solve these problems. Using the basis of the dynamic model, the no-jamming and no-wedging assembly strategies can be obtained.

To realize a peg in hole insertion with a multi degree of freedom manipulator, you would normally need the precise position of the hole, this is obtained using cameras or with force/torque sensors. Park et al. [20] provided an intuitive assembly strategy that does not use any of those; instead, it first pushes the peg towards the hole, once it touches the hole, the peg is dragged in a pattern until it matches the hole, and then, the peg is inserted into it. For this experiment, a simulation was done to verify the procedure, after that, it was physically tested with a Kitech Arm.

Tsuruoka et al. [26] presented contact analysis in a 3 dimensional space, map regions of the contacts are presented for analysis. The simulations took in consideration the orientation of the peg and how it makes contact in the hole.

Callegari et al. [2] described the architecture of the virtual prototyping environments that can be presently set up to try to make the best from a concurrent mechatronic design of mechanical devices and control systems. Integration of different software modules can do the job.

Callegari and Suardi [3] proposed a new parallel kinematics machine for the assembly task. The architecture of the system was explained and the dynamic behavior was tested. A position/force controller was developed for the purpose. The robot used was a 3-RCC parallel machine.

Reinhart and Radi [23] implemented a telepresence system to make an assembly. The system is composed of three parts: the human operator side, the robot side, and the communication between them. For this paper, a peg-and-hole assembly is planned for the task. First the movements are fast, until the position of the robot is close to the hole, in which the movements are changed to be slower and more precise. Once the peg touches the hole, the user receives feedback from the robot and controls the movements of the robot using a joystick to complete the insertion. A KUKA industrial robot is used for this paper.

Zhou *et al.* [30] conducted a 3D modeling simulation of the contact forces occurring during peg-in-hole assembly operations. The orientation of the peg should be explicit in the force/torque output function since it affects the feedback perception.

Second Group: Machine Learning

Cervera [4] described a robot programming architecture for learning fine motion tasks. Learning is an autonomous process of experience repetition, with the goal being completing the task in with the minimum amount of steps. The sensor data was analyzed, and it determined the route that the robot should take.

Balletti *et al.* [1] showed how to achieve an accurate peg-in-hole insertion using only position sensors when resourcing to Variable Impedance Actuator. For this, the CubeBot, a 13 DOF Variable Stiffness Actuator is used. The robot uses a search algorithm to drive the position of the peg and the hole in the same plane, after that, the peg is inserted with an oscillation movement to solve orientation uncertainties and jamming.

Lopez *et al.* [13] demonstrated that robotic agents can be benefited from integration of perceptual learning in order to modify its behavior against changing environments. Camera perception and force sensing are of big help for the learning process, and using those, the robot can adapt and be a flexible system. The robot used is a KUKA KR15.

While robot assembly operations can be performed by specifying the name of the operation, this is not recommended because of uncertainties in the operation. Lopez *et al.* [15] developed a Neural Network Controller consisting of two stages to adapt and decide the best way to complete the assembly. The robot used is a Puma 761.

Lopez *et al.* [14] created self-adapting robots using a Neural Network Controller. A force/torque sensor was used by the robot to get data and adapt its movement and orientation on the line, using previously obtained data. The robot used is a Puma 761.

A biology multimodal architecture called MARTMAP, based on the biological model of sensorial perception, was integrated in a robot by Lopez *et al.* [16] so that it can adapt to the environment. This method, while slower in practice, has other benefits that make it practical for certain situations.

Lopez *et al.* [17] used a method using 2D image object representation for grasping. The method used only two image patterns from a regular or irregular object for training. From this, it was possible to recognize a lot of objects achieving invariance to: rotation, scale, and location.

Sharma *et al.* [25] analyzed and compared different mathematical optimization models for peg insertion. The main problem being that it must work without specifications of peg and hole. A neural network strategy based on moments and descend of the peg was generalized for tilted pegs.

Yun [29] investigated the usefulness of passive compliance in a manipulator that learns contact motion. The robot learnt the policy for peg in hole insertion using a gradient descending method. The compliance helped with the contact motion and it yielded more stability and a slower sampling time.

Third Group: Vision Sensors

Choi *et al.* [5] solved an assembly task by using different sensor data. Vision and proximity sensors were mainly used for gross motion control, and the force/torque sensor was used for fine motion control of the robot. Each data of the sensor was evaluated to see the usefulness of each sensor.

Kim and Cho [9] used vision sensors to solve for misalignments of the peg because of deformation. An algorithm is designed and tested, and proved to be effective in detecting misalignments and fixing the errors.

Xue *et al.* [28] introduced and used a new type cell of Self Organizing Manipulator for dual-peg-in-hole insertion. A camera and a force/torque sensor is used to complete this process, using the results obtained from an analysis of geometric and force conditions in performing that work.

Newman *et al.* [19] implemented intelligent methods to deal with an assembly task. The reason is that they work faster and better than blind search. For this, sensory data is gathered and interpreted; furthermore, pattern matching can be used for some cases to improve greatly the time required for completion.

In this research, we used computer vision based algorithms to automate the "peg-hole" insertion task. Towards achieving this goal, we first implement template matching algorithm to match the peg-hole pair which provides the image coordinates of the center position and rotation of the peg, hole and the position of the gripper. Then calibration algorithm converts the image coordinates to the world coordinates which are used as an input to the robot kinematics algorithm. Different well-known methods of template matching and calibration algorithm are mentioned in the next section.

3   Related Computer Vision Algorithms

3.1   Template Matching Algorithms

Different template matching algorithms are available in literature [21]. Some of them are explained below.

Naive Template Matching. In this method, we are provided with the pattern image representing the reference object we are looking for and the input image to be inspected. To perform the search, the pattern is positioned over the image at every possible location, and each time we will compute some numeric measure of similarity between the pattern and the image segment it currently overlaps. Finally we will identify the positions that yield the best similarity measures as the probable pattern position.

Grayscale-Based Matching. This is an advanced algorithm that extends the original idea of correlation-based template detection enhancing its efficiency and allowing to search for template occurrences regardless of its orientation. To do this, it uses a process called "Image pyramids", this process reduces the scale of both, the template and the second image, while this removes fine details of the original pictures, the template is still identifiable on the second image. Therefore, we first identify matches in the highest level, and then we search on a lower level of the pyramid, performing the search again considering only the template positions that scored high on the previous level. Grayscale-Based Matching uses this pyramid search to allow for multi-angle matching by computing a set of pyramids, one for each possible rotation of the template. During the search, the algorithm identifies both, position and orientation.

Edge-Based Matching. Edge-based Matching enhances grayscale-based matching using one crucial observation, that the shape of any object is defined mainly by the shape of its edges. Therefore, instead of matching the whole template, we could extract its edges and match only the nearby pixels, thus avoiding some unnecessary computations. In common applications, the achieved speed up is usually significant. In edge-based matching, the gradient direction of the edge pixels is what is matched, not their intensity, as this would cause a match anywhere wherever there is a large enough blob of the appropriate color. There are two important properties associated with the gradient: (1) the vector $G|f(x,y)|$ points in the direction of the maximum rate of increase of the function $f(x,y)$, and (2) the magnitude of the gradient, given by: $G|f(x,y)| = \sqrt{G_x^2 + G_y^2}$ equals the maximum rate of increase of $f(x,y)$ per unit distance in the direction G. From vector analysis, the direction of the gradient is defined as: $\alpha(x,y) = tan^{-1}(\frac{G_y}{G_x})$, where the angle α is measured with respect to the x axis.

Cross-Correlation. The fundamental method of calculating the image correlation is called cross-correlation, which essentially is a simple sum of pairwise multiplications of corresponding pixel values of the images. The cross-correlation function plays an important role in matching the characteristic features of the object to match. Its main drawback is that it is biased by changes in global brightness of the images, so changing the brightness of the image may increase or reduce the value of the cross-correlation, even if the second image is not similar at all.

Normalized Cross-Correlation. The equation of cross-correlation for template matching is motivated by the distance measure (squared Euclidean distance)

$$d_{f,t}^2(u,v) = \sum_{x,y}[f(x,y) - t(x - u, y - v)]^2$$

where f is the query image and the sum is over (x,y) under the window containing the template t positioned at (u,v). Expanding d^2

$$d_{f,t}^2(u,v) = \sum_{x,y}[f^2(x,y) - 2f(x,y)t(x - u, y - v) + t^2(x - u, y - v)]$$

The term $\sum_{x,y}[t^2(x - u, y - v)]$ is constant. If the term $\sum_{x,y}[f^2(x,y)]$ is approximately constant, then the remaining cross-correlation term

$$c(u,v) = \sum_{x,y}[f(x,y)t(x - u, y - v)] \tag{1}$$

is a measure of the similarity between the image and the feature. There are several disadvantages to using (1) for template matching:

- If the image brightness varies with position, matching (1) can fail. The correlation of the feature and a bright spot may be higher than the feature and an exactly matching region.
- The range of $c(u, v)$ is dependant on the size of the feature.

The correlation coefficient overcomes these difficulties by normalizing the image and feature vectors to unit length, yielding a cosine-like correlation coefficient.

$$NCC(u,v) = \frac{\sum_{x,y}[f(x,y) - \bar{f}_{u,v}][t(x-u, y-v) - \bar{t}]}{\sqrt{\sum_{x,y}[f(x,y) - \bar{f}_{u,v}]^2 \sum_{x,y}[t(x-u, y-v) - \bar{t}]^2}}$$

3.2   Calibration Algorithms

To understand the calibration algorithm we describe here how an image is formed through calibration algorithm [8]. Figure 1 illustrates how an image is created. Figure 1 illustrates the following:

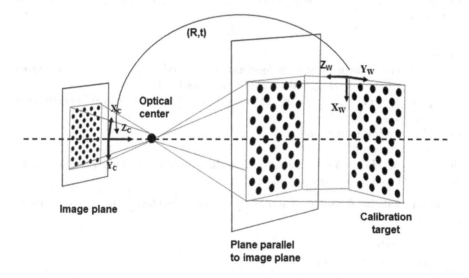

Fig. 1. How the image is formed in a Calibration technique

- The calibration target is represented in a real-world coordinate system (X_w, Y_w, Z_w).
- The camera coordinate system is represented as (x_c, y_c, z_c), with the z axis aligned with the optical axis and the x and y axes aligned with the horizontal and vertical axes of the image plane.

- An intermediate plane, parallel to the image plane, illustrates the shape of the calibration target in an image.

A camera coordinate axis is displaced from a real-world coordinate axis by the following transformation:

$$P_c = R(P_w - T)$$

where,

P_w equals a point in the real-world coordinate system,

P_c equals the homogeneous point in the camera coordinate system,

R equals the rotation matrix between the real-world coordinate axis and the camera coordinate axis, and

T equals the origin of the real-world coordinate axis minus the camera coordinate axis.

Homography. A physical projection, or homography, defines a geometric mapping of points from one plane to another. In calibration, a homography can describe the conversion of 3D coordinates in the real world to pixel coordinates in the image.

A physical projection transformation maps the real-world point $P(X_w,\ Y_w,\ Z_w)$ to the image point $p(x_w,\ y_w)$ A typical homography can be expressed as

$$p = sHP,$$

where

p equals the image plane projection expressed in camera coordinates $[Xc\ \ Yc\ \ 1]^T$ that correspond to $2D$ image coordinates.

P equals a real-world point expressed in $3D$ real world coordinates $[X_w\ \ Y_w\ \ Z_w\ \ 1]^T$

s equals a scaling factor, and

H equals homography.

Homography (H) is a 3×3 matrix which is the product of two matrices: a camera matrix (M) and a homography matrix (W).

Camera Matrix. A camera matrix (M) describes the following internal camera parameters:

- Focal length
- Principle point position
- Pixel size
- Pixel skew angle

Internal camera parameters are represented with the following matrix:

$$M = \begin{bmatrix} f_x & \alpha f_x & c_x \\ 0 & f_y & c_y \\ 0 & 0 & 1 \end{bmatrix}$$

where, f_x equals $\frac{F}{S_x}$

f_y equals $\frac{F}{S_y}$ and

F equals the focal length, in millimeters

S_x equals the horizontal size of a pixel in the camera sensor, in pixels per millimeter

S_y equals the vertical size of a pixel in the camera sensor, in pixels per millimeter

C_x equals the horizontal displacement of the imager from the optical axis, in millimeters

C_y equals the vertical displacement of the imager from the optical axis, in millimeters, and

α equals the pixel skew angle of y with respect to x. α is typically equal to 0.

The camera focal length (F) and pixel dimensions (S_x, S_y) cannot be directly calculated. Camera calibration can only calculate the derivative focal length and pixel dimension combinations (f_x, f_y).

Homography Matrix. A homography matrix (W) consists of the rotation matrix and translation vector that relate a point in a real-world plane and a point in an image plane. The physical projection transformation matrix can be expressed as

$$W = [R \quad t]$$

where

R equals the rotation matrix and

t equals the translation vector

The rotation matrix (R) can be expressed as 3 separate 3×1 matrices, so that $R = [r1 \quad r2 \quad r3]$

Thus, the original homography $p = sHP$ can be expressed as,

$$\begin{bmatrix} x \\ y \\ 1 \end{bmatrix} = sM[r1 \ r2 \ r3 \ t] \begin{bmatrix} X \\ Y \\ 0 \\ 1 \end{bmatrix}$$

Because calibration is performed with a planar calibration target, we can generalize that $Z = 0$ to further simplify the homography as,

$$\begin{bmatrix} x \\ y \\ 1 \end{bmatrix} = sM[r1 \ r2 \ t] \begin{bmatrix} X \\ Y \\ 1 \end{bmatrix}$$

Different calibration algorithms [8, 12, 24] are available in literature. One of the well-known methods are Tsai two-step method, in which the process of calculating the camera parameters is divided into two steps. The first step is to solve linear equations to get parts of the external parameters. The focal length and distortion correction coefficients will be figured out in the second step. It only needs one image to get the rotation and translation matrix of the camera model, and most equations in this method are linear, so that reduces the calculation complexity.

4   Proposed Methodolody

Proposed methodology for peg-hole insertion task consists of two sequential step: (i) vision control and (ii) robot kinematics as shown in Fig. 2. Two cameras were mounted to capture the top and side view of the peg and hole. Vision control returns the three dimensional world coordinate of the center position and rotation of the peg, hole and gripper. From this position, the robot kinematics can compute the number of rotations required for the encoder of the robot arm servomotor so that robot gripper can reach to the peg position, then pick pulse are sent to the gripper servomotor to pick the peg and then the arm servomotor provides the linear motion for the gripper to reach to the hole position, then insert pulse are sent to the gripper servomotor to insert the peg into the hole. After that release pulse are sent to the gripper servomotor to release the peg and then return pulse are sent to the robot arm servomotor to return the gripper to its initial position. The mathematical model used by vision control and robot kinematics are given below.

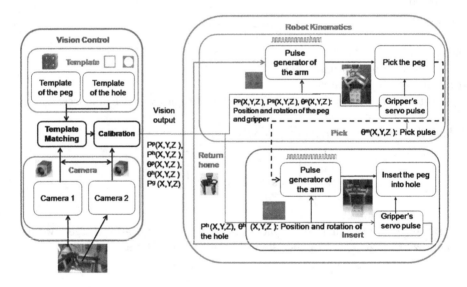

Fig. 2. Block diagram of the proposed vision controlled peg-hole insertion task

4.1   Vision Control

The vision control consists of two sequential steps: (i) Template Matching, and (ii) Calibration.

(i) Template matching. We exploit normalized cross correlation technique for matching the expected peg and hole shapes. Normalized cross-correlation is an enhanced version of the classic cross-correlation method that introduces two improvements over the original one: The results are invariant to the global brightness changes, i.e. consistent brightening or darkening of either image has no effect on the result (this is accomplished by subtracting the mean image brightness from each pixel value). The final correlation value is scaled to $[-1, 1]$ range, so that NCC of two identical images equals 1.0, while NCC of an image and its negation equals -1.0.

(ii) Calibration. We exploit distortion model (grid) calibration. Distortion modelling is typically used to correct radial distortion introduced by a lens, or telecentric distortion introduced by sensor misalignment. The Calibration Training Interface also corrects for perspective distortion during distortion modelling. Given a set of calibration points, the projections of the calibraion points in the image plane are determined, the error in the projected positions are calculated, and these errors are used to solve for the camera calibration parameters. The actual camera calibration parameters are obtained and can be used regardless of where the camera is later located in scene. The principle behind the solution to the camera calibration problems is to measure the locations (x'_i, y'_i) of the projections of the calibration points onto the image plane, calculate the deviations $(\delta x_i, \delta y_i)$ of the points from the correct positions, and plug this measurements into equations that model the camera parameters. Each calibration point yields two equations. The solution requires at least enough equations to cover the unknowns, but for increased accuracy more equations that unknowns are used and the overdetermined set of equations is solved using nonlinear regression.

Assume that the approximate position and orientation of the camera in absolute coordinates is known. The parameters of the regression problem are the rotation angles θ, ω, k; the position of the camera in absolute coordinates p_x, p_y, and p_z; the camera constant f; the corrections to the location of the principal point (x_p, y_p); and the polynomial coefficients for radial lens distortion k_1, k_2 and k_3. Since we have initial estimates for the rotation angles, we can formulate the exterior orientation problem in terms of the Euler angles in the rotation matrix using the next equations:

$$r_{xx} = cos\theta * cosk$$
$$r_{xy} = sin\omega * sin\theta * cosk + cos\omega * sink$$
$$r_{xz} = -cos\omega * sin\theta * cosk + sin\omega * sink$$
$$r_{yx} = -cos\theta * sink$$
$$r_{yy} = sin\omega * sin\theta * sink + cos\omega * cosk$$
$$r_{yz} = -cos\omega * sin\theta * sink + sin\omega * sink$$
$$r_{zx} = sin\theta$$
$$r_{zy} = -sin\omega * cos\theta$$
$$r_{zz} = -cos\omega * cos\theta$$

The equations for the exterior orientation problem are:

$$\frac{x'}{f} = \frac{r_{xx}x_a + r_{xy}y_a + r_{xz}z_a + p_x}{r_{zx}x_a + r_{zy}y_a + r_{zz}z_a + p_z}$$

$$\frac{y'}{f} = \frac{r_{yx}x_a + r_{yy}y_a + r_{yz}z_a + p_y}{r_{zx}x_a + r_{zy}y_a + r_{zz}z_a + p_z}$$

Replace x' and y' with the corrected positions of the camera model,

$$\frac{(\tilde{x} - x_p)(1 + k_1 r^2 + k_2 r^4 + k_3 r^6)}{f} = \frac{r_{zz}x_a + r_{xy}y_a + r_{xz}z_a + p_x}{r_{zx}x_a + r_{zy}y_a + r_{zz}z_a + p_z}$$

$$\frac{(\tilde{y} - y_p)(1 + k_1 r^2 + k_2 r^4 + k_3 r^6)}{f} = \frac{r_{zz}x_a + r_{xy}y_a + r_{xz}z_a + p_x}{r_{zx}x_a + r_{zy}y_a + r_{zz}z_a + p_z}$$

The regression algorithm will require good initial conditions. If the target is plane, the camera axis is normal to the plane, and the image is roughly centered on the target, then the initial conditions are easy to obtain. These are:

$\theta = \omega = k = 0$

$x = $ translation in x from the origin

$y = $ translation in y from the origin

$z = $ distance of the camera from the calibration plane

$f = $ focal length of the lens

$x_p = y_p = 0$

$k_1 = k_2 = k_3 = 0.$

4.2   Robot Kinematics

The Cartesian coordinate system uses the pulse-width modulation (PWM) and movement control signals for the actuators, i.e. the number of revolutions achieved by the servomotor will be linked to the number of pulses that are sent as a reference signal. To approach $X = \frac{N}{R}T$ the linear distance traversed by the robot arm in millimeters, where $X = P^g(X, Y, Z) - P^h(X, Y, Z)$, $N = $ number of pulses required to send to servo drivers for the encoder to traverse the distance X, $R = $ constants for number of pulses required for one revolution of the encoder, $T = $ ball screw pitch. Hence we get,

$$N = \frac{XR}{T} \tag{2}$$

Figure 3 shows how the encoder does work. Figure 7 shows the implementation of the gantry robot kinematics through LabVIEW.

5   Experimental Results

Gantry Robot. We conducted the peg hole insertion task experiment using gantry robot. A gantry robot consists of a manipulator mounted onto an over-head system that allows movement across a horizontal plane. Gantry robots are also called Cartesian or linear robots. They are usually large systems that per-form pick and place applications, but they can also be used in welding and other applications. Unlike other industrial robots, gantry robots have one additional feature that give them a leg, or rather an arm, up on other systems. Because they are mounted from above, they are capable of reach angles and crevices that even standard floor mounted robots may have trouble reaching during an appli-cation. Along with their reach and all position capability, gantry robots are also fundamental in packaging and other material handling applications. Because of their track, they can pick up items or boxes of items and move them to another work station or space down the line, something a floor-mounted robot could never achieve. It is this kind of versatility that makes gantry robotics attractive to manufacturers in several different industries [22]. The gantry robot used in this experiment has three degrees of motion and have one servomotor for each of this motion as shown in Fig. 3.

Camera Used in this Experiment. The camera used for this experiment is a Basler acA640-90gm with resolution 659×494 px, frame rate 90 fps, pixel bit depth 12 bits.

Advantages of LabVIEW for Robot Programming. We executed the code in LabVIEW environment [11]. For the robot control we exploited LabVIEW in

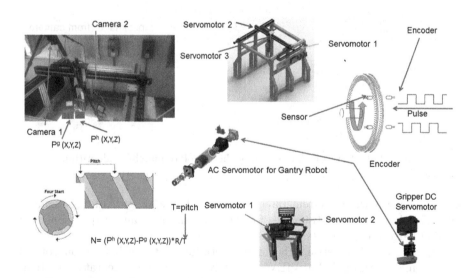

Fig. 3. Diagram of the experimental set up with gantry robot, servomotor of the arm and gripper as well as ball-screw pitch

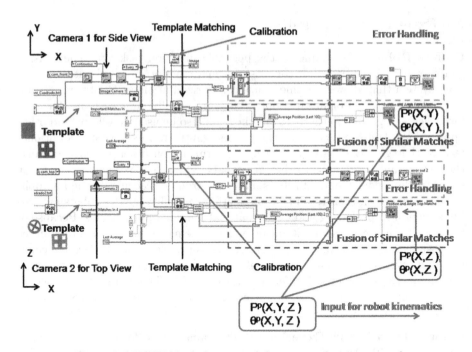

Fig. 4. LabVIEW block diagram of the proposed vision control

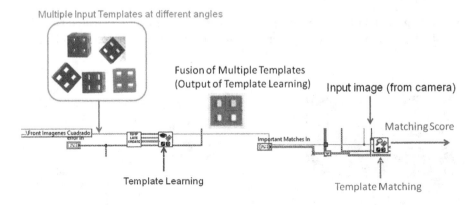

Fig. 5. LabVIEW block diagram of the template matching algorithm

order to have a whole system integrated in just one programming language. LabVIEW has a lot of advantages for data transmission and acquisition from external hardware due to its libraries.

Figures 4 and 7 illustrate the implementation of the robot vision control and kinematics through LabVIEW respectively. The implementation of template matching and calibration are demonstrated in Figs. 5 and 6 respectively. Figure 5 shows that we use multiple input templates at different angles and

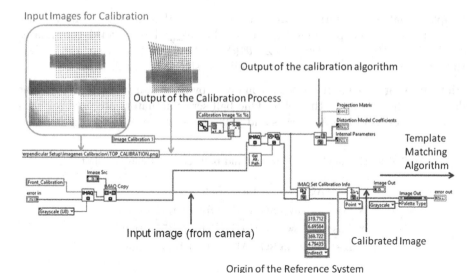

Fig. 6. LabVIEW block diagram of the calibration technique

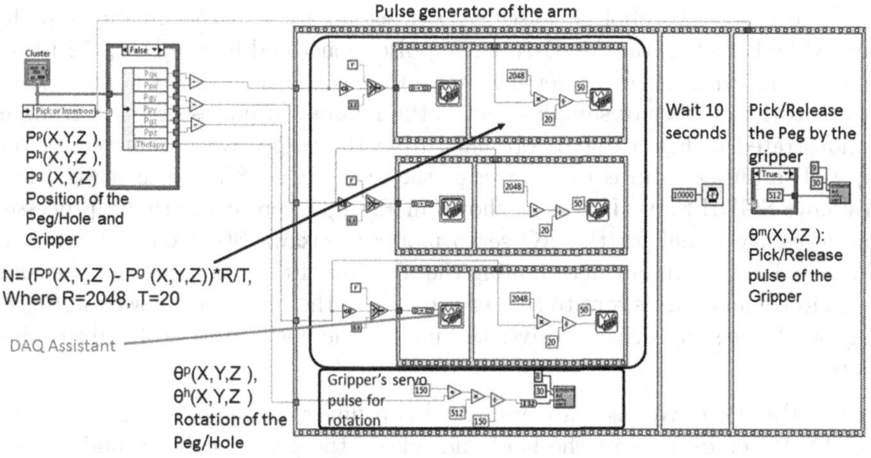

Fig. 7. LabVIEW block diagram of the gantry robot kinematics

brightness as the input of template learning and then fuse these templates which use as an input for template matching algorithm. Fusion of multiple templates increases the accuracy of template matching algorithm. Figure 6 demonstrates that multiple images of circular dots and the distances among them are used as the input of the calibration algorithm. The output of the calibration algorithm is the inverse of the homography matrix as discussed in Sect. 3.2 which is used as the input of the template matching algorithm. The pixel coordinate of the center position of the peg, hole and gripper found from template matching algorithm are multiplied with this inverse of the homography matrix which provides their three dimensional real world coordinates $P^p(X, Y, Z), P^h(X, Y, Z), \theta^p(X, Y, Z), \theta^h(X, Y, Z), P^g(X, Y, Z)$ that are used as the input of the robot kinematics controller as shown in Fig. 2.

Pick the Peg. The gantry robot is composed by three ball screw actuators that determine the motion of the robot. One ball screw actuators are used for each axis. The models of the AC servos and ball screws are given in the Table 1.

Table 1. Models of AC servos and ball screws of gantry robot.

	AC servo motor	Ball screw
X axis	Yaskawa SGMAH	THK SKR55 20 mm
Y axis	Yaskawa SGMAH	THK SKR55 20 mm
Z axis	Yaskawa SGMAH	THK KR33 10 mm

In order to control the position of each axis of the gantry robot we have to operate the servo drivers on position control. For the purpose of generating the pulses to move the robot, we use DAQ Assistant to send the pulses from the card NI SCB-68A to the AC Drivers. N pulses generated by the DAQ Assistant as shown in Eq. 2 where we set high time that is the time that the pulse is on high and the number of samples that is the number of pulses or pulse train as demonstrated in Fig. 9 that is obtained from the respective parameters of the Eq. 2. The pulses train is driven out of the DAQ SCB-68A to the servo driver (Yaskawa SGDH Servo Driver as shown in Fig. 8) where it internally processes the necessary signal for the AC servo motor (Yaskawa SGMAH AC Servo as illustrated in Fig. 8). For determining the rotation of the servo motion is needed an digital signal that is sent to the servo driver as the same way showed in Fig. 8. In general, the servo driver receives two inputs: the position control and rotation control.

Insert the Peg. We used a commercial two fingers gripper composed by two DC AX-18 servos, one for the hold and release the peg and the second one for

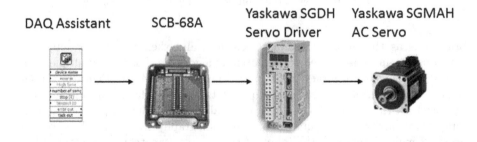

Fig. 8. Robot kinematics for the arm servo motor

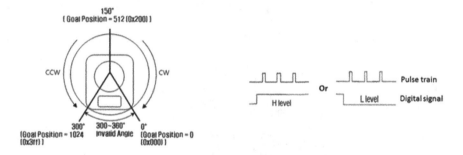

Fig. 9. Robot kinematics for the gripper servo motor

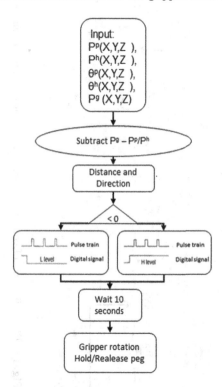

Fig. 10. Flow chart of the gantry robot kinematics

the roll axis. In order for a better grip and for the pick and insertion task, the gripper has to have the same rotation as the peg/hole from the respective Y axis. Given that angle as θ_p/θ_h, we calculated the necessary input for the DC servo. Where θ_p and θ_h are the decimal numbers from 0 to 1023 where the unit is 0.29° in that way we obtain the roll axis for the gripper. For the hold and release task of the gripper it uses two gears with a 1:1 gear ratio for the motion of each finger. For hold the peg the servo could rotates to 30° or 270° and for the release of the peg the servo has to rotate to 150° as illustrated in Fig. 9.

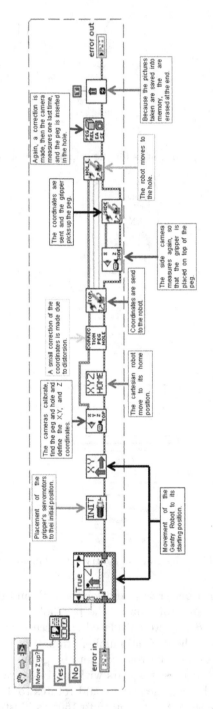

Fig. 11. Block diagram of computer vision guided peg hole insertion task

Table 2. Experimental error.

Name of the algorithm	Error
Template matching	
Cross correlation	10%
Normalized cross correlation	5.0%
Calibration	
Point Coordinates	±4.5 mm
Distortion model (grid)	±2.5 mm

Return Home. Return home consists of release pulse for gripper servo motor as shown in Fig. 9 and return pulse for arm servo motor as shown in Fig. 8. Figure 10 shows the flowchart of the gantry robot kinematics. The average errors of template matching and calibration algorithms are illustrated in Table 2.

The block diagram of the implementation of computer vision guided peg hole insertion task through labview is demonstrated in Fig. 11.

6 Conclusion and Future Work

Peg hole insertion task is an open long standing problem for computer vision and artificial intelligence community. In this research we implemented a peg and hole template matching algorithm followed by camera calibration algorithm to find the real world co-ordinates of the center position of the peg and hole. To find the three dimensional real world co-ordinates of the center of the peg and hole we mounted two cameras capturing the top and side view of the peg and hole. We implemented normalized cross correlation based template matching algorithm using different shape and size of the peg and hole in different illumination conditions and different positions. Then we implemented a distortion model (grid) camera calibration algorithm which can incorporate lens distortion and angular view of the peg and hole. The pulse required for the encoder to provide linear and rotational displacement of the arm and gripper of the robot so that the robot can grab and insert the peg into the hole is computed by a linear equation. We conducted the peg hole insertion task experiment in the gantry robot. We used Gantry robot because gantry robot is easier to program, with respect to motion, because they work with an X, Y, Z coordinate system. Another advantages of gantry robot are that they are less limited by floor space constraints that provides the advantage of large work areas, ability to reach at different angles and better positioning accuracy. We conducted the experiment in LabVIEW environment. A decent amount of accuracy was achieved with an error of 5% error for template matching and an ±2.5 mm error for calibration algorithm.

Our work provides several interesting avenues for future work. One of our future directions is to teach the robot so that the robot can insert the peg into the hole more efficiently. Towards achieving this goal, we plan to implement the force and torque sensor in the finger of the gripper of the robot so that the robot can change the direction and angle of the motion while inserting the peg into the hole based on the signal captured by the force and torque sensor. Then we plan to incorporate visual sensor with the force torque sensor to compute the misalignment of the peg with the hole and decrease the overall experimental error by identifying the location of the marks [9]. We would also plan to modify the calibration algorithm to reduce the calibration error as well. We plan to implement a linear algebra based novel cost function which is constructed in real-world coordinates which makes calibration error uniform for different types of geometric primitives and perspective invariant that makes non sensitive to image resolution or camera-object distance. In the cost function formulation back projection will be casted as a minimization problem, such that the re-projection of the estimated world-space position, from world space to image space, achieves a minimum difference from the annotated image position [7].

References

1. Balletti, L., Rocchi, A., Belo, F., Catalano, M., Garabini, M., Grioli, G., Bicchi, A.: Towards variable impedance assembly: the VSA peg-in-hole. In: 2012 12th IEEE-RAS International Conference on Humanoid Robots (Humanoids 2012), pp. 402–408. IEEE (2012)
2. Callegari, M., Gabrielli, A., Palpacelli, M.-C., Principi, M.: Design of advanced robotic systems for assembly automation. Int. J. Mech. Control 8(1), 3–8 (2007)
3. Callegari, M., Suardi, A.: On the force-controlled assembly operations of a new parallel kinematics manipulator. In: Proceedings of the Mediterranean Conference on Control and Automation, pp. 18–20 (2003)
4. Cervera Mateu, E.: Perception-based learning for fine motion planning in robot manipulation (1997)
5. Choi, J.W., Fang, T.H., Yoo, W.S., Lee, M.H.: Sensor data fusion using perception net for a precise assembly task. IEEE/ASME Trans. Mech. 8(4), 513–516 (2003)
6. Dietrich, F., Buchholz, D., Wobbe, F., Sowinski, F., Raatz, A., Schumacher, W., Wahl, F.M.: On contact models for assembly tasks: Experimental investigation beyond the peg-in-hole problem on the example of force-torque maps. In: 2010 IEEE/RSJ International Conference on Intelligent Robots and Systems (IROS), pp. 2313–2318. IEEE (2010)
7. Ismail, K.A.: Application of computer vision techniques for automated road safety analysis and traffic data collection. Ph.D. thesis, University of British Columbia (2010). https://open.library.ubc.ca/cIRcle/collections/24/items/1.0062871
8. Jain, R., Kasturi, R., Schunck, B.G.: Machine Vision. McGraw-Hill Inc., New York (1995)
9. Kim, J., Cho, H.S.: Visual sensor-based measurement for deformable peg-in-hole tasks. In: Proceedings of the 1999 IEEE/RSJ International Conference on Intelligent Robots and Systems, IROS 1999, vol. 1, pp. 567–572. IEEE (1999)
10. Kwon, K., Ready, S.: Practical Guide to Machine Vision Software: An Introduction with LabVIEW. Wiley (2015). https://books.google.com.mx/books?id=_jiCoAEACAAJ

11. Kwon, K., Ready, S., Sons, J.W.: Practical Guide to Machine Vision Software: An Introduction with LabVIEW. Wiley-VCH (2014). https://books.google.ca/books?id=yXkKrgEACAAJ

12. Li, W., Gee, T., Friedrich, H., Delmas, P.: A practical comparison between Zhang's and Tsai's calibration approaches. In: Proceedings of the 29th International Conference on Image and Vision Computing New Zealand, IVCNZ 2014, pp. 166–171 (2014) http://doi.acm.org/10.1145/2683405.2683443

13. Lopez-Juarez, I., Corona-Castuera, J., Peña-Cabrera, M., Ordaz-Hernandez, K.: On the design of intelligent robotic agents for assembly. Inf. Sci. **171**(4), 377–402 (2005)

14. Lopez-Juarez, I., Howarth, M.: Learning manipulative skills with art. In: Proceedings of the 2000 IEEE/RSJ International Conference on Intelligent Robots and Systems (IROS 2000), vol. 1, pp. 578–583. IEEE (2000)

15. Lopez-Juarez, I., Howarth, M., Sivayoganathan, K.: An adaptive learning approach to control contact force in assembly. In: Proceedings of the 1998 IEEE/RSJ International Conference Intelligent Robots and Systems, vol. 3, pp. 1443–1448. IEEE (1998)

16. Lopez-Juarez, I., Ordaz-Hernández, K., Peña-Cabrera, M., Corona-Castuera, J., Rios-Cabrera, R.: On the design of a multimodal cognitive architecture for perceptual learning in industrial robots. In: Gelbukh, A., Albornoz, Á., Terashima-Marín, H. (eds.) MICAI 2005. LNCS, vol. 3789, pp. 1062–1072. Springer, Heidelberg (2005). doi:10.1007/11579427_108

17. López-Juárez, I., Rios-Cabrera, R., Peña-Cabrera, M., Méndez, G.M., Osorio, R.: Fast object recognition for grasping tasks using industrial robots. Computación y Sistemas **16**(4), 421–432 (2012)

18. Navarro-Gonzalez, J., Lopez-Juarez, I., Rios-Cabrera, R., Ordaz-Hernández, K.: On-line knowledge acquisition and enhancement in robotic assembly tasks. Robot. Comput. Int. Manuf. **33**, 78–89 (2015)

19. Newman, W.S., Zhao, Y., Pao, Y.H.: Interpretation of force and moment signals for compliant peg-in-hole assembly. In: Proceedings of the 2001 IEEE International Conference on Robotics and Automation, ICRA 2001, vol. 1, pp. 571–576. IEEE (2001)

20. Park, H., Bae, J.H., Park, J.H., Baeg, M.H., Park, J.: Intuitive peg-in-hole assembly strategy with a compliant manipulator. In: 2013 44th International Symposium on Robotics (ISR), pp. 1–5. IEEE (2013)

21. Perveen, N., Kumar, D., Bhardwaj, I.: An overview on template matching methodologies and its applications. IJRCCT **2**(10), 988–995 (2013)

22. Ratcliffe, J.D., Lewin, P.L., Rogers, E., Htnen, J.J., Owens, D.H.: Norm-optimal iterative learning control applied to gantry robots for automation applications. IEEE Trans. Robot. **22**(6), 1303–1307 (2006). http://dblp.uni-trier.de/db/journals/trob/trob22.html#RatcliffeLRHO06

23. Reinhart, G., Radi, M.: Some issues of integrating telepresence technology into industrial robotic assembly. In: Proceedings of the International Conference on Control and Automation, Dubai. Citeseer (2009)

24. Samper, D., Santolaria, J., Brosed, F.J., Majarena, A.C., Aguilar, J.J.: Analysis of Tsai calibration method using two- and three-dimensional calibration objects. Mach. Vis. Appl. **24**(1), 117–131 (2013)

25. Sharma, K., Shirwalkar, V., Pal, P.K.: Intelligent and environment-independent peg-in-hole search strategies. In: 2013 International Conference on Control, Automation, Robotics and Embedded Systems (CARE), pp. 1–6. IEEE (2013)

26. Tsuruoka, T., Fujioka, H., Moriyama, T., Mayeda, H.: 3D analysis of contact in peg-hole insertion. In: 1997 IEEE International Symposium on Assembly and Task Planning, ISATP 1997, pp. 84–89. IEEE (1997)

27. Xia, Y., Yin, Y., Chen, Z.: Dynamic analysis for peg-in-hole assembly with contact deformation. Int. J. Adv. Manuf. Technol. **30**(1–2), 118–128 (2006)

28. Xue, G., Fukuda, T., Arai, F., Asama, H., Kaetsu, H., Endo, I.: Dynamically reconfigurable robotic systemassembly of new type cells as a dual-peg-in-hole problem. In: Asama, H., Fukuda, T., Arai, T., Endo, I. (eds.) Distributed Autonomous Robotic Systems, pp. 383–394. Springer, Tokyo (1994). doi:10.1007/978-4-431-68275-2_34

29. kook Yun, S.: Compliant manipulation for peg-in-hole: is passive compliance a key to learn contact motion? In: ICRA, pp. 1647–1652. IEEE (2008) http://dblp.uni-trier.de/db/conf/icra/icra2008.html#Yun08

30. Zhou, J., Georganas, N.D., Petriu, E.M., Shen, X., Marlic, F.: Modelling contact forces for 3D interactive peg-in-hole virtual reality operations. In: Proceedings of the Instrumentation and Measurement Technology Conference, IMTC 2008, pp. 1397–1402. IEEE (2008)

Object Tracking Based on Modified TLD Framework Using Compressive Sensing Features

Tao Yang$^{(\boxtimes)}$, Cindy Cappelle$^{(\boxtimes)}$, Yassine Ruichek$^{(\boxtimes)}$,
and Mohammed El Bagdouri

Université de Technologie Belfort-Montbéliard, 90010 Belfort, France
{tao.yang,cindy.cappelle,yassine.ruichek,
mohammed.el-bagdouri}@utbm.fr

Abstract. Visual object tracking is widely researched but still challenging as both accuracy and efficiency must be considered in a single system. CT tracker can achieve a good real-time performance but is not very robust to fast movements. TLD framework has the ability to re-initialize object but can't handle rotation and runs with low efficiency. In this paper, we propose a tracking algorithm combining the CT into TLD framework to overcome the disadvantages of each other. With the scale information obtained by an optical-flow tracker, we select samples for detector and use the detection result to correct the optical-flow tracker. The features are extracted using compressive sensing to improve the processing speed. The classifier parameters are updated by online learning. Considering the situation of continuous loss of object, a sliding window searching is also employed. Experiment results show that our proposed method achieves good performances in both precision and speed.

Keywords: Visual tracking · Compressive sensing · TLD framework · Multi-scale · Multi-object

1 Introduction

Visual tracking is an important research topic in computer vision. It has wide applications in the areas of surveillance, intelligent vehicle navigation and human-computer interaction. The tracking process estimates the position of object in the subsequent frame based on the positions in previous frames. Although a number of algorithms have been proposed over past several decades, object tracking remains a challenging problem because of the appearance changes of object caused by pose variation, illumination changes, drift, occlusion, background clutter and so on [1]. In addition to these aspects, the computational efficiency of algorithms also needs to be considered for real-time processing, especially for multi-object tracking. According to appearance model of object, the tracking algorithms of the literature can be divided into generative methods [2, 3] and discriminative methods [4, 5]. The generative methods are based on previous frames to generate an appearance model of target for estimating the reconstruction errors of the object candidates in the next frame. The generative model can be

© Springer International Publishing AG 2017
G. Sidorov and O. Herrera-Alcántara (Eds.): MICAI 2016, Part I, LNAI 10061, pp. 459–470, 2017.
DOI: 10.1007/978-3-319-62434-1_37

trained off-line in initialization phase [2] and updated online to adapt itself to the appearance changes [6]. However, the background information isn't utilized to improve tracking stability and accuracy. The discriminative methods treat tracking as binary classification problem. The current region is composed of the object and background. Classifier is updated by positive and negative samples in the current frame. There are two main challenges to build such a tracking-by-detection system [7]: (1) Finding a good and effective feature representation for object tracking; (2) Developing an efficient learning algorithm to train the detector. Besides, an ensemble post-processor, which fuses the information of different trackers, also influents results a lot, especially when the trackers have high diversity.

Compressive tracking (CT) proposed by Zhang [8] is an efficient tracking algorithm with a discriminative model. This algorithm uses sparse representation and compressive sensing to decrease the dimension of features. Thus, the computation time is significantly reduced. However, the robustness still needs to be improved for fast movements and occlusion. In addition, although the CT tracker utilizes multi-scale rectangle filter to obtain the features of multi-scale object, the size of the tracked bounding box always remains fixed, which is a significant drawback when object changes significantly in scale. In [9], Wu modified the rectangle filter and the measurement matrix to make the compressive sensing suitable to multi-scale object, and used Bootstrap filter to produce the scales and locations of candidate objects. However, this algorithm reduces the processing speed and can't handle the situation when object disappears and reappears. Tracking-Learning-Detection (TLD) framework [10] improves tracking performance by combining a detector to an optical-flow tracker. The detector is used to correct the drift of tracker and to re-initializes the tracking after an occlusion. It uses a sliding window based algorithm to scan the input image by various window sizes to detect whether the patch contains the object. However, most of the checked grids are negative samples, so detecting these girds consumes a lot of processing time and reduces efficiency [11].

In this paper, we propose an approach which combines compressive tracking (CT) into TLD framework to enhance the TLD detector and overcome the disadvantages of the CT algorithm simultaneously. Figure 1 visualizes the whole framework. We use compressive sensing features instead of the original ones used in TLD to improve the processing speed without loss of accuracy. The features and the measurement matrix are modified to be adapted to the various sizes of bounding boxes. The tracker uses optical-flow tracking algorithm to estimate the position and scale of target for each frame. Then, we provide the scale information to the detector to sample nearby the tracked position of previous frame. The samples are discriminated by a trained Naïve Bayes classifier to find out the bounding box of maximum classification score as the detected object. The final position is acquired through integrating the information of tracker and detector. In case the object disappears and reappears from different position, we also build a cascade classifier to re-initialize the object from samples of different scales acquired by a global sliding window. Classifiers are updated by online learning. Finally, we extend this algorithm to multi-object tracking.

The contributions of this paper are twofold: First, we show how to combine the CT tracker into TLD framework with the scale information provided by optical-flow tracker. Second, we select the candidate samples for detector with two motion models,

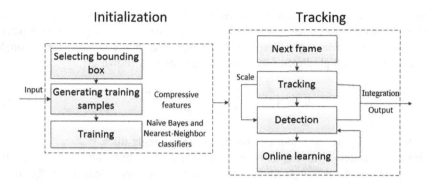

Fig. 1. Flow diagram of the proposed method

radius search window and global sliding window, depending on different tracking situations, and the advantage of our method with respect to original methods is shown.

This paper is organized as follows. In Sect. 2, we present related works about compressive tracking and TLD framework. Section 3 describes in details our approach. Section 4 shows experimental results with common datasets. Section 5 summaries the paper and prospects future improvements.

2   Related Works

2.1   Compressive Tracking

Compressive sensing theory [12] indicates that if a signal is sparse in a transform domain, we can use an observation matrix unrelated to the transform basis to project the signal from high-dimension space to low-dimension space. The original signal can be reconstructed precisely through solving an optimization problem. That means that the projection already contains enough information of original signal. This dimension reduction process can be expressed as $v = Rx$. $v \in \mathbb{R}^n, x \in \mathbb{R}^m$ are the m, n-dimension vectors respectively, where $n \ll m$, and $R \in \mathbb{R}^{n \times m}$ is the random measurement matrix.

Zhang [8] found a very sparse random measurement matrix $R_0 \in \mathbb{R}^{n \times m}$ satisfying the restricted isometry property (RIP) required by compressive sensing, whose matrix element is defined as:

$$r_{i,j} = \sqrt{s} \times \begin{cases} 1 & \text{with probability } \frac{1}{2s} \\ 0 & \text{with probability } 1 - \frac{1}{s} \\ -1 & \text{with probability } \frac{1}{2s} \end{cases} \tag{1}$$

Where s is set to be $m/4$. The matrix is very easy to calculate with a uniform random number generator.

Using a set of rectangle filters to convolve the input image, compressive tracking provides multi-scale feature representation of selected image patch. These features actually are equivalent to the sum of the pixels in the corresponding rectangles.

Therefore, the convolution can be efficiently calculated by the integral image. The result of each convolution is a matrix with the same size as the original image patch. All the matrices are arranged into column vectors and then combined into a single feature vector with high-dimension. The rectangle filter is shown as:

$$h_{i,j}(x, y) = \begin{cases} 1 & 1 \leq x \leq i, 1 \leq y \leq j \\ 0 & \text{otherwise} \end{cases} \tag{2}$$

Where i and j are the width and height of the rectangle filter.

With the random measurement matrix R_0, when we extract the features, we only need to compute the rectangle filters corresponding to nonzero elements in R_0, so the computation load is very light. Each element of final feature vector can be expressed as $v_i = \sum_j r_{ij}x_j$. The matrix R_0 needs to be computed only once and will keep fixed during the tracking process. A Naïve Bayes classifier is trained with the lower dimension features to model the tracking process. Positive samples nearby the target and negative samples far away from the target are selected to update the classifier parameters in each frame. To predict the object position, samples are extracted within a predefined search radius surrounding the object location in the previous frame, and the patch with the maximum classification score will be selected as the most probable tracking position.

2.2   TLD Framework

TLD framework, also known as Predator and Tracking-Modelling-Detection (TMD), is a long term single object tracking algorithm proposed by Zsenek Kalal during his PhD [10]. Traditional short-term trackers always drift away from their objects over time. The process of TLD is to use a tracker as the supervisor to train a detector, and use the trained detector to correct the tracker and re-initialize when the tracker fails. The only prior knowledge about the object is a bounding box in the initial frame. The detector is trained online via semi-supervised learning. The algorithm can be divided into four modules: tracking module, detector module, integrator module and learning module. The detailed block-diagram of the TLD framework is shown in Fig. 2.

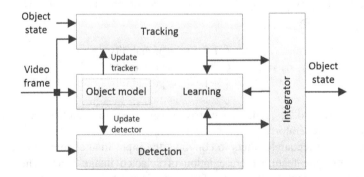

Fig. 2. The detailed block-diagram of the TLD framework [10]

The tracker utilizes a median-flow tracking algorithm [10] based on Lucas-Kanade optical-flow to estimate the position and scale changes of the object. Firstly, a uniform set of feature points in previous frame are tracked with Lucas-Kanade. Then, the error of each tracked point is estimated using both Forward-Backward error and Normalised Cross-Correlation. Filtering out the invalid points, the remaining points are utilized to estimate the bounding-box at time $t + 1$.

The detector uses a sliding window to scan the entire frame and classifies each patch with a cascade classifier. The cascade classifier has three components: variance filter, ensemble classifier and Nearest-Neighbor classifier. The patch will be rejected if the variance is less than half the variance of the object. The ensemble classifier is a random forest classifier including 10 trees, and each tree has 13 nodes. The Nearest-Neighbor classifier evaluates the relative similarity and conservative similarity between the patch and the positive patch set, the patch and negative patch set respectively. These two sets represent the object model and are updated by P-N learning [14].

The integrator combines the outputs of the tracker and detector into a single output through similarity comparison. If there is no output bounding box in neither the tracker nor the detector, the object will be declared to be invisible.

The learning module is implemented by the P-N learning algorithm [14]. The purpose of P-N learning is to correct the classification errors. P-expert is mainly based on the consideration of temporal structure and increases the robustness of the classifier. N-expert mainly considers the space structure and increases the discriminative ability of the classifier.

3 Proposed Method

In this section, we present our method in details. The tracking framework is initialized in the first frame. The compressive features are extracted to train the classifiers with a modified rectangle filter and a measurement matrix adapted to different scales. During the initialization phase, we firstly consider the first frame and select the bounding box manually for the initial position of object. The patches nearby and far away from this position are selected as the positive and negative samples respectively. The negative samples are split into a training set and a test set. After training, the test set will be the input into each classifier, and we will use the maximum classification value to correct the initial classification threshold. In each frame, the tracker estimates the location and scale information of object. According to the scale information, we obtain the detection candidates surrounding the object position of the previous frame, and the Naïve Bayes classifier will look for the patch of the maximum classification score as the detected object from the samples. The integrator combines the results provided by the tracker and detector. In order to prevent the failure of tracking, we re-initialize the target location using a sliding window and a cascade classifier after low reliability of several continuous frames. Classifier parameters are updated by online learning.

3.1 Tracking and Detection

We use a median-flow tracker as in TLD framework. To get the Forward-Backward error, a set of feature points are tracked by Lucas-Kanade optical-flow from frame t to frame $t + 1$, then the same points are backward tracked from frame $t + 1$ to frame t with the same method. The distances between the backward tracked points and the original points are the measured errors. Normalised Cross-Correlation is the measurement of the image similarity between the two patches of each point at times t and $t + 1$. Filtering out 50% of points with the largest errors, tracker will use the remaining points to estimate the position and scale of the tracking box.

The detector is coupled with the tracking by detecting samples around the selected region of the previous frame within a fixed radius. However, with fixed size of searching windows, when the selected region drifts or the scale of target changes more background will be contained in the window, which would lead to inaccuracy of classification [11]. Thus, we change the size of the searching windows in each frame following the output of tracker to improve the detection accuracy. In response to the wrong value of the scale information when the tracker fails, the scale input to the detector is limited between 0.5 – 1.5. Although the rectangle filter uses different sizes of rectangles to obtain multi-scale representation of the object, the rectangle features are not suitable to scale changes of sampled patches, because when the rectangle regions are zoomed in and zoomed out, the sum of pixels will not be the same. We modify the rectangle filter and the random measurement matrix in the same way as [9]. Equation (2) is then modified as:

$$h_{i,j}(x, y) = \begin{cases} \frac{1}{ij} & 1 \leq x \leq i, 1 \leq y \leq j \\ 0 & \text{otherwise} \end{cases} \tag{3}$$

Where the nonzero elements become $\frac{1}{ij}$, and the rectangle features still can be calculated by the integral image. Because of the changing dimension of the original high-dimension features, the random measurement matrix R_0 also needs to be changed. For sampling with scale s, the positions and sizes of the rectangles corresponding to the nonzero elements of R_0 will be zoomed in or zoomed out by the same scale. We calculate R_0 once in the initialization phase, and modify it according to s in each frame.

After extracting the compressive low-dimension features from the positive and negative samples, a Naïve Bayes classifier and a Nearest-Neighbor classifier are both trained. The Naïve Bayes classifier is a simple but effective choice to get the classification score of each sample. The feature of i th sample is denoted by $v^{(i)} = \left(v_1^{(i)}, v_2^{(i)}, \ldots, v_n^{(i)} \right)$, with a label $y^{(i)} = 1$ if it corresponds to object, $y^{(i)} = 0$ if it corresponds to background. For the k th element of $v^{(i)}$, we assume $p(v_k^{(i)} | y^{(i)} = 1) \sim \mathcal{N}\left(\mu_k^1, \sigma_k^1 \right)$ and $p(v_k^{(i)} | y^{(i)} = 0) \sim \mathcal{N}\left(\mu_k^0, \sigma_k^0 \right)$. $\mu_k^1, \sigma_k^1, \mu_k^0, \sigma_k^0$ are the classifier parameters updated in each frame by maximal likelihood estimation with the learning parameter λ [8]. The classifier response is:

$$H(v^{(i)}) = \sum_{k=1}^{m} \log(\frac{p(v_k^{(i)}|y^{(i)} = 1)}{p(v_k^{(i)}|y^{(i)} = 0)}) \tag{4}$$

The Nearest-Neighbor classifier measures the relative similarity and conservative similarity of each input patch. Relative similarity is defined as: $S^T = \frac{S^+}{S^+ + S^-}$, where S^+ and S^- are the feature similarities between input patch and positive sample set and between input patch and negative sample set respectively. Conservative similarity is defined as: $S^c = \frac{S_{50\%}^+}{S_{50\%}^+ + S^-}$, where $S_{50\%}^+$ is the feature similarity between input patch and first 50% of positive sample set [10].

In the general situation, the Naïve Bayes classifier is used to find the detected object from sampled candidates and the Nearest-Neighbor classifier is used to evaluate the results of both tracker and detector by measuring the relative similarity. In order to deal with the situation where the object disappears from the view and reappears at another position, when the tracker and the detector both fail over ten consecutive frames, we will use a sliding window of various scales for global sampling, and detect the object with a cascade classifier. All the patches will pass Naïve Bayes classifier and Nearest-Neighbor classifier. If there is only one output bounding box from the clustering of the positive patches utilizing the conservative similarity, this bounding box will be used for re-initialization.

3.2   Integration and Learning

The outputs from the tracker and detector will be integrated into a single output according to the following strategy:

(a) When the tracker has an output, if the relative similarity is higher than detection result, then we use the bounding box provided by the tracker as the final output. Or we use the bounding box provided by the detector as the final output.
(b) If the tracker hasn't an output, then we use detection result as the final output.
(c) If the tracker and the detector both fail for ten consecutive frames, we start a sliding window scanning. Once the object is found successfully, back to (a).

In each frame, when the relative similarity of the final output is higher than a threshold set manually, online learning will be activated. Samples nearby the target and samples far away from the target are stored to the positive set and negative set respectively to update the classifiers. Besides, when tracker is valid to provide the final result, the patches with positive classification scores but low overlap rates with the target will be added to the negative set. The whole algorithm can be summarized as following:

```
Initialize the tracker and detector;
Correct the classification thresholds thr_nb, thr_nn;
for i = 2 to M (M is the length of the image sequence.)
if k<= 10 (kcounts the consecutive failed frames.)
Track using median-flow, and output the tracking boxtBB,
        scale s, relative similaritytConf;
Select samples of scale s surrounding the object of
        previous frame. Extractcompressive features;
        Use NaïveBayes classifier to detect the object
        cBBwith the relative similarity ofcConf;
Intergrate tBB and cBB to a single output BBby comparing
        tConf and cConf;
if(BBisempty) k ←k + 1;
elsek ←0;
else
Detect the object using a sliding window with the cascade
        classifier;
Cluster the positive patches;
if(there is only one output cBB)BB←cBB, k←0;
Update classifier parameters byonline learning;
```

3.3 Extension to Multi-object Tracking

We extend our algorithm to two or more objects tracking by parallel processing of each object. For each object, a data structure is created to store the parameters and the sample sets. Every object is tracked by independent tracker and detector. The processing flowchart is shown in Fig. 3.

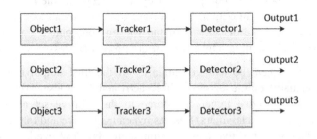

Fig. 3. Parallel Processing for multi-object tracking

Multi-core CPU parallel processing technology can be considered to further improve the processing speed.

4 Experiments

This section details the results of our algorithm. We compare our results with those of compressive tracking and TLD used alone. We use the image sequence from the videos of TLD dataset [10] and the website http://www.visual-tracking.net. The metrics we use to evaluate the results are the PASCAL overlap measure [15] and the center location error [16], which are both widely used as evaluation metrics for tracking precision. The bounding box overlap measure is defined as:

$$S = \frac{|B_t \cap B_{gt}|}{|B_t \cup B_{gt}|} \tag{5}$$

Where B_t is the tracking bounding box, and B_{gt} is the ground truth in each frame. If the overlap ratio of bounding box with the ground truth is bigger than 0.25 [10], we consider the tracking is successful.

The center location error is defined as the average Euclidean distance between the center of the tracked object and the ground truth. We define the error within 20 pixels [16] to be successful.

We also measure the processing average frames per second (FPS) for both single-object tracking and multi-object tracking to evaluate the processing speed. The learning rate λ is set to 0.85 [8], and the number of rectangle filters is set to 100 to be a good balance between accuracy and speed. The threshold to active online learning is set to 0.3 which is acquired by experiments. We implement our algorithm with Matlab, C++ hybrid programming based on the open source code of CT and TLD running at a desktop with a quad-core CPU i7-3770 3.40 Ghz.

The tracking precision is defined as the percentage of frames with valid bounding box among all the predictions. We calculate the precision using both the overlap measure and the center location error. As shown in Table 1, the values in each column are the precision based on overlap, precision based on location error and the average FPS. According to the experiment results, our algorithm achieves a good performance. For the dataset 'David', corresponding to the situation of illumination changes, all these three algorithms perform well. We can see that the CT tracker drifts in image sequence 'Carchase' because it hasn't the ability to re-initialize its procedure when object is lost, and in the 'ClifBar', TLD loses the target because it can't handle object rotation. However, our tracker has a high tracking precision in these datasets. 'Tiger2' and 'Couple' correspond to occlusion and camera shaking situations respectively. The center location error of our tracker is high in 'Tiger2' but still better in overall. For dataset 'Football', all the methods track wrongly by estimating another similar target at the end. We can summarize that our method proposes a complementary between CT and TLD, allows a great improvement of the FPS to TLD and has the ability to preserve the tracking precision. Figure 4 shows some screenshots of the tracking results.

Finally, we test our method to multi-object tracking on 291×217 images sequence with three objects. Without any acceleration technology, the FPS is around 27, and we note that when the sliding window is activated to re-initialize, the processing speed decreases significantly. The screenshots of the tracking results are shown in Fig. 5.

Table 1. Comparison of our algorithm with CT and TLD. (The numbers in each column are the precision based on overlap, precision based on location and the average frames per second)

Datasets	Frames	Our algorithm	CT	TLD
David	462	0.989/0.947/44	0.955/0.998/69	0.975/0.975/24
Carchase	200	0.965/0.965/55	0.055/0.010/78	0.940/0.940/30
ClifBar	329	0.982/0.967/43	0.933/0.945/69	0.450/0.450/30
Tiger2	365	0.759/0.271/25	0.721/0.249/37	0.200/0.238/24
Couple	140	0.964/0.936/43	0.643/0.643/70	0.607/0.607/44
Football	362	0.779/0.790/34	0.798/0.798/51	0.790/0.790/20

Fig. 4. Screenshots of the tracking results (From top to bottom: **a.** David **b.** ClifBar **c.** Tiger2)

Fig. 5. Screenshots of the multi-object tracking

5   Conclusion

In this paper, we proposed a tracking algorithm integrating compressive tracking into TLD framework to complement and overcome disadvantages of each other. Giving the scale information acquired by tracker to detector, the detection result is more accurate to correct the tracker. The modified rectangle filter and random measurement matrix are used to extract the sparse compressive features of multi-scale patches. We also considered the situation of losing target and extended our algorithm to multi-object tracking. Experiment results demonstrated that our method has good performance in both precision and speed compared to CT and TLD. However, the processing speed drops significantly when activating the re-initialization with a sliding window. In the further work, we envision employing moving object detection to initialize our tracker and improve the performance of re-initialization.

Acknowledgements. The authors gratefully acknowledge financial support from China Scholarship Council.

References

1. Yilmaz, A., Javed, O., Shah, M.: Object tracking: a survey. ACM Comput. Surv. (CSUR) **38**(4), 13 (2006)
2. Black, M.J., Jepson, A.D.: Eigentracking: robust matching and tracking of articulated objects using a view-based representation. Int. J. Comput. Vis. **26**(1), 63–84 (1998)
3. Wang, D., Lu, H., Yang, M.H.: Least soft-threshold squares tracking. In: Proceedings of the IEEE Conference on Computer Vision and Pattern Recognition, pp. 2371–2378 (2013)
4. Grabner, H., Grabner, M., Bischof, H.: Real-time tracking via on-line boosting. In: BMVC, vol. 1, p. 6 (2006)
5. Avidan, S.: Support vector tracking. IEEE Trans. Pattern Anal. Mach. Intell. **26**(8), 1064–1072 (2004)
6. Ross, D.A., Lim, J., Lin, R.S., Yang, M.H.: Incremental learning for robust visual tracking. Int. J. Comput. Vis. **77**(1–3), 125–141 (2008)
7. Wang, N., Shi, J., Yeung, D.Y., Jia, J.: Understanding and diagnosing visual tracking systems. In: Proceedings of the IEEE International Conference on Computer Vision, pp. 3101–3109 (2015)
8. Zhang, K., Zhang, L., Yang, M.-H.: Real-time compressive tracking. In: Fitzgibbon, A., Lazebnik, S., Perona, P., Sato, Y., Schmid, C. (eds.) ECCV 2012. LNCS, vol. 7574, pp. 864–877. Springer, Heidelberg (2012). doi:10.1007/978-3-642-33712-3_62
9. Wu, Y., Jia, N., Sun, J.: Real-time multi-scale tracking based on compressive sensing. Vis. Comput. **31**(4), 471–484 (2015)
10. Kalal, Z., Mikolajczyk, K., Matas, J.: Tracking-learning-detection. IEEE Trans. Pattern Anal. Mach. Intell. **34**(7), 1409–1422 (2012)
11. Li, Q., Ge, X., Wang, G.: An improved TLD tracking method using compressive sensing. In: 18th International Conference on Advanced Information Technologies and Applications, San Diego, pp. 259–262 (2016)
12. Baraniuk, R.G.: Compressive sensing. IEEE Sig. Process. Mag. **24**(4), 118–121 (2007)

13. Achlioptas, D.: Database-friendly random projections. In: Proceedings of the Twentieth ACM SIGMOD-SIGACT-SIGART Symposium on Principles of Database Systems, pp. 274–281. ACM (2001)
14. Kalal., Z., Matas, J., Mikolajczyk, K.: PN learning: bootstrapping binary classifiers by structural constraints. In: 2010 IEEE Conference on Computer Vision and Pattern Recognition (CVPR), pp. 49–56. IEEE (2010)
15. Everingham, M., Van Gool, L., Williams, C.K., Winn, J., Zisserman, A.: The pascal visual object classes (VOC) challenge. Int. J. Comput. Vis. **88**(2), 303–338 (2010)
16. Wu, Y., Lim, J., Yang, M.H.: Online object tracking: a benchmark. In: Proceedings of the IEEE Conference on Computer Vision and Pattern Recognition, pp. 2411–2418 (2013)

Parameter Characterization of Complex Wavelets and its use in 3D Reconstruction

Claudia Victoria Lopez$^{(\boxtimes)}$, Jesus Carlos Pedraza,
Juan Manuel Ramos, Elias Gonzalo Silva,
and Efren Gorrostieta Hurtado

Universidad Autonoma de Queretaro, Queretaro, Mexico
azul.cielo.2007@gmail.com

Abstract. Fringe projection is an optical method used to perform three-dimensional reconstruction of objects by applying structured light and phase detection algorithms. Some of these algorithms make use of the wavelet transform, which is a function that splits a signal into sub-signals with different scales at different levels of resolution. However, despite the above characteristics, the use and implementation of the wavelet transform requires good parameterization of the many variables involved for each wavelet function (scale and translation coefficient variation), in addition to analyze different wavelet functions such as Morlet, Paul Mother, and Gaussian, among others. Based on these requirements, the present paper aims to develop an in-depth analysis of the most suitable parameters for the Shannon, B-Spline and Morlet Wavelets that ensure the most efficient 3D reconstruction. The experimental results are presented using a set of virtual objects and can be applied to a real object for the purpose of validation.

Keywords: Wavelet transform · Profilometry · Morlet · B-Spline · Shannon · 3D reconstruction

1 Introduction

In the past 30 years, many investigations in Computer Vision have made inference of 3D information in scenes, meaning extracting the useful depth information in 2D images [1]. This dimensional measurement has different applications, such as industrial inspection of manufactured parts, reverse engineering (digitization of complex, free-form surfaces), object recognition, 3D map building, biometrics, and clothing design, among others. For this kind of investigations there are two different techniques, which are of contact or non-contact [2]. We choose the non-contact technique, since nondestructive and noninvasive testing systems play a key role in many industrial applications [3].

In particular, optical methods such as fringe projection, projecting a line of light and projection of a beam have been used to reconstruct the 3D shape of fixed and rotated objects. These structured light techniques make the system very reliable and the acquired data are easier to understand and interpret. Specifically, in the fringe projection method, the object surface is obtained by applying a phase detection algorithm

G. Sidorov and O. Herrera-Alcántara (Eds.): MICAI 2016, Part I, LNAI 10061, pp. 471–481, 2017.
DOI: 10.1007/978-3-319-62434-1_38

since phase varies according to its profile [4]. The best known method for the fringe pattern analysis is called Fourier Transform Profilometry [5].

This first approach has multiple derived variations, such as the technique called Wavelet Profilometry, which is considered an extension of Fourier Profilometry. It takes advantage of a wavelet function, where the transition from one to more dimensions is immediate. It is possible to obtain a better simultaneous concentration in time and frequency, achieving efficient characterization of non-stationary and fast transient local signals. This is a mathematical tool capable of decomposing a signal into sub-signals with different scales at different levels of resolution [6]. The results vary according to the Wavelet function selected and its parameters.

However, only a few studies give a quantitative evaluation and analytic information of the parameters and functions used in the process. For example, Gorthi et al. [7] analyze the effects of non-periodic fringe patterns on the errors-of-phase calculation and give some qualitative comparisons in the discontinuities of the Wavelet Transform (WT). Li et al. [8] make full use of the amplitude information of wavelet coefficients in order to keep the phase unwrapping error limited to local minimum areas, with wavelets in 1D and 2D for phase recovery on a hemispherical object. Huang et al. [9] make comparisons between Windowed Fourier Transform (WFT) and WT methods for phase extraction from a single fringe pattern on a smooth surface. Quan et al. [10] examine the performance of phase calculation at discontinuities. Zhang et al. [11] explore an evaluation and analysis of the discontinuities of a single fringe pattern in WFT and WF algorithms.

Nevertheless, as the examples described above in other research, there is not a formal study of the parameters for each function selected, and these functions are limited in most cases to Morlet, Gaussian, and Paul Mother functions, which are well known in the literature [12, 13], and usually do not include wavelet functions such as Shannon or B-Spline.

In order to formally analyze both parameters, and work with other transforms commonly not used, the present work proposes the use of the complex wavelet in one dimension, working with a projected fringe pattern to obtain the 3D depth of virtual shapes varying parameters in the functions Morlet, Shannon, and B-Spline.

This paper is organized as follows: In Sect. 2 we introduced the principle of the WT and analytical wavelets. Simulated data varying the parameters is presented in Sect. 3. Section 4 shows the experimental results obtained using the selected variations. Finally, Sect. 5 contains the conclusion.

2 Wavelet Transform Principle and its use in 3D Reconstruction

The Continuous Wavelet Transform (CWT), developed in the 80's, is efficient for the analysis of non-stationary signals and fast transients. The wavelet maps the signal with a time-scale representation and provides a multi-resolution analysis, enabling the representation of the signal in both time and frequency simultaneously.

The Continuous Wavelet Transform (CWT) of a function $f(x)$ is the decomposition of the function into a set of functions $\psi_{s,\tau}(x)$, such that these form a basis and are called the "Wavelets". The Wavelet Transform is defined as:

$$W_f(S, \tau) = \int f(x)\psi^*_{S,\tau}(x)dx \tag{1}$$

where, s is a scale value, τ is the translation value, and * denotes complex conjugation.

The wavelets or daughter wavelets are generated from translations, dilations, and scale changes of the same wavelet function $\psi(x)$, called the "Mother Wavelet," defined as:

$$\psi_{\tau,s}(x) = \frac{1}{\sqrt{|s|}}\left(\frac{x-\tau}{s}\right) \tag{2}$$

where, s is a scale value, τ is the translation value, both factors being continuous variables.

The changes made to the Mother Wavelet give us several variants, enabling us to modify the parameters of the Wavelet itself and the domain in which it is located.

A classification of these methods is based on the way in which the translation and scale parameters are quantized, resulting in three types of Wavelet Transform: Continuous (CWT), Semi-discrete (SWT) and Discrete (DWT). Similarly, a secondary classification can be generated based on the nature of the wavelet function, i.e., complex or not complex, whichever is the case. In the present case we apply only Continuous CWT and inside it, the complex. The complex wavelet has real and imaginary parts which are used to handle the amplitude and phase information. In particular, for this study we analyze only the Complex Wavelets because we want to get the amplitude and phase information of the object to be reconstructed. Figure 1 shows the plots of some Complex Wavelets.

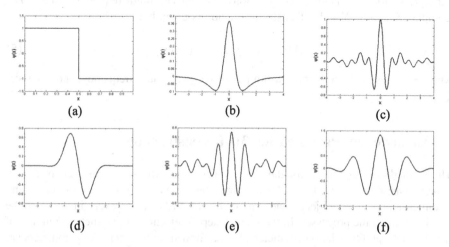

Fig. 1. Mother wavelet transforms; (a) Haar, (b) Paul, (c) Shannon, (d) Gaussian first derivative, (e) B-Spline, (f) Morlet.

2.1   Complex Morlet Wavelet

Complex Morlet is part of the Continuous family of wavelets, frequently used because it is very responsive to vibration signals. It is defined by:

$$\Psi(x) = \pi^{-1/4} \, exp(i2\pi w_0 x) exp\left(-x^2/2\right) \tag{3}$$

where, i is equal to $\sqrt{-1}$, w_0 is the frequency of Morlet wavelet.

Using the complex version of wavelets allows us to separate the phase and amplitude components within the signal.

2.2   B-Spline Wavelet

Signal processing has a range of data that is better described as a group of local features, followed by a single global feature. The B-Spline has its roots in a generation of curves and computer aided geometric design, and it is defined for a polynomial by parts with a compact support, the general equation is given by:

$$\Psi(x) = \sqrt{f_b} \, exp(2\pi i f_c x) \left[\left(sinc\left(\frac{f_b x}{m}\right) \right) \right]^m \tag{4}$$

where, f_b corresponds to the bandwidth parameter, f_c to central frequency, m is the integer order of the wavelet and i is equal to $\sqrt{-1}$.

2.3   Shannon Wavelet

The Shannon wavelet is studied in conjunction with its distinctive properties, known as the connection coefficients. The Shannon sampling theorem can be considered more appropriate for the analysis of functions ranging in multi-frequency bands. The Complex Shannon Wavelet Transform function is given by:

$$\Psi(x) = \sqrt{f_b} \, exp(2\pi i f_c x)(sinc(f_b x)) \tag{5}$$

where f_b corresponds to the bandwidth parameter, f_c o central frequency, and i is equal to $\sqrt{-1}$.

3   Methodology Proposed for 3D Reconstruction

The methodology proposed for the 3D reconstruction process is presented in Fig. 2, which consists of eight steps. In the first step, a virtual object is obtained and re-dimensioned to an object inside an image of 512×512 pixels in order to be consistent in all the processes. In the second step, a selection of parameters (number of fringes, scale and translation coefficients) is performed. In this step, the parameters are varied heuristically for each transform selected (3 for B-Spline, and 2 for the others). In step three, a fringe pattern with frequency f_o is added to the object. In the fourth step, the selected wavelet transform (B-Spline, Morlet, and Shannon) is applied for processing the 3D reconstruction. The fifth step determines the number of fringes added to the object. This number is important because it serves to find the spatial frequency f_o, which is used in the filtering process. In the sixth step, once the filtering in the frequency f_o has been carried out, the inverse wavelet transform is obtained. By detecting the amplitude value at each position of higher coefficients of Wavelet Transform, the modulating phase of the fringe pattern added can be recovered, thereby obtaining the desired information. Once the corresponding inverse transforms are obtained, the phase map of the object is obtained in step seven. In step eight, the unwrapped phase is obtained. This unwrapped phase corresponds to the 3D reconstruction. With this reconstruction it is possible to calculate the difference with the original object. This difference provides the error as a result. The result is saved for use in a statistical analysis, in order to find the best parameters for 3D reconstruction.

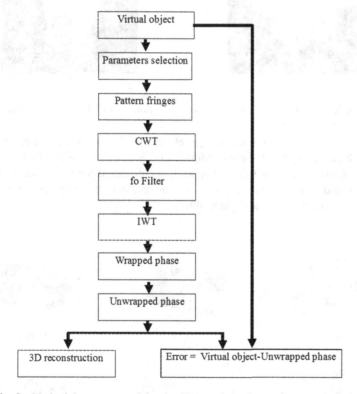

Fig. 2. Methodology proposed for the 3D reconstruction and error calculation.

The purpose of the variation of these parameters is to identify those that provide minimal error, i.e., the result of reconstruction is nearest to the original object. This variation was used, taking all the possible values of the parameters mentioned beforehand, i.e., for the bandwidth, we took the values in a range of 0.5 to 2 with an increment of 0.5. The same procedure was applied for all parameters.

4 Experimental Results

For this proposed methodology, we selected two virtual objects shown in Fig. 3. We obtain a quantitative error for each point in a depth plane. These values can be computed independently or as statistical error over the entire shape, meaning the average over each point in the shape.

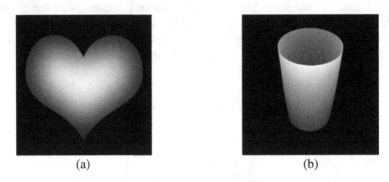

(a)   (b)

Fig. 3. Objects used for the proposed methodology: (a) Heart and (b) Glass.

Once the objects to be processed were selected, all the possible errors are calculated for each object, using the B-Spline, Morlet, and Shannon wavelets. Figures 4 and 5 show the minimum error, which in this work is considered the best case. In the same way Figs. 6 and 7 show the maximum error, the results in these figures are considered the worst case for the heart and glass object.

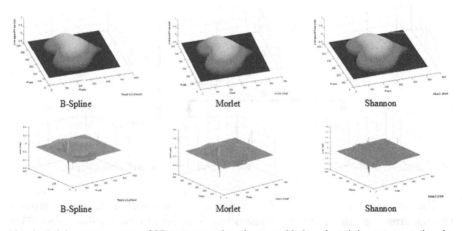

Fig. 4. Minimum error case of 3D reconstruction above, and below the minimum error using the heart object with B-Spline, Morlet and Shannon wavelets.

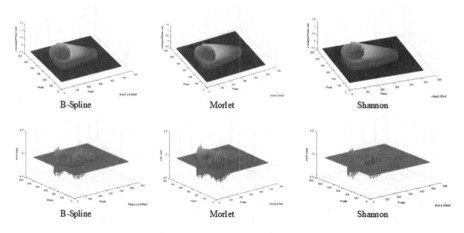

Fig. 5. Minimum error case of 3D reconstruction above, and below the minimum error using glass object with B-Spline, Morlet and Shannon wavelets.

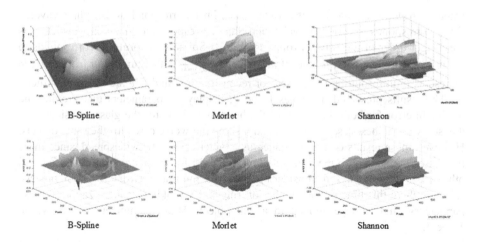

Fig. 6. Maximum error case of 3D reconstruction above, and below the maximum error using the heart object with B-Spline, Morlet and Shannon wavelets.

It is necessary to establish a standard of the parameters between the heart and glass virtual objects, due to these parameters are different in both cases. In Tables 1 and 2, we present the parameters used in obtaining the values previously shown, represented as follows:

$$'wavelet'\ 'm' - 'fb' - 'fc'\ 'f' \frac{1}{fringes}\ 'e'\ 'scale'$$

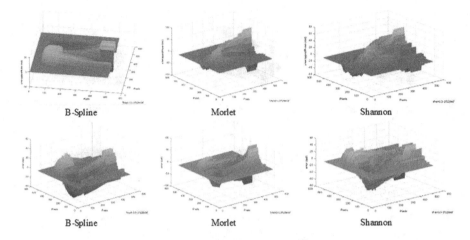

Fig. 7. Maximum error case of 3D reconstruction above, and below the maximum error using the glass object with B-Spline, Morlet and Shannon wavelets.

where, *wavele* t is the name of the wavelet, i.e., Fbsp corresponds to B-Spline wavelet, Cmor corresponds to Morlet wavelet, and Shan corresponds to Shannon wavelet, m is the integer order of the wavelet (only apply to B-Spline transform), fb corresponds to the bandwidth parameter, fc to central frequency, $\frac{1}{fringes}$ is the number of fringes, *scale* represents multiresolution scale used for reconstruction, and f, e are string identifiers.

The results presented in Tables 1 and 2, display all parameters that provide the minimum error for both the object of the heart as well as for the glass, considered in this study as the best cases. Tables 3 and 4 show the worse cases for the same objects. However, these results do not guarantee us a better case to be widespread, since these best cases are subject to the number of fringes used for reconstruction. Therefore, all other cases were analyzed considering only the minimum errors for both objects, selecting them this time by the number of fringes. By looking standardization of these parameters, they can be applied to a real object. These parameters are shown in Table 5.

Table 1. Minimum error in the 3D reconstruction of the heart shape

CWT	Wavelet	m	fb	fc	fringes	Scale	Min. error
B-Spline	Fbsp	3	1.5	2	f128	e16	0.00176
Morlet	Cmor	n/a	1	1	f128	e8	0.00246
Shannon	Shan	n/a	2	2	f128	e8	0.00325

Table 2. Minimum error in the 3D reconstruction of the glass shape

CWT	Wavelet	m	fb	fc	Fringes	Scale	Min. error
B-Spline	Fbsp	3	1	0.5	f128	e8	0.002324
Morlet	Cmor	n/a	1	1	f128	e8	0.003583
Shannon	Shan	n/a	2	2	f128	e8	0.004813

Table 3. Maximum error in the 3D reconstruction for the heart shape

CWT	Wavelet	m	fb	fc	Fringes	Scale	Max. error
B-Spline	Fbsp	4	2	1	f4	e64	18.158673
Morlet	Cmor	n/a	2	1.5	f4	e8	27.822529
Shannon	Shan	n/a	0.5	2	f4	e32	12.429766

Table 4. Maximum error in the 3D reconstruction for the glass shape

CWT	Wavelet	m	fb	fc	Fringes	Scale	Max. error
B-Spline	Fbsp	5	0.5	1	f4	e16	7.990961
Morlet	Cmor	n/a	2	1.5	f4	e16	9.18
Shannon	Shan	n/a	0.5	1	f4	e8	7.653576

Table 5. Standard parameters used for a minimum error for any amount of fringes patterns.

Standard paramters			
B-Spline	Fbsp3−1−0.5fXeY	Fbsp3−2−1fXeY	Fbsp4−1−0.5fXeY
Morlet	Cmor1−1.5fXeY	Cmor0.5−1.5fXeY	Cmor1.5−1fXeY
Shannon	Shan0.5−0.5fXeY	Shan2−2fXeY	Shan1−1fXeY

where, in all cases X corresponds to the number of fringes, and Y corresponds to one scale of 16, 32 or 64. The results presented are the three with minimum error ordered by best performance. This selection made according to the highest number of times that the parameters appear in the results, i.e., how many times each parameter was repeated for both objects (the heart and glass), taking into account their minimum error. For the case of Morlet a study in this field has been developed before in [14] and the results do not contrast with the result obtained in this work.

The minimum values present in Fig. 4 were applied to a real object, using a fringe pattern of 128 fringes, which is shown in Fig. 8.

Fig. 8. Real object with 128 fringes.

Figure 9 shows the 3D reconstruction with the parameters obtained for minimum error. It is important to mention that the real object has some external factors to be

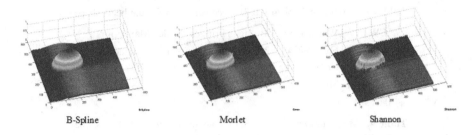

B-Spline   Morlet   Shannon

Fig. 9. 3D reconstruction of a real object using the parameters obtained.

considered in the reconstruction, such as the shadow of the object created by the light at the time of projecting the fringe pattern, the object opacity, the light of the environment, among others. These factors are decisive to obtain a good 3D reconstruction.

The methodology used in Fig. 2, shows some variations when applied to the real object. Since this object already has the projected fringe pattern. On the other hand, the comparison between the object and its 3D reconstruction cannot be performed, since the measurement of the original object is unknown.

5   Conclusions

In this paper a parameter characterization was presented considering three different wavelets: B-Spline, Morlet, and Shannon, which was applied to virtual objects. The parameter variation includes scale, number of fringes, and displacement coefficients. It is important to note that the number of fringes is directly proportional to the quality of the reconstruction, i.e., the greater the number of fringes, the better the reconstruction. On the other hand, these parameters provide a set of quantifiable values for a statistical analysis to identify which of these values are appropriate for getting the best 3D reconstruction of a real object. With the results obtained it is possible establish a standard of values for any number of fringes projected over an object, continuing with scales of 16 to 64 for a minimal error. Likewise, we deduced which type of wavelet produced best results. The B-Spline produces a more successful reconstruction even in the worst case. (See Fig. 6.) The results obtained with Morlet confirm the work presented by Abdulbasit-Zaid [14], supporting with theory the practical experimentation developed in the present work.

Acknowledgments. This research was supported by "Consejo Nacional de Ciencia y Tecnologia" (CONACYT) through the project 590661 and also we would like to thank Universidad Autonoma de Queretaro.

References

1. Pedraza Ortega, J.C., Rodriguez Moreno, J.W., Barriga Rodriguez, L., Gorrostieta Hurtado, E., Salgado Jimenez, T., Ramos Arreguin, J.M., Rivas, A.: Image processing for 3D reconstruction using a modified fourier transform profilometry method. In: Gelbukh, A., Kuri Morales, Á.F. (eds.) MICAI 2007. LNCS, vol. 4827, pp. 705–712. Springer, Heidelberg (2007). doi:10.1007/978-3-540-76631-5_67
2. Salvi, J., Fernandez, S., Pribanic, T., Llado, X.: A state of the art in structured light patterns for surface profilometry. Pattern Recogn. **43**, 2666–2680 (2010)
3. Ambrosini, D., Paoletti, D., Rashidnia, N.: Overview of diffusion measurements by optical techniques. Opt. Lasers Eng. **46**, 852–864 (2008)
4. Fernandez, S., Gdeisat, M.A., Salvi, J., Burton, D.R.: Automatic window size selection in windowed Fourier transform for 3D reconstruction using adapted mother wavelets. Opt. Commun. **284**(12), 2797–2807 (2011)
5. Su, X., Chen, W.: Fourier transform profilometry. Opt. Lasers Eng. **35**, 263–284 (2001)
6. Gdeisat, M.A., Abid, A., Burton, D.R., Lalor, M.J., Liley, F., Moore, C., Qudeisat, M.: Spatial and temporal carrier fringe pattern demodulation using the one-dimensional continuous wavelet transform: recent progress, challenges, and suggested developments. Opt. Lasers Eng. **47**(12), 1348–1361 (2009)
7. Gorthi, S.S., Lolla, K.R.: Wavelet transform analysis of truncated fringe patterns in 3D surface profilometry. In: Proceeding of SPIE, vol. 5856, pp. 265–273 (2005)
8. Li, S., S., Su, X., Y., Chen, W.: Spatial carrier fringe pattern phase demodulation by use of a two dimensional real wavelet. Appl. Opt. **48**, 893–906 (2009)
9. Huang, L., Qian, K.M., Pan, B., Asundi, A.K.: Comparison of Fourier transform, and wavelet transform methods for phase extraction from a single fringe pattern in fringe projection profilometry. Optic. Lasers Eng. **48**, 141–148 (2010)
10. Quan, C., Chen, W., Tray, C.: Phase-retrieval techniques in fringe projection profilometry. Optic. Lasers Eng. **48**, 235–243 (2010)
11. Zhang, Z., Jing, Z., Wang, Z., Kuang, D.: Comparison of Fourier transform, windowed Fourier transform, and wavelet transform methods for phase calculation at discontinuities in fringe profilometry. Optic. Lasers Eng. **50**, 1152–1160 (2012)
12. Forster, B., Blu, T., Unser, M.: Complex B-splines. Appl. Comput. Harmon. Anal. **20**, 261–282 (2006)
13. Cattani, C.: Shannon wavelets theory. Mathematical Problems in Engineering, pp. 1–24, (2008)
14. Abid, A..Z., Gdeisat, M.A., Burton, D.R., Lalor, M.J., Abdul-Rahman, H.S., Lilley, F.: Fringe pattern analysis using a one-dimensional modified Morlet continuous wavelet transform. In: Photonics Europe. International Society for Optics and Photonics, p. 70000Q (2008)

Methodology for Automatic Collection of Vehicle Traffic Data by Object Tracking

Jesús Caro-Gutierrez[1]([✉]), Miguel E. Bravo-Zanoguera[2],
and Félix F. González-Navarro[1]

[1] Engineering Institute, Autonomous University of Baja California,
Ensenada, Mexico
c17jesus@gmail.com, fernando.gonzalez@uabc.edu.mx
[2] Engineering Faculty, Autonomous University of Baja California,
Ensenada, Mexico
mbravo@uabc.edu.mx

Abstract. Traffic monitoring is carried out both manual and mechanically, and is subject to problems of subjectivity and high costs due to human errors. This study proposes a methodology to collect vehicle traffic data (counts, speeds, etc.) on video in an automated fashion, by means of object tracking techniques, which can help to design and implement reliable and accurate software. The development of this methodology has followed the design cycle of all tracking system, namely, preprocessing, detection, tracking and quantification. The preprocessing stage attenuated the noise and increased the classification percentage by an average of 10%. The object detection algorithm with better performance was Gaussian Mixture Models with an execution time of 0.06 s per image and a classification percentage of 86.71%. The Computational cost of the object tracking was reduced using Template Matching with Search Window. Finally, the quantification stage got to successfully collect the vehicular traffic data on video.

Keywords: Traffic monitoring · Video processing · Object detection and tracking

1 Introduction

Studies about vehicle traffic are crucial for the analyzing and decision-making related to the development of transportation systems. Volume and composition of traffic, velocity studies, travel times and movement directions are some of the statistics collected by traffic monitoring systems in Transportation Departments, where volume and complexity must be manage in order to avoid delays in daily activities in most modern cities [1].

Currently, most of traffic monitoring is done manually and mechanically. In the first case, a group of people keeps track of the count and vehicles type by using sheet papers. In periods of high-volume traffic, observers are overloaded with huge amount of data that cannot be registered with required accuracy and

© Springer International Publishing AG 2017
G. Sidorov and O. Herrera-Alcántara (Eds.): MICAI 2016, Part I, LNAI 10061, pp. 482–493, 2017.
DOI: 10.1007/978-3-319-62434-1_39

reliable standards. In the second case, tools such as pneumatic tube counters and loop detectors are used to obtain the monitoring data, which tend to be very expensive [2].

In order to avoid or minimize errors, a methodology that can help to create reliable and accurate software in traffic data acquisition is proposed. Aiming to solve subjectivity problems in human observers, an automated fashion proposal by means of object tracking techniques is described in this paper. This would be a more economical solution in cases where the traffic data collection is carried out by expensive tools.

Some objectives that guided the design of the methodology presented in this paper were: identify noise causes in traffic videos that affect the vehicle tracking and propose strategies to reduce it; quantitatively compare the detection and tracking methods of vehicles to select and implement the most appropriate; and design a set of methods to collect the traffic monitoring data from videos.

The remainder of the work is organized as follows: Sect. 2 describes the material and the methodology used for the experiments, the results and their discussion are shown in Sects. 3 and 4 respectively, finally in Sect. 5 the conclusions are presented.

2 Materials and Methods

Data (video sequences) were selected as follows: from (i-Lids dataset for AVSS 2007), the easy and night videos were taken; from [3], mit; from [4], passat, inter and kwbb; and from [5], farley and simple. These videos were edited so that they had the characteristics: avi format, size 160×120 pixels and a 25 fps velocity (see Table 1). These sequences have been used to test and evaluate vehicle detection algorithms [6], in the development of a vision system to recognize objects and movements of vehicular traffic [7] and in the creation of algorithms to segment vehicles of their respective shadows [8].

Table 1. Technical details of video sequences.

Video name	Duration (s)	Images number	Video size
easy	201	5025	42.9 MB
night	234	5850	49.9 MB
mit	276	6900	58.9 MB
passat	51	1275	10.8 MB
inter	11	275	2.35 MB
kwbb	57	1425	12.1 MB
farley	676	16900	144.4 MB
simple	66	1650	14.1 MB

The experimental part and software development were carried out by using the software MATLAB R2013a, running on Windows 7 operative system, and a CPU @ 64-bit AMD TO6-3600 APU @ 2.10 GHz and a 6 GB RAM memory.

The methodology proposed in [9] was developed in this study, which corresponds with the design cycle of an object tracking system. The activities carried out in each of its stages are described below.

2.1   Video Preprocessing

A qualitative study was carried out with images of variance of the passat, night, mit, easy, inter and kwbb videos. It was found that the main noise causes were the capture device malfunction, its vibrations and the false movement produced by the branches and leaves of trees (dynamic background). Noise reduction strategies were proposed: smoothing operations, video stabilization and the use of low-resolution images respectively.

2.2   Object Detection

Background subtraction methods were quantitatively compared for the vehicles detection: Temporal Mean Filter (TMF), Gaussian Mixture Models (GMM) and Eigenbackgrounds (EB) [10]. Methods comparison was performed by using videos with noise (simple, passat, easy and kwbb), without and with the preprocessing stage and measuring the following features: execution time, memory consumption and correct classification percentage. To calculate classification percentages was necessary to estimate false positives and negatives.

2.3   Object Tracking

Template Matching (TM) method was used to track vehicles in a traffic scene. A quantitative comparison of the TM method and its variant Template Matching with Search Window (TMSW) took place. The comparison was made according to the number of blocks compared. Only at this stage we worked with other resolutions of the video sequences to clearly show which method had a lower computational cost.

2.4   Movement Quantification

This is the stage that allows the collection of vehicle traffic data. Among the main data are the following: vehicles counting, average velocity, average travel time, vehicular traffic composition and vehicular traffic volume. Below is an explanation of how the data were computed and collected.

Vehicle Counting. One of the main parameters is the count of the vehicles that have traveled for each lane of the road, this parameter is obtained by a counter that increases every time that a vehicle centroid enters in the region of interest (ROI), i.e. an image specific area.

Average Velocity. For its computation are necessary the numbers of the input and output images of a vehicle in the ROI, the elapsed time in crossing this region and the video frames per second (fps). Knowing how many frames passed between the input and output of a vehicle (Δc), single-vehicle velocity can be approximated by the following expression:

$$V_i = \frac{d}{\Delta c_i * fps} \tag{1}$$

It is necessary to know in advance the ROI distance (d), a good approximation of this means greater accuracy in velocity. If there is more than one vehicle, the average velocity is obtained as follows:

$$V_a = \frac{1}{n} \sum_{i}^{n} v_i \tag{2}$$

where n is the total number of vehicles.

Average Travel Time. This parameter is reciprocal of the previous, since a higher velocity means a lower travel time. It allows to know how much time is added to the travel of a vehicle, for example, by a given maintenance of the road. To calculate this parameter simply applies the following equation:

$$ATT = \frac{1}{n} \sum_{i}^{n} \Delta c_i * fps \tag{3}$$

where Δc_i is the number of frames that exists between the input and output of i-th vehicle, fps the video frame rate and n the total number of vehicles that have passed until that moment.

Vehicular Traffic Composition. This data is obtained as follows: first, for each detected vehicle its area in pixels units is calculated. Next, this area is compared against predefined ranges of pixels corresponding to the different types of vehicles. Finally, the vehicle is classified as a motorcycle, small, medium or large vehicle. It is very important to achieve good image segmentation because it can affect the areas in pixels of vehicles and as a result the vehicular traffic composition.

Vehicular Traffic Volume. Vehicular traffic volume can be defined as the number of vehicles that travel by a certain lane per unit of time, this data can be obtained by using the following equation:

$$VTV = \frac{n(t + \Delta_t) - n(t)}{\Delta_t} \tag{4}$$

where t is the time, Δ_t is a determined time interval and n is the total number of vehicles up to that time.

486   J. Caro-Gutierrez et al.

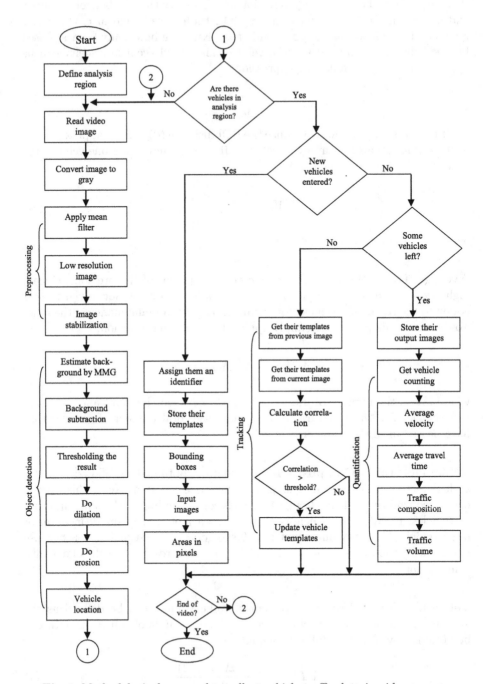

Fig. 1. Methodological proposal to collect vehicle traffic data in video scenes.

The complete methodology to collect vehicle traffic data in video scenes by object tracking can be seen in Fig. 1.

3   Results

Figure 2 presents the variance images of noisy videos and captured by cameras with vibration (Fig. 2a and b). Also the variance images of these same videos after the preprocessing stage are seen in Fig. 2c and d.

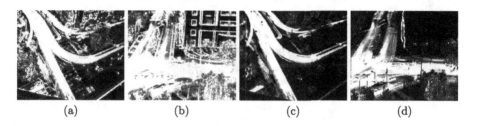

| (a) | (b) | (c) | (d) |

Fig. 2. Variance images of videos with noise and vibration (a and b) and variance images of the same videos after apply them preprocessing stage (c and d).

Table 2 shows information about execution time and memory consumption per image for three algorithms selected without (wo/p) and with preprocessing (w/p).

Table 2. Execution time and memory consumption for three algorithms selected.

Algorithm	Execution time per image (s)		Memory consumption (KB)	
	wo/p	w/p	wo/p	w/p
TMF	0.040	0.051	5480	7422
GMM	0.055	0.066	2936	4889
EB	0.083	0.100	22760	24815

The Correct Classification Percentages (CCP) in the the four scenarios without and with preprocessing is given in Table 3.

The data in Table 4 correspond to average percentages of False Positives (FP) and False Negatives (FN) in the four scenarios without and with preprocessing.

Table 5 shows the number of blocks compared when applying the template matching methods without and with search window to different image sizes, the search template had a size of 50×50 pixels. The value of the p parameter is the search window width and determines the estimation precision and the computational complexity.

Finally, some results of the vehicular traffic data collection from the simple video are shown in Fig. 3. The data obtained are: vehicles counting, average velocity, vehicular traffic volume and vehicular traffic composition.

Table 3. Correct classification percentages in the four scenarios.

Algorithm	Simple	passat	easy	kwbb
CCP without preprocessing				
TMF	75.03	65.32	63.29	62.80
GMM	84.36	75.19	72.76	72.14
EB	72.97	71.78	62.49	65.23
CCP with preprocessing				
TMF	80.24	75.64	73.83	77.11
GMM	90.48	86.43	85.32	84.64
EB	78.28	81.76	73.69	75.85

Table 4. Percentages of false positives and negatives in the four scenarios.

Alg	simple		passat		easy		kwbb	
	FP	FN	FP	FN	FP	FN	FP	FN
FP and FN without preprocessing								
TMF	13.2	11.6	11.5	23.1	26.8	9.8	20.1	17.0
GMM	8.1	7.5	8.8	15.9	19.0	8.2	14.4	13.3
EB	13.0	14.0	11.7	16.5	25.5	11.9	19.4	15.3
FP and FN with preprocessing								
TMF	9.4	10.3	7.8	16.5	16.4	9.7	10.8	12.0
GMM	5.3	4.2	5.9	7.6	7.9	6.7	8.3	7.0
EB	8.8	12.8	9.5	8.6	16.9	9.3	13.5	10.5

Table 5. Blocks number compared of the TM and TMSW methods.

Data	TM: $(M - m + 1)(N - n + 1)$	TMSW: $(2p + 1)^2$
Image: 80×60, p: 10	341	441
Image: 160×120, p: 20	7881	1681
Image: 200×250, p: 30	30351	3721
Image: 250×275, p: 40	45426	6561
Image: 300×300, p: 50	63001	10201

4   Discussion

As can be seen in the variance images in Fig. 2, the proposed preprocessing stage in this study allowed attenuate the noise present in traffic videos. Smoothing operation i.e. the mean filtering, reduced the video noise and improved the contrast between moving and static areas. Image stabilization attenuated the variance produced at the edges of static objects due to vibration, being the most notorious case the Fig. 2b and d. The use of low-resolution images decreased the movement regions produced by the branches and leaves of trees, as seen in the Fig. 2a and c.

According to Table 2, the background subtraction algorithm with the best execution time per image was TMF with 0.040 and 0.051 s without and with preprocessing stage respectively, the worst was EB with 0.083 and 0.100 s. In the case of memory consumption, the GMM algorithm got the best with 2936 KB and 4889 KB without and with preprocessing stage respectively, the worst was

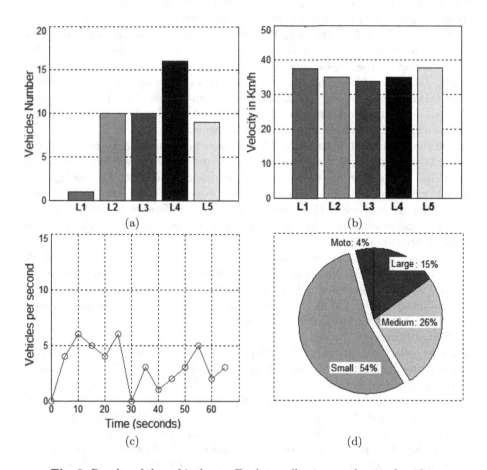

Fig. 3. Results of the vehicular traffic data collection on the simple video.

EB with 22760 KB and 24815 KB. The use of the proposed preprocessing stage in this paper raised the execution time per image in 0.013 s and the memory consumption in 1983 KB on average.

The main reason why EB is an algorithm with high computational cost and memory consumption is because while TMF and GMM build their background models by the application of statistical measures such as mean and covariance from the original image of dimensions $m \times n$, EB makes it but on a new space of dimension $m \times n^2$ of eigenvectors, which becomes a high dimensionality problem when EB requires build and update its background model.

The results in Table 3 show that GMM is the algorithm with the best correct classification percentages with an average in the four scenarios of 76.11% and 86.71% without and with preprocessing stage respectively, the worst was TMF with 66.61% and 76.70%, EB obtained results very close to these. The preprocessing stage increased the classification percentage by an average of 10%. According with this result and previous, GMM is the background subtraction algorithm with the best performance under the metrics: execution time per image, memory consumption and classification percentage, followed by TMF and EB.

Based on Table 4, in the passat video the average percentages of false negatives were higher in most of the cases (5 of 6) than the false positives; this result is due to the appearance similarity challenge, i.e. intensity levels very similar between vehicles and background. When the background subtraction is done this difference is very small, and if a certain threshold to this difference is applied, most of the vehicle pixels will not exceed the threshold, and as a result they are labeled as background pixels (false negatives).

On the other hand, in the easy video the false positives percentages are higher to the false negatives, this may be due to the presence of the vehicles shadows in the video. During the day shadows make strong contrast with the background model, which remains after the subtraction because their intensity levels are very different, and when the thresholding of the difference is performed, the shadow pixels exceed the threshold and therefore are labeled as vehicle pixels (false positives).

As shown in Table 5, in most cases the number of blocks compared by TMSW is much less than TM, therefore also its computational cost. A template in the image k should be searched only in a small region of the image $k + 1$ and not in the full image as the TM method does. Now we know that a lot of comparisons that this method performs are unnecessary.

Figure 3 presents the results of applying the proposed methodology in this study to collect vehicle traffic data from the simple video scene. Let us remember that the methodology consists of a preprocessing stage, the background subtraction algorithm with the best performance (GMM), the tracking technique with less execution time (TMSW) and the set of formulas for quantification. It can be observed that the application achieved to extract the traffic monitoring parameters. The most difficult parameter to extract was the vehicular traffic composition, this is obtained from the areas in pixels of detected vehicles, and these areas are affected by the false positives (shadow pixels labeled as vehicle pixels). To solve this problem, an image processing is performed using dilation and erosion morphological operations.

Finally, Fig. 4 shows a screenshot of the graphical user interface (GUI) of a developed software with the proposed methodology in this paper.

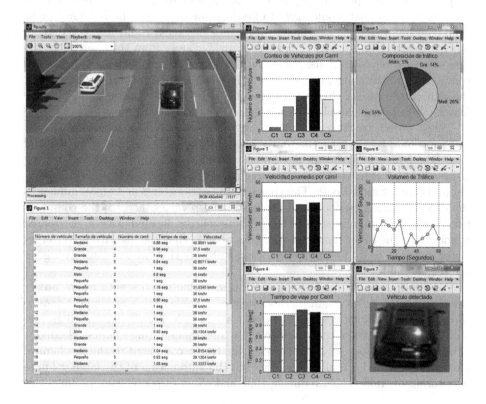

Fig. 4. Software screenshot.

5   Conclusions

The proposed preprocessing stage in this study achievement attenuate the noise present in the input videos that affected the performance of the object detection algorithms. It demonstrated quantitatively that the use of the preprocessing stage increased by an average of 10% the classification percentages of the background subtraction algorithms, with their respective increase in execution time per image and memory consumption of 0.013 s and 1983 KB. Experiments showed how the challenges of appearance similarity and shadows presence increased the averages of false negatives and positives respectively, this result guides us on how improve the preprocessing stage by means of the inclusion of specific strategies to face these challenges, it must take into account that the increase in the computational cost of the preprocessing could do less possible the development of a realtime application.

The preprocessing stage misuse can bring certain disadvantages. The image stabilization algorithm does use of the template matching method that can be very expensive computationally if the video is very unstable, because the comparisons number that would have to be done for detecting the reference point would be high. Reduce the image resolution in excess could affect the small objects monitoring, such as vehicles that are far away from the camera. In the case of smoothing operations, remember that these attenuate the high frequency components in the image, i.e. not only affect the noise but also the object edges; the unnecessary use of these operations in videos with low noise could blur the moving objects and complicate their detection and tracking.

When object tracking is carried out by TM method, it incurs in a great computational cost due to the unnecessary blocks comparisons. An analysis of objects maximum displacement allowed to define a search window for locating objects in small regions of image, thus achieving to reduce the comparisons number and computational cost. The choice of the parameter p in TMSW influences the object tracking performance, because large p-values increase the computational cost and guarantee that the objects will be located within the search window. On the other hand, small values of p do that the algorithm converges faster, however could be imprecise locating objects that are not entirely within the search window.

An application for quantifying motion in traffic video scenes where object tracking is used as the main methodology is a viable option as support tool to carry out the traffic monitoring. Firstly, it would collect traffic data with greater reliability and accuracy compared to the manual monitoring method. Secondly, it would be a cheaper way for studying the traffic compared to the mechanical monitoring method. Finally, would help in the automation of the large volumes monitoring of traffic video reducing time and effort to people who perform this task.

References

1. Tran, B., Tran, C., Scora, G., Manubhai, M., Barth, M.: Real-time video-based traffic measurement and visualization system for energy/emissions. IEEE Trans. Intell. Transp. Syst. **13**, 1667–1678 (2012)
2. Bennett, C., Chamorro, A., Chen, C., Solminihac, H., Flintsch, G.: Data Collection Technologies for Road Management, Washington D.C. (2005)
3. Wang, X., Ma, X., Grimson, E.: Unsupervised activity perception in crowded and complicated scenes using hierarchical Bayesian models. IEEE Trans. Pattern Anal. Mach. Intell. **31**, 539–555 (2009)
4. Dahlkamp, H., Nagel, H., Ottlik, A., Reuter, P.: A framework for model-based tracking experiments in image sequences. Int. J. Comput. Vis. **73**, 139–157 (2006)
5. Vezzani, R., Cucchiara, R.: Video Surveillance Online Repository (ViSOR): an integrated framework. Multimedia Tools Appl. **50**, 359–380 (2010)
6. Maddalena, L., Petrosino, A.: A 3D neural model for video analysis. In: Proceedings of Neural Nets WIRN 2009, pp. 101–109 (2009)

7. Haag, M., Nagel, H.: Incremental recognition of traffic situations from video image sequences. Image Vis. Comput. **18**, 137–153 (2005)
8. Prati, A., Mikic, M., Trivedi, M.: Detecting moving shadows: algorithms and evaluation. IEEE Trans. Pattern Anal. Mach. Intell. **25**, 918–923 (2003)
9. Maggio, E., Cavallaro, A.: Video Tracking: Theory and Practice. Wiley (2011)
10. Piccardi, M.: Background subtraction techniques: a review. In: IEEE International Conference on Systems, Man and Cybernetics, pp. 3099–3104 (2004)
11. Chih-Hsien, Y., Yi-Ping, Y., Tsung-Cheng, W., Jen-Shiun, C.: Low resolution method using adaptive LMS scheme for moving object detection and tracking. In: Proceeding of Intelligent Signal Processing and Communication Systems (2010)
12. Sugandi, B., Kim, H., Kooi, J.: A block matching technique for object tracking based on peripheral increment sign correlation image. In: Proceedings of the International Conference on Innovative Computing, Information and Control (2007)

Robotics

GPS-Based Curve Estimation for an Adaptive Pure Pursuit Algorithm

Citlalli Gámez Serna(✉), Alexandre Lombard(✉), Yassine Ruichek(✉),
and Abdeljalil Abbas-Turki(✉)

Le2i FRE2005, CNRS, Arts et Métiers, University Bourgogne Franche-Comté,
UTBM, 90010 Belfort, France
{citlalli.gamez-serna,alexandre.lombard,yassine.ruichek,
abdeljalil.abbas-turki}@utbm.fr

Abstract. Different algorithms for path tracking have been described and implemented for autonomous vehicles. Traditional geometric algorithms like Pure Pursuit use position information to compute vehicle's steering angle to follow a predefined path. The main issue of these algorithms resides in cutting corners since no curvature information is taken into account. In order to overcome this problem, we present a sub-system for path tracking where an algorithm that analyzes GPS information offline classifies high curvature segments and estimates the ideal speed for each one. Additionally since the evaluation of our sub-system is performed through a simulation of an adaptive Pure Pursuit algorithm, we propose a method to estimate dynamically its look-ahead distance based on the vehicle speed and lateral error. As it will be shown through experimental results, our sub-system introduces improvements in comfort and safety due to the extracted geometry information and speed control, stabilizing the vehicle and minimizing the lateral error.

Keywords: Autonomous vehicle · Path tracking · Look-ahead distance · Lateral error · Curvature estimation · Pure Pursuit

1 Introduction

Autonomous vehicle navigation has become a challenged field of study during the last three decades. One of the main tasks consists in trajectory tracking. The goal of path tracking is to minimize the lateral distance between the vehicle and defined path. There are different methods to perform this task which can be classified into geometric, kinematic and dynamic models [22].

Kinematic models [7,16] neglect vehicle dynamics as well as geometric ones, but its performance is worse than simple geometric models. Dynamic models [15], on the other hand, take into account vehicle dynamics impacting tracking performance when speed increases or curvature varies. The problem with these kind of models is their complexity, since most of the time, they are non-linear and computationally expensive. Geometric models [2,11,20,21] are one of the most popular due to their good accuracy and easy implementation.

© Springer International Publishing AG 2017
G. Sidorov and O. Herrera-Alcántara (Eds.): MICAI 2016, Part I, LNAI 10061, pp. 497–511, 2017.
DOI: 10.1007/978-3-319-62434-1_40

Geometric models, as their name suggest, are based on geometric relationships between the vehicle and the path. They make use of a look-ahead distance to measure error ahead of the vehicle and can extend from simple circular arc calculations to more complicated ones involving screw theory [24]. Pure pursuit, vector pursuit and Stanley methods belong to these models. A comparison between geometric models is performed in [22] leading us to the conclusion of using Pure Pursuit as our path tracking algorithm.

The original pure pursuit method is a pure path tracking algorithm which does not consider vehicle speed to define the distance for the target point [2]. This definition results in two kind of problems: (1) when the distance is too small, it causes the vehicle to return to the path more aggressively (oscillations), and (2) when it is too big, curvature information is neglected (cutting corners). In order to calculate a convenient look-ahead distance, different factors need to be considered. One of them is speed, which is the main parameter when no visual information is used [15,20]. On the contrary, there are studies which tend to understand how humans define their fixation points (look-ahead fixations) to drive safely [12,13] based on time, horizon and speed. The work presented here focuses only on GPS information, and the look-ahead distance definition takes into account current vehicle speed, path geometry (curvature information) and feedback error (lateral error) of the path tracker.

This paper proposes a curve safety sub-system for path tracking (see Fig. 1) based on the Pure Pursuit algorithm and a dynamic look-ahead distance definition based on vehicle current speed and lateral error. The aim of this sub-system is to analyze the geometric information of the planned path and to define the convenient speed and look-ahead distance that the vehicle needs to perform more stable path tracking and reduce the lateral error. Our solution pre-processes GPS data through Ramer-Douglas-Peucker algorithm [3] to reduce the number of points. The GPS points are then analyzed to define segments which belong to a curve or a tangent line. For each curve segment, the radius, angle, length and convenient driving speed are computed. The idea behind the curve estimation relies on overcoming the cutting corners problem of the pure pursuit tracking algorithm. In other words, if a segment is detected as part of a curve, the vehicle will need to decrease speed and consider a shorter look-ahead distance; otherwise it will increase speed until reaching the maximum one and consequently considering a long look-ahead distance. Even though curvature estimation performs good, right threshold value needs to be tuned.

The rest of the paper is organized as follows. Section 2 presents a review of similar works. Section 3 introduces the basics of the Pure pursuit algorithm. Section 4 explains how curvature information is extracted with our sub-system. This information will be considered in Sect. 5 for velocity planning module and definition of look-ahead distance. In Sect. 6, analysis and discussion of the results with and without the improvements of our sub-system are presented. Finally, Sect. 7 concludes our work and introduces future ideas to implement.

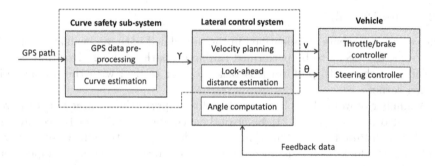

Fig. 1. Overall work-flow of the vehicle path tracking system. Blue dotted lines highlight our contributions. (Color figure online)

2 Related Works

The main related issues taken into account in our sub-system can be classified into 2 parts: (1) Curve estimation, and (2) Pure pursuit control modification. Important state of the art studies in these fields are outlined below.

2.1 Curve Estimation

Road shape estimation has been considered as an essential function for road following and other applications in Advanced Driving Assistance System (ADAS).

Several studies have tried to estimate road geometry. Some of them are based on the motion analysis of other vehicles when poor visibility is present (weather changes, road hills) [4,17,18]. The idea behind this comes from assuming that observed leading vehicles are likely to keep following their lane [4]. Mostly, these works use different sensors like video cameras, infrared and radar sensors, as well as steering wheel and wheel speed sensors.

Some other works proposed to extract curvature information from GPS data and GIS maps with the aim to calculate the road ahead of the vehicle through a flexible road model [23]. In other cases, they are used to identify critical curves where accidents occur frequently [5,8].

Also, researchers have focused on methods to identify curves and measure safety-related parameters using again GPS data, and GIS information. These with the objective to estimate curve radius, length and angle through the identification of straight line, clothoid and circular curves [8,14].

There are a lot of methods to identify road geometry, nevertheless, only a few of them have focused on considering convenient velocities to perform safe trajectory with actual tracking algorithms for Unmanned Ground Vehicles (UGVs) [19–21]. Our work is based on curvature estimation [14] considering only off-line GPS information to detect curves and estimate reference velocities of each segment of the path. This estimation is calculated by considering various properties such as curvature, flatness and side friction coefficient [21].

2.2 Pure Pursuit

Once curved segments are identified in the predefined path, an evaluation of the safe trajectory needs to be performed through a path tracking algorithm. Pure pursuit was chosen to perform this task in order to deal with the problem of cutting corners.

A number of works have been developed to improve the accuracy of the pure pursuit algorithm [11,15,20,21]. Some of them combining a PID or PD controller together with Pure Pursuit [20,21] in order to decrease the tracking error. Others modifying the look-ahead distance [11,15,20,21], since it is the most important parameter of this algorithm.

The idea of a dynamic look-ahead distance started with [11] in which they sum up every second the distance between vehicle and path (lateral error) and the fixed look-head distance. In the original Pure Pursuit method, the definition of the look-ahead distance was a fixed term [2].

Some other authors have defined the look-ahead distance based on a certain weight and speed limits [15,20,21]. The magnitude of the look-ahead distance is dynamically adjusted considering min and max values for certain speed thresholds, and a weight value for a speed range. The minimum distance is defined according to what the vehicle needs to respond safely when there is an emergency stop [15]. The weight applied to certain vehicle speeds is an adjustable parameter. Usually, this parameter is fixed as presented in [15,20,21], but the aim of our work is to make it dynamic according to lateral error and vehicle speed.

An adaptive Pure Pursuit algorithm will be considered for our test paths modifying the distance to the goal point (target point) and taking into account the curvature information. Through simulations we will compare the results with DGPS (Differential Global Positioning System) data.

3 Path Tracking Algorithm

The geometric-based pure pursuit method consists in defining a goal point in the path at a certain distance ahead of the vehicle actual position, and reaching it drawing a circular arc. This algorithm iterates continuously with the goal point sliding along the path, forming a smooth tracking trajectory, as shown in Fig. 2(left). It operates in a similar way humans drive, in which we fix a point at some distance ahead on the road and attempt to follow it.

The goal point is determined by the look-ahead distance (l) which is the only parameter the pure pursuit depends on. In Fig. 2 (G_x, G_y) represent the goal point in xy coordinates, (P_x, P_y) the projected point, R the radius, θ_{err} the heading angle needed it to reach the point.

Estimating circular arc for Pure pursuit algorithm depends only on the look-ahead distance, as seen in Eq. 1. For this reason, this algorithm is easy to implement. Even though it is easy, tuning the look-ahead distance could be a bit tricky since it could lead to problems defining it too small or too big [6] as mentioned previously.

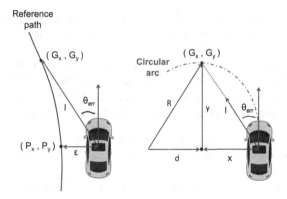

Fig. 2. Pure pursuit geometry diagram showing the path to be tracked(left) and the calculated steering curvature(right).

$$\gamma = \frac{2\theta_{err}}{l} \tag{1}$$

4 Curve Safety Sub-system

Detection of curves along a recorded GPS path for an unnamed ground vehicle (UGV) will help path tracking algorithms to perform a safer and more accurate route.

In order to start analyzing the path, GPS data needs to be preprocessed before to detect the points which belong to a curvature. Once the points are detected, an estimation of the radius, angle and length will be performed for each horizontal curve based on the work of Li et al. [14] with minor modifications.

4.1 GPS Pre-processing

The accuracy of GPS data (15 m) can vary depending on different factors. Among them are the quality of the GPS receiver, the environmental surroundings (tall buildings, trees, tunels, valleys, etc.) and even the weather itself.

Differential Global Positioning System (DGPS) was used for data collection due to the improved accuracy it provides (about 10 cm). Even though the recorded data is supposed to be trust-able, there is a lot of noise which needs to be considered before trying to detect curves. In our case noisy points were removed manually in order to have a reliable route. At the same time, the amount of information to be processed for curve analysis is huge and in consequence the performance of the method will be time consuming and storage capacity dependent.

Since a recorded path is described as a sequence of points, it is possible to reduce its number considering line simplification algorithms. Douglas-Peucker

(DP) algorithm is among the most accurate line simplification algorithms with minimum shape distortions according to a comparison made with different algorithms in Ivanov et al. work [9].

DG algorithm [3] finds a similar curve to the original with less number of points. The algorithm is based on a threshold value which determines the distance at which the point should be kept or discarded for the new simplified curve. It divides recursively the line according to the following manner:

1. At the beginning, the first and last points are kept.
2. Find the point located farther away from the line segment drawn between these two points.
3. Evaluate the furthest point (best point) with the threshold (ε). If the distance between the farthest point and line segment is greater than ε, the point must be kept or discarded otherwise.
4. Recursively evaluate the points between the first and best points and between the best and end points repeating steps 2 and 3.

The drawbacks of this algorithm are its complexity and the definition of its threshold value. Its average complexity is $O(n^2 \log m)$, and in the best case $O(n \log n \log m)$, where n is the total number of points and m is the number of points retained [9]. The threshold ε is user defined. The number of output points will vary depending on its value. For this reason, the user needs to tune this value according to the desired number of points. In our case, a value of 0.05 reduced the number of points around 8.5 times and kept the information needed to evaluate curvature information.

4.2   Curve Estimation

PC and PT Identification Method. Horizontal curve identification is represented by its point of curvature (PC), point of tangency (PT), point of intersection (PI), curve length (L), radius (R) and central angle (θ). An illustration of these curve parameters is shown in Fig. 3a.

Identifying the start and end points (PT and PC) is critical for curve classification. We identify and classify the curve segments according to the method

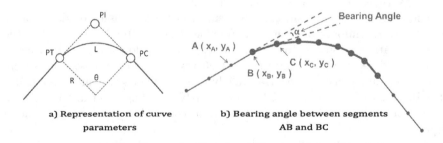

a) Representation of curve   b) Bearing angle between segments
        parameters   AB and BC

Fig. 3. Curve parameters representation

proposed by Li et al. [14], where a large central angle describes sharp curves (dangerous curves) and large radius describes less severe curves.

The critical step for this method is how to choose the ideal threshold value (bearing angle) to identify curves between two consecutive segments. An illustration of bearing angle is presented in Fig. 3b.

A,B and C are consecutive points. The computation of this angle between 2 consecutive segments is performed following the formula:

$$\alpha = cos^{-1} \left(\frac{(x_B - x_A)(x_C - x_B) + (y_B - y_A)(y_C - y_B)}{\sqrt{(x_B - x_A)^2 + (y_B - y_A)^2} \times \sqrt{(x_C - x_B)^2 + (y_C - y_B)^2}} \right) \times \frac{180}{\pi} \tag{2}$$

If the angle is greater than the threshold value, the center point is considered as part of a curve. Tuning this threshold value is very important since for long and smooth curves the bearing angle could be very small (less than 1°) and will tend to confuse the curved segments with tangent ones. Different threshold values were evaluated ending up following the optimal one as proposed in [14] (1.25°).

Secondly, and different from Li et al. work, where a compound curve (multiple curves) is considered as long as the distance between curves is less than 183 m; we defined the minimum number of consecutive points equal to 3, in order to have a candidate curve and we do not considered length between them. An evaluation with their criteria was performed and our whole path was considered a compound curve. The reasons behind this behavior could be due to: (1) their definition was given for roadway maps and in our datasets, only urban environments were considered; and (2) our datasets are still not completely free from noisy information.

Curve Parameters Estimation. The geometric information of each curve will be computed once the initial and ending points are identified (PC and PT). These information includes the radius (R), length (L) and central angle(θ). In order to perform these computations, the center point of the curve (O) needs to be found. These parameters can be computed following the work [14].

Besides Li et al. classification, we went further identifying sharp curves. Sharp curves deserve special attention due to the fact that it's a location where the vehicle needs to decrease speed in order to take the curvature as if a human was driving, keeping the lateral error as smaller as possible. The aim of identifying these kind of curves is related to safety issues, which is a very important point for intelligent vehicle systems [10].

Curves are classified as sharp if the radius is small or the curve angle is big. An angle range from 30°–180° defines a dangerous curve with radius from 5–18 m according to American Association of State Highway and Transportation Officials' (AASHTO's) "A Policy on Geometric Design of Highways and Streets" [1]. In our datasets, any curve with angle bigger than 30° is considered a sharp curve.

5   Lateral Control System

Lateral control system is a path tracking system based on the pure pursuit algorithm [2]. We divided it into three units: velocity planning, look-ahead distance estimation, and steering angle computation. Our work covers only the first two units, since the aim is to show how tracking accuracy is improved taking into account path geometry.

The velocity planning component estimates the ideal speed of the vehicle taking into account the curvature information obtained previously in Sect. 4. The look-ahead distance unit computes the distance considered to define the goal point depending on the vehicle speed and lateral error. A more detailed description of these units is explained in the following section.

5.1   Velocity Planning

Velocity planning module calculates the ideal speed needed when the vehicle moves around a horizontal curve. When the vehicle drives in a curve, the force that makes it follow the curve is called centripetal force. This force does not depend on the gravity but instead on the friction between tires and the roadway. Opposite to this force, centrifugal one tries to move the vehicle outwards the curve. Centrifugal force can be reduced inclining the road into the center of the circle modeling the curve. This inclination is also known as banked angle (θ) or super-elevation angle (e). In other words, the ideal speed will be computed depending on the curvature of the path, friction coefficient and banked angle as shown in Fig. 4. N is the normal force, f is the friction force, μ is the friction coefficient, m is the vehicle mass, g is the gravity and F_{net} is the net force.

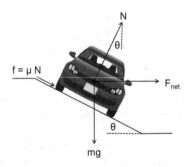

Fig. 4. Centripetal force diagram

The estimation of the ideal speed is be given by Eq. 3 where k represents the curvature information which is the inverse of the curve radius $R = \frac{1}{k}$.

$$v = \sqrt{\frac{(e + \mu)g}{k}} \tag{3}$$

Super-elevation is defined to be between 6%–12% for rural and urban roads according to American Association of State Highway and Transportation Officials' (AASHTO's) "A Policy on Geometric Design of Highways and Streets" [1].

The side friction factor depends on the road surface conditions and vehicle speed. It is usually limited from 0.1 to 0.16 [21]. We compute the ideal speed for all the curves identified in Sect. 4 and limit the max velocity for the path tracking algorithm to 36 kmph. Only sharp curves ended up with a speed smaller than the maximum one.

5.2   Look-Ahead Distance Definition

The look-ahead distance value determines the accuracy of the pure pursuit algorithm. In other words, if the look-ahead distance is too short for the current speed, vehicle will be unstable, ending up in a lot of oscillations. On the other hand, if it is too long, the tracking performance will be deteriorated, resulting in the well-known problem of 'cutting corners'.

In this paper, we defined a dynamic look-ahead distance based on the vehicle speed and the lateral error as:

$$L = \begin{cases} L_{min} + v, & \text{if } T \leq 1 \\ L_{min} + Tv, & \text{otherwise} \end{cases} \tag{4}$$

where L_{min} is the minimum look-ahead distance, v is the current vehicle speed and T is a gain value. The gain value is a dynamic parameter defined according to the lateral error and the maximum speed ($T = \frac{L}{v_{max}}$). The maximum speed is 36 kmph.

The idea behind the gain T is to stabilize the vehicle faster when the distance from the vehicle to the path is big, and in consequence, removing the lateral error faster. This improved look-ahead distance definition is useful only if the tracking precision is low, otherwise there wont be much difference. A similar idea was presented in [15] but without a dynamic gain value. Most of the state of the art works which consider a dynamic look-ahead distance definition use a fixed gain value depending on speed thresholds [15,20,21]. The main drawback of these works is related to their accuracy because as soon as the vehicle speed increases, the lateral error will also increase.

6   Experimental Results

In this section we present simulation results performed on real datasets collected in Belfort, France with our experimental platform shown in Fig. 5. This vehicle is based on an electric GEM car equipped with several sensors, among them a GPS receiver and a RTK-GPS receiver, together with an embedded hard disk and a computer system (PC) to log the acquired data.

Two datasets were considered containing GPS data with different lengths and curvature information. A small description of the datasets is listed below.

Fig. 5. Equipped experimental platform.

- **Dataset UTBM-1.** This path contains 7,803 original points (pts) and 882 pts after pre-processing. The vehicle was driven in urban environments through a distance of about 3.8 km. A number of 40 curves were detected following Liu et al. classification [15] and 15 sharp curves (dangerous curves) came out after our analysis. For the final evaluation, our proposed curve safety sub-system (Sect. 4) passes this information to the lateral control system to calculate the ideal driving speed for each one.
- **Dataset UTBM-2.** The path contains 4,963 original GPS pts and only 540 after pre-processing. The distance of this track is about 2.2 km. Following Liu et al. classification [15], 22 curves were detected and only 6 sharp curves resulted after our classification. The ideal driving speed for each curve was computed once in the lateral control system and applied for the simulations.

Path tracking simulations were performed with and without considering curvature information for both datasets. When considering curves, the lateral control system knows exactly where the curves are located and estimates the necessary distance to start decelerating ($2\,\mathrm{m/s^2}$) before arriving to them, until reaching the desired speed at the beginning and throughout the curves. In these simulations, a maximum speed of 36kph was used.

Figures 6 and 7 show the results of UTBM-1 and UTBM-2 datasets comparing the obtained simulations against the original GPS information. Table 1 shows the complete results regarding lateral errors obtained in each curve.

The performance of our curve safety sub-system showed significant improvements for most of the curves, but similar or inclusive less accuracy in some others. At the same time it is remarkably to note that standard deviation (SD) decrease by half in each path (see Table 1) which makes our proposed subsystem more reliable.

For UTBM-1 dataset, tracking error is reduced by about 25% and around 35% for UTBM-2 dataset. While accuracy is improved for most of the curves in last dataset (see Table 1), error in curve 4 increased around 34%. The same behavior occurred in curves 5, 8, 11 and 14 of UTBM-1 dataset (see Table 1). The reason behind this increment is due to the fact that the lateral control

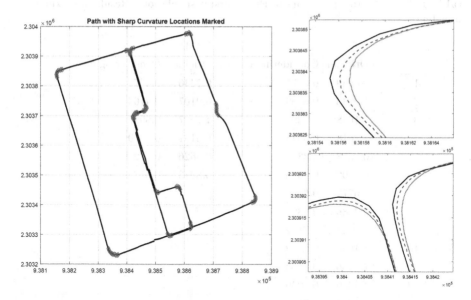

Fig. 6. Lateral errors comparison for UTBM-1 dataset. Solid black line (—) represents the original path, dotted blue line (· · ·) is the simulated path, and dashed red line (− −) is the simulated path considering curvature information. (Color figure online)

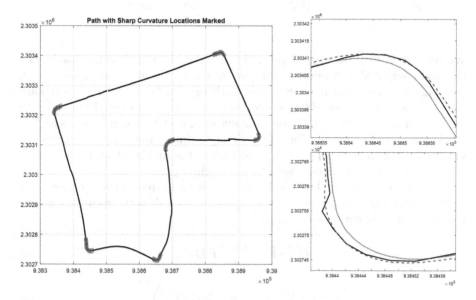

Fig. 7. Lateral errors comparison for UTBM-2 dataset. Solid black line (—) represents the original path, dotted blue line (· · ·) the simulated path, and dashed red line (− −) the simulated path considering curvature information. (Color figure online)

Table 1. Lateral errors according to Pure Pursuit simulations. Results are expressed in meters.

Curve	UTBM-1		UTBM-2	
	Original	Considering curves	Original	Considering curves
1	0.6649	0.6577	0.7446	0.4672
2	1.0043	0.6409	0.9107	0.4163
3	1.1658	0.7097	1.1627	0.5916
4	1.2618	0.6535	0.5161	0.6919
5	0.2658	0.3346	0.8626	0.4823
6	0.5092	0.4508	0.8013	0.6172
7	0.6772	0.6135		
8	0.4286	0.4393		
9	1.2744	0.7112		
10	1.1698	0.9222		
11	0.2656	0.2763		
12	1.1369	0.8036		
13	0.8694	0.5742		
14	0.5402	0.6990		
15	0.9733	0.6803		
Average	0.8138	0.6111	0.833	0.5444
SD	0.3455	0.1665	0.1936	0.0962

system (without considering curvature information) reaches smaller speeds than the ones computed as convenient for the curves. As a result of low speed, small look-ahead distance is defined, reducing tracking error but emerging oscillations. These oscillations are one of the problems of the pure pursuit algorithm and with our system we have proven, through simulations, that they can be reduced.

Another problem of the Pure Pursuit algorithm is the 'cutting corners'. A visual comparison is shown in Figs. 6 and 7 where the simulated path, considering curvature information, sticks closer to the original path.

In order to compare both methods, the average root mean square error (RMSE) and standard deviation (σ) per method are calculated regarding lateral errors obtained in curves for each path.

$$\overline{RMSE} = \frac{1}{2} \sum RMSE \tag{5}$$

$$\sigma = \left(\frac{1}{2} \sum (RMSE - \overline{RMSE})^2 \right)^{\frac{1}{2}} \tag{6}$$

The comparison results are shown in Fig. 8. The tracking errors with our subsystem improved significantly **32%** over the pure pursuit without considering

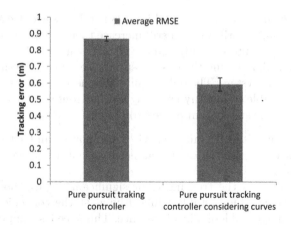

Fig. 8. Average and standard deviation of the lateral errors.

curvature information. Here the standard deviation only tells us that errors depend on the characteristics of the path itself.

With the aim to prove that a wrong definition of the look-ahead distance can affect considerably the accuracy of the tracking algorithm, we compared our definition (Sect. 5.2) with the one of Liu and Duan [15]. Our curvature system was active for both simulations with a max speed of 36 kmph. The test was made with UTBM-2 dataset and the average lateral error resulted in 1.51 m with Liu and Duan's definition; almost 3 times more than with our look-ahead distance definition (0.54 m).

Even though our implementation have proven to be easy, robust and reliable; some limitations still remain. The main one refers to the data preprocessing for smoothing the GPS path and getting rid of noisy information. Since the curvature identification depends on the path itself, a bad or noisy track will end up with really bad results.

Another limitation is the look-ahead distance definition. Our proposal makes the vehicle reach the path faster (but more stable) when the lateral error is big, otherwise, the look-ahead distance definition depends only on the vehicle speed. Although most of the literature share the same idea of defining the look-ahead distance based on the speed, tuning this parameter could result tricky and hence an improved definition should be considered taking into account more information.

7 Conclusions

We have proposed a look-ahead definition, convenient speed estimation and curve safety sub-system for path tracking algorithms based only on GPS information. Our sub-system, which works off-line, is capable to reduce significantly tracking errors and solve the well known problem of cutting corners for Pure Pursuit.

The main advantage of our method is its generality, since it can be adopted for different tracking algorithms and still increase their accuracy. Since the path geometry is analyzed automatically and the ideal driving speed is computed with the output obtained; applying the desired speed at each curve results in an easy task for the tracking system. The only requirement needed is a set of GPS points free of noise to be able to identify correctly the horizontal curves.

In conclusion, our sub-system proved to be:

1. Simple and robust: it works only with GPS information and detects accurately sharp curves which are the ones that need special attention for safety and comfort issues.
2. Accurate: it reduces the tracking error significantly throughout the curves making the vehicle more stable while driving at the convenient speed and considering an optimal look-ahead distance. This speed is computed following physics laws and considering the friction coefficient and super-elevation angle for urban roads [1].
3. Safe: the aim of any intelligent vehicle is to provide safety to the user. If the accuracy of the path tracking algorithm is good enough, we assure the user that the vehicle will not deviate and will reach its destination without any problems.

At the moment, only simulations were executed, but the sub-system will be tested in real vehicle to prove its performance. An interesting direction for future research would be to try different methods to remove GPS noise and simplify the path, like RANSAC and variations of Douglas Peucker algorithm. Also, more sensors (like cameras, lidar, or radar) need to be considered in case that unwanted moving objects appear in the predefined path. Consequently, methods to avoid obstacles and plan new trajectory will be necessary.

Acknowledgments. Special thanks to National Council of Science and Technology (CONACYT) for the financial support. CONACYT is Mexico's entity in charge of the promotion of scientific and technological activities, granting scholarships for graduate studies (masters and doctoral) in Mexico and foreign countries.

References

1. Green Book: A policy on Geometric Design of Highways and Streets. AASHTO, 5th edn., vol. 49 (2004). ISBN 1–56051
2. Coulter, R.C.: Implementation of the pure pursuit path tracking algorithm. Technical report, DTIC Document (1992)
3. Douglas, D.H., Peucker, T.K.: Algorithms for the reduction of the number of points required to represent a digitized line or its caricature. Cartogr. Int. J. Geogr. Inf. Geovis. 10(2), 112–122 (1973)
4. Eidehall, A., Pohl, J., Gustafsson, F.: Joint road geometry estimation and vehicle tracking. Control Eng. Pract. 15(12), 1484–1494 (2007)
5. Fitzsimmons, E.J., Lindheimer, T.E., Schrock, S.D., Gonterwitz, K.: Evaluation of large truck crashes at horizontal curves on two-lane rural highways in kansas. In: Transportation Research Board 92nd Annual Meeting, No. 13–2340 (2013)

6. Giesbrecht, J., Mackay, D., Collier, J., Verret, S.: Path tracking for unmanned ground vehicle navigation. DRDC Suffield TM 224 (2005)
7. Girbés, V., Armesto, L., Tornero, J., Solanes, J.E.: Continuous-curvature kinematic control for path following problems. In: 2011 IEEE/RSJ International Conference on Intelligent Robots and Systems, pp. 4335–4340. IEEE (2011)
8. Hans, Z., Souleyrette, R., Bogenreif, C.: Horizontal curve identification and evaluation. Technical report (2012)
9. Ivanov, R.: Real-time GPS track simplification algorithm for outdoor navigation of visually impaired. J. Netw. Comput. Appl. **35**(5), 1559–1567 (2012)
10. Kannan, S., Thangavelu, A., Kalivaradhan, R.: An intelligent driver assistance system (I-DAS) for vehicle safety modelling using ontology approach. Int. J. Ubicomp **1**(3), 15–29 (2010)
11. Kelly, A.: A feedforward control approach to the local navigation problem for autonomous vehicles. Carnegie Mellon University, The Robotics Institute (1994)
12. Lehtonen, E., Lappi, O., Koirikivi, I., Summala, H.: Effect of driving experience on anticipatory look-ahead fixations in real curve driving. Accid. Anal. Prev. **70**, 195–208 (2014)
13. Lehtonen, E., Lappi, O., Kotkanen, H., Summala, H.: Look-ahead fixations in curve driving. Ergonomics **56**(1), 34–44 (2013)
14. Li, Z., Chitturi, M., Bill, A., Noyce, D.: Automated identification and extraction of horizontal curve information from geographic information system roadway maps. Transp. Res. Rec. J. Transp. Res. Board **2291**, 80–92 (2012)
15. Liu, R., Duan, J.: A path tracking algorithm of intelligent vehicle by preview strategy. In: 2013 32nd Chinese Control Conference (CCC), pp. 5630–5635. IEEE (2013)
16. Low, C.B., Wang, D.: GPS-based path following control for a car-like wheeled mobile robot with skidding and slipping. IEEE Trans. Control Syst. Technol. **16**(2), 340–347 (2008)
17. Lundquist, C., Schon, T.B.: Road geometry estimation and vehicle tracking using a single track model. In: 2008 IEEE Intelligent Vehicles Symposium, pp. 144–149. IEEE (2008)
18. Lundquist, C., Schön, T.B.: Joint ego-motion and road geometry estimation. Inf. Fusion **12**(4), 253–263 (2011)
19. Park, B., Han, W.Y.: Reference velocity estimation method for on-road unmanned ground vehicle. In: 2013 10th International Conference on Ubiquitous Robots and Ambient Intelligence (URAI), pp. 230–231. IEEE (2013)
20. Park, M.W., Lee, S.W., Han, W.Y.: Development of lateral control system for autonomous vehicle based on adaptive pure pursuit algorithm. In: 2014 14th International Conference on Control, Automation and Systems (ICCAS), pp. 1443–1447. IEEE (2014)
21. Park, M., Lee, S., Han, W.: Development of steering control system for autonomous vehicle using geometry-based path tracking algorithm. ETRI J. **37**(3), 617–625 (2015)
22. Snider, J.M.: Automatic steering methods for autonomous automobile path tracking. Robotics Institute, Pittsburgh, PA, Technical report, CMU-RITR-09-08 (2009)
23. Wang, C., Hu, Z., Uchimura, K.: Precise curvature estimation by cooperating with digital road map. In: 2008 IEEE Intelligent Vehicles Symposium, pp. 859–864. IEEE (2008)
24. Wit, J.S.: Vector pursuit path tracking for autonomous ground vehicles. Technical report, DTIC Document (2000)

Collective Motion of a Swarm of Simulated Quadrotors Using Repulsion, Attraction and Orientation Rules

Mario Aguilera-Ruiz$^{(\boxtimes)}$, Luis Torres-Treviño, and Angel Rodríguez-Liñán

Universidad Autónoma de Nuevo León, Facultad de Ingeniería Mecánica y Eléctrica,
San Nicolás de Los Garza, Mexico
mario.a01@gmail.com

Abstract. Coordination of large groups of robots can be a difficult task, but recent approaches, like swarm robotics, offer an alternative based on the behaviors observed in social animals. In this paper, the collective behaviors of the model proposed by Iain Couzin et al. are implemented in a swarm of 10 simulated quadcopters. The simulations are carried with a dynamic model of the quadcopter and a PID controller for stable flight. Collective behaviors are obtained with local rules of repulsion, orientation and attraction, based on the relative position of neighbors.

Keywords: Swarm robotics · Quadcopter simulation · Collective behavior · Repulsion · Orientation · Attraction

1 Introduction

Swarm robotics focuses on the coordination of large groups of relatively simple robots, taking inspiration from the emergent behavior in social animals like ants, bees, birds and fish.

As observed in nature swarms, a collective behavior can emerge from the interaction between individuals and the interaction with the environment. This emergent collective behavior is robust, scalable and flexible, allowing the swarm to perform complex tasks, beyond the individual skills of each member [1].

Robotic swarms are of great interest in tasks involving large space and time, and tasks potentially dangerous to humans or robots themselves. Examples of potential applications are search and rescue tasks in collapsed buildings or fires, exploration and 3D mapping of unknown buildings, target tracking, surveillance, cooperative transportation, etc. [2,3].

Aerial robots are preferred for this type of tasks, due to higher speed to cover large terrain in less time. The use of quadrotors has increased in the last decade, thanks to its maneuverability in narrow spaces, vertical take off and landing, and the capacity of stationary flight over an interest point [4].

This paper intends to implement repulsion, orientation and attraction rules, to coordinate 10 simulated aerial robots. Each robot is represented by a quadcopter dynamic model, opposed to the massless particles in Couzin's model.

© Springer International Publishing AG 2017
G. Sidorov and O. Herrera-Alcántara (Eds.): MICAI 2016, Part I, LNAI 10061, pp. 512–521, 2017.
DOI: 10.1007/978-3-319-62434-1_41

This work will help us to determine the viability of a physical implementation and the considerations needed to achieve a proper behavior to allow indoor navigation of a fleet of autonomous robots.

1.1 Related Work

There are several works on the coordination of multiple flying robots. Hoffmann et al. presented an autonomous flock of three quadcopters which communicate with each other to generate collision-free trajectories [5]. Kushleyev et al. implemented a flock of 20 micro quadrotors with a central computer that calculates the trajectory of each drone [6]. Stirling et al. presented an autonomous group of three quadcopters using infrared sensors to obtain the relative position of near robots. Two of the robots remain stationary as reference points for the third robot flying [7]. Vásárhely et al. implemented a swarm of ten autonomous quadcopters based on local interactions between robots. A communication system transmit the position of each robot to the neighbors in the range of communication. Repulsion rules allow collision avoidance and the definition of a bounded area keeps the robots together [8]. Saska utilizes three quadrotors with an on board camera for estimation of relative position of neighbors. Repulsion and attraction rules keep an equilibrium in the detection range of the visual system, and a virtual target with respect to the center of the swarm allows the navigation in a predefined trajectory [9].

2 Behavior Rules

Couzin et al. investigated the dynamics of animal groups such as birds or fish, and developed a self-organizing model of group formation, based on local repulsion, alignment and attraction rules [10].

They proposed three spherical zones around each individual. The desired direction of each individual is computed based on the number of neighbors in each of the zones of behavior. If at least one neighbor $n_r \geq 1$ is in the zone of repulsion (zor), individual i will turn to maintain a minimum distance:

$$d_r(t + \tau) = -\sum_{j \neq i}^{n_r} \frac{r_{ij}(t)}{|r_{ij}(t)|} \tag{1}$$

if no neighbors are detected in the zone of repulsion, desired direction is calculated according to the neighbors in the zones of orientation and attraction:

$$d_o(t + \tau) = \sum_{j \neq i}^{n_o} \frac{v_j(t)}{|v_j(t)|} \tag{2}$$

$$d_a(t + \tau) = \sum_{j \neq i}^{n_a} \frac{r_{ij}(t)}{|r_{ij}(t)|} \tag{3}$$

where c_i is the position vector, v_i is the unit direction vector, $r_{ij} = c_j - c_i$ is the vector pointing in the direction of neighbor j.

3   Simulation Platform

Simulations are used to test the Couzin model on the swarm of quadcopters. The simulation let us evaluate the performance of the swarm without the high cost involved in time and resources of a physical implementation.

3.1   Quadrotor Dynamic Model

A dynamic model was used to represent each quadcopter in the simulation. A quadcopter is a rotorcraft propelled by four rotors as shown in Fig. 1. The structure of the quadcopter is considered rigid and symmetric, and the center of gravity coincide with the origin of the body reference frame.

Absolute linear position $\xi = [x\ y\ z]^T$ and angular position $\eta = [\phi\ \theta\ \psi]^T$ are defined in the inertial frame $\{X, Y, Z\}$, while angular velocities $\nu = [p\ q\ r]^T$ are given in the body frame $\{x_B, y_B, z_B\}$.

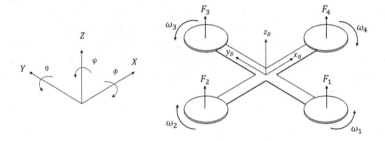

Fig. 1. Inertial and body reference frames of the quadcopter.

The system can be written as follows [11]:

$$
\begin{bmatrix} \ddot{x} \\ \ddot{y} \\ \ddot{z} \\ \ddot{\phi} \\ \ddot{\theta} \\ \ddot{\psi} \end{bmatrix} = \begin{bmatrix} (C_\phi S_\theta C_\psi + S_\phi S_\psi)\frac{1}{m}U_1 - K_d\dot{x} \\ (C_\phi S_\theta S_\psi - S_\phi C_\psi)\frac{1}{m}U_1 - K_d\dot{y} \\ -g + (C_\theta C_\phi)\frac{1}{m}U_1 - K_d\dot{z} \\ \frac{1}{I_{xx}}U_2 - \frac{I_{yy}-I_{zz}}{I_{xx}}\dot{\theta}\dot{\psi} \\ \frac{1}{I_{yy}}U_3 - \frac{I_{zz}-I_{xx}}{I_{yy}}\dot{\phi}\dot{\psi} \\ \frac{1}{I_{zz}}U_4 - \frac{I_{xx}-I_{yy}}{I_{zz}}\dot{\phi}\dot{\theta} \end{bmatrix} \tag{4}
$$

with the inputs:

$$
\begin{aligned}
U_1 &= T = k(\omega_1^2 + \omega_2^2 + \omega_3^2 + \omega_4^2) \\
U_2 &= \tau_\phi = lk(\omega_1^2 - \omega_3^2) \\
U_3 &= \tau_\theta = lk(\omega_2^2 - \omega_4^2) \\
U_4 &= \tau_\psi = d(\omega_1^2 - \omega_2^2 + \omega_3^2 - \omega_4^2)
\end{aligned} \tag{5}
$$

where m is the mass of the quadcopter, K_d is the air friction coefficient, g is the gravity, T is the vertical thrust, τ is the torque on each axis, k is the thrust coefficient, d is the drag coefficient, l is the arm length and ω_i is the rotor speed.

3.2 PID Controller

For stable flight, a PID controller (Fig. 2) is used for each control input, similar as in [12]:

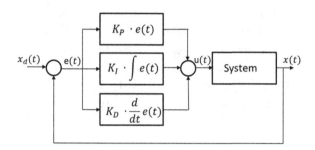

Fig. 2. PID controller block diagram.

$$T = \left(g + K_D(\dot{z}_d - \dot{z}) + K_P(z_d - z) + K_I \int_0^T (z_d - z)dt \right) m/C_\phi C_\theta$$

$$\tau_\phi = \left(K_D(\dot{\phi}_d - \dot{\phi}) + K_P(\phi_d - \phi) + K_I \int_0^T (\phi_d - \phi)dt \right) I_{xx}$$

$$\tau_\theta = \left(K_D(\dot{\theta}_d - \dot{\theta}) + K_P(\theta_d - \theta) + K_I \int_0^T (\theta_d - \theta)dt \right) I_{yy} \qquad (6)$$

$$\tau_\psi = \left(K_D(\dot{\psi}_d - \dot{\psi}) + K_P(\psi_d - \psi) + K_I \int_0^T (\psi_d - \psi)dt \right) I_{zz}$$

The angular speed of each rotor ω_i is calculated from Eq. 5 with values from Eq. 6:

$$\omega_1^2 = T/4k - \tau_\psi/4d - \tau_\theta/2lk$$
$$\omega_2^2 = T/4k + \tau_\psi/4d - \tau_\phi/2lk$$
$$\omega_3^2 = T/4k - \tau_\psi/4d + \tau_\theta/2lk \qquad (7)$$
$$\omega_4^2 = T/4k + \tau_\psi/4d + \tau_\phi/2lk$$

For simulation, the physical parameters shown in Table 1 were taken from [13].

Each quadcopter in the simulation uses the behavior rules shown in Sect. 2, to determinate the desired direction. This desired direction is adapted as inputs for the PID's controllers to achieve the desired movement. Figure 3 illustrates the general concept of each individual.

Table 1. Physical parameters of a quadcopter.

Parameter	Symbol	Value	Units
Mass	m	0.650	Kg
Arm lenght	l	0.23	m
Gravity	g	9.81	m/s^2
Inertia on x axis	I_{xx}	7.5×10^{-3}	$Kg\ m^2$
Inertia on y axis	I_{yy}	7.5×10^{-3}	$Kg\ m^2$
Inertia on z axis	I_{zz}	1.3×10^{-2}	$Kg\ m^2$
Thrust coefficient	k	3.13×10^{-5}	$N\ s^2$
Drag coefficient	d	7.5×10^{-7}	$N\ m\ s^2$
Friction coefficient	k_d	0.25	$Kg\ s$

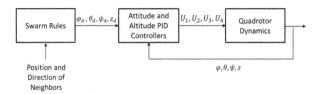

Fig. 3. Control diagram of each quadcopter.

4   Results

Experiments with ten quadrotors were simulated changing the widths of the zones of repulsion $\Delta r_r = r_r$, orientation $\Delta r_o = r_o - r_r$, and attraction $\Delta r_a = r_a - r_o$. Table 2 shows the width of the zones for each simulation. Each quadcopter starts in a random xy position and random initial orientation ψ. The initial altitude is set in 2 m and the PID controller keeps this altitude over the simulation.

The group polarization p_{group} is used to measure the level of alignment between quadcopters, which maximum value equals 1 when all members of the group are aligned in the same direction.

$$p_{group}(t) = \frac{1}{N} \left| \sum_{i=1}^{N} v_i(t) \right| \tag{8}$$

In the first experiment, the zones of behavior have small values and just few members are detected by each robot. Figure 4 shows that collective alignment is not achieved. It can be seen from Fig. 5 that small groups of nearby robots are formed and is noted that after 140 s there are 3 groups of aligned robots. Figure 6 shows the trajectories and final positions of the quadrotors.

In the experiment 3 shown in Fig. 7, the zone of orientation has a bigger value and the quadcopters quickly organize themselves turning to a collective

Table 2. Width of repulsion, orientation and attraction zones in the experiments. Units in meters.

Exp	Δr_r	Δr_o	Δr_a
1	1	5	5
2	1	5	20
3	1	20	5
4	1	20	20
5	5	5	5
6	5	5	20
7	5	20	5
8	5	20	20

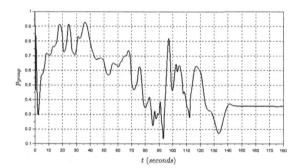

Fig. 4. Polarization of the swarm in simulation 1.

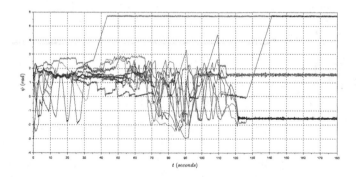

Fig. 5. Orientation ψ of the ten quadcopters in simulation 1.

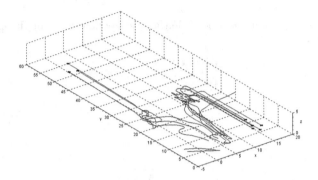

Fig. 6. Trajectories and final position after 180 s of simulation 1, with $\Delta r_r = 1$, $\Delta r_o = 5$ and $\Delta r_a = 5$.

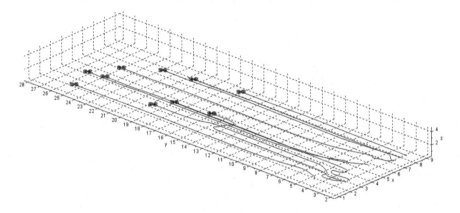

Fig. 7. Trajectories and final position after 90 s of simulation 5, with $\Delta r_r = 1$, $\Delta r_o = 20$ and $\Delta r_a = 5$.

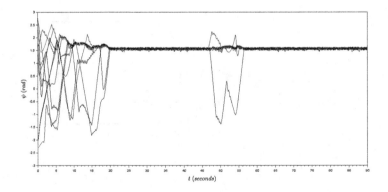

Fig. 8. Orientation ψ of the ten quadcopters in simulation 3.

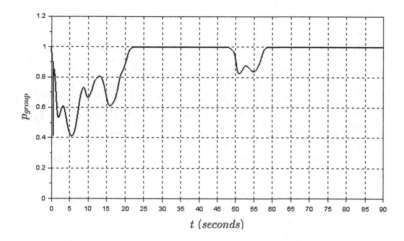

Fig. 9. Polarization of the swarm in simulation 3.

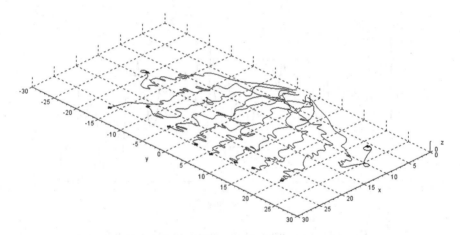

Fig. 10. Trajectories and final position after 180 s, with $\Delta r_r = 5$, $\Delta r_o = 5$ and $\Delta r_a = 5$.

direction. From Fig. 8 it is noted that after 20 s the robots are moving in the same direction. Figure 9 shows the polarization of the swarm which reach a value of 1 after 25 s, meaning that all the robots move in the same direction. At 50 s, the group polarization decreases as a result of some quadcopters turning to keep the minimum distance with the neighbors.

Increasing the zone of repulsion as in experiments 5 to 8, causes that quadcopters move whit some oscillations. Regardless of orientation and attraction values, the results are very similar when using high repulsion. An example is shown in Fig. 10 corresponding to the experiment 5. Even that most af the quadcopters advance in the same direction, Figs. 11 and 12 show that the orientation angle is continuously changing to avoid other robots in the zone of repulsion.

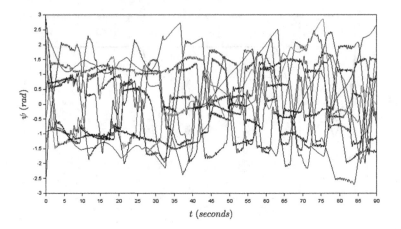

Fig. 11. Orientation ψ of the ten quadcopters in simulation 5.

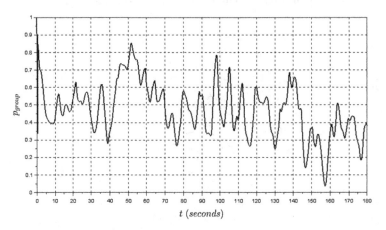

Fig. 12. Polarization of the swarm in simulation 5.

5   Conclusions

From the preliminary results, it can be concluded that the model of animal groups proposed by Couzin can be used for the coordination of a group of quadrotors. Changes in the sizes of repulsion, orientation and attraction zones can produce a different behavior in the swarm. This behaviors can be applied in the realizations of some task where the coordination of large groups are needed. For example, when the value of repulsion is low and the value of orientation is high, the robots can move as a compact group in the same direction for quick navigation. Not all the emergent behaviors displayed by the Couzin model are achieved in this paper, since there are other factors that need to be considered as the number of robots, field of perception and speed.

References

1. Brambilla, M., Ferrante, E., Birattari, M., Dorigo, M.: Swarm robotics: a review from the swarm engineering perspective. Swarm Intell. **7**, 1–41 (2013)
2. Tan, Y., Zheng, Z.Y.: Research advance in swarm robotics. Def. Technol. **9**, 18–39 (2013)
3. Şahin, E.: Swarm robotics: from sources of inspiration to domains of application. In: Şahin, E., Spears, W.M. (eds.) SR 2004. LNCS, vol. 3342, pp. 10–20. Springer, Heidelberg (2005). doi:10.1007/978-3-540-30552-1_2
4. Gupte, S., Mohandas, P.I.T., Conrad, J.M.: A survey of quadrotor unmanned aerial vehicles. In: 2012 Proceedings of IEEE Southeastcon, pp. 1–6. IEEE (2012)
5. Hoffmann, G.M., Huang, H., Waslander, S.L., Tomlin, C.J.: Precision flight control for a multi-vehicle quadrotor helicopter testbed. Control Eng. Prac. **19**, 1023–1036 (2011)
6. Kushleyev, A., Mellinger, D., Powers, C., Kumar, V.: Towards a swarm of agile micro quadrotors. Auton. Robot. **35**, 287–300 (2013)
7. Stirling, T., Roberts, J., Zufferey, J.C., Floreano, D.: Indoor navigation with a swarm of flying robots. In: 2012 IEEE International Conference on Robotics and Automation (ICRA), pp. 4641–4647. IEEE (2012)
8. Vásárhelyi, G., Virágh, C., Somorjai, G., Tarcai, N., Szorenyi, T., Nepusz, T., Vicsek, T.: Outdoor flocking and formation flight with autonomous aerial robots. In: 2014 IEEE/RSJ International Conference on Intelligent Robots and Systems (IROS 2014), pp. 3866–3873. IEEE (2014)
9. Saska, M.: Mav-swarms: Unmanned aerial vehicles stabilized along a given path using onboard relative localization. In: 2015 International Conference on Unmanned Aircraft Systems (ICUAS), pp. 894–903. IEEE (2015)
10. Couzin, I.D., Krause, J., James, R., Ruxton, G.D., Franks, N.R.: Collective memory and spatial sorting in animal groups. J. Theor. Biol. **218**, 1–11 (2002)
11. Luukkonen, T.: Modelling and control of quadcopter. Independent research project in applied mathematics, Espoo (2011)
12. Gibiansky, A.: Quadcopter dynamics, simulation, and control (2010)
13. Bouabdallah, S.: Design and control of quadrotors with application to autonomous flying. PhD thesis, Ecole Polytechnique Federale de Lausanne (2007)

Design and Simulation of a New Lower Exoskeleton for Rehabilitation of Patients with Paraplegia

Fermín C. Aragón[1], C. Hernández-Santos[1(✉)],
José-Isidro Hernández Vega[1], Daniel Andrés Córdova[1],
Dolores Gabriela Palomares Gorham[2],
and Jonam Leonel Sánchez Cuevas[2]

[1] División de Estudios de Posgrado e Investigación,
Instituto Tecnológico de Nuevo León,
Avenue Eloy Cavazos #2001, Guadalupe, Nuevo León, Mexico
fermin.aragon91@gmail.com,
carlos.hernandez@itnl.edu.mx
[2] Departamento de Ingeniería Eléctrica-Electrónica,
Instituto Tecnológico de Nuevo León,
Avenue Eloy Cavazos no. 2001, Colonia Tolteca,
67170 Guadalupe, Nuevo León, Mexico

Abstract. The paper proposes a new architecture for a lower exoskeleton with five degrees of freedom (DOF) per each leg, where, the design and synthesis of the kinematic chains is based on human leg parameters in terms of ratios, range of motion, and physical length. This research presents the design and simulation of lower limb exoskeleton for rehabilitation of patients with paraplegia. This work presents close equation for the forward and inverse kinematics by geometric and Denavit-Hartenberg (D-H) approach. Also, the dynamic model is approached by applying the principle of Lagrangian dynamics. The paper contains several simulations and numerical examples to prove the analytical results.

Keywords: Exoskeleton · Mechanical design · Simulation · Paraplegia · Rehabilitation

1 Introduction

In Mexico since 2010, exist over 5, 739, 270 million persons with some disability, that represents 5.1% of the total population. Limitation of mobility is the greatest suffering among the population of the country; the 58.3% limiting the declared relate to walk or move. One disease that affects walking mobility is paraplegia, which affects more than 20 million people in the world, where these people have no or partial capacity for mobility in your lower extremities [1].

The growing number of people with motor disabilities has been launched to develop new engineering techniques to assist walking. One of the techniques under development are driving exoskeletons. These devices are intended to give patients the

© Springer International Publishing AG 2017
G. Sidorov and O. Herrera-Alcántara (Eds.): MICAI 2016, Part I, LNAI 10061, pp. 522–534, 2017.
DOI: 10.1007/978-3-319-62434-1_42

opportunity to regain mobility and thus actively integrated into society, overcoming physical limitations associated with the inability to walk. Exoskeletons are a technological alternative to wheelchairs or passive orthosis in which the patient performs support and supported rolling walkers, crutches or canes.

Some research centers around the world (Japan with HAL 3 and 5, Israel with rewalk, the US with Sarcos XOS, rex bionics, HULC, Mexico with OAMI) have developed exoskeletons for rehabilitation of some paralysis in the lower limbs, all for the same purpose, optimize man performance machine interaction, and provide a better lifestyle to patients suffering from these diseases.

This paper proposes a new architecture for an exoskeleton with five DOF per each leg, also, the work presents close equation for the forward and inverse kinematics by geometric and D-H approach. Also, the dynamic model is approached by applying the principle of Lagrangian dynamics. The paper contains several simulations and numerical examples to prove the analytical results.

2 Mechanical Model of the Lower Exoskeleton

The design of an exoskeleton is a subject of high complexity due to the different considerations and issues exist simultaneously. The proposed prototype for exoskeleton is developed by CAD software as shown in Fig. 1. The exoskeleton has a five DOF and a range of movement equivalent to that of human leg with restrictions on the movements of flexion, extension, abduction and adduction movements for the lower limb, Table 1 presents the rank of motion for the human leg versus the exoskeleton, where, the range of movement of the exoskeleton is shown in comparison with that of an average human being, however a safety factor was determined to define the range of movement of the exoskeleton to prevent an accident in case of technical failure.

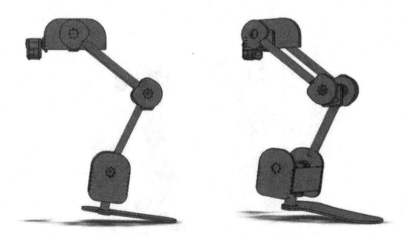

Fig. 1. Exoskeleton designed by CAD software

Table 1. Rank of motion human leg versus the exoskeleton

Joint	Rank of motion in the human leg	Rank of motion in exoskeleton
Hip:		
flexion	0° to 90°	0° to 80°
extension	0° to −15°	0° to −15°
Abduction/adduction	−30° to 130°	−20° to 120°
Knee:		
Flexion/extension	0° to −135°	0° to −120°
Ankle:		
Flexion/extension	25° to −60°	25° to −20°
Abduction/adduction	25° to −25°	25° to −25°

3   Forward and Inverse Kinematics for the Exoskeleton

There are two fundamental problems to solve in the kinematics of the robot which are the direct and inverse kinematics. In direct kinematic joint values are known, the geometric parameters and the location of them on the same plane this will allow us to determine the position and orientation on the same plane [3].

The forward kinematic is developed by D-H convention, where the parameters are taken from Fig. 2. It consists of five DOF leg, namely 2-DOF hip, 1-DOF knee and 2-DOF ankle. The exoskeleton can be modeled as a chain with trhee links (L1…L3) connected by five revolute joints ($q_1...q_5$). The synthesis of the kinematic chains is based on human body parameters in terms of ratios, range of motion, and physical length. The frames are assigned to each joint and all the variables are found by following the D-H convention in order to define the position and orientation of link coordinate frames (X_i, Y_i, Z_i) [12]. Consider the base frame (X_0, Y_0, Z_0) at the center of the waist as the global reference frame.

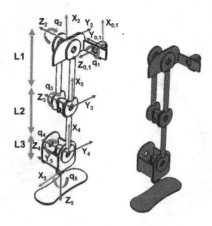

Fig. 2. View from the sagittal plane of the exoskeleton of 5 DOF with frameworks

Table 2 shows the DH parameters where q_i is the angle between axes measured in the x plane is perpendicular to z, d_i is z angle distance between the x-axis (variable parameter in prismatic joints), a_i is distance along the x-axis with respect to the z axis intersection, α_i is the separation angle of the z axis measured in a plane perpendicular to the x axis.

Table 2. D-H parameters

Link	d_i	q_i	a_i	α_i
1	0	q1	0	0
2	0	q2	0	90
3	0	q3	L1	0
4	0	q4	L2	0
5	0	q5	L3	-90

With the D-H parameters, the homogeneous matrix are obtained as shown in Eqs. 1 to 5:

$$^0A_1 = \begin{bmatrix} Cq1 & Sq1 & 0 & 0 \\ Sq1 & Cq1 & 0 & 0 \\ 0 & 0 & 1 & 0 \\ 0 & 0 & 0 & 1 \end{bmatrix} \tag{1}$$

$$^1A_2 = \begin{bmatrix} Cq2 & 0 & Sq2 & 0 \\ Sq2 & 0 & -Cq2 & 0 \\ 0 & 1 & 0 & 0 \\ 0 & 0 & 0 & 1 \end{bmatrix} \tag{2}$$

$$^2A_3 = \begin{bmatrix} Cq3 & -Sq3 & 0 & L1Cq3 \\ Sq3 & Cq3 & 0 & L1Sq3 \\ 0 & 0 & 1 & 0 \\ 0 & 0 & 0 & 1 \end{bmatrix} \tag{3}$$

$$^3A_4 = \begin{bmatrix} Cq4 & -Sq4 & 0 & L2Cq4 \\ Sq4 & Cq4 & 0 & L2Sq4 \\ 0 & 0 & 1 & 0 \\ 0 & 0 & 0 & 1 \end{bmatrix} \tag{4}$$

$$^4A_5 = \begin{bmatrix} Cq5 & 0 & -Sq5 & L3Cq5 \\ Sq5 & 0 & Cq5 & L3Sq5 \\ 0 & -1 & 0 & 0 \\ 0 & 0 & 0 & 1 \end{bmatrix} \tag{5}$$

Where: $Cq1 = Cos(q_1)$, $Cq2 = Cos(q2)$, $Cq3 = Cos(q3)$, $Cq4 = Cos(q4)$, $Cq5 = Cos(q5)$, $Sq1 = Sin(q1)$, $Sq2 = Sin(q2)$, $Sq3 = Sin(q3)$, $Sq4 = Sin(q4)$, $Sq5 = Sin(q5)$.

With the five homogeneous matrices, the Eqs. 6–8 represent the position for the hip until foot for exoskeleton.

$$px = L1Cq3C(q3 - q2) + L2C(q1 - q2) + L3C(q1 - q2)Cq5 - (q3 + q4) \quad (6)$$

$$py = L1Cq3S(q1 + q2) + L2S(q1 + q2)C(q3 - q4) + L3Sq1 + q2C(q5 - (q3 + q4)) \quad (7)$$

$$pz = L1Sq3 + L2S(q3 - q4) + L3S(q5 - (q3 + q4)) \quad (8)$$

Where: $Cq1 = Cos(q_1)$, $Cq2 = Cos(q2)$, $Cq3 = Cos(q3)$, $Cq4 = Cos(q4)$, $Cq5 = Cos(q5)$, $Sq1 = Sin(q1)$, $Sq2 = Sin(q2)$, $Sq3 = Sin(q3)$, $Sq4 = Sin(q4)$, $Sq5 = Sin(q5)$.

Inverse Kinematics

The inverse kinematics for exoskeleton is divide in two parts; geometric method and solution for homogeneous matrix. The strategy of the decomposition of the inverse kinematics is simplify the complexity presents an ordinary calculation of inverse kinematics in robotic manipulators with more than three DOF.

The first approach is to obtain $q2$, $q3$ and $q4$ angles by geometrical method, Fig. 3 show the angles $q2$, $q3$, and $q4$, where $q2$ represent the angle between the reference global an axis Y, $q3$ represent the angle between links $L1$ and $L2$ and $q4$ represents the angle between the links $L2$ and $L3$, X and Y are the global references. The approach that this paper follows for finding the inverse kinematics solution for the $q2$, $q3$ and $q4$ is a geometrical method, as shown in Fig. 4.

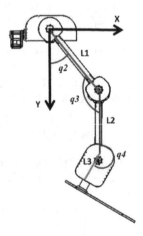

Fig. 3. Sagittal plane view of the exoskeleton of 5 DOF

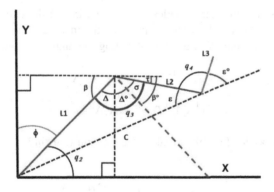

Fig. 4. Representation of 3 DOF located in the sagittal plane

Assuming that the value q_2 is known a solution to find the values of β, ϕ, τ and Δ are:

$$\phi = 90 - q_2 \tag{9}$$

$$\beta = \sin^{-1}\left(\left(\frac{L1Cos\phi}{L1}\right)\right) \tag{10}$$

$$\Delta = \sin^{-1}\left(\left(\frac{L1Cosq_2}{L1}\right)\right) \tag{11}$$

$$\Delta = \Delta° \tag{12}$$

$$\beta = \beta° \tag{13}$$

$$\tau = 180 - \beta - \beta° - \Delta - \Delta° \tag{14}$$

$$\beta° - \tau = \sigma \tag{15}$$

$$q_3 = 2\left(\sin^{-1}\left(\left(\frac{L1Cosq_2}{L1}\right)\right)\right) + \sigma \tag{16}$$

Where: $\beta°$, $\Delta°$ were obtained by symmetry in angles shown in Fig. 4.

Starting to find the value of C from Fig. 4 and subsequently by the law of cosines $q4$ value was found as shown in Eqs. 17 and 18.

$$C = \sqrt{L1^2 + L2^2 - 2L1L2Cosq_3} \tag{17}$$

$$q_4 = 180 - \sin^{-1}\left(\left(\frac{L1}{\sqrt{L1^2 + L2^2 - 2L1L2Cosq_3}}\right)(Sinq_3)\right) \tag{18}$$

After obtaining the first three angles ($q2$, $q3$ and $q4$) in the exoskeleton, the two remaining angles is obtained from the proposal by the method of homogeneous matrix solution. Equations 19 and 20 is used to obtaining the angles $q1$ and $q5$:

$$\left(^{0}A_{1}\right)^{-1}T = {}^{1}A_{2}{}^{2}A_{3}{}^{3}A_{4}{}^{4}A_{5} \tag{19}$$

$$\left(^{4}A_{5}\right)^{-1}T = {}^{1}A_{2}^{2}A_{3}^{3}A_{4}^{0}A_{1} \tag{20}$$

Solve the product for Eq. 19 and taken the element (2,4) in both sides of equation to find q_1:

$$q_{1} = q_{3} - \left(cos^{-1}\left(\frac{Cq_{4}}{C(q_{2} - q_{3})}\right)\right) \tag{21}$$

As the same approach from Eq. 22, match the element (1,4) in both sides find $q5$.

$$q_{5} = q_{3} - \left(cos^{-1}\left(\frac{L1Cq3C(q1 - q2) + L3Cq3Cq5C(q1 - q2) - L3Sq3Sq5C(q1 - q2)}{L3C(q1 - q2)}\right)\right) \tag{22}$$

4 Dynamic Model

One of the most frequent methods for obtaining the dynamic models of the robot manipulators, in closed form, is based on the Lagrangian dynamics equations [3]. The approach followed in this paper applies the principles of Lagrangian dynamics for determining the close equations for obtaining the torque in each joint of the exoskeleton.

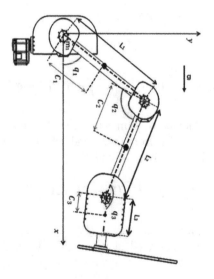

Fig. 5. Sagittal plane for dynamic analysis

In Fig. 5 show the sagittal plane exoskeleton where *L1*, *L2* and *L3* are the length of links, q_1, q_2 and q_3 joint in the exoskeleton g is gravity, *x* and *y* is the global reference, C_1, C_2 and C_3 are the mass centers each of the links, *m1*, *m2*, and *m3* are the mass of each link.

The determination of the equations of kinetic energy and potential energy for each joint is calculated by Eqs. 23 and 24.

$$K(q,\dot{q}) = \frac{1}{2}m_n v_n^2 + \frac{1}{2}I_n \dot{q}_n^2 \tag{23}$$

$$U(q) = m_n g l_n \tag{24}$$

The position of the links is obtained to later derive these and found the kinetic and potential energy, see the Eqs. 26 to 32.

$$x_1 = l_1 cos q_2 \tag{25}$$

$$y_1 = l_1 sen q_2 \tag{26}$$

$$x_2 = l_1 cos q_2 + l_2 cos(q_2 - q_3) \tag{27}$$

$$y_2 = l_1 sen q_2 + l_2 sen(q_2 - q_3) \tag{28}$$

$$\alpha = q_2 - q_3 \tag{29}$$

$$x_3 = l_1 cos q_2 + l_2 cos(q_2 - q_3) + l_3 cos(\alpha + q_4) \tag{30}$$

$$y_3 = l_1 sen q_2 + l_2 sen\alpha + l_3 sen(\alpha + q_4) \tag{31}$$

The kinetic and potential energy in the links is determined by the Eqs. 34 to 39

$$k_2(q_2, \dot{q}_2) = \frac{1}{2}m_1 v_1^2 + \frac{1}{2}I_1 \dot{q}_2^2 \tag{32}$$

$$k_3(q_3, \dot{q}_3) = \frac{1}{2}m_2 v_2^2 + \frac{1}{2}I_2(\dot{\alpha})^2 \tag{33}$$

$$k_4(q_4, \dot{q}_4) = \frac{1}{2}m_3 v_3^2 + \frac{1}{2}I_3(\dot{\alpha} - \dot{q}_4)^2 \tag{34}$$

$$u_2(q_2) = -m_1 g l_1 sen q_2 \tag{35}$$

$$u_3(q_3) = -m_2 g l_1 sen q_2 - m_2 l_2 g sen\,\alpha \tag{36}$$

$$u_4(q_4) = -m_3 g l_1 sen q_2 - m_3 l_2 g sen\alpha - m_3 l_3 g sen(\alpha - q_4) \tag{37}$$

To obtain the dynamics, this work considers the Lagrange formulation, whose unconstrained equation is given as follows.

$$\tau_i = \frac{d}{dt}\left(\frac{\partial L}{\partial \dot{q}_i}\right) - \frac{\partial L}{\partial q_i} \tag{38}$$

$$i = 1\ldots 3$$

where L = K-P, and K denotes the rotational kinetic energy, P is the potential energy, and τ_i is the unconstrained force determined by the Eqs. 39-41 which allow us to obtain the value of mechanical torque in each of the joints, resulting τ_1 for link in the hip, τ_2 for link in the knee and τ_3 for link in the ankle.

$$
\begin{aligned}
\tau_1 =\ & m_3 l_1 C_3 C(q_2 - q_3)(\ddot{q}_1 - \ddot{q}_2 + \ddot{q}_3) - m_3 l_1 C_3 S(q_2 - q_3)(q_1 - q_2 + q_3)(\dot{q}_2 - \dot{q}_3) \\
& + m_3 l_1 C_3 C(q_2 - q_3)\ddot{q}_1 - m_3 l_1 C_3 S(q_2 - q_3)(\dot{q}_2 - \dot{q}_3)\dot{q}_1 \\
& + [-m_3 l_2 C_3 S(q_3)\dot{q}_3 - 2l_1(m_2 C_2 + m_3 l_1 S(q_2)\dot{q}_2]\dot{q}_1 \\
& + [2m_3 l_2 C_3 C(q_3) + 2l_1(m_2 C_2 + m_3 l_2)C(q_2) \\
& + m_3(l_1^2 + l_2^2 + l_3^2) + m_1 C_1^2 + m_2 l_1^2 + m_2 C_2^2 + I_1 + I_2 \\
& + I_3]\ddot{q}_1 + [2m_3 l_2 C_3 S(q_3)\dot{q}_3 + l_1(m_2 C_2 + m_3 l_2)S(q_2)\dot{q}_2]\dot{q}_2 \\
& - [2m_3 l_2 C_3 C(q_3) + l_1(m_2 C_2 + m_3 l_2)C(q_2) + m_3(l_2^2 + C_3^2) \\
& + m_2 C_2^2 + I_2 + I_3]\ddot{q}_2 + \left[m_3 l_2 C_3 C(q_3) + m_3 C_3^2 + I_3\right]\ddot{q}_3 \\
& - m_3 l_2 C_3 S(q_3)\dot{q}_3^2 - (m_1 c_1 - m_2 l_1 - m_3 l_1)gS(q_1) \\
& + (m_2 C_2 + m_3 l_2)gS(q_1 - q_2) + m_3 C_3 gS(q_1 - q_2 + q_3)
\end{aligned}
$$
$$\tag{39}$$

$$
\begin{aligned}
\tau_2 =\ & -m_3 l_1 C_3 C(q_2 - q_3)\ddot{q}_1 + m_3 l_1 C_3 S(q_2 - q_3)(\dot{q}_2 - \dot{q}_3)\dot{q}_1 + [2m_3 l_2 C_3 S(q_3)\dot{q}_3 \\
& + l_1((m_2 C_2 + m_3 l_2)S(q_2)\dot{q}_2]\dot{q}_1 \\
& - [2m_3 l_2 C_3 C(q_3) + l_1(m_2 C_2 + m_3 l_2)C(q_2) + m_3(l_2^2 + C_3^2) \\
& + m_2 C_2^2 + I_2 + I_3]\ddot{q}_1 - 2m_3 l_2 C_3 S(q_3)\dot{q}_2 \dot{q}_3 \\
& + [2m_3 l_2 C_3 C(q_3) + m_3(l_2^2 + C_3^2) + m_2 C_2^2 + I_2 + I_3]\ddot{q}_2 \\
& - \left[m_3 l_2 C_3 C(q_3) + m_3 C_3^2 + I_3\right]\ddot{q}_3 + m_3 l_2 C_3 S(q_3)\dot{q}_2 \\
& + l_1(m_2 C_2 + m_3 l_2)S(q_2)[\dot{q}_1^2 - \dot{q}_1 \dot{q}_2] \\
& - (m_2 C_2 + m_3 l_2)gS(q_1 - q_2) \\
& + m_3 l_1 C_3 S(q_1 - q_2)(\dot{q}_1 - \dot{q}_2 + \dot{q}_3)\dot{q}_1 - m_3 C_3 gS(q_1 - q_2 + q_3)
\end{aligned}
$$
$$\tag{40}$$

$$
\begin{aligned}
\tau_3 =\ & m_3 l_1 C_3 C(q_2 - q_3)\ddot{q}_1 + m_3 l_1 C_3 S(q_2 - q_3)(\dot{q}_2 - \dot{q}_3)\dot{q}_1 + [m_3 C_3^2 \\
& + I_3]\ddot{q}_3 - m_3 l_2 C_3 S(q_3)(\dot{q}_1 - \dot{q}_2)\dot{q}_3 + [m_3 l_2 C_3 C(q_3) + m_3 C_3^2 \\
& + I_3](\ddot{q}_1 - \ddot{q}_2) - m_3 C_3\{-gS(q_1 - q_2 + q_3) \\
& + [l_1 S(q_2 - q_3)\dot{q}_1 - l_2 S(q_3)(\dot{q}_1 - \dot{q}_2)](\dot{q}_1 - \dot{q}_2 + \dot{q}_3)\}
\end{aligned}
$$
$$\tag{41}$$

5   Numerical Examples and Simulation

This work used Maple for producing the numerical examples of the analytical solutions to the kinematics and dynamics of the exoskeleton. In addition, this paper used SolidWorks and the SimMechanics toolbox from MATLAB for modelling and simulating mechanical systems that use the standard Newtonian laws [24].

To validate the kinematics, the CAD model of exoskeleton of SolidWorks is exported to SimMechanics. In order to verify the mobility of each joint of the leg a repeating sequence to move each joint to a reference position as shown in Fig. 6 shows the block diagram for the exoskeleton where each block represents one of the links and the conditions to generate the movement of the exoskeleton and Fig. 7 shows the simulation of the behavior of the block diagram in SimMechanics.

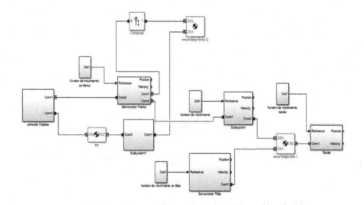

Fig. 6. Block diagram representing the exoskeleton

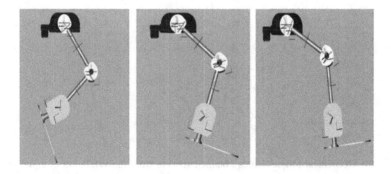

Fig. 7. Exoskeleton motion simulation shown in Simulink

To validate the dynamic equations, the parameters for the exoskeleton as mass, inertia, length and center of mass are obtained from Solidworks data, as shown in Table 3.

Table 3. Exoskeleton parameters obtained from Solidworks

	Moment of inertia (kg*m^2)	Mass (kg)	Center of mass (kg*m^2)	Lengths (m)
Link 1	0.000315	1.148	0.043722	0.44
Link 2	0.000200	0.29	0.162788	0.41
Link 3	0.000300	1.913	0.036	0.19

With the information obtained in Table 3 and the equations of Lagrangian, the values of torque and position for each DOF is obtained as shown in Figs. 8 and 9.

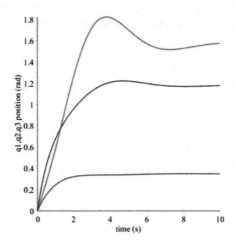

Fig. 8. Position values from the dynamic equations

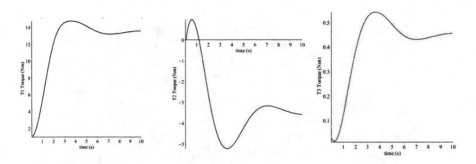

Fig. 9. Mechanical torque values obtained starting from the validation of equations

The results shown in Figs. 8 and 9 are the behavior of position and the mechanical torque across of time in each links, where *T1* and *q1* represents the torque and position in hip, *T2* and *q2* is the torque in knee and *T3* and *q3* is the torque in ankle, in Table 4 shows the torques for each joint when the desired position is achieving.

Table 4. Mechanical torque values obtained starting maple simulation

Joint	Mechanical torque proposed
hip	20 N/m
Knee	15 N/m
Ankle	5 N/m

6   Conclusions and Future Work

In this paper the forward and inverse kinematics and dynamics of a new five DOF exoskeleton are presented. The paper shows a new architecture for a biped robot with five DOF per each leg.

This work obtained closed-form solutions for the kinematic equations through the analytical method, where forware kinematic was solved by D-H metodology and the inverse kinematic was solved by geometrycal method and homogeneous matrix. Also the principle of Lagrangian dynamics was recurred in order to find the torque in the joints for the desired position for each joint.

Simmechanics was used to verify the rank of motion for each DOF of the Exo-skeleton, where the rank of motion proposed for the architecture is achieved in eac joint and numerical examples were provided for found the desired position and torque for each joint in the sagittal plane.

Future work of this paper will focus on the fabrication of exoskeleton proposed and the implementation of a control system using the human leg workspace as some target parameters.

Acknowledgments. This study was supported by Consejo Nacional de Ciencia y Tecnología (CONACYT), located at Insurgentes 1582, Zip Code 03940, CDMX, México.

References

1. Instituto Nacional de estadística y geografía: Las personas con discapacidad en México una visión al 2010, Mexico (2013)
2. Pedro, V.L.: Biomecánica de la marcha normal y patológica, Instituto de Biomecánica de Valencia
3. Cortes, F.R.: Robotica. Alfaomega Grupo Editor (2011)
4. Kelly, R., Santibáñez, V., Loría, A.: Control of Robot Manipulators in Joint Space. Springer, London (2005)
5. Perry, J.: Gait Analysis: Normal and Pathological Function. Slack Incorporated, New York (1992)
6. Kawamoto, H., Sankai, Y.: Power assist system HAL-3 for gait disorder person. Institute of Engineering Mechanics and Systems, University of Tsukuba (2010)
7. Agrawal, S.K., Banala, S.K., Fattah, A., Sangwan, V., Krishnamoorthy, V., Scholz, J.P., Hsu, W.-L.: Assessment of motion of a swing leg and gait rehabilitation with a gravity balancing exoskeleton. IEEE Trans. Neural Syst. Rehab. Eng. **15**(3), 410–420 (2007)

8. Ekkelenkamp, R., Veltink, P., Stramigioli, S., van der Kooij, H.: Evaluation of a virtual model control for the selective support of gait functions using an exoskeleton. In: IEEE 10th International Conference on Rehabilitation Robotics, ICORR 2007, pp. 693–699, June 2007

9. Gomez-Ferrer Sapiña, R.: Estudio biomecánico de la marcha humana, Tesis Doctoral, Universidad de Valencia, Departamento de medicina, Valencia España (2004)

10. Chávez Cardona, M.A.: Exoesqueletos para potenciar las capacidades humanas y apoyar la reabilitación. Revista Ingeniería Biomédica 7(4), 63–73 (2010). Universidad del Valle

11. Kessler Foundation and Ekso Bionics: kurzweilai. http://www.kurzweilai.net/ekso-exoskeleton-allowing-traumatic-spinal-cord-injury-patients-to-walk. Accessed Nov 2015

12. Argo Medical Technologies Inc. (2012). http://rewalk.com/

13. Ekkelenkamp, R., Veltink, P., Stramigioli, S., van der Kooij, H.: Evaluation of a virtual model control for the selective support of gait functions using an exoskeleton. In: IEEE 10th International Conference on Rehabilitation Robotics, ICORR 2007, pp. 693–699, June 2007

14. Kazerooni, H.: (2010). bleex.me.berkeley.edu/research/exoskeleton/elegs/

15. Pinto Palmero, R.: Diseño cinemático para mejorar la ergonomía en humano-maquina, Avance de Tesis de Maestría, UNAM, Facultad de Ingeniería (2014)

16. Jaime, A.L.: Control automático de un exoesqueleto de marcha para pacientes con discapacidad motora. Tesis de Maestría, Universidad Nacional de Colombia, Colombia Bogota (2013)

17. Kajita, S., Kanehiro, F., Kaneko, K., Fujiwara, K., Harada, K., Yokoi, K., Hirukawa, H.: Biped walking pattern generation by using preview control of zero-moment point. In: ICRA, pp. 1620–1626. IEEE (2003)

18. Choi, Y., Kim, D., You, B.-J.: On the walking control for humanoid robot based on the kinematic resolution of com jacobian with embedded motion. In: Proceedings 2006 IEEE International Conference on Robotics and Automation, ICRA 2006, pp. 2655–2660, May 2006

19. Onen, U., Botsali, F., Kalyoncu, M., Tinkir, M., Yihnaz, N., Sahin, Y.: Design and actuator selection of a lower extremity exoskeleton. IEEEIASME Trans. Mechatron. 19(2), 623–632 (2013)

20. Hernández-Santos, C., Rodriguez-Leal, E., Soto, R., Gordillo, J.L.: Kinematics and dynamics of a new 16 DOF humanoid biped robot with active toe joint. Int. J. Adv. Robot. Syst. 9, 190 (2012). ISSN 1729-8806

Sensorial System for Obtaining the Angles of the Human Movement in the Coronal and Sagittal Anatomical Planes

David Alvarado, Leonel Corona$^{(\boxtimes)}$, Saúl Muñoz, and José Aquino

Instituto Politécnico Nacional, Mexico City, Mexico
{dalvarador1000, jmunozr1002}@alumno.ipn.mx,
lcoronaramirez@hotmail.com, jaquinor@gmail.com

Abstract. This paper presents the construction of a system composed by inertial sensors and the linkage with a biped robot, our main aim is the obtaining, quantification and analysis of human body posture (in rest or in motion). To achieve this, we have three objectives:

1. Determination and obtaining, of kinematics and dynamic of the body joints,
2. Imitation of body movements (biped robot prototype)
3. Quantification of anomalies presented in the human gait.

For this purpose, we present the development a sensorial system capable to obtaining the angles in the human body.

Keywords: Human gait · Body posture · Inertial sensors · Movements of human joints · Biped robot

1 Introduction

From the point of view clinical the analysis of the body has a considerable importance. Considering the body posture and motions are result from interaction of three organizations (muscular system, skeletal and nervous system).

In the area of biomechanical, traditionally to monitor and analyze the dynamic of the patients, were utilize video systems and markers, placed in strategic points. These systems imply some limitations because cameras are not portable, furthermore, analysis of motion in exteriors proves to be complex locate the markers, due they are confused with external factors. In the other hand, analyses by cameras are usually done in rooms delimited and designed to eliminate noise signals, in addition to own a determined illumination. For another thing, measurements delivered by these systems presented errors if do not consider techniques of stereoscopic vision, because the camera is only able to capture images in one plane delimiting the field of vision. The systems of digital processing have a high cost in hardware and software [1, 2]. Exist some acoustic systems for evaluation of motion that are another alternative, in tracking of objects. These systems characterize themselves for the use of more of three receivers and transmitters, commonly located in a space delimited and controlled, allowing the receiver and transmitter always being in contact. However, it is necessary consider the

G. Sidorov and O. Herrera-Alcántara (Eds.): MICAI 2016, Part I, LNAI 10061, pp. 535–547, 2017.
DOI: 10.1007/978-3-319-62434-1_43

dissipation of the sound wave through the surroundings to obtain one adequate calibration of the system.

The studies of motion from mechanical systems are able to obtain measurements directly between the limbs, but it requires a rigid system to subjection (exoskeletons).

In some cases, motion of the extremities is conditioned, modifying measurements [3].

A system of inertial sensors presents some similarities respect to the before-mentioned systems, assuming that these systems can perceive the displacement angles in the three space axes, it does not need small rooms, the use of markers and cameras is not necessary, also it can achieve bigger sampling rates and data processing [4].

These sensors are constituted by accelerometers, gyroscopes and magnetometers, they need an implementation of filters, their measurements are gotten from algorithms based in the cinematic.

In this work is performed the design and the construction of a structure conformed by twelve inertial sensors (accelerometers and gyroscopes), this system is a tool for diagnosis of anomalies in the human gait, it can be used for study of body posture, improvement in athletic performance, validation of mechanical systems like prosthesis, orthosis or exoskeletons, with the purpose to enhance patient biomechanics.

The system designed can be used in robotics area for control of engines, this system is proved for the operation of a biped robot with eighteen degrees of freedom, where is obtained 84% relationship in human gait.

2 Design of Sensorial System

2.1 System Devices

This inertial system consists of twelve sensors with 3-axis accelerometer and 3-axis gyroscope (MPU6050), the sensors are capturing the motions in the sagittal and frontal anatomic plane, it works using the I2C protocol and a digital decoder 4×16 (47HC154). These devices are synchronizing with a microcontroller (ATmega48) of architecture RISC (Reduced Instruction Seth Computer) and send the processed data by protocol UART (Universal Asynchronous Receiver Transmitter), toward a Bluetooth® device 2.0 (HC 05), it allows have a fast data transmission toward a mobile device, PC or hardware for the later processing.

For the power supply it has been chosen a battery of 7.4 V and 1000 mA, it gives 3 h of duration. In the Fig. 1 is described the block diagram the system.

It is necessary know the cinematic of every one of the sensors MPU6050. Referring to the recommended position of sensors (Fig. 4) the cinematic of the system is represent by the matrix of rotation, for this case were used Eqs. 1, 2 and 3 to represent the rotations on the X, Y y Z-axes in the sensor [5] (Fig. 2). The trigonometric functions sine and cosine are abbreviated with the S and C respectively.

$$R_{X,\theta} = \begin{bmatrix} 1 & 0 & 0 \\ 0 & C\theta & -S\theta \\ 0 & S\theta & C\theta \end{bmatrix} \tag{1}$$

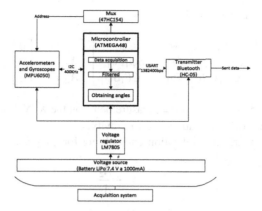

Fig. 1. Block diagram of the sensory system.

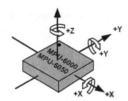

Fig. 2. Sensor reference system MPU6050.

$$R_{Y,\theta} = \begin{bmatrix} C\theta & 0 & S\theta \\ 0 & 1 & 0 \\ -S\theta & 0 & C\theta \end{bmatrix} \tag{2}$$

$$R_{Z,\theta} = \begin{bmatrix} C\theta & -S\theta & 0 \\ S\theta & C\theta & 0 \\ 0 & 0 & 1 \end{bmatrix} \tag{3}$$

Calculations are performed in accord to the position of the sensors, it is shows in Fig. 4. We are considering three cases for the obtaining of angles in accordance with the sagittal and frontal planes.

For the first case, the reference and back sensors are conducting the following rotations.

$$R_{Y,90}R_{Z,\theta_1}R_{Y,\varphi_1}$$

Therefore, the sensor model is:

$$
\begin{bmatrix}
-S\varphi_1 & 0 & C\varphi_1 \\
C\varphi_1 S\theta_1 & C\theta_1 & S\varphi_1 S\theta_1 \\
-C\varphi_1 C\theta_1 & S\theta_1 & -C\theta_1 S\varphi_1
\end{bmatrix}
\begin{bmatrix}
A_X \\
A_Y \\
A_Z
\end{bmatrix}
=
\begin{bmatrix}
0 \\
0 \\
g
\end{bmatrix}
\tag{4}
$$

Where A_X, A_y y A_z are acceleration measurements on the X, Y, Z accelerometer axis and g is the constant of acceleration due to gravity.

Performing the matrix multiplication and solving for φ_1 y θ_1.

$$
\tan \varphi_1 = \frac{-A_z}{-A_x}
\tag{5}
$$

$$
\tan \theta_1 = \frac{A_Y}{-A_x \cos \varphi_1 - A_z \sin \varphi_1}
\tag{6}
$$

For the second case, the left inferior and superior limbs are performing the following rotations.

$$
R_{Y,90} R_{X,90} R_{Z,\theta_2} R_{Y,\varphi_2}
$$

Therefore, the sensor model is:

$$
\begin{bmatrix}
S\varphi_2 & C\varphi_2 & 0 \\
C\varphi_2 S\theta_2 & -S\varphi_2 S\theta_2 & -C\theta_2 \\
-C\varphi_2 C\theta_2 & -C\theta_2 S\varphi_2 & -S\theta_2
\end{bmatrix}
\begin{bmatrix}
A_X \\
A_Y \\
A_Z
\end{bmatrix}
=
\begin{bmatrix}
0 \\
0 \\
g
\end{bmatrix}
\tag{7}
$$

Performing the matrix multiplication and solving for φ_2 y θ_2.

$$
\tan \varphi_2 = \frac{-A_Y}{A_x}
\tag{8}
$$

$$
\tan \theta_2 = \frac{-A_Z}{-A_X \cos \varphi_2 + A_Y \sin \varphi_2}
\tag{9}
$$

For the third case, the right inferior and superior limbs are performing the following rotations.

$$
R_{Y,90} R_{X,-90} R_{Z,\theta_3} R_{Y,\varphi_3}
$$

Therefore, the sensor model is:

$$
\begin{bmatrix}
S\varphi_3 & -C\varphi_3 & 0 \\
-C\varphi_3 S\theta_3 & S\varphi_3 S\theta_3 & C\theta_3 \\
-C\varphi_3 C\theta_3 & C\theta_3 S\varphi_3 & -S\theta_3
\end{bmatrix}
\begin{bmatrix}
A_X \\
A_Y \\
A_Z
\end{bmatrix}
=
\begin{bmatrix}
0 \\
0 \\
g
\end{bmatrix}
\tag{10}
$$

Performing the matrix multiplication and solving φ_3 y θ_3.

$$\tan \varphi_3 = \frac{A_Y}{-A_X} \tag{11}$$

$$\tan \theta_3 = \frac{A_Z}{A_X \cos \varphi_3 - A_Y \sin \varphi_3} \tag{12}$$

2.2 Search of Recurrence Equation for Obtaining Angles

It is important consider, that the inertial sensors are delivering angles of inclination in relation to the gravitational axis. For this, it is necessary find an equation that permits getting the separation between the members of the body and the angles, so that is proposed a three-link system E_1, E_2 y E_3 which are united for articulations A_1, A_2 y A_3. Each link contains a sensor S which measures an angle θ_s concerning the gravitational axis g, and requires to find the angle θ_E between links (Fig. 3).

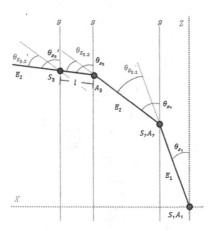

Fig. 3. Three links system for find the recurrence equation.

Of previous graphical analysis were obtained three points:

1. The recurrence equation where find the angle between links (Eq. 13).

$$\theta_{E_{k_p, k_{p-1}}} = \theta_{s_{k_p}} - \theta_{s_{k_p-1}}, K \in \mathbb{N}^* \tag{13}$$

Where k is the number of link that takes the measurement and p is the reference plane, with it is granted the measurement, this plane could be coronal or sagittal. (φ o θ).

2. If the sensor S is not located exactly in the A_3 joint and the measurement is located distance L of the rotational joints, it does not prove to be affected (Eq. 14).

$$\theta'_{E_{3,2}} = \theta_{E_{3,2}} \tag{14}$$

3. Sensor has located parallel to the link, if this not occurs the measurement not be correct.

2.3   Location of Inertial Sensors

The principal function of sensorial system is detecting the angles between the inferior limbs, superiors and appendicular of a person. Sensors are located in such a way that detect flexion, extension, abduction and adduction (Fig. 4).

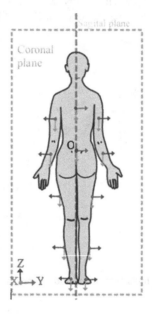

Fig. 4. Recommended location of sensors.

The specific functions of the sensors are the detection of inclination of the back, flexion-extension of the forearms and flexion-extension and abduction-adduction of humerus, leg, thigh and foot. On the other hand, this system has a reference sensor, it positions itself between the fifth lumbar vertebra and the sacrum, this with the purpose to give better precision.

3   Communication I^2C and Crosstalk Elimination

Every one of sensors is communicated by protocol I^2 C, this protocol requires that the system has a capacitance lower to 20 pF, with the purpose of avoiding electromagnetic interferences between the canals SCL and SDA for their oscillation (crosstalk).

We used a cable 28AWG with a separation of 0.00127 m between leads. This type of cable presents inconveniences with the phenomenon of crosstalk if it is not configured correctly. Therefore, it was calculated the capacitance between every one of the cables using the Eq. 15.

$$C = \frac{\varepsilon_r \times \varepsilon \times 2\pi \times R \times L}{D} \tag{15}$$

Where C is considered a cable with length (L) of 4 m, and a distance of separation D of 1.651 cm, radius R of 1.905e-4 m and a relative permissiveness ε_r of 7,465, In this way is obtains a capacitance C of 19,16 pF what proves to be inferior to the maximum value of capacitance. With this configuration, it is got a data transmission of 400 kbits/s.

4   Kalman Filter

The MPU6060 need an additional filtering, therefore Kalman filter is implemented, with the aim to obtaining a better measurement between accelerometers and gyroscopes. For the implementation of the filter, it takes the model of the accelerometer gives an angle θ_M shaped by the real angle θ_T and plus a random noise n_θ, to obtain the Eq. 16.

$$\theta_M = \theta_T + n_\theta \tag{16}$$

It is also necessary know the behavior of the gyroscope, the sensor have an angular speed represented by ω_M, this is compound by the real measurement of angular speed ω_T and with a constant angular velocity ω_b and a random noise n_ω. ω_b is considered that is caused by a noise $n_\propto$ from the angular acceleration ω_b, with this information the Eqs. 17 and 18 are obtained [6].

$$\omega_M = \omega_T + \omega_b + n_\omega \tag{17}$$

$$\dot{\omega}_b = n_\propto \tag{18}$$

To apply the Kalman filter is necessary represent a discrete system and state-space equations, these are show in Eqs. 19 and 20.

$$X_{k+1} = A_{X_k} + B_{U_k} + \omega_k \tag{19}$$

$$Z_k = H_{X_k} + V_k \tag{20}$$

Where X is state vector of the system, A is matrix of states, B is input matrix, U is input vector or control, Z is output vector, H is output array, w is resulting noise and V is measurement noise.

According to Eqs. 19 and 20, the accelerometer-gyroscope system state space equations is described by Eqs. 21 and 22.

$$\begin{bmatrix} \theta_{k+1} \\ \omega_{b,k+1} \end{bmatrix} = \begin{bmatrix} 1 & -dt \\ 0 & 1 \end{bmatrix} \begin{bmatrix} \theta_k \\ \omega_{b,k} \end{bmatrix} + \begin{bmatrix} dt \\ 0 \end{bmatrix} \omega_{M,k} + dt \begin{bmatrix} n_{\omega,k} \\ n_{\alpha,k} \end{bmatrix} \tag{21}$$

$$\theta_{M,k} = [1 \ 0] \begin{bmatrix} \theta_k \\ \omega_{b,k} \end{bmatrix} + n_{\theta,k} \tag{22}$$

The model in state variables is described a Kalman filter algorithm, which divides into two parts, prediction and correction.

In the prediction are performed two processes:

1. Estimation a priori (Eq. 23).

$$\widehat{X}_{k+1}^- = A\widehat{X}_k + Bu_{k+1} \tag{23}$$

2. Calculation the error of covariance associated with the estimate a priori. Is necessary to consider the matrix Q is the covariance matrix of the noise sensor).

$$P_{k+1}^- = AP_k A^T + Q \tag{24}$$

In the correction process are performed three steps:

1. Calculation of the Kalman gain where it is required the noise covariance matrix R measurement (Eq. 25).

$$K_{k+1} = P_{k+1}^- H^T \left(HP_{k+1}^- H^T + R \right)^{-1} \tag{25}$$

2. Posterior estimation (Eq. 26).

$$\widehat{X}_{k+1} = \widehat{X}_{k+1}^- + K_{k+1} \left(Z_{k+1} - H\widehat{X}_{k+1}^- \right) \tag{26}$$

3. Calculation of error associated with estimating posteriori (Eq. 27).

$$P_{k+1} = (I - K_{k+1}H)P_{k+1}^- \tag{27}$$

In the implementation of algorithm is considered the noise covariance matrix of sensor Q:

$$Q = \begin{bmatrix} 3.497697246e - 3 & 2.669997898e - 5 \\ 2.669997898e - 5 & 3.497697246e - 3 \end{bmatrix} \tag{28}$$

And the noise covariance vector R:

$$R = 3.497697246e - 3 \tag{29}$$

5 Calibration of the System

Calibration of the system is to calculate the angular compensation of each of the MPU6050 sensors, this offset appears because exist an error in the position of sensors on the person. The calibration algorithm presents four steps.

1. Calculation of offset sensor located in the hip.
2. Calculation of offset sensors back and leg.
3. Calculation of offset sensors humerus and tibia.
4. Calculation of offset sensors forearm and foot.

Each stage has a duration of 10 s, the calibration algorithm runs at a sampling frequency of 50 Hz and applying the Kalman filter. Furthermore, the person must have fitted sensors like in Fig. 4 and must stand and in anatomical position without moving until the calibration process ends.

6 System Control Implemented with a Microcontroller ATmega48

This control program programmed into the microcontroller ATmega48 has thirteen steps:

1. Declaration of variables to be used throughout the program implementation process.
2. Setting all ports to use (I^2C, UART and port dedicated to the decoder).
3. The MPU6050 a sampling frequency to 1 kHz are set, the sensitivity of the gyroscope and accelerometer to 131 LSB/°/s and 16384 LSB/g respectively is set.
4. It runs a sensor calibration algorithm.
5. Timer microcontroller is configured to detect when 20 ms has elapsed program execution.
6. The timer is reset.
7. Acceleration data and angular velocity of each of the sensors are obtained by the address sent to the decoder.
8. Angles through Eqs. 5, 6, 8, 9, 11 and 12 are calculated.

9. It is obtained the filtering value from the sensor.
10. Calculating angles between links are performed according to Eq. 13.
11. The data is sent by the Bluetooth® to UART port at a rate of 1382400 bauds.
12. Compare if the execution time is equal and waits 20 ms.
13. Return to the step six.

It is important to take in count the speeds of processing of the microcontroller, for this work is considered a speed of 22,1184 MHz, it is provided a frequency of sampling 50 Hz. It is possible to increase the frequency sampling of 1 kHz, that is the maximum frequency sampling of the sensors, but it is necessary consider have a powerful hardware, to grant more speeds processing.

7   Testing of Sensorial System

To perform the tests, we designed and built twelve boards, eleven have a function to support for MPU6050 sensors, the remaining board contains all the processing unit and power supply.

For attachment system, they were designed and built twelve bases foamed PVC. Furthermore, these bases were added nylon tapes with Velcro inch and plastic clips for attaching the sensors to the extremities of the person. In Fig. 5 the results of this process are shown.

Fig. 5. Parts that form the sensorial system.

To validate the system, is produced a joint of two degrees of freedom which contains two resistive angular linear sensors (potentiometers) with a detection range of 0 to 280°. Both sensors have an analog output between 0 and 5 V depending on the angle at which they are, to display the angular behavior, is implemented a validation system (see Fig. 6), this performs tasks such as converting the analog values to digital values, converts the value bits to angular values using Eqs. 30 and 31, sends the result by the serial port to a PC using the Labview®2015 software for the data processing.

The converter analog-digital has a resolution of 10 bits, therefore, it is capable to detecting angular variations of 0.27°, In Fig. 7 is presented the characteristic curves of potentiometers, Eqs. 30 and 31 represent their behavior, where ADC0 is the value from

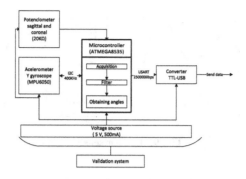

Fig. 6. Block diagram of the system validation.

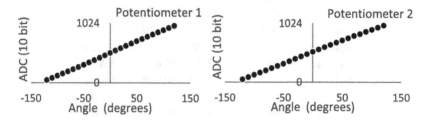

Fig. 7. Response curve of potentiometers.

potentiometer located in coronal plane, and ADC1 is the value from potentiometer located in the sagittal plane.

$$\varphi = 0.25248294 \times ADC0 - 129.7762313 \tag{30}$$

$$\theta = 0.252360992 \times ADC1 - 132.5500873 \tag{31}$$

The results show that the coronal plane potentiometer has an error 0.52° and sagittal plane potentiometer has a variation of 0.56°. This system works as a first test for the Kalman filter and the signals obtained from the accelerometer and gyroscope, these tests were very helpful because, with that information we found the R (Eq. 29) and Q (Eq. 28). In Fig. 8 is presented the results of the input signals like filtered signal and the unfiltered signal respect to sagittal and coronal plane, the sampling frequency is 50 Hz.

After obtaining the parameters R and Q of Kalman filter is performed a comparison between the validation system and devices. Then we obtain behavior the correlation C (Eq. 32) and error RMSE (Eq. 33), compared to calibrated system. Figure 9 show the

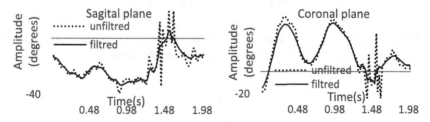

Fig. 8. Signals acquired in the sagittal and coronal plane filtered and unfiltered.

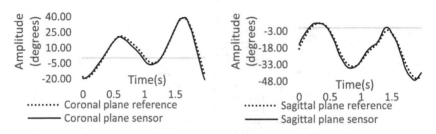

Fig. 9. Lumbar sensor.

Table 1. Correlation and error of sensors.

Sensor	Plane sagittal		Plane coronal	
	Correlation	RMSE	Correlation	RMSE
Lumbar	99.51%	2.8289°	99.17%	2.8317°
Right femur	99.67%	2.9497°	98.77%	3.9029°
Left femur	99.45%	3.6994°	97.66%	5.2059°
Right tibia	99.77%	2.7383°	98.90%	5.8452°
Left tibia	99.35%	3.3121°	97.84%	6.2241°
Right ankle	99.57%	3.0009°	99.09%	4.4343°
Left ankle	99.57%	3.1545°	99.73%	3.6771°
Right humerus	99.36%	3.699°	97.31%	7.2164°
Left humerus	99.75%	1.777°	98.90%	7.7526°
Right radius	99.25%	3.6215°	99.12%	5.0106°
Left radius	99.34%	1.968°	98.57%	3.4625°
Reference	99.82%	2.9541°	99.38%	2.9411°

result of the above described experiment, with this is obtained the relationship between both signals. On the other hand, the error is finds to determine performance of MPU6050.

$$c = \frac{\sum_{i=1}^{n}(x_i - \bar{x}) \cdot (y_i - \bar{y})}{\sqrt{\sum_{i=1}^{n}(x_i - \bar{x})} \cdot \sqrt{\sum_{i=1}^{n}(y_i - \bar{y})}} \tag{32}$$

From Eq. 32, x and y are the samples of signals, $\bar{x}$ and $\bar{y}$ are the average of the signals and n is the number of signal samples.

$$RMSE = \sqrt{\frac{1}{n}\sum_{i=1}^{n}(S_P - S_R)^2} \tag{33}$$

For Eq. 33, S_P is the signal from the potentiometer and S_R is the signal from the inertial sensor, both signals belong to the same reference plane.

8   Conclusions

For the 12 sensors of this system is obtained the behavior by applying a random motion for 10 s and average of 50 samples/second. Table 1 shows the correlation and the corresponding error to each sensor.

From Table 1 is possible find the correlation and average error of the entire system, resulting in an average correlation of 99.12% and average error of 3.92°.

References

1. Yang, Z., Ka-Chun, C., Charlie, C.: Pedalvatar: an IMU-based real-time body motion capture system. In: International Conference on Intelligent Robots and Systems, Chicago, IL, pp. 4130–4135 (2014)
2. Diana, C., Mihaela, B.: Biomechanical analyzes of human body stability and equilibrium. In: Proceedings of the World Congress on Engineering 2010, London, vol. II (2010)
3. William, F., Michael, Z., Robert, M., Bill, C.: Off-the-Shelf, Real-Time, Human Body Motion Capture for Synthetic Environments. Computer Science Department Naval Postgraduate School, Monterey, California (1996)
4. Daniel, R., Henk, L., Per, R.: Xsens MVN: Full 6DOF Human Motion Tracking Using Miniature Inertial Sensors. Xsens Technologies (2013)
5. Mark, W., Seth, H., Vidyasagar, V.: Robot Modeling and Control. Rigid Motions and Homogeneous Transformations, pp. 29–64. Wiley, New York (2010)
6. Walter, T., Higgins J.: A comparison of complementary and Kalman filtering. In: IEEE Tranactions on Aerospace and Electronic Systems, Arizona State University (1975)

Author Index

Printed in the United States
By Bookmasters